Communications
in Computer and Informa2

Natarajan Meghanathan   Brajesh Kumar Kaushik
Dhinaharan Nagamalai (Eds.)

Advances in Networks and Communications

First International Conference on Computer Science
and Information Technology, CCSIT 2011
Bangalore, India, January 2-4, 2011
Proceedings, Part II

 Springer

Volume Editors

Natarajan Meghanathan
Jackson State University
Jackson, MS, USA
E-mail: nmeghanathan@jsums.edu

Brajesh Kumar Kaushik
Indian Institute of Technology
Roorkee, India
E-mail: bkk23fec@iitr.ernet.in

Dhinaharan Nagamalai
Wireilla Net Solutions PTY Ltd
Melbourne, Victoria, Australia
E-mail: dhinthia@yahoo.com

Library of Congress Control Number: 2010941308

CR Subject Classification (1998): H.4, C.2, I.2, H.3, D.2, I.4

ISSN	1865-0929
ISBN-10	3-642-17877-4 Springer Berlin Heidelberg New York
ISBN-13	978-3-642-17877-1 Springer Berlin Heidelberg New York

springer.com

© Springer-Verlag Berlin Heidelberg 2011
Printed in Germany

Typesetting: Camera-ready by author, data conversion by Scientific Publishing Services, Chennai, India
Printed on acid-free paper   06/3180

Preface

The First International Conference on Computer Science and Information Technology (CCSIT-2011) was held in Bangalore, India, during January 2–4, 2011. CCSIT attracted many local and international delegates, presenting a balanced mixture of intellect from the East and from the West.

The goal of this conference series is to bring together researchers and practitioners from academia and industry to focus on understanding computer science and information technology and to establish new collaborations in these areas. Authors are invited to contribute to the conference by submitting articles that illustrate research results, projects, survey work and industrial experiences describing significant advances in all areas of computer science and information technology.

The CCSIT-2011 Committees rigorously invited submissions for many months from researchers, scientists, engineers, students and practitioners related to the relevant themes and tracks of the workshop. This effort guaranteed submissions from an unparalleled number of internationally recognized top-level researchers. All the submissions underwent a strenuous peer-review process which comprised expert reviewers. These reviewers were selected from a talented pool of Technical Committee members and external reviewers on the basis of their expertise. The papers were then reviewed based on their contributions, technical content, originality and clarity. The entire process, which includes the submission, review and acceptance processes, was done electronically. All these efforts undertaken by the Organizing and Technical Committees led to an exciting, rich and a high-quality technical conference program, which featured high-impact presentations for all attendees to enjoy, appreciate and expand their expertise in the latest developments in computer network and communications research.

In closing, CCSIT-2011 brought together researchers, scientists, engineers, students and practitioners to exchange and share their experiences, new ideas and research results in all aspects of the main workshop themes and tracks, and to discuss the practical challenges encountered and the solutions adopted. We would like to thank the General and Program Chairs, organization staff, the members of the Technical Program Committees and external reviewers for their excellent and tireless work. We also want to thank Springer for the strong support, and the authors who contributed to the success of the conference. We sincerely wish that all attendees benefited scientifically from the conference and wish them every success in their research.

It is the humble wish of the conference organizers that the professional dialogue among the researchers, scientists, engineers, students and educators continues beyond the event and that the friendships and collaborations forged will linger and prosper for many years to come.

Natarajan Meghanathan
B.K. Kaushik
Dhinaharan Nagamalai

Organization

General Chairs

David C. Wyld   Southeastern Louisiana University, USA
Selwyn Piramuthu   University of Florida, USA

General Co-chairs

Michal Wozniak   Wroclaw University of Technology, Poland
Jae Kwang Lee   Hannam University, South Korea

Steering Committee

Eric Renault   Institut Telecom–Telecom SudParis, France
Natarajan Meghanathan   Jackson State University, USA
Nabendu Chaki   University of Calcutta, India
Khoa N. Le   Griffith University, Australia
Kamalrulnizam Abu Bakar   Universiti Teknologi Malaysia, Malaysia
Abdul Kadhir Ozcan   The American University, Cyprus
John Karamitsos   University of the Aegean, Samos, Greece
Dhinaharan Nagamalai   Wireilla Net Solutions PTY Ltd., Australia
Brajesh Kumar Kaushik   Indian Institute of Technology - Roorkee, India

Program Committee Members

Sajid Hussain   Acadia University, Canada
Seungmin Rho   Carnegie Mellon University, USA
Emmanuel Bouix   iKlax Media, France
Charalampos Z. Patrikakis   National Technical University of Athens, Greece
Chin-Chih Chang   Chung Hua University, Taiwan
Yung-Fa Huang   Chaoyang University of Technology, Taiwan
Jeong-Hyun Park   Electronics Telecommunication Research Institute,
                               South Korea
Abdul Kadir Ozcan   The American University, Cyprus
Al-Sakib Khan Pathan   Kyung Hee University, South Korea
Andy Seddon   Asia Pacific Institute of Information Technology,
                               Malaysia
Atilla Elci   Eastern Mediterranean University, Cyprus

B. Srinivasan	Monash University, Australia
Balasubramanian K.	Lefke European University, Cyprus
Boo-Hyung Lee	KongJu National University, South Korea
Chih-Lin Hu	National Central University, Taiwan
Cho Han Jin	Far East University, South Korea
Cynthia Dhinakaran	Hannam University, South Korea
Dhinaharan Nagamalai	Wireilla Net Solutions Pty Ltd., Australia
Dimitris Kotzinos	Technical Educational Institution of Serres, Greece
Dong Seong Kim	Duke University, USA
Farhat Anwar	International Islamic University, Malaysia
Firkhan Ali Bin Hamid Ali	Universiti Tun Hussein Onn Malaysia, Malaysia
Ford Lumban Gaol	University of Indonesia
Girija Chetty	University of Canberra, Australia
H.V. Ramakrishnan	MGR University, India
Henrique Joao Lopes Domingos	University of Lisbon, Portugal
Ho Dac Tu	Waseda University, Japan
Hoang, Huu Hanh	Hue University, Vietnam
Hwangjun Song	Pohang University of Science and Technology, South Korea
Jacques Demerjian	Communication & Systems,Homeland Security, France
Jae Kwang Lee	Hannam University, South Korea
Jan Zizka	SoNet/DI, FBE, Mendel University in Brno, Czech Republic
Jeong-Hyun Park	Electronics Telecommunication Research Institute, South Korea
Jivesh Govil	Cisco Systems Inc. - CA, USA
Johann Groschdl	University of Bristol, UK
John Karamitsos	University of the Aegean, Samos, Greece
Johnson Kuruvila	Dalhousie University, Halifax, Canada
Jose Enrique Armendariz-Inigo	Universidad Publica de Navarra, Spain
Jungwook Song	Konkuk University, South Korea
K.P.Thooyamani	Bharath University, India
Khoa N. Le	Griffith University , Australia
Krzysztof Walkowiak	Wroclaw University of Technology, Poland
Lu Yan	University of Hertfordshire, UK
Luis Veiga	Technical University of Lisbon, Portugal
Marco Roccetti	University of Bologna, Italy
Michal Wozniak	Wroclaw University of Technology, Poland
Mohsen Sharifi	Iran University of Science and Technology, Iran
Murugan D.	Manonmaniam Sundaranar University, India
N. Krishnan	Manonmaniam Sundaranar University, India

Nabendu Chaki	University of Calcutta, India
Natarajan Meghanathan	Jackson State University, USA
Nidaa Abdual Muhsin Abbas	University of Babylon, Iraq
Paul D. Manuel	Kuwait University, Kuwait
Phan Cong Vinh	London South Bank University, UK
Ponpit Wongthongtham	Curtin University of Technology, Australia
Rajendra Akerkar	Technomathematics Research Foundation, India
Rajesh Kumar P.	The Best International, Australia
Rajkumar Kannan	Bishop Heber College, India
Rakhesh Singh Kshetrimayum	Indian Institute of Technology-Guwahati, India
Ramayah Thurasamy	Universiti Sains Malaysia, Malaysia
Sagarmay Deb	Central Queensland University, Australia
Sanguthevar Rajasekaran	University of Connecticut, USA
Sarmistha Neogyv	Jadavpur University, India
Sattar B. Sadkhan	University of Babylon, Iraq
Sergio Ilarri	University of Zaragoza, Spain
Serguei A. Mokhov	Concordia University, Canada
SunYoung Han	Konkuk University, South Korea
Susana Sargento	University of Aveiro, Portugal
Salah Š. Al-Majeed	University of Essex, UK
Vishal Sharma	Metanoia Inc., USA
Wei Jie	University of Manchester, UK
Yannick Le Moullec	Aalborg University, Denmark
Yeong Deok Kim	Woosong University, South Korea
Yuh-Shyan Chen	National Taipei University, Taiwan
Sriman Narayana Iyengar	VIT University, India
A.P. Sathish Kumar	PSG Institute of Advanced Studies, India
Abdul Aziz	University of Central Punjab, Pakistan.
Nicolas Sklavos	Technological Educational Institute of Patras, Greece
Shivan Haran	Arizona State University, USA
Danda B. Rawat	Old Dominion University, USA
Khamish Malhotra	University of Glamorgan, UK
Eric Renault	Institut Telecom – Telecom SudParis, France
Kamaljit I. Lakhtaria	Atmiya Institute of Technology and Science, India
Andreas Riener	Johannes Kepler University Linz, Austria
Syed Rizvi	University of Bridgeport, USA
Velmurugan Ayyadurai	Center for Communication Systems, UK
Syed Rahman	University of Hawaii-Hilo, USA

Sajid Hussain	Fisk University, USA
Suresh Sankaranarayanan	University of West Indies, Jamaica
Michael Peterson	University of Hawaii at Hilo, USA
Brajesh Kumar Kaushik	Indian Institute of Technology, India
Yan Luo	University of Massachusetts Lowell, USA
Yao-Nan Lien	National Chengchi University, Taiwan
Rituparna Chaki	West Bengal University of Technology, India
Somitra Sanadhya	IIT-Delhi, India
Debasis Giri	Haldia Institute of Technology, India
S.Hariharan	B.S. Abdur Rahman University, India

Organized By

ACADEMY & INDUSTRY RESEARCH COLLABORATION CENTER (AIRCC)

Table of Contents – Part II

Networks and Communications

Network and Communications Security

Wireless and Mobile Networks

Table of Contents – Part III

Soft Computing (AI, Neural Networks, Fuzzy Systems, etc.)

Distributed and Parallel Systems and Algorithms

Security and Information Assurance

Ad Hoc and Ubiquitous Computing

Wireless Ad Hoc Networks and Sensor Networks

Table of Contents – Part I

Distributed and Parallel Systems and Algorithms

DSP/Image Processing/Pattern Recognition/ Multimedia

Software Engineering

Database and Data Mining

Soft Computing (AI, Neural Networks, Fuzzy Systems, etc.)

XXVI   Table of Contents – Part I

Analysis of Successive Interference Cancellation in CDMA Systems

G.S. Deepthy[1] and R.J. Susan[2]

[1] Department of Electronics and Communication
Rajagiri School of Engineering and Technology, Ernakulam, Kerala, India
guddy_13@yahoo.co.in
[2] Department of Electronics and Communication
College of Engineering, Trivandrum, India
susanrj@rediffmail.com

Abstract. In DS/CDMA systems, overcoming near/far effects and fading is imperative for satisfactory performance. One way to combat the near/far effect is to use stringent power control, as is done in most of the commercial systems. Another approach is multi-user detection (MUD). In addition to mitigating the near/far effect, MUD has the more fundamental potential of raising capacity by canceling MAI. This paper analyses the convergence behavior and performance of successive interference cancellation (SIC) for CDMA systems this analysis will be generalized in this paper for parallel interference cancellation (PIC) also. In this paper a hybrid interference cancellation receiver is designed by combining the successive and parallel interference cancellation algorithms, so that the advantages of both the schemes are utilized effectively. The hybrid interference cancellation scheme results in a simple, faster and reliable receiver. With the help of simulations, it is shown that this hybrid approach outperforms the other multi-user detection schemes.

Keywords: Multi-user detection, SIC, PIC, HIC MAI.

1 Introduction

Code Division Multiple Access (CDMA) has emerged as the technology of choice for the wireless industry because of its attractive features over the other multiple access schemes – Time Division Multiple Access (TDMA) and Frequency Division Multiple Access (FDMA) – to meet the high capacity and other performance requirements for the emerging Personal Communication Services (PCS). Some of the prominent features are spectrum sharing, rejection of multipath signal components or utilizing them for recombining, and having a frequency reuse factor of one, in the cellular case. However, the capacity of CDMA systems employing the conventional matched filter detector at the receiver end is often limited by interference due to other users in the system, known as multiple-access interference (MAI).

Multiple Access Interference (MAI) is a factor, which limits the capacity and performance of CDMA system. The conventional detector does not take into account

N. Meghanathan et al. (Eds.): CCSIT 2011, Part II, CCIS 132, pp. 1–9, 2011.

the existence of MAI. Hence, a multi-user detection strategy is used for mitigating the effects of MAI. Novel receiver structures that take advantage of knowledge of MAI signal parameters are termed as Multi-user receivers and are more complex than conventional ones. The complexity arises because of their capability of using MAI signal information to help recover the desired user. Interference cancellation receivers have received a great deal of attention due to its advantages when compared with the other multi-user detectors. The interference cancellation techniques can be broadly broken into successive and parallel schemes for canceling multiple access interference.

A major problem with multi-user detectors and interference cancellers is the maintenance of simplicity. Certain schemes where the users' signals are detected collectively turn out to have a complex parallel structure. An alternative to parallel cancellation is to perform successive cancellation. The successive cancellation requires less hardware and is more robust in doing cancellations.

The SIC (Successive Interference Cancellation) is a form of multi- user detection in which signals are detected in the order of perceived reliability. The SIC approach successively cancels strongest users but assumes no knowledge of the users' powers. The outputs of conventional correlation receivers are utilized to rank the users.

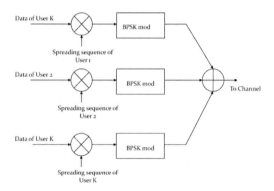

Fig. 1. Multiuser DS/CDMA Transmitter

A simple method of interference cancellation is to estimate and cancel interference successively using feedback. In this approach users are first ranked according to their received powers, then estimated and cancelled in order from strongest to weakest. This cancellation approach has two advantages. First, the strongest users cause the most interference. Second, the strongest users provide the most reliable estimates and thus cause the least error in cancellation. The result is that each user is estimated and only cancelled once as opposed to times in the parallel cancellation approach. The performance relative to parallel cancellation is dependent on the spread of user powers. That is, for the equal power case the successive cancellation scheme performs significantly worse than the parallel approach. However, as the user powers get more widely distributed, the relative performance of the successive scheme improves.

2 System Analysis

2.1 Transmitter Section

A specific user in the K user communication system transmits a binary information-symbol bi $\in$ {-1, 1}. The data of a specific user is then multiplied with a spreading sequence unique to each user. The resultant of the obtained sequence is then BPSK modulated and the same process is applied to the rest of the users'. The outputs of all the BPSK modulated signals are then added up and transmitter over an AWGN channel. The AWGN channel adds zero-mean complex white Gaussian noise with variance $\sigma^2 = No/2$ where No is the single-sided noise power spectral density.

2.2 Receiver Section

In the SIC receiver, users are detected in succession. The estimated interference detected from initial users is cancelled before detection of the next user.

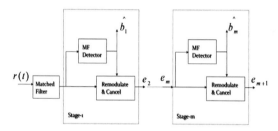

Fig. 2. SIC Receiver

2.3 SIC Algorithm

The SIC works by first attempting to detect and demodulate the strongest user signal, among those present in the overall received signal (also called the original baseband signal). After this user has been detected and demodulated, its contribution to the original baseband signal is regenerated and subtracted from the overall received signal - producing a new baseband signal. The algorithm then repeats except the strongest user from the new baseband signal (which has one less user signal) is detected, demodulated, regenerated, and subtracted.

When making a decision about the transmitted information of the kth user we assume that the decision of users k+1,...,K are correct and neglect the presence of users 1,...,k-1.Therefore the decision for the information bit of the kth user, for synchronous transmission is

$$\hat{b}_k = \text{sgn}\left[r_k - \sum_{j=k+1}^{K} \sqrt{\varepsilon_j} \rho_{jk}(0) \hat{b}_j \right] \tag{1}$$

Where r_k is the output of the correlator or matched filter corresponding to the kth user's signature sequence.

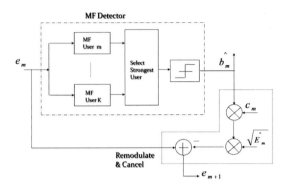

Fig. 3. m^{th} stage in SIC

The SIC multiuser detector for the above case is also a suboptimal detector, since the signals of weaker users are treated as additive interference. The jointly optimum interference canceller for synchronous transmission computes the decisions $\hat{b}_k$ as

$$\hat{b}_k = \text{sgn}\left[r_k - \sum_{j \neq k} \sqrt{\varepsilon_j} \rho_{jk}(0)\hat{b}_j \right] \tag{2}$$

2.4 Parallel Interference Cancellation Scheme

In contrast to the SIC receiver, the PIC receiver estimates and subtracts out all of the MAI for each user in parallel.

The hard decision corresponds to the estimates of a conventional receiver. For each user, the corresponding interference signal replicas are subtracted from the receiver signal, generating interference mitigated signal. The main advantage of PIC is its fastness. But it suffers from the disadvantage that lower power users will have their BER very high, since detection is with less SIR and hardware complexity of receiver is high. Hence, the performance of PIC is inferior to SIC.

2.5 Hybrid Interference Cancellation Scheme

The SIC yields better performance with lot of processing time, but the PIC is superior to SIC in terms of computation time but is inferior in terms of BER. So a mix of SIC and PIC will yield an optimal result. The main idea behind HIC is that instead of canceling all K users either in series or in parallel, they are cancelled partially in parallel and partially in series .The configuration for cancellation will be K-P-S, where K is the total number of users and the number cancelled in parallel and in series at each stage is denoted by P and S, respectively. The signals of the first P stronger users (out of K) are chosen to perform PIC between them. As a result of this action, the most reliable P users are chosen, and their signals reconstructed in order to subtract them from the buffered version of the received signal.

Due to the rapid changing characteristics of the Rayleigh fading process, an estimate of local mean power is obtained by averaging the samples X. The average of the received samples is given by the equation below,

$$E_{SA} = 1/N \sum_{j=1}^{N} X_j \tag{3}$$

Where N is the window size, X_j is the received power measurement.

Noise power estimate is found by finding the difference between the noisy received signal and the noiseless signal.

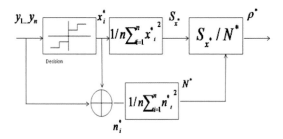

Fig. 4. SNR Estimation

3   Simulation Results

For ideal power control case the comparison of BER vs. SNR for the matched filter, SIC and PIC were been done for 10 users. For AWGN channel, figure shows that PIC outperforms SIC when all the users are received with equal power.

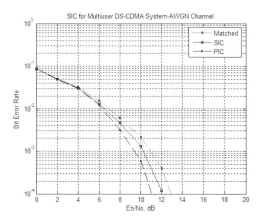

Fig. 5. SIC for Multiuser DS-CDMA System-AWGN channel

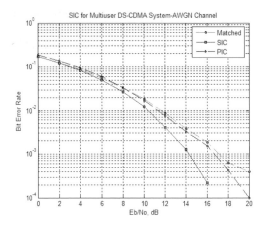

Fig. 6. SIC for Multiuser DS-CDMA System-AWGN channel

For AWGN channel, simulation result shows that SIC outperform PIC when all the users have unequal power distribution.

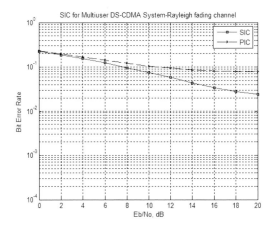

Fig. 7. SIC for Multiuser DS-CDMA System-Rayleigh fading channel

For the case of Rayleigh fading channel with users having unequal power levels simulation result that SIC is better in performance than PIC

Fig.8 shows the BER performance of the DS-CDMA system with HIC scheme. The HIC scheme is an optimal scheme, a good tradeoff between SIC and PIC scheme. The hybrid interference cancellation receiver, as seen from the Fig.3, nearly matches the performance of the SIC receiver.

Fig.9 shows the BER performance of the DS-CDMA system with HIC scheme for Rayleigh fading channel.

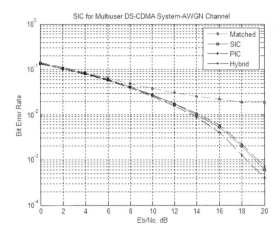

Fig. 8. HIC for Multiuser DS-CDMA system-AWGN channel

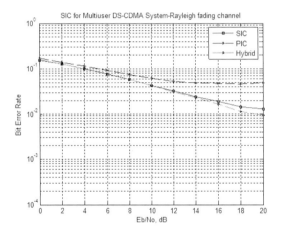

Fig. 9. HIC for Multiuser DS-CDMA system-Rayleigh fading channel

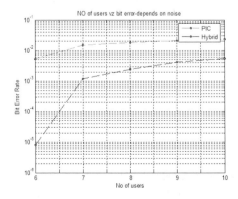

Fig. 10. HIC for Multiuser DS-CDMA system-AWGN channel

Fig. 10 shows the plot between Number of users and Bit error rate. As the number of users increase, the error rate also increases. Here again, the performance of the conventional receiver and the PIC receiver are poor whereas the performance of HIC nearly approaches the performance of SIC.

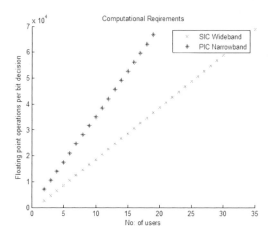

Fig. 11. Computational Complexity

Fig. 11 shows the plot for computational complexity of wideband SIC and PIC schemes.

4 Conclusion

In this paper on Hybrid Interference Cancellation receiver has been proposed and the performance of the receiver were obtained using simulations. The performance of the proposed receiver was compared with the other interference cancellation receivers. From the results obtained, it is concluded that, the performance of the Hybrid Interference Cancellation receiver matches the Successive Interference Cancellation scheme with much lesser number of correlations and hence with less computational time. The complexity of the HIC receiver is comparatively greater than that of the SIC receiver, and lesser than that of the PIC receiver. Hence a perfect tradeoff between the computation time and receiver complexity is achieved.

Acknowledgement

The author would like to thank Mrs. Susan R.J. for her supervision and guidance of the work presented in this thesis. The author would also like to thank Prof. S. Shabu and the Department of Electronics and Communication faculty for their hinding support. Finally, this work would never have been completed without the blessings of almighty.

References

[1] Patel, P., Holtzman, J.: Analysis of a simple successive cancellation scheme in a DS/CDMA system. IEEE Jour. on Sel. Areas in Comm. 12(5), 796–807 (1994)
[2] Weitkemper, P., Zielinski, K., Kammeyer, K.-D., Laur, R.: Optimization of Interference Cancellation in coded CDMA by means of Differential Evolution. In: Turbo Coding 2006, Munich, April 3-7 (2006)
[3] Wang, T.F.: Spread Spectrum & CDMA. Multi-user Detection
[4] Reed, M.C., Alexander, P.D.: Iterative Multi-user Detection for CDMA with FEC: Near-Single-User Performance. IEEE Transactions on Communications 46(12) (December 1998)
[5] Benvenuto, N., Carnevale, G., Tomasin, S.: Energy Optimization of CDMA Transceivers using Successive Interference Cancellation
[6] Tan†, P.H., Rasmussen†, L.K., Lim, T.J.: Iterative Interference Cancellation as Maximum-Likelihood Detection in CDMA. Centre for Wireless Communications, National University of Singapore
[7] Buehrer, R.M., Correal-Mendoza, N.S., Woerner, B.D.: A Simulation Comparison of Multiuser Receivers for Cellular CDMA. IEEE Transactions on Vehicular Technology 49(4) (July 2000)
[8] Rasmussen, L.K., Lim, T.J., Johansson, A.-L.: A Matrix Approach to Successive Interference Cancellation in CDMA. Submitted to IEEE Transactions on Communications (May 14, 1997) (revised June 1998)
[9] Sivakumar, B., SubhaRani, S., Shanmugam, A.: A New Methodology for Switching Multi-user Detector for DS CDMA Systems. GVIP Journal 5(8) (August 2005)
[10] Li, W., Aaron Gulliver, T.: Successive Interference Cancellation for DS-CDMA Systems with Transmit Diversity. EURASIP Journal on Wireless Communications and Networking 1, 46–54 (2004)
[11] Seskar, I., Pederson, K.I., Kolding, T.E., Holtzman, J.M.: Implementation Aspects for Successive Interference Cancellation in DS/CDMA Systems. Wireless Networks 4, 447–452 (1998)

Scenario Based Performance Analysis of AODV and DSDV in Mobile Adhoc Network

S. Taruna and G.N. Purohit

Computer Science Department,
Banasthali University,
Rajasthan, India
{staruna,pgopal}@mail.banasthali.in

Abstract. A mobile Adhoc network(MANET) is formed by a group of autonomous mobile nodes connected by wireless link without centralized control or established infrastructure. Routing protocols for adhoc networks are typically evaluated using simulation, since the deployment of adhoc network is relatively rare. In this paper, using a simulation tool ns-2 we make a comparison between AODV and DSDV protocols for CBR traffic in mobile ad hoc networks. We analyze the performance of the routing protocol after extracting data from trace file. There are many languages which can be used for analyzing data. We have used AWK scripting language and Java code for extracting data from trace file. The analysis is done for generating various performance metrics like packet delivery fraction, average end-to-end delay, packet loss, packet delay, routing overhead, throughput, route acquisition time.

Keywords: Ad Hoc Network, routing protocol, network simulation, AWK, DSDV, AODV.

1 Introduction

The maturity of wireless transmission and the popularity of portable computing devices have to satisfy personal communication desire , that is " in any time and in any area", which is an important issue in the next generation network. Users can move around, while at the same time still remaining connected with the rest of the world. It is because of this that wireless adhoc network is one of the hot topics of research in networks these days.

In adhoc network, each host must act as router since routes are mostly 'multi-hop' Nodes in such a network move arbitrarily , thus network topology changes frequently and unpredictably. Since wireless adhoc network does not need span network establishment, scalability is fast, immunity is strong and hence it is becoming the core technology in tactical internet. It is used in automated battlefields, disaster recovery , intelligent transportation and other areas.

Mobile adhoc network provides a method of building a distributed communication network in rapidity for the environment which has no fixed communication establishment and need extemporaneous communication. Since an adhoc network has

N. Meghanathan et al. (Eds.): CCSIT 2011, Part II, CCIS 132, pp. 10–19, 2011.

the advantages of building network fast, flexible and does not require wire circuitry, it has an expansive application foreground.

In this paper we make a comparison between AODV and DSDV routing protocols in NS-2, regarding performance metrics which includes various comparison factors like packet delivery fraction, average end-to-end delay, packet loss, packet delay, routing overhead, throughput, route acquisition time etc. The simulation of routing protocol is shown using Network Animator (NAM) and the performance of routing protocol is shown by way of graphical display.

2   Literature Review

Adhoc routing protocols can be classified based on different criteria. Depending upon the routing mechanism employed by a given protocol, it may fall under more than one class. Routing protocols for ad-hoc networking can be classified into four categories viz. (i) Based on routing information update routing mechanism (proactive or table-driven, reactive or on-demand and hybrid protocols), (ii) Based on the use of Temporal information (Past Temporal and Future Temporal) for routing, (iii) Based on routing topology (Flat Topology, Hierarchical Topology), (iv) Based on the Utilization of Specific Resources (Power Aware Routing and Geographical Information Assisted Routing)[5-7].

2.1   Pro-active Routing Protocol

In pro-active routing protocol[6], every node in the network are distributed through the periodically broadcast routing message. The typical pro-active routing protocol includes destination sequence distance vector routing protocol DSDV, wireless routing protocol WRP, fish eyes status routing protocol FSR.

In DSDV, every route collects the routing information from all its neighbors, and then computes the shortest path to all nodes in the network. After generating a new routing table, the router broadcasts this table to all its neighbors. This may trigger other neighbors to re-compute their routing tables, until routing information is stable. DSDV performance is enhanced due to freedom from loops and differentiation of stale routes from new routes by sequence numbers. Each mobile host maintains a sequence number by increasing it each time the host sends an update message to its neighbors. A route will be replaced only when the destination sequence number is less than the new one, or two routes have the same sequence number but one has a lower metric.

The advantage of DSDV is it's principle and operation are simple, using destination sequence number loop routing is avoided and speeding up the velocity in convergence. It's disadvantage is that periodically broadcasting messages add cost to the network.

2.2   On-Demand Routing Protocol

An on- demand routing protocol is also called reactive protocol, as it tries to discover/ maintain routes when necessary. When a source node wants to deliver data to a destination node, it has to find a route first, then data packets can be delivered.

2.2.1 Dynamic Source Routing Protocol (DSR)

The DSR is a simple and efficient routing protocol designed specifically for use in multi-hop wireless ad hoc networks of mobile nodes [6,7,8,9]. DSR allows the network to be completely self-organizing and self-configuring, without the need for any existing network infrastructure or administration. The protocol is composed of the two main mechanisms of "Route Discovery" and "Route Maintenance', which work together to allow nodes to discover and maintain routes to arbitrary destinations in the ad hoc network All aspects of the protocol operate entirely on DSR protocol which include easily guaranteed loop-free routing, operation in networks containing unidirectional links, use of only "soft state" in routing, and very rapid recovery when routes in the network change. In DSR, Route Discovery and Route Maintenance each operate entirely "on demand". In particular, unlike other protocols, DSR requires no periodic packets of any kind at any layer within the network.

2.2.2 On Demand Distance Vector Protocol (AODV)

The AODV [1,6]algorithm is an improvement of DSDV protocol described above. It reduces number of broadcast by creating routes on demand basis, as against DSDV that maintains routes to each known destination [4,5,14]. When source requires sending data to a destination and if route to that destination is not known then it initiates route discovery. AODV allows nodes to respond to link breakages and changes in network topology in a timely manner. Routes, which are not in use for long time, are deleted from the table. Also AODV uses Destination Sequence Numbers to avoid loop formation and Count to Infinity Problem.

An important feature of AODV is the maintenance of timer based states in each node, regarding utilization of individual routing table entries. A routing table entry expires if not used recently. A set of predecessor nodes is maintained for each routing table entry, indicating the set of neighboring nodes which use that entry to route data packets. These nodes are notified with RERR packets when the next-hop link breaks. Each predecessor node, in turn, forwards the RERR to its own set of predecessors, thus effectively erasing all routes using the broken link. Route error propagation in AODV can be visualized conceptually as a tree whose root is the node at the point of failure and all sources using the failed link as the leaves.

2.3 On-Level (Hybrid) Routing Protocol

The Zone routing protocol (ZRP)[10] is a hybrid of proactive and reactive approaches. With respect to each node, the set of nodes within r hops is called a zone, where r is pre-defined value. For each host, routing information inside its zone is constantly collected in a proactive fashion. To do so, whenever a node's link state is changed, a notice will be sent as far as r hops away based on DSDV[16]. Hence, a node always knows how to reach a node inside its zone. This also limits the number of updates triggered by a link state change to a local range.

On the other hand, inter-zone routing is done in a reactive fashion. A modified DSR protocol is used as follows, when a node needs a route to a node outside its zone, it performs a border casting by sending a route request to each node on the 'border' of its zone. On receiving such a packet at a border node, it first checks its intra-zone routing table for existence of a route to the requested destination node. If found, a route reply can be sent; otherwise it performs other border casting in its zone. The performance of ZRP depends on the radius of the zone.

3 Simulation Model and Building a Scenario

3.1 Simulation Model

In this section, the network simulation are implemented using the ns-2 [13] simulation tool. The network simulator NS-2 is a discrete event simulator, which means it simulates such events as sending, receiving forwarding and dropping packets. For simulation scenario and network topology creation it uses OTCL (Object Tool Command Language).

To create new objects, protocols and routing algorithm or to modify them in NS-2, C++ source code has to be changed. It provides support for simulation of TCP, UDP, routing and multicast protocols over wired and wireless networks. The simulation were conducted on Xeon processor at speed 1.0 GhZ,512 MB RAM running Linux.

3.2 Building the Scenario

The scenario need to indicate the region[10-12], the number of nodes, the whole time of node moving, the node's moving affair in the process including indicating from one moment to start, a certain node moving into a target with a velocity, how long time it stays after arrived in the target and perform the next step of moving. The user just need to fix the node number, the max of velocity the time of staying and other parameters, stochastically according to requirement. Thecommand is as follows:

setdest[-n num_of_nodes] [-P pausetime] [-s maxspeed] [- - t simtime] [-x maxi] [-y maxy]>[movementfile]; For instance, in this evaluation, the scenario is build up including 10,20,35 nodes, the average time of staying is 0 second(no staying), the max of velocity is 10 meter per second, the average velocity is 10m/s, the time of simulation is 150 second, the borderline is 1000×1000. *For example, we have used it as* ./setdest −n 10 −p 2.0 −s 10.0 −t 150 −x 1000 −y 1000 > Dsecn-10.

The Scenario is created for AODV, DSDV protocol on the area 1000* 100 with simulation time of 150 seconds on 10, 20, 35 nodes with CBR traffic each of 512 bytes and with a data rate of 2Mbps and a packet rate of 4 packets/seconds.

4 Result and Analysis

a) *Packet Delivery Fraction (Pdf):* Also known as ratio of the data packets delivered to the destinations to those generated by the CBR sources. This metric states the robustness, completeness, and correctness of the routing protocol and its reliability.

The performance metrics obtained from analysis of trace file generated by simulation of DSDV and AODV routing protocol states that for 10 nodes AODV performs best, for 20 and 35 nodes DSDV performs well. Thus it states that, in case of higher node density, DSDV performs well, delivering of data packets increases, but for lower node density AODV performs better, as represented in table 1.

Table 1. Experimental Result of Various Performance Metrics

NO OF NODES	10		20		35	
Comparison Factors	AODV	DSDV	AODV	DSDV	AODV	DSDV
Packets Send	2905	2921	6543	6578	8210	8201
Packets Received	2905	1929	2601	3381	5119	5926
Packet Delivery Fraction	100	66.04	39.75	51.40	62.35	72.26
Throughput	80.71	53.61	72.26	93.93	142.22	164.69
Routing Overhead	21262	17053	33668	37043	101869	103440
Normalized Routing Load	7.32	8.84	12.94	10.96	25.76	17.46
Packet Loss	0	992	3942	3197	3091	2275
Average end-to-end Delay	10.37	11.62	18.67	17.59	586.06	1013.82
Packets Dropped	2	977	3543	3263	3936	3441
Bytes Dropped	1180	519844	1885166	1741832	2132812	1856488

b) *Throughput:* Also known as percentage of packets that reach their destination successfully. This metric states the scalability of the routing protocol.

The performance metrics obtained from analysis of trace file and study of graph generated by simulation of DSDV and AODV routing protocols, states that for 10 nodes AODV performs best in comparison to DSDV but in case of 20 nodes DSDV performs better compare to AODV and in case of 35 nodes, DSDV and AODV performs relatively close. Thus it states that in case of higher node density, DSDV performs well and is more scalable, but for lower node density AODV performs well, .as represented in Fig -1, 2.

c) *Normalized Routing Load (Nrl):* It is defined as the no. of routing packets transmitted per data packet delivered at the destination. This metric states the efficiency of the routing protocol in terms of the extra load introduced to the network.

The performance metrics obtained from analysis of trace file generated by simulation of DSDV and AODV routing protocol states that for 10 nodes AODV and DSDV performs closely but for 20 nodes NRL value increases for AODV in comparison to DSDV and in case of 35 nodes AODV NRL value increases relatively very high compare to DSDV. Thus it states that in case higher node density, AODV performs well and is more efficient, but for lower node density DSDV and AODV perform relatively close, as represented in table 1.

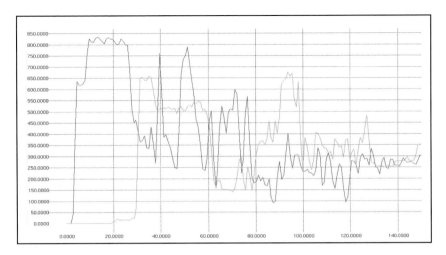

Fig. 1. Throughput in AODV and DSDV for 10 nodes

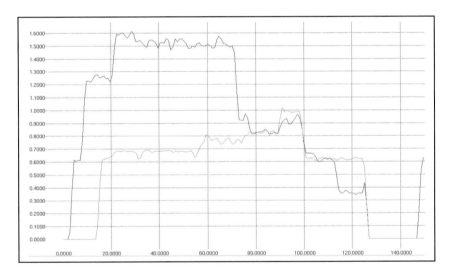

Fig. 2. Throughput in AODV and DSDV for 35 nodes

d) Average End-To-End Delay: It includes all possible delays caused by queuing for transmission at the node, buffering data for detouring, retransmission delays at the MAC, propagation delay and transmission time. This metric states the quality of the routing protocol.

The performance metrics obtained from analysis of trace file and study of graph generated by simulation of DSDV and AODV routing protocol states that for 10 nodes AODV and DSDV has relatively close delay value and for 20 nodes too delay value is relatively close for AODV and DSDV but in case of 35 nodes, DSDV has more delay which is relatively high compare to AODV. Thus it states

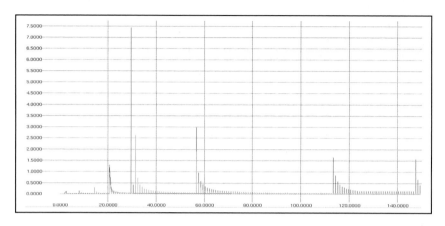

Fig. 3. Packet. delay in AODV and DSDV with 10nodes

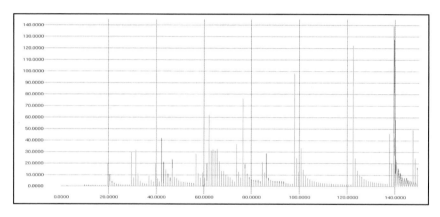

Fig. 4. Packet. delay in AODV and DSDV with 35nodes

that in case of higher node density, DSDV has more delay that its quality deteriorates, but for lower node density DSDV and AODV perform relatively close, as represented in fig-3, 4.

e) Routing Overhead: It is defined as the total no of routing packets transmitted during the simulation The number of control packets per mobile node. Control packet includes route request, replies, and error messages. This metric states the efficiency of the routing protocol.

The performance metrics obtained from analysis of trace file generated by simulation of DSDV and AODV routing protocol states that for 10 nodes, AODV has more overhead in comparison to DSDV, but for 20 nodes overhead value increases for DSDV in comparison to AODV but are relatively very close and in 35 nodes DSDV overhead value increases relatively very high compare to AODV. Thus it states that, DSDV has more overhead value for more no. of nodes and is less efficient, but for low node density DSDV and AODV overhead value is relatively close, as represented in table1.

h) Packet Loss: It occurs when one or more packets being transmitted across the network fail to arrive at the destination.

The performance metrics obtained from analysis of trace file and study of graph generated by simulation of DSDV and AODV routing protocols states that for 10 nodes, AODV has more packet loss in comparison to DSDV and in case of 20 nodes AODV has more packet loss compare to DSDV but in case of 35 nodes, DSDV has high packet loss compare to AODV. Thus it states that in case of higher node density, DSDV has more packet loss but in lower node density AODV has more packet loss as represented in figure-5,6,7.

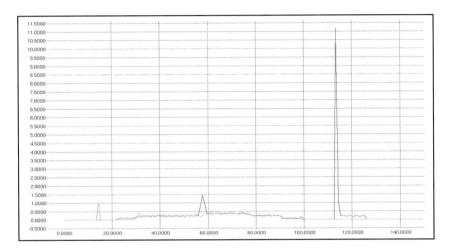

Fig. 5. Packet. loss in AODV and DSDV with 10 nodes

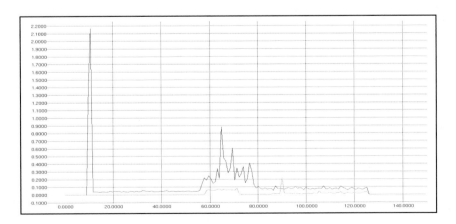

Fig. 6. Packet. loss in AODV and DSDV with 20 nodes

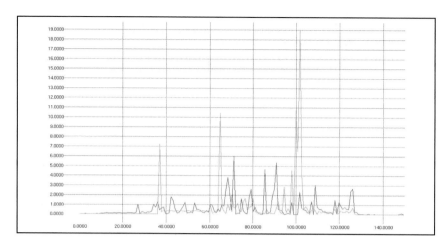

Fig. 7. Packet. loss in AODV and DSDV with 35 nodes

i) Packet Dropped: It occurs in wireless simulation, when one or more packets being dropped by source node when receiver node is not in its wireless range.

The performance metrics obtained from analysis of trace file generated by simulation of DSDV and AODV routing protocols states that for 10 nodes, DSDV drop more packets in comparison to AODV but in case of 20 nodes, AODV has more packets dropped compare to DSDV and in case of 35 nodes, AODV has more no. of packets dropped in compare to DSDV. Thus it states that in case of higher node density AODV drops more packets but in low node density DSDV drops more packets, as represented in table 1.

j) Route Acquisition Time: The time it takes, a source node to find a route to a destination node. Since DSDV is a table routing protocol, every node maintains the network topology information in the form of routing tables, so DSDV has very low route acquisition time in any scenario in comparison to AODV routing protocol which finds the necessary path when it is required by using a connection establishment process. Thus this metrics state that DSDV is best in case of route acquisition time, as represented in table 1.

5   Conclusion

In this paper analysis and investigations are carried out on two prominent protocols, AODV and DSDV using NS-2. DSDV is selected as representative of proactive routing protocol while AODV is the representative of reactive routing protocols. AODV performed better in dense environment except packet loss. AODV is proved to be better than DSDV. Though it is not very clear that which one protocol is best for all the scenarios, each protocol is having its own advantages and disadvantages and may be well suited for certain scenarios.

We found similarities in the results from prior simulation studies using ns-2 as well as differences, This indicates that the simulation results serve as good reference for studying protocol features and for comparing different protocols , but are not accurate enough for deriving conclusions about the expected performance of a given protocol in a real network.

Although the field of adhoc network is rapidly growing and new developments are coming day by day. We are planning for a new protocol which performs well in all scenario.

Acknowledgement. We gratefully acknowledge the financial support provided by Department of Science and Technology (DST), New Delhi for the project "Banasthali Centre for Education and Research in Basic Sciences" under their CURIE (Consolidation of University Research for Innovation and Excellence in Women Universities) progamme.

References

1. Perkins, E., Belding, R., Das, S.: Ad hoc on demand distance vector (AODV) routing. IETF RFC3561 (2003)
2. Xie, J.: AM route: Ad Hoc multicast routing protocol. Mobile Networks and Applications 7, 429–439 (2002)
3. Lee, S.J., Gerla, M., Chiang, C.C.: On-demand multicast routing protocol in multi hop wireless mobile networks. Mobile Networks and Applications 7, 441–453 (2002)
4. Gerasimov, I., Simon, R.: Performance analysis for ad hoc QoS routing protocols. In: Proc. IEEE Computer Society Mobility and Wireless Access Workshop (AobiWac). IEEE Press, Los Alamitos (2002)
5. Xiong, Y., Miao, F.Y., Wang, X.P.: LSCR: A link statebased cluster routing protocol of mobile ad hoc network. Acta Electronica Sinica 31, 645–648 (2003)
6. Zang, W.Y., Yu, M., Xie, L., Sun, Z.X.: A survey of on demand routing protocols for ad hoc mobile networks. Chinese Journal of Computers 25, 1009–1017 (2002)
7. Lee, S., Su, W., Hsu, J.: A performance comparison study of ad hoc wireless multicast protocols. In: Israel (ed.) 19th Annual Joint Conference of the IEEE Computer and Communications, Societies (2000)
8. Moyer, M.J., Abamad, M.: Generalized Role-based Access Control. In: Proc. of the 21st International Conference on Distributed Computing Systems, pp. 391–398 (2001)
9. Zheng, T., Shi, X.R., Yi, P.B.: A new method of solution in mobile Ad Hoc network safety. Computer Engineering 32, 144–145 (2006)
10. Zhou, W.M., Zhou, X.Y.: A method of classify used in Ad Hoc network. Computer Transaction 28, 864–869 (2005)
11. Wang, H.T., Tian, C., Zheng, S.R.: A new method of classify arithmetic and performance simulation of Ad Hoc network. System Simulation Transaction 15, 193–197 (2003)
12. Zheng, S.R., Wang, H.T.: Ad Hoc network technology. Beijing: people mail and telephone, pp. 93–129 (2005)
13. Network Simulator- ns-2, http://www.isi.edu/nsnam/ns/
14. Royer, E., Toh, C.K.: A Review of current routing protocols for Adhoc Mobile wireless network. RFC 2409, IEE personal communication (1999)
15. Perkins, C.E.: Ad Hoc Networking. Dorling Kindersley (India) Pvt. Ltd. (2008)
16. Pan, Y.: Design Routing Protocol Performance Comparison in NS2: AODV Comparing to DSR as Example, Deptt of CS, SUNY Binghamton, Vestal NY 13850
17. Lakshmikant, G., Gaiwak, A., Vyavahare, P.D.: Simulation Based Performance Analysis of Adhoc Routing Protocols. In: Proceedings of TENCON 2008 (2008)
18. Perkins, C.E., Bhagwat, P.: Highly Dynamic Destination- Sequenced Distance-Vector Routing (DSDV) for Mobile Computers. In: Proceedings of the SIGCOMM 1994 (August 1994)

Web Service Based Sheltered Medi Helper

Priya Loganathan, Jeyalakshmi Jeyabalan, and Usha Sarangapani

Department of Information Technology, Rajalakshmi Engineering College,
Chennai, TamilNadu, India
priya.l@rajalakshmi.edu.in,
jeyalakshmi.j@rajalakshmi.edu.in,
usha.s@rajalakshmi.edu.in

Abstract. The veracity and secrecy of medical information which is transacted over the Internet is vulnerable to attack. But the transaction of such details is mandatory in order to avail the luxury of medical services anywhere, anytime. Especially in a web service enabled system for hospital management, it becomes necessary to address these security issues. This paper presents a VDM++ based specification for modelling a security framework for web services with non repudiation to ensure that a party in a dispute cannot repudiate, or refute the validity of a statement or contract. This model presents the procedure and technical options to have a secure communication over Internet with web services. Based on the model, the Medi - Helper is developed to use the technologies of WS-Security and WS-Policy, WSRN in order to create encrypted messages so that the Patient's medical records are not tampered with when relayed over Internet, and are sent in a reliable manner. In addition to authentication, integrity, confidentiality, as proposed in this paper security framework for healthcare based web services is equipped with non repudiation which is not inclusive in many existing frameworks.

Keywords: Web Services, WS-Policy, METRO, WS-Security, Web Services Security, e – Healthcare, SOAP, VDM++, Security Framework, Formal Modelling.

1 Introduction

Web services are considered as self-contained, self-describing, modular applications that can be published, located, and invoked across the Web. Nowadays, an increasing amount of companies and organizations implement their core business and outsource other application services over Internet like healthcare applications which have a large customer base and wide application. Perimeter-based [25] network security technologies like firewalls are inadequate to protect SOAs. Moreover, Transport Layer Security (TLS), which is used to authenticate and encrypt Web-based messages, is inadequate for protecting SOAP messages because it is designed to operate between two endpoints. TLS cannot accommodate Web services' inherent ability to forward messages to multiple other Web services simultaneously.

The healthcare services [2,5] are widely used, when a user travels to different places it is necessary that the person's medical history is also available anywhere for easy access. But when it comes to the mode of transferring medical records [8] online,

N. Meghanathan et al. (Eds.): CCSIT 2011, Part II, CCIS 132, pp. 20–32, 2011.

it is necessary to think about the security of the document as well, else it can be misused. The major security challenges are making the documents available to the right people and keeping the document from being viewed by anyone else. Keeping these challenges in mind, a platform-neutral way for sharing medical records is proposed in this paper. It also becomes mandatory that the solution built is scalable and extensible making way for services like QOS and Security. To provide a fast secured medical services by making use of the fast growing web services [9], a medical assistant is developed using METRO STACK on jdk1.6. Though Web service processing model can handle most attacks it needs to be further strengthened by means of enhancing and improving security. This paper presents a security framework in session II, to handle authentication, authorization, confidentiality, integrity and especially non-repudiation mechanisms. It is presented as a specification in VDM++ so that it can be verified and proof analysis can also be done over the services. The Medi - Helper discussed in this paper is deployed to transfer the medical document across Internet in a secured manner and it is made available only to authorized people by providing good security.

2   Related Work – Web Service Based Medi Helper

Web services expose the valuable XML-encoded healthcare information. Tampering the existing history or record will lead to heavily built problem even it may cause death without security[17]. Web services might even make this situation worse. The reason is that Web services can be thought of as allowing in strange, new users who might take the existing hospital management system and may spoil the accessible database which is not likely to happen in case of the Medi – Helper due to the Single Sign On capability. The [20] Medi – Helper may be are prone to following attacks and they have to be prevented against them. Message alteration, Loss of confidentiality, Falsified messages ,Man in the middle, Principal spoofing ,Forged claims, Replay of message, Replay of message parts and Denial of service .Prevention needs focus on Integrity, Confidentiality, Authentication, Authorization, Non-repudiation as suited for multi -tiered security. The following is a course of action proposed in order to secure the Medi – Helper which is in general applicable to any web service based application. The data flow of the same is presented in Figure 1.

The course of action is explained as below.

1. Message Level Security is ensured by keeping the SOAP messages from being viewed or modified by attackers as the messages traverse the Internet. The credentials are acquired from the user by the service which is left to the designer.There are several options available for securing Web service messages[20]

- HTTP over SSL/TLS (HTTPS) Because SOAP messages are transmitted using HTTP, it is trivial to modify a Web service to support HTTPS.
- XML Encryption and XML Signature These XML security standards developed by W3C allow XML content to be signed and encrypted. Because all SOAP messages are written in XML, Web service developers can sign or encrypt any portion of the SOAP message using these standards, but there is no standard mechanism for informing recipients how these standards were applied to the message.

- WS-Security WS-Security was developed to provide SOAP extensions that define mechanisms for using XML Encryption and XML Signature to secure SOAP messages.
- SAML Authentication of SOAP Headers.

2. Identity Management may follow any of the following architectures[20].

- Isolated identity management is the architecture used by most Web applications on the Internet. In isolated identity management, service providers act both as a credential provider and identity provider.
- In identity federation, a group of providers agrees to recognize user identifiers from one another. Each service provider acts as a credential and identity provider for a subset of requesters.
- In centralized identity management, providers rely on a single TTP to provide credentials and identifiers to requesters. Centralized identity management is similar to federated identity management in that the identity and credential providers supply assertions directly to service providers, allowing requester access without authenticating a second time.

3. Session Management is proposed to use the credentials of the user which are already secured but along with de identification. [13,22] Identification of medical records involves 2 steps:(1) the identification of personally identifying references within medical text(2) the masking, coding, and/or replacing of these references with values irreversible to unauthorized personnel.4 Some computation methods have been described previously to achieve this goal in medical text documents.

4. Resource Management [20] is done by ensuring that they are adequately protected. Usually, Web services are intended to be accessible only to authorized requesters, requiring mechanisms for access control. Several different methods are available, including transport layer authentication, token authentication via the WS-Security specification using SAML assertions or other tokens, and the SOAP authentication header.

5. Trust Management [20] Each trust model provides different benefits and drawbacks, allowing trust to be supported in a wide variety of environments.

- The **pair wise trust model** is the simplest of all trust architectures, but the least scalable. In the pair wise architecture, each Web service is provided—at configuration—the security information of all other Web services that will be interacted with so that those transactions and Web services can be trusted.
- In the **brokered trust model**, an independent third party acts as a trusted third party (TTP) for the Web service. The requester and provider interface with the third party for a variety of security services. Unlike the pair wise trust model, Web services using the brokered trust model need to be designed with the broker's interface in mind, so that identity information can be properly retrieved by the Web service.

6. Policy Framework - WS-Policy represents a set of specifications that describe the capabilities and constraints of the security (and other business) policies on intermediaries and end points (for example, required security tokens, supported encryption algorithms, and privacy rules) and how to associate policies with services and end points. Application and domain specific policies need to be designed.

7. The documents representing patient's medical history need to be encrypted or signed appropriately.

8. Establishing a secure communication channel is necessary. [24]Secure Web communication protocols provide a way to authenticate clients and servers on the Web and to protect the confidentiality of communication between clients and servers. A variety of secure communication standards that use public key technology have been developed, including Secure Hypertext Transfer Protocol (SHTTP), IP Security (IPSec), PPTP, and L2TP. The leading general-purpose, secure Web communication protocols are SSL 3.0 and the open TLS protocol that is based on SSL. The SSL and TLS protocols are widely used to provide secure channels for confidential TCP/IP communication on the Web.

9. Web Services Security: Non–Repudiation This specification extends the use of XML Digital Signature in the context of WSS[14]: SOAP Message Security to allow senders of SOAP messages to request message disposition notifications that may optionally be signed to prove that the receiver received the SOAP message without modification. The specification also defines a method for embedding SOAP message dispositions in a SOAP message header. This specification constitutes a protocol for voluntary non-repudiation of receipt that when used systematically provides cryptographic proof of both parties participation in a transaction. This specification does not define any mechanism to prove receipt of a message by a non-conformant implementation.

The formal specification of the procedure is presented as a VDM++ snippet herein generated using Overture.

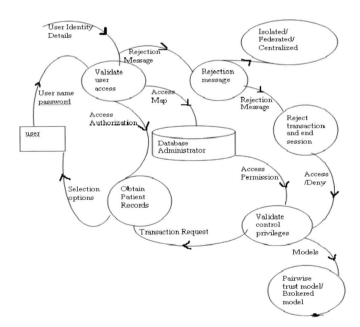

Fig. 1. Context Layout Showing Medi – Helper

```
service.vdmpp
class service
types
id_management =  <Isolated> | <Federated> |  <Centralized> | <nil>;
securing_credentials = <HTTPS> | <xml_enc_or_dsig> | <WS_Security> | <other> | <nil>;
session_management =<authenticated_with_deidentification> | <nil> | <othercredentials> ;
repository_acl = <access> | <deny> | <nil> ;
trust_management = <pairwise> | <Brokered> | <nil>;
Security_Policy = <rolebasedaccess> | <encryption> | <authentication> | <nil>;
encrypt_document = <yes> | <no> ;
secure_comm_channel = <yes> | <no> ;
ws_non_repudiation = <wsrn> | <others> | <nil>;
endstatus = <true> | <false> ;
instance variables
public pid : map service to set of PatientInfo;
identity_scheme : id_management := <Isolated>;
securing_scheme : securing_credentials :=  <WS_Security>;
repoacl_scheme : repository_acl := <deny>;
trust_scheme : trust_management := <pairwise>;
session_scheme : session_management := <authenticated_with_deidentification> ;
policy_choice : Security_Policy := <authentication>;
encryption : encrypt_document := <yes>;
comm_channel : secure_comm_channel := <yes>;
repudiation_scheme : ws_non_repudiation := <wsrn>;
status : endstatus := <false>;
operations
functions
request(service: service , PatientInfo: PatientInfo) status:endstatus
pre service.pid = PatientInfo.pid
post
if securecredentials(service) = nil then
(
if manageid(service) = nil    then
(
if managesession(service) = nil then
(
if aclauthorization(service) = nil then
(
if managetrust(service) = nil then
(
if policyapplication(service) = nil then
(
if encryptdoc(service) = nil then
(
if securecommchannel(service) = nil then
(
if addnonrepudiation(service) = nil then status = <true>  else status = <false>
) else status = <false>
) else status = <false>
) else status = <false>
) else status = <false>
) else status = <false>
```

```
) else status = <false>
) else status = <false>
) else status = <false> ;
manageid(service: service) status:endstatus
pre nil
post if service.identity_scheme = <nil> then status = <false> else status = <true> ;
securecredentials(service: service) status:endstatus
pre nil
post if service.securing_scheme = <nil> then status = <false> else status = <true> ;
aclauthorization(service: service) status:endstatus
pre nil
post if service.repoacl_scheme = <nil> then status = <false> else status = <true> ;
managetrust(service: service) status:endstatus
pre nil
post if service.trust_scheme = <nil> then status = <false> else status = <true> ;
policyapplication(service: service) status:endstatus
pre nil
post if service.policy_choice = <nil> then status = <false> else status = <true> ;
encryptdoc(service: service) status:endstatus
pre nil
post if service.encryption = <no> then status = <false> else status = <true> ;
securecommchannel(service: service) status:endstatus
pre nil
post if service.comm_channel = <no> then status = <false> else status = <true> ;
addnonrepudiation(service: service) status:endstatus
pre nil
post if service.repudiation_scheme = <nil> then status = <false> else status = <true> ;
managesession(service: service) status:endstatus
pre nil
post if service.session_scheme = <nil> then status = <false> else status = <true> ;
end service
```

Fig. 2. Specification of service class which has the pid mapped with pid of Patient Info class

The specification stated in VDM++ in Figure 2 makes sure all the attributes of security like authentication, confidentiality, integrity and non repudiation are met by the service and returns true if not. There are two classes namely service and PatientInfo which are mapped to each other on a one – to – one basis with the help of pid attribute.Using the WS-Security Specification presented here, service end-points have a standard means for securing SOAP messages using XML Signature and XML Encryption. In this paper, in addition to usage of WS – Security for securing messages, a technique for negotiating a mutually-acceptable security policy based on WSDL is proposed. The Medi – Helper discussed in session III shows a secure architecture for transacting healthcare information over the Internet.

3   Integrated Secure Medi Helper Architecture

In this section we propose how to implement the security mechanisms and integrate the security framework into Web services in order to make Web services robust against the attacks. This framework shown in Figure 3 shows three layer architecture. They are legacy layer, integrated service layer and application layer. Legacy Layer consists of Server management system and server(s) for data storage and manipulation. These are updated to the Log Server in a standard format. It plays a vital role in making the medical history of a Patient available anywhere anytime. The role of infrastructure services renders the services for Patients like X-Ray, ECG, and ICU etc. The data obtained is transferred to the integrated services layer for creating WS Policy. Wherein, the data is synchronized by the data source. MIS component manipulates, filters the data over the data source and provides a view of the medical history of user to the Doctor. It hides the underlying complexity attributed by the Legacy Layer and provides an integrated view of the data.

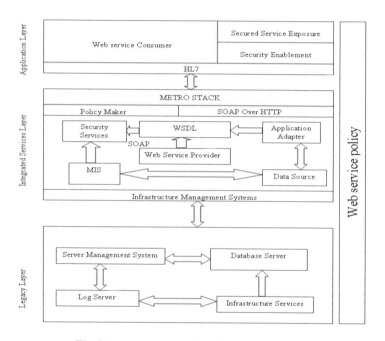

Fig. 3. Integrated Secure Web Service Architecture

The WS-Security and integrated security services that come along with METRO stack are made available to the application. The Application Adapter accesses and updates the data source for user oriented information, with configuration details on WSDL and generates the SOAP messages for the application. This Layer depicts the practical aspect of web service deployment where the messages are based on SOAP technologies, which is definitely not capable of replacing HTTP, because of its wide acceptability and usage. So it is good to extend the existing framework with SOAP messages over HTTP using METRO STACK .The METRO is the Middleware that offers the underlying technologies like WS-POLICY and WS-SECURITY. Medi – Helper uses the non–profit HL7[6] effort for healthcare systems, to manipulate to the full extent the capability of XML for a standard globally accepted messaging syntax and document structure. The security can be provided by selective policy assertion and WS – Security. Web services are being successfully used for interoperable solutions across various industries. One of the key reasons for interest and investment in Web services is that they are well-suited to enable service-oriented systems.

3.1 Middleware and Its Technologies

3.1.1 Username Authentication with Symmetric Key Mechanism

The Medi - Helper uses "Username Authentication with Symmetric Key mechanism". It protects the application for integrity and confidentiality. Symmetric key cryptography relies on a single, shared secret key that is used to both sign and encrypt a message. Symmetric keys are usually faster than public key cryptography. For this mechanism, the client does not possess any certificate/key of his own, but instead sends its username/password for authentication. The client shares a secret key with the server. The shared, symmetric key is generated at runtime and encrypted using the service's certificate. The client must specify the alias in the trust store by identifying the server's certificate alias. Using the existing AES encryption algorithm, mixing of data re-encryption is done. The following a code snippet from the security parameter configuration files used intheapplication.<xenc:EncryptionMethodAlgorithm="http://www.w3.org/2001/04/ xmlenc#aes128-cbc" />

3.1.2 WS-Security

IBM and Microsoft have begun a joint initiative to define an architecture and roadmap to address gaps between existing security standards ,Web Services and SOAP. The model serves as a means to unify formerly dissimilar security technologies such as PKI and Kerberos. The Medi – Helper uses Binary Security Token with X.509 Certificates. A security token[18] asserts claims and can be used to assert the binding between authentication secrets or keys and security identities. Message signatures are also used by message producers to demonstrate knowledge of the key, typically from a third party, used to confirm the claims in a security token and thus to bind their identity (and any other claims represented by the security token) to the messages they create.

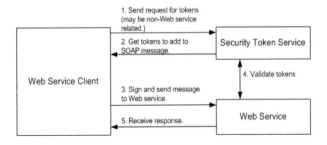

Fig. 4. WS-Security Message Flow

The Message Flow [19] of WS- Security is shown in the Figure 4. WS-Security seeks to encapsulate the security interactions described above within a set of SOAP

Headers. WS-Security handles credential management in two ways. It defines a special element, Username Token, to pass the username and password if the Web service is using custom authentication. WS-Security also provides a place to provide binary authentication tokens such as Kerberos Tickets and X.509 [18,15] Certifications: Binary Security Token. The Security Token service might be Kerberos, PKI, or a username/password validation service. When using X.509 certificates, the message can be signed using the private key. The message should contain the certificate in a Binary Security Token. When using X.509, anyone who knows the X.509 public key can verify the signature.

3.1.3 WS-Policy

WS-Policy provides a flexible and extensible grammar for expressing the capabilities, requirements, and general characteristics of entities in an XML Web services-based system [8, 15]. WS-Policy defines a framework and a model for the expression of these properties as policies. The WS-Policy and WS-Policy Attachment specifications extend this foundation and offer mechanisms to represent the capabilities and requirements of Web services as Policies.

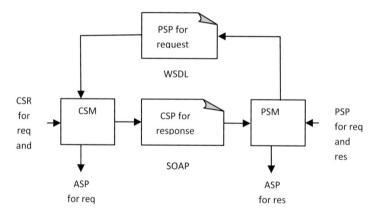

Fig. 5. Sheltered Medi - Helper Policy Assertion

```
SecureWebServiceService.xml
<wsp:Policy wsu:Id="SecureWebServicePortBindingPolicy">
<wsp:ExactlyOne>
<wsp:All>
...........
<sc:CallbackHandlerConfiguration wspp:visibility="private">
<sc:CallbackHandler default="12345" name="usernameHandler"/>
<sc:CallbackHandler default="54321" name="passwordHandler"/>
</sc:CallbackHandlerConfiguration>
</wsp:All>
</wsp:ExactlyOne>
</wsp:Policy>
```

Fig. 6. Client File Showing Ws-Policy Code for Carrying Username and Password

CSR:Consumer Security Policy for request and response; CSM:Consumer Security Manager; CSP: Consumer Security Policy for request; PSM:Provider Security Manager; SP: Provider Security Policy; ASP: Applied Security Policy; SOAP: Simple Object Access Protocol ; WSDL :Web Services Description Language;

The Medi - Helper uses the authentication oriented policies. The policies used by client and server are shown in Figure 6 and Figure 7.

```
Wsit-test.SecureWebService.xml
<wsp:Policy>
………..
<sp:X509Token
sp:IncludeToken="http://schemas.xmlsoap.org/ws/2005/07/securitypolicy/IncludeToken/
Never">
<wsp:Policy>
<sp:WssX509V3Token10/>
……………….
</wsp:Policy>
</sp:Layout>
<sp:IncludeTimestamp/>
………….
</wsp:Policy>
</sp:AlgorithmSuite>
</wsp:Policy>
……
<sp:EncryptedParts>
<sp:Body/>
</sp:EncryptedParts>
```

Fig. 7. Server Side File Showing Policy To Accept Binary Security Tokens And Encrypting Body Segment

```
<S:Body wsu:Id="_5007">
<xenc:EncryptedDataxmlns:ns17="http://docs.oasis-open.org/ws-sx/ws-
secureconversation/200512" xmlns:ns16="http://www.w3.org/2003/05/soap-envelope"
Type="http://www.w3.org/2001/04/xmlenc#Content" Id="_5008">
<xenc:EncryptionMethod Algorithm="http://www.w3.org/2001/04/xmlenc#aes128-cbc" />
<ds:KeyInfo
……..
</wsse:SecurityTokenReference>
</ds:KeyInfo>
<xenc:CipherData>
<xenc:CipherValue>
…………..
</xenc:CipherData>
</xenc:EncryptedData>
</S:Body>
```

Fig. 8. Request - SOAP Body

```
<S:Body wsu:Id="_5006">
<xenc:EncryptedData
xmlns:ns17="http://docs.oasis-open.org/ws-sx/ws-secureconversation/200512" xmlns
:ns16="http://www.w3.org/2003/05/soap-envelope" Type="http://www.w3.org/2001/04/
xmlenc#Content" Id="_5007">
<xenc:EncryptionMethod
Algorithm="http://www.w3.org/2001/04/xmlenc#aes128-cbc" />
<ds:KeyInfo xmlns:xsi="http://www.w3.org/2001/XMLSch
ema-instance" xsi:type="keyInfo"><wsse:SecurityTokenReference>
<wsse:KeyIdentifier
…………
</wsse:KeyIdentifier>
</wsse:SecurityTokenReference>
</ds:KeyInfo>
<xenc:CipherData>
………..
</xenc:CipherValue>
</xenc:CipherData>
</xenc:EncryptedData>
</S:Body>
```

Fig. 9. Response - SOAP Body

4   Results and Discussions

In Medi - Helper the web service messages are subjected to the policy check and
then are allowed to access the actual web services. The messages are encrypted for
Security purpose. The output of the web service which registers the details of the
patient is shown in Figure 10. The web service client enters the username and
password and passes the details of personal identification, disease indication and
remedial treatments undergone. The details are not visible to the onlooker of the
SOAP messages [18] since they are encrypted as shown in Figure 10. They are
only visible to the server as shown in Figure10, as printed on the server console.
The WS-POLICY code for the server and client are shown in Figure 6 and Figure
7. The client embeds the username and password information on the
SecureWebServiceService.xml file. If the entry becomes wrong the service shows
errors and is not invoked as shown in Figure 11.

The graph shown in Figure 12 shows the benefits of proposed security
framework in terms of securing the web services against several attacks. It clearly
states that, the proposed approach is providing good security by making use of
METRO – STACK and the HL7[6] document structures meant for critical services
like healthcare. The table 1 shows that the Medi – Helper uses the technologies of
XML Encryption, Signatures and WS-Security Tokens and HTTP Authentication
and its comparative study. Together they prevent against almost all attacks except
Denial of Service.

Fig. 10. The Web Service Client And Server Consoles

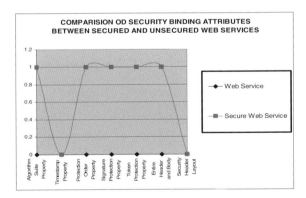

Fig. 11. Output Incurred From Wrong Username Password

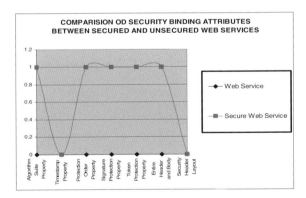

Fig. 12. Performance Analysis

5 Conclusion and Future Work

The Web Service Based Secure Medical Assistant serves as a platform for the transfer of medical documents and also ensuring confidentiality and integrity of the same data in conformance to the Security Framework. The framework is a proposal for optimal security, which may be suitable generally for any domain. It is also scalable to use any web service related technology for acquiring features like QOS and Security. The Secure Medical Assistant can be used with standards like HL7 which are created to depict medical information in terms of XML so that the documents can be interchanged in a standard manner. The service can be implemented with Third Party Authentication mechanisms like Kerberos so that we can manage large number of patient's details and in a secure manner. By incorporating the proposed technology with UDDI it is better to have a good time-stamp.

References

1. Institute of Medicine, Crossing the Quality Chasm: A New Health System for the 21st Century. National Academy Press, Washington (2001)
2. Field, M.J., Lohr, K.N.: Guidelines for Clinical Practice: From Development to Use. Institute of Medicine, National Academy Press, Washington (1992)
3. Boyer, J., et al.: Exclusive Canonicalization Version 1.0. World Wide Web Consortium (January 18, 2002), http://www.w3.org/TR/xml-exc-c14n/
4. Shiffman, R.N., Liaw, Y., Brandt, C.A., Corb, G.J.: Computer-based guideline implementation systems: A systematic review of functionality and effectiveness. J. Amer. Med. Informat. Assoc. 6(2), 104–114 (1999)
5. Entwistle, M., Shiffman, R.N.: Turning guidelines into practice: Making it happen with standards—Part. In: Healthcare and Informatics Review Online. Enigma, Auckland (March 2005)
6. http://www.hl7.org/implement/standards/index.cfm
7. Seyfang, A., Miksch, S., Marcos, M.: Combining diagnosis and treatment using Asbru. Int. J. Med. Informat. 68(1-3), 49–57 (2002)
8. Peleg, M., Ogunyemi, O., Tu, S.: Using features of Arden syntax with object-oriented medical data models for guideline modeling. In: Proc. AMIA Symp., pp. 523–527 (2001)
9. Ciccarese, P., Caffi, E., Boiocchi, L., Quaglini, S., Stefanelli, M.: A guideline management system. In: Proc. MedInfo 2004, pp. 28–32 (2004)
10. Stein, M.: Medical Education and the Internet: This Changes Everything. JAMA 285(6), 809 (2001)
11. Evenhaim, A.: Taking e-Health Relationship Management into the next Millennium. Medical Marketing and Media 36(2), 104–110 (2001)
12. Booth, D., Haas, H., McCabe, F., Newcomer, E., Champion, M., Ferris, C., Orchard, D.: Web services architecture. W3C (February 2004), http://www.w3.org/TR/ws-arch/
13. Improving Web Application Security: Threats and Countermeasures on MSDN, http://msdn.microsoft.com/library/default.asp?url=/library/en-us/dnnetsec/htmlThreatCounter.asp
14. http://msdn.microsoft.com/en-us/library/ms788756.aspx
15. Singhal, A., Winograd, T., Scarfone, K.: Guide to Secure Web Services NIST
16. Larsen, P.G.: Tutorial for Overture/VDM-SL - Overture – Open-source Tools for Formal Modelling TR-2010-01 (March 2010)
17. Gupta, D., Melissa Saul2, M., Gilbertson, J.: Evaluation of a Deidentification (De-Id) Software Engine to Share Pathology Reports and Clinical Documentsfor Research
18. http://en.wikipedia.org/wiki/Formal_specification
19. http://technet.microsoft.com/en-us/library/cc962039.aspx
20. Zhang, W.: Integrated Security Framework for Secure Web Services. In: Third International Symposium on Intelligent Information Technology and Security Informatics

Reliable Neighbor Based Multipath Multicast Routing in MANETs

Rajashekhar C. Biradar and Sunilkumar S. Manvi

Reva Institute of Technology and Management, Bangalore-560064, India
{raj.biradar,sunil.manvi}@revainstitution.org

Abstract. In this paper, we propose a scheme for multipath multicast routing in MANETs using reliable neighbor selection (MMRNS) mechanism. MMRNS operates in following phases. (1) Computation of reliability pair factor based on node power level, received differential signal strength between the nodes and mobility, and pruning neighbor nodes that have reliability pair factor lesser than a threshold. (2) Discovery of multipath multicast mesh routes with the help of request and reply packets. (3) Multipath priority assignment based on minimum value of reliability pair factor of a path and information transfer from source to multicast destination. (4) Route maintenance against link failures. The simulation results for packet delivery ratio and control overhead demonstrate the effectiveness of MMRNS scheme.

Keywords: MANET, neighbor node selection, reliability pair factor, multipath multicast routes.

1 Introduction

The reliable routing in Mobile Adhoc Networks (MANETs) must ensure that the nodes participating in route establishment and route maintenance have links with higher reliability making reliable routing protocol design as a challenging research problem in MANETs[1][2]. Link reliability of multicast routes depend upon node power, received signal strength, mobility and physical conditions. Two classes of multicast routing based on topology are tree and mesh based multicast routing protocols. Tree-based schemes establish a single path between any two nodes in the multicast group and they are bandwidth efficient. However, as mobility increases, link failures trigger the reconfiguration of the entire tree. Mesh-based schemes establish a mesh of alternate paths interconnecting the source and destinations.

Multipath routing consists of finding multiple routes between a source and destination node. In the literature, multipath routing protocols in MANETs mainly concentrate on designing redundant routes between source-destination pairs[3][4]. To provide higher reliability in routing multicast packets, multipaths with different priorities may be a better choice such that data are routed on one of the priority paths according to significance of the data (i.e., higher significant data may be sent on top priority path). The work given in [5] proposes that the

N. Meghanathan et al. (Eds.): CCSIT 2011, Part II, CCIS 132, pp. 33–43, 2011.

neighbor node stability is dependent upon link lifetime estimation where received signal strength of a node is monitored continuously using Newton Interpolation to estimate link lifetime. In [6], strength based neighbor selection procedure is implemented to test the causes for failures of routing protocol due to fading channels and unreliable network links. In [7], a QoS aware routing problem is proposed by maximizing the link stability and lifetime while minimizing the link cost. Agent based reliable ring multicast routing scheme is proposed in [8] that employs reliable ring backbone construction with the help of convex hull algorithm and multicast routes are established using the backbone. The work given in [9] uses a mesh structure, which is capable of quick recovery from mobility by utilizing node locality to reduce the overhead of route failure recovery and mesh maintenance.

In this paper, we propose a multipath multicast routing scheme that employs neighbor node pruning mechanism to establish a mesh of multipath routes based on reliability of connection.

2   Reliable Neighbor Node Selection

Reliable neighbor node selection mechanism is given in our previous work [10] and the concept is used for establishing multipath multicast routes using reliability pair. Reliability pair is defined as a set of two connected reliable nodes. Reliability pair factor (F_{RP}) defines the link connectivity status. In order to compute F_{RP}, let us assume F as the full battery capacity of a node, then remaining battery power of node i at time t ($W_i^{rem}(t)$) is given by Eq. 1.

$$W_i^{rem}(t) = W_i^{rem}(t-1) - P \times B(t-1,t) - P_I(t-1,t) \qquad (1)$$

where P is the power required to transmit a bit, $B(t-1,t)$ is the number of bits transmitted from time $t-1$ to t and $P_I(t-1,t)$ is the power required to perform node i's internal operations for the duration t to $t-1$. At $t=0$, $W_i^{rem}(t)=F$. It is assumed that $W_i^{rem}(t)$ lies in two ranges based on *Power ratio* defined by Eq. 2

$$Power\ ratio = \frac{W_i^{rem}(t)}{F}, \qquad (2)$$

such that $W_i^{rem}(t)$ of node i is either in *Low range* or in *High range*, as given in Eq. 3.

$$W_i^{rem}(t) = \begin{cases} Low\ range & if\ 0 < Power\ ratio < 0.1 \\ High\ range & if\ 0.1 < Power\ ratio \le 1 \end{cases} \qquad (3)$$

The ranges of $W_i^{rem}(t)$ of node i decides transmission power and connectivity status of reliability pair nodes. Reliability pair is augmented as follows. Let initial positions of nodes i and j have coordinate values $(x1, y1)$ and $(x2, y2)$, respectively located at a distance d meters apart. At time $T = 0$, the distance between the nodes is $d_{(ij,0)}$, and at time $T = t$, nodes move to new positions

$(x1', y1')$ and $(x2', y2')$ with new distance between them as $d_{(ij,t)}$. The successful transmission of packets between nodes i and j is defined with F_{RP} which is directly proportional to the minimum remaining battery power level of either nodes (W_i^{rem}, W_j^{rem}), differential signal strength (D_S) calculated at either node and inversely proportional to the distance between them $(d_{(ij,0)}, d_{(ij,t)})$. The F_{RP} at $T = 0$ is given by Eq. 4.

$$F_{RP} = K \frac{Min(W_i^{rem}, W_j^{rem}) + D_S}{d_{(ij,0)}} \qquad (4)$$

where K is a proportionality constant. At $T = t$, the F_{RP} is obtained by replacing $d_{(ij,0)}$ by $d_{(ij,t)}$ in Eq. 4.

3 Multipath Multicast Routing with Reliable Neighbor Selection

Multipath multicast routes are constructed using neighbor node selection method and the system operates in following phases. (1) Pruning neighbor nodes and multipath multicast mesh route discovery, (2) multipath priority assignment and information transfer and (3) route maintenance.

Initially, the node willing to initiate route set up, identifies its neighbors. The F_{RP} corresponding to each neighbor is computed using Eq. 4. We wish to establish multicast routes using non-pruned nodes that have $F_{RP} \geq F_{RP}^{Th}$. Here, F_{RP}^{Th} is the threshold of F_{RP} and is fixed by system administrator as per the application and routes are established through only non-pruned neighbors.

The components of request packet (RQ) and reply packet (RP) that are used to establish multicast routes are shown in Table 1. The components are explained.

RQ Packet details: *Source address (S_{addr}):* It is the address of source willing to set up multicast mesh route to group members. *Multicast address (MC_{addr}):* It is the group address. *Sequence number (Seq no):* It is the RQ packet number originated at source to establish a path and helps in identification of duplicate RQ packets. *Request flag (RQF):* This one bit flag identifies RQ packet. $RQF = 1$ implies RQ packet. *Path information (PT_{infm}):* This field stores node addresses a packet has visited in sequence. It stores all node addresses the packet visits while traveling from source to destination, i.e., visited node appends its address to this field at tail end of the field. $F_{RP_{min}}$: This is the minimum value of F_{RP} for a path. The field is updated (at every visited node) if previous node F_{RP} ($F_{RP_{Prevnode}}$) is less than $F_{RP_{min}}$. It helps in deciding the priority level of a path. This is updated at every visited node. *Hop count (HC):* It is set to maximum value (number of hops RQ packet can travel) by source. The value is decremented by one for every visited node. This helps in preventing orphan packets, i.e., with hop count as zero, packet is discarded and the source of the packet is informed about it.

Table 1. RQ/RP Packet details

RQ Packet		RP Packet	
Parameter	**Value**	**Parameter**	**Value**
S_{addr}	128.54.22.3	S_{addr}	128.54.22.3
MC_{addr}	228.45.63.4	MC_{addr}	Same as in RQ
		DN_{addr}	124.12.83.25
$Seq\ no$	2	$Seq\ no$	4
RQF	1	RQF	0
PT_{infm}	128.54.22.3, –,	PT_{infm}	128.54.22.3, –,
			,–, 124.12.83.25
$F_{RP_{min}}$	3.2	$F_{RP_{min}}$	2.1
HC	20	HC	11

RP Packet details: *Source address (S_{addr})*: It is the address of the source (as given in RQ packet) to which RP packet is routed from a destination. *Destination address (D_{addr})*: It is the destination address of a member in a multicast group where RP packet is generated and routed to source. *Multicast address(MC_{addr})*: It is the group address. *Sequence number ($Seq\ no$)*: Same as in RQ. This helps the source to identify RP for a RQ packet. *Request flag (RQF)*: Setting $RQF = 0$ implies RP packet. *Path information (PT_{infm})*: Same as in RQ. The sequence of addresses stored in this field are used by RP packet to route it to the source from destination node. The route traced is through the sequence of addresses starting from tail end address to front address. $F_{RP_{min}}$: This is the final value of a path brought by RQ packet at destination. For RP packet, this value is unchanged until delivered to the source. *Hop count (HC)*: This field is set at destination with total number of addresses in PT_{infm} brought by RQ packet. It is decremented at every visited node while traveling to source.

There are three types of database maintained at a node: (1) neighbor information (*NI*) to identify pruned and non-pruned neighbors, (2) temporary RQ information (*TI*) - it is created temporarily at a node to keep track of RQ packets visited at a node for multicast group. The *TI* from RQ is purged when respective RP packet visits the node and (3) routing information (*RI*) - it helps in transmitting packets through mesh of multicast routes.

The components of *NI* are shown in Table 2). It includes: F_{RP} for all neighbor nodes and a pruned node flag (*PNF*) that indicate whether the node is either pruned or non-pruned. A pruned node can not participate in routing.

Table 2. Neighbor information

Neighbor node	F_{RP}	PNF
128.45.63.4	2.8	0
128.36.23.42	1.1	1
129.0.0.99	3.1	0
128.34.45.95	2.3	0
–	–	–

Table 3. Temporary information

MC_{group}	$Seq\ no$	PT_{infm}
128.45.63.4	5	128.45.63.4, $-$, $-$, $-$, 124.12.83.25
128.36.23.42	8	128.45.63.4, $-$, $-$, $-$, 132.53.21.102
$-$	$-$	$-$

The components of TI are shown in Table 3). They are: MC_{group} - multicast group address, $Seq\ no$ - sequence number and PT_{infm} - path information. Entries in Table 3 are updated at every node for each received RQ packet. This information is purged when RP packet corresponding to RQ packet is received at the node. Components of routing information (RI) at a node are shown in Table 4. It includes: MC_{group} - multicast group address, DN_{addr} - multicast destination address, $Next\ hop$ - address of next hop for forwarding data packet, DN - destination node, $F_{RP_{min}}$ - the minimum F_{RP} value of a path and Normalized priority ($P_{DN}^{(N,i)}$) - the normalized priority of ith next hop at node N for a DN.

And they utilize only one among those redundant routes at any given time to transmit the data.

Table 4. Routing information

MC_{group}	DN_{addr}	**Next hop**	$F_{RP_{min}}$	**Normalized** priority ($P_{DN}^{(N,i)}$)
224.12.83.0	138.33.0.6	138.33.0.6	2.6	0.68
		138.33.0.6	3.8	1.0
		182.0.56.7	1.9	0.5
	129.0.0.99	129.0.0.99	1.8	0.85
		128.34.45.95	2.1	1.0
$-$	$-$	$-$	$-$	$-$

In request phase, every node identifies its non-pruned neighbors using F_{RP} in NI and broadcasts RQ packet until either it reaches the other end of the network or hop count is zero. While traversing from source, RQ packet is appended with address of visited node in PT_{infm} at tail end of RQ packet and $F_{RP_{min}}$ of path is updated. For every RQ visited at a node, TI components are updated to keep track of duplicate packets and path information. The processing of request packet is shown in Algorithm 1. Nomenclature used in algorithm 1 are as follows. $F_{RP_{min}}$ = path F_{RP}, PT_{infm} = path information, S = source node, NPn = non-pruned node, $Prevnode$ = previous node from where RQ arrived, TI = temporary information, MC_{group}= multicast group address, NPn_{addr}= address of NPn, DUP = duplicate packet, $F_{RP_{Prevnode}}$= F_{RP} with previous node from where RQ arrived and HC = hop count.

Essentially, Algorithm 1 uses RQ packets to compute mesh of multicast paths to all group members in a network from source. By the time RQ packet reaches

---

Algorithm 1. Processing of RQ packet at a node

1: **Begin**
2: Initialize $F_{RP_{min}} = 100$, $PT_{infm}[\ ] = [S, --, --,]$ and other fields of RQ at S;
3: S broadcasts RQ to non-pruned neighbors;
4: **for** Every RQ arrived at NPn **do**
5:     **if** There are no neighbors to NPn except $Prevnode$ **then**
6:         Goto line 30;
7:     **else**
8:         Update TI for MC_{group};
9:         Compare MC_{group} in RQ with MC_{group} of NPn_{addr};
10:        **if** MC_{group} in RQ$\neq MC_{group}$ of NPn_{addr} **then**
11:            **if** $[RQ \neq DUP\ ]\vee[(RQ == DUP)\wedge$ (has different PT_{infm})] **then**
12:                $HC = HC - 1$;
13:                **if** $HC > 0$ **then**
14:                    **if** $F_{RP_{Prevnode}} < F_{RP_{min}}$ of RQ **then**
15:                        $F_{RP_{min}} = F_{RP_{Prevnode}}$;
16:                    **end if**
17:                    Append NPn_{addr} to $PT_{infm}[\ ]$ in RQ;
18:                    Rebroadcast RQ to non-pruned neighbors;
19:                **else**
20:                    Discard RQ and goto line 30;
21:                **end if**
22:            **else**
23:                Discard RQ and goto line 30;
24:            **end if**
25:        **else**
26:            Repeat steps 11 to 24; CALL Algorithm 2;
27:        **end if**
28:    **end if**
29: **end for**
30: **End**

---

destination, individual route information such as PT_{infm} and $F_{RP_{min}}$ are available. During request phase, if a node does not find its non-pruned neighbors (due node and link failures), RQ packet is not re-broadcasted.

In reply phase, RP packet is generated at each multicast destination and it is routed to S through the path defined in PT_{infm} brought by RQ packet. At every visited node, RI is updated by RP packet for DN, $Next\ hop$ (using path information) and $F_{RP_{min}}$ components. For RP packet traveling from destination to source, RP packet updates $Next\ hop$ by node address $PT_{infm}[HC]$. Visited node purges its TI for corresponding RP packet (based on sequence number of RQ and RP packets).

The processing of RP packet at a node is shown in algorithm 2. Nomenclature used in the algorithm 2 are as follows. $DN=$ destination node, $MC_{group} =$ multicast group address, and $DN_{addr} =$ address of DN.

In reply phase, if a node does not find its next hop due to node or link failure, RP packet is made to wait for some time at the visited node and after timeout,

---

Algorithm 2. Processing of RP packet at a node

1: **Begin**
2: Generate RP packet using received RQ packet at DN;
3: Initialize $HC \leftarrow$ number of addresses in PT_{infm}, $RQF \leftarrow 0$, $DN_{addr} \leftarrow$ node
    address generating RP packet, and other fields same as in received RQ packet;
4: **for** $HC > 0$ **do**
5:     $HC = HC - 1$;
6:     Purge TI for MC_{group} in the node;
7:     Update RI;
8:     **if** $PT_{infm}[HC] \neq S$ **then**
9:         Transmit RP to node at addr $PT_{infm}[HC]$;
10:    **else**
11:        Deliver RP to S and goto line 14;
12:    **end if**
13: **end for**
14: **End**

---

it can be resent. If a node does not find next hop even after timeout, RP packet is dropped and informed to destination who generated the RP packet. However, nodes are fairly stable in the path and thus RP packet dropping rate may be low because reliable nodes are selected.

3.1 Multipath Priority Assignment and Information Transfer

After receiving RP packet from each multicast destination, source assigns priority to all multiple paths to a destination. Sequence of operations performed by source are as follows: (a) receive RP packets from all destinations, (b) assign normalized priority to multiple paths based on $F_{RP_{min}}$ brought by RP packets, (c) segregate information to be transmitted to multicast destinations into different streams and assign the priority level to each stream and (d) transmit high priority information on high priority path and subsequent priority information on next priority paths.

The normalized priority of ith next hop of a node N for a destination DN is computed as, $P_{DN}^{(N,i)} = \frac{F_{RP_{min}}^{(N,i)}}{F_{RP_{min}}^{(N,H)}}$, where $0 < P_{DN}^{(N,i)} < 1$. $F_{RP_{min}}^{(N,i)}$ is $F_{RP_{min}}$ of ith next hop of a node N and $F_{RP_{min}}^{(N,H)}$ is highest $F_{RP_{min}}$ of all next hop nodes of node N.

Figure 1 shows an arbitrary network topology with three multicast destinations ($D1$, $D2$ and $D3$) and one source (S). In Figure 1, there are two paths from S to $D3$: the first priority path being $[S - 1 - 2 - D3]$ and the second priority path being $[S - 1 - 6 - 5 - 4 - D3]$. Likewise, there are two paths to $D2$ from S with first priority path as $[S - 1 - 2 - 10 - 24 - D2]$ and second priority path as $[S - 7 - 8 - 9 - 18 - 17 - D2]$. Since there are two paths to each destination $D2$ and $D3$, the source segregates data into two priority levels $P1$ (high priority) and $P2$ (next priority) and transmits the streams in following manner.

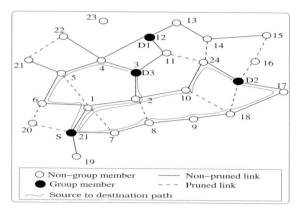

Fig. 1. Multipath multicast routes

The multicast routing scheme balances various streams on different priority paths (mesh routes) so as to reduce the burden on a single route. As the number of multiple paths to a destination increase, the route reliability increases since different streams flow on different priority paths.

3.2   Route Maintenance

Due to node mobility and node/link failure, a link may be unavailable. This situation can be handled by either of the following mechanisms: (1) local recovery of failed link through non-pruned neighbor nodes and (2) entire reconstruction of routes. Whenever a link fails on a path from source to destination, the failed link divides the path into two segments: one segment is from source to the source side node of a failed link and the other segment is from receiver to the receiver side node of a failed link.

In local recovery mechanism, RQ packet is generated by the source side node of a failed link using source address as its own address and destination address as the receiver side node of a failed link. Route discovery takes place as explained in section 3 to patch-up the path between nodes of a failed link. However, the receiver side node generates only one RP packet needed to patch-up the failed link. If many links fail simultaneously, mesh routes are reconstructed from source to destination since local recovery overhead will be more than overhead of reconstruction of routes.

Whenever a new node wishes to join multicast group, it uses RQ and RP packets to join to multicast group using its non-pruned neighbors existing on multipath. Whenever a node is willing to leave the group, it simply does not respond to any control messages (RQ/RP packets) and its neighbor nodes remove this node from their list when the network is refreshed.

4   Simulation Model

The routing scheme is simulated in various network scenarios to assess the performance and effectiveness of the approach. Simulation environment for the proposed work consists of five models: (1) *Network model*: An ad hoc network is generated in an area of $l \times b$ square meters. It consists of N number of mobile nodes that are placed randomly in an area. Every node sets F_{RP}^{Th}, (2) *Power model*: Every node is assumed to have its remaining battery power in two randomly distributed ranges, *Low range* and *High range*. A node has full battery power, F. P is the power required to transmit a bit and P_I is the power required to perform node's internal operations. Differential received signal strength D_S is randomly distributed. *Propagation model*: Free space propagation model is used with propagation constant β. Transmission range of a node is r for a one-hop distance. *Mobility model*: Random way-point (RWP) mobility model based upon three parameters is used where speed of movement, direction and time of mobility. In RWP, each node picks a random destination within a geographical area, and travels with a speed v whose values are decided by initial velocity v^s and final velocity v^f. Node pause time at destination is Z. Eight directions are considered for node movement: east, west, north, south, north-east, north-west, south-east and south-west and *Traffic model*: A multicast group may comprises of M members. Constant bit rate model is used to transmit constant sized packets, Tr_{pkts}. Coverage area around each node has a bandwidth, $BW_{single-hop}$, shared among its neighbors.

4.1 Simulation Procedure

The proposed scheme is simulated using following simulation inputs. $l = 450$ meters, $b = 460$ meters, $N = 50$ to 200. $F_{RP}^{Th} = 1.2$, *Low range* $=0$ to 100mW, *High range* $=100$mW to 1000mW, $D_S =10$nW to 100nW, $F = 1000mW$, $P = 10nW$, $P_I = 20nW$. $\beta = 2.5$, $r = 350$ meters, $v^s = 0m/s$, $v^f = 24m/s$, $Z = 0.1ms$, $M= 5$ to 25, $Tr_{pkts} =$ in multiples of 1000, $BW_{single-hop} = 20Mbps$.

The following performance parameters are assessed. *Packet delivery ratio (PDR)*: It is defined as the average of ratio of packets received to the number of packets sent from a sender at the receivers. *Control overhead*: It is defined as number of control packets (RQ/RP packets) needed to establish routes to all destinations from a source. *Memory overhead*: It is the total number of bytes to be stored in node database (RI and NI) to establish and maintain the routes for a multicast group.

5 Results

The analysis of performance parameters are given in this section.

Figure 2 shows three types of results, namely, the effect of group size on PDR for various mobility patterns, control overhead with increase in number of nodes and memory overhead for 50 and 100 node topology at discrete simulation time.

For static pattern of nodes (no mobility), PDR is fairly high compared to mobility of 5 m/s and 10 m/s. The fall in PDR is due to change of non-pruned node's pattern under mobility condition, thus creating different set of end-to-end multipaths.

For given number of nodes, the control overhead (control packets) increase with increase in group size. As network size increases (beyond 150 nodes), the control overhead decreases at higher multicast group sizes due to the possibility of establishing multiple paths by many number of same non-pruned nodes to receivers since these non-pruned nodes happen to be on the path for all those receivers. and they utilize only one among those redundant routes at any given time to transmit the data.

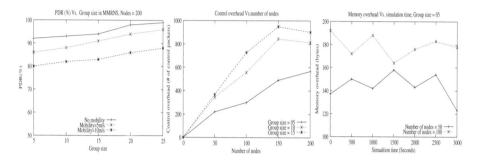

Fig. 2. Results for PDR, control overhead and memory overhead

The memory overhead in 100 node topology is more than that of 50 node topology. As the number of nodes increase, there are chances that more number of neighbors satisfy F_{RP}^{Th} condition and there are more entries in node database increasing the memory overhead.

6 Conclusions

In this paper, we proposed a scheme for multipath multicast routing in MANETs that used reliable neighbor node selection mechanism. Neighbor nodes are selected that satisfy certain threshold of reliability pair factor to find non-pruned neighbors. Non-pruned neighbors are used to establish reliable multipath multicast routes with assigned priority levels using request and reply control packets along with node database comprising of neighbor and routing information. Prioritized multipaths carry various priority data to multicast destinations. Robust route maintenance mechanism is provided to handle link and node failure situations. The results of simulation for packet delivery ratio, control and memory overheads illustrate the effectiveness of the scheme.

Acknowledgements

Authors thank Visvesvaraya Technological University (VTU), Karnataka, INDIA, for funding the part of the project under VTU Research Scheme (Grant No. VTU/Aca./2009-10/A-9/11624, Dated: 4 Jan. 2010).

References

1. Junhai, L., Danxia, Y., Liu, X., Mingyu, F.: A Survey of multicast routing protocols for mobile ad-hoc networks. IEEE Communications Surveys and Tutorials 11(1), 78–91 (2009)
2. Torkestania, J.A., Meybodib, M.R.: Mobility-based multicast routing algorithm for wireless mobile Ad-hoc networks: a learning automata approach. Computer Communications 33(6), 721–735 (2010)
3. Mueller, S., Tsang, R.P., Ghosal, D.: Multipath routing in mobile ad hoc networks: issues and challenges. In: Calzarossa, M.C., Gelenbe, E. (eds.) MASCOTS 2003. LNCS, vol. 2965, pp. 209–234. Springer, Heidelberg (2004)
4. Sarma, N., Nandi, S.: A route stability based multipath qos routing (SMQR) in MANETs. In: First International Conference on Emerging Trends in Engineering and Technology (ICETET), Nagpur, India, pp. 193–198 (2008)
5. Wu, D.-p., Wu, M.-q., Zhen, Y.: Reliable routing mechanism based on neighbor stability for MANET. The Journal of China Universities of Posts and Telecommunications 16(3), 33–39 (2009)
6. Chin, K.-W., Judge, J., Williams, A., Kermode, R.: Implementation experience with manet routing protocols. ACM SIGCOMM Computer Communications Review 32(5), 49–59 (2002)
7. Mamun-Or-Rashid M., Hong, C.S.: LSLP: link stability and lifetime prediction based qos aware routing for MANET. In: Joint Conference on Communications and Information, JCCI (2007)
8. Biradar, R.C., Manvi, S.S.: Reliable ring based multicast routing scheme in MANET: an agent based approach. In: Proc. IEEE Conference on Automation Science and Engineering (IEEE CASE), Bangalore, India, pp. 507–512 (2009)
9. Lee, S., Kim, C.: Neighbor supporting ad hoc multicast routing protocol. In: Proceedings of the 1st ACM International Symposium on Mobile Ad Hoc Networking and Computing, pp. 37–44 (2000)
10. Biradar, R.C., Manvi, S.S.: Channel condition and mobility based choice of neighbor node for routing in MANET. In: International Conference on Advances in Computer Engineering (ACE), Bangalore, India, June 21-22, pp. 74–78 (2010)

Ad-Hoc On Demand Distance Vector Routing Algorithm Using Neighbor Matrix Method in Static Ad-Hoc Networks

Aitha Nagaraju[1], G. Charan Kumar[2], and S. Ramachandram[3]

[1,2] Vaagdevi Collage of Engineering, Warangal, A.P, India
[3] Osmania University, Hyderabad, A.P, India

Abstract. The existing Ad-Hoc On demand Routing Protocol (AODV) for MANETs is more suitable for highly dynamic networks, but in generally ad-hoc networks many of the situations topology changes slowly. In this scenario finding the shortest path using AODV making use of RREQ and RREP is quite over head and consumes much of the existing bandwidth. In this paper we have proposed neighbor matrix approach to find the shortest path in static Ad-hoc Networks. In the proposed approach whenever a node wants to find path to the destination it evaluate the neighbour matrix of the existing ad-hoc network which is helpful in finding the path to the destination using incremental neighbour searching till the destination has reached. This approach avoids the frequently sending Route Request Phase of existing AODV reactive routing protocol for MANETs. The Proposed algorithm uses the neighbour matrix more effectively and evaluates the path.

Keywords: AODV, Neighbor Matrix, Ad-Hoc Networks.

1 Introduction

Now-a-Days MANETs [2] play a key role in the society because of rapid increasing in the mobile devices. The users need the services on demand manner. One of the special types of the Ad-Hoc Network is static ad-hoc network in which node pause time is considerably large. The existing routing algorithms in the literature such as AODV [4], DSR [10] and TORA [11] are designed for highly dynamic networks. But in many of the situations structure of the network is varying very slowly. So the researchers have been introduced several mechanisms to provide the services to the existing mobile users [8]. In this project we have made an attempt to improve the efficiency of existing routing algorithms for MANETs such as AODV, DSR and TORA. In the literature many researchers made an attempt to the same. But they have tried to reduce the existing redundant broadcasting in MANETs. In this paper we made an attempt to use the proactive and reactive concepts integrated to reduce the redundant broadcasting [12,13,14].

2 Related Work

The limited resources in MANETs have made designing of an efficient and reliable routing strategy a very challenging problem. An intelligent routing strategy is

N. Meghanathan et al. (Eds.): CCSIT 2011, Part II, CCIS 132, pp. 44–54, 2011.

required to efficiently [9] use the limited resources while at the same time being adaptable to the changing network conditions such as: network size, density and network partitioning. In parallel with this, the routing protocol may need to provide different levels of QoS to different types of applications and users. Prior to the increased interests in wireless networking, in wired networks two main algorithms were used. These algorithms are commonly referred to as the link-state and distance vector algorithms. In link-state routing, each node maintains an up-to-date view of the network by periodically broadcasting the link-state costs of its neighboring nodes to all other nodes using a flooding strategy. When each node receives an up-date packet, they update their view of the network and their link-state information by applying a shortest-path algorithm to choose the next hop node for each destination.

The distance vector information is updated at each node by a periodical dissemination of the current estimate of the shortest distance to every node. The traditional link-state and distance vector algorithm do not scale in large MANETs. This is because periodic or frequent route updates in large networks may consume significant part of the available bandwidth, increase channel contention and may require each node to frequently recharge their power supply. To overcome these problems associated with the link-state and distance-vector algorithms [5] a number of routing protocols have been proposed for MANETs.

These protocols can be classified into three different groups: global/proactive, on-demand/reactive and hybrid. In proactive routing protocols, the routes to all the destination (or parts of the network) are determined at the start up, and maintained by using a periodic route update pro-cess. In reactive protocols, routes are determined when they are required by the source using a route discovery process. Hybrid routing protocols combine the basic properties of the first two classes of protocols into one. That is, they are both reactive and proactive in nature. Each group has a number of different routing strategies, which employ a flat or a hierarchical routing structure.

3   Description of AODV

The AODV algorithm is inspired from the Bellman-Ford algorithm like DSDV [3]. The principal change is to be On Demand. The node will be silent while it does not have data to send. Then, if the upper layer is requesting a route for a packet, a "ROUTE REQUEST" packet will be sent to the direct neighbourhood.

If a neighbor has a route corresponding to the request, a packet "ROUTE REPLY" will be returned. This packet is like a "use me" answer. Otherwise, each neighbour will forward the "ROUTE REQUEST" to their own neighborhood, except for the originator and increment the hop value in the packet data. They also use this packet for building a reverse route entry (to the originator). This process occurs until a route has been found. Another part of this algorithm is the route maintenance. While a neighbour is no longer available, if it was a hop for a route, this route is not valid any more.

AODV uses "HELLO" packets on a regular basis to check if they are active neighbours. Active neighbours are the ones used during a previous route discovery process. If there is no response to the "HELLO" packet sent to a node, then, the originator deletes all associated routes in its routing table. "HELLO" packets are similar to ping requests. While transmitting, if a link is broken (a station did not receive acknowledgment from the layer 2), a "ROUTE ERROR" packet is unicast to all previous forwarders and to the sender of the packet.

3.1 Routing Tables

Each routing table entry contains the following information:

- Destination Address
- Next hop Address
- Number of hops
- Destination sequence number
- Active neighbours for this route
- Expiration time for this route table entry

Expiration time also called lifetime, is reset each time the route has been used. The new expiration time is the sum of the current time and a parameter called active route timeout. This parameter, also called route caching timeout, is the time after which the route is considered as invalid, and so the nodes not lying on the route determined by RREPs delete their reverse entries. If active route timeout is big enough route repairs will maintain routes.

3.2 Route Request

When a route is not available for the destination, a route request packet (RREQ) is flooded throughout the network. Table 1 RREQ contains fields the request ID is incremented each time the source node sends a new RREQ, so the pair (source address, request ID) identifies a RREQ uniquely. On receiving a RREQ message each node checks the source address and the request ID. If the node has already received a RREQ with the same pair of parameters the new RREQ packet will be discarded. Otherwise the RREQ will be either forwarded (broadcast) or replied (unicast) with a RREP message:

Table 1. RREQ contains fields

Source Address	Request ID	source sequence No.	destination address	destination sequence No.	hop count

If the node has no route entry for the destination or it has one but this is no more an up-to-date route, the RREQ will be re broadcasted with incremented hop count. If the node has a route with a sequence number greater than or equal to that of RREQ, a RREP message will be generated and sent back to the source. The number of RREQ messages that a node can send per second is limited. There is an optimization of AODV using an expanding ring (ESR) [7] technique when flooding RREQ messages.

Every RREQ carries a time to live (TTL) value that specifies the number of times this message should be rebroadcast. This value is set to a predefined value at the first transmission and increased at retransmissions. Retransmissions occur if no replies are received. Historically such floodings used a TTL large enough – larger than the diameter of the network - to reach all nodes in the network, and so to guarantee successful route discovery in only one round of flooding. However, this low delay time approach causes high overhead and unnecessary broadcast messages. Later, it was shown that the minimal cost flooding search problem can be solved via a sequence of floodings with an optimally chosen set of TTLs.

3.3 Route Replay

If a node is the destination, or has a valid route to the destination, it unicasts a route reply message (RREP) back to the source. This message has the following format Source destination destination hop life- Address Address sequence No. count time.

Table 2. RREP fields

Source	destination	destination	hop	life-
Address	address	sequence No.	count	time

The reason one can unicast RREP back is that every node forwarding a RREQ mes-sage caches a route back to the source node.

3.4 Route Error

All nodes monitor their own neighbourhood. When a node in an active route gets lost, a route error message (RERR) is generated to notify the other nodes on both sides of the link of the loss of this link.

3.5 Neighbor Matrix Approach in RREQ

In the existing routing protocol AODV consisting of three phases which are called RREQ, RREP and RERR. AODV protocol to find the path if it is not established previously in route table. But it is going to consume more battery power during RREQ process to each and every of its neighbor node. In this paper we are going to present a new approach to find a path using a neighbor matrix which is calculated at source node. The Fig 1 shows the evaluation of neighbor matrix evaluation. Source node using this matrix and evaluates the path to the destination node which is shown in Fig 2.

48   A. Nagaraju, G. Charan Kumar, and S. Ramachandram

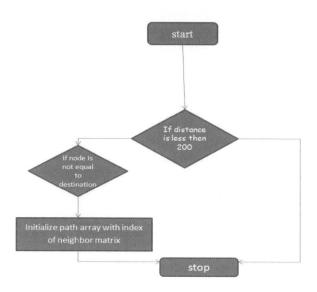

Fig. 2. Finding Path from Source to Destination

3.5.1 Neighbor Matrix Evaluation

In this neighbor matrix approach we are going to find the distance between each and every node if the node is between the vicinity then neighbor matrix is initialized with value '1' if not '0' and by using this neighbor matrix we are going to find the path to destination.

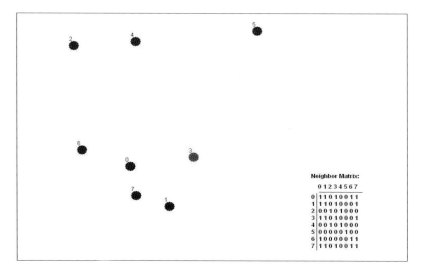

Fig. 3. Neighbour Matrix example

In the above example (figure 3) we have shown the neighbor matrix for each and every node. In this if any two nodes has the distance as less than 200 then we have initialized the neighbor matrix with its corresponding index as '1' if the distance is greater then 200 then it is initialized as '0'. In the above example the distance between the nodes 1 and 7 is less then 200 so the 1st row and 7th column in the matrix is initialized as 1. In the similar way 1-0, 1-3, 2-4 etc rows and columns are initialized with 1's and 0's and these values are going to be used in path discovery process for AODV protocol which is going to save much energy with out sending route request to each and every neighbor node.

3.5.2 Path Finding Using Bellman Ford Algorithm [1]

BellmanFord (v, cost, dist, n)

{

for i:=1 **to** n **do**

dist[i]:= cost[v,i]; // initialize dist

for k:=2 to n-1 **do**

for each u such that u != v and u has atleast one

incoming edge **do**

for each <i,u> in the graph **do**

if dist[u]>dist[i]+cost[i,u] **then**

dist[u]:=dist[i] +cost[i,u];

else

return

}

3.5.3 Path Finding Using Neighbor Matrix Using Various Metrics

In this paper we are going to find the best path according to battery power consumption. In this we are going to choose the path which consumes less battery power comparing to all the paths which we have. So that we are going to save energy with out sending RREQ to all neighbor nodes. In the similar way we can go for different approaches such as path which consumes less time and etc. So that the energy consumption for the path discovery process will be saved to much extent and an efficient path will be discovered from source node to destination node.

4 Implementation Details

Classes used:

Class node

{

}

Usage: This is the class used to create a node and where each node will have the data values which differ from each and every node. It consists of a constructor to initialize the data values for each and every node

Class SampleFrame

{

}

Usage: This class is used to create a frame where the nodes are created and moved according to time factor.

Data Members used:

Node ID: It stores the ID of each and every node

Battery power: It stores the battery power of each and every node.

Speed: It stores the speed of each and every node.

Time: It stores the time period of each and every node.

cordX : It stores the X-Coordinate of each and every node.

cordY : It stores the Y-Coordinate of each and every node.

5   Results

We have implemented neighbor matrix approach using applets in java language the following table shows the simulation parameters used in the simulation. Fig 4 to Fig 8 shows the results of the simulation in GUI format.

Simulation Parameters:

Table 3. Simulation Parameters

Simulation area	1000 X 1000
Number of nodes	12
Simulation Time	∞
Source Node	2
Destination Node	4
Pause time	Randomly allot each node by the simulator
Battery Power	Randomly allot each node by the simulator
Node velocity	Randomly allot each node by the simulator
Bandwidth	Randomly allot each node by the simulator

Applet window with empty fields:

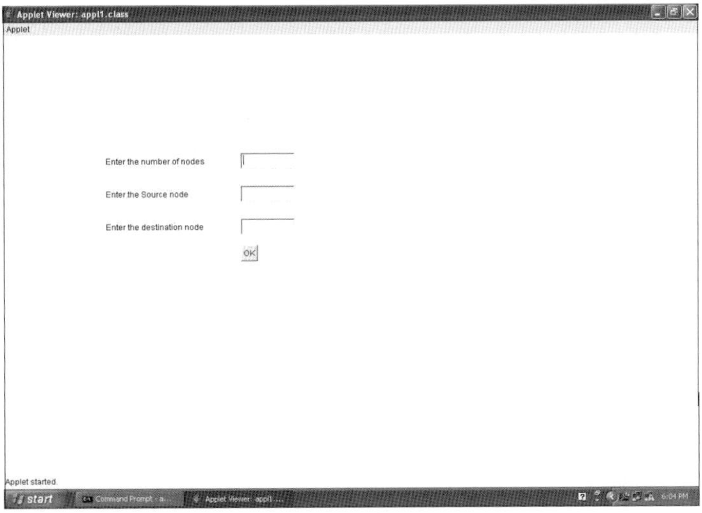

Fig. 4. Opening applet window to enter the input

Applet window with entered fields:

Fig. 5. Filled fields of applet window

Frame window showing links:

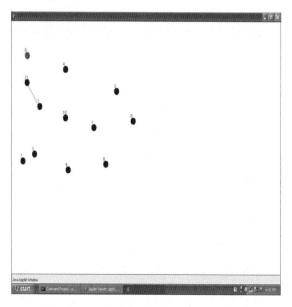

Fig. 6. Created nodes and link a between nodes in frame window

Frame window showing links:

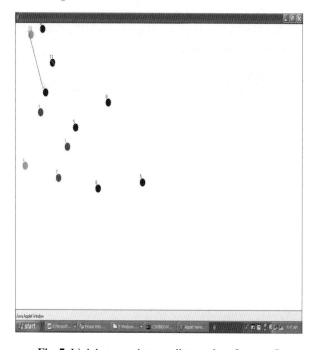

Fig. 7. Link between intermediate nodes of source 5

Command prompt with result:

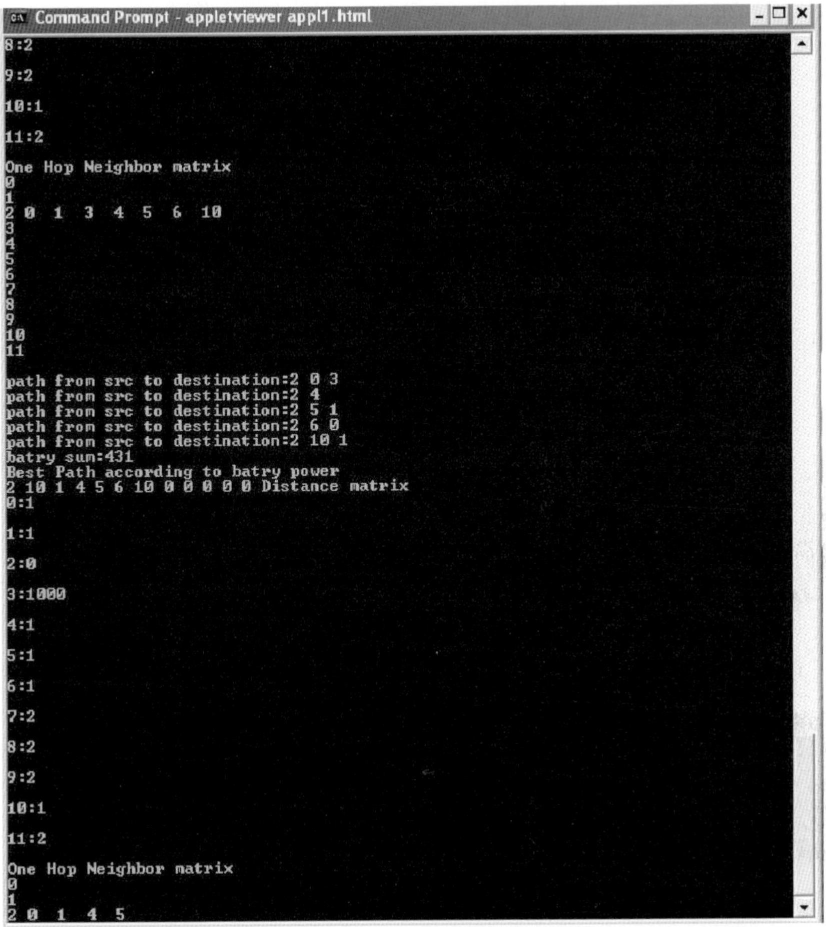

Fig. 8. Showing one hop matrix, path from source and destination and best path in command prompt

6 Conclusions and Future Scope of the Work

In this paper we have implemented neighbor matrix approach to existing AODV routing protocol for static MANETs. We simulated the proposed approach using java applet concepts. We designed an applet to create the simulation environment. Nodes are randomly placed and we allowed the movement of the nodes. In this project we consider the functionalities network layer and we assumed the remaining layers in TCP/IP are ideal. It means except network layer all the other layers are ideal.

References

[1] Tanenbaum, A.S.: Computer Networks. 3 edn.
[2] Schiller, J.H.: Mobile Communications, mobile network layer
[3] Perkins, C.E., Bhagawat, P.: Highly dynamic Destination Sequnced Distance- Vector routing (DSDV) for mobile computers. In: Proceedings of the Conference on Communications Architectures, Protocols and Applications. ACM Press, London (October 1994)
[4] Perkins, C.E., Royer, E.M.: Ad Hoc On-Demand Distance Vector Routing. In: Precedings of the 2nd IEEE Workshop on Mobile Computing Systems and Applications (February 1999)
[5] Royer, E.M., Toh, C.-K.: A Review of Current Routing Protocols for Ad Hoc Mobile Wireless Networks. IEEE Personal Communications
[6] Maltz, D.A.: On-Demand Routing in Multi-hop Wireless Mobile Ad Hoc Networks. A research report sponsored by NSF under CAREER Award NCR
[7] Kumar, M., Ramamurthy, S.: Mobile Communications, 2nd edn. Pearson Education, Inc., Dorling Kindersly (2008)
[8] Nagaraju, A., Ramachandram, S.: Rough Set Based Adhoc On demand Routing Algorithm for MANETs. In: Procedings of ACM Banglore Chapter Compute 2009 (2009)
[9] Ali, H.A., Saleh, M.S., Sadik, M.A.: An Efficient Reliable Broadcast Algorithm in Ad-hoc Networks Based On Self-Pruning. The Journal of IJICS 5(1) (July 2005)
[10] Johnson, D.B., et al.: The dynamic source routing protocol for mobile ad-Hoc networks, Internet Draft (1999), http://www.ietf.org/internetdrafts/draftietf-manet-dsr-02.txt
[11] Park, V.D., Corson, M.S.: Temporally-Ordered Routing Algorithm (TORA) Version 1: Fundamental Specification. Internet Draft (1997)
[12] Wu, J., Li, H.: On Calculating Connected Dominating Sets for Efficient Routing in Ad Hoc Wireless Networks. In: Proc., ACM Int'l Workshop Discrete Algorithms and Methods for Mobile Computing 1999, pp. 7–14 (August 1999)
[13] Nagaraju, A., Ramachandram, S.: Rough Set Based Ad-hoc On demand Routing Algorithm for MANETs. In: Procedings of ACM Banglore Chapter Compute 2009 (2009)
[14] Nagaraju, A., Ramachandram, S.: Adaptive Pritial Dominating Pruning Algorithm for MANETs. In: Proceedings of ACM Bangalore Chapter Compute 2009 (2009)

Improving QoS for Ad-Hoc Wireless Networks Using Predictive Preemptive Local Route Repair Strategy

G.S. Sharvani, T.M. Rangaswamy, Aayush Goel, B. Ajith,
Binod Kumar, and Manish Kumar

Computer Science and Engineering,
RV College of Engineering, Bangalore, India
sharvanim@yahoo.com, dr.tmrswamy@rediffmail.com,
aayush_rv@yahoo.co.in, ajithmdh@gamil.com,
vinod.tiwary@gmail.com, manishrvce1173@gmail.com

Abstract. Ad-hoc wireless networks comprise of sets of nodes connected by wireless links that form arbitrary wireless network topologies without the use of any centralized access point. Ad-hoc wireless networks are inherently self-creating, self-organizing and self-administering. The proposed model is designed to alleviate the impediments to real-time event-based communication that are characteristics of an ad-hoc wireless environment, for example, dynamic connectivity, unpredictable latency and link failures and limited resources and it improves the performance of the routing process significantly and increases the Quality of Service (QoS). It can reduce communication overhead (by avoiding unnecessary warning messages), decrease the number of breaks in active links (by prior prediction), reduce end-to-end packet delays, and improve packet delivery ratio (by segmentation of packets).

Keywords: Ad-Hoc Wireless Networks, QoS, Lagrange Interpolation, power, predictive preemptive approach.

1 Introduction

A wireless ad-hoc network is a self-configuring network of routers connected by wireless links – the union of which forms an arbitrary topology. The nodes are free to move randomly and organize themselves arbitrarily. Thus the network's topology may change rapidly and unpredictably. These kinds of networks are very flexible and they do not require any existing infrastructure or central administration and are suitable for temporary communication links. The biggest challenge in these kinds of networks is to find a path between the communication end points of nodes that are mobile. Due to the limited transmission range of wireless interfaces, the communication traffic has to be relayed over several intermediate nodes to enable the communication between two nodes. Therefore, these kinds of networks are also called multi-hop ad-hoc networks. Every node acts as both, a host and as a router. Another limitation associated with wireless devices is the power constraint of the

N. Meghanathan et al. (Eds.): CCSIT 2011, Part II, CCIS 132, pp. 55–62, 2011.

nodes i.e. each node has only limited battery power which should be used judiciously for the node to survive longer and to provide its services within the network.

Nodes cooperate with their neighbors to route data packets to their final destinations. As intermediate nodes may fail, routes between sources and destinations need to be determined and adjusted dynamically. Routing protocols for ad-hoc networks typically include mechanisms for route discovery and route maintenance.

The route discovery mechanism is invoked to determine a route between a sender and a receiver.

The performance of these protocols depends on the route maintenance mechanism they use. Schemes that use Global Positioning System (GPS) information for detecting and handling expected link failures early have been proposed [1], [2], and [3].A node on a route from a source to a destination may become unreachable from its predecessor node because of node movement or node failure. In this paper, route maintenance is initiated when a link break is expected rather than waiting for the break to happen. The route maintenance mechanism finds new valid routes as substitutes for broken active routes. Several approaches to route maintenance have been proposed. In this paper, a predictive preemptive local route repair strategy is used. Its aim is to find an alternative path before the cost of a link failure is incurred. A link is considered likely to break when the power of either of the nodes that it connects is close to the minimum detectable power. Route repair (finding sub-path to the destination) is the responsibility of a source node after receiving a warning about the imminence of a link break on an active route to a destination.

Quality of Service (QoS) is the performance level of a service offered by the network to the user. It is the collective set of service performance which determines the degree of satisfaction of the user of the service. Providing QoS in MANETs is a challenging and difficult task where nodes may leave or join the network and move around dynamically. Our approach aims to improve the QoS by predicting a link failure before its occurrence thereby routing packets through an alternative path.

Applications and Challenges

Commercial scenarios [4] for ad-hoc wireless networks include:

- Conferences/meetings/lectures
- Emergency services
- Law enforcements

Current challenges for ad-hoc wireless networks include:

- Multicast
- QoS support
- Power-aware routing
- Location-aided routing

2 Major Challenges In Ad-Hoc Wireless Networks

Major challenges [5] in ad-hoc wireless networks are:

1. Mobility: One of the most important properties of ad-hoc wireless networks is the mobility associated with the nodes. The mobility of nodes results in frequent path breaks, packet collisions, transient loops, stale routing information and difficulty in resource reservation.
2. Bandwidth constraint: Since the channel is shared by all nodes in the broadcast region, the bandwidth available per wireless link depend on the number of nodes and traffic they handle.
3. Error-prone and shared channel: The bit error rate (BER) in a wireless channel is very high, compared to that in its wired counterparts.
4. Lack of centralized control: The major advantage of an ad-hoc network is that it can be set up spontaneously without the need for centralized control. Routing and resource management are done in a distributed manner in which all the nodes cooperate to enable communication among them.
5. Resource constraints: The constraints on resources such as computing power, battery power, and buffer storage also limit the capability of the network.

3 Quality of Service (QoS)

Quality of Service (QoS) [5] is the performance level of a service offered by the network to the user. The goal of QoS provisioning is to achieve a more deterministic network behavior, so that information carried by the network can be better delivered and network resources can be better utilized. QoS [6] is the collective set of service performance which determines the degree of satisfaction of the user of the service.

The dynamic nature of ad-hoc networks makes QoS a challenging and difficult task where nodes may leave or join the network or move around anytime. To support QoS, the link state information such as delay, bandwidth, cost, loss rate, and error rate in the network should be available and manageable.

QoS Parameters in Ad-Hoc Wireless Networks

A service can be characterized by a set of [5] measureable service requirements such as bandwidth, delay, delay jitter, power etc. Military applications have stringent security requirements while emergency operations should operate with minimal overhead.

4 Proposed Algorithm

Step 1: Use Lagrange Interpolation method to continuously determine the power of each node in the established network [7].

P=Use_Lagrange_interpolation ();

Lagrange interpolation has the following general form:

$$y = \sum_{i=0}^{n} \left[\frac{\prod_{\substack{j=0 \\ j \neq i}}^{n} (x - x_j)}{\prod_{\substack{j=0 \\ j \neq i}}^{n} (x_i - x_j)} \times y_i \right]$$

Lagrange Interpolation generates a random value by which the power of every node keeps on decreasing continuously in time.

Step 2: When the power P of a node N is lower than the minimum acceptable power, a warning message is first propagated to the predecessor node and in case the predecessor node is unable to find an alternative path to the destination [8][9], then the link failure warning message is further propagated to all upstream sources that make use of this node. The routing table is also updated to notify the nodes in the network about the change in the network topology that is expected to take place as a result of node failure.

Predict ()
{
  If (P <= Min_Acc_Power) then
    {
       Send warning (predecessor node);
       Find_Alternative_path ();
    }
}

Step 3: The predecessor of node N then initiates a local route repair procedure to find an alternative path to the destination by consulting the updated routing table. The proposed approach also accounts for the segmentation of packets.ie. the source sends only the remaining data packets which had not been transmitted earlier through the path in which the link failure had occurred thereby leading to its abandoning, through an alternative route, to the destination.

Step 4: When the power of the node N becomes zero, then the node is removed from the network and all links attached to it are broken.

5 Sequence of Activities

In the Predictive Preemptive Local Route Repair Strategy for improving QoS, we have proposed the following sequence of steps that occur for the routing process as shown in Figure 1.

1. The user requests for the creation of a node in a specified cell of the pre-defined grid.

2. The deploy network option responds by asking the user for the (X,Y) location of the the center of the circular node.

3. The user then replies with the (X,Y) location and as a result, the deploy network process successfully creates the node and assigns a node number to it.

4. In this way, the user can deploy several nodes in the network.

5. Upon the creation of every node, the node value is forwarded to the Routing process, which in turn updates the routing table and checks for the presence of nodes which lie within the range of a given node. This is the Route Discovery mechanism.

6. Every node has a pre-defined range, in which it can detect the presence of other nodes. The following strategy is adopted when a node needs to find a path to an unknown destination.

7. We adopt 4 techniques to determine the nodes which lie within the range of the concerned node and can hence be detected by the concerned node,

    i.) Check the range of the concerned node in clockwise direction.
    ii.) Check the range of the concerned node in anti- clockwise direction.
    iii.) Check the range of the concerned node in down clockwise direction.
    iv.) Check the range of the concerned node in down anti-clockwise direction.

8. This approach is particularly useful in determining the shortest path (minimum number of hops) to the destination.

9. Next, the user requests for the transmission of data from the source to the destination.

10. The Deploy network process responds, by asking the user for the source and destination and in turn, the user specifies the desired source and destination node.

11. The Send Data Process then finds an optimal path (consisting of least number of hops) between the source and destination by consulting the routing table.

12. Next is the Route Maintenance and Route Failure Handling phase.

13. Link failure may occur due to the crashing of certain nodes because of the depletion of their battery power. Such failures are handled by the route failure handling phase. On reaching the source, route discovery phase is restarted.

14. We propose a predictive preemptive local route repair strategy to increase Quality of Service (QoS) in the network. Its aim is to find an alternative path before the cost of a link failure is incurred.

15. The power of the node is used to estimate when a link is expected to break. A link is considered likely to break when the power of either of the nodes that it connects is close to the minimum detectable power.

16. When the power of a node becomes lower than the minimum acceptable power, a warning message is sent to the predecessor node which then attempts to find an alternative path to the destination. This is the local route repair strategy adopted.

17. If a link should fail, the node whose power has decreased below the pre-defined threshold power is simply removed from the routing table, the next-hop probabilities are recomputed for the remaining set (ie. the routing table contents are updated) and the remaining packets which were not transmitted earlier through the route which has failed are sent through an alternative path.

18. If no nodes lie within the range of the source node or any of the intermediate nodes to route packets, the packet is dropped.

19. Finally, data is successfully transmitted through the alternative path to the destination.

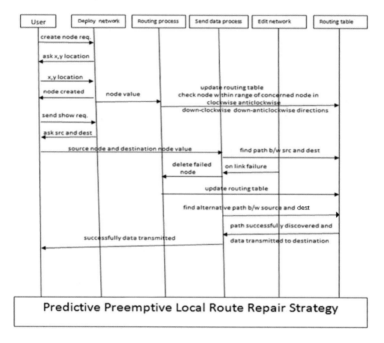

Fig. 1. Sequence of steps that occur for the routing process

6 Related Route Maintenance Mechanisms

Route failures have a significant negative impact on packet delivery. Packet dropping and higher delays are the main consequences of route failures. The time elapsed between link break detection and alternative path establishment can be high. Therefore, many studies have focused on improving route repair.

In [2], Crisòstomo et al. propose a Preemptive Local Route Repair (PLRR) extension to AODV. Nodes trigger the preemptive local route repair procedure when they predict that a link on the route to a destination is about to break. All packets are modified so as to contain node positions and motion information obtained using GPS receivers that nodes are equipped with. The problems with this approach are the cost associated with using a GPS and the need for synchronization between the internal clocks of nodes.

Cahill et al. [1] propose the use of node position and mobility information in the route discovery mechanism of DSR. When multiple routes to a destination exist, route selection is based on route stability and hop count. Moreover, nodes upstream of links that are predicted to break carry out preemptive local repair. This proposal uses DSR caching [10]. Therefore, it is not applicable to AODV. Moreover, a GPS is used.

In [3], Goff et al. propose a preemptive route maintenance extension to on-demand routing protocols. Its aim is to find an alternative path before the cost of a link failure is incurred. The received transmission power is used to estimate when a link is expected to break. A link is considered likely to break when the power of the signal received over it is close to the minimum detectable power. Route repair is the responsibility of a source node after receiving a warning about the imminence of a link break on an active route to a destination. This mechanism has been applied to DSR; AODV is also considered, but only superficially.

7   Improvisation in QoS

The model is designed for best effort delivery of data (higher packet delivery ratio).

- The aim of the application is to build an optimal path from the source to the destination (based on least hop count) and maintain it.
- It results in minimum overhead as it does not propagate unnecessary warning messages in the network to upstream nodes.
- It results in fewer broken active links due to prior prediction of link failure based on the power calculation for each node.
- It results in lower end-to-end delay.
- Route discovery is efficiently achieved by finding the nodes which lie within the range of the concerned node.

8   Scope and Motivation

Routing in wireless ad-hoc networks has always been a challenging task, mainly due to the high degree of the dynamic nature involved in the network. The basic algorithms involve a lot of overhead due to exchange of routing tables among the nodes and every node maintaining the routing information about every other node. Predictive Preemptive Local Route Repair algorithm was chosen to be implemented due to following reasons:

- The application is designed for best effort delivery of data (higher packet delivery ratio).
- The aim of the application is to build an optimal path from the source to the destination (based on least hop count) and maintain it.
- It results in minimum overhead as it does not propagate unnecessary warning messages in the network to upstream nodes.

- It results in fewer broken active links due to prior prediction of link failure based on the power calculation for each node.
- It results in lower end-to-end delay.
- Route discovery is efficiently achieved by finding the nodes which lie within the range of the concerned node.

References

[1] Cahill, A., et al.: Link cache extensions for predictive routing and repair in ad hoc wireless networks. In: Proceedings of the 4th IEEE Conference on Mobile and Wireless Communication Networks (MWCN), pp. 43–52 (September 2002)
[2] Crisòstomo, S., et al.: Improving AODV with Preemptive Local Route Repair. Technical Report Series: DCC-2003-0, Universidad do Porto, Portugal (2003)
[3] Su, W.J., et al.: Mobility Prediction and Routing in Ad hoc Wireless Networks. International Journal of Network Management (2000)
[4] Royer, E.M., Toh, C.-K.: A Review of Current Routing Protocols for Ad Hoc Mobile Wireless Networks. IEEE Personal Communications (April 1999)
[5] Siva Ram Murthy, C., Manoj, B.S.: Ad Hoc Wireless Networks Architectures and Protocols, 2nd edn. Pearson Education, London (2005)
[6] Inayatullah, M., Ahmad, S., Salam, A.: Optimized QOS Protocols for Small-Sized Manets. In: 2nd International Conference on Emerging Technologies, IEEE-ICET 2006, Peshawar, Pakistan, November 13-14 (2006)
[7] Hacene, S.B., Lehireche, A., Meddahi, A.: Predictive Preemptive Ad Hoc On-Demand Distance Vector Routing. In: Evolutionary Engineering and Distributed Information Systems Laboratory, EEDIS, Computer Science Department, Sidi Bel Abbes University, Algeria
[8] Belding-Royer, E., Perkins, C.: Evolution and future directions of the ad hoc on-demand distance-vector routing protocol. Ad Hoc Networks Journal 1(1), 125–150 (2003)
[9] Belding-Royer, E., et al.: Ad hoc On-Demand Distance Vector (AODV) Routing. Draft-ietf- manet-aodv-13.txt, INTERNET DRAFT (2003)
[10] Goff, T., et al.: Preemptive routing in ad hoc networks. Journal of Parallel and Distributed Computing, 123–140 (2003)

Improving Energy Efficiency in Wireless Sensor Network Using Mobile Sink

K. Deepak Samuel, S. Murali Krishnan, K. Yashwant Reddy, and K. Suganthi

Department of Information Technology, Anna University Chennai
{dpksam1989,krishnan39,kyrmit,suganthi.kamal}@gmail.com

Abstract. Wireless Sensor Networks have been deployed for various purposes like military applications, surveillance in volcanic or remote regions, etc. But one of the major challenges in Wireless Sensor Network (WSN) that is yet to be sorted out is the lack of energy efficiency which retards the lifetime of the network. In this paper, we propose an approach that can be deployed for small sensor networks to achieve maximum energy efficiency using a single mobile sink. The mobile sink does not have a wide range as a base station but has a rechargeable battery and so it can act as a collector for getting data from sensor nodes and transmitting it to base station via internet or cellular network. We have analysed the optimum speed of the mobile sink for minimal delay. The proposed approach includes clustering followed by data gathering and forwarding by mobile sink. In this paper, we evaluate and compare network performance using delay parameter upon varying the speed of the mobile sink. Knowing the number of sensor nodes and its distribution in the network, there is a need to ensure that the energy wastage is minimal with acceptable levels of delay depending on the application. We have compared the energy efficiency of the proposed approach with that of the traditional approach in this paper.

Keywords: Wireless Sensor Networks; Delay; Energy Efficiency; Clustering; Basestation; Mobile Sink.

1 Introduction

Major challenge in Wireless Sensor Network (WSN) is the lack of energy efficiency in the network and as a result shorter network lifetime due to failure of the sensors as they have limited energy. In this paper we propose an approach to provide both energy efficiency and analyse the delay to determine the optimum speed of mobile sink. We use mobile sinks along with the static sensors to enhance the performance of the network in terms of its lifetime. In the case of a complete static sensor network where there is no mobile sink involved, traditionally multiple hop technique is usually used. But the nodes near the base station die quickly. And also since each and every sensor dissipates some amount of energy during the exchange of information at some stage, the node tends to die. The rate at which a sensor node dissipates energy depends on its distance from the sink and also the number of times it's been accessed. Therefore it is important to reduce the energy consumed by energy-limited sensor nodes to increase the efficiency of the network as mentioned in [2] and [5].

N. Meghanathan et al. (Eds.): CCSIT 2011, Part II, CCIS 132, pp. 63–69, 2011.
© Springer-Verlag Berlin Heidelberg 2011

This problem can only be resolved by the use of a sink which is mobile and can periodically obtain information from the sensors near its range. The clustering using mobile sinks is performed by taking into account connectivity of the sensor nodes. Connectivity of a sensor node refers to the number of its neighbouring nodes that are within its range.

2   Related Work

Unlike the previous approaches where mobile sink was used instead of static sink, we propose a dual sink approach that uses one-hop clusters for effective data gathering. The concept of one-hop clusters makes the dual sink approach more energy efficient than specified in [3]. This approach provides the facility to use the sleep mode operation of sensor nodes as specified in [6] thus making the network as much energy efficient as possible. The amount of time the sensor node must operate in sleep mode is decided based on the application. For example for applications like temperature monitoring at a particular time in a particular place, sleep mode operation is very useful to prevent energy wastage caused due to idle listening as specified in [10].

A detailed study of the different ways of conserving sensor node energy is discussed in [7]. The use of multiple mobile sinks for energy efficiency is used in [4], but the cost of deployment is very high for small networks. The proposed approach provides energy efficient data collection using single mobile sink and hence more cost efficient. The following section describes the steps involved in the proposed approach.

3   Approach

The two major possible energy losses that a sensor node exercises in a sensor network is energy lost during sensing and communication cost.The energy loss in communication is much higher than the energy loss in sensing as specified in [7].But communication cost is the major loss that can be efficiently reduced. So the proposed approach aims at reducing the communication cost as much as possible using dual sink thereby providing energy efficiency. The main stages of the proposed approach include:

    A. Formation of one-hop clusters (Clustering)
    B. Notification to mobile sink and sink mobility
    C. Sensing of mobile sink by cluster heads
    D. Cluster head energy conservation
    E. Monitoring Cluster heads

3.1   Formation of One Hop-Clusters (Clustering)

Based on the location of the sensor nodes and hence their connectivity, the base station performs various computations and groups sensor nodes into clusters. Cluster with maximum connectivity becomes head of each cluster. The information about the list of cluster heads after clustering is sent to mobile sink by the base station at the end of the clustering process. The use of mobile sink helps to overcome the challenges in data collection discussed in [11].

Initially the base station sorts the all the sensor nodes based on their connectivity i.e. the number of neighbors' of that sensor. Then flag is set for that node and all its neighbors. They form a cluster and a unique cluster head which has the maximum connectivity is set as the cluster head by the base station. These sensors should not be used for further clustering as they are already part of a cluster. This procedure is followed for all the remaining sensors. For this purpose flags are used. As a result, a number of one-hop clusters are formed.

The result of clustering is first sent by the base station to all sensor nodes so that each sensor node can identify its head. Next, the cluster information (cluster head list) is sent to the mobile sink by base station after notifying static sensor nodes.

Algorithm:

Step 1:
Base station gets the location of all static nodes and also knows the   sensing range of all sensor nodes.

Step 2:
Nodes are arranged in descending order of their connectivity and one hop clusters are formed.

Step 3:
While forming one-hop clusters flags are used to ensure that no node becomes part of more than one cluster.

Step 4:
Repeat steps 2 and 3 until all nodes become part of a cluster.

Step 5:
Base station sends this cluster head information to all sensor nodes.

Step 6:
Sensor nodes in turn send a packet to their corresponding heads, where data aggregation is done.

Step 7:
At last, the list of cluster heads is sent to the mobile sink which upon receiving the packet starts its motion.

The cluster head receives packet from all the members of the cluster which send their individual packet to the head node. This phase avoids multiple hop approach as one-hop clusters are formed as a result of clustering in the previous step. The use of one-hop clusters makes the process more energy efficient as explained in [1].

3.2 Notification to Mobile Sink and Sink Mobility

Now the mobile sink has to be notified by the base station about the cluster heads so that the mobile sink can initiate its movement. On receiving the notification from base station, the mobile sink follows a particular mobility model (in this case constant speed mobility) and starts sensing the cluster heads within its range.

3.3 Sensing of Mobile Sinks by Cluster Heads

When the mobile sink starts sensing cluster heads and finds them within its range while moving it sends a MOBSINK packet to these heads. The mobility model of

mobile sink is chosen based on various factors as said in [9]. Also the velocity must
be optimum for maximum efficiency as explained in [8]. Upon receiving this packet
the cluster heads immediately checks whether the moving mobile sink is within their
range (since range of cluster head < range of mobile sink). This sensing of mobile
sink by head is possible only when the mobile sink is within range at that instant as
illustrated in [1].

If (Mobile sink is within its range) then

{
Cluster heads forwards the aggregated packet of its members to the mobile sink
which in turn sends it to base station via internet or cellular network.
}

Else

Cluster head ignores the packet prom mobile sink.

3.4 Cluster Head Energy Conservation

Once the packet is sent by the cluster head to the mobile sink, the cluster head can go
to sleep mode or remain idle irrespective of incoming packets for some time t, which
is the minimum interval or time gap between successive transmissions of packet to the
mobile sink by a cluster head. Thus unwanted energy wastage for sending duplicate
packet immediately by cluster head to mobile sink is avoided. During this time
interval the cluster head can change to sleep mode to avoid idle listening. This time
interval length can be decided based on the application.

3.5 Monitoring Cluster Heads

Irrespective of the cluster heads' response, the mobile sink sends MOBSINK packet
to them if they fall within its range. In case of failure of any cluster the total process
must be initiated once again by base station. Thus each cluster is monitored through
its cluster head.

4 Simulations

The configuration of the network chosen for implementation is shown in figure 1
below:

1. Total number of static sensors = 40
2. Total number of mobile sinks = 1
3. Area of playground = 400m X 400m
4. Speed of mobile sink = 10 m/sec
5. Mobility model = Constant speed mobility
6. Range of mobile sink = 80m
7. Range of sensor nodes = 55m
8. Minimum possible delay > 5 sec

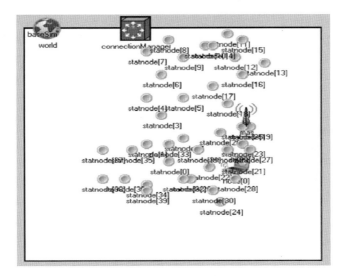

Fig. 1. Topology considered

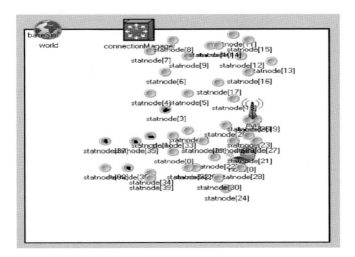

Fig. 2. Topology showing nodes considered for energy efficiency

If energy required for 1 hop is 1 joule, then the nodes with black dots as shown in figure 2 require,

1. 27 joules in traditional approach
2. 5 joules in our approach to send packet to base station.
3. So there is a decrease of 81.5% when compared to the traditional approach.

The larger the network, this percentage will improve at the cost of delay.

There is a trade-off between energy efficiency and delay upon using mobile sinks in a sensor network. The delay associated with a cluster head can be controlled by two methods:

1. By using appropriate speed of motion of mobile sink so that delay is reduced
2. By increasing the number of mobile sinks.

The second method is not preferred as the cost increases and also there are chances of few cluster heads getting depleted quickly as a result of multiple mobile sinks. We have analyzed the delay experienced by a cluster head for different speeds of mobile sink. Delay associated with a cluster head which is a bit far off from initial position of mobile sink was studied against varying speeds of mobile sink. In the given topology head node 5 is considered. The following figure 3 shows the result.

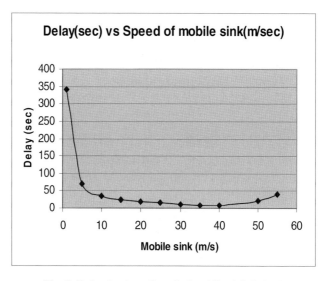

Fig. 3. Delay (sec) vs. Speed of mobile sink (m/sec)

The following can be inferred from the graph,

1. As the speed of mobile sink is increased the delay decreases up to a certain level.
2. On further increasing the speed (in this case >35m/sec) the delay starts increasing again because the mobile node moves so quickly that it moves out of the range of head when the head is ready to deliver the packet.
3. Depending on the size of network, the optimum speed for minimum delay should be selected. For small networks (~40 sensors) speeds in range 10-35m/sec is suitable.

5 Conclusions and Future Work

As the number of sensor nodes gets increased the energy efficiency improves at the cost of delay in the proposed approach. The proposed approach can be extended for large scale sensor networks using multiple mobile sinks by effectively handling individual sink mobility considering both the cost involved and delay associated with heads. Thus energy is conserved by using the proposed cluster based approach along with mobile sink compared to traditional approach which uses multiple hop approach. The speed of the mobile sink should be optimal for better efficiency.

References

1. Ren, B., Ma, J., Chen, C.: The Hybrid Mobile Wireless Sensor Networks for Data Gathering. In: IWCMC 2006 (July 2006)
2. Jeon, H., Park., K., Hwang, D.-J., Choo, H.: Sink oriented dynamic location service protocol for mobile sinks with an energy efficient grid based approach. In: Sensors 2009 (March 2009)
3. Wu, X., Chen, G.: Dual Sink: Using Mobile And Static Sinks For Life Improvement. In: Wireless Sensor Networks, China NFS Grant (2006)
4. Kim, J., In, J., Hong, S., Kim, B., Lee, H., Eom, D.: A efficient Agent Based Routing Algorithm For Multiple Mobile Sink. In: Wireless Sensor Networks, Korea University IT Research Center (2004)
5. Aktildiz, I.F., Su, W., Sankarasubramaniam, Y., Cayirci, E.: Wireless Sensor Networks: a Survey
6. Pantazis, N.A., Vergados, D.J., Vergados, D.D., Douligeris, C.: Energy efficiency in wireless sensor networks using sleep mode TDMA scheduling. Adhoc Networks, Journal Homepage, http://www.elsevier.com/locate/adhoc
7. Anastasi, G., Conti, M., Di Francesco, M., Passarella, A.: Energy conservation in wireless sensor networks: A survey. Adhoc Networks Journal
8. Chen, C., Ma, J., Yu, K.: Designing Energy-Efficient Wireless Sensor Networks with Mobile Sinks
9. Vincze, Z., Vass, D., Vida, R., Vidács, A., Telcs, A.: Adaptive Sink Mobility in Event-driven Multi-hop Wireless Sensor Networks
10. Demirkol, l., Ersoy, C.: Energy and delay optimized contention for wireless sensor networks. Journal Homepage, http://www.elsevier.com/locate/comnet
11. Lian, J., Naik, K., Agnew, G.B.: Data Capacity Improvement of Wireless Sensor Networks Using Non-Uniform Sensor Distribution

Transformed Logistic Block Cipher Scheme for Image Encryption

I. Shatheesh Sam[1], P. Devaraj[2], and R.S. Bhuvaneswaran[1]

[1] Ramanujan Computing Centre, College of Engineering, Guindy
Anna University, Chennai, India
shatheeshsam@yahoo.com, bhuvan@annauniv.edu
[2] Department of Mathematics, College of Engineering, Guindy,
Anna University, Chennai, India
devaraj@annauniv.edu

Abstract. A transformed logistic block cipher scheme for image encryption is proposed. It includes three major parts, pixel position permutation, block cipher scheme and XORing the resultant values with chaotic key. The key is generated using transformed logistic maps. The proposed chaotic block cipher scheme encrypts blocks of bits rather than blocks of pixels. It encrypts 256-bits of plain image to 256-bits of cipher image with four 32-bit registers. The key space of the proposed method is large enough to protect the system against any brute force, chosen-plaintext/ciphertext, differential and statistical attacks. From the information entropy analysis it is found that, the entropy is very close to the theoretical value which shows that the information leakage is negligible and so the scheme is secure. The simulation results show that the efficient encryption speed is achieved.

Keywords: Transformed Logistic Map, Permutation, Block Cipher.

1 Introduction

Nowadays, the security of digital images becomes more vital since web attacks are more serious. Image encryption is somehow different from text encryption due to inherent features of images such as bulk data capacity and high correlation among pixels, which are generally difficult to handle. Many image content encryption algorithms have been proposed in the recent past [1-3]. Plethora [4-5] of research have been made on image encryption with chaotic based algorithms. Due to the cryptographic properties such as sensitivity to initial conditions and random like behavior. The major core of these encryption systems consists of one or several chaotic maps serving the purpose of either just encrypting the image or shuffling the image and subsequently encrypting the resulting shuffled image.

Chaos block cipher algorithm is proposed by Xinag and Liao [7]. Their idea is described as follows. Firstly they generate random binary sequences with logistic system; and scramble plaintext with the part of generated sequences. Lastly they make the remaining part of sequences using XOR operation with blocked

N. Meghanathan et al. (Eds.): CCSIT 2011, Part II, CCIS 132, pp. 70–78, 2011.

plaintext to produce ciphertext. This encryption algorithm not only improves the speed of encryption, but also makes the length of plaintext and ciphertext equal. XBC [8] is a typical representative of chaotic encryption algorithms which transforms the points of the chaotic trajectory and directly participate in the process of encryption. In the process of encryption, the key stream sequence has nothing to do with the plaintext, which is similar to synchronous stream encryption mechanism. However, its sequence has nothing to do with the explicit, which easily leads to chosen-plaintext attack.

Huaqian Yang et al. [10] used tent map and keyed hash function for fast image encryption and authentication. A modified architecture for fast image encryption [6] has been proposed by Wong et al. In this architecture, certain diffusion effect is introduced in the substitution stage by simple sequential add-and-shift operation. Wang Xing-yuan and Chen Feng [11] proposed a block encryption for image using combination of confusion and diffusion. The major challenge in designing effective image encryption algorithms is that it is rather difficult to shuffle and diffuse image data efficiently by traditional cryptographic means.

The aforesaid image encryption schemes have several disadvantages such as less security level, low speed and weak key. In this paper, we propose a new transformed logistic block cipher scheme (TLBCS) to improve the key space, security and speed.

The paper is organized as follows: Section 2 describes the chaotic logistic map and its transformed maps. The proposed image encryption scheme is introduced in Section 3. Section 4 discussed the experimental results and security analysis. Finally, Section 5 gives the conclusion.

2   Logistic Map

Logistic is a simple example of a map with an extremely complicated behavior for some values of the parameter μ. The dynamics of the map have been studied extensively, and there are many important results that have been generalized to one dimensional dynamical systems.

It is described as follows:

$$x_{k+1} = \mu x_k (1 - x_k)$$

where μ is system parameter, $0 < \mu \leq 4$ and x_k is a floating number in (0,1), $k = 0, 1, 2, 3 \ldots$. When $\mu > 3.569945672$, this system become chaotic in behavior, in other words, the sequence $\{x_k, k = 0, 1, 2, \ldots\}$ is produced based on logistic map with the initial value x_0 which is neither periodic nor convergent. Its bifurcation diagram is shown in Figure 1.

Among the special features of logistic map, its high sensitivity to initial value and parameter makes suitable for image encryption. If they are taken as security key, it will meet the security which is requirement of encryption algorithm, sensitivity property.

Though, the logistic map is better for image encryption it has common problems such as stable windows, blank windows, uneven distribution of sequences

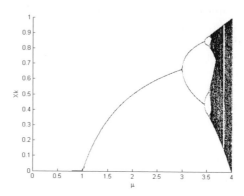

Fig. 1. Bifurcation Diagram of Logistic Map

and weak key [9]. New types of transformed logistic maps have been proposed in this paper to alleviate the problems in the logistic map. The maps are mixed together so as to achieve larger key space and to attain chaotic behavior.

2.1 Transformed Logistic Maps

We have attempted to improve logistic map by chaotic transformation. These maps are used to generate the keys for the block cipher scheme(BCS). The proposed transformed logistic maps are defined as follows:

$$x_{n+1} = [(a \times y_n \times (1 - x_n + z_n)] \, mod \, 1$$

$$y_{n+1} = [a \times y_n \times (k_1 \times sin(z_n)) \times x_{n+1}] \, mod \, 1$$

$$z_{n+1} = [a \times z_n + y_{n+1} + x_{n+1}] \, mod \, 1$$

where $0 < a \leq 3.999$, $\mid k_1 \mid > 37.7$. In order to increase the key size, k_1 can be used as another set of keys. The k_i improves the distribution of the keys. Mod 1 operation limits the data values which are above 1 to the range of (0,1). which helps to check the data from going unbounded.

3   The Proposed TLBCS

A new image encryption scheme has been proposed which performs pixel position permutation, block encryption scheme using primitive operations and XORing the resultant values with secret key.

3.1   Position Permutation

The chaos based image encryption schemes are mainly consisting of image pixel permutation stage otherwise called as *confusion stage* and pixel value diffusion stage. Confusion refers to making the relationship between the key and the cipher text as complex as possible. Generally, the confusion effect is considered by permutation stage. Our new confusion stage is composed of position permutation. The method is defined by:

$$C[i, j] = P[1 + (51 \times i + 3) mod\, 256, 1 + (31 \times j + 3) mod\, 256]$$

where $P[i, j]$ represents the $(i, j)^{th}$ pixel of the plainimage and $C[i, j]$ denotes the $(i, j)^{th}$ pixel of the cipherimage. This method uses two constant values to improve the pixel scrambling of image.

3.2 Key Generation

The key has been generated as follows:

$$
\begin{aligned}
&for\ i = 1\ to\ 256\\
&for\ j = 1\ to\ 256\\
&\quad x_{i,j+1} = (3.935 \times y_{i,j} \times (1 - x_{i,j}) + z_{i,j})\ mod\ 1\\
&\quad y_{i,j+1} = (3.986 \times y_{i,j} \times (k_1 \times sin(z_{i,j})) \times x_{i,j+1})\ mod\ 1\\
&\quad z_{i,j+1} = (3.928 \times x_{i,j+1} + y_{i,j+1} + z_{i,j})\ mod\ 1\\
&\quad X_{i,j} = \lfloor x_{i,j+1} \times 256 \rfloor\\
&\quad Y_{i,j} = \lfloor y_{i,j+1} \times 256 \rfloor\\
&\quad Z_{i,j} = \lfloor z_{i,j+1} \times 256 \rfloor\\
&end\\
&\quad x_{i+1,1} = x_{i,j+1}\\
&\quad y_{i+1,1} = y_{i,j+1}\\
&\quad z_{i+1,1} = z_{i,j+1}\\
&end
\end{aligned}
$$

3.3 Block Cipher Scheme (BCS)

A new block cipher scheme (BCS) is specified as BCS-$w/r/b$ where w is the word size (32 bits), r is the number of encryption rounds (0...255), and b denotes the length of the encryption key (0...255) in bytes. The proposed BCS-$w/r/b$ works with four w-bit words as input (plaintext) and four w-bit words as (ciphertext) output block size. This scheme uses primitive operations and lg(x) to denote the base two logarithm of x.

Encryption operation is defined as:

$$
\begin{aligned}
&for\ i = 1\ to\ r\ do\\
&\{\\
&\quad A = A + S[4i - 3]\\
&\quad B = B + S[4i - 2]\\
&\quad T_1 = (A \times B + k_2) \lll lgw\\
&\quad T_2 = (C \times B + k_3) \lll lgw\\
&\quad C = ((C \oplus T_1) + 1) \lll lgw + S[4i - 1]\\
&\quad D = ((D \oplus T_2) + 1) \lll lgw + S[4i]\\
&\quad (A, B, C, D) = (B, C, D, A)\\
&\}
\end{aligned}
$$

The encrypted block of 128 bits is stored in the four 32 bit (A, B, C, D) registers. $\mid k_2 \mid > 27.3, \mid k_3 \mid > 29.1$ are used as set of keys. The actual key array size of 8-bit is converted into 32 bit. $S[4i-3], S[4i-2], S[4i-1], S[4i]$ are the four 32 bit key array register. The above process is continued till the whole image is ciphered. The stored blocks is again converted into 8-bit pixel values and XORing with set of secret key.

3.4   BCS for Decryption

The decryption algorithm is just the reverse of encryption one. In order to get the original image, XORing encrypted image pixel values with the same set of secret key which we used in the encryption process.

The below operation is used for decrypting the blocks.

$for \; i = r \; downto \; 1 \; do$
$\quad \{$
$\qquad (A, B, C, D) = (D, A, B, C)$
$\qquad T_1 = (A \times B + k_2) \lll lgw$
$\qquad C = (((C - S[4i-1]) \ggg lgw) - 1) \oplus T_1$
$\qquad T_2 = (C \times B + k_3) \lll lgw$
$\qquad D = (((D - S[4i]) \ggg lgw) - 1) \oplus T_2$
$\qquad A = A - S[4i-3]$
$\qquad B = B - S[4i-2]$
$\quad \}$

The permutation is replaced by inverse permutation values. The inverse method is described by:

$$P[i, j] = C[1 + (251 \times i - 4) mod \, 256, 1 + (253 \times j - 4) mod \, 256]$$

The original image can be recovered once the above decryption process is completed.

4   Experimental Result

A good encryption scheme should be robust against all kinds of cryptanalytic, statistical and brute force attacks. Some experimental results are given in this section to demonstrate the efficiency of our scheme. All the experiments are performed on a PC with Intel Core 3.0GHz CPU, 4G RAM with Windows Vista Business Edition. The compiling environment is MATLAB 7.4.

4.1   Statistical Analysis

In order to resist the statistical attacks, which are quite common nowadays, the encrypted images should possess certain random properties. A detailed study has been undergone and the results are summarized in the next section. Different images have been tested, and we found that the intensity values are similar.

4.2   Histogram Analysis

Histograms may reflect the distribution information of the pixel values of an image. An attacker can analyze the histograms of an encrypted image by using some attacking algorithms to get some useful information of the original image. Thus, the histograms of an encrypted image should be as smooth and evenly distributed as possible, and should be very different from that of the plaintexts.

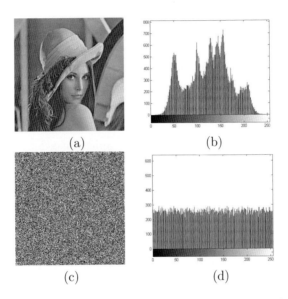

(a)   (b)

(c)   (d)

Fig. 2. Histogram of Analysis of Plain Image and Ciphered Image

Figure 2 shows a comparison of the histograms between plaintext and encrypted images. Figure 2(a) is the plaintext (original image), Figure 2(b) is the histogram of the plaintext, Figure 2(c) is the ciphertext, and Figure 2(d) is the histogram of the ciphertexts. By comparing Figure 2(b) to Figure 2(d), it is clear that the two histograms are very different, in which the histogram of the ciphertext is much more smooth and much more evenly distributed.

4.3   Correlation Coefficient Analysis

We use the 256 gray levels image Lena (256× 256 pixels) as the original image. Experiment shows that image scrambling effect is inverse ratio to the correlation coefficient function of the adjacent pixels. Correlation coefficient function is used as follows.

$$D(x) = \frac{1}{k}\sum_{i=1}^{k}[x_i - E(x)]^2$$

where x is the grey value of pixel point; k is the number of pixel point; E(x) is mathematical expectation of x and D(x) is variance of x.

$$Conv(x, y) = \frac{1}{k}\sum_{i=1}^{k}[x_i - E(x)][y_i - E(y)]$$

where x is grey value of the former pixel point; y is grey value of the latter pixel point;

$cov(x, y)$ is the covariance of x, y.

$$r_{xy} = cov(x, y)/\left(\sqrt{D(x)}\sqrt{D(y)}\right)$$

where r_{xy} is the related coefficients. Carrying out the experiment analysis on the adjacent pixel points of the primitive image: the final result is presented in Table 1.

Table 1. Correlation Coefficients of Two

Direction	Plain image	Cipher image
Horizontal	0.9329	0.0029
Vertical	0.9691	0.0050
Diagonal	0.9414	0.0011

4.4 Differential Analysis

Differential attack would become ineffective even if a single pixel change in the plaintext causes a significant difference in the ciphertext. In order to measure this capability quantitatively, the following measures are usually used: number of pixels change rate (NPCR) and unified average changing intensity (UACI). They are defined as follows:

$$D_{ij} = \begin{cases} 1, & if\ C_{ij} \neq C'_{ij} \\ 0, & otherwise \end{cases}$$

The NPCR is defined as

$$NPCR = \frac{\sum_{i,j} D_{ij}}{M \times N} \times 100\%$$

The UACI is defined as

$$UACI = \frac{1}{M \times N}\left[\sum_{i,j} \frac{C_{ij} - C'_{ij}}{M \times N}\right] \times 100\%$$

where C_{ij} and C'_{ij} are the two cipherimages at position (i, j) whose corresponding plainimages have only one pixel difference and M and N are the number of rows and columns of images. The results of NPCR and UACI are listed in Table 2.

In order to assess the influence of changing a single pixel in the original image on the encrypted image, the $NPCR$ and the $UACR$ is computed in the proposed

Table 2. Sensitivity to Ciphertext

	NPCR%	UACI%
Lena	99.6291	33.4992
Baboon	99.6343	33.4821
House	99.6352	33.4811
Tree	99.6327	33.4812

scheme. It can be found that the NPCR is over 99.3% and the UACI is over 33.4%. The results show that a small change in the original image will result in a significant difference in the cipherimage, so the scheme proposed has a good ability to anti differential attack.

4.5   Key Space Analysis

There are series of transformed maps parameters, initial values, and k_i values that can be used as key in our scheme. The key space is as large as the range between 192 to 380 bits.

4.6   Information Entropy Analysis

Information entropy is one of the criteria to measure the strength of the cryptosystem in symmetric cryptosystem. The entropy $H(m)$ of a message m can be calculated as

$$H(m) = \sum_{i=0}^{2^N-1} p(m_i) log \frac{1}{p(m_i)}$$

where $p(m_i)$ represents the probability of occurrence of symbol m_i and log denotes the base 2 logarithm. If there are 256 possible outcomes of the message m with equal probability, it is considered as random. In this case, that $H(m)$ is 8 is an ideal situation. The final round of proposed scheme has found that the value is 7.9963. This means that information leakage in the encryption process is negligible and the encryption system is secure upon entropy attack.

5   Conclusion

In this paper, transformed logistic block cipher scheme for image encryption has been proposed. Based on the pixel position permutation, block cipher scheme and XORing the resultant values with chaotic key, the scheme encrypts 256-bits input plaintext to 256-bits output ciphertext, using 256-bits key. Experimental results show that the proposed scheme has a high security level and can withstand against known/chosen plain text, brute force, statistical and differential attacks and able to encrypt large data sets efficiently. The proposed method is expected to be useful for real time image encryption and transmission applications.

Acknowledgement

The first author is partially supported by the All India Council for Technical Education(AICTE), New Delhi, India.

References

1. Chen, G., Mao, Y., Chui, C.K.: A symmetric image encryption scheme based on 3D chaotic cat maps. Chaos, Solitons & Fractals 21, 749–761 (2004)
2. Zhang, L., Liao, X., Wang, X.: An image encryption approach based on chaotic maps. Chaos, Solitons and Fractals 24, 759–765 (2005)
3. Jakimoski, G., Kocarev, L.: Chaos and cryptography: block encryption ciphers based on chaotic maps. IEEE Trans. Circuits Syst. I 48(2), 163–169 (2001)
4. Gao, T.G., Chen, Z.Q.: Image encryption based on a new total shuffling algorithm. Chaos, Solitons & Fractals 38, 213–220 (2008)
5. Li, C., Chen, G.: On the security of a class of image encryption schemes. In: Proceedings of the IEEE International Symposium on Circuits and Systems, pp. 3290–3293 (2008)
6. Wong, K.W., Bernie, S.H.K., Law, W.S.: A Fast Image Encryption Scheme based on Chaotic Standard Map. Physics Letters A 372, 2645–2652 (2008)
7. Xiang, T., Liao, X.F.: A novel block cryptosystem based on iterating a chaotic map. Physics Letters A 349(2), 109–115 (2006)
8. Yu, W., Cao, J.: Cryptography based on delayed neural networks. Physics Letters A 356(3), 333–338 (2006)
9. Jianquan, X., Chunhua, Y., Qing, X., Lijun, T.: An Encryption Algorithm Based on Transformed Logistic Map. In: IEEE International Conference on Network Security, Wireless Communications and Truested Computing, pp. 111–114 (2009)
10. Yang, H., Wong, K.W., Liao, X., Zhang, W., Wei, P.: A Fast Image Encryption and Authentication Scheme based on Chaotic Maps. Communications in Nonlinear Science and Numerical Simulation 15(11), 3507–3517 (2010)
11. Wang, X.Y., Chen, F., Wang, T.: A new compound mode of confusion and diffusion for block encryption of image based on chaos. Communications in Nonlinear Science and Numerical Simulation 15(9), 2479–2485 (2010)

Context Management Using Ontology and Object Relational Database (ORDBMS) in a Pervasive Environment

B. Vanathi and V. Rhymend Uthariaraj

Ramanujan Computing Centre, Anna University Chennai
Chennai, Tamil Nadu, India
mbvanathi@yahoo.co.in, rhymend@annauniv.edu

Abstract. Applications must adjust their behavior to every changing surroundings. Adjustment means proper capture, management and reasoning of context. This paper proposes representation of context in a hierarchical form and storing of context data in an object relational database than an ordinary relational database. Semantic of the context is managed by Ontology and context data is handled by Object relational database. These two modeling elements are associated to each other by semantics relations build in the ontology. Loading appropriate data into the reasoner improves the reasoning process performance.

Keywords: Context, Ontology, Relational Database, Object Relational Database.

1 Introduction

A smart device maintains information about their locations, the contexts in which they are being used and relevant data about their users. Portable and wireless appliances play a major role. Personal data assistances (PDA's), smart phones and global positioning systems (GPSs) are only the first precursors of new devices and services that will emerge. The continuing technical progress in computing and communication lead to an all-encompassing use of networks and computing power called ubiquitous or pervasive computing [1]. Pervasive computing system targets at constantly adapting their behavior in order to meet the needs of users within every changing physical, social, computing and communication context. Pervasive devices make ad-hoc connections among them and may be connected to different types of sensors to capture changes in the environment. In the evolution chain from centralized computing to pervasive computing [2] [3] context awareness is at the heart of pervasive computing problems. Context can be defined as an operational term whose definition depends on the intension for which it is collected and the interpretation of the operations involved on an entity at a particular time and space rather than the inherent characteristics of the entities and the operations themselves according to Dey & Winogards [4, 5].The complexity of such problems increases in multiplicative fashion rather than additive with the addition of new components into the chain. Context aware computing has three major basic components: pervasive environment, Context management modeling and context-aware service [6]. Pervasive environment

N. Meghanathan et al. (Eds.): CCSIT 2011, Part II, CCIS 132, pp. 79–87, 2011.

is characterized by dynamicity, heterogeneity and ubiquity of users, devices and other computing resources, ad-hoc connection among the devices and existence of hardware and software sensors. Context management modeling deals with how context data is collected, organized, represented, stored and presented to the reasoning module. Context aware service performs context reasoning and decisions about the actions to be triggered. Proper modeling, specification and definition of context and its management are essential for efficient reasoning, interpretation, and utilization of context data. In this paper special emphasize on context data representation which can be further used in the development of collaborative context application is proposed.

2   Related Research

Dynamic adaptation of application to a changing environment leads to an enhancement of the user satisfaction. Managing and use of contextual information in pervasive environment is still a challenge. Data required for modeling are obtained from the applications using sensors. Sensors can be physical, virtual or logical sensors [6].Many earlier works based on context aware computing system focused on application specific systems. *ParcTab, Cyberguide, Project CoolTown, The cricket Compass* are some few examples of context aware computing systems. After collecting the data from the application, it has to be represented in a suitable way for processing. Various context management and modeling approaches are introduced to present context for reasoning in different application area. Data from the sensors are presented using any of the following modeling approaches. Major classifications of context management modeling approaches are key-value-pair modeling, Graphical modeling, Object Oriented modeling, logic based modeling, Mark up scheme modeling and Ontology modeling.

2.1   Overview of Context Modeling Approaches

Context representation and management modeling is an important aspect of pervasive computing. Context-aware applications must adapt to changing situations like users' activities and entities in the surroundings that share users' perception of real world. These entities have different meanings associated with them in different environments. In order to have similar meanings of these entities, when used at different times, in different situations, by different applications their semantics must be formalized. This helps to store context data for future use and to communicate context universally with other systems. The basic steps in the development of context-aware applications are to provide formalized representation and standardized access mechanisms to context information.

Earlier context management modeling approaches are based on context widgets, networked services and blackboard models. Context Widgets are derived from techniques in GUI development.GUI is a software component that provides a public interface for a hardware sensor and separate application from the context acquisition process. Networked services use the data source-discovery techniques instead of a global widget manager to find networked services. Blackboard approach, processes post messages to a shared media called blackboard and subscribe to it to be notified when some specifies events occur.

Context models that use markup scheme approaches are used for profile data representation. Among all the modeling approaches ontology based context model is more suitable for context aware computing [3].

2.2 Ontology Based Context Model and Restrictions

Ontology is defined as explicit specification of a shared conceptualization [5].Context is modeled as concepts and facts using ontology. Some context aware systems that use this approach are discussed below.

CONON [7] is based on treatment of high-level implicit contexts that are derived from low-level explicit context. It supports interoperability of different devices. CONON defines generic concepts regarding context and provides extensibility for adding domain specific concepts. Logic reasoning is used to perform consistency checks and to calculate high-level context knowledge from explicitly given low-level context information. CONON consists of an upper ontology which is extended by several domain specific ontologies for intelligent environments such as "home", "office" or "vehicle". The upper ontology holds general concepts which are common to the sub domains and can therefore be flexibly extended. CONON is implemented using OWL. Context reasoning in pervasive environment is time-consuming but is feasible for non-time-critical applications. For time-critical applications like navigation systems or security systems, the data size and rule complexity must be reduced. Context reasoning is dissociated from context usage. A server does the reasoning and tiny devices like mobile phones get the pre-calculated high-level context from the server for direct use. This is an infrastructure based environment.

CoBrA-ONT [8] is a context management model that enables distributed agents to control the access to their personal information in context-aware environments. CoBrA-ONT is a collection of OWL ontologies for context-aware systems. CoBrA-ONT is designed to be used as a common vocabulary in order to overcome the obstacle of proprietary context models that block the interoperability of different devices. Semantics of OWL are used for context reasoning. CoBrA-ONT is central part of CoBrA, a "broker-centric agent architecture in smart spaces" where it supports context reasoning and interoperability. The center of this architecture is context broker agent, which is a server that runs on a resources rich stationary computer. It receives and manages context knowledge for a set of agents and devices in its vicinity, which is the "smart space". Agents and devices can contact the context broker and exchange information by the FIPA Agent Communication Language. The architecture of CoBrA-ONT is based on the upper ontology and domain specific ontology that extends the upper ontology .CoBrA-ONT is defined using the Web Ontology Language (OWL) to model the counts of people, agents, places and presentation events. It also describes the properties and relationships between these concepts. CoBrA-ONT depends on the assumption that there always exists a context-broker server that is known by all the participants. CoBrA is infrastructure-centric and is not fit for pervasive computing whereas the platform proposed in this work is mobile device-centric, where no additional equipment for a mobile device itself is required for system operation.

SOUPA (Standard Ontology for Ubiquitous and Pervasive Applications) [9] is designed to model and support pervasive computing applications. The SOUPA ontology is expressed using the Web Ontology Language OWL and includes modular component vocabularies to represent intelligent agents with associated beliefs, desires and intension, time, space, events, user profiles, actions and policies for security and privacy. SOUPA is more comprehensive than CoBrA-ONT because it deals with more areas of pervasive computing. It also addresses CoBrA-ONT because it deals with more areas of pervasive computing and also addresses problems regarding ontology reuse. The SOUPA sub-ontologies map many of its concepts using owl: equivalentClass to concepts of existing common ontologies.

GAS ontology [10] is ontology designed for collaboration among ubiquitous computing devices. The basic goal of this ontology is to provide a common language for the communication and collaboration among the heterogeneous devices that constitute these environments. The GAS Ontology also supports the service discovery mechanism that a ubiquitous computing environment requires.

Context aware systems are based on ad-hoc models of context, which causes lack of the desired formality and expressiveness. Existing models do not separate processing of context semantics from processing and representation of context data and structure. Ontology representation tools are suitable for statically representing the knowledge in a domain. They are not designed for capturing and processing constantly changing information in dynamic environment in a scalable manner. Existing ontology languages and serialization formats are test-based (xml/rdf/owl) and not designed for efficient query optimization, processing and retrieval of large context data. The main drawbacks of pure ontological approaches are low performance and data throughput.

3 Proposed Work

The proposed context aware system has three layers as shown in fig 1. They are context acquisition layer, context middleware and application layer. Context acquisition layer gathers the context from the environment using sensors, active badges, camera, Wi-Fi devices etc. Context middleware has three components. They are representation layer, context management layer and decision layer .Context representation layer represents context as entity relation hierarchy form. For example context defined using predicates like ownedby are inactive and context defined using predicates like locatedIn are active. Inactive context are stored in Object relational database and active context are stored in Ontology. The persistent data about static context in the database are selectively populated as context instances into the ontology structure at runtime.

In the middleware rules learned or rules derived from other rules are also maintained. Rules play an important role in the process of reasoning about contexts. Rules come from either rules defined by user, rules derived from organizational policies and rules derived from history data of past decisions. Reasoning is performed based on two reasoning sources:

Ontology reasoning is based on rules that are integrated in the Web Ontology Language semantics, like using transitive and inverse relations.

User-defined reasoning which are stated outside of Web Ontology Language, like if *person* is *locatedIn bedroom* and *electricLight is dim* conclude *the person is sleeping*. Implicit rules are derived from the ontology and explicit rules are defined by the user based on the specific domain of application. Table 2 shows some of these rules into two categories: ontology based and user defined rules. Using the rules, relevant context from database and ontology are forwarded to the reasoning component. From reasoning layer appropriate context is sent to user in the application layer.

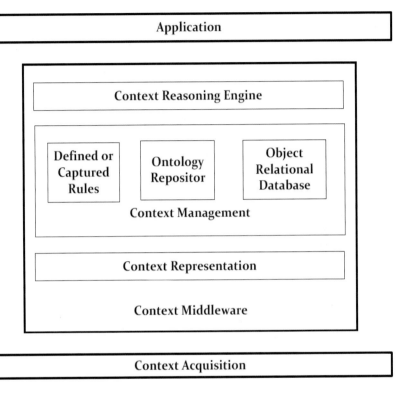

Fig. 1. Block Diagram

Table 1. Ontology Based and user defined rules Example

Rule	Category
(? a property ?b) (?b property ?c) → (?a property ?c) Eg. locatedIn, subCalssOf, contains… (transitive property)	Ontology
(?a property1 ?b) → (?b property2 ?a) Eg. ownerOf and OwnedBy, locatedIn and contains… (inverse property)	
(?a property ?b) → (?b property ?a) coLocatedWith, friendOf … (symmetric)	
(?device locatedIn ?location) (?device ownedBy ?person) → (?person locatedIn ?location)	User defined
(?student locatedIn Library) (?student owns ?phone) → (?phone "switchMode" "Silent")	

3.1 Context Representation

Context defined as characteristics of the entities, their relationships and properties of the relationships [4, 5]. Context representation needs a model that supports easy transaction of piece wise tiny but voluminous and dynamic context data. It is important to aggregate and interpret the context data with respect to its semantics it to make it ready for reasoning and decision.

In the context management layer context is further classified as inactive context and active context. Predicates are used to decide the inactive context. Context can be personal context, device context, physical context, activity context, network context, location context etc. Personal entity provides contexts like person's identity, address, activity; location etc. Context can be represented as Entity, Hierarchy, Relation, Axiom and Metadata [11].

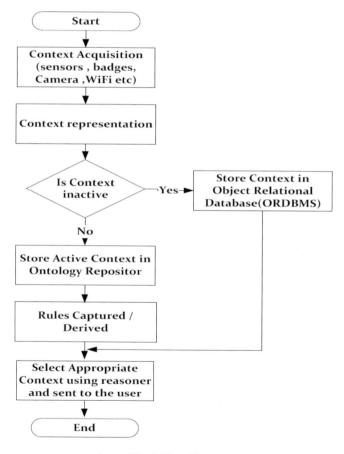

Fig. 2. Flow Chart

Hierarchy is a set of binary relations that form an inversely directed acyclic graph on entities. Nodes of the graph represent entities and arcs of the graph represent hierarchical relations. The root entity at the top of the hierarchy graph is a global entity known as ContextEntity. Relation is union of set of binary relations. Relation can be either entity relation or attribute relation. Entity relation has a set of binary relations having either its domain or range from the set of entity. Attribute relation is the set of binary relations defined from set of entities to set of literals.

Example *hasEndTime, hasMemory, hasStartTime and hasBodyTemp are attribute relations.* Relations like *hasDoctor, locatedWith and owns are entity relations.* SubEntityOf relation, SubPropertyOf, domain, range etc is some relations used to link entities. Entities and relations are sources of context data. Relation can be generic or domain based.

For example in a generic level, relation is defined as person isLocatedIn Location and in a domain level, relation is defined as Student isLocatedIn Class. Axiom is the axiomatic relations. Some of the generic level axiomatic relations are sameAs, inverse, symmetric and transitive. Meta data are information about a defined relation instance. Information like time of occurrence, precision, source of data can be a part of Meta information. Example, Student isLocatedIn Class at a given time t. Here t is metadata.

3.2 Comparing Object Relational Database and Relational Database

Relational models provide standard interfaces and query optimization tools for managing large and distributed context database or receive and send notification on context changes. Relational models are not designed for semantic interpretation of data.

Table 2. Comparision of Relational Database and Object Relational Database (ordbms)

Necessary Feature	Relational Approach	Ontology Approach	Object Relational Approach
Semantic Support	No	Yes	No
Ease of transaction (large data)	Yes	No	Yes
Query optimization	Yes	No	Yes
Reasoning Support	No	Yes	No
Formality	Yes	Yes	Yes
Scalability	Yes	Yes	Yes

Relational database alone cannot be used to represent context in a pervasive environment. For semantic interpretations, ontology is used along with relational database. The table 2 above summarizes the appropriateness of both approaches in relation to the necessary features [14]. Both approaches have strong and weak sides with respect to features for context management modeling. Best of two worlds are combined to form a hybrid context management model. Both relational approach and object relational approach are in the same level.

Object Relational Approach is more suitable than Relational approach because of the following advantages: Object relational database supports several storage units like collection list, arrays, types and UDTs (User defined data types) and most of them are represented as objects arrays. Object relational approach ensures large storage capacity, which is an important part in web based development. The access speed is fairly quick. Object relational database have a massive scalability compared to relational approach. Object relational database boast excellent manipulation power of object databases. It supports rich data types by adding a new object-oriented layer. The systems are initially implemented by storing the inactive context to a relational database and active context to an ontology. Then the response time to get the relevant time is noted. Then system is implemented by replacing the storing of inactive context to relational database by object relational database. Then appropriate service can be provided to the user using service discovery [12] [13].

3.3 Storing Context to an Relational Database

Context represented in entity relation hierarchy form is stored in a relational database using the algorithm steps mentioned below. The attributes used in the relational table are: CEntity stores name of context entities. An attribute that stores name of the entity one step above in the hierarchy is called isa relation. Layer field stores whether an entity is in the generic or domain layer. Relation field stores name of relations .An attribute that stores persistence of the relation when applied to an entity can be inactive or active. Values of relations with static persistence are stored in the persistent context repository and values with dynamic persistence are stored temporarily for immediate use in the field named Persistence. ValueForm field stores source of value as a context entity or as a "Litral"..Structure of the relational table is shown below:

Step 1 : Create Entity table with fields Context Entity, direct hierarchy relation Like isa, isinstanceof and Layer is whether generic or domain.
Step 2 : Create Relation table with Relation, Persistence where the context is static or dynamic.
Step 3 : Create Relation Instance table with fields Relation name, Context Entity, And its Value.
Step 4 : Create Entity Instance table with fields Entity Instance and Context Entity.
Step 5 : Create Context Instance table with fields Entity Instance, Relation, Value, Time Stamp, Context Source and Context Precision .Time Stamp, Context Precision are the Meta data.

An attribute that stores name of instances is EInstance. Value is an attribute that stores value of the relation after applied to the instance. Timestamp field stores context timestamp. Source field stores source of context. Precision field stores precision of the context.

4 Conclusion

A hierarchical representation is used to represent the context using a directed acyclic graph. This representation is used to separate context as domain dependent or domain independent. Here it is focused on context representation and storage using ontology and object relational database. Future work includes a reasoner to decide the context obtained from the context management and provide the appropriate service to the user.

References

1. Mattern, F., Sturn, P.: From Distributed Systems to Ubiquitous Computing- State of the Art. Trends and Prospects of Future Networked systems. In: Fachtagung Kommunication in Verteilten Systems (KiVS), Leipzig, pp. 3–25. Springer, Berlin (2003)
2. Satyanarayanan, M.: Pervasive Computing Vision and Challenges. IEEE Personal Communications, 10–17 (2000)
3. Strang, T., LinnhoPopien, C.: A Context Modeling Survey. In: The Proceedings of the First International Workshop on Advanced Context Modeling, Reasoning and Management, 6th International Conference on UbiComp 2004, Nottingham, England (2004)
4. Winograd, T.: Architectures for Context. Human-Computer Interaction 16(2-4), 401–419 (2001)
5. Dey, A.K., Abowd, G.D.: Towards a Better Understanding of Context and Context Awareness. In: Proceedings of the CHI Workshop on the What, Who, Where and How of Context-Awareness, The Hague, the Netherlands (2000)
6. Baldauf, M.: A survey on context aware Systems. Int. J. Ad hoc and Ubiquitous Computing 2(4), 263–277 (2007)
7. Wang, X., Zhang, D., Gu, T., Pung, H.K.: Ontology Based Context Modeling and Reasoning using OWL, workshop on context modeling and reasoning. In: IEEE International Conference on Pervasive Computing and Communication, Orlando, Florida (2004)
8. Chen, H.: An Intelligent Broker Architecture for Pervasive Context-Aware Systems. PhD Thesis University of Maryland, Baltimore Country, USA (2004)
9. Chen, H., Perich, F., Finin, T., et al.: SOUPA: Standard Ontology for Ubiquitous and Pervasive Applications. In: International Conference on Mobile and Ubiquitous Systems: Networking And Services, Boston, USA (2004)
10. Christopoulou, E., Kameas, A.: GAS Ontology: ontology for collaboration among ubiquitous Computing devices. International Journal of Human-Computer Studies 62(5), 664–685 (2005)
11. Ejigu, D., Scuturi, M., Brunie, L.: An Ontology Based Approach to Context Modeling and Reasoning in Pervasive Computing. In: 5th IEEE International Conference on Pervasive Computing and Communications Workshops, pp. 14–19 (2007)
12. Vanathi, B., Rhymend Uthariaraj, V.: Ontology based service discovery for context aware computing. In: 1st IEEE International Conference on Advanced Computing. IEEE Computer Society, Chennai (2009)
13. Vanathi, B., Rhymend Uthariaraj, V.: Context Representation and Management in a Pervasive Environment. In: International Conference on Advances in Information and Communication Technologies, pp. 543–548. Springer, Heidelberg (2010)
14. Vanathi, B., Rhymend Uthariaraj, V.: Context representation using hierarchical method and heuristic based context selection in context aware computing. In: Conference of Women in Computing in India Proceedings of the 1st Amrita ACM-W Celebration on Women in Computing in India (2010)

Path Optimization and Trusted Routing in MANET: An Interplay between Ordered Semirings

Kiran K. Somasundaram and John S. Baras*

Insitute for Systems Research and
Department of Electrical and Computer Engineering
University of Maryland,
College Park, MD 20742
kirans@umd.edu, baras@umd.edu

Abstract. In this paper, we formulate the problem of trusted routing as a transaction of services over a complex networked environment. We present definitions from service-oriented environments that unambiguously capture the difference between trust and reputation relations. We show that the trustworthiness metrics associated with these relations have a linear order embedded in them. Identifying this order structure permits us to treat the trusted routing problem as a bi-objective path optimization problem. We consider bottleneck trust and present polynomial time algorithms to obtain the optimal routing paths in various bi-objective settings. In developing these algorithms, we identify an interesting decomposition principle for $(\min, +)$ and $(\min, \max)$ semirings, which yields a distributed solution.

Keywords: Pareto Optimality, Lexicographic Optimality, Max-Order Optimality, Semirings.

1 Introduction

Mobile Ad Hoc Networks (MANETs) have been envisioned as self-organising networks requiring little or no pre-established infrastructure. The proposed ability of the hosts to dynamically associate themselves with the network in an ad-hoc manner has fuelled a number of application ideas for these networks. However, recent research ([1], [2]) has revealed that this flexibility bears with it several security and survivability threats.

In this paper, we address the problem of trusted routing in MANETs. The lack of pre-installed trust relations in MANETs has steered the networking community to adopt mechanisms from reputation technology for trusted routing ([3],[4], [5]).

* This material is based upon work supported by the Communications and Networks Consortium sponsored by the U.S. Army Research Laboratory under the Collaborative Technology Alliance Program, Cooperative Agreement DAAD19-01-2-0011 and the MURI Award Agreement W911-NF-0710287 from the Army Research Office.

N. Meghanathan et al. (Eds.): CCSIT 2011, Part II, CCIS 132, pp. 88–98, 2011.

However, there has been many inconsistencies in defining these trust concepts ([1]). Therefore, we introduce precise definitions of trust concepts from the literature on reputation systems, which has been well established and applied in e-services and e-businesses [6].

In this paper, we consider an additive performance metric and a bottleneck trust metric. We show that the trustworthiness metrics used in the literature have a linear order embedded in them. Such order structures are fundamental to optimization ([7]) and help formulate the performance-trust routing problem as a bi-objective optimization problem. We also present distributed polynomial time algorithms which can solve these problems. Our methods find efficient trade-off points between performance and trust for routing. For a more detailed version, see our technical report [8].

The two main contribution of this paper are the following: modeling the performance-trust problem as a bi-objective problem, and providing distributed solutions to the corresponding $(\min, +)$ and $(\min, \max)$ semiring problems.

This paper is organized as follows. In Section 2, we introduce trust and reputation concepts and their application to MANET routing protocols. In Section 3, we present an order-theoretic modeling of trustworthiness metrics. We then develop path metrics for routing in Section 4. Finally, in Section 5, we use the metrics to formulate several bi-objective optimization problems and present algorithms to solve them.

2   Trust and Reputation Inspired Routing Paradigm

Several reputation schemes that mitigate the selfish behaviour in MANET were proposed (e.g., [9], [3],[10], [4]). The concepts of trust and reputation have been developed and applied in diverse areas such as social sciences, e-business and computer science, which resulted in many inconsistent definitions. It has been observed that there is no formal definition of trust and reputation in communication networking literature ([1]). In this paper, we adopt definitions from the literature on *service-oriented environments* because we find a clear distinction between the trust and the reputation concepts. We introduce these concepts in the forthcoming subsections. A detailed introduction is available in our technical report [8].

2.1   Trust and Reputation Concepts

Most trust relations are between a *trusting agent* and a *trusted agent*. Every trust relation involves a *context C* and *time t*. Such a binary relation is called a *direct trust relation*. However, in some scenarios it is not possible for a trusting agent to initiate a direct trust relation with the trusted agent due to spatial or temporal limitations. In such scenarios, the trusting agent requests for recommendations from a third party. The recommendations from this third party about the trusted agent forms the initial trust for bootstrapping the transactions. Such a ternary trust relation, is called a *indirect trust* or *reputation* relation. Associated with every trust relation (direct or indirect) is a trustworthiness measure which captures the strength of a trust relation. We show in Section 3, that these trustworthiness metrics live in an ordered space. This order captures the strength of the trust relations (direct trust, opinion credibility, etc.). To illustrate these relations in a MANET setting, consider any reputation based routing scheme such as *CONFIDANT* ([9]) or *LARS* ([5]). In these protocols, every station performs *self-policing*: trust monitoring, trustworthiness update, and response routing. In this setting, the context of relation is *C=Packet Forwarding*. However, not all trust contexts are restricted *Packet Forwarding*, e.g., the context can be *C=Strength of the Encryption Key*.

2.2 Trust and Reputation in Self-organised Networks

Reputation systems have already proven useful in e-businesses and e-services [6]. These systems, such as Amazon and eBay, have a centralized architecture for the reputation system where the decision makers are usually humans who look at the trustworthiness metrics and make decisions. However, in self-organized networks, the decision making must be automated [1]. The automated decision making component must be capable of interpreting the trustworthiness metrics.

This decision making component is called the *response routing* component in MANET routing ([11]). A trust-aware routing component should provide two services:

1. Exploit the trusted paths for routing traffic, i.e., for paths which have unambiguous trustworthiness metrics, the decision maker should route traffic without any subjective judgement.
2. Penalize the stations which do not conform to the packet forwarding protocol.

In this paper, we consider only the former as an objective for trusted routing.

3 Trustworthiness and Orders

In this section, we show that most trustworthiness metrics defined in literature form an *ordered set* and in particular they contain a linearly ordered subset that we can exploit for the routing protocols. In this paper we work with trustworthiness metrics which live in a finite set. Such metrics encompass a large body of literature on trust and reputation systems ([12], [13],[14], [15],[16], Amazon, eBay, etc). Again, for detailed definitions of linear orders and their relations to trustworthiness metrics, see [8].

4 Routing Metrics

Most of the works on routing inspired from trust and reputation mechanisms use only the trustworthiness measure to find the optimal routes for packet forwarding ([3], [4], [5]). In all the mechanisms, the trust context *C=Packet Forwarding*. In MANETs, such an approach might route packets through high delay (length) paths. In many scenarios, such high lengths might be intolerable for the application traffic. In this paper, we define two semiring metrics for the path to capture the length and the trustworthiness of a path. We address this problem as a *bi-objective* graph optimization problem.

4.1 Trustworthiness of a Path

Let us consider a path $p = S \to i_1 \to i_2 \to \cdots i_{n-1} \to T$ in G_c. Associated with every directed arc (i_m, i_n) is a trustworthiness $x(i_m, i_n) \in \mathcal{X}$. In defining the trustworthiness of a path, it is reasonable to adhere to the adage that the strength of a chain (path) is limited to the strength of its weakest link. This is called as bottle-neck trust. If the trustworthiness of a link along a path is unknown, the trustworthiness of this path is also unknown. Since the routing controller works only on the exploitable paths, it suffices to consider paths containing only links whose trustworthiness is exploitable. Let us denote these paths as $\mathcal{P}^L_{ST} = \{p \in \mathcal{P}_{S,T} : \forall (i_m, i_n) \in p, x(i_m, i_n) \in \mathcal{X}^L\}$. Then the trustworthiness of path $p \in \mathcal{P}^L_{S,T}$ is

$$x_p \leq x(i_m, i_n), \forall (i_m, i_n) \in p$$
$$\Rightarrow x_p \leq \min_{(i_m, i_n) \in p} x(i_m, i_n)$$

We use this upper bound as the trustworthiness of the path: $x_p = \min_{(i_m,i_n)\in p} x(i_m, i_n)$. This metric is called the bottleneck trust. Note, the trust in the context $C=Packet$ *Forwarding* cannot be modeled as bottleneck trust. In this context, the trust metric is multiplicative along a path. The bottleneck trust is applicable in contexts such as *C=Strength of the Encryption Keys*.

The duality principle of ordered sets provides an equivalent metric in terms of the dual ordered set. If we impose the dual order on $\mathcal{X}$, the order relation on $\mathcal{X}^\partial$ induces an equivalent dual trust metric

$$x_p^\partial = \max_{(i_m, i_n) \in p} x^\partial(i_m, i_n)$$

4.2 Length of a Path

For legacy routing schemes such as ARPANET ([17]) or IP ([18]), we associate a length l_p for path p. This could be a simple metric such as the hop count or more complicated average delay statistic which captures the delay of the path. In the wireless multi-hop scenario, the delays are primarily due to the congestion in the local MAC. Let us denote the queue congestion metric at station i_m for packets destined to the neighbouring node i_n by $d(i_m, i_n)$. Then,

$$l_p = \sum_{(i_m, i_n) \in p} d(i_m, i_n)$$

The algorithms in this paper are generic and invariant to the path length metric. However, we do assume that the path length composition is an additive composition along the path.

5   Route Selection - A Bi-objective Optimization Problem

In Subsections 4.1 and 4.2, we introduced the trust and length metrics for the path. A good design criteria for a routing controller is to construct routes that have *high trustworthiness* and *low length*. However, in general these two objectives may be opposing in nature, which results in a trade-off analysis problem. This is the primary object of study in multi-criteria optimization. A summary of the various multi-criteria methods can be found in [19].

The two objectives of the routing controller to constructs routes for a source target pair S, T are: $\{ \min_{p \in \mathcal{P}^L_{S,T}} l_p, \max_{p \in \mathcal{P}^L_{S,T}} x_p \}$. The dual trustworthiness transforms the problem into a bi-metric minimization problem: $\{ \min_{p \in \mathcal{P}^L_{S,T}} l_p, \min_{p \in \mathcal{P}^L_{S,T}} x_p^\partial \}$. This bi-objective optimization problem is represented as a Multi-Criteria Optimization Problem (MCOP) class ([19]):

$$(\mathcal{P}^L_{S,T}, \begin{bmatrix} l_p \\ x_p^\partial \end{bmatrix}, \mathbb{R}^+ \times \mathcal{X}^{L^\partial}, \leq^2) \tag{1}$$

where $\mathcal{P}^L_{S,T}$ is the set of decision alternatives, $\begin{bmatrix} l_p \\ x_p^\partial \end{bmatrix}$ is a vector valued objective function that maps the decision alternatives to the *length-dual-trust* $(\mathbb{R}^+ \times \mathcal{X}^{L^\partial})$ objective space. There are various $\leq^2$ orders that can be considered for vectors. Table 1 shows the most commonly used orders for two-dimensional vectors $\underline{x}$ and $\underline{y}$. Among these orders, the *Max order* is valid only when $\mathcal{X}^{L^\partial}$ is comparable with $\mathbb{R}^+$.

Table 1. Table of Orders

Notation	Definition	Name
$\underline{x} < \underline{y}$	$x_i \leq y_i \quad i = 1, 2$ and $\underline{x} \neq \underline{y}$	Componentwise
$\underline{x} \leq_{lex} \underline{y}$	$x_k < y_k \quad or \quad \underline{x} = \underline{y} \quad k = \min\{i : x_i \neq y_i\}$	Lexicographic
$\underline{x} \leq_{MO} \underline{y}$	$\max\{x_1, x_2\} \leq \max\{y_1, y_2\}$	Max-order

5.1   Length and Trust Semirings

The presented *MCOP* involves two semiring structures ([20]). The length optimization problem corresponds to a $(\mathbb{R}^+, \min, +)$ semiring. The trust optimization problem corresponds to a $(X^l, \max, \min)$ semiring. Both of these semiring structures have been independently studied and extensively used in the optimization community ([20]). In the theory of MCOP classes, there are many possible methods to combine objectives to obtain solutions ([19]). However, to the best of our knowledge, no theory has combined these two semirings in the various MCOP settings. In the forthcoming subsections, we present distributed polynomial-time algorithms to solve the various bi-objective optimization formulations.

5.2   Pareto Optimal Routing Strategy

The Pareto class for the bi-objective optimization problem is given by

$$(\mathcal{P}_{S,T}^{L}, \begin{bmatrix} l_p \\ x_p^{\partial} \end{bmatrix}, \mathbb{R}^{+} \times \mathcal{X}^{L^{\partial}}, <) \tag{2}$$

where $<$ is the component-wise order defined in Table 1. A path $p^{efficient} \in \mathcal{P}_{S,T}^{L}$ is Pareto optimal if there exists no path $p \in \mathcal{P}_{S,T}^{L}$ and $p \neq p^{efficient}$ such that $\begin{bmatrix} l_p \\ x_p^{\partial} \end{bmatrix} < \begin{bmatrix} l_{p^{efficient}} \\ x_{p^{efficient}}^{\partial} \end{bmatrix}$. For a general decision problem, there are many *Pareto efficient points* ([19]). One of the common methods to compute efficient points is using the *Haimes-ϵ constraint* method ([21], [22]), which converts all but one of the objectives into constraints and solves the single-objective constraint optimization problem. By considering various relaxations of the Haimes method, we obtain all the Pareto solutions.

Semiring Decomposition: In our case, we show that the Haimes-ϵ constraint method lends itself to a natural decomposition which separates the length and trust semiring. The Haimes formulation is:

$$\min_{p \in \mathcal{P}_{S,T}^{L}} l_p$$

$$x_p^{\partial} \leq \epsilon, \quad \epsilon \in \mathcal{X}^{\partial L}$$

The constraint $x_p^{\partial} \leq \epsilon \Rightarrow \max_{(i_m, i_n) \in p} x^{\partial}(i_m, i_n) \leq \epsilon$

$$\Rightarrow x^{\partial}(i_m, i_n) \leq \epsilon, \forall (i_m, i_n) \in p.$$

This implication gives the following decomposition.
Subproblem 1(ϵ): Find a subset of paths in $\mathcal{P}_{S,T}^{L}$ whose paths have a trustworthiness less than ϵ. This corresponds to finding a pruned subset:

$$\mathcal{P}_{S,T}^{L\text{-}Pruned\text{-}\epsilon} = \{p \in \mathcal{P}_{S,T}^{L} : x^{\partial}(i_m, i_n) \leq \epsilon, \forall (i_m, i_n) \in p\}$$

Subproblem 2(ϵ):

$$\min_{p \in \mathcal{P}_{S,T}^{L\text{-}Pruned\text{-}\epsilon}} l_p$$

The decomposition is evident as *Subprob 1(ϵ)* involves only the trust semiring and *Subprob 2(ϵ)* involves only the length semiring. This decomposition yields an *edge exclusion* and *shortest path* procedure to solve Eqn. (2). Algorithm 1 builds on these ideas to obtain all the Pareto efficient paths between a source destination pair S, T. It runs on every $i \in V$ and requires only local neighbourhood information ($\mathcal{N}_i$). The routine call Covered Element(x) returns the covered element of x. The proofs of convergence and correctness are available in our technical report [8].

Algorithm 1. Compute All Pareto Paths
***

$\mathcal{P}_{S,T}^{L\text{-}Frontier} \leftarrow \emptyset$

$\epsilon \leftarrow \top$

repeat

    $E_r \leftarrow E_c$

    for $j \in \mathcal{N}_i$ **do**

        if $x(i,j) > \epsilon$ **then**

            $E_r \leftarrow E_r \backslash \{(i,j)\}$

        end if

    end for

    $G_r \leftarrow G_r(V, E_r)$

    $\mathcal{P}_{S,T}^{L\text{-}Pruned\text{-}\epsilon} \leftarrow$ Set of paths betweenS, T pair in $G_r(V, E_r)$

    $\mathcal{P}^{candidate}(\epsilon) \leftarrow arg \min_{p \in \mathcal{P}_{S,T}^{L\text{-}Pruned\text{-}\epsilon}} l_p$

    $p^{efficient} \leftarrow arg \min_{p \in \mathcal{P}^{candidate}} x_p^\partial$

    $\mathcal{P}_{S,T}^{L\text{-}Frontier} \leftarrow \mathcal{P}_{S,T}^{L\text{-}Frontier} \cup p^{effecient}$

    $\epsilon \leftarrow$ **Covered element**$(x_{p^{effficient}}^\partial)$

until $\mathcal{P}_{S,T}^{L\text{-}Pruned\text{-}\epsilon} \neq \emptyset$

return $\mathcal{P}_{S,T}^{L\text{-}Frontier}$
***

5.3 Biased Routing Strategy

A shortcoming of using the Pareto optimality approach is that the number of paths optimal in the Pareto sense is large. One popular approach to prune the Pareto set is *Lexicographic Ordering* ([19]). This method assumes that one metric is superior to other and tries to optimize with respect to the superior metric. Only if two or more feasible solutions are equally optimal in the superior measure, the other measure is considered. This *MCOP* class is represented as

$(\mathcal{P}_{S,T}^L, \begin{bmatrix} l_p \\ x_p^\partial \end{bmatrix}, \mathbb{R}^+ \times \mathcal{X}^{L^\partial}, \leq_{lex})$

Based on the lexicographic ordering that we choose, we obtain length or trust biased routing strategies. The strategies consider length or trust as the superior metric respectively. To obtain these paths, we introduce two semiring algebras.

Length-Lexicographic Semiring: $(\mathbb{R}^+ \times \mathcal{X}^{L^\partial}, \oplus_d, \otimes)$. The semiring operations are defined as follows. For $(d1, x1^\partial), (d2, x2^\partial) \in (\mathbb{R}^+ \times \mathcal{X}^{L^\partial})$ we define:

$$(d1, x1^\partial) \oplus_l (d2, x2^\partial)$$
$$= \begin{cases} (d1, x1^\partial) & \text{if} \quad d1 < d2 \\ (d2, x2^\partial) & \text{if} \quad d2 < d1 \\ (d1, \min(x1^\partial, x2^\partial)) & \text{if} \quad d1 = d2 \end{cases}$$

$$(d1, x1^\partial) \otimes (d2, x2^\partial) = (d1 + d2, \min(x1^\partial, x2^\partial))$$

Trust-Lexicographic Semiring: $(\mathbb{R}^+ \times \mathcal{X}^{L^\partial}, \oplus_x, \otimes)$. The semiring operations are defined as follows. For $(d1, x1^\partial), (d2, x2^\partial) \in (\mathbb{R}^+ \times \mathcal{X}^{L^\partial})$ we define:

$$(d1, x1^{\partial}) \oplus_x (d2, x2^{\partial})$$

$$= \begin{cases} (d1, x1^{\partial}) & \text{if} \quad x1^{\partial} < x2^{\partial} \\ (d2, x2^{\partial}) & \text{if} \quad x2^{\partial} < x1^{\partial} \\ (\min(d1, d2), x1^{\partial}) & \text{if} \quad x1^{\partial} = x2^{\partial} \end{cases}$$

$$(d1, x1^{\partial}) \otimes (d2, x2^{\partial}) = (d1 + d2, \min(x1^{\partial}, x2^{\partial}))$$

Defining these semirings facilitates the development of a generic distributed algorithm (i.e., Algorithm 2) to obtain lexicographic optimal paths between the source target pair S, T. Again, the algorithm runs at every $i \in V$ and needs only local information. The stations locally store and exchange a dynamic pair $(l, x^{\partial})[T]_i^n \in (\mathbb{R}^+ \times \mathcal{X}^{L^{\partial}})$ which represents the cost of the best lexicographic path from i to T that the algorithm can construct in n iterations.

Algorithm 2. Compute Lexicographic/Biased Path

---

repeat
$$(l, x^{\partial})[T]_i^{n+1} = \bigoplus_{k \in \mathcal{N}_i^+} (d_{i,k}, x^{\partial}(i, k)) \otimes (l, x^{\partial})[T]_k^n$$
until $(l, x^{\partial})[T]_i^n$ converges

The $\bigoplus$ used in Algorithm 2 is $\oplus_l$ and $\oplus_x$ for length and trust biased routing, respectively. We omit the Proof of Lexicographic Optimality of Algorithm 2 due to space limitations; the proof is presented in our technical report [8].

5.4 Conservative Routing Strategy

Another formulation in bi-objective optimization is the *Max-Ordering* (MO) method ([19]). However, this method is applicable to our problem only if the trust values and the path lengths are comparable. If they are, then we obtain a conservative routing strategy. This belongs to the *MCOP* class: $(\mathcal{P}_{S,T}^L, \begin{bmatrix} l_p \\ x_p^{\partial} \end{bmatrix}, \mathbb{R}^+ \times \mathcal{X}^{L^{\partial}}, \leq_{MO})$.

The above MCOP class tries to select paths which are optimal in the worst-case sense of trust and delay. Thus it is a conservative strategy for routing, where the cost of the path is governed by the worst-case value of its trust and delay. The problem is stated as

$$\min_{p \in \mathcal{P}_{S,T}^L} \max\{l_p, x_p^{\partial}\} \tag{3}$$

Semiring Decomposition: The MO problem involves the trust and length semirings. We present decomposition method to separate the semirings. Eqn. (3) can be written as

$$\min_{p \in \mathcal{P}_{S,T}^L} z$$

$$\text{subject to} \quad l_p \leq z$$
$$x_p^{\partial} \leq z$$

Again, the decomposition yields an *Edge Exclusion* and a *Shortest Path* procedure to obtain the MO paths. This is illustrated in Algorithm 3 which is carried out at every $i \in V$. The algorithm assigns an infinite cost to a non-existent path. The routine `Covering Element`(x) returns the covering element of x. The proofs of convergence and optimality are presented in our technical report [8].

Algorithm 3. Compute MO paths

$z \leftarrow \bot$
while True **do**
    $E_r \leftarrow E_c$
    for $j \in \mathcal{N}_i$ **do**
      if $x(i,j) > \epsilon$ **then**
        $E_r \leftarrow E_r \backslash \{(i,j)\}$
      end if
    end for
    $G_r \leftarrow G_r(V, E_r)$
    $\mathcal{P}_{S,T}^{L\text{-}Pruned\text{-}\epsilon} \leftarrow$ Set of paths between(S,T) pair in $G_r(V, E_r)$
    $p^{candidate} \leftarrow arg \min_{p \in \mathcal{P}_{S,T}^{L\text{-}Pruned\text{-}\epsilon}} p$
    if $l_{p^{candidate}} \leq \epsilon$ **then**
      return $p^{candidate}$
    end if
    if $\epsilon =?\top$ **then**
      return No path found
    end if
    $\epsilon \leftarrow$ `Covering Element`(ϵ)
end while

The three algorithms proposed use the `Shortest path` subroutine and `Edge Exclusion` subroutine repeatedly. This is a manifestation of the Semiring decomposition principle. There are many efficient polynomial-time distributed implementations for both of these subroutines ([23]). Thus all these algorithms can be efficiently implemented in a self-organised MANET.

6 Conclusion

In this paper, we present an order-theoretic modeling of the trustworthiness metrics used in different trust and reputation systems. We then treat the trusted routing for a bottleneck trust as a bi-objective path optimization problem involving length and trust metrics. We solve the corresponding Pareto class, which yields the efficient paths. We also solve the Lexicographic and MO classes. In all three cases, we present distributed polynomial-time algorithms that can be implemented in a self-organized MANET.

References

1. Buchegger, S., Mundinger, J., Boudec, J.-Y.L.: Reputation systems for self-organized networks. IEEE Technology and Society Magazine 27, 41–47 (2008)
2. Yau, P., Mitchell, C.: Security vulnerbilities in ad hoc networks. In: 7th International Symposium on Communication Theory and Applications (2003)
3. Buchegger, S., Boudec, J.-Y.L.: A robust reputation system for p2p and mobile ad-hoc networks. In: Proceedings 2nd workshop on the Economics of P2P Systems (2004)
4. Bansal, S., Baker, M.: Observation-based cooperation enforcement in ad hoc networks. Stanford University, Tech. Rep. (2003)
5. Hu, J., Burmester, M.: Lars: a locally aware reputation system for mobile ad hoc networks. In: 44th ACM Annual Southeast Regional Conference, pp. 119–123 (2006)
6. Chang, E., Hussain, F., Dillon, T.: Trust and Reputation for Service-Oriented Environments: Technologies For Building Business Intelligence And Consumer Confidence. Wiley, Chichester (2006)
7. Davey, B., Priestley, H.: Introduction to lattices and order. Cambridge University Press, Cambridge (1990)
8. Somasundaram, K., Baras, J.S.: Path optimization techniques for trusted routing in mobile ad-hoc networks: An interplay between ordered semirings, Institute for Systems Research Technical Report (2008), http://hdl.handle.net/1903/9785
9. Buchegger, S., Boudec, J.-Y.L.: Performance analysis of confidant protocol: Cooperation of nodes - fairness in dynamic ad-hoc networks. In: Proceedings MobiHoc (2002)
10. Buchegger, S., Boudec, J.-Y.L.: The effect of rumour spreading in reputation systems for mobile ad-hoc networks. In: Proceedings of WiOpt (2003)
11. Resnick, R.Z.P.: Trust among strangers in internet transactions: Emperical analysis of ebay's reputation system. In: Advances in Applied Microeconomics: The Economics of the Internet and E-Commerce, vol. 11, pp. 127–157 (November 2002)
12. Aberer, K., Despotovic, Z.: Managing trust in a peer-2-peer information system. In: Proceedings of the Tenth International Conference on Information and Knowledge Management, pp. 310–317 (2001)
13. Xiong, L., Liu, L.: A reputation-based trust model for peer-to-peer ecommerce communities. In: IEEE Conference on E-Commerce, CEC 2003 (2003)
14. Chen, R., Yeager, W.: Poblano: A distributed trust model for peer-to-peer networks. Sun Microsystems, Tech. Rep. (2001)
15. Rahman, A., Hailes, S.: A distributed trust model. In: Proceedings of the 1997 Workshop on New Security Paradigms (1998)
16. Cornelli, F., Damiani, E., Di, S.D.C., Paraboschi, S., Samarati, P.: Choosing reputable servants in a p2p network. In: Proceedings of the 11th World Wide Web Conference, pp. 376–386 (2002)
17. McQuillan, J., Richer, I., Rosen, E.: The new routing algorithm for the arpanet. IEEE Transactions of Communication 28, 711–719 (1980)
18. Malkin, G.: Rip version 2. RFC 2453, Network Working Group (November 1998), http://www.ietf.org/rfc/rfc2453.txt

19. Ehrgott, M.: Multicriteria Optimization. Springer, Heidelberg (2000)
20. Rote, G.: Path problems in graphs. In: Computing Supplementum, vol. 7, pp. 155–189 (1990)
21. Haimes, Y., Lasdon, L., Wismer, D.: On a bicriterion formulation of the problems of integrated system identification and system optimization. IEEE Transactions on Systems, Man and Cybernetics 1, 296–297 (1971)
22. Chankong, V., Haimes, Y.: Multiobjective Decision Making: Theory and Methodology. Elsevier Science Publishing Co., Inc., Amsterdam (1983)
23. Kleinberg, J., Tardos, E.: Algorithm Design. Addison Wesley, Reading (2005)

LEAD:
Energy Efficient Protocol for
Wireless Ad Hoc Networks

Subhankar Mishra, Sudhansu Mohan Satpathy, and Abhipsa Mishra

Department of Computer Science and Engineering,
National Institute of Technology Rourkela, Odisha, India
{cse.vicky,findsudhansu,titliabhipsa}@gmail.com
http://nitrkl.ac.in

Abstract. Wireless Ad Hoc Networks comprise a fast developing research area with a vast spectrum of applications. Wireless sensor network systems enable the reliable monitoring of a variety of environments for both civil and military applications. The Energy efficiency continues to be a key factor in limiting the deployability of ad-hoc networks. Deploying an energy efficient system exploiting the maximum lifetime of the network has remained a great challenge since years. The time period from the instant at which the network starts functioning to the time instant at which the first network node runs out of energy, i.e. the network lifetime is largely dependent on the system energy efficiency. In this paper, we look at energy efficient protocols, which can have significant impact on the lifetime of these networks. The cluster heads get drain out maximum energy in the wireless ad hoc networks . We propose an algorithm that deals with minimizing the rate of dissipation of energy of cluster heads. The algorithm LEAD deals with energy efficient round scheduling of cluster head allocation of nodes and then followed by allocation of nodes to the cluster heads maximizing network lifetime using ANDA [1,2]. We compare our results with the previous works.

Keywords: Clustering, ANDA, energy efficiency, LID, energy factor, network lifetime, LEACH, LEAD.

1 Introduction

The greatest challenge manifesting itself in the design of wireless ad-hoc networks is the limited availability of the energy resources. These resources are quite significantly limited in wireless networks than in wired networks.

The network lifetime is defined as the time instant at which the network starts functioning to the time instant at which the first network node runs out of energy. In this paper we basically deal with the design of techniques to maximize the network lifetime in case of cluster-based systems, which represent a significant subset of ad-hoc networks. We present our work in stages where we first study and implement the ANDA. Then we implement the LID along with the ANDA

N. Meghanathan et al. (Eds.): CCSIT 2011, Part II, CCIS 132, pp. 99–106, 2011.

and finally we propose our own original algorithm for improving upon the ANDA and maximizing the network lifetime. Our proposed algorithm uses a concept of the traditional LEACH for the maximization of the network lifetime. We hence show in our paper that our Algorithm quite outperforms the traditional Algorithms proposed till date.

CLUSTERING, in general is defined as the grouping of similar objects or the process of finding a natural association among some specific objects or data. In sensor networks, clusters are used to transmit processed data to base stations. In cluster-based systems the network nodes are partitioned into several groups. In each group one node becomes the cluster-head and the rest of the nodes act as ordinary nodes. The process of cluster-formation consists of two phases : cluster-head election and assignment of nodes to cluster-heads[4,5]. The cluster-head needs to coordinate all transmissions within the cluster, so also it handles the inter-cluster traffic, delivers the packets destined for the cluster etc. Hence these cluster-heads experience high-energy consumption and thereby exhaust their energy resources more quickly than the ordinary nodes. It is therefore required that the cluster-heads. energy consumption be minimized (optimal) thus maximizing the network lifetime [1].

We first discuss the previous work done in this field like the anda, lid and leach and then move on for our algorithm lead, its detailed algorithm and our simulation environment.

2   Related Works

2.1   ANDA

ANDA [1] algorithm allocates the ordinary nodes to the cluster heads [1] in a way such that the cluster heads sustain for a longer period thereby increasing the overall lifetime of the network. Here a single node is assigned to a cluster head if this allocation increases the lifetime of the network. ANDA algorithm basically comprises two algorithms, one the covering algorithm [1] which is applied to the static and dynamic case and second, the reconfigure algorithm [1] which applies only to the dynamic scenario. Covering performs the optimal assignment of nodes to cluster-heads that presents the longest functioning time. Reconfigure algorithm makes use of Δ to obtain new nodes assignment every time the network configuration changes. But this algorithm deals with a fixed set of cluster-heads which continuously dissipate energy throughout the network functioning time. We came with the idea of having dynamic set of cluster-heads, thereby distributing the energy dissipation among the set of nodes for a better lifetime.

2.2   LID

The LID Algorithm is the Lowest ID Algorithm [2,3]. The LID algorithm is used to determine cluster heads and the nodes that constitute the cluster. The basic approach is that we used the LID algorithm[6,11] to choose the cluster-head and then implemented ANDA to cover the nodes. We assign a unique ID to each node in the network. The LID algorithm chooses arbitrarily the node with the lowest ID as the cluster-head and declares all the nodes within the range of this cluster-head as its members. This process continues until all nodes in the network have been grouped into cluster-heads. We calculated the network lifetime using our simulator and then compared with the ANDA. This whole thing is basically implemented in a dynamic scenario. The above scenario was implemented on a simulation platform. We took a dynamic scenario whereby nodes were also changing their positions at regular intervals, thereby considering speed of nodes. Basing on these factors the LID and ANDA algorithms were applied, to calculate lifetime.

3   LEAD

LEAD deals with dynamic selection of cluster heads among the set of nodes in the network and then allocation of the rest ordinary nodes to the cluster-heads dynamically. It adapts to the network and selection and allocation is done according to the current status of the network.

LEAD achieves three goals. First, we select a set of cluster heads among the nodes randomly which is very practical in case of wireless ad hoc networks instead of having a fixed set of cluster heads. Second, set of cluster heads are selected dynamically after a time Δ in a round schedule balancing the load (energy dissipation) throughout the nodes of the network thus increasing the lifetime. Third, dynamically allocates the nodes to the cluster heads using the enhanced feature of ANDA thereby reducing the load on each cluster head to sustain them for other rounds.

LEAD is proactive: each node periodically broadcasts HELLO messages that contain the nodes status (i.e., whether or not the node is currently a cluster head), its current energy, no of nodes under it, its range. From these HELLO messages the nodes calculate the lifetime if it is pseudo assigned to a particular cluster head and thus calculating final allocation of the node. The nodes together form the matrix of the ANDA using these messages. The state of the nodes change every Δ time so they periodically send the HELLO messages after every Δ time.

3.1   Cluster Head Selection

Let $S_C = \{1...C\}$ be the set of cluster-heads, $S_N = \{1...N\}$ be the set of ordinary nodes to be assigned to the clusters. Initially, when clusters are being created, each node decides whether or not to become a cluster-head for the current round according to the table created periodically updated every N/C rounds. This decision is based on the suggested percentage of cluster heads for the network (determined a priori) and the number of times the node has been a cluster-head so far. After a broadcast of HELLO messages the total network data is clubbed together and the nodes are sorted according to their current residual energy.

```
Selectcluster
    If (N/C divides Δ )
        Begin nodeSort
        for (every i∈S_C)
            for (every j∈S_N)
                if(energy[i] > energy[j])
                swap(i ,j)
            end for
        end for
        end nodeSort
    end if
```

3.2 Node Assignment

Let $S_C = \{1...C\}$ be the set of cluster-heads, $S_N = \{1...N\}$ be the set of ordinary nodes to be assigned to the clusters. We choose the set of cluster-heads SC Major Contributions to power consumption in nodes are: power consumed by the digital part of the circuitry, Power consumption of the transceiver in transmitting and receiving mode and output transmission power. The lifetime is calculated according to the following equation:-

$$L_i = \left(\frac{E_i}{\alpha r_i^2 + \beta|n_i|} \right) \qquad (1)$$

where E_i is the initial amount of energy available at cluster-head i, r_i is the coverage radius of cluster-head i, n_i is the number of nodes the control of cluster-head i, and α and β are constants. Considering that the limiting factor to the network lifetime is represented by the cluster-heads functioning time, the lifetime is defined by

$$L_S = min_{i\in S_C}\{L_i\} \qquad (2)$$

We need to devise techniques to maximize L_S. The Algorithm for assignment of the nodes is as follows:

```
Begin Assignnodes
    for (every i∈S_C)
        set Ei=initial energy of cluster-head i
        for (every j∈S_N)
            Compute d_ij,|n_ij|,l_ij
        end for
    end for
    L_S(new)= L_S(old)= L_S
    Δ=0
    while(L_S(new).L_S(old)-Δ)
        Δ=Δ+1
        for (every i∈S_C)
            for (every j∈S_N)
```

```
            Recompute Eᵢ=Eᵢ-Δ( αr²ᵢ+β|nᵢⱼ|)
            Update lᵢⱼ ∀ i∈S_C, j∈S_N
        end for
    end for
    Call Selectcluster and update L_S
    L_S(new)=L_S
 end while
endAssignnodes
```

4   Numerical Results

The performance of LEAD is derived in terms of the network life time measured at the time instant at which the first cluster head runs out of energy. We derived results by using a software tool designed by us using Java. We simulated an ad hoc network composed of slowly changing network topology. The network nodes are randomly distributed. The simulated area is a 1000 x 1000 matrix. The nodes can attain a maximum speed of 5m/sec and the mobility of nodes is random. We assumed that the initial energy of all the nodes in the network is 5000J and it can support up to 1000 nodes and even if a node is not a cluster head it loses some amount of energy due to radio transceiver and transmission amplifier.

Figure 1 shows the variation between the percentage of nodes becoming cluster heads and lifetime of the network in LEAD.

First, we compare the performance of LEAD with the results obtained by using ANDA (Ad hoc network design algorithm) in which cluster heads are known apriori. Figure 2 shows the network lifetime as a function of the number of nodes, for a percentage of cluster heads P=0.05. The life-time decreases as

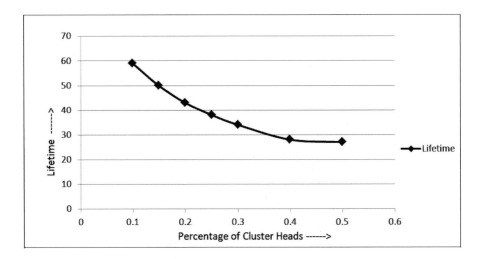

Fig. 1. Lifetime as a function of the number of nodes becoming cluster heads. The result is obtained through LEAD.

the number of nodes grow; however for a number of nodes greater than 100, the life-time remains almost constant as the number of nodes increases. Lifetime decreases because Clusterheads have to cover more nodes as the number of nodes in the network size increases. But LEAD shows significant improvement over ANDA, this is because in ANDA the cluster-heads are determined apriori but in case of LEAD cluster-heads are chosen in a random basis and each node becomes a cluster head in 1/P rounds i.e.the nodes that are cluster-heads in round 0 cannot be cluster-heads for the next 1/P rounds. From the comparison with the performance of ANDA, we observe that the improvement achieved through LEAD is equal to 35 %. Energy is uniformly drained from all the nodes and hence the network life-time is significantly increased.

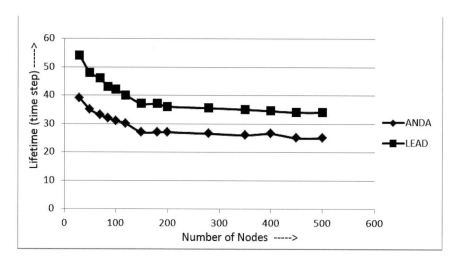

Fig. 2. Lifetime as a function of the number of nodes, for a percentage of nodes becoming cluster heads equal to 0.05. Results obtained through ANDA and LEAD scheme are compared.

Figure 3 shows the network life-time as the number of cluster-heads, C. Curves are obtained for N=1000 and nodes distributed randomly over the network area. In ANDA we observe that as the number of cluster heads increases for a given number of nodes, the life-time is increased ,this is due to the fact that increasing C , cluster heads now have to cover less number of nodes and energy of each node is drained at a slower rate. But, in case of LEAD we observe that network life-time decreases with the increase in percentage of nodes becoming cluster-heads (P). For less percentage of nodes becoming cluster-heads the time interval between successive election of a node as cluster-head is large but if percentage of nodes becoming cluster-heads is high, the time interval is small i.e a node is again elected as a cluster-head in less number of rounds. So, energy is drained early resulting in a decreased network life-time.

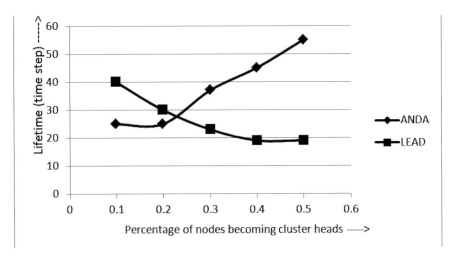

Fig. 3. Lifetime as a function of the percentage of nodes becoming cluster heads. Results obtained through ANDA and LEAD scheme are compared.

5   Conclusion

This paper mainly deals with the problem of maximizing the life-time of a wireless ad hoc network, i.e the time period during which the network is fully working. We presented an original solution called LEAD which is basically an improvement on ANDA. After making a brief comparative study of our work, we see that as we move on from ANDA to our proposed Algorithm, we gradually get an increased network lifetime. From the various graphs and tables, we can successfully prove that our Algorithm quite outperforms the traditional energy-efficient algorithms in an obvious way. The LEAD algorithm outperforms the original ANDA algorithm by 35%.

References

1. Chiasserini, C.-F., Chlamtac, I., Monti, P., Nucci, A.: Energy Efficient Design of Wireless Ad Hoc Networks. In: Gregori, E., Conti, M., Campbell, A.T., Omidyar, G., Zukerman, M. (eds.) NETWORKING 2002. LNCS, vol. 2345, pp. 376–386. Springer, Heidelberg (2002)
2. Ephremides, A., Wieselthier, J.E., Baker, D.J.: Proc. IEEE 75(1) (January 1987)
3. Baker, D.J., Ephremides, A.: The architectural organization of a mobile radio network via a distributed algorithm. IEEE Transactions on Communications, 1694–1701 (November 1981)
4. Kwon, T., Gerla, M.: Clustering with Power Control. In: Proc. MILCOM 1999 (November 1999)
5. Heinzelman, W.B., Chandrakasan, A., Balakrishnan, H.: Energy-Efficient Communication Protocols for Wireless Microsensor Networks. In: Proceedings of Hawaiian International Conference on Systems Science (January 2000)

6. Heinzelman, W.B.: Application-Specific Protocol Architectures for Wireless Networks, PhD thesis, Massachusetts Institute of Technology (June 2000)
7. Akyildiz, I.F., et al.: Wireless sensor networks: a survey. Computer Networks 38, 393–422 (2002)
8. Hill, J.: System Architecture for Wireless Sensor Networks, PhD Thesis (Spring 2003)
9. Manjeshwar, A., Agrawal, D.P.: TEEN: A Protocol for Enhanced Efficiency in Wireless Sensor Networks. In: 1st International Workshop on Parallel and Distributed Computing Issues in Wireless Networks and Mobile Computing, San Francisco, CA (April 2001)
10. Jiang, M., Li, J., Tay, Y.C.: Cluster Based Routing Protocol, Internet Draft (1999)
11. Royer, E.M., Toh, C.K.: A Review of Current Routing Protocols for Ad-Hoc Mobile Wireless Networks. IEEE Personal Communications Magazine, 46–55 (April 1999)
12. Intanagonwiwat, C., Govindan, R., Estrin, D.: Directed Diffusion: A Scalable and Robust Communication Paradigm for Sensor Networks. In: Proceedings of the 6th Annual ACM/IEEE International Conference on Mobile Computing and Networking (MOBICOM), pp. 56–67 (August 2000)

Scale-Down Digital Video Broadcast Return Channel via Satellite (DVB-RCS) Hub

N.G. Vasantha Kumar, Mohanchur Sarkar, Vishal Agarwal, B.P. Chaniara,
S.V. Mehta, V.S. Palsule, and K.S. Dasgupta

Space Applications Centre, ISRO
Ahmedabad, India
{vasant,msarkar,vagarwal,bpchaniara,
vilaspalsule,ksd}@sac.isro.gov.in

Abstract. This paper discusses in-house designed and developed scale-down DVB-RCS hub intended to support the Satellite Based e-Learning initiative in India. The scale-down DVB-RCS HUB is implemented around a single PC with other subsystems making it very cost effective and unique of its kind. Due to the realization of this scale-down hub the total cost of realization of a Satellite based Education Network has drastically been reduced as very low cost commercially available Satellite Interactive Terminals (SITs) complying to open standard could be used at remote locations. The system is successfully tested to work with a commercial SIT using a GEO satellite EDUSAT which is especially dedicated for satellite based e-Learning.

Keywords: DVB-RCS, GEO, VSAT, HUB, MPEG, MFTDMA.

1 Introduction

Indian Space Research Organization (ISRO) has launched an exclusive satellite viz., EDUSAT (GSAT-3), to meet the demand for an interactive satellite based distance education system in the country. This reflects India's strong commitment to use space technology for national development, especially for the development of the population in remote and rural areas. EDUSAT is primarily meant for providing connectivity to school, college and higher levels of education and also to support non-formal education including developmental communication.

Education technology has undergone a sea change with the convergence of computers and communications. Much more versatile systems are now available and this calls for a fresh look at the communication segment of distance education [8]. In terms of technology, it is necessary to use commercially available technologies on the ground so as to reduce costs. These technologies must be simple and easy to deploy and operate. They must be fully multimedia capable and Internet enabled. The **D**igital **V**ideo **B**roadcast-**R**eturn **C**hannel via **S**atellite (**DVB-RCS**) [1] is an open standard defined by ETSI in late 2000. It is a potential technology for supporting the goals set by EDUSAT. The intent of the open standard is to accelerate economies of scale, thereby generating lower-cost solutions and opening the market in a shorter timeframe than could be possible with competing proprietary solutions.

N. Meghanathan et al. (Eds.): CCSIT 2011, Part II, CCIS 132, pp. 107–116, 2011.

Keeping in view of these advantages, of inter operability and growth potential it is decided to use the DVB RCS standard for our proposed EDUSAT network. Commercially off-the-shelf DVB-RCS Hubs and terminals are available. However these HUBS very costly for the sophisticated features it provides and the IPR of their manufactures. All the sophisticated features of a commercial HUB may not be needed in network dedicated for education. There is a need to provide multiple Hubs as in our country education is a state policy and each state or university may need its own HUB. This calls for realization of a cost effective scaled down version of DVB RCS HUB, which can work with the commercially available terminals thereby encouraging the growth potential of the EDUSAT network.

In order to support distance education application (Lecture broadcast and interaction of student with teacher one-at-a-time), a scale-down DVB-RCS hub is proposed with support of Constant Rate Assignment (CRA) and MPEG option only [14]. The support of CRA eliminates the development of complex network resource allocation and MPEG option eliminates the development of AAL5 decapsulation at Hub side. The other functionalities AAL5 and capacity management features will be added at a later stage to make a full-fledged hub utilizing the efficient usage of return link bandwidth.

In section II an overview is given about the scale-down DVB-RCS hub. In section III the implementation and realization of the scale-down DVB-RCS system is described. Section IV describes the test and evaluation of the implemented system using live satellite link.

2   Overview of Scale-Down DVB-RCS Hub

The basic building blocks of the scale-down DVB-RCS hub consists of a Forward link sub system (FLSS), Return link subsystem (RLSS) and Hub Management. Fig. 1 gives an overview of the system architecture for scale-down DVB-RCS hub and cross marked subsystems are not implemented in the scale-down version from the full-fledged DVB-RCS hub. Internet facility can be provided at the remote end through the Internet connection provided at the hub. The scale-down DVB-RCS hub supports MPEG in Return link and CRA in capacity management. The FLSS consists of Static tables [1] generator, IP Encapsulator, DVB Mux (data stream), Program Clock Reference (PCR) inserter and the DVB modulator. The RLSS consists of Multi channel Multi carrier burst demodulator (MCD), IP Decapsulator and IP router. The hub management includes burst processing (control), dynamic tables [1] generation and capacity management. The static tables like Superframe Composition Table (SCT), Frame Composition Table (FCT), Timeslot Composition Table (TCT), Satellite Position Table (SPT), Broadcast Terminal Information Message (TIM-B) are generated in FLSS. The dynamic tables Unicast Terminal Information Message (TIM-U), Correction Message Table (CMT) and Terminal Burst Time Plan (TBTP) are generated in RLSS and forwarded to the FLSS. These tables are generated on-the fly for the proper operation of the total network. The IP based traffic corresponding to all the users are multiplexed into a conventional DVB/MPEG-2 data broadcast stream at the Hub and relayed to all the Satellite Interactive Terminals (SITs). The return link traffic received from SITs is either sent to the local LAN of the HUB or forwarded to the

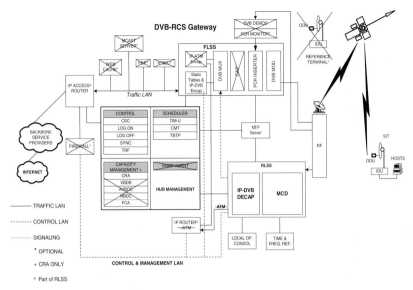

Fig. 1. DVB-RCS Scaled Down Version

FLSS for sending it to other SITs based on the destination IP address. The total network is synchronized using a Network Clock Reference (NCR). The NCR is similar to Program Clock Reference (PCR) which is used for MPEG audio video synchronization [3]. A stable clock reference source is required for maintaining the clock stability to be around 5 ppm [1]. A Global Positioning System (GPS) based Network Time Protocol (NTP) Server is used to synchronize with all individual subsystems of the hub and the total network. The outdoor unit at the hub consists of RF elements like BUC / HPA, LNBC / LNA and antenna.

2.1 Forward Link Sub System (FLSS)

The FLSS Software performs four main functions (I) SITable Generation, (ii) IP Encapsulation, (iii) NCR Generation and (iv) Multiplexing.

2.1.1 SI Table Generation

DVB RCS Forward Link Packet Generator software provides a flexible way of generating the Forward link Signaling as per user requirement and fully compliant with the DVB-RCS standard [1]. A highly user interactive GUI takes the relevant information from the network operator and generates the static DVB RCS Service Information tables like Network Information Table (NIT) [17], Program Association Table (PAT), Program Map Table (PMT), RCS Map Table (RMT), SCT, FCT, TCT, SPT[1]. All generated tables are packed inside Private Sections and then converted to MPEG2-TS as per the DVB RCS standards. Tables of length more than 1024 bytes are segmented into multiple Private Sections using the section number and last section number fields of SI Header. The software also generates all the descriptors specified in the standard [1]. These descriptors are sent through a Broadcast Terminal Information Message to the terminals. The GUI of the Forward Link generator takes the input from the user to generate the tables like the Name of network, forward link symbol rate, frequency in which the forward link is transmitted, the pids of the other tables and the way the forward link is arranged in terms of pids and all other files necessary for the generation of the tables as per the standard [1].

2.1.2 IP Encapsulation

IP Encapsulation into DVB is done using the Multi-protocol Encapsulation as specified [2]. The software module for IP Encapsulation performs the following major functions:

(i)   The software takes the IP data through socket and packs it into DSMCC Sections with the appropriate MAC address of the destination SIT. The IP Address to MAC translation is done using lookup table whose size depends on the number of terminals registered in the network.
(ii) The DSMCC sections can take a maximum of 4KB of IP data. So IP data with larger length is to be segmented by the software into multiple DSMCC Sections using the section number and last section number fields of DSMCC [1].
(iii) The software distributes DSMCC Sections containing IP Packets into 188 bytes MPEG2-TS packets which act as containers of the IP data. In case the length of the DSMCC Section does not match with the 184 bytes payload of MPEG2 TS the remaining space is stuffed with 0xFF(FFh).

2.1.3 NCR Generation

The Forward link Packet generator sends the NCR packets with the same syntax as PCR packets [3] on a separate PID. This PID is indicated to the network in the Program Map Table. The NCR is sent every 10 milliseconds taking the time from the system clock. The system clock is stabilized by installing a NTP Client in the Forward link Packet generator PC which takes NTP time from the GPS integrated NTP Server [12] to synchronize its own system clock. This stabilized clock is used to generate the NCR.

2.1.4 Multiplexing

The major functions of Multiplexing [18] module are as follows:

(i)   Take multiple inputs like static tables, encapsulated IP packets, dynamic tables from RLSS, PCR [20] [21] packets and generate a single output transport stream.
(ii) For constant data rate output NULL packets are added as and when required.

2.2   Return Link Sub System and Hub Management

The RLSS & Hub Management Software performs following main functions:

(i)   Handle SIT logon / logoff
(ii) SIT Synchronization, Dynamic table Generation and capacity management
(iii) IP Decapsulation

2.2.1 SIT Log ON / Log OFF Procedure

After receiving Forward link, if any SIT wants to interact with hub, it sends CSC burst using S-Aloha random access. On receiving CSC Burst, hub checks whether SIT is authorized, by seeing its MAC address. Then it assigns Logon ID and Group ID to the SIT and SIT may go for coarse synchronization.

The logOFF procedure is initiated as a normal session termination or as a failure (abnormal) case. Abnormal log-off is initiated in case of loss of synchronization. When terminal is logged off, its logon ID, group ID and SYNC slots are released.

2.2.2 SIT Synchronization, Dynamic Table Generation and Capacity Management

The synchronization of the SIT is an important feature of any satellite interactive network. This is required to obtain efficient TDMA (here MF-TDMA) operation with maximum throughput and minimum interference. The SIT synchronization scheme operates on the Clock Reference and signaling information received through the forward link, which is MPEG2-TS. The Network Clock Reference (NCR) [1] is derived from the HUB reference clock (27 MHz) and distributed through the forward link with a separate PID in the MPEG2 transport stream. This enables all terminals in the network to receive the reference clock at 27 MHz for synchronization [20]. The 27MHz clock is slaved with the GPS based NTP server[12]. Since the MFTDMA operation requires a high precision in timing and frequency accuracy there is a need for periodic correction of the terminals when they are in communication. The HUB manages terminal synchronization through a set of messages exchanged between HUB and terminal on reserved time slots. It allows the fine-tuning of the synchronization parameters like, frequency offsets and time offsets between the terminal and the HUB. It also controls the SITs transmit power. This is achieved using the dynamic tables TIM-U and CMT. For terminal synchronization dynamic tables like TIM and CMT are used sent on forward link and CSC, ACQ and SYNC bursts are used on the return link. The ACQ and SYNC bursts are special bursts containing symbols dedicated for the HUB to be able to measure frequency and timing offset.

The HUB requests a terminal to transmit a sequence of ACQ bursts via the TIM by assigning a BTP ACQ timeslot for a limited number of repeats. The HUB also requests terminal to transmit SYNC burst periodically via the TIM by signaling a SYNC time slot once every N super frames. By receiving the ACQ and SYNC bursts, the HUB determines the power, frequency, and burst time error of the terminal. Corrections for frequency and burst time are sent in CMT for correction by the terminal.

A SIT can request for TRF slots based on its requirement either in SYNC burst or as in-band data of TRF burst. The hub receives the requests from all the logged in SITs in the network and allocate the time slots in the MF-TDMA structure. The assignment of timeslots is sent from the HUB using TBTP table. A SIT will receive this information and transmits the TRF burst based on the assignment received from the HUB.

2.2.3 IP Decapsulation

The IP packets are received in the HUB as IP-MPE packets in the TRF slots assigned to the SIT, which are to be either sent to other SITs by forwarding them through Forward link or on the local LAN of the hub. These IP packets are received in fragments and are to be combined to build a proper IP packet. If the IP packet is destined for other SITs it is forwarded to the Forward link. If the IP packet is destined for the local LAN it is sent through the Ethernet card of the system.

3 Implementation

A scale-down DVB-RCS hub prototype is implemented and is tested via satellite using a single SIT. The Transponder used in the testing is Western beam of EDUSAT. The total test setup diagram is shown in Fig2. The NTP server, MCD, DVB Modulator, Servers etc. are the COTS items on the hub side. The SIT, the PC etc. are the COTS items on the remote side. This implementation is based on one frame in one super frame with a single carrier frequency in Return Link The timeslots defined in the frame are 1 CSC, 1 ACQ, 2 SYNC and 11 MPEG TRF[1] slots with a data rate of 624.3 Kbps using Turbo code of 2/3[1]. All the burst types are as per the DVB-RCS standard specifications [1]. The burst formats used in the test setup are defined in the TCT. The NTP [12] server based on GPS can provide a frequency stability of $2x10^{-11}$.

The forward and return link software runs on a standard server running Linux O.S.. These two software are running as independent programs on the same server. The MCD ver 1.0 used in this set up is from M/S Alcatel Bell Space. The demodulated data is distributed in the multicast IP packets on the local LAN of the hub. The return link software uses a socket to obtain the information regarding the start time of the first superframe, in the network, from the forward link software. This is the critical information as all the dynamic tables generated are based on the current superframe number. All the subsystems of the hub i.e., MCD, Forward link and return link software uses the NCR as reference. The most critical part in this system is the generation of proper time stamp [9]. A GPS based NTP server is used for disciplining all the clocks used within the total system. The NTP client services running on the Server and the MCD get disciplined with the NTP server time. A system call is used for getting the current time and this time is converted in to the NCR time. The Golden Rule is applied in calculation of NCR time [3]. The NCR rollover has also be taken into account while calculating the current NCR time. The Hub Management software is also part of the return link software.

An Object Oriented Design approach is adopted in designing the forward link software. More details on the forward link software are given in [10]. All the Service Information tables, Descriptors, IP Encapsulated data and NCR are coded as separate objects, with associated routines of generating them as member functions. The general SI Header's objects and DSMCC Sections [1] objects are inherited by SI Table and IP Encapsulation objects. The return link software is developed on multithreading environment for handling different tasks at the same time. The main objective of the RLSS software is to receive the bursts sent by MCD at multicast IP address, identify the bursts and distribute them to the appropriate software module threads for further processing. More details on the return link software are given in [11]. The functionalities of different threads that are developed in the RLSS software are as follows:

1. Receive data from MCD
2. Burst identification
3. CSC burst processing
4. TIM-U generation
5. ACQ burst processing
6. CMT generation
7. SYNC burst processing

8.   CMT generation
9.   TRF burst processing & IP Decapsulation.
10. TBTP generation.
11. Sending IP packets in to the network using raw sockets.

The IP packet handling method in this implementation does not require a router at the hub and a patent [13] has been filed on this concept. This method can be adopted in any application where there are different paths for sending and receiving IP packets at the hub.

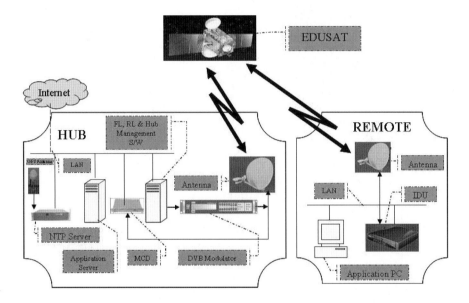

Fig. 2. Test Setup of Scale-down DVB-RCS system

4   Test and Evaluation

The scaled-down DVB-RCS hub was operated with 4.3404 MSPS with FEC ½ rate using western beam (Ku-band) of EDUSAT (GSAT-3) in the forward link. A 1.2m Antenna with 2 W SSPB was used for up linking from the hub. A 1.2m Antenna with 2 W SSPB and a COTS SIT. A snapshot showing the various states of the SIT which it has undergone to become active is shown in figure 3. For traffic, multicast broadcasting of multiple video streams aggregating to the 3.5 Mbps were used and found to be working satisfactorily. The TCP/IP throughput was obtained by assigning all the traffic slots to the SIT as shown in Table 1 for the commercial hub and in Table 2 for the in-house developed hub. The results obtained using in-house developed hub, are comparable with the results obtained using the commercial hub.

The results obtained using the in house HUB is seen to perform 10%-20% lower than the commercial HUB when the size of the file increases. This is attributed because of the fact that the commercial HUB uses dedicated commercial router and uses

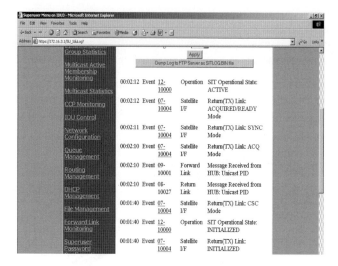

Fig. 3. Log of SIT showing the various states

Table 1. FTP Throughput with commercial HUB

Sr. No.	File Size (in bytes)	With 11 CRA	With 1 CRA
		Throughput (KB/Sec)	Throughput (KB/Sec)
1	1M	133.47	127.00
2	2M	174.06	159.07
3	5M	204.93	191.40
4	50M	237.28	214.42
5	100M	239.51	216.18
6	200M	240.87	216.88

Table 2. FTP Throughput with in house developesd HUB

Sr. No.	File size (in bytes)	With 11 CRA	With 1 CRA
		Throughput (KB/Sec)	Throughput (KB/Sec)
1	1M	132.13	128.76
2	2M	172.91	157.54
3	5M	206.48	184.09
4	50M	214.25	191.95
5	100M	200.26	188.67
6	200M	203.78	193.45

hardware based solutions for forward and return link processing. The in house developed HUB uses a total software based PC centric approach for the generation of the forward link and return link processing. The hardware based solution being dedicated performs faster than a totally software based solution.

5 Conclusion

A scale-down DVB-RCS hub has been realized and functionally tested with a COTS SIT. This implementation does not require a router at the hub thereby reducing the-cost of the overall system. It uses a totally software based PC centric solution in the generation of the Forward and Return Link. The in-house HUB developed uses COTS items for Modulator, NTP Server and Multi Channel Demodulator and all other functionalities are realized in house using indigenous technology. This provides the 50% cost savings when compared to a commercial HUB. The TCP/IP throughput obtained with in house developed hub is comparable with that of the commercial hub.

Acknowledgment

The authors wish to thank Mr. Peter Amendusan, Mr. Oyvin Slungard, Mr. Hallvard of M/s Verisat, Norway for providing the Hub emulation software, analyzers, active technical support, and advises without which we could have not achieved this. We also would like to thank all the staff members of Advanced Communication Technology Division for their advice and active technical support towards the realization of this work.

References

1. ETSI EN 301 790 V1.4.1 Digital Video Broadcasting (DVB); Interaction channel for satellite distribution systems (2005-2009)
2. ETSI TR 101 202 V1.2.1 – Digital Video Broadcasting Implementation Guidelines for Data Broadcasting
3. ISO / IEC 13818 - Information technology – Generic coding of moving pictures and associated audio information: Systems
4. Richard, S.W.: TCP/IP Illustrated: The Protocols, vol. 1, 2, 3. Addison Wesley, Reading (1994)
5. DVB-RCS Study Team – Proposal on Study, Simulation and Proof-of- concept of DVB-RCS
6. Video LAN Client Software, http://www.videolan.org
7. Multi-Channel Multi-Frequency Burst Mode Demodulator Version 1.1 Specification. Doc: BMD-ABSP-SPE-0004 from Alcatel Bell Space N.V
8. Project Report on GSAT-3 (EDUSAT) Applications Programmer, Space Applications Centre (March 2003)
9. Fibush, D.K.: Timing and synchronization using MPEG-2 Transport Stream. SMPTE Journal (July 1996)

10. Sarkar, M., Vasantha Kumar, N.G., Palsule, V.S., Dasgupta, K.S.: DVB-RCS Compliant Forward Link Packet Generator. In: National Conference on Communication NCC (2005)
11. Sarkar, M., Vasantha Kumar, N.G., Mehta, S.V., Palsule, V.S., Dasgupta, K.S.: Implementation of Application Specific DVB-RCS Hub. In: International Conference On Communication ADCOM (2006)
12. References of Tym Server, from Symmetricom (2000),
    http://www.symmetricom.com
13. Vasantha Kumar, N.G., Agarwal, V., Sarkar, M.: A method for processing a plurality of Internet Protocol (IP) packets of a DVB-RCS Hub
14. Proposal on Study Simulation & Proof of Concept of DVB-RCS, DVB-RCS Task Team, SAC/SITAA/TP/16 (October 2002)
15. SatLabs System Recommendations (January 2004)
16. ETSI ETS 300 802: Digital Video Broadcasting (DVB); Network-independent protocols for DVB Interactive services
17. ETSI EN 300 468: Digital Video Broadcasting (DVB) Specification for Service Information (SI) in DVB systems
18. Longfei, L., Songyu, Y., Xingdong, W.: Implementation of a New MPEG-2 Transport Stream Processor for Digital Television Broadcasting. IEEE Transactions on Broadcasting 48(4) (December 2002)
19. Lee, S.i., Cho, S.B.: Implementation of MPEG2 TS Remultiplexer and data transport unit for HDTV Satellite Broadcasting. IEEE Transaction on Consumer Electronics 43(3) (August 1997)
20. Terminal timing synchronization in DVB-RCS systems using on-board NCR generation by Neale and Guy Begin Space Communications 17 (2001)
21. Fibush, D.K.: Timing and synchronization using MPEG-2 Transport Stream. SMPTE Journal (July 1996)

Reconfigurable Area and Speed Efficient Interpolator Using DALUT Algorithm

Rajesh Mehra[1] and Ravinder Kaur[2]

[1] Faculty of Electronics & Communication Engineering Department
rajeshmehra@yahoo.com
[2] ME Student of Electronics & Communication Engineering Department
National Institute of Technical Teachers' Training & Research,
Sector-26, Chandigarh, India
rk_sid@yahoo.co.in

Abstract. In this paper an efficient method has been presented to implement high speed and area efficient interpolator for wireless communication systems. A multiplier less technique is used which substitutes multiply-and-accumulate operations with look up table (LUT) accesses. Interpolator has been implemented using Partitioned distributed arithmetic look up table (DALUT) technique. This technique has been used to take an optimal advantage of embedded LUTs of the target FPGA. This method is useful to enhance the system performance in terms of speed and area. The proposed interpolator has been designed using half band polyphase FIR structure with Matlab, simulated with Modelsim XE, synthesized with Xilinx Synthesis Tools (XST) and implemented on Spartan-3E based 3s500efg320-4 FPGA device. The proposed LUT based multiplier less approach has shown a maximum operating frequency of 61.6 MHz as compared to 52.1 MHz in case of MAC based multiplier approach by consuming considerably less resources to provide cost effective solution for wireless communication systems.

Keywords: DALUT, FIR, LUT, MAC, XST.

1 Introduction

The widespread use of digital representation of signals for transmission and storage has created challenges in the area of digital signal processing. The applications of digital FIR filter and up/down sampling techniques are found everywhere in modem electronic products. For every electronic product, lower circuit complexity is always an important design target since it reduces the cost. There are many applications where the sampling rate must be changed. Interpolators and decimators are utilized to increase or decrease the sampling rate. Up sampler and down sampler are used to change the sampling rate of digital signal in multi rate DSP systems [1]. This rate conversion requirement leads to production of undesired signals associated with aliasing and imaging errors. So some kind of filter should be placed to attenuate these errors.

N. Meghanathan et al. (Eds.): CCSIT 2011, Part II, CCIS 132, pp. 117–125, 2011.
© Springer-Verlag Berlin Heidelberg 2011

Today's consumer electronics such as cellular phones and other multi-media and wireless devices often require multirate digital signal processing (DSP) algorithms for several crucial operations in order to increase speed, reduce area and power consumption. Due to a growing demand for such complex DSP applications, high performance, low-cost Soc implementations of DSP algorithms are receiving increased attention among researchers and design engineers [2]. Although ASICs and DSP chips have been the traditional solution for high performance applications, now the technology and the market demands are looking for changes. On one hand, high development costs and time-to-market factors associated with ASICs can be prohibitive for certain applications while, on the other hand, programmable DSP processors can be unable to meet desired performance due to their sequential-execution architecture. In this context, embedded FPGAs offer a very attractive solution that balance high flexibility, time-to-market, cost and performance. Therefore, in this paper, an interpolator is designed and implemented on FPGA device. An impulse response of an FIR filter may be expressed as:

$$Y = \sum_{k=1}^{K} C_k x_k \tag{1}$$

where $C_1, C_2 \ldots\ldots C_K$ are fixed coefficients and the $x_1, x_2 \ldots\ldots x_K$ are the input data words. A typical digital implementation will require K multiply-and-accumulate (MAC) operations, which are expensive to compute in hardware due to logic complexity, area usage, and throughput. Alternatively, the MAC operations may be replaced by a series of look-up-table (LUT) accesses and summations. Such an implementation of the filter is known as distributed arithmetic (DA).

2 Interpolator

Up sampler is basic sampling rate alteration device used to increase the sampling rate by an integer factor. An up-sampler with an *up-sampling factor L*, where L is a positive integer, develops an output sequence $x_u[n]$ with a sampling rate that is L times larger than that of the input sequence $x[n]$. The up sampler is shown in Figure 1. Up-sampling operation is implemented by inserting equidistant zero-valued samples between two consecutive samples of $x[n]$. The input and output relation of up sampler can be expressed as

$$x_u[n] = \begin{cases} x[n/L], & n = 0, \pm L, \pm 2L, \\ 0, & \text{otherwise} \end{cases} \tag{2}$$

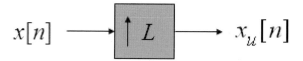

Fig. 1. Up Sampler

The zero-valued samples inserted by the up-sampler are replaced with appropriate nonzero values using some type of filtering process called *interpolation* [3]. The input-output relation of an up-sampler with factor of 2 in the time-domain is given by:

$$x_u[n] = \begin{cases} x[n/2], & n = 0, \pm 2, \pm 4, \\ 0, & \text{otherwise} \end{cases} \tag{3}$$

The z transform of input output relation is given by

$$X_u(z) = \sum_{n=-\infty}^{\infty} x_u[n] z^{-n} = \sum_{\substack{n=-\infty \\ n \text{ even}}}^{\infty} x[n/2] z^{-n} \tag{4}$$

$$= \sum_{m=-\infty}^{\infty} x[m] \ z^{-2m} = X(z^2) \tag{5}$$

In a similar manner, we can show that for a *factor-of-L up-sampler*

$$X_u(z) = X(z^L) \tag{6}$$

On the unit circle, for $z = e^{j\omega}$, the input-output relation is given by

$$X_u(e^{j\omega}) = X(e^{j\omega L}) \tag{7}$$

A factor-of-2 sampling rate expansion leads to a compression of $X(e^{j\omega})$ by a factor of 2 and a 2-fold repetition in the baseband $[0, 2\pi]$. This process is called *imaging* as we get an additional "*image*" of the input spectrum. Similarly in the case of a factor-of-*L* sampling rate expansion, there will be L-1 additional images of the input spectrum in the baseband. Interpolator is used as low pass filter to remove the $x_u[n]$ images and in effect "fills in" the zero-valued samples in $x_u[n]$ with interpolated sample values [4]-[6].

3   DA Algorithm

DISTRIBUTED ARITHMETIC (DA) is an efficient method for computing inner products when one of the input vectors is fixed. It uses look-up tables and accumulators instead of multipliers for computing inner products and has been widely used in many DSP applications such as DFT, DCT, convolution, and digital filters [7]. The example of direct DA inner-product generation is shown in Eq. (1) where x_k is a 2's-complement binary number scaled such that $|x_k| < 1$. We may express each x_k as:

$$x_k = -b_{k0} + \sum_{n=1}^{N-1} b_{kn} 2^{-n} \tag{8}$$

where the b_{kn} are the bits, 0 or 1, b_{k0} is the sign bit. Now combining Eq. (1) and (8) in order to express *y* in terms of the bits of x_k ; we see

$$Y = \sum_{k=1}^{K} C_k[-b_k + \sum_{n=1}^{N-1} b_{kn} 2^{-n}] \tag{9}$$

The above Eq.(9) is the conventional form of expressing the inner product. Interchanging the order of the summations, gives us:

$$Y = \sum_{n=1}^{N-1} [\sum_{k=1}^{K} C_k b_{kn}] 2^{-n} + \sum_{k=1}^{K} c_k(-b_{k0}) \tag{10}$$

Eq.(10) shows a DA computation where the bracketed term is given by

$$\sum_{k=1}^{K} C_k b_{kn} \tag{11}$$

Each b_{kn} can have values of 0 and 1 so Eq.(11) can have 2^K possible values. Rather than computing these values on line, we may pre-compute the values and store them in a ROM. The input data can be used to directly address the memory and the result. After N such cycles, the memory contains the result, y. The term x_k may be written as

$$x_k = \frac{1}{2}[x_k - (-x_k)] \tag{12}$$

and in 2's-complement notation the negative of x_k may be written as:

$$-x_k = -\overline{b_{k0}} + \sum_{n=1}^{N-1} \overline{b_{kn}} 2^{-n} + 2^{-(N-1)} \tag{13}$$

where the over score symbol indicates the complement of a bit. By substituting Eq.(8) & (13) into Eq.(12), we get

$$x_k = \frac{1}{2}[-(b_{k0} - \overline{b_{k0}}) + \sum_{n=1}^{N-1} (b_{kn} - \overline{b_{kn}}) 2^{-n} - 2^{-(N-1)} \tag{14}$$

In order to simplify the notation later, it is convenient to define the new variables as:

$$a_{kn} = b_{kn} - \overline{b_{kn}} \quad \text{for } n \neq 0 \tag{15}$$

and

$$a_{k0} = b_{k0} - \overline{b_{k0}} \tag{16}$$

where the possible values of the a_{kn}, including $n=0$, are ± 1. Then Eq.(14) may be written as:

$$x_k = \frac{1}{2}[\sum_{n=0}^{N-1} a_{kn} 2^{-n} - 2^{-(N-1)}] \tag{17}$$

By substituting the value of x_k from Eq.(17) into Eq.(1), we obtain

$$Y = \frac{1}{2}\sum_{k-1}^{K} C_k [\sum_{n=0}^{N-1} a_{kn}2^{-n} - 2^{-(N-1)}]$$

$$Y = \sum_{n=0}^{N-1} Q(b_n)2^{-n} + 2^{-(N-1)}Q(0)$$

(18)

where

$$Q(bn) = \sum_{k=1}^{K} \frac{C_k}{2a_{kn}} and Q(0) = \sum_{k=1}^{K} \frac{C_k}{2}$$

(19)

It may be seen that $Q(b_n)$ has only $2^{(K-1)}$ possible amplitude values with a sign that is given by the instantaneous combination of bits. The computation of y is obtained by using a $2^{(K-1)}$ word memory, a one-word initial condition register for $Q(O)$, and a single parallel adder sub tractor with the necessary control-logic gates.

4   Matlab Based Proposed Design

Equiripple window based half band polyphase interpolator has been designed and implemented using Matlab [9]. The order of the proposed interpolator is 66 with interpolation factor of 2, transition width of 0.1 and stop band attenuation of 60 dB whose output is shown in Figure 2.

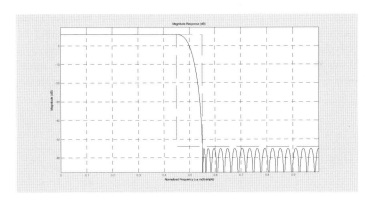

Fig. 2. Interpolator Response

Nyquist interpolators provide same stop band attenuation and transition width with a much lower order. An Lth-band Nyquist filter with $L = 2$ is called a half-band filter. The transfer function of a half-band filter is thus given by

$$H(z) = \alpha + z^{-1}E_1(z^2)$$

(20)

with its impulse response as

$$h[2n] = \begin{cases} \alpha, & n = 0 \\ 0, & \text{otherwise} \end{cases} \qquad (21)$$

In Half band filters about 50% of the coefficients of $h[n]$ are zero. This reduces the computational complexity of the proposed interpolator significantly. The first interpolator design is has been implemented by using MAC based multiplier technique where 67 coefficients are processed with MAC unit as shown in Figure 3.

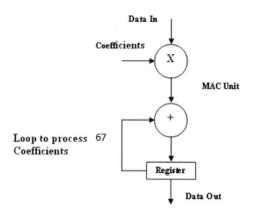

Fig. 3. MAC Based Multiplier Approach

The second interpolator design has replaced MAC unit with LUT unit which is proposed multiplier less technique. Here 67 coefficients are divided in two parts by using polyphase decomposition. The proposed 2 branch polyphase interpolator structure is shown in Figure 4 where interpolation takes place after polyphase decomposition to reduce the computational complexity and can be expressed as:

$$H(z) = E_0(z^2) + z^{-1} E_1(z^2) \qquad (22)$$

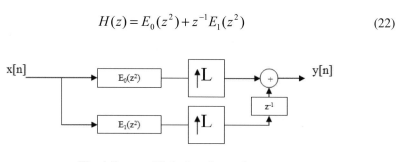

Fig. 4. Proposed Polyphase Interpolator

The coefficients corresponding to 2 branches $E_0(z^2)$ and $E_1(z^2)$ are processed by using partitioned distributed arithmetic look up table technique as shown in Figure 5.

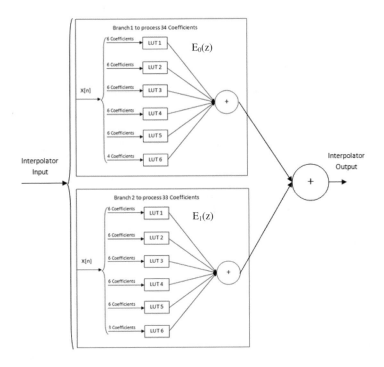

Fig. 5. Proposed LUT based Multiplier Less Approach

Each branch is processing the required coefficients using six partitions consisting of 6 LUTs. The two branches process the required coefficients in 6 6 6 6 6 4 and 6 6 6 6 6 3 manner respectively.

5   Hardware Implementation

The MAC based and DA based interpolator designs have been synthesized and implemented on Spartan-3E based 3s500efg320-4 target device and simulated with modelsim. Simulator.

The modelsim simulator based output response of proposed LUT based multiplier less interpolator with 16 bit input and output precision is shown in Figure 6. The area and speed comparison of both techniques has been shown in table 1. The proposed LUT based multiplier less approach has shown a maximum operating frequency of 61.6 MHz as compared to 52.1 MHz in case of multiplier based approach. The proposed multiplier less interpolator has consumed only 6% slices, 2% flip flops and 5% LUTs and 0% multipliers out of available on target device which is considerably less as compared to multiplier based design.

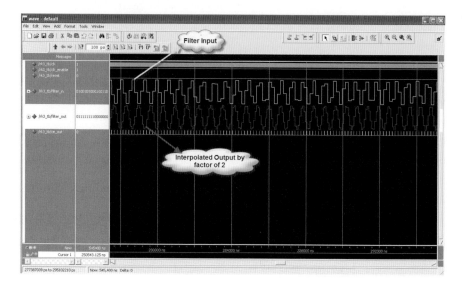

Fig. 6. Modelsim Based Proposed Interpolator Response

Table 1. Area and Speed Comparison

Logic Utilization	Multiplier Approach	Multiplier Less Approach
# of Slices	590 out of 4656 (12%)	309 out of 4656 (6%)
# of Flip Flops	643 out of 9312 (6%)	268 out of 9312 (2%)
# of LUTs	568 out of 9312 (6%)	485 out of 9312 (5%)
# of Multipliers	1 out of 20 (5%)	0 out of 20 (0%)
Speed (MHz)	52.100	61.607

6   Conclusion

In this paper, an optimized equiripple based half band polyphase decomposition technique is presented to implement the proposed interpolator for wireless communication systems. The proposed interpolator has been designed using partitioned distributed arithmetic look up table approach to further enhance the speed and area utilization by taking optimal advantage of look up table structure of target FPGA. The proposed LUT based multiplier less approach has shown a maximum frequency of 61.6 MHz as compared to 52.1 MHz in case of multiplier based approach. The proposed multiplier less interpolator has consumed only 6% slices, 2% flip flops, 5% LUTs and no multiplier of target device which is considerably less as compared to multiplier based design to provide cost effective solution for wireless and mobile communication systems.

References

1. Jou, S., Jheng*, K.-Y., Chen, H.-Y., Wu, A.-Y.: Multiplierless Multirate Decimator *I* Interpolator Module Generator. In: IEEE Asia-Pacific Conference on Advanced System Integrated Circuits, pp. 58–61 (August 2004)
2. Sundararajan, V., Parhi, K.K.: Synthesis of Minimum-Area Folded Architectures for Rectangular Multidimensional. IEEE Transactions On Signal Processing 51(7), 1954–1965 (2003)
3. Mitra, S.K.: Digital Signal Processing, 3rd edn. Tata McGraw Hill, New York (2006)
4. AI-Haj, A.: An Efficient Configurable Hardware Implementation of Fundamental Multirate Filter Banks. In: 5th International Multi-Conference on Systems, Signals and Devices, IEEE SSD 2008, pp. 1–5 (2008)
5. Luo, B., Zhao, Y., Wang, Z.: An Area-efficient Interpolator Applied in Audio -DAC. In: Third International IEEE Conference on Signal-Image Technologies and Internet-Based System, pp. 538–541 (2008)
6. Zawawi, N.M., Ain, M.F., Hassan, S.I.S., Zakariya, M.A., Hui, C.Y., Hussin, R.: Implementing WCDMA Digital Up Converter In FPGA. In: IEEE International Rf And Microwave Conference, RFM 2008, pp. 91–95 (2008)
7. Allred, D.J., Yoo, H., Krishnan, V., Huang, W., Anderson, D.: A Novel High Performance Distributed Arithmetic Adaptive Filter Implementation on an FPGA. In: Proc. IEEE Int. Conference on Acoustics, Speech, and Signal Processing (ICASSP 2004), vol. 5, pp. 161–164 (2004)
8. Longa, P., Miri, A.: Area-Efficient FIR Filter Design on FPGAs using Distributed Arithmetic. In: IEEE International Symposium on Signal Processing and Information Technology, pp. 248–252 (2006)
9. Mathworks, Users Guide Filter Design Toolbox 4 (March 2007)

Performance Evaluation of Fine Tuned Fuzzy Token Bucket Scheme for High Speed Networks

Anurag Aeron[1], C. Rama Krishna[1], and Mohan Lal[2]

[1] NITTTR-Chandigarh, India
[2] IIT-Roorkee, India
anuragaeron@gmail.com, rkc_97@yahoo.com,
mluccfcc@iitr.ernet.in

Abstract. The dynamic nature of the bursty traffic of high speed ATM networks may cause severe network congestion. Thus, to assure QoS, policing is required as the preventive congestion control mechanism. The fuzzy token bucket scheme was proposed for predicting and policing the token generation rate for congestion control in a high speed networks. In this paper, fuzzy-token bucket scheme is compared with token bucket scheme on the basis of two parameters: Average Delay and Throughput. A simulation study was performed for the fuzzy logic predictor using MATLAB-Simulink simulator. The simulation results show that the fuzzy logic based token bucket scheme achieve high throughput and offer lower average delay as compared to the a non-fuzzy token bucket scheme.

Keywords: Fuzzy Predictor, Available Bandwidth, Average Rate, Average Delay, Throughput, Token Generation Rate.

1 Introduction

Asynchronous Transfer Mode (ATM) has been recommended by CCITT as the solution for the future Broadband Integrated Services Digital Network (B-ISDN) in 1988 because it offers an attractive way of supporting multimedia services. In an ATM networks, if bandwidth is available along the route from source to destination, as required by the new connection, the connection is accepted for the transmission. Otherwise the connection is rejected. In leaky bucket algorithm for congestion control, instead of outrightly rejecting an ATM connection, some restriction is put over the maximum number of cells that can be put by a source in the network. This is done by using a buffer and a token pool in the switch.

1.1 Token Bucket Scheme

The basic idea of this approach is that a cell, before entering the network, must obtain a token from a token pool [9]. This scheme is specified by two parameters: token generation rate r, bucket size s.

N. Meghanathan et al. (Eds.): CCSIT 2011, Part II, CCIS 132, pp. 126–136, 2011.

As shown in Fig.1, tokens are generated at a fixed rate of r and stored in a token pool. If the token pool is empty, then the cell must wait for a token before it is delivered to the network. The pool has a finite buffer size of s. Tokens arriving to the pool are discarded after filling the pool.

The token generation rate r is a measure of the average bit rate of the connection or it quantifies the allowed rate of admissions. The token pool size s corresponds to the maximum allowable burst rate of the traffic admitted. Thus, it is guaranteed that the long term average bit rate does not exceed the pre-specified average rate of the connection [11]. This scheme only ensures that the user is not using more than the allocated peak bandwidth.

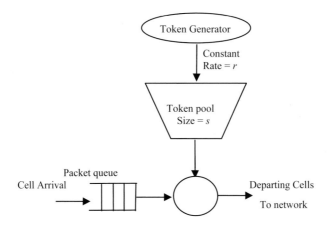

Fig. 1. Token Bucket Scheme

2 Traffic Model

ATM network is considered as a distributed discrete system in the analysis of arrival process, and time is assumed to be "slotted". Each time slot, either with cell or without cell corresponds to the time it takes to transmit one cell in the media. Here, p represents the probability of observing a cell in a slot over long duration, and $0 \leq p \leq 1$. This falls into Bernoulli arrival process. Its analog in continuous time domain is the Poisson arrival process [4].

2.1 Bernoulli Arrival Process

In Bernoulli arrival process, a knowledge of the past arrival pattern does not help in present or future arrivals. Another important property is multi and demulti-plexing. If N Bernoulli processes with identical p's and slot widths are interleaved together then the resulting process is also a Bernoulli process, and it is N times faster. On the other hand if a Bernoulli process is demultiplexed into N arrival processes and these are also Bernoulli through each is N times slower.

2.2   Interarrival Time – Geometric Distribution

The probability of the next slot at which an arrival occurs. If the current slot is slot 0 and the next arrival occurs in slot i then

$$Prob(arrival\ in\ slot\ i) = Prob(i - 1 empty\ slots)Prob(1\ arrival)$$

$$Prob(arrival\ in\ slot\ i) = (1 - p)^{i-1} P$$

$$i = 1, 2...$$

This geometric distribution is the discrete time analogy to the continuous time exponential distribution. Like the exponential distribution, the geometric distribution is memory-less and it is the only discrete time distribution to do so.

2.3   Arrivals - Binomial Distribution

Consider cells arriving to a discrete time sequence according to a Bernoulli arrival process. If the probability of a single arrival in a single slot is p, what is the probability that i out of N consecutive slots contain arrivals? This corresponds to the ATM switching scenario that if a virtual path (VP) switch has N input virtual channel (VC) queues, what is the probability of i arrivals in a single slot to the VP switch. This complies with binomial distribution with parameters (i, N, p).

$$b(i, N, p) = \frac{N!}{(N-i)!i!} p^i (1 - p)^{N-i}$$

$$i = 0\ 1\ 2\ ...\ N$$

3   Fuzzy Token Bucket Scheme

In an ordinary LB scheme without threshold in data buffer, rate of token generation in token pool is kept constant irrespective of arrival rate of the traffic. This results in large cell loss whenever there is a rush at the input of the switch, as switch is unaware of the traffic arrival and has been told to generate tokens at a constant rate [10]. It has been suggested to set a threshold in data buffer in a modified scheme. Whenever the number of cells in buffer is more than the set threshold value, token generation rate is kept a little more than the otherwise case.

3.1   Fuzzy Token Bucket Algorithm

In token bucket with threshold scheme, a gradual change in token generation rate is more suitable than the abrupt change. This can be done with Fuzzy logic control as shown in Fig.2. Fuzzy logic is helpful whenever there is need to handle processes not clearly defined through rigorous models. In fixed threshold case, two states of token generation can be replaced by fuzzy logic controlled generation rate where decision regarding the Token generation rate is based upon the state of Available bandwidth and Average rate at the input of buffer. There can be several token generation rates depending upon the complexity of fuzzy system and the number of membership functions taken.

The fuzzy logic predictor predicts the token generation rate required based on the average rate and available bandwidth. The fuzzy inputs are the ratio of the average measured rate over the peak rate denoted by Avgrate and the ratio of available bandwidth over the peak bandwidth denoted as Avaibw. The output is the new token generation rate denoted by NewRate.

The fuzzy logic based token bucket policer comprise of a rate estimator, a fuzzy predictor, a subtraction and a divisor. A rate estimator is used to get the running average bandwidth. The fuzzy logic predictor is used to predict the bandwidth based on the available bandwidth and average rate. The difference of token generated and burst length is used to find the loss of data. The average rate and the available bandwidth are then used to find the new rate based on the rules defined in the fuzzy inference system. So the adaptive token generation rate value is the current token bucket rate value. The adaptive rate value will take on the value of New Token Bucket Rate after each evaluation cycle. This process is a continuous real time process.

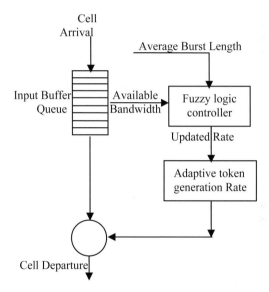

Fig. 2. Fuzzy Token Bucket Scheme

The other parameter is *delay*; it refers to the time which a cell takes more than the usual time to reach the destination. If a cell could not get a token, then it will discard by the network and the sender must resend it. So the additional time for resending the data cell and successfully received by the receiver is considered as the delay. The average delay is defined as

$$Avgdelay = total\ number\ of\ cell\ loss\ during\ unit\ time \\ \times average\ time\ to\ resend\ a\ cell$$

The number of cell losses can be find as

$$Total\ number\ of\ cell\ loss\ during\ unit\ time$$
$$= \frac{total\ number\ of\ cell\ loss\ during\ a\ calculated\ time}{Total\ duration\ of\ calaulated\ time}$$

Actually the cells which are lost during some time period are those cells which do not get tokens at that time. So those cells must resend to the receiver by the sender; and the time it takes to resend, is the delay for this message.

Throughput: It is defined as the work done in a unit time. Therefore with reference to the network characterization; throughput is the amount of successful transmission of data in a unit time.

$$Throughput = \frac{number\ of\ cells\ reach\ in\ total\ time\ duration}{total\ time}$$

The fuzzy token rate, available bandwidth, average cell loss are used to find and compare the average delay and throughput for the different kind of congestion control schemes.

4 Simulation Methodology

MATLAB Simulink software is used to implement the fuzzy token bucket scheme. Available bandwidth and average rate are the two fuzzy inference system (FIS) input variables. The output is the token generation rate. A triangular shaped membership function is chosen to represent the rate of token generation corresponding to different combinations of available bandwidth and average rate. As the number of linguistic values for different membership functions becomes higher, the accuracy will become higher in predicting the new token generation rate.

4.1 Fuzzy Logic Based Token Generator

The fuzzy logic predictor predicts the token generation rate required based on the average rate and available bandwidth [1]. The fuzzy inputs are the 'Avgrate' and 'Avaibw'. The output is the new token generation rate denoted by 'Newrate'. The parameter, Y, for the fuzzy predictor is represented by the following linguistic variables,

$$Y = \{Avgrate, Avaibw, Newrate\}$$

And the linguistic values are given below:

$$S\ (Avgrate) = \{VL, LO, BA, AV, AA, HI, VH\}$$
$$S\ (Avaibw) = \{VL, LO, BA, AV, AA, HI, VH\}$$
$$S\ (Newrate) = \{VL, LO, BA, AV, AA, HI, VH\}$$

where VL = Very Low, LO = Low, BA = Below Average, AV = Average, AA = Above Average, HI = High and VH = Very High.

These values are normalized between 0 and 1. The membership functions use triangular, S-shaped and Z-shaped functions again based on the simplicity of these kinds of functions.

In MATLAB Simulink the mamdani type model is used for fuzzy inference system. The parameters are shown in Table 1.

Table 1. FIS parameters

Parameter	Value
AND method	Min
OR method	Max
Implication	Min
Aggregation	Max
Defuzzification	Centroid

After declaring input and output variables, the membership functions are plotted i.e, the range is defined between 0 and 1 in a normalized form [12]. There are seven membership functions for each FIS variable. The value of each variable is increasing from very low to very high. The lower value is VL and the higher value is VH. So the name of variable is given according to the strength of variable. These are shown in Table 2.

Table 2. Membership function parameters

Name	Type	Parameter
VL	zmf	0 0.2
LO	trimf	0.1 0.2 0.3
BA	trimf	0.26 0.36 0.46
AV	trimf	0.42 0.52 0.62
AA	trimf	0.58 0.68 0.78
HI	trimf	0.74 0.84 0.94
VH	smf	0.8 1

As shown in Fig. 3, the input variable 'Avgrate' has seven membership functions which are of three types: Membership function VL is of Z – shaped, membership function VH is of S – shaped and from LO to HI triangular shaped membership function. The input and output variables also has same seven membership functions.

The linguistic variables are those variables whose values are words rather than numbers. Much of fuzzy logic may be viewed as a methodology for computing with words rather than numbers [13]. Fuzzy sets and fuzzy operators are the subjects and verbs of fuzzy logic. These "if-then rule" statements are used to formulate the conditional statements that comprise fuzzy logic. A single fuzzy if-then rule i.e. If (Avgrate is LO) and (Avaibw is BA) then (Newrate is LO); where LO and BA are linguistic values defined by fuzzy sets on the ranges (universes of discourse) Low and Below Average respectively. The if-part of the rule "Avgrate is LO and Avaibw is

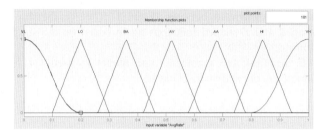

Fig. 3. Membership Function for Avgrate

BA" is called the antecedent or premise, while the then-part of the rule "Newrate is LO" is called the consequent or conclusion. The fuzzy engine has forty nine rules that relate the two inputs with the fuzzy output. The constructions of the rules are based on logical reasoning of how the system can track bandwidth usage.

It is the normalized form of inputs and output. It is observed that the z-axis variable smoothly varies from 0 to 1 i.e. the new token generation rate is varying in continuous form [5]. In token bucket with threshold scheme, there was a sudden change in the token generation rate, and this problem is overcome in fuzzy token bucket scheme as seen by above figure. Hence this fuzzy scheme works more efficiently than the earlier token bucket scheme.

The circuit is designed in MATLAB Simulink. This circuit consists of following components:

- Fuzzy Logic Controller
- Traffic Generator
- Average Rate
- Available Bandwidth
- Data Loss through Fuzzy Scheme

- *Fuzzy Logic Controller:* The main part of fuzzy scheme is Fuzzy Logic Controller. All the 49 rules are connected through the circuit. This circuit controls the output according to the rules defined in the rule editor. The implication and aggregation methods are done by this circuit.
- *Traffic Generator:* The traffic is generated by Bernoulli Random Generator. Here the number is generated by specifying the initial seed and probability of a zero. Different values are given to both for various rounds of simulation. So a random output is occurring for different values.
- *Avgrate:* The average rate is calculated by using a random number generator, a switch and a pulse generator. The random number is generated by function generator and it is similar to the main burst generator. A pulse generator is used to take the value of random generator at each pulse tick. So the average of two generators is taken and it will be sent to the Fuzzy Logic Controller as an 'Avgrate'.
- *Available Bandwidth:* The available bandwidth is calculated by using add subtract function block, a constant, a random number generator and a switch. The constant is set to 30 megabytes. At each pulse tick, arrived data length is

subtracted from channel capacity, so it sends the available bandwidth which is available to the next pulse. By this method the 'Avaibw' value is provided to the Fuzzy Logic Controller. The output of Fuzzy Logic Controller is the updated token generation rate. An add-sub function block is used to find the data loss with this new token generation rate. This circuit gives the new token generation rate as well as the data loss with this new rate.

- *Data Loss through fuzzy scheme:* The data loss due to token bucket scheme is calculated by an add-sub function block and an integrator.

5   Results and Discussion

5.1   Generated Bursty Traffic

Fig.4 shows the Bursty Data. In Fig.4, the time is depicted at x-axis in seconds and the length of data is shown on y-axis. The burst length is in megabytes. This random length is generated by random number generator in MATLAB Simulink software. As it is already discussed in earlier   section II, that the traffic is generated through the Bernoulli random generator which is purely random arrival process and its memory less property is unique in the sense that the knowledge of past arrival pattern does not help in present or future arrivals. Therefore it can be clearly seen by the graph that the traffic is purely random with reference to time. The height of each bar represents the size of data at that particular moment of time. So each bar is of different height as it is obvious in real time environment.

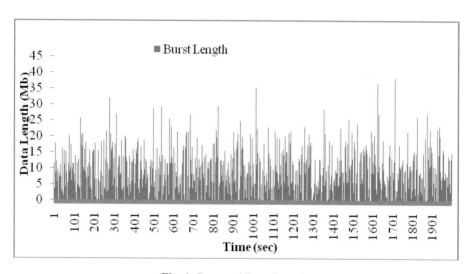

Fig. 4. Generated Burst Length

5.2   Comparison of Data Loss with and without Fuzzy Scheme

Fig.5 compares the data loss by using fuzzy logic controller to without fuzzy scheme. The time is shown on x-axis and data size is shown at y-axis. Blue line depicts the data loss with token bucket scheme and red line depicts the data loss with fuzzy token bucket scheme. Here it is observed that the data loss by fuzzy scheme is negligible compared to the token bucket (non-fuzzy) scheme. The blue line shows the data loss increases as the time passes, but in fuzzy scheme it raises little. As it is seen in the graph that the data loss is increases rapidly if the burst increases rapidly. But it can be controlled in the fuzzy token bucket scheme. So the fuzzy token bucket scheme is performed well and work outstanding compare to non-fuzzy scheme.

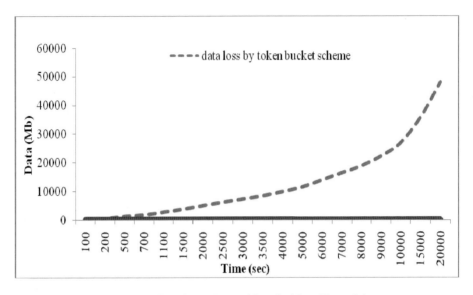

Fig. 5. Comparision of Data Loss with and without Fuzzy Scheme

5.3   Comparison of Delay between Token Bucket and Fuzzy Token Schemes

In Fig.6 the graph shows the average delay due to the loss of data cell. When a data cell could not get the token then it is discarded by the network. So this data cell must be send again by the sender. The time it takes to reach successfully is considered as the delay for that cell. The total delay divided by the number of cells discarded is measured as average delay. Here in this graph x-axis shows the time duration for simulation and the y-axis shows the average delay due to the loss of data cell. Here it is observed that the average delay is very high for token bucket scheme compared to the fuzzy token scheme. Therefore it is observed that the fuzzy token scheme can achieve the lower delay compare to token bucket scheme.

5.4   Comparison of Throughput between Token Bucket and Fuzzy Token Schemes

In fig.7 the x-axis represents the duration of simulation and the y-axis shows the throughput in terms of the successful packets per unit of time. Throughput value can get by calculating the successful packets which can reach to the destination in a unit

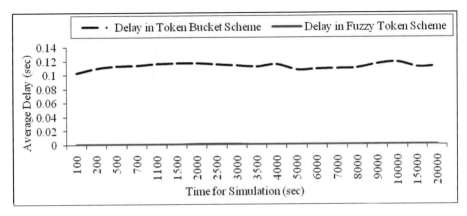

Fig. 6. Comparison of Average Delay between Token Bucket and Fuzzy Token Schemes

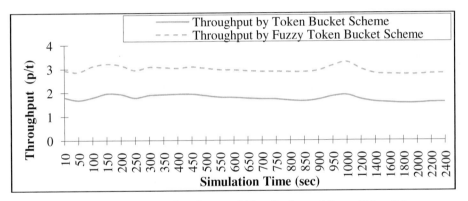

Fig. 7. Comparison of Throughput between Token Bucket and Fuzzy Token Schemes

time without delay. Here in graph for 2400 seconds duration of simulation; the throughput of token bucket scheme is 1.5 (approx.) whereas the throughput of fuzzy token scheme is 2.8 (approx.). On calculating the average throughput, it is observed that the fuzzy token scheme is achieved 2.96 and the token bucket scheme achieved 1.76. It is clear by graph that the throughput of fuzzy token scheme is approximately double as compared to the token bucket scheme.

6 Conclusion

This work compares the performance of fuzzy token bucket scheme and token bucket (non-fuzzy) scheme; after performing simulations in MATLAB Simulink. The proposed fuzzy based token bucket scheme has the added advantage that it is adaptive to network conditions. This scheme outperforms the previously existing token bucket scheme. According to the results it is concluded that the fuzzy token scheme is able to achieve lower average delay and higher throughput. Another advantage of fuzzy based scheme is that, instead of having two token generation rates as in token bucket scheme with threshold, it has several token generation rates and is capable of shifting much more smoothly than without fuzzy scheme. Therefore it is able to achieve higher throughput and lower average delay for high speed networks. Future work is to analyze the performance of fuzzy based token bucket scheme with different input parameters.

References

[1] Anurag, A.: Fine Tuning of Fuzzy Token Bucket Scheme for Congestion Control in High Speed Networks. In: IEEE Second International Conference on Computer Engineering and Applications, vol. 1, pp. 170–174 (March 2010)
[2] Chen, Y.-C., Xu, X.: An Adaptive Buffer Allocation Mechanism for Token Bucket Flow Control. In: Vehicular Technology Conference, vol. 4, pp. 3020–3024 (August 2004)
[3] Chang, C.-J., Chang, C.-S., Eul, Z., Lin, L.-F.: Intelligent Leaky Bucket Algorithms for Sustainable-Cell-Rate Usage Parameter Control in ATM Networks. In: IEEE International Conference on Information Networking, pp. 453–460 (August 2001)
[4] Dubois, J.P.: Congestion Control Mechanism of ATM Traffic using Leaky Bucket VP Shaping. In: IEEE International Conference on Trends in Communications, pp. 500–507 (January 2001)
[5] Dimyati, K., Chin, Y.T.: Policing mechanism and cell loss priority control on voice cells in ATM networks using fuzzy logic. IEEE Proceedings of Communications 147(4), 239–244 (2000)
[6] Bensaou, B., Lam, S.T.C., Chu, H.-W., Tsang, D.H.K.: Estimation of the Cell Loss Ratio in ATM Networks with a Fuzzy System and Application to Measurement-Based Call Admission Control. IEEE/ACM Transactions on Networking 5(4), 572–584 (1997)
[7] Choi, B.D., Choi, D.I.: Discrete-time analysis of the leaky bucket scheme with threshold-based token generation intervals. IEEE Proceedings of Communications 143(2), 105–111 (1996)
[8] Yamanaka, N., Sato, Y., Sato, K.-I.: Performance Limitation of the Leaky Bucket Algorithm for ATM Networks. IEEE Transactions on Communications 43(8), 2298–2300 (1995)
[9] Zadeh, L.A.: Fuzzy Logic: Issues, Contentions and Perspectives. In: IEEE International Conference on Acoustics, Speech, and Signal Processing, ICASSP 1994, vol. 5, p. 183 (1994)
[10] Catania, V., Ficili, G., Palazzo, S., Panno, D.: A Comparative Analysis of Fuzzy Versus Conventional Policing Mechanisms for ATM Networks. IEEE/ACM Transactions on Networking 4(3), 449–459 (1996)
[11] Turner, J.: New directions in communications (or which way to the information age?). IEEE Communication Magazine 24(10), 17–24 (1986)
[12] Hunt, B.R., Lipsman, R.L., Rosenberg, J.M.: A Guide to MATLAB. Cambridge University Press, Cambridge (2001)
[13] User's Guide, Version-2, Fuzzy Logic Toolbox-For Use with MATLAB, The MathWorks, Inc. (2005)

A Survey on Video Transmission Using Wireless Technology

S.M. Koli[1], R.G. Purandare[2], S.P. Kshirsagar[3], and V.V. Gohokar[4]

Dept. of Electronics and Telecommunications
[1] Smt. Kashibai Navale College of Engineering
smkoli.skncoe@sinhgad.edu
[2] Vishwakarma Institute of Information Technology
radhika.purandare@viit.ac.in
[3] AnchorTek Techno Consultancy Pvt. Ltd.
Pune, Maharashtra, India
shirish@anchorteksys.com
[4] Sant. Gajanan Maharaj College of Engineering, Shegaon, Maharashtra, India
vngohokar@ssgmce.ac.in

Abstract. The video transmission using wireless technology is an important functionality in multimedia communication. Video coding/compression and real time transmission are the key indicators to select the appropriate techniques and needs very careful designing of the parameters. The extra efforts taken at the encoder side allows the decoding of the video on a less powerful hardware platform, where the issues like client buffer capacity and computational time are very critical. This article surveys and appraises available literature on various video encoding and wireless transmission techniques. It also discusses various parameters of wireless medium like reliability, QoS, transmission rate, transmission delay for video transmission as a key element of wireless multimedia communication.

Keywords: Video coding, video compression, wireless video transmission.

1 Introduction

In present era of technology wireless video services are broadly deployed with the fast growth of wireless network. Wireless multimedia services like video conference, video telephony, home entertainment, internet protocol television (IPTV), video on demand (VoD), real time video transmission needs to be offered by the network service provider in addition to voice and low bit rate data services. For real time and interactive applications, the home video systems are likely to be deployed with a limited number of users within a household, including a single TV with a set-top-box and several computers and/or media adapters, including personal digital assistant (PDAs), multimedia mobile phones, each accessing a video server connected to the core network via a wireless Access Point [1]. These forthcoming wireless multimedia services pose several challenges, including limited bandwidth, bandwidth variation, time-varying characteristics of IP network channels. To provide satisfied quality of service (QoS) for video applications under current best-effort network becomes a crucial

N. Meghanathan et al. (Eds.): CCSIT 2011, Part II, CCIS 132, pp. 137–147, 2011.
© Springer-Verlag Berlin Heidelberg 2011

issue, due to heavy traffic of encoded video data along with its timing constraints. These issues involved two aspects of high-efficiency video coding techniques and high-quality adaptive network transmission [2]. Intermittent loss and excessive delay have a negative impact on perceived video quality, and these are typically caused by network congestion. A congestion control mechanism is required at the end systems to reduce packet loss and delay. For conferencing and streaming video, congestion control typically takes the form of rate control. Rate control endeavors to minimize the possibility of network congestion by matching the rate of the video stream to the available network bandwidth. QoS support is a multidisciplinary topic comprising of several contingents, compassing from applications, terminals, networking architectures to network management, business models, and ultimately the end users [3]. On these accounts, it appears that the energy efficient video transmission over a wireless link proposed by Ye Li *et al.* [2] and reliable video transmission using codes close to the channel capacity by Reza Dianat *et al.* [4] are the most promising and pragmatic approach for video transmission and coding respectively.

In this paper, various video coding and wireless transmission techniques are discussed. Various such techniques available in the literature are catalogued and review of video coding technique is provided. Section III describes transmission of video over wireless links. The article highlights the summary in section IV.

2   General Review of Video Coding

The advanced video coding and compression standard H.264 from ITU-T offers good coding efficiency. It saves 48.8% and 38.62% bit rate as compared to previous standards H.263++ and MPEG respectively, as proposed by Zhikao Ren *et al.*(2009) [5].

Reza Dianat *et al.* [4], proposed a class of Reed–Solomon (RS) channel codes over prime fields GF $(2^{16}+1)$ that have excellent performance with low complexity and archives nearly error free video transmission system. It is a low overhead channel code for reliable transmission of video over noisy and lossy channels, if the delay is tolerable. They also, proposed a nearly error free transmission system for Gaussian channels.

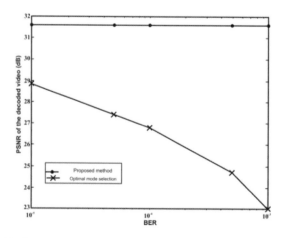

Fig. 1. Performance comparison using the QCIF "Foreman" sequence [4]

Fig. 1 and 2 shows the performance of the proposed method in literature [4] against that of the optimal mode selection and sync insertion [6] for a wide range of bit error rates for two video test sequences of Foreman and News for Binary symmetric channel (BSC).

Fig. 3 shows the performance of the proposed method with the method of joint source channel in [7], for the "Mother and Daughter" QCIF 150-frame sequence for bursty channel with the average burst length of 8 symbols.

Fig. 4 shows the performance of the proposed method [4] with the method of adaptive mode selection in [8], for the "Foreman" QCIF 150-frame sequence for packet loss channel in 250 kbps with 96 bytes in each packet. The method relies on nearly exact error estimation and correction using long RS codes over the field GF (65537).

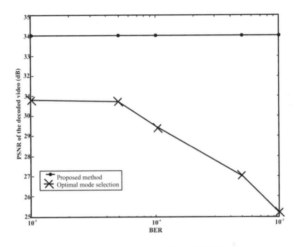

Fig. 2. Performance comparison using the QCIF "News" sequence [4]

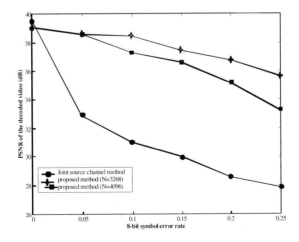

Fig. 3. Performance comparison using the QCIF "Mother and Daughter" 150-frame sequence [4]

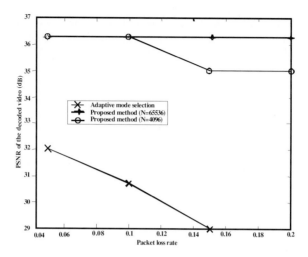

Fig. 4. Performance comparison using the QCIF "Foreman" in 250kbps [4]

Bernd Girod, *et al.* [9], presented feedback-based low bit-rate video coding techniques for robust transmission in mobile multimedia networks. It is called as channel-adaptive source coding; where intelligent processing of acknowledgment information by the coding control is used to adapt the source encoder to the channel. But the transcoders used here significantly increases complexity and add unacceptable delay. These feedback schemes are suitable for interactive, individual communications, but they have inherent limitations outside this domain.

3   Transmission over Wireless Link

With respect to the real-time transmission of video streams, the transmitting delay should be minimal. The high transmitting delay may cause the video packets not to been decoded. Adjustment of the bit rates of video stream is required for a reliable video transmission.

In order to guarantee the reliable real-time video transmission of overlay multicast network (OMN), a layered multicast tree with three-level is proposed by Deqiang Cheng *et al.*(2008) [10]. It uses NICE protocol to manage multicast service nodes which improves the data-transmitting efficiency and minimize the redundant packets in OMN.

Also, for the reliable video transmission in bandwidth-limited links of OMN, a QoS algorithm is analyzed by discarding the redundant frames of the video sequences according to the detected network condition. The packet loss rate is looked as an important parameter to reflect the network quality. So, the frame loss rates is used between multicast service nodes (MSNs) and nodes to detect the network quality.

Dalei Wu *et al.* (2009) [11], suggests a quality driven decision engine for live video transmission under service oriented architecture (SOA). The various kinds of data processing services are jointly considered and optimized by the proposed decision engine [11], as shown in fig. 5 below.

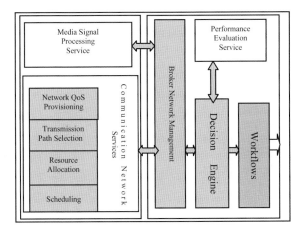

Fig. 5. The proposed SOA system model for live video communication [11]

With the expected end-to-end user-perceived quality as the objective function, various services such as video encoding, transmission path selection, and packet scheduling for foregrounds /backgrounds are put together in a systematic way. The most significant component of SOA is the decision engine, which creates a workflow. It is a performance evaluation component.

For Video streaming applications, the media server resides at a different location from router/gateway and the video is pre-encoded and packetized at the same server. The video encoding cannot be adapted to changes in the network such as network congestions and/or channel variations. For interactive video applications like video conferencing, video instant messaging and live broadcasting, the captured videos are coded on-the-fly, the source content and network conditions are jointly considered to determine the optimal source encoding modes.

In the proposed SOA [11], key data processing components for live video transmissions is multimedia signal processing which includes video trans-coding, content analysis, extracting region of interest (RIO) (foreground part) information of a video sequence, down-sampling a frame, filtering high frequency components of a frame and summarizing a video sequence. For smooth video display experience, the delay deadline is imposed on the transmission of each packet like frame decoding deadline T^{max}. Here, T^{max} indicates that all the packets needed to decode a frame must be received at the decoder buffer prior to the playback time of that frame.

To compare the received quality of different video contents, two schemes are considered. The first uses the content analysis service to perform the identification of ROI (IRI), while the second does not use the content analysis service, considering the requested video sequence as a whole part under no IRI. These two schemes have different PSNR performance; with and without using the service of priority scheduling. The single-packet delay deadline T^{max} is 0.01 s. It has been observed that without using the service of priority scheduling, the average PSNRs of the whole video under no IRI, the foreground, and the background are the same. However, when the service of priority scheduling is used, the foreground has a 4.5 dB and 9.5 dB PSNR improvement over the whole video under no IRI and the background, respectively. This indicates that the proposed [11] decision engine provides a guarantee for the received quality of ROI in a delay stringent or rate-limited multi-hop wireless network.

Yubo Tan *et al.* (2008) [12], presented a self-adapted feedback algorithm (SAFA) for video transmission which is based on the forward error correction (FEC) coding technology and the KALMAN filter theory. By modifying the rate using the adapted KALMAN filter, this algorithm efficiently solves the problem of rate fluctuation caused by the lost packets. It reduces the network load caused by the retransmission of lost packets using the state model, based on Gilbert model, about the quantity of FEC packets which need to be sent as follows (figure 6) [12].

The status *0* means that the variable *b* is fixed and the server sends packets normally. The status *1* means that the receiver successfully receives packets for *s* times, then the server decreases the value of variable *b*. The state *2* means that the receiver losses packet for *t* times, then the server increases the value of *b*. The parameter *p* is the probability of successfully received packet, while *q* is the probability of loss ($q=1-p$). Yubo Tan guarantee the satisfied performance of the video transmission in the high-packet-lost networks. SAFA only encodes the elementary-layer packets and some important data using the packet-level FEC method and greatly reduces the quantity of the ack-packets.

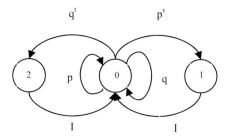

Fig. 6. SAFA state model (t>1, s>1) [12]

The structure of peer-to-peer real time video transmission system is shown in Fig. 7 and is proposed by Zhikao Ren *et al.* [4]. The compressed video flows-divided into the RTP packages and transmitted.

At the receiver, RTCP control packages are send to the sender for feedback the current situations of networks, which separates the effective data, decodes these encoded images and also, displays. The sender will adjust flows and the modes of transmission by analyzing RTCP. Zhikao Ren also has suggested fine control methods of video transmission system, which is a comprehensive control methods of real time transmission. The video coding is divided in two layers, firstly the basic layer, used for large network load, which does the basic display of videos and secondly the expand layer, which considers RTCP feedback, network load situations and carries dynamic control of data flows by the selective sending of the data. It adjusts the size of RTP data packets automatically and realigns dis-ordered data packages.

Zhikao Ren has implemented the algorithm for experimentation into H.264 reference software JM86 realized by JVT. The algorithm of realigning disordered data packages is used to calculate the amount of disordered and lost RTP packages. Thus, a real time video transmission system is successfully implemented.

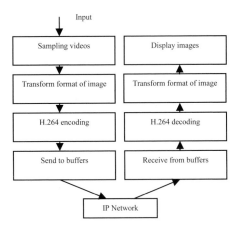

Fig. 7. Diagram of Transmission System [5]

Ye Li *et al.* [2], suggests energy efficient video transmission system for single user and multiuser. Ye Li have given emphasize on energy minimization in radio frequency (RF) front end devices by adjusting parameters in PHY and MAC layers. The PHY parameters considered are modulation level, bit rate, bit error rate, multiple access interface and the MAC (link layer) parameters are buffer status, idle time, active time.

For single user system the authors have suggested four energy efficient schemes as,

A. *Frame by frame transmission*
B. *GoP (Group of pictures) by GoP transmission*, which transmits at optimal data rate and saves energy. Both these techniques considers a slow –fading channel with constant attenuation factor over the duration of frame/GOP. It uses ideal adaptive transmission scheme which considers parameters affecting optimal modulation levels like distance and channel conditions and are updated regularly. The modulation level is adjusted for every video frame (or GOP) to save energy. Above techniques do not consider the effect of the client buffer size and client buffer occupancy.
C. *Client buffer related energy efficient video transmission (CBEVT)*, where energy savings of upto 85% is achieved in RF front end by considering client buffer occupancy and the video delay constraints. Knowing the client buffer capacity, the transmitter keeps track of the client buffer occupancy by tracking its transmissions and the size of the video frames that were retrieved from the buffer for play-out. For frame loss on wireless link an acknowledgement (ACK) / Negative ACK (NACK) is required for keeping track of successfully received video frames. It gives superior performance, consumes less energy and reduces the peak data rate.
D. *Energy Efficient Optimal Smoothing Scheme.*
   It reduces the peak data rate in video transmission and avoids the overflow and starvation in the client buffer. To achieve this, the constant bit rate (CBR) transmission should be as smooth as possible, so the smoothing algorithm must make

the CBR transmission segments as long as possible and if the client buffer is close to overflowing or starvation, the transmission rate (C_{max} and C_{min}) must be changed as early as possible. For low energy consumption, data rate should be between [C_{max} and C_{min}]. The algorithm considers the effect of the energy consumption, peak data rate, client buffer status and queuing delay.

For multi-user based energy efficient video transmission (MBEVT) system, the entire system energy consumption is reduced by considering number of active users, client buffer sizes and delays. Video communication has two characteristics [11]; firstly, different bits in a video stream have different levels of importance in terms of their contribution to user-perceived video quality. Secondly, error resilience and error concealment (EC) techniques used in the process of video encoding and decoding allow multimedia applications to recover from a certain degree of packet losses. The key component in transmission is communication network which does the job of transmission path selection, network resource allocation, scheduling and network QoS provisioning. For live video transmission, frame decoding deadlines T^{max} [11] is linked with frame rate r as

$$T^{max} \cong \frac{1}{r} \qquad ..\text{equ.}(1)$$

The authors [12], proposed a novel SAFA algorithm to support video transmission. The algorithm automatically modifies the sending rate and the quantity of FEC encoded packets through self-adapted feedback. It can avoid the collapse caused by the mass ACK packets and the rate fluctuation caused by the retransmission lost packets. The algorithm can guarantee video transmission quality even in the high- packet-lost network, which may leads to loss of the elementary layer and the PSNR [13] ratio is shown in Fig. 8.

In order to transmit multimedia contents more robust and effectively the communication systems to provide selectable and/or adaptive link qualities in accordance with the transmitted contents. Unequal error protection (UEP) is one of the techniques to meet such demands [14]. To improve the robustness of MPEG-4 transmission different error performance is provided for each of MPEG-4 data partitions in accordance with their error sensitivity. By assigning the more important partitions to the bit levels of multiple block coded modulation (MBCM) that provide a smaller bit error rate (BER), the quality of the whole MPEG-4 video transmission can be increased. As a result, the transmission becomes more robust against channel errors and a higher reliability can be achieved than the case of without UEP.

Huan-Bang Li et al. [14], implemented a codec to cope with a UEP-enabled modem for MPEG-4 video transmission. Their results for the video picture showed that some parts or a whole picture froze sometime at the link without UEP while this was not observed at the link with UEP. A much better video quality was obtained at the link with UEP.

Tomi Raty et al. 2007 [15], have constructed a scalable QoS (SQoS) middleware system. During the initial video transmission from the network camera through the SQoS server to the ultimate destination, the smart phone, the bit-rate of the utilized protocol, the Real-time Transport Protocol (RTP), over the wireless network is

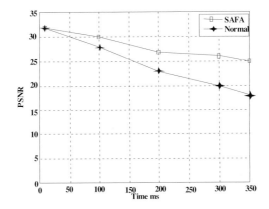

Fig. 8. Diagram of Transmission System [10]

evaluated. The video transmission by a network camera to a smart phone routed through a SQoS server. Both monitoring user agents monitor the video transmission's bit-rate. The monitoring user agents transmit their evaluation to the leader agent. Then the leader agent deducts whether to ordain the network camera to scale the QoS values down or up. Tomi Raty shows improvement in the control of the video transmission over a mobile system by innovative theories like, the SQoS middleware system's architecture, passive monitoring paradigm, calculation, deduction methods and optimize the video transmission rate to a smart phone over a wireless network. The intent of the theories is to optimize or improve, the video transmission rate to a smart phone over a wireless network.

In the implemented SQoS middleware system, the problem of connection fluctuation can be solved by three options of actions: 1) downgrading the quality of the video data transmission at the source, if the quality requirements of the client are transgressed, 2) upgrading the quality of the video data transmission at the source, if the quality requirements of the client are surpassed or 3) maintaining the current video data transmission at its current level. The decision of downgrading, upgrading or maintaining the data transmission is conducted by the leader agent, e.g., a user agent that conducts and controls the quality level of the video data transmission based on the QoS information of the connection received from the monitoring user agent client and the monitoring user agent server.

The implemented leader agent is an integration of the monitoring user agent server and the leader agent. The initial predictions, according to which the SQoS server adapts its video transmission, are the default preferences of the SQoS server. This initial method is then refined by the leader agent's calculations based on the information collected or evaluations of the monitoring user agent client and the monitoring user agent server. Once the connection has been formed, the video data transmission from the SQoS server to the smart phone client may commence.

The functionality of the middleware system indicates that the video transmission rate from a network camera to a smart phone over a wireless network has improved.

4 Conclusion

Supporting video communication over lossy channels such as wireless networks and the internet is a challenging task due to the stringent QoS required by video applications and also affected by many channel impairments. By using a fast mode decision algorithm for H.264 intra prediction and an adaptive transmission control methods of video can gain good QoS and achieves 30% to 60% computation reduction on aspects of video coding, so that the stability and good qualities of video transmission can be ensured [5].

Using Long Reed–Solomon codes over the prime field GF $(2^{16} + 1)$ it is possible to have a class of nearly error free video transmission systems for reliable transmission of video over noisy and lossy channels. Multiple energy-efficient transmission schemes for prerecorded continuous media (e.g., streaming video and audio) in single-user and multiuser systems is obtained by adjusting parameters in the PHY and MAC layers namely 1) the frame-by-frame transmission; 2) the GOP-by-GOP transmission; and 3) the CBEVT. The CBEVT reduces the reception energy consumption by completing the video transmission sooner and thus, achieves the lowest energy consumption among the considered schemes.

Based on the above investigation the work can be continued in the following areas which includes efficient video coding, reliable wireless transmission, QoS, transmission rate, energy efficiency of handheld devices to improve the overall wireless video transmission system.

References

1. Ferre, P., Doufexi, A., Chung-How, J., Nix, A.R., Bull, D.r.: Robust video transmission over wireless LANs. IEEE Trans. Veh. Technol. 57(4), 2596–2602 (2008)
2. Li, Y., Reisslein, M., Chakrabarti, C.: Energy-efficient video transmission over a wireless link. IEEE Trans. Veh. Technol. 58(3), 1229–1244 (2009)
3. Zhang, Q., Zhu, W., Zhang, Y.: End-to-End QoS for video delivery over wireless Internet. Proc. of the IEEE 93(1), 124–234 (2005)
4. Dianat, R., Marvasti, F., Ghanbari, M.: Reliable video transmission using codes close to the channel capacity. IEEE Trans. Circuits and Systems for Video Technol. 16(12), 1550–1556 (2006)
5. Ren, Z., Liu, M., Ye, C., Shao, H.: Real time video transmission based on H.264. In: International Conf. on Web Information Systems and Mining, Shanghai, China, pp. 270–274 (2009)
6. Cote, G., Shirani, S., Kossentini, F.: Optimal mode selection and synchronization for robust video communications over error-prone networks. IEEE J. Sel. Areas Commun. 18(6), 952–965 (2000)
7. Stuhlmuller, K., Farber, N., Link, M., Girod, B.: Analysis of video transmission over lossy channels. IEEE J. Sel. Areas Commun. 18(6), 1012–1032 (2000)
8. He, Z., Cai, J., Chen, C.W.: Joint source channel rate-distortion analysis for adaptive mode selection and rate control in wireless video coding. IEEE Trans. Circuits Sys. Video Technol. 12(6), 511–523 (2002)
9. Girod, B., Farber, N.: Feedback based error control for mobile video transmission. Proc. of the IEEE 87(10), 1707–1723 (1999)

10. Cheng, D., Jin, Y., Qian, J.: A layered multicast tree for reliable real-time video transmission of OMN. In: International Conf. on Intelligent Computation Technology and Automation, pp. 69–72 (2008)
11. Wu, D., Ci, S., Luo, H., Wang, H., Katsaggelos, A.: A quality driven decision engine for live video transmission under Service Oriented Architecture (SOA). IEEE Trans. Wireless communication, 48–54 (2009)
12. Tan, Y., Wang, H., Wang, X., Zhang, Q.: A video transmission algorithm over the internet based on FEC and Kalman. In: Proc. of IEEE International Symposium on IT in Medicine and Education, pp. 263–267 (2008)
13. Yongjun, Z., Zhangyi, P.: Error control and recovery technology in real-time media stream transmission. Journal of National University of Defense Technology 3(6), 75–76 (2003)
14. Li, H.-B., Taira, S.: MPEG-4 video transmission using unequal error protection for mobile satellite communication, IEEE paper (2005)
15. Raty, T., Oikarinen, J., Sihvonen, M.: A scalable quality of service middleware system with passive monitoring agents over wireless video transmission. In: International Conf. on the Quality of Information and Communication Technology, pp. 123–129 (2007)

Cluster Localization of Sensor Nodes Using Learning Movement Patterns

R. Arthi and K. Murugan

Ramanujan Computing Centre, Anna University, Chennai,
Chennai 25, Tamilnadu, India
darthi73@gmail.com, murugan@annauniv.edu

Abstract. In Wireless Sensor Networks (WSN), localization system is required in order to provide position information to sensor nodes. The cost and limited energy resource associated with common, mobile nodes prohibits them from carrying relatively expensive devices such as Global Positioning System (GPS). This paper proposes a mechanism that allows non-GPS-equipped nodes in the network to derive their approximated locations from a limited number of GPS-equipped nodes. A Non-GPS equipped node uses Received Signal Strength Indicator (RSSI) to know the position of the node using Hidden Markov Model (HMM). To enhance lifetime, an efficient clustering scheme is used for localizing the nodes of HMM with Random Walk Mobility (RWM) model. Coverage Preserving Clustering Protocol (CPCP) approach is compared with existing LEACH protocol for localization with HMM combined mobility through NS2 simulation. Simulation analysis shows that our cluster localization out performs well with Learning Movement Patterns.

Keywords: Cluster Localization, HMM, RWM, LEACH, CPCP, Estimation Error.

1   Introduction

In most of the WSN applications, sensors are deployed in the large physical environment where location information of each sensor is critical to the applications e.g. habitat monitoring, target tracking, location based routing, etc., however localization remains a challenging problem in wireless sensor networks. Due to low energy constraints in WSN, the network is divided in to clusters and cluster heads are used to collect the current location information of the sensor node.

There are many considerations for using the clustering protocol in WSN nodes like considering the characteristics of WSN, energy resource of node should be managed wisely to extend the lifetime of sensors. This is very important to prolong the lifetime of entire sensor networks. In order to guarantee low energy consumption and a uniform load distribution over the network, there have been many schemes that sensor nodes are organized into clusters in Wireless Sensor Network.

This paper proposes a cluster based localization approach which requires very few cluster heads that acts like an anchor nodes (GPS nodes) to work well in a decentralized fashion. The protocol used for clustering is Coverage preserving

N. Meghanathan et al. (Eds.): CCSIT 2011, Part II, CCIS 132, pp. 148–157, 2011.

Clustering protocol (CPCP) and it is compared with LEACH protocol. In this paper non-GPS-equipped nodes in the network derive their approximated locations from cluster heads that act as GPS-equipped nodes. In this method, all nodes periodically broadcast their estimated location, in terms of learning movement model. Non-GPS nodes estimate the distance to their neighbors by measuring the received signal strength of incoming messages. Learning Movement Pattern along with the RWM model is then used to estimate the approximated location from the sequence of distance estimates and has wide applications in Military and Defense. With the help of NS-2, the Estimation error, Average energy dissipated, Control Overhead, with respect to node density, transmission range and speed is simulated and analyzed.

The organization of the paper is as follows: Section 2 reviews the Related Work in WSN localization and Clustering. Section 3 discusses the System Architecture of proposed System. Section 4 gives the Simulation Results. The Conclusion is presented in Section 5.

2   Related Work

In [1] the author has proposed the various types of sensors used in localization such as AoA sensors and RSSI sensors. Both AoA sensors as well as the RSSI sensors do not work well when the network connectivity or the anchor ratio is low. In [2] the author has proposed localization of sensor nodes using HMM combined with Reference Point Group Mobility model and Semi Markov Smooth Mobility model to study the performance based on Estimation Error.

In [3] numerical results show that the HMM method improves the accuracy of localization with respect to conventional ranging methods, especially in mixed LOS/NLOS indoor environments. In [4] the author has proposed a practical target tracking system based on the HMM in a distributed signal processing framework.

In [5] the author has proposed the balanced energy among the cluster head nodes throughout the network lifetime. This mainly deals with coverage aware cost metrics for the selection of cluster head nodes. Coverage redundancy problem can also be eliminated by using clustering protocol in wireless sensor network. In [6] the author has proposed the dealing of load balancing, node deployment, tolerating the failure of Cluster Head (CH). These all can be possible only by use of categorization of clusters such as cluster properties, cluster head capabilities and clustering process. Main objective of this cluster categorization which includes the inter cluster connectivity, mobility of cluster head and node grouping.

3   System Architecture

The focus of the proposed architecture is to obtain better location accuracy using the clustering approach and to minimize the low energy constraints in WSN. The proposed system architecture is shown in the Figure 1. The main System Architecture Components are Cluster configuration, where the Clusters are formed with the use of Clustering protocol. Then HMM system [2] is useful for localizing the nodes sequence and satisfies the parameters of HMM.

The proposed system architecture shows that dynamic node is deployed around the network randomly. With the help of Clustering Protocol, the CH is selected as Anchor nodes (GPS nodes) and the rest are considered as Non-anchor nodes that need to be localized. After the election of CH, which knew its initial position is given to the HMM system .Knowing the location estimation of Anchor Nodes [2] is considered as initial state sequence (π). From initial position, the node movement takes place by the random walk mobility model [9] and those probabilities form the transition matrix (A).The hidden state sequence (nodes) are localized by the Observation matrix (B). The HMM parameter set is satisfied by the various problems of HMM.

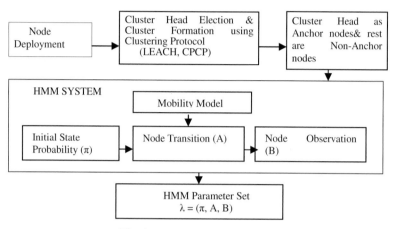

Fig. 1. Proposed System Architecture

3.1 Node Deployment Phase

In the node deployment phase, assume the nodes are spread dynamically over an area of network. The node localization is achieved through limited number of anchor nodes (GPS nodes) using RSSI measurement. Any message from a node is sent to all the neighbors within its transmission region with a delay d where d is (Distance between the communicating Sensor Nodes) / Speed of Light. Various Radio Propagation models are used to predict the received signal power of each packet. The wireless channel derives these models affect the communicating region between any two nodes. The wireless channel considers the Two Ray Ground Propagation Model that takes RSSI measurement for node localization.

3.2 Clustering Approach

Clustering [7] is an effective topology control approach in WSNs which can increase network scalability and lifetime. A clustering scheme can effectively prolong the lifetime of wireless sensor networks by using the limited energy resources of the deployed sensor nodes efficiently. The routing protocol LEACH and CPCP is designed such that it groups the balanced energy nodes in the clustering of WSN nodes.

3.2.1 LEACH Protocol
LEACH is an energy efficient protocol designed for sensor networks with continuous data delivery mechanism. With LEACH [7], cluster heads are randomly selected from

sensor nodes biased by their experience in serving as heads. Sensor nodes transmit data to their cluster heads according to the time slot assigned by cluster heads. Cluster heads send aggregated data to base station by single hop transmission. The system repeats the clustering and transmission for each round. Since LEACH is a traditional algorithm that does not support mobility of nodes.

In order to support mobility in sensor node by adding its membership declaration to the LEACH protocol [8].The idea behind this membership declaration is to confirm the inclusion of sensor nodes in a specific cluster in steady state phase. The cluster head will send data request to its member nodes, however, packet be considered loss when the cluster head does not receive data from its member nodes. The membership of the sensor node under this cluster head will be lost. Sensor node that does not receive request from its cluster head realizes that it has moved out from its cluster. It then sends the join message to nearby cluster heads in order to join into the new cluster and avoid losing more packets. LEACH's operation consists of multiple rounds. Each round has two phases those are

3.2.1.1   A Setup Phase. All sensor nodes compute the value of T (n) in equation (1) according to the following formula at the beginning of all rounds:

$$T(n) = P / 1 - P \times (r \bmod P^{-1}) \forall n \in G$$
$$T(n) = 0 \, otherwise$$

(1)

Where *n* is a random number between 0 and 1. *P* is the Cluster head probability. *G* is the set of nodes were not the cluster heads in the previous rounds.

3.2.1.2   A Steady State Phase. Cluster heads will plan and broadcast the time division multiple access (TDMA) schedule for those nodes included in the cluster. After sensor nodes receive TDMA information, they will send data to cluster head at the time slot assigned by the cluster heads. Notice that each sensor nodes will turn on the transmitter and receiver only at the time slot assigned to it. At other time slots, they can turn off the transmitter and receiver to save energy.

3.3   CPCP (Coverage Preserving Clustering Protocol)

In many of the clustering algorithm used in Wireless Sensor Network, range of coverage plays the main role. By using the clustering techniques available will lead to an undesirable situation such that cluster head nodes gets overcrowded in densely populated parts of the network, while the scarcely covered areas will be left without any cluster head nodes. In this situation, it may be possible for the high cost sensors from poorly covered areas perform expensive data transmissions to distant cluster head nodes, thereby reducing their lifetime. In order to overcome this problem, the clustering method called coverage- preserving clustering protocol (CPCP) is used. The idea is hired from CPCP [5] and considers only two phases for clustering Localization process. By limiting the maximum cluster area, CPCP spreads cluster head nodes more uniformly throughout the network.

The cluster radius is tuned such that it determines the minimum distance between any two-cluster head nodes in the network. This parameter helps to prevent the appearance of non-uniformly distributed clusters within the network. As per CPCP, the information update phase is skipped because the energy-aware cost C_{ea} metric is used and this does not depend on the neighboring nodes' remaining energy. C_{ea} evaluates the sensors' ability to take part in the sensing task based solely on its remaining energy E (s_i).

In this work, CPCP uses two important phase for cluster localization namely, Cluster Head Election and Cluster formation, Sensor Activation Phase.

3.3.1 Cluster Head Election and Cluster Formation

In this phase, every sensor determines its "activation time"- an amount of time proportional to its current cost C_{ea}. In order to decide the new cluster head for the upcoming communication round, each sensor waits until the expiration of its "activation time". If a node does not hear an announcement message from any other sensor node during the "activation time", then, after expiration of it's "activation time" it declares itself to be a new cluster head, by sending an announcement message to all the nodes within the cluster range. The announcement message contains information about the new cluster head's location. All cluster head from where it receives the announcement message so far, as well as the distance to each cluster head node maintain a table. In this manner, the cluster head election takes place and moves to form the cluster.

Each non-cluster head node decides to join the closest cluster head node in order to form the cluster. By sending the JOIN messages to the selected cluster head nodes, a node becomes a member of the cluster for the upcoming round. Upon this activation message cluster uses low energy for the cluster formation. There are no restrictions on the number of cluster members in cluster. Based on cluster range the nodes join less than one CH in the network. In this way, the cluster formation takes place around cluster head nodes in the network to   enhance lifetime of the network.

3.3.2 Sensor Activation Phase

In the sensor activation phase [5], each sensor node assigns itself an activation delay that is proportional to its current application cost C_{ea}. In this way, sensor nodes with smaller cost waits for a period of time before deciding whether it has to stay awake during the next communication round. While waiting for its activation delay to expire, the sensor node can receive the ACTIVATION messages from its neighboring nodes, which have smaller activation delays (smaller cost), if they decide to become active during the upcoming communication round.

After its activation delay time expires, the sensor node determines that its sensing area is completely covered by its neighbouring nodes; it turns itself off for the upcoming round. Otherwise, the sensor node broadcasts an ACTIVATION message to inform its neighbors about its decision to remain active. In this way, the lower cost nodes have priority to decide whether they should be active.

Using the following algorithm the sensor range in the sensor activation phase is obtained, where T_a (s) is time of activation.

   1. Initializing S =E(s) where E(s) is the residual energy of node S and T_a (s) α C(s), C(s) $\in$ {C_{ea}}.

   2. During period $T_a(s)$, S can receive ACTIVATION messages from its neighboring nodes.

   3. Once $T_a(s)$ is expired, S checks whether its sensing range is fully covered.

   4. if sensing range of node S is not fully covered then   send "ACTIVATION message" to its neighboring nodes end if.

3.4 Hidden Markov Model

Hidden Markov Models extend Markov models by assuming that the states of the markov chain were not observed directly, i.e., the Markov chain itself remains hidden. Hence this model shows how the states (nodes) relate to the actual observations (localizations).The advantage of representing the HMM as a graphical model is that it can easily write down the joint probability distributions over all the variables.

A Hidden Markov Model (HMM) [5] consists of a set of N states, each of which is associated with a set of M possible observations. The parameters of the HMM include:

An initial matrix of state probabilities is known by assumption

$$\Pi = [P_1, P_2, \ldots\ldots P_N]^T \tag{2}$$

whose elements P_i, $i \in [1, N]$, describe the position distribution probabilities of the node over the initial state set at the beginning $t = 1$.The Transition Probability is the matrix A that depends on the speed distribution of the node, on the geographical feature of the area and on the allowed transition. The Probability distribution from the observed signals is the matrix B.

Finally, the HMM parameter set is denoted by $\lambda = (A, B, \pi)$. As usual, the HMM have three problems [5]: First is the Evaluating problem, what is the probability of the observation O, given the model λ, i.e. $P(O/\lambda)$? => Solution: Forward or Backward algorithm. For the decoding problem, the solution for the most likely state sequence given the observation O. For Estimating problem, the estimate parameters given for the training observation sequences, $\lambda * = \arg_\lambda [\max P \ O/ \ \lambda]$, the solution is Baum-Welch algorithm.

4 Simulation Results

The proposed work was implemented using NS- 2, in order to evaluate and validate the performance of the HMM based localization. The network area has been set to 1000 X 1000m^2. The network area consists of 250 nodes and 5% of the total nodes are considered as anchor nodes, which know their position. All the nodes in the network have transmission range of 250m.Initally the energy level of each node is set to 5.1 joules. The transmission rate is 500Kb/sec of control packet size 512 bytes. The simulation was conducted for Random Walk Mobility Model with speed of 5m/sec. The performance metrics of Estimation Error, Average Energy Dissipated and Control Overhead are considered to validate the algorithm.

The effect of node density on the estimation error is shown in Fig. 2. The error estimate of CPCP-HMM proves to be better. As expected; higher node density lowers the estimation error. The reason is that when there is higher number of nodes, each sensor nodes has more anchors that has multihop neighborhood and gets more location information, so the localization improves.

The effect of transmission range on the estimation error is shown in Fig.3. CPCP-HMM seems to be good since the effect of coverage becomes high when the network is sparse, i.e., increase in transmission range. The estimation error increases due to increase in the transmission range.

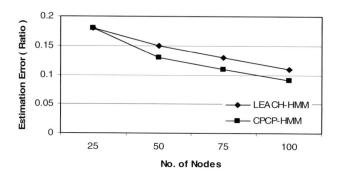

Fig. 2. Impact of Node Density over Estimation Error

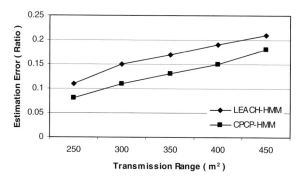

Fig. 3. Impact of Transmission Range over Estimation Error

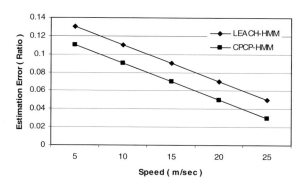

Fig. 4. Impact of Speed over Estimation Error

The effect of speed on the estimation error is shown in Fig. 4. CPCP-HMM proves that increase in the speed reduces the estimation error. The reason for this behavior is that increased random movement in the network can increase the chance of visiting more sensors and getting more information from the environment. However, at high speed past location is no longer useful and the error decreases. At constant speed, HMM predicts location of the non-anchors by learning movement profile.

Average Energy dissipated over the node density is shown in Fig. 5. This shows energy consumption gets varied due to increase in the node density. CPCP-HMM consumes less energy because the election of cluster is based on cost energy aware metric when compared with LEACH-HMM.

In Fig. 6. CPCP-HMM consumes less energy when compared with LEACH-HMM. The energy consumption is increased as the transmission range becomes more due to sparse connectivity of the sensor nodes.

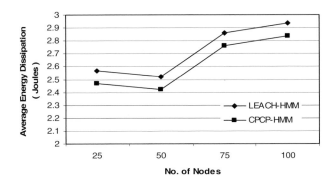

Fig. 5. Impact of Node Density over Average Energy Dissipation

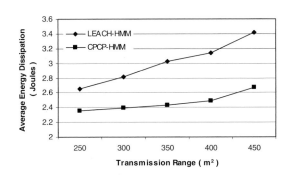

Fig. 6. Impact of Transmission Range over Average Energy Dissipation

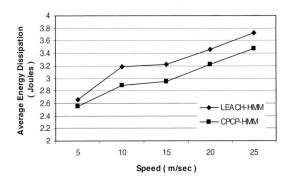

Fig. 7. Impact of Speed over Average Energy Consumption

In Fig. 7. the energy gradually increases as the speed increases.CPCP-HMM consumes less energy based on cost energy aware metric for cluster head election than LEACH-HMM depends on the time slot for cluster head election.

The Fig. 8. shows the performance of Control Overhead on Node density. With the node density growing, the control overhead gradually decreases and reaches consistent in CPCP-HMM. More denser the nodes, the anchor node becomes closer to the unknown nodes.

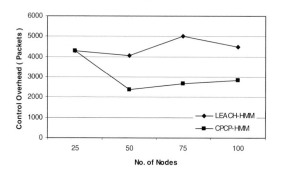

Fig. 8. Impact of Node Density over Control Overhead

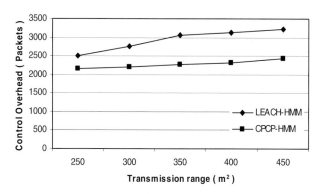

Fig. 9. Impact of Transmission Range over Control Overhead

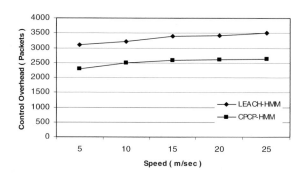

Fig. 10. Impact of Speed over Control Overhead

The control overhead packets are increased as shown in Fig.9. due to sparse node availability with increase in Transmission Range. As usual CPCP-HMM takes less control overhead packets than LEACH-HMM.

Fig.10. shows that the control overhead becomes gradually consistent as the speed increases. CPCP-HMM takes less control overhead packets than LEACH-HMM.

5 Conclusions

The Cluster based localization through HMM with Mobility Model was implemented for the sensor nodes using NS-2 Simulator. The focus of this work is to obtain the better Location precession. The simulation results shows that CPCP-HMM gives better result for random walk model scenario. Since this work is carried out for random deployment of node, it can be analyzed for uniform and non-uniform deployment of the node for further improvement of the location precession.

References

1. Huang, R., Zaruba, G.V.: Incorporating Data from Multiple Sensors for Localizing nodes in Mobile Ad Hoc Networks. IEEE Trans. Mobile Computing 6(9), 1090–1104 (2007)
2. Arthi, R., Murugan, K.: Location Estimation of Sensor Nodes Using Learning Movement Patterns. In: Proc. IEEE Students' Technology Symposium, pp. 146–150 (April 2010), doi:10.1109/TECHSYM.2010.5469217
3. Morelli, C., Nicoli, M., Member, IEEE, Rampa, V., Spagnolini, U., Senior Member, IEEE: Hidden Markov Models For Radio Localization In MixedLos/NlosConditions. IEEE Transactions On Signal Processing 55(4), 1525–1541 (2007)
4. Hieu, H.Q., Thanh, V.D.: Ground Mobile Target Tracking By Hidden Markov Model. Science & Technology Development 9(12) (2006)
5. Soro, S., Heinzelman, W.B.: Cluster head election techniques for coverage preservation in wireless sensor networks. Elsevier Ad hoc Networks, 955–972 (2009), doi:10.1016/j.adhoc.2008.08.006
6. Abbasi, A.A., Younis, M.: A survey on clustering algorithms for wireless sensor networks. Elsevier Computer Communications, 2826–2841 (June 2007), doi:10.1016/j.comcom.2007.05.024
7. Dimokas, N., Katsaros, D., Manolopoulos, Y.: Energy efficient distributed clustering in wireless sensor network. Elsevier J. of Parallel Distrib. Comput., 1–10 (2009), doi:10.1016/j.jpdc.2009.08.007
8. Awwad, S.A.B., Ng, C.K., Noordin, N.K., Rasid, M.F.A.: Cluster Based Routing Protocol for Mobile Nodes in Wireless Sensor Network, pp. 233–241. IEEE Computer Society, Los Alamitos (2009)
9. Camp, T., Boleng, J., Davies, V.: A Survey of Mobility Models for Ad Hoc Network Research. Wireless Communication & Mobile Computing 2(5), 483–502 (2002)

Improving TCP Performance through Enhanced Path Recovery Notification

S. Sathya Priya and K. Murugan

Ramanujan Computing Centre, Anna University Chennai
Chennai, Tamil Nadu, India
sathyapriya80@yahoo.co.in, murugan@annauniv.edu

Abstract. Handoff in wireless networks causes temporal link disconnection which introduces consecutive packet losses in the network. This degrades the performance of the Transmission Control Protocol and forces it to aggravate the bandwidth utilization of wireless networks. TCP Path Recovery Notification mechanism recovers the lost packets during handoff by keeping the congestion window and slow start threshold unaltered to maintain its throughput. The losses that occur due to handoff cannot be distinguished from that due to congestion by TCP-Path Recovery Notification. The proposed protocol, Enhanced Path Recovery Notification, classifies the packet losses into congestion loss and link error loss. The protocol measures the one way delay, if measured one way delay is less than that of the Delay Threshold, then it is identified as link failure and Path Recovery Notification is immediately invoked to retransmit the lost packets. If measured one way delay is greater than that of Delay Threshold then it is identified as congestion loss and slow start procedure in TCP is initiated to retransmit the lost packet. The result of Enhanced Path Recovery Notification shows that it outperforms both Path Recovery Notification and TCP-SACK in terms of throughput.

Keywords: One way delay, Packet loss differentiation, Path recovery notification, Tolerance margin.

1 Introduction

TCP is the most reliable transport protocol in internet applications. Although TCP is very reliable in wired networks, its performance deteriorates in wireless environments. In addition to network congestion, which has been the primary reason for packet loss, bit error corruption due to an unreliable wireless link easily induces packet loss at the TCP receiver. A Path Recovery Notification [PRN] mechanism is used to prevent performance degradation during disconnection period. PRN executes immediate recovery of lost packets during a handoff and keeps congestion window (cwnd) and slow start threshold (ssthresh) to maintain its throughput. An access point attached with a TCP receiver sends a special acknowledgement, during disconnection period. The special acknowledgement consists of two components namely PRN option and TCP SACK option which contains information on the sequence numbers of the lost packets. The network congestion is intensified with the appearance of PRN.

N. Meghanathan et al. (Eds.): CCSIT 2011, Part II, CCIS 132, pp. 158–168, 2011.

The main reason for the performance degradation is the protocol's inability to distinguish congestion losses from wireless losses.

The proposed protocol, Enhanced Path Recovery Notification (EPRN) is used for classifying the packet loss into congestion loss and link error loss. EPRN measures one way delay, if the measured one way delay is less than that of Delay Threshold (DT), then it is considered as a link failure and PRN is immediately invoked to retransmit the lost packets. If measured one way delay is greater than that of DT then it is considered as a congestion loss, and the slow start procedure of TCP is immediately initiated to retransmit the lost packets. The result shows that the proposed protocol, EPRN outperforms both the PRN and the TCP SACK in terms of throughput when simulated using ns-2 simulator.

2 Related Work

A useful survey of TCP enhancements for wireless networks is provided in [8]. TCP receiver which is attached to a new access point after a disconnection period or handoff sends a special acknowledgement. This acknowledgement consist of two components namely TCP SACK option and PRN option. TCP SACK option contains information on the sequence number of the lost packets and PRN option is used to retransmit the lost packets [1].

Loss differentiation algorithms such as Biaz, mBiaz, Spike, ZigZag, ZBS, PLC, SPLD, and TD are used in wireless networks to detect congestion or link error [2]. The slow start and congestion avoidance must be used by a TCP sender to control the amount of outstanding data being injected into the network [3]. In TCP HMM [5] and MLTCP [6], the authors collect data pertaining to different parameters through simulations and train a classifier to classify the cause of packet loss at the sender. The former approach employs a Hidden Markov Model whereas the latter approach employs a Decision Tree classification algorithm.

In TCP IAT [4], the loss cause is classified at the receiver by using the measured values of inter-arrival time (IAT); the assumption being that the last hop link is a wireless link and is a bottleneck.

3 TCP SACK and PRN

3.1 TCP SACK

A Selective Acknowledgment (SACK) mechanism, combined with a selective repeat retransmission policy, can help to overcome the limitation of multiple dropped segments efficiently and re-transmission of more than one lost packet per RTT is also possible. SACK retains the same slow-start and fast retransmit. TCP SACK requires that segments not be acknowledged cumulatively but should be acknowledged selectively. Thus each ACK has a block which describes which segments are beingïacknowledged. Thus the sender has a picture of which segments have been acknowledged and which are still outstanding.

3.2 PRN

PRN is to recover the adverse impact of the temporal link disconnection due to handoff. When a TCP receiver is attached to a new access point after a disconnection period or handoff it sends a special acknowledgement. This consist of two components namely PRN option and other is a TCP SACK. PRN option plays a role in notifying the sender that a wireless link was temporarily disconnected and reconnected. The option is set to one of three condition flags. They are reconnection (RC), partial loss (PL) and no packet arrival (NPA). TCP SACK contains information on the sequence numbers of the lost packets. This acknowledgement notifies a TCP sender that which packets are lost due to the temporal link disconnection. Once the receiver knows that the wireless link has been reconnected, it informs the sender with this information by sending an acknowledgement with a PRN option set to the condition flag. Before the PRN timer expires if new packet arrival at the receiver, it is possible that they includes gaps in the sequence numbers. In that case the receiver sends an acknowledgement packet with a PRN option set to PL flag. This ensures that the sender only transmits the lost packets. Then the receiver cancels the PRN timer. If no new packets arrive at the receiver and the PRN timer expires, the receiver sends an acknowledgement packet with only the PRN option set to NPA. This forces the sender to send all unacknowledged packets to perform the process.

4   Cross Layer Design

The concept of cross-layer design is about sharing of information among different protocol layers for adaptation purposes and to increase the interlayer interactions. In wireless networks there is tight interdependence between layers. Cross-layer design can help to exploit the interactions between layers and promotes adaptability at various layers based on information exchanged. However, such a design process needs to be carefully coordinated to avoid unintentional and undesirable consequences.

Cross layer design allow interactions between various protocols of non-adjacent layers through introduction of new interfaces and keep the impact of design violations as small as possible. They violate the traditional layer architecture by creation of new interfaces, merging of adjacent layers and sharing of variables and parameters among multiple layers.

5   The Proposed Protocol

The architecture of the proposed protocol, Enhanced Path Recovery Notification [EPRN] is shown in figure 1. It is used for classifying the packet loss into congestion loss and link loss. The sender sends packets to the receiver. The receiver acknowledges the packet received. Based on the Duplicate Acknowledgement (DACK) sent by the receiver, the sender knows that there is a packet loss. The packet loss may be either due to Congestion or due to link error. On receiving the DACK, the algorithm classifies the packet loss accordingly.

If the loss is identified as link loss, immediately PRN is invoked to retransmit the lost packets. If the loss is due to congestion, TCP slow start algorithm is initiated to retransmit the lost packets.

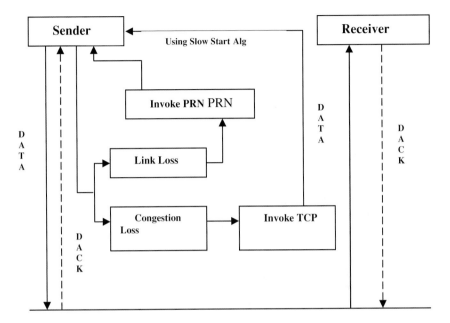

Fig. 1. EPRN Architecture

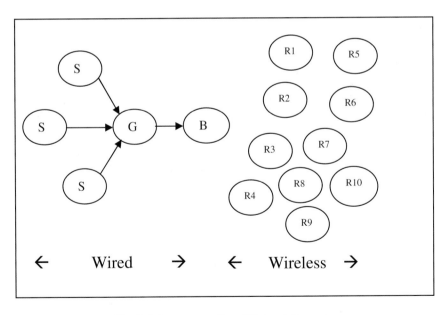

Fig. 2. Infra-structure Based Network Scenario

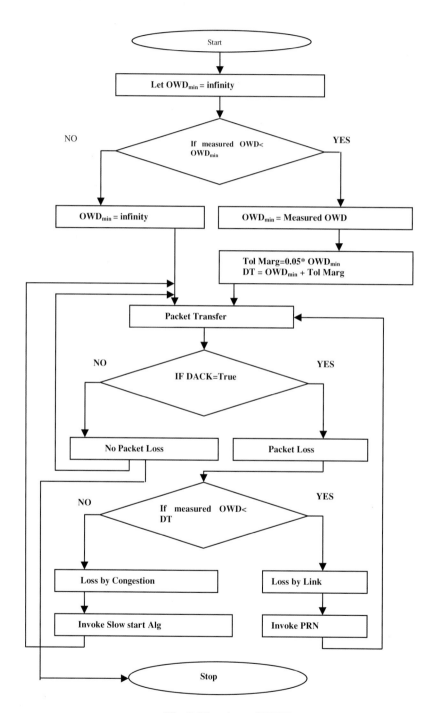

Fig. 3. Flowchart of EPRN

The network scenario taken is infra-structure based with three different senders (S_1, S_2 and S_3) and ten different receivers (R_1, $R_{2...}$ R_{10}) and is shown in figure 2. The flows from different senders are destined to the corresponding receivers through the Base Station (BS).

Let P_{di} be the propagation delay of each link and Q_{dj} be the queuing delay of each link. EPRN will measure one way delay (OWD). OWD is calculated by,

$$OWD = \sum P_{di} + \sum Q_{dj} \qquad (1)$$

If there is no congestion, the queuing delay will be zero, then

$$OWD = \sum P_{di} \qquad (2)$$

The variability in the propagation delay should be counted as it will vary in wireless environment. A small margin called the tolerance margin is added up to the end to end delay.

In that measured OWD, minimum of OWD is taken as OWD_{min}. Using that OWD_{min}, delay threshold (DT) is calculated by the sum of OWD_{min} and tolerance margin (Tol Marg) where,

$$\text{Tol Marg} = 0.05 * OWD_{min} \qquad (3)$$

$$DT = OWD_{min} + \text{Tol Marg} \qquad (4)$$

If the measured OWD is less than that of DT, then link failure has occurred and immediately PRN is invoked to retransmit the lost packet. If measured OWD is greater than that of DT then it is a congestion loss, immediately slow start procedure in TCP is initiated to retransmit the lost packet. The concept is indicated as flow chart in Figure 3.

6   Performance Evaluation

The proposed protocol was evaluated using the Network Simulator (NS-2). The performance of EPRN is compared with existing SACK and PRN. The performance is evaluated in two different scenarios involving both wireless loss and congestion loss. The scenario1 evaluates the performance of the protocols with only wireless loss and scenario 2 with both wireless and congestion loss.

The simulation is carried out considering the various parameters- simulation time, packet loss fraction and disconnection period, and the parameters are shown in Table 1.

Table 1. Simulation Parameters

Propagation Model	Two ray ground
Transmission Range	75m
Packet size	200 Bytes
Simulation time	25s to 200s
Disconnection Period	2s to 4s
Queue Delay	10ms
Bandwidth	5MB
Protocols	Sack1, PRN, EPRN

6.1 Scenario 1

This scenario is simulated by setting the queue size of the router (10 packets) to be equal or greater than the maximum receiver window size (7 packets). This setting guarantees that there is no loss due to queue overflow (congestion loss) during the simulation.

The figure 4 shows the determination of delay with respect to simulation time of wireless loss obtained at EPRN. Here the OWD is measured. The minimum of OWD is taken as OWD_{min}. Using the OWD_{min}, delay threshold and tolerance margin are calculated using the equation (4) and (3) in section V. The inference made from the graph is that the delay increases from OWD to delay threshold. The points which are below the delay threshold value are detected as wireless loss.

The figure 5 shows throughput variations of protocols with respect to packet loss fraction. The inference made from the graph is that as packet loss fraction increases, the throughput is degraded. The result shows throughput of EPRN is higher than TCP SACK and PRN. The figure 6 shows throughput variations of protocols with respect to disconnection period. The inference made from the graph is that as disconnection

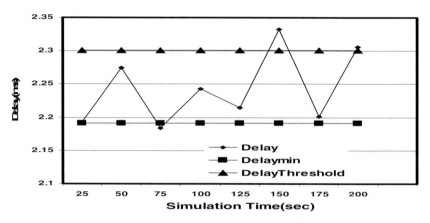

Fig. 4. Simulation Time with respect to Delay

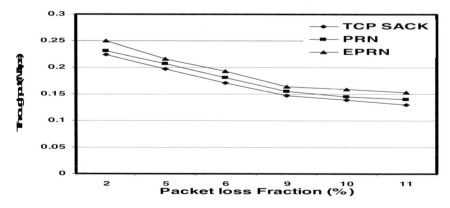

Fig. 5. Packet Loss Fraction with respect to Throughput

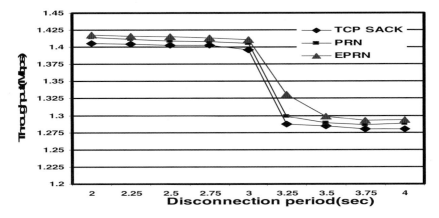

Fig. 6. Disconnection Period with respect to Throughput

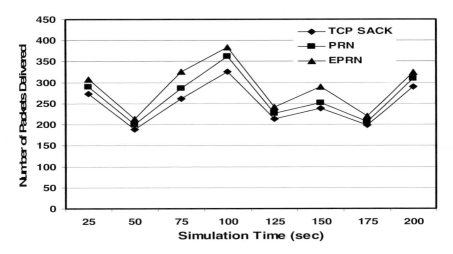

Fig. 7. Simulation Time with respect to Packets Delivered

period increases, the throughput is degraded. The result shows throughput of EPRN is higher than TCP SACK and PRN. The figure 7 shows the number of packets delivered with respect to simulation time. The result shows that the number of packets delivered by EPRN is higher than that of TCP SACK and PRN.

6.2   Scenario 2

This scenario is simulated by setting the queue size of the router (7 packets) to be less than the maximum receiver window size (10 packets). This setting guarantees that there is loss due to queue overflow (congestion loss) during the simulation.

The figure 8 shows the determination of delay with respect to simulation time of wireless loss and congestion loss obtained at EPRN. Delay threshold and tolerance margin are calculated using the equation (4) and (3) in section V. The inference made from the graph is that delay increases from OWD through delay threshold. The points which are below the delay threshold values are detected as wireless loss and above the threshold level are detected as congestion loss.

The figure 9 shows throughput variations of protocols with respect to packet loss fraction. The inference made from the graph is that as packet loss fraction increases, the throughput is degraded. The result shows throughput of EPRN is higher than TCP SACK and PRN. The figure 10 shows throughput variations of protocols with respect to disconnection period. The inference made from the graph is that as disconnection period increases, the throughput is degraded. The result shows throughput of EPRN is higher than TCP SACK and PRN. The figure 11 shows the number of packets delivered with respect to simulation time. The result shows that the number of packets delivered by EPRN is higher than that of TCP SACK and PRN.

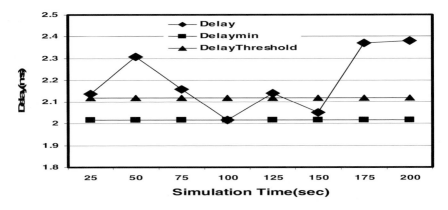

Fig. 8. Simulation Time with respect to Delay

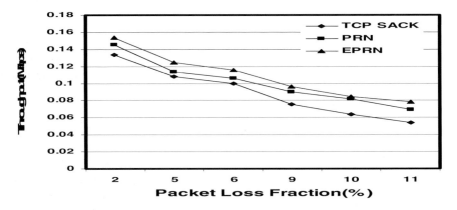

Fig. 9. Packet Loss Fraction with respect to Throughput

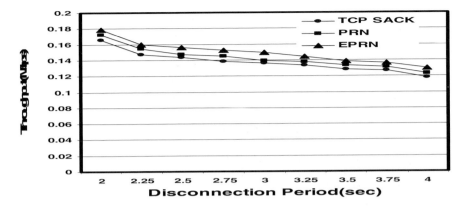

Fig. 10. Disconnection Period with respect to Throughput

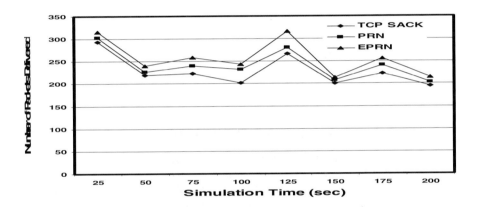

Fig. 11. Simulation Time with respect to Packets Delivered

7 Conclusions

This work mainly focuses on loss differentiation to differentiate the loss as congestion loss and link loss using EPRN protocol with respect to OWD. If the measured OWD is less than that of DT, then link failure has occurred. If measured OWD is greater than that of DT then it is a congestion loss. Finally wireless loss and congestion loss has been identified using EPRN. The simulation results show that EPRN protocol has better performance with respect to throughput, disconnection period, packet loss fraction and number of packets transferred when compared to TCP SACK and PRN Protocol. The machine learning techniques can be used along with EPRN protocol to further increase the performance of the network by focusing on congestion loss.

References

1. Lee, M., Kang, M., Kim, M., Mo, J.: A Cross Layer Approach for TCP Optimization Over Wireless and Mobile Networks. Computer Communication, 2669–2675 (March 2008)
2. Boukerche, A., Jia, G., Pazzi, R.W.N.: Performance Evaluation of Packet Loss Differentiation Algorithms for Wireless Networks. In: PM2HW2N 2007, pp. 50–52 (October 2007)
3. Allman, M., Paxson, V., Stevens, W.: RFC-2581 TCP Congestion Control. Tech. Rep., IETF (April 1999)
4. Biaz, S., Vaidya, N.: Discriminating Congestion Losses from Wireless Losses using Inter-Arrival Times at the Receiver. In: IEEE Symposium on Application-Specific Systems and Software Engineering and Technologies, Richardson, TX, pp. 10–17 (March 1999)
5. Liu, J., Matta, I., Crovella, M.: End-to-End Inference of Loss Nature in a Hybrid Wired/Wireless Environment. In: Modeling and Optimization in Mobile, Ad Hoc and Wireless Networks (WiOpt), France (March 2003)
6. Geurts, P., Khayat, E., Leduc, G.: A Machine Learning approach to Improve Congestion Control over Wireless Computer Networks. In: IEEE International Conference on Data Mining ICDM, Brighton, UK (November 2004)
7. NS-2 simulator tool home page, http://www.isi.edu/nsnam/ns
8. Chen, X., et al.: A Survey on Improving TCP Performance over Wireless Networks. Network Theory and Applications 16 (July 2006)
9. Priya, S.S., Murugan, K.: Cross Layer Approach to Enhance TCP Performance over Wireless Networks. In: Proc. IEEE Students' Technology Symposium, pp. 171–176 (April 2009), doi:10.1109/TECHSYM.2010.5469175

The Replication Attack in Wireless Sensor Networks: Analysis and Defenses

V. Manjula and C. Chellappan

Department of CSE, Anna University, Chennai, India
manjuvv@yahoo.com, drcc@annauniv.edu

Abstract. Security is important for many sensor network applications. Wireless sensor networks (WSN) are often deployed in hostile environments, where an adversary can physically capture some of the nodes. Once a node is captured, adversary collects all the credentials like keys and identity etc. The attacker can re-program it and replicate the node in order to eavesdrop the transmitted messages or compromise the functionality of the network. Identity theft leads to two types attack: clone and Sybil. In particularly a harmful attack against sensor networks where one or more node(s) illegitimately claims an identity as replicas is known as the Node Replication attack.

The replication attack can be exceedingly injurious to many important functions of the sensor network such as routing, resource allocation, misbehavior detection, etc. This paper analyzes the threat posed by the replication attack, several novel techniques to detect and defend against the replication attack, and analyzes their effectiveness.

Keywords: Security, Clone, Sybil, Node Replication Attack, wireless sensor network.

1 Introduction

A Wireless Sensor Network (WSN) is a collection of sensors with limited resources that collaborate in order to achieve a common goal. Sensor nodes operate in hostile environments such as battle fields and surveillance zones. Due to their operating nature, WSNs are often unattended, hence prone to several kinds of novel attacks.

The mission-critical nature of sensor network applications implies that any compromise or loss of sensory resource due to a malicious attack launched by the adversary-class can cause significant damage to the entire network. Sensor nodes deployed in a battlefield may have intelligent adversaries operating in their surroundings, intending to subvert damage or hijack messages exchanged in the network. The compromise of a sensor node can lead to greater damage to the network. The resource challenged nature of environments of operation of sensor nodes largely differentiates them from other networks. All security solutions proposed for sensor networks need to operate with minimal energy usage, whilst securing the network.

We classify sensor network attacks into three main categories [7]: Identity Attacks, Routing Attacks & Network Intrusion. Fig 1 shows the attack taxonomy in wireless sensor network. Identity attacks intend to steal the identities of legitimate nodes

N. Meghanathan et al. (Eds.): CCSIT 2011, Part II, CCIS 132, pp. 169–178, 2011.
© Springer-Verlag Berlin Heidelberg 2011

operating in the sensor network. The identity attacks are *Sybil attack and Clone (Replication) attack.* In a Sybil attack, the WSN is subverted by a malicious node which forges a large number of fake identities in order to disrupt the network's protocols. A node replication attack is an attempt by the adversary to add one or more nodes to the network that use the same ID as another node in the network.

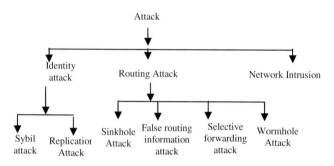

Fig. 1. Attack Taxonomy

Routing attack intend to place the Rogue nodes on a routing path from a source to the base station may attempt to tamper with or discard legitimate data packets. Some of the routing attacks are *Sinkhole Attack, False routing information attack, Selective forwarding attack, and Wormholes.* The adversary creates a large sphere of influence, which will attract all traffic destined for the base station from nodes which may be several hops away from the compromised node which is known as *sinkhole attack.* *False routing attack* means that injecting fake routing control packets into the network. Compromised node may refuse to forward or forward selective packets called as *Selective forwarding attack.* In the *wormhole attack,* two or more malicious colluding nodes create   higher level virtual tunnel in the network, which is employed to transport packets between the tunnel end points.

Network intrusion is an unauthorized access to a system by either an external perpetrator, or by an insider with lesser privileges.

In this paper we are concentrating on an identity attack called replication attack where one or more nodes illegitimately claim an identity of legitimate node and replicated in whole WSN network as shown Fig 2. Reason for choosing this attack is that it can form the basis of a variety attacks such as Sybil attack, routing attacks and link layer attacks etc. also called as denial of service attacks.

The detection of node replication attacks in a wireless sensor network is therefore a fundamental problem. A few centralized and distributed solutions have recently been proposed. However, these solutions are not satisfactory. First, they are energy and memory demanding: A serious drawback for any protocol that is to be used in resource constrained environment such as a sensor network. Further, they are vulnerable to specific adversary models introduced in this paper.

The rest of this paper is organized as follows; section 2 presents the significance of replication attack nature; section 3 studies analysis of detection and countermeasure of replication attacks and presents discussion and summary. In section 4 presents our proposed model and in section 5 concludes the paper.

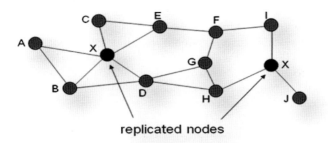

replicated nodes

Fig. 2. Replication Attack

2 Significance of Replication Attack and Background

2.1 Goals

For a given sensor network, we assume that sensor node not tamper proof and deployed in unattended location. The adversary can capture the node collect all the secret keys, data, and code stored on it. All the credentials are exposed to the attacker. The attacker can easily replicate it in a large number of clones and deploy them on the network. This node replication attack can be the basis for launching a variety of attacks such as DoS attacks and Sybil attacks [7]. If there are many replicated nodes, they can multiply the damage to the network. Therefore, we should quickly detect replicated nodes. The scheme should also revoke the replicated nodes, so that nonfaulty nodes in the network cease to communicate with any nodes injected in this fashion. We evaluate each protocol's security by examining the probability of detecting an attack given that the adversary inserts L replicas of a subverted node. The protocol must provide robust detection even if the adversary captures additional nodes. We also evaluate the efficiency of each protocol. The Communication (for both sending and receiving) among nodes requires at least an order of magnitude power than any other operation. So our first priority to minimize the communication cost for both whole network and individual nodes (hotspots quickly exhausts power), which one of the limitation of WSN. Another limitation is memory. Thus any protocol requiring a large amount of memory will be impractical.

2.2 Sensor Network Environments

A sensor network typically consists of hundreds, or even thousands, of small, low-cost nodes distributed over a wide area. The nodes are expected to function in an unsupervised fashion even if new nodes are added, or old nodes disappear (e.g., due to power loss or accidental damage). While some networks include a central location for data collection, many operate in an entirely distributed manner, allowing the operators to retrieve aggregated data from any of the nodes in the network. Furthermore, data collection may only occur at irregular intervals.

For example, many military applications strive to avoid any centralized and fixed points of failure. Instead, data is collected by mobile units (e.g., unmanned aerial units, foot soldiers, etc.) that access the sensor network at unpredictable locations and utilize the first sensor node they encounter as a conduit for the information accumulated by the network. Since these networks often operate in an unsupervised fashion for long periods of time, we would like to detect a node replication attack soon after it occurs. If we wait until the next data collection cycle, the adversary has time to use its presence in the network to corrupt data, decommission legitimate nodes, or otherwise subvert the network's intended purpose.

We also assume that the adversary cannot readily create new IDs for nodes. Newsome et al. describe several techniques to prevent the adversary from deploying nodes with arbitrary IDs. For example, we can tie each node's ID to the unique knowledge it possesses. If the network uses a key predistribution scheme, then a node's ID could correspond to the set of secret keys it shares with its neighbors (e.g., a node's ID is given by the hash of its secret keys). In this system, an adversary gains little advantage by claiming to possess an ID without actually holding the appropriate keys. Assuming the sensor network implements this safeguard, an adversary cannot create a new ID without guessing the appropriate keys (for most systems, this is infeasible), so instead the adversary must capture and clone a legitimate node.

3 Solutions to Replication Attacks and Countermeasurements

Solutions to replication attack should follow three key design goals for replica detection schemes. First, replica nodes should be detected with minimal communication, computational, and storage overheads. Second, the detection schemes should be robust and highly resilient against an attacker's attempt to break them. More specifically, the schemes should detect replicas unless the attacker compromises a substantial number of nodes. Finally, there should be no false positives, meaning that only compromised and replica nodes would be detected and revoked. This is important to prevent the attacker from turning a replica detection scheme into a tool for denial of service attacks.

Replication attack detection protocols classified as in the Fig. 3 are two categories: Centralized and Distributed approaches. These approaches have their own merits and demerits. The main idea of these schemes are to have nodes report location claims that identify their positions and attempt to detect conflicting reports that signal one node in multiple locations. This requires every node to sign and send a location claim, and verify and store the signed location claim of every other node.

3.1 Centralized Detection Approaches

3.1.1 Simple Approach
In a simple Centralized approach, the Base Station (BS) acts as centralized entity, each node sends a list of its neighbor nodes and their claimed locations to a base station. If the base station finds that there are two far distant locations for one node ID, then the node clone must have occurred. The BS simply broadcasts through the whole network to expel the cloned nodes. Then, the BS will revoke the replicated nodes. This solution has several drawbacks, for instance: Single point of failure (BS) or any compromise to BS, and high communication cost due to the relevant number of exchanged messages. Furthermore, the nodes closest to the base station will receive

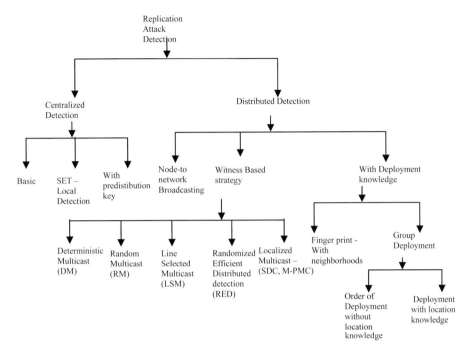

Fig. 3. Replication Attack Detection Taxonomy

the brunt of the routing load and will become attractive targets for the adversary. The protocol also delays revocation, since the base station must wait for all of the reports to come in, analyze them for conflicts and then flood revocations throughout the network. A distributed or local protocol could potentially revoke replicated nodes in a more timely fashion.

3.1.2 Local Detection (SET)

Next proposed solutions rely on local detection [4]; using localized voting mechanism, a set of neighbors can agree on the replication of a given node that has been replicated within the neighborhood. However, this kind of method fails to detect replicated nodes that are not within the same neighborhood. SET manages to reduce the communication cost of the preceding approach by computing set operations of exclusive subsets in the network. First, SET launches an exclusive subset maximal independent set (ESMIS) algorithm which forms exclusive unit subsets among one-hop neighbors in an only one disjointed subset which are controlled by a randomly decided leader.

Then those subsets, as in the basic scheme, are transmitted by leaders to the base station such that it can construct all nodes locations and detect clones. Since the subset division procedure eliminates redundancy in the node location reports, SET lowers the communication cost. However, in order to prevent malicious nodes in the ESMIS algorithm, an authenticated subset covering protocol has to be performed, which increases the communication overload and complicates the detection procedure. SET also employs a tree structure to compute non-overlapped set operations and integrates interleaved authentication to prevent unauthorized falsification of subset information during forwarding. Randomization is used to further make the exclusive subset and tree formation unpredictable to an adversary.

3.1.3 With the Context of Random Key Predistribution

Brooks et al. [9] propose a clone detection protocol in the context of random key predistribution. The basic idea is that keys that are present on the cloned nodes are detected by looking at how often they are used to authenticate nodes in the network. First each node makes a counting Bloom filter of the keys it uses to communicate with neighboring nodes and appends a nonce. Then Bloom filter and nonce are transferred to base station, which will count the number of times each key is used in the network. Key usage exceeds a threshold can be thought of as suspicious. In fact, it is detecting cloned keys rather than cloned nodes. In the protocol, every node reports its keys to a base station and then the base station uses a statistical approach to find cloned keys. A big problem in this kind of approaches is the high false negative and positive rates. Furthermore, honesty of the malicious nodes while reporting their keys is uncertain.

3.2 Distributed Detection Approaches

Distributed detection approaches can be classified broadly in to three categories: *Node-to network Broadcasting, Witness Based strategy, and With Deployment knowledge.*

3.2.1 Node-to Network Broadcasting

This detection approach utilizes a simple broadcast protocol. Basically, each node in the network uses an authenticated broadcast message to flood the network with its location information. Each node stores the location information for its neighbors and if it receives a conflicting claim, revokes the offending node. This protocol achieves 100% detection of all duplicate location claims if the broadcasts reach every node. This assumption becomes false when the adversary jams key areas or otherwise interferes with communication paths through the network. Nodes could employ redundant messages or authenticated acknowledgment techniques to try to thwart such an attack. In terms of efficiency, this protocol requires each node to store location information about its d neighbors. One node's location broadcast requires $O(n)$ messages, assuming the nodes employ a duplicate suppression algorithm in which each node only broadcasts a given message once. Thus, the total communication cost for the protocol is $O(n^2)$. Given the simplicity of the scheme and the level of security achieved, this cost may be justifiable for small networks. However, for large networks, the $O(n^2)$-factor is too costly, so we investigate schemes with a lower cost.

3.2.2 Witness Based Strategy

Most of the existing distributed detection protocols [1], [4], [5] adopt the *witness finding* strategy, in which each node finds a set of sensor nodes somewhere as the *witnesses* for checking whether there are the same IDs used at different locations, to detect the replicas.

In *Deterministic Multicast (DM) [1]*, to improve on the communication cost of the previous protocol, we describe a detection protocol that only shares a node's location claim with a limited subset of deterministically chosen "witness" nodes. When a node broadcasts its location claim, its neighbors forward that claim to a subset of the nodes called 'witnesses'. The witnesses are chosen as a function of the node's ID. If the Adversary replicates a node, the witnesses will receive two different location claims for the same node ID. The conflicting location claims become evidence to trigger the revocation of the replicated node.

In the *Random Multicast* (RM) [1], when a node broadcasts its location, each of its neighbors sends (with probability p) a digitally signed copy of the location claim to a set of randomly selected nodes. Assuming there is a replicated node, if every neighbor randomly selects $O(\sqrt{n})$ destinations, then exploiting the birthday paradox, there is a non negligible probability at least one node will receive a pair of non coherent location claims. The node that detects the existence of another node in two different locations within the same time-frame will be called witness. The RM protocol implies high communication costs: Each neighbor has to send $O(\sqrt{n})$ messages.

In the *Line Selected Multicast* (LSM)[1]protocol, uses the routing topology of the network to detect replication, each node which forwards claims also saves the claim. That is, the forwarding nodes are also witness nodes of a node which has the node ID in a claim. Therefore, LSM gives a higher detection rate than that of RM. However, both protocols have relatively lower detection rates compared with RED.

In the *Randomized Efficient Distributed detection* (RED) protocol [5], a trusted entity broadcasts a one-time seed to the whole network. The location of the witness node of a node is determined from the node ID and the seed. Because the seed changes every time, an attacker cannot specify the location of a witness node in advance. The authors of RED said one can also use distributed protocol without a trusted entity such as a local leader election mechanism to create a one-time seed. However, the authors did not mention how to create it; moreover, the local leader election mechanism creates a local leader from a small number of sensor nodes. Even worse, the method does not consider the existence of compromised nodes. Therefore, we cannot use it to create a global leader of a sensor network composed of a large number of nodes with some of them compromised.

In *Localized Multicast – (SDC, M-PMC)[4]* scheme, each node sends a location claim message to a predetermined cell which is grouped in a geographically separated region. Upon arriving at a cell, this message is broadcasted and stored probabilistically at the witness nodes within the cell. Therefore, the detection rate and the communication overhead are tightly related to the number of nodes and the fraction of witness nodes, which store the location claim message in a cell. However, this scheme is not robust when all nodes within a predetermined cell are compromised.

In the Single Deterministic Cells (SDC) and Parallel Multiple Probabilistic Cells (PMPC) approaches [4], a set of witness nodes located in the vicinity are chosen for each node by using a public known Hash function. Based on the assumption that there is a very efficient way to broadcast a pseudorandom number to all of the sensor nodes periodically, RED [5] also adopts the witness finding strategy to detect the node replication attacks but with less communication cost. The sensor network is considered to be a geographic grid. In the SDC protocol, witness nodes candidates of one node are all nodes of a grid. The grid is statically determined by the node ID, but which nodes in the grid actually become witness nodes are determined randomly. In P-MPC, to increase resiliency to many compromised nodes, the candidate witness nodes for one node are all nodes of several grids.

3.2.3 With Deployment Knowledge

Bekara and Laurent-Maknavicious proposed a new protocol for securing WSN against nodes replication attacks by limiting the *order of deployment* [9] and no knowledge of nodes deployment locations. Their scheme requires sensors to be deployed progressively in successive generations. Each node belongs to a unique generation. In their scheme, only newly deployed nodes are able to establish pair-wise keys with their neighbors, and all nodes in the network know the number of highest deployed generation. Therefore, the clone nodes will fail to establish pair-wise keys with their neighbors since the clone nodes belong to an old deployed generation.

Xing et al. [10] proposed an approach that achieves real-time detection of clone attacks in WSN. In their approach, each sensor computes a fingerprint by incorporating the neighborhood information through a superimposed s-disjunct code. Each node stores the fingerprint of all neighbors. Whenever a node sends a message, the fingerprint should be included in the message and thus neighbors can verify the fingerprint. The messages sent by clone nodes deployed in other locations will be detected and dropped since the fingerprint does not belong to the same "community".

Group deployment knowledge scheme [6] is based on the assumption that nodes are deployed in groups, which is realistic for many deployment scenarios. By taking advantage of group deployment knowledge, the proposed schemes perform replica detection in a distributed, efficient, and secure manner. The sensors can be preloaded with relevant knowledge about their own group's membership and all group locations. Then, the sensors in the same group should be deployed at the same time in the location given to that group. Three schemes have been discussed: Basic, Location claim and multi-group approaches. A basic way to stop replica attack , each node only accept the messages from the member's of their own group(trusted nodes) not from other groups (untrusted nodes). It stops inter communication between groups. Advantage of this basic scheme is low communication and computational or memory overhead. But the problem is even honest nodes suffers for communication due to deployments points far away from their group. The network becomes poorly connected and not suitable for high resilient applications. To solve this problem, scheme 2 also forwards messages from untrusted nodes as long as they provide provable evidence that they are not replicas, but based on only predetermined locations for replica detection. Scheme 2 Achieves high replication detection capability with less communication, computational and storage overheads than scheme 1. But there is risk of DoS by flooding fake claims.

To protect against this kind of aggressive adversary, every sensor node sends its neighbor's location claims to multiple groups rather than a single group. This greatly improves our scheme's robustness, while this scheme has higher communication overhead. It can provide a trade-off between the overhead and resilience to attack. This scheme provides very strong resilience to node compromise. Since Attacker needs to compromise multiple groups of nodes to prevent replicas being undetected. Disadvantage of this scheme is more overheads than scheme 2.

3.3 Summary of Replication Attack

Table 1. Summary of Detection Mechanisms performance overheads

Schemes	Communication cost	Memory
SET	$O(n)$	$O(d)$
Node –to – Network (Broadcast)	$O(n^2)$	$O(d)$
Deterministic Multicast	$O(g \ln g \sqrt{n} \ / d \ )$	$O(g)$
Randomized Multicast	$O(n^2)$	$O(\sqrt{n})$
Line-Selected Multicast (LSM)	$O(n\sqrt{n})$	$O(\sqrt{n})$
RED	$O(r \ \sqrt{n})$	$O(r)$
SDC	$O(r_f \ \sqrt{n}) + O(s)$	g
P-MPC	$O(r_f \ \sqrt{n}) + O(s)$	g
With Deployment Order Knowledge (no location knowledge)	$< O(n\sqrt{n})$	$< O(\sqrt{n})$
With Neighborhood knowledge - Fingerprint	$O(num_m \ \sqrt{n}) \cdot \log 2M$	$O(d) + \min(M , \omega \cdot \log 2 \ M)$
With group Deployment Knowledge(basic, location claim, multi-group approach)	$O(m)$	$O(m)$
	$O(m+d)$	$O(d+2m)$
	$3O(m+d)$	$O(d+2m(1+D_{max}))$

Where ,

n – No. of nodes in the network
d – Degree of neighboring nodes
g - no. of witness nodes
r- Communication radius
r_f – No of neighboring nodes forwards location claims
s - The number of sensors in a cell

m –group size
num_m - total number of regular data messages generated during network lifetime
M - the number of rows in the superimposed s-disjunct code
ω - the column weight in the superimposed s-disjunct code.
D_{max} - maximum no. of times that a group servers as the detector group

4 Conclusion

Table 1 shows the communication cost and storage cost for each technique. In this paper we discussed classification of detection mechanisms for replication attack. Distributed detection approach is more advantages than centralized approaches since single point failure. In witness based strategy of distributed approaches, randomness introduced in choosing witnesses at various levels like whole network and limited to geographical grids to avoid prediction of future witnesses. If chosen witness node itself compromised node or cloned node then detection of replication attack is uncertain. There may be tradeoff between memory, communication cost overhead and detection rate. All the approaches dealt with static WSN. With the deployment knowledge (like order, neighborhoods, and group members with locations) all the nodes in the network should know highest deployed generation which impractical and cannot move join other groups since neighbors or fingerprints vary. Some WSN application requires mobile nodes. The entire approaches become complex when considering for mobile nodes which dealt with location claims and Deployment knowledge are not suitable for mobile WSN, since location changes time to time in mobile wireless sensor network.

References

1. Parno, B., Perrig, A., Gligor, V.: Distributed Detection of Node Replication Attacks in Sensor Networks. In: Proceedings of the IEEE Symposium on Security and Privacy, pp. 49–63 (2005)
2. Choi, H., Zhu, S., La Porta, T.F.: SET: Detecting node clones in sensor networks. In: Third International Conference on Security and Privacy in Communications Networks and the Workshops (SecureComm 2007), pp. 341–350 (2007)
3. Brooks, R., Govindaraju, P.Y., Pirretti, M., Vijaykrishnan, N., Kandemir, M.T.: On the Detection of Clones in Sensor Networks Using Random Key Predistribution. IEEE Transactions on Systems, Man, and Cybernetics, Part C: Applications and Reviews 37(6), 1246–1258 (2007)
4. Zhu, B., Addada, V.G.K., Setia, S., Jajodia, S., Roy, S.: Efficient Distributed Detection of Node Replication Attacks in Sensor Networks. In: Choi, L., Paek, Y., Cho, S. (eds.) ACSAC 2007. LNCS, vol. 4697, pp. 257–267. Springer, Heidelberg (2007)
5. Conti, M., Di Pietro, R., Mancini, L.V., Mei, A.: A randomized, efficient, and distributed protocol for the detection of node replication attacks in wireless sensor networks. In: ACM MobiHoc, pp. 80–89 (2007)
6. Ho, J.-W., Liu, D., Wright, M., Das, S.K.: Distributed detection of replica node attacks with group deployment knowledge in wireless sensor networks. Ad Hoc Networks 7, 1476–1488 (2009)
7. Baig, Z.A.: Distributed Denial of Service Attack Detection in Wireless Sensor Networks, thesis (2008)
8. Sei, Y., Honiden, S.: Distributed Detection of Node Replication Attacks resilient to Many Compromised Nodes in Wireless Sensor Networks. In: ICST 2008 (2008)
9. Bekara, C., Laurent-Maknavicius, M.: A new protocol for securing wireless sensor networks against nodes replication attacks. In: Proceedings of the 3rd IEEE International Conference on Wireless and Mobile Computing, Networking and Communications, WiMob (2007)
10. Xing, K., Liu, F., Cheng, X., Du, D.H.C.: Real-time detection of clone attacks in wireless sensor networks. In: Proceedings of the 28th International Conference on Distributed Computing Systems, ICDCS (2008)

New Distributed Initialization Protocols for IEEE 802.11 Based Single Hop Ad Hoc Networks

Rasmeet S. Bali and C. Rama Krishna

Department of Computer Science and Engineering, NITTTR,
Chandigarh 160 019, India
rasmeetsbali@gmail.com, rkc_97@yahoo.com

Abstract. Leader election and initialization are important fundamental tasks to set up an ad hoc network, which involves assigning each station, a distinct ID (e.g. IP address). IEEE 802.11 is extensively used in simulation studies or developing testbeds for ad hoc networks. Existing solutions to leader election and initialization diverge considerably from IEEE 802.11 standard and thus require major modifications in the IEEE 802.11 standard. In this paper, contention based leader election and initialization protocols for IEEE 802.11 based single hop ad hoc networks have been proposed and their performance is evaluated using extensive simulations. A method for estimating the remaining number of stations to be initialized (when the number of stations is unknown in a network) using the number of packet collisions within a fixed time period is also presented. The simulation results indicate that the proposed protocols have comparable performance with existing schemes and can be incorporated into the IEEE 802.11 standard with minor modifications.

Keywords: IEEE 802.11; Ad hoc network; Initialization; Leader Election.

1 Introduction

Ad hoc networks have a great potential in a variety of applications. It is a distributed system consisting of many stations (STAs) with no pre-determined topology or central control [1]. Such networks can be used in situations where either there is no other wireless communication infrastructure present or where such infrastructure cannot be used such as battlefields, search and rescue operations and disaster environments [2]. The characteristics that distinguish mobile ad hoc networks from existing distributed networks include concurrent and unpredictable topology changes due to arbitrary mobility pattern of STAs, dynamic wireless link formation and removal, network partitioning and disconnections, limited bandwidth and energy, and highly variable message delay. These characteristics signify mobile ad hoc network as a challenging domain for implementing distributed algorithms [3].

Typically, the mobile STAs in the ad hoc network are small, inexpensive, bulk produced, commodity devices running on batteries and we assume that it is impossible or impractical to distinguish individual machines by serial or manufacturing numbers [4]. Hence, leader election and initialization of ad hoc networks is of fundamental importance, which is discussed in [1], [4-7]. The initialization protocol assigns a

N. Meghanathan et al. (Eds.): CCSIT 2011, Part II, CCIS 132, pp. 179–190, 2011.

unique ID to each station so that each station can execute ID based protocols. The leader serves as a coordinator for smooth running of group communication protocols and the other processes in ad hoc network.

The initialization problem was first studied in [4]. These randomised protocols are not practical as they are based on impractical assumption that the sending station can detect the status of its own transmission which is not valid in case of ad hoc networks. In [5], an efficient hybrid method is proposed for the initialization. However, carrier sensing has not been utilised and suitable acknowledgement schemes have not been proposed. In [1], distributed randomized initialization algorithms are developed. These algorithms also use an acknowledgement scheme to notify a transmitting station if its transmission is successful or not. In [6-7], contention based leader election and initialization protocols are proposed for IEEE 802.11 based single hop mobile ad hoc networks (MANETs). Although these protocols are efficient but also require modifications in IEEE 802.11 standard. These protocols use election rounds for leader election and initialization. The IEEE 802.11 standard does not employ rounds so implementing these protocols would involve making considerable modifications in the standard.

This paper presents two leader election and initialization protocols for IEEE 802.11 based single hop ad hoc networks when the number of STAs is known as well as when the number of STAs is unknown. In the proposed protocols, all the STAs attempt to transmit a packet in a given time slot using modified IEEE 802.11 DCF. If more than one packet is transmitted in a time slot, the packets collide and are rendered useless. If a single packet is transmitted during a time slot, the transmission is declared successful. The first station that successfully transmits a packet obtains an ID 1.This station will also be designated as a leader. The second successful transmitter will get an ID of 2. This process continues until all the STAs do not obtain their IDs.

Rest of the paper is organized as follows. Section 2 presents some background material related to our work. In Section 3, we describe Hsu's protocol. Section 4 presents the proposed protocol and the results of our simulation are given in Section 5. We finally draw our conclusions in Section 6.

2   Background

2.1   IEEE 802.11 MAC Protocol

The IEEE 802.11 WLAN medium access (MAC)/PHY specification [8] is one of the standards for WLANs that defines detailed functions for both MAC and physical layers. In the DCF mode, STAs contend for the channel in distributed manner using carrier sense multiple access with collision avoidance (CSMA/CA) mechanism [6]. This scheme has been widely used in test-beds and simulations of MANETs, as it does not require a central controller for coordination [9, 10].

2.2   Initialization in Adhoc Networks

Ad hoc networks are formed by the collection of mobile wireless STAs. The communication links form and disappear as STAs come into and go out of each other's communication range. It is often assumed that the address of a station in both wired networks and in wireless networks is either permanently stored in its local memory or is received at start up time. This assumption is not always appropriate in some cases. The requirement for initialization protocol is to assign each of the n STAs a distinct and short ID from 1 to n.

In a n-station single hop ad hoc network, any station can hear the transmission from all the other STAs. The time is divided into equal length slots and the transmission channel is assumed to be error free [1]. A station can identify the channel status as either *BUSY* or *IDLE*. However, a transmitting station cannot sense the channel while it is transmitting a packet.

3   Existing Initialization Protocols

The problem of initializing ad hoc networks has been researched a lot but there have been very few attempts to perform initialization using IEEE 802.11. As per our knowledge Hsu's protocols are the only initialization protocols based on IEEE 802.11. However, Hsu's protocols require major modifications to be made in the IEEE 802.11 standard. The proposed initialization protocols are more practical than Hsu's protocols as they can be incorporated in the IEEE 802.11 standard with minor modifications.

3.1 Hsu's Protocol

Hsu et al. proposed two leader election and initialization protocols for IEEE 802.11 based single hop ad hoc networks for two cases: when the number of STAs in the network is known and when the number of STAs in the network is unknown.

In Hsu's protocol, every station follows IEEE 802.11 DCF procedure to contend for the medium. However, unlike IEEE 802.11, where the backoff window grows exponentially, Hsu's protocol uses the concept of election rounds. The value of *CW* is set according to number of STAs in the ad hoc network i.e. if there are n STAs in the network; *CW* is set to $n-1$. Each station contends only once for the medium in an election round. When any STA's backoff time expires, that station will broadcast a message. Irrespective of whether the broadcast is successful or results in a collision, this station will not contend for the medium again in this round and wait for all the other STAs to broadcast their messages. The election round is said to be over if the nth backoff time slot has expired. If the leader election or initialization is not completed in the present round, the above procedure is repeated again in the subsequent rounds.

Although Hsu's protocols are efficient but there implementation demands major changes to IEEE 802.11 as they diverge from IEEE 802.11 which is discussed in section 1.

4   Proposed Leader Election and Initialization Protocol

This work focuses on the initialization of IEEE 802.11 based single hop ad hoc networks. Two leader election and initialization protocols are proposed here. One set of protocols are for ad hoc networks where the number of STAs are known and the other set is for ad hoc networks where the number of STAs are not known. The proposed protocols use a modified IEEE 802.11 DCF.

4.1 Modified IEEE 802.11 DCF

According to modified IEEE 802.11 DCF, a station having a packet to transmit must initially listen to the channel before transmitting its packet. If no transmission takes place for distributed inter frame space (DIFS) time interval, the transmission may proceed. If the medium is busy, the station will wait until the end of current transmission. It will then wait for an additional DIFS time and then generate a random delay called the contention window (CW) before transmitting its packet. If there are transmissions from other STAs during this time period, a station will freeze its backoff timer until the end of current transmission. Then the station resumes decrementing its timer value after channel is found idle for DIFS time. Whenever the backoff value of a station reaches 0, it broadcasts its initialization query packet (IQP) whose format is shown in figure 1.

Broadcast Address	Time stamp of IQP being transmitted	Timestamp of recent successfully transmitted packet

Fig. 1. Format of Initialization Query Packet (IQP) format

We illustrate working of our protocol using IEEE 802.11 by assuming that our network contains three STAs: A, B and C. Suppose STAs A, B and C chooses a backoff value of 2, 4 and 1 respectively. First station C becomes successful in broadcasting its IQP after waiting for one slot time, as this station is having a backoff value of 1 only. Then station A becomes successful in transmitting its IQP after waiting for one additional time slot after the transmission of C's IQP. When station A transmits its IQP, station C will understand that its earlier IQP was successful and becomes the leader with an ID of 1. Then immediately after time interval equal to SIFS, station C (leader) will transmit an initialization response packet (IRP) which having format shown in figure 2.

Broadcast Address	Leader _ID	Timestamp of recent successfully transmitted IRP

Fig. 2. Format of Initialization Response Packet (IRP) format

IRP is used by the leader to assign IDs to un-initialized STAs.

The station C's IRP will contain an ID of 2 which is the ID be to be assigned to station A, as this was the station which transmitted its IQP successfully immediately after station C. Subsequently station B gets an ID of 3 from the leader after it transmits its IQP successfully. Figure 3 illustrates the leader election and initialization process using the modified IEEE 802.11 DCF.

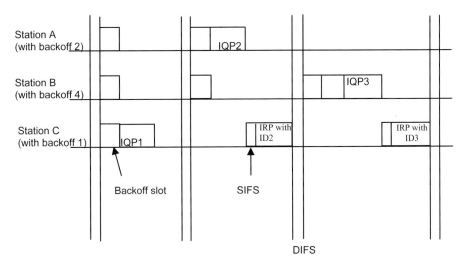

Fig. 3. Modified DCF used during leader election and initialization of STAs

4.2 Proposed Initialization Algorithm 1 (When the Number of Stations Is Known)

It is assumed that no network exists initially and a group of STAs (say n) are willing to form an ad hoc network. Initialization is done in two steps. First anyone out of n STAs is elected as a leader. Then the elected leader assists all other STAs to obtain their IDs.

4.2.1 Leader Election Algorithm

It is assumed that all STAs have equal opportunity to become a leader. All the STAs contend for the channel using modified IEEE 802.11 DCF. However the value of CW is uniformly chosen in the range $(0, W-1)$ where the value of W is initially fixed and is based on [9]. The size of W is computed using [10]

$$W \approx \sqrt[n]{2T} \tag{1}$$

where T is the total packet transmission time measured in time slot. The algorithm for proposed leader election protocol is shown as follows:

Leader Election algorithm for known n

n: number of STAs
CW : initial value of backoff window calculated using Bianchi's formula
S_L : indicates the first station that transmits a packet successfully *i.e.* leader
Leader = false
while (leader not elected)
each station contends for the channel using modified IEEE 802.11 DCF
while a station's backoff value does not reach zero.
      if the channel is continuously free for DIFS
        decrement backoff value by 1
      else
        freeze the backoff value to its current value
      endif
endwhile

if any station's backoff value reaches zero
    if (leader==false)
        station S_i transmits an IQP containing its own timestamp
    else
        station S_i transmits an IQP containing S_L's own timestamp
    endif
endif
if a station's S_j receives an IQP from some other station S_i
    if (S_i received time stamp==S_j previously transmitted timestamp)
        station S_j waits for a period of time equal to SIFS
        S_j announces itself as leader by transmitting an IRP.
    else
        leader=true
        $S_L=S$
    endif
else   //unsuccessful transmission
  station S_i randomly generates a new backoff value
endif
endwhile

4.2.2 Initialization of Remaining Nodes

Once the leader has been elected, the initialization process can go on smoothly. This is because leader is responsible for transmitting IRPs immediately after a SIFS for each successful transmission of IQP by any other station in the network. The initialization process is implemented as follows: After waiting for a time interval equal to SIFS, the leader will give the next available ID (i.e. 2) to the station that successfully transmitted its time stamp in the leader election process by broadcasting an IRP. Now all the STAs except the leader and already initialized STAs contend for the channel using modified IEEE 802.11 DCF. This process will continue till all the STAs obtain their ID's. The algorithm for proposed initialization protocol is shown as follows:

Initialization algorithm for known n

n : number of STAs
m : initial value of *CW* calculated using eq (1) in [10]
$ID=2$
leader S_L transmits an IRP containing the timestamp of second station that successfully transmitted IQP.
while (ID<=n)
    each station except the leader randomly generates a backoff value and contends
    for the channel using modified IEEE 802.11 DCF
while a station's backoff value does not reach zero
    if channel continuously free for DIFS
        decrement backoff value by 1.
    else
        freeze backoff value to its current value
    endif
endwhile

if any station's backoff value reaches zero
    station S_i transmits an IQP
endif
if leader S_L receives an IQP from some station
    leader waits for a period of time equal to SIFS
    ID=ID+1
    leader transmits an IRP that contains the timestamp of S_i IQP and its ID.
else
    station H_i again generates a new backoff value
endif
endwhile

4.3 Proposed Initialization Algorithm 2 (When the Number of Stations Is Unknown)

It is assumed that no network exists and a group of STAs are ready to be initialized and that the the number of STAs is not known in advance.

4.3.1 Leader Election Algorithm

Leader election is first performed using the same procedure that was used when the number of STAs was known. However to elect a leader the value of CW is fixed at 255 using (1). After the leader is elected, we then estimate the number of STAs in the network based on average number of collisions that occurs in the leader election process. The simulation result shows that the number of collisions within any given time period is related to the number of STAs. Table 1 lists the average number of collisions for different number of STAs for a period of time equal to 1ms.

Table 1. Number of collisions in the network for various number of stations using simulations

Number of Stations	Average number of collisions for 25 simulations
10	10
20	20
30	31
40	41
50	50
60	60
70	71
80	82
80	93
100	101

The proposed initialization protocol use table 1 to predict the uninitialized STAs. Let us assume that for a period of time equal to 1ms, the number of collisions in the network is 43. When we compare this value (i.e. 43) to the values in the table, it is observed that the nearest value is found to be 40. This becomes the current value of remaining number of STAs in the network. Thus for a period of time equal to 1 ms the relationship between number of collisions in network and number of competing STAs can be formulated as

$$\text{Number of Collisions} \approx n \qquad\qquad (2)$$

4.3.2 Initialization of Rest of Nodes

The STA(s) that need to be initialized will try to send their IQP by competing with other uninitialized STAs. When a station transmits its IQP successfully, the leader will transmit an IRP after waiting for one SIFS. This procedure will be repeated until all the STAs obtain an ID. However to accurately compute the value of remaining STAs to be initialized, the protocol repeatedly estimates this value every 1ms using (2). When the number of collisions becomes zero, initialization process stops indicating that all the STAs have been initialized.

5 Comparison of Results with Hsu's Work

We compare the proposed protocol with Hsu's protocol using simulations. The simulator is developed using C++ programming language. The simulated ad hoc network consists of following parameters: Transmission rate of 2 Mbps, DIFS is 50 µs, SIFS is 10 µs, ST is 20 µs and slot is of 200 µs respectively. The size of IQP and IRP is 352 bits. The number of STAs in the network varies from 20 to 100. Our initialization protocol follows Modified IEEE 802.11 DCF, while Hsu's protocols are simulated using election rounds to initialize a given network.

We have simulated four leader election protocols. These protocols are proposed leader election protocol when the number of STAs is known (PRLE(K)), and when the number of STAs is unknown (PRLE(U)), Hsu's leader election protocol when the number of STAs is known (HSLE(K)) and when the number of STAs is unknown (HSLE (U)). Figure 4 and Figure 5 presents the relationship between average time and the corresponding number of STAs for the above Hsu's and proposed leader election protocols.

The proposed leader election protocols are found to be better than Hsu's protocols. A leader election requires two successful broadcasts for electing a leader. In Hsu's protocols election rounds are used and a station can broadcast only once in an election round. If a broadcast by a station is not successful, that station does not contend for the channel again in that election round. This reduces the probability of successful transmission by a station during leader election. In contrast, in the proposed leader election protocols, if a station is unsuccessful in broadcasting IQP, it can again contend for the channel immediately after its unsuccessful transmission. Thus the proposed protocols have higher probability of success as compared to Hsu's protocols.

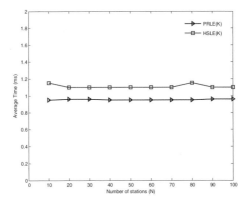

Fig. 4. Average Time required for Hsu's and Proposed Leader Election Protocol when number of stations is known

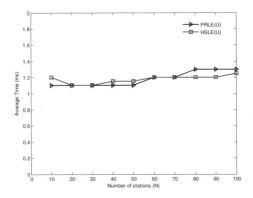

Fig. 5. Average Time required for Hsu's and Proposed Leader Election Protocol when number of stations is unknown

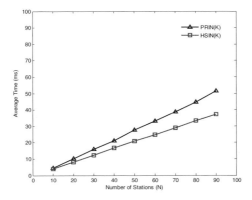

Fig. 6. Average Time required for Hsu's and Proposed Initialization Protocol when number of stations is known

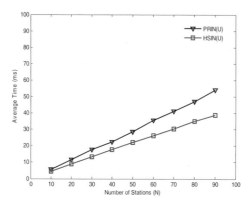

Fig. 7. Average Time required for Hsu's and Proposed Initialization Protocol when number of stations is unknown

We have simulated four initialization protocols. These protocols are proposed initialization protocols when the number of STAs is known (PRIN (K)) and when the number of STAs is unknown (PRIN (U)), Hsu's initialization protocol when the number of STAs is known (HSIN (K)) and when the number of STAs is unknown (HSIN (U)). Figure 6 and Figure 7 present the relationship between average time and the corresponding number of STAs for both Hsu's and proposed initialization protocols.

Figure 8 illustrates the performance of Hsu's initialization protocols and the proposed initialization protocols for both the cases.

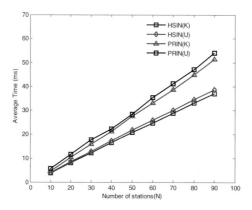

Fig. 8. Average Time required for Hsu's and Proposed Initialization Protocol for both cases

The graphs indicate that Hsu's initialization protocols perform marginally better than proposed initialization protocols. In Hsu's protocols a station contends for the channel only once in an election round even if its broadcast is unsuccessful. The value of *CW* in an election round is also optimized by equating it to remaining number of STAs to be initialized. These assumptions although unrealistic increase the probability of a station successfully transmitting a packet in a time slot. In the proposed protocols a station repeatedly contends for the channel until it is successful in obtaining its ID. Thus the number of contending STAs only decreases after a station obtains an ID. Although the performance of proposed initialization protocols are slightly worse than Hsu's protocol but the proposed protocols are more practical for IEEE 802.11based single hop ad hoc network. The proposed protocols require minor modification and can be easily implemented in IEEE 802.11 standard.

6 Conclusion and Future Work

The main contribution of this work is to propose two leader election and initialization protocols for IEEE 802.11 based single hop ad hoc networks. We have proposed a new approach for the initialization problem using IEEE 802.11 and also evaluated their performance through extensive simulations. Simulation results indicate that proposed initialization protocols are more practical than Hsu's protocols as they can be incorporated in the IEEE 802.11 standard with minor modifications. It is observed that the proposed leader election protocols takes less time to elect a leader in a network than Hsu's protocols. However, the average time taken by proposed initialization protocols to initialize the remaining nodes in the network is marginally higher than Hsu's protocols, but our schemes can be easily incorporated into 802.11 standard.

References

1. Cai, Z., Lu, M., Wang, X.: Distributed Initialization Algorithms for Single-Hop Ad Hoc Networks with Minisloted Carrier Sensing. IEEE Transaction an Parallel and Distributed System 14(5), 516–527 (2003)
2. Hass, Z.J., Gerla, M., Johnson, D.B., Perkins, C.E., Pursley, M.B., Steenstrup, M., Toh, C.K., Hayes, J.F.: Guest Editorial Wireless Ad Hoc Networks. IEEE Journal Selected Areas in Communication 17(8), 1329–1332 (1999)
3. Masum, S.M., Ali, A.A., Bhuiyan, M.T.I.: Asynchronous Leader Election in Mobile Ad Hoc Networks. In: Proceedings of 20th International Conference on Advanced Information Networking and Applications, vol. 02, p. 5 (2006)
4. Nakano, K., Olariu, S.: Randomized Initialization Protocols for Ad Hoc Networks. IEEE Trans. Parallel and Distributed Systems 11(7), 749–759 (2000)
5. Micic, A., Stojmenovic, I.: A Hybrid Randomized Initialization Protocol for TDMA in Single-Hop Wireless Networks. In: Proc. Int'l Parallel and Distributed Processing Symp., pp. 147–154 (2002)
6. Chih-Shun, H., Jang-Ping, S.: Initialization Protocols for IEEE 802.11-based Ad Hoc Networks. In: Proceedings of Ninth International Conference on Parallel and Distributed Systems (2002)
7. Chih-Shun, H., Jang-Ping, S.: Design and performance evaluation of the leader election and initialization protocols. Technical Report of HSCC Lab (2002)
8. LAN MAN Standards Committee of the IEEE Computer Society. IEEE Std 802.11-1999, Wireless LAN Medium Access Control (MAC) and Physical Layer (PHY) specifications. IEEE (1999)

190   R.S. Bali and C. Rama Krishna

9. Rama Krishna, C., Chakrabarti, S., Datta, D.: A Modified Backoff Algorithm for IEEE 802.11 DCF based MAC protocol in Mobile Ad Hoc Network. In: TENCON 2004, vol. B(2), pp. 664–667 (2004)
10. Bianchi, G., Fratta, L., Oliveti, M.: Performance evaluation and enhancement of the CSMA/CA MAC protocol for 802.11 wireless LAN's. In: Proceedings of IEEE PIMRC, Taipei, Taiwan, pp. 392–396 (1996)
11. Nakano, K., Olariu, S.: Uniform leader election protocols for radio networks. In: IEEE International Conference on Parallel Processing, pp. 240–248 (2001)
12. Myoupu, J.F.: Dynamic Initialization Protocols for Mobile Ad Hoc Networks. In: IEEE International Conference On Networks (ICON 2003), Sydney, Australia, pp. 149–154 (2003)

Deployment of GSM and RFID Technologies for Public Vehicle Position Tracking System

Apurv Vasal, Deepak Mishra, and Puneet Tandon

PDPM Indian Institute of Information Technology, Design and Manufacturing,
Jabalpur, Madhya Pradesh, India
{apuvas,deemish,ptandon}@iiitdmj.ac.in

Abstract. Low occupancy rate is one of the major problems faced by public transport systems. One reason for low occupancy rate is that a passenger normally does not know the public vehicle scheduling information and its arrival timing information at predefined stops. Trends in wireless technology like Global System for Mobile communication (GSM) and Radio Frequency Identification (RFID) have resulted in easier and faster communication. We propose a new cost effective public vehicle tracking system by integrating both of the above mentioned technologies. By providing reliable public vehicle arrival information to the passengers at predefined stops, it is expected to improve the public vehicle occupancy. Thus, this system provides the facility to know about the time for arrival at different stops and the location of public vehicles having predefined routes.

Keywords: Vehicle Tracking, GSM, RFID.

1 Introduction

Efforts are being made by public transport corporations to improve public vehicle occupancy by requesting the public to use public transport over other modes of transport. It is possible to motivate a passenger to opt for public vehicles having predefined routes by providing the vehicle location and time of arrival at respective stoppage along with scheduling information, thus, in the process reducing the wastage of public time.

Therefore, there is a need of a system that can provide the passengers the information about the location of a public bus in a city. The future intelligent transportation system (ITS) will rely predominantly on several vehicle communication systems [1] including peer-to-peer and peer-to-base station communications. It can be noted that if the passenger knows with high confidence that the bus is going to come, he/she will definitely wait rather than opting for other modes of transport. So, we believe that more passengers opt for bus transport, if we provide the arrival timing information of bus (to the bus-stops) and route information in a real-time manner. This paper introduces a system that:

(i) offers a very cost-effective solution as compared to existing technologies for tracking vehicles for public transports, and

(ii) offers an open architecture that can be easily expanded to other applications.

N. Meghanathan et al. (Eds.): CCSIT 2011, Part II, CCIS 132, pp. 191–201, 2011.

In this paper, however, we have dealt with vehicles traveling in two-dimensional object space. In two-dimensional object space, vehicles may follow two types of routes like static or predetermined and dynamic. Trains usually follow static routes moving through intermediate stations up to destination station. These routes are fixed in the form of rail tracks. Public Bus transport generally uses national highways or fixed intra-city routes that are predetermined. On the other side private vehicles are free to choose their path; they can deviate from a predetermined path and hence their routes are dynamic.

The development and validation of the system in the present work is carried out for the city of Jabalpur (India) and the public transport system here, is referred as Metro buses. In this paper, we present an extensible public vehicle position tracking system (PVPTS) that exploits data transmission capabilities of the Global System for Mobile Communication (GSM). Our design is extensible to big cities where many buses will need to be simultaneously tracked and monitored. The bus, train arrival information can be provided to the passengers using this system. A background of the relevant technologies is given in Section 2. Section 3 contains the methodology; while existing technologies are discussed in Section 4. Section 5 describes the implementation of PVPTS. Section 6 discusses on low cost solution. Section 7 contains system testing and results. Section 8 compares and contrasts this system with other PVPTS systems and concludes with a discussion on future directions for this research project.

2 Background

One of the possible reasons for people preferring private vehicles over public vehicles is that a passenger normally does not have exact information about the public vehicle arrival timing at their stops. Proper public vehicle arrival information can, therefore, guide them to choose a cheaper and convenient mode of transportation over private vehicles and thus in process can increase the occupancy rate of public vehicle. This is beneficial to both the passengers and public transport corporations. Tracking of a vehicle can be expressed as continuously monitoring of a vehicle. Tracking of buses can be useful for the automation of existing transportation systems [2]. By the use of tracking the required efficient information about bus-arrival timing can be provided to the passengers.

The different wireless technologies available today have resulted in the reliable and faster communication. GSM is an open, digital cellular technology used for transmitting mobile voice and data services [3]. GSM has become the world's fastest growing mobile communication standard. It allows for seamless and secure connectivity between networks on a global scale. Digital encoding is used for voice communication, and time division multiple access (TDMA) transmission methods provide a very efficient data rate content ratio.

Radio-Frequency Identification (RFID) is a wireless sensor technology which is based on the detection of electromagnetic signals [4]. There is emission of radio waves from the transmitter in ranges which can reach up to 100 feet or more, depending on its power output and the radio frequency used. RFID can be employed for different applications. RFID is used successfully in a variety of industries, such as aeronautics and medicine. In the construction industry, RFID is used successfully for the tracking of pipe spools, structural steel members and as an on-site support system [5, 6].

3 Existing Technologies

There are lots of tracking applications available for tracking of various public vehicles. One simple cost-effective technique for vehicle tracking is the 'vehicle card' technique [7], which uses STD phone booths and a specially designed vehicle-card. Vehicle owner has to carry a card to the nearest tracking point, basically a designated STD booth on vehicle routes, at major stops and petrol bunks. The card is coded with details of the vehicle; these details and a simple numbered message are transferred to a local telephone number. The receiver uploads all incoming messages by email to a central server, where it is processed and placed on a website. In this way a vehicle can be tracked. But this scheme is not so useful for a large scale implementation of a fully automated real-time system. Another scheme for tracking has been proposed using odometer and inertial sensors [8]. But this technique is proposed specifically for train transport. It does not provide a generalized solution for all the public transports. Similarly one more technique employing distance-meter (odometer) and cellular infrastructure is used for tracking vehicles in public domain [9].

One popular technique on which most of the moving objects tracking schemes rely is GPS (Global Positioning System). GPS provides specially coded satellite signals that can be processed in a GPS receiver, enabling the receiver to compute position, velocity and time. Four GPS satellite signals are used to compute positions in three dimensions and the time offset in the receiver clock.

GPS is the most accurate and popular positioning system. It provides a position accuracy of around 15 meters. A clear line of sight to at least four GPS satellites is necessary for high accuracy. GPS was developed by the U.S. Department of Defense. The system consists of a constellation of 24 satellites orbiting around 12,000 miles above the Earth's surface, shown in Fig. 1. GPS was dedicated solely for military use and has recently been declassified for civilian use. To acquire GPS information, a wireless receiver capable of the civilian frequency of 1575.42 MHz is required. The GPS receiver measures distances to four or more satellites simultaneously. GPS receivers take this information and use triangulation to calculate the user's exact location [10, 11]. Factors that can degrade the GPS signal and thus affect accuracy include following:

(i)   Ionosphere and troposphere delays – On passing through atmosphere the satellite signal slows down. Significantly larger delays occur for signals emitted from low elevation satellites.

(ii)   Signal multi path - Satellite navigation receivers operate by line of sight with global positioning satellites. When GPS signal is reflected off big objects such as tall buildings or any large mountain before it reaches the receiver there is increase in the travel time of the signal, thereby causing errors.

Evaluation of currently available technologies has found that each technology affords unique advantages for vehicle tracking applications while also facing distinctive challenges to overcome so as to satisfy the practical requirements in terms of   reliable performance and cost effectiveness.

Fig. 1. GPS consists of 24 satellites of which at least 5 can be seen from any point on the globe [10]

4 Proposed System

The tracking of any public vehicle involves the frequent and fast communication of vehicle's location information. For the purpose of vehicle tracking the information is required to be sent simultaneously at different locations so that passengers can get timely information for different public transport vehicles. In all the techniques stated previously, either hardware or software overhead is often needed at cell-site. If routes on most of the places under tracking are known in advance, a mapping system can easily trace a specific location on any route. The proposed tracking system eliminates the need of additional hardware or software at cell-site. This proposed system relies on GSM system and RFID for its operation. In our research, we have employed the text-based data via the short message service enabled by the standard cellular phone communication network of GSM which provides a low-cost, effective solution in an urban area with an extensive coverage of mobile phone networks and has overcome the drawbacks of conventional walkie-talkie systems. The main limitations of data transmission on walkie-talkie or voice radios are:

(i)   the possibility of losing packets of data since data from multiple vehicles occupy the same radio channel

(ii)   the limited range the voice radio can cover.

In the proposed tracking system, two technologies RFID and GSM communication are integrated. In proposed system 8 channel Radio transmitter and receiver with short range of few meters are used to get information about the presence of vehicle near the bus stop, which is further communicated through GSM module. In this way the system provides the information about the timing of bus arrival/departure in an online manner. Table 1 compares the proposed scheme with other schemes such as Vehicle-card technique and Pure GPS/GPS–GPRS mixed.

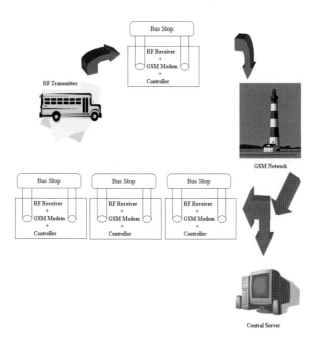

Fig. 2. Architecture of the proposed system

Table 1. Comparison of vehicle tracking schemes

Parameter	Technique		
	Vehicle-card technique	Pure GPS/ GPS–GPRS mixed	Proposed GSM and RFID technique
Accuracy of location detection	Lower	Accurate	Accurate
Cost of installation	Very low	Highest	Much lesser than GPS based techniques
Suitability for real-time applications	May be adopted	Suitable	Suitable
Environmental susceptibility	Not applicable	Moderate	Most Suited
Scope of human intervention	High	Not at all	Not at all

The PVPTS prototype consists of two underlying technologies: GSM and RFID. Fig. 2, shows the architecture of the proposed system. The proposed system can be divided into three parts: Vehicle addressing and identification system, Information routing system and Display and data analysis system.

Every vehicle is provided an identifier so that it can be recognized and tracked easily. Every vehicle has an 8 bit RF transmitter which is preset different for different vehicles. The RF transmitter always remains ON so that it can be identified by RF receivers located at every bus stop, whenever it is in proximity of few feets. The buses of same route may have same or different transmitting code. Thus, buses of 256 different bus routes can be tracked simultaneously if buses of same route are given the same code. In another case where particular public vehicle has to be tracked among the other vehicles of the same route, 2 or more bits out of 8 bits can be reserved for differentiating them.

There are different modules at different bus stops to transfer the identified vehicle information from one location to another and display units to display the expected time of arrival of public vehicle. The PVPTS uses Short Message Service (SMS) sent over GSM networks for communication between different public vehicle stops. The signals from the GSM modem are sent to nearest Base Transceiver Station (BTS) that in turn are transferred to Mobile Switching Center (MSC) through Base Station Controller (BSC). The GSM modem equipment has a Subscriber Identity Module (SIM) security and authentication. The SIM is a detachable smart card containing the user's subscription information and phone book. This allows the user to retain his or her information after switching handsets. The BTS and BSC together constitute the Base Station Subsystem (BSS) and perform all the functions related to the radio channel for data signaling and frequency hopping control and power level control. All of the elements in the system combine to produce many GSM services such as voice calls and SMS. Basic architecture of GSM network is shown in Fig. 3. GSM uses a variation of Time Division Multiple Access (TDMA) scheme developed for mobile radio systems and is the most widely used among the digital wireless telephony technologies. LED displays are low cost, low power device capable of displaying text. Every Bus stop is provided with an LED display device, displaying the route number and time of arrival of a bus at bus stop. The location information is updated by GSM Modem placed at bus stop which in turn is connected to a microcontroller unit which sends data to LED displays. The LED display periodically displays information of different buses along with time of arrival. Data stored at the central server can be analyzed through an application. It receives, processes, analyzes and stores the incoming SMS messages. The tracking of buses at central server is easily carried out by having a GSM modem connected to server which updates the vehicle's location upon receiving the messages from different GSM modems placed at bus stops.

5 Implementation

Several components were used to assemble our tracking system. For identification, every vehicle has been provided with 8 bit RF transmitter. The transmitter on buses of different routes transmits different 8 bit word. The buses of same route may have same transmitting code. For information routing system we have used the microcontroller unit which integrates RFID receiver and GSM unit placed at every bus stop. Every bus stop has 8 bit RF receiver along with GSM modem to send and receive data. Whenever some bus comes within the range of about 100 feet of the bus stop, the receiver receives the 8 bit word sent by the transmitter in a bus. For information routing system we have used the microcontroller unit which integrates RFID receiver and GSM unit placed at every bus.

The microcontroller placed at different bus stops are programmed such that they contain GSM number of the modems placed at further bus stops. Communication between microcontroller and modem is done using USART (Universal Synchronous Asynchronous Receiver and Transmitter) module. The interfacing of RF receiver with GSM modem is done using microcontroller unit. The eight bits signal received at receiver are then sent to microcontroller which decodes it and depending on the bits received sends the command to the GSM modem which is also placed at every bus stop. The standard 'AT' commands which microcontroller unit sends to the GSM modem are as follows:

(i)   AT (Testing for AT commands)
(ii)   ATE0 (Command used to determine whether or not the modem echoes characters received by an external application)
(iii)   AT+CMGF=1 (command to set text mode)
(iv)   AT+CMGR=1 (command to read a message)
(v)   AT+CMGS=<Number><CR><Text><ctrl-Z> (Command to send a message in text mode)
(vi)   AT+CNMI=2, 1,0,0,0 (command to select the procedure for message reception according to the values)

'AT' commands given to GSM modem sends the SMS containing the 8 bit code of the bus and bus stop id to the next 3 or more bus stops. Thus, the information about location of bus is passed to next bus stops. We have designed, implemented and tested the system in our lab. The system prototype set up and some of its components are shown in Figure 3. To test the functionality of the system we placed the prototype in a mobile vehicle. While the vehicle was moving vehicle's current location was reported as SMS messages to the further stops as well as to the central server. The SMS received by the modems located at different bus-stops is sent to the microcontroller unit. The microcontroller unit acknowledges the received message through GSM modem and decodes the information being sent in the form of message. The information about bus arrival is finally sent to the LED display board connected to microcontroller unit. LED display boards have clear visibility and thus are placed at

Fig. 3. RF Receiver and GSM/GPRS modem used for lab testing

different bus stops. The LED board displays the message about bus with estimated time of arrival of bus at that bus stop. The LED boards display the time of arrival of different buses as different messages are sent to it through the microcontroller unit. Some useful information is also displayed on the display boards as message can be also be routed from the central server having database of phone numbers allotted to different SIM placed inside the modems. Thus, useful information can be circulated to the public in different situations.

6   Discussion on Low Cost Solution

Efforts have been taken to reduce the total cost of the system including devices and services. Starting from small transport systems to large transport systems, the devices and services cost can be made affordable.

The RF transceivers are now available at low prices in the range of INR 1000 – 1500. The GSM modems are available in the range of INR 3000 - 4000 from different vendors. The controller made using 8051 microcontroller costs around INR 500. The LED displays are available in the range of INR 5000-6000. Thus, the overall cost of the system is cheaper than GPS based public vehicle tracking systems ranging from INR 15,000 - 20,000 available in the market.

By using SMS for communication, the service cost has been reduced drastically. Most operators are providing SMS services at very cheap rates (SMS service costs about 1paisa/SMS). Thus services cost of the system is much lesser than other tracking systems.

7   System Testing and Results

System design is verified by testing after integration of all components of the system. The hardware used in the implementation of the system includes 8 channel Radio frequency transmitter and receiver, GSM modem, interfacing controller unit and display unit which make the overall system cost effective. Debugging serial port of microcontroller was connected to a PC's COM port to see the results on HyperTerminal during its operation as shown in the Figure 4.

Fig. 4. Hyperterminal image showing simulation results

The LED/LCD board displays the location of bus with estimated time of arrival of bus at that bus stop, as shown in Fig. 5. The tracking of buses at some server located at a particular place is easily carried out by having a modem connected to server. The location information of different buses is updated, as GSM modems located at each bus stop forwards an SMS containing vehicle location information to this central server. Thus the server keeps tracks of different buses. Figure 6 shows the application

Fig. 5. LED display unit

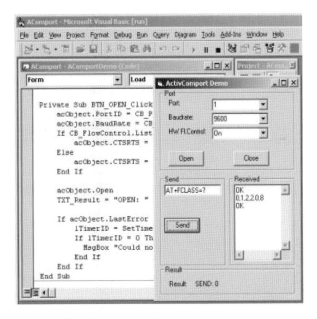

Fig. 6. Application interface at the server

interface build using Microsoft Visual Basic at the server. It receives the different messages, thus keeps track of public vehicle's current location. The application interface receives and analyzes the data received by it and thus tracking of all the buses can be done at the central server providing more information which can be used for analysis of traffic and other information.

8   Conclusion

The key feature of this system is its relatively simple mode of communication. The tracking of different local buses or local train can be done easily. The project involves the use of GSM and RFID technology which is used to send and receive information for locating any vehicle. Our proposed system is vulnerable to network congestions as the SMS sent to other locations may get delayed. Thus, the efficiency of the proposed system depends on the congestion free working of GSM networks. The use of GSM technology as compared to other existing techniques used for tracking makes it more cost efficient and innovative. Our system design has an open architecture that can be easily expanded to other applications. These capabilities and attributes make the device ideally suited for public vehicle tracking applications because:

(i)   low cost opens up a new segment of the market.
(ii)   use of GSM permits vehicle reports in high density urban areas and along interstate corridors.
(iii)   operation does not require human intervention.

This system can be further extended for central tracking system to keep track of all the public vehicles. Thus, the program size of microcontrollers can be reduced as the vehicle's location information routing can be done via central server application. Data stored at the control center can be analyzed through a software application. Trends in wireless technology have resulted in most of the passengers owning mobile phones. We believe that by providing bus-route and arrival information to passengers' cell phones in a timely manner, it is possible to improve the bus occupancy. Thus, this system can be integrated with internet which maintains the vehicle's current location database so that people owing mobiles can enter vehicle route number and bus-stop ID and get the time arrival of respective bus on their mobile. Using a GSM/GPRS modem connected to server, various parameters can be tracked for further analysis. Due to easily available means like LCD displays, mobile phones, laptops, Personal Digital Assistants (PDAs), passengers would not have to rely on old manual enquiry terminals. Thus, the system can be beneficial for both passengers and the bus operators.

References

1. Figueiredo, L., Jesus, I., Machado, J.A.T., Ferreira, J.R., Martins de Carvalho, J.L.: Towards the Development of Intelligent Transportation Systems. In: IEEE Intelligent Transportation Systems Proceedings, Oakland, CA (2001)
2. Lee, K., Ryu, H.Y.: Automatic circuity and accessibility extraction by road graph network and its application with high resolution satellite imagery. In: Proceedings of the IEEE International Geosciences and Remote Sensing Symposium, IGARSS 2004, September 20-24, vol. 5, pp. 3144–3146 (2004)
3. GSM ~ GSM World,
   http://www.gsmworld.com/technology/gsm/index.htm
4. Landt, J.: The history of RFID. IEEE Potentials 24(4), 8–11 (2005)
5. Domdouzis, K., Kumar, B., Anumba, C.: Radio-Frequency Identification (RFID) applications: A brief introduction. Advanced Engineering Informatics 21(4), 350–355 (2007)

6. Kim, M., Chong, N.Y.: RFID-based mobile robot guidance to a stationary target. Mechatronics 17(4-5), 217–229 (2007)
7. Rus, C., Bilcu, R.C., Egiazarian, K., Rusu, C.: Scanned maps processing using wavelet domain hidden Markov models. In: First International Symposium on Control, Communications and Signal Processing, pp. 451–454. IEEE, Los Alamitos (2004)
8. Ernest, P., Mazl, R., Preucil, L.: Train locator using inertial sensors and odometer. In: IEEE Intelligent Vehicles Symposium 2004, June 14-17, pp. 860–865 (2004)
9. Kane, L., Verma, B., Jain, S.: Vehicle tracking in public transport domain and associated spatio-temporal query processing. Elsevier: Computer Communications 31(12), 2862–2869 (2008)
10. Garmin | What is GPS?, http://www.garmin.com/aboutGPS/index.html
11. Global Positioning System Overview, http://www.colorado.edu/geography/gcraft/notes/gps/gps.html

Type of Service, Power and Bandwidth Aware Routing Protocol for MANET

Divyanshu, Ruchita Goyal, and Manoj Mishra

Department of Electronics and Computer Engineering,
Indian Institute of Technology Roorkee, India
divyanshu26@gmail.com, goyal.ruchita@gmail.com,
manojfec@iitr.ernet.in

Abstract. Quality of Service (QoS) provisioning is important in MANET in order to deploy multimedia applications over it. Limited battery power, other resource constraints and mobility of nodes make QoS provisioning difficult in MANET. Only a cross-layer approach for routing can handle the resource constraints of MANET. In [1] Patil et al., proposed a cross-layer routing protocol named Cost Based Power Aware Cross Layer – AODV (CPACL-AODV) which overcomes the resource constraint related to limited battery power of nodes. Though many energy efficient and cross-layer routing protocols have been proposed for MANET, none of them handles QoS. In this paper a novel MANET routing protocol named Type of Service, Power and Bandwidth Aware AODV (TSPBA-AODV) is proposed that overcomes resource constraints and simultaneously provides QoS guarantees using a cross-layer approach. In this paper the performance of TSPBA-AODV, the newly proposed protocol, is compared with the performance of CPACL-AODV [1] for different network traffic scenarios. As shown by the results of simulations performed, the proposed protocol performs better than the CPACL-AODV for MANET in which nodes move with small speeds (speeds up to 40 Km/hr approx.).

Keywords: QoS provisioning; MANET; ad-hoc network; cross-layer; routing protocol.

1 Introduction

MANET has been of great interest in research community over the last decade because of its highly dynamic nature and usefulness. It forms an infrastructure-less network on the fly without need of any central administration. Earlier the use of MANET was limited to emergency situations such as natural disasters, military conflicts, emergency medical facilities, etc. However with proliferation of multimedia applications over internet, it has become necessary to provide proper support for deployment of multimedia applications on MANET too.

Deployment of multimedia applications on MANET requires proper QoS support at network layer of MANET. So, the routing protocol should be designed in such a way that it can provision QoS. Earlier the cost function used for making routing

N. Meghanathan et al. (Eds.): CCSIT 2011, Part II, CCIS 132, pp. 202–214, 2011.
© Springer-Verlag Berlin Heidelberg 2011

decisions in MANET was hop count. However since, MANET works under various constraints, such as limited battery power and frequently changing topology, the routing protocol can be effective only if it is designed by taking care of cross-layer parameters such as battery lifetime, application type, bandwidth, etc. Several cross-layer aware routing cost functions have been proposed by researchers for routing in MANET. Such cost functions can be divided into three types:

(1) Type 1 - *Monotonically increasing function*: A cost function which increases monotonously with time for a node. For example fraction of initial battery power utilized, etc.

(2) Type 2 – *Fluctuating function*: A cost function which doesn't show monotonic variation, but rather shows fluctuations by either increasing or decreasing. For example bandwidth utilization, fraction of message queue occupied, etc.

(3) Type 3 – *Hybrid function*: A cost function which is combination of Type 1 and Type 2 cost functions.

Whatever be the cost function, if we take nodes as identical and overall cost function of path as sum of cost function of nodes along a path (taking average is not much justified as a very long path can have better average) then in the beginning hop count will implicitly come into picture as cost function for individual nodes will be almost in same range. However in case of cost function of the Type 1, due to monotonous increase in cost function with time, at a later stage routing will no more be dependent on hop count, but this can't assure quality of service. For example - a path with better sum of battery utilization can be longer and congested compared to a path with sustainable battery power but having lesser congestion or length and so lesser delay. On the other hand if cost function is taken to be of the second type then we are actually ignoring the resource constraints of MANET such as limited power supply.

In this paper we propose a novel protocol named Type of Service, Power and Bandwidth Aware AODV (TSPBA-AODV) that uses a Type 3 cost function. The scenario we are assuming is that we have a large No. of mobile nodes in a small area, so that hop count is not a matter of concern but rather QoS provisioning in dynamic environment is the matter of concern. Earlier most of the protocols use either Type 1 or Type 2 cost function. Recently a protocol named CPACL-AODV [1] was proposed by Patil et al., which uses cost function of Type 1, based on battery utilization. We compared performance of our protocol (TSPBA-AODV) with CPACL-AODV (implemented with assumption that energy loss due to transmission or receipt is directly proportional to size of the packet dealt with).

Rest of the paper is organized as follows. Section 2 gives a brief overview of related works. Section 3 describes TSPBA-AODV. Section 4 discusses about the simulation environment used, performance metrics evaluated and the results obtained. Finally, section 5 concludes our paper.

2 Related Works

Extensive research has been done in finding a cost function that is most suitable for routing in MANET.

Table 1. Classification of Recent Cross-layer Routing Protocols on the Basis of Type of Cost Function Used

Type 1	Type 2	Type 3
SNR/RP aware routing protocol [3] in case RP is used; CPACL–AODV [1];	SNR/RP aware routing protocol [3] in case SNR is used; ALW protocol [6];	TSPBA-AODV (discussed in section 3); TEA – AODV [5]
Protocol proposed in [2];	TSLA protocol [7]	
SQ–AODV [4]		

Table 1 classifies recent cross-layer routing protocols on the basis of type of cost function (types as described in section 1) used.

Earlier a cost function that accounted for the utilization of battery of a node was proposed by Patil et al., [1]. However Patil et al., assumed that transmit power of a node is fixed which doesn't occur in real life situation. Power lost due to transmission depends upon the size of the message transmitted. Moreover they accounted only for battery power during routing, but it is possible that a route that has better battery life can have high delay due to high congestion or more length, whereas a route with sustainable battery power can provide better delay. Moreover the path selected by considering battery life only may not be capable of providing minimum bandwidth guarantee to multimedia applications. So this protocol is not suitable for multimedia applications. In another protocol, the authors Enneya et al., accounted for mobility only in their cost function for routing [2]. However, it is possible that a bit more mobile path than the least mobile path can give better bandwidth and delay guarantees. Moreover they didn't consider the major constraint of limitation of battery power of nodes. Alnajjar et al., proposed a protocol that uses either SNR or remaining power (RP) to determine route [3]. Accounting only for SNR can't provide bandwidth and delay guarantees required by multimedia applications. Moreover it accounts either for SNR or RP but not for both. Veerayya et al., proposed a protocol that accounts for battery power available at nodes for routing [4]. So, only Type 1 cost function is used, ignoring the QoS requirements of applications. Pushpalatha et al., proposed a protocol which uses trust based on forwarding frequency as a cost function [5]. However, trust alone can't guarantee QoS provisioning. Al-Khwildi et al., proposed a protocol that considers cost function on the basis of type of application [6]. However, the protocol is entirely new rather than being an extension to an existing protocol. Moreover as per Al-Khwildi et al., the protocol provides advantage over AODV only in terms of network load and route discovery time. Mbarushimana et al., proposed a protocol that takes into account the type of service and load in network while routing [7], both these parameters give the cost function corresponding to Type 2 and ignore the limitation of battery power of nodes.

3 Type of Service, Power and Bandwidth Aware AODV (TSPBA-AODV)

TSPBA-AODV is an extension to AODV. In this section the changes made over AODV to obtain TSPBA-AODV are discussed.

TSPBA-AODV divides applications into following two categories on the basis of their requirements:

(1) Type-1 – Loss tolerant applications that are not delay sensitive. For example – DNS service, etc.

(2) Type-2 – Loss tolerant applications that are delay sensitive. For example – instant messaging, etc.

Each node maintains two different routing tables Table-1 and Table-2 for Type-1 and Type-2 types of applications, respectively. For an application, the type of application is decided from the above two types and then corresponding routing table and corresponding control packets are used. However, algorithm used is same for both types of application.

3.1 Format of Packets and Route Table Entry

New fields are added to RREQ, RREP, RERR and route table entry. They are as follows:

1) For RREQ packet:
   a) Boolean field named isComputeCost, whose purpose is described in subsection 3.2
   b) Integer field named appType to identify the type of application (Type-1 or Type-2) to which RREQ packet belongs.
   c) Double field named cumulativeCost, which is updated from hop to hop. It denotes the cost of route from the origin to the hop forwarding the RREQ.
2) For RREP packet:
   a) Integer field named appType to identify the type of application (Type-1 or Type-2) to which RREP packet belongs.
   b) Double field named cumulativeCost, which is kept constant from hop to hop. It denotes the cost of route from origin to destination.
3) For RERR packet:
   a) Integer field named appType to identify the type of application (Type-1 or Type-2) to which RERR packet belongs.
4) For route table entry:
   a) Double field named cumulativeCost, which represents cost of the route.

Here wherever cost of a route is talked about it is the sum of costs of each node in the route including end points of it also.

3.2 Route Discovery and Maintenance

The protocol is reactive. Whenever a node has to send data to another node it searches the route table corresponding to the application for entry corresponding to the destination. If the entry is found it sends the packet to the corresponding next hop. If entry is not found then it broadcasts RREQ packet with isComputeCost field reset, cumulativeCost set to cost of the source node corresponding to the type of application and appType given the value corresponding to the application type. A node receiving the RREQ takes following actions:

1) If the node has battery power less than a threshold value it discards the packet. If the appType of the RREQ is Type-2 but the queue of the node is filled to more than half of its maximum capacity then the RREQ is discarded. If more than one RREQ with same RREQ id are received by the node then the newly received RREQ is discarded if its cumulativeCost is more than the cumulativeCost of the previously received one.

2) If the corresponding route table at the node has route to the origin of RREQ with lesser sequence No. than the origin sequence No. in RREQ or if the RREQ represents a lower cost route to origin as compared to the route to the origin already known to the node and has sequence number of its origin same as the sequence number stored in route table for the origin or if the node doesn't have any entry in its corresponding routing table for the origin of RREQ, then the node updates the route table entry for the origin of RREQ with next hop as the last hop of the RREQ and cumulativeCost as the sum of cumulativeCost of the RREQ and the cost of the node corresponding to the appType of the RREQ.

3) If the node is destination of the RREQ then RREP is generated with cumulativeCost as sum of cumulativeCost of the RREQ and the cost of the node corresponding to the appType of the RREQ, and appType as the appType of the RREQ, and is unicasted to the last hop of the RREQ. The RREP is further unicasted hop by hop back to the source of RREQ using route tables of intermediate nodes.

4) If the node is neither the destination nor it knows a path to destination (even if it knows the path, the sequence No. of destination known to the node is less than the sequence No. of destination present in the RREQ) then it broadcasts the RREQ after changing its cumulativeCost to sum of its cumulativeCost and the cost of the node corresponding to appType of the RREQ.

5) If the node is not the destination but the node knows path to destination (with the sequence No. of destination known to the node as more than or equal to the sequence No. of destination present in the RREQ) then the node sets the isComputeCost field of the RREQ and unicasts it to the next hop known to the node for the destination and the appType. RREQ with isComputeCost set is handled in the same way as RREQ with isComputeCost reset except for that if it is discarded as in step 1 then the entry for the destination in corresponding route table of the node is deleted and RERR packet is sent to the last hop of the RREQ, and that it is unicasted to its destination rather than being broadcasted. RREQ packet with isComputeCost set is basically used to compute the current cost of a known route and to know whether the route is capable of handling the traffic any more or a new route discovery process should be initiated.

3.3 Cost Calculation

Cost of a node has following three components:

1) BandwidthCost $(B_i(t))$ – It is the utilization of radio of node-i at time t.
2) DelayCost $(D_i(t))$ – It is fraction of queue of node-i occupied at time t.
3) PowerCost $(P_i(t))$ – It is equal to the fraction of initial power that has been consumed till the point of time at node-i.

Cost of a node is weighted mean of all three of these costs but the weightings depend upon the type of application in the way shown in Table 2. The values of the weightings were decided experimentally in order to optimize performance.

Table 2. Weightings Related to Components Depending Upon the Type of Application

Application type / Weighting for component	b	d	p
Type-1	0.33	0.33	0.33
Type-2	0.30	0.40	0.30

Overall cost of a node at time t, i.e., $C_i(t)$, is given by (1) as

$$C_i(t) = b* B_i(t) + d* D_i(t) + p* P_i(t). \tag{1}$$

$$C(\pi, t) = \sum_{i \in \pi} C_i(t) \tag{2}$$

$C(\pi, t)$ in (2) represents cost of a route and is likely to be least for the path having minimum hop count because each of the cost components is a proper fraction. The protocol assumes that the field has a lot of nodes and the basic requirement is to effectively provision QoS. This assumption is made in order to ensure that change in one cost component may not subvert the change in other cost components. Thus, there are multiple routes between a source and a destination, each with almost similar hop count (around the minimum hop count), but with different QoS parameters and the problem is to find the most efficient path which can provision QoS.

If there are 2 routes with costs $C_1(\pi, t)$ and $C_2(\pi, t)$ such that $C_j(\pi, t) = b*\sum B_{ij}(t) + d*\sum D_{ij}(t) + p*\sum P_{ij}(t)$ for j=1, 2. So now when we are comparing $C_1(\pi, t)$ and $C_2(\pi, t)$ then we are not comparing the overall cost but rather we are comparing $\sum B_{i1}(t)$ and $\sum B_{i2}(t)$, i.e., we are concentrating on $\Delta(\sum B_i(t))$ and similarly on Δ values of other cost components. So, for delay sensitive traffic if we give more weighting to $D_i(t)$ then we are actually giving more weighting to $\Delta (\sum D_i(t))$, so we are more interested in difference created by $\Delta(\sum D_i(t))$ than by any other parameter. Thus, we are giving priority to our interest. To account for the case in which path corresponding to $C_1(\pi, t)$ has less battery power left than the path corresponding to $C_2(\pi, t)$, PowerCost component of $C_1(\pi, t)$ will become high and $C_1(\pi, t)$ will not be comparable to $C_2(\pi, t)$, until its other components give better cost. Similarly, the case in which path corresponding to $C_1(\pi, t)$ has less available bandwidth than the path corresponding to $C_2(\pi, t)$ is taken care of by BandwidthCost.

4 Simulations and Results

All simulations were performed using JiST-SWANS-1.0.6. Simulations were run 10 times for each case and then the average of the results was taken.

4.1 Simulation Environment

Sixty nodes were taken in a 2D field of 1000m *1000m. Each of the simulations was run for 600 sec. The initial battery capacity of each node was taken 100 units. This initial energy was progressively reduced by data transmission/reception. When it reached zero units for a node, then the node could no more take part in the communication and was regarded as dead. The mobility model used was random waypoint with pause time as 10 sec and granularity as 10 sec. Rest of the parameters were varied to assess performances of protocols as mentioned in subsection 4.3.

4.2 Performance Metrics

Four performance metrics were used to compare the protocols. They are as follows:

1) Average end to end delay - It includes all delays possible namely, transmission delay, processing delay, queuing delay and propagation delay.

2) Throughput - This metric gives the number of bits that are successfully delivered to corresponding destinations in unit time in the network.

3) Packet Delivery Ratio - It is the ratio of the number of data packets successfully delivered to the destinations to the number of data packets generated by the sources.

4) Control Overhead - The number of routing packets transmitted per data packet delivered at the destination. Each hop wise transmission of a routing packet is counted as one transmission.

4.3 Results

This section discusses and compares the performances of the reference protocol (CPACL-AODV) and the proposed protocol (TSPBA-AODV).

Effect of Variation in Node Speed
Rate of sending data packets was kept at 1 packet/sec/node. Range of speeds of nodes was varied and performances of the two protocols were compared for different types of traffic. This section deals with these comparisons.

UDP Traffic
The traffic used for simulation in this subsection was taken to be loss tolerant and delay insensitive with packets arriving in the network at constant bit rate.

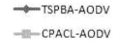

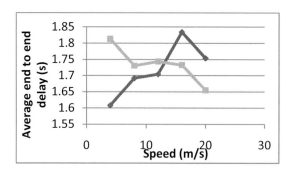

Fig. 1. Delay vs. Speed for UDP Traffic

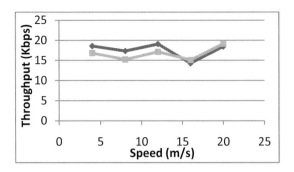

Fig. 2. Throughput vs. Speed for UDP Traffic

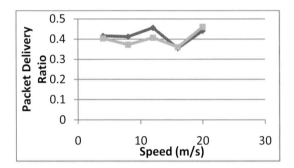

Fig. 3. Packet Delivery Ratio vs. Speed for UDP Traffic

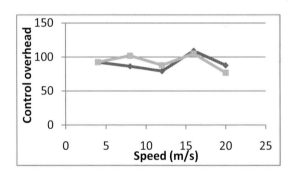

Fig. 4. Control Overhead vs. Speed for UDP Traffic

As it can be seen in Fig. 1 to Fig. 4, maximum percentage improvement of TSPBA-AODV over CPACL-AODV are 11.32% for delay, 14.02% for throughput, 12.04% for packet delivery ratio, 15.25% for control overhead.

UDP Delay Sensitive Traffic
The traffic used for simulation in this subsection was taken to be loss tolerant and delay sensitive with packets arriving in the network at constant bit rate.

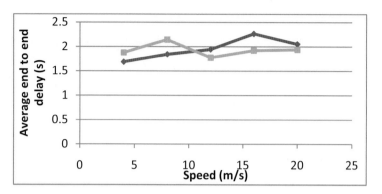

Fig. 5. Delay vs. Speed for UDP Delay Sensitive Traffic

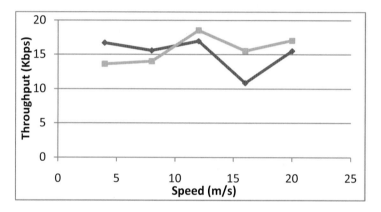

Fig. 6. Throughput vs. Speed for UDP Delay Sensitive Traffic

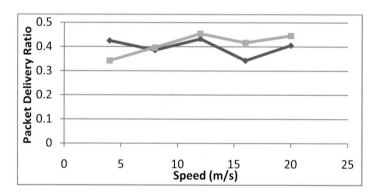

Fig. 7. Packet Delivery Ratio vs. Speed for UDP Delay Sensitive Traffic

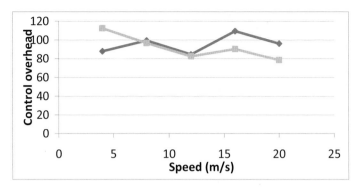

Fig. 8. Control Overhead vs. Speed for UDP Delay Sensitive Traffic

As it can be seen in Fig. 5 to Fig. 8, maximum percentage improvement of TSPBA-AODV over CPACL-AODV are 14.08% for delay, 22.55% for throughput, 24.07% for packet delivery ratio, 21.92% for control overhead.

UDP Burst Traffic
The traffic used for simulation in this subsection was taken to be loss tolerant and delay insensitive with packets arriving in the network as burst.

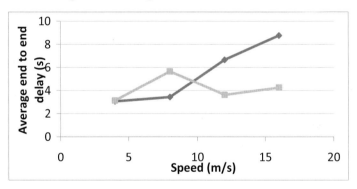

Fig. 9. Delay vs. Speed for UDP Burst Traffic

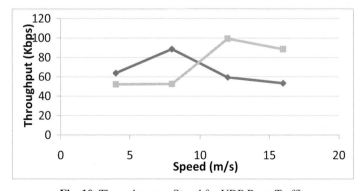

Fig. 10. Throughput vs. Speed for UDP Burst Traffic

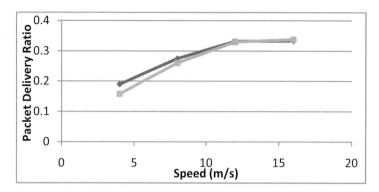

Fig. 11. Packet Delivery Ratio vs. Speed for UDP Burst Traffic

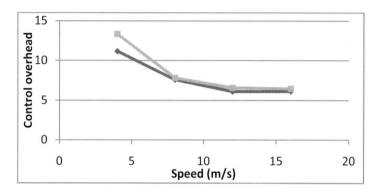

Fig. 12. Throughput vs. Speed for UDP Burst Traffic

As it can be seen in Fig. 9 to Fig. 12, maximum percentage improvement of TSPBA-AODV over CPACL-AODV are 2.11% for delay, 69.05% for throughput, 20.13% for packet delivery ratio, 16.36% for control overhead.

As it can be seen in Fig. 1 to Fig. 12, at low speeds performance of TSPBA-AODV is better than that of CPACL-AODV for UDP traffic, UDP delay sensitive traffic and UDP burst traffic because the cost function used for selecting the optimal path in case of TSPBA-AODV comprises of delay, bandwidth and power cost components, due to which the route chosen has following features:

(1) It has optimal value of power cost. So the route lasts long. Since the route lasts long, number of control packets is less in the network and so the control overhead is less. Long life of selected routes also decreases average end to end delay because a route once established lasts long and less time is wasted in maintenance and rediscovery of route between same source and destination nodes.

(2) It has optimal value of delay cost. So the path chosen has optimal congestion along it, due to which there is decrease in average end to end delay. Moreover there will be less packet loss due to congestion and so packet delivery ratio and throughput will increase.

(3) It has optimal value of bandwidth cost. So path chosen has optimal potential to deliver data, due to which there is increase in throughput, packet delivery ratio and decrease in average end to end delay.

However, the performance of the TSPBA-AODV degrades when nodes are highly mobile (speed more than 40 Km/hr approx.). This happens because when nodes are highly mobile then route breakage occurs frequently and the nodes along the established routes send control packets for route maintenance frequently, resulting in less availability of bandwidth, message queue and power for nodes along established routes which thereby results in selection of otherwise non-optimal route.

5 Conclusion

In this paper we proposed TSPBA-AODV, a cross-layer MANET routing protocol capable of provisioning QoS in MANET. Extensive simulations were performed. The results show that the proposed routing protocol TSPBA-AODV performs better than CPACL-AODV [1] in case the speeds of nodes in the MANET are small (up to approx. 40 Km/hr). The performance is improved in terms of average end to end delay, throughput, packet delivery ratio and control overhead for all three types of traffic namely UDP traffic, UDP delay sensitive traffic, UDP burst traffic. However, the performance of the proposed protocol degrades in scenario in which nodes are highly mobile (speed more than 40 Km/hr). So, the proposed protocol is better than the reference protocol for applications where mobility of nodes is small (up to 40 Km/hr). Few situations where the proposed protocol can be used are as follows:

1) Vehicles running at speed less than 40 Km/hr and using MANET for communication

2) In PANs because PAN devices generally move with speed much less than 40 Km/hr

3) In meeting rooms, sports stadium, airports, airplane, etc because at these places devices generally move with speed much less than 40 Km/hr

4) In search and rescue, policing and fire fighting because the members of rescue team generally move at speed much less than 40 Km/hr

5) For military usage of MANET because there communication needs to be facilitated between soldiers, slowly moving bulky tanks, stationary tents and stationary head quarters. All these communicating parties have speed much below 40 Km/hr.

References

1. Patil, R., Damodaram, A.: Cost Based Power Aware Cross Layer Routing Protocol For Manet. IJCSNS International Journal of Computer Science and Network Security 8(12), 388–393 (2008)
2. Enneya, N., Koutbi, M.E., Berqia, A.: Enhancing AODV Performance based on Statistical Mobility Quantification. IEEE Xplore, 2455–2460 (2006)

3. Alnajjar, F., Chen, Y.: SNR/RP Aware Routing Algorithm: Cross-Layer Design for MANETS. International Journal of Wireless & Mobile Networks (IJWMN) 1(2), 127–136 (2009)
4. Veerayya, M., Sharma, V., Karandikar, A.: SQ-AODV: A Novel Energy-Aware Stability-based Routing Protocol for Enhanced QoS in Wireless Ad-hoc Networks, pp. 1–7. IEEE, Los Alamitos (2008)
5. Pushpalatha, M., Venkataraman, R., Ramarao, T.: Trust Based Energy Aware Reliable Reactive Protocol in Mobile Ad Hoc Networks. World Academy of Science, Engineering and Technology 56 (2009)
6. Al-Khwildi, A.N., Khan, S., Loo, K.K., Al-Raweshidy, H.S.: Adaptive Link-Weight Routing Protocol using Cross-Layer Communication for MANET. WSEAS Transactions on Communications 6(11), 833–839 (2007)
7. Mbarushimana, C., Shahrabi, A.: TSLA: A QoS-Aware On-Demand Routing Protocol for Mobile Ad Hoc Networks. In: Coudert, D., Simplot-Ryl, D., Stojmenovic, I. (eds.) ADHOC-NOW 2008. LNCS, vol. 5198, pp. 265–278. Springer, Heidelberg (2008)

Energy Efficiency in Wireless Network Using Modified Distributed Efficient Clustering Approach

Kaushik Chakraborty[1], Abhrajit Sengupta[2], and Himadri Nath Saha[2]

[1] Department of Computer Science and Engineering, Jadavpur University, Kolkata-700032
{Kaushik.chakraborty9,abhrajit.sengupta}@gmail.com
[2] Dept. of Computer Sc. & Engg., Institute of Engineering &
Management, Salt Lake, Sec-V, Kolkata – 700091,
West Bengal, India
him_shree_2004@yahoo.com

Abstract. A wireless network consisting of a large number of small sensors with low-power transceivers can be an effective tool for gathering data in a variety of environments. The data collected by each sensor is communicated through the network to a single processing center that uses all reported data to determine characteristics of the environment or detect an event. But due to limitation of battery power WSNs are highly energy constrained. So the protocols used in WSN for communication and message passing must be energy efficient to make better utilization of these low power sensors and to enhance the network life time. The DECA protocol which is an elegant solution to this problem try to minimize the overall energy dissipation by the nodes in the network by providing a robust clustering approach to form subgroups in a hierarchical structure. Though DECA offers certain amount of resilience towards node mobility it fails to take into account the remaining battery power of the nodes. As a result as the network grows older the cluster head becomes more and more feeble to transmit. In our modified version of DECA a score is calculated for each node taking into account various parameters like leftover battery power, node connectivity, probability of failure and mobility of the nodes with certain weights and based on the score calculated clusterheads are formed. It leads to enhancement of network lifetime in achieving its goal towards equalizing energy dissipation by each node. Extensive simulations have been carried out which shows that significant improvement over DECA.

Keywords: Wireless Sensor Network, DECA, MDECA, Data Gathering, Cluster, Node Mobility.

1 Introduction

Wireless Sensor Network consists of spatially distributed autonomous sensors that are deployed over a particular area for the purpose of monitoring certain physical or environmental condition or to detect an event. The nodes perform certain measurements and needs to transmit all the collected information to a base station over a wireless channel. The data are then processed in the base station to draw some

N. Meghanathan et al. (Eds.): CCSIT 2011, Part II, CCIS 132, pp. 215–222, 2011.

conclusions about the current activity in the area. To keep the cost and size of these sensors small, they are equipped with small batteries that can store at most 1 Joule [6]. This puts significant constraints on the power available for communications, thus limiting both the transmission range and the data rate. Thus a sensor can communicate directly with others which are within its transmission range. But to establish communication between distant ones a multi-hop communication network is needed.

One of the fundamental solution to this problem is forming of clusters. Since the cost of transmitting a bit is higher than a computation [4] it is advantageous to organize nodes into groups. In this clustered environmental the data gathered by the nodes are transmitted to the base station through a hierarchy of cluster heads. As the sensors now communicate over a small range in a cluster rather than directly communicating with the central information processing center the energy spent is much lower.

The distributed efficient clustering approach (DECA) provides robust clustering to form subgroups. Communications are generally restricted within a subgroup at a tier. In earlier strategies clustering decisions were based on static views of the network topology; none of the proposed schemes, even equipped with local maintenance schemes, is satisfactorily resistant to node mobility beyond trivial node movement. DECA clustering protocol is resilient against mild to moderate mobility where each node can potentially move.

In the hybrid energy-efficient distributed clustering approach (HEED), cluster head selection is primarily based on the residual energy of each node. The clustering process entails a number of rounds of iterations; each iteration exploiting some probabilistic methods for nodes to elect to become a cluster head. While HEED is one of the most recognized energy-efficient clustering protocols, DECA is an improvement. The protocol terminates without rounds of iterations as required by HEED, which makes DECA a less complex and more efficient protocol.

2 Related Work

Among clustering mechanisms in ad hoc and sensor networks, dominating-set-based clustering [8-10] surfaces as one of the most promising approaches. A subset of vertices in an undirected graph is a dominating set if every vertex not in the subset is adjacent to at least one vertex in the subset. Moreover, this dominating set should be connected for ease of the routing process.

Siva Kumar et al. [8–10] proposed a series of 2-level hierarchical routing algorithms for ad hoc wireless networks. The idea is to identify a sub network that forms a minimum connected dominating set (MCDS). In this approach, a connected dominating set is found by growing a tree T starting from a vertex with the maximum node degree. Then, a vertex v in T that has the maximum number of neighbors not in T is selected. Finally, a spanning tree is constructed and non-leaf nodes form a connected dominating set.

Ref. [11] proposed localized algorithms that can quickly build a backbone directly in ad hoc networks. This approach uses a localized algorithm called the marking process where hosts interact with others in restricted vicinity. This algorithm is simple, which greatly eases its implementation, with low communication and computation cost; but it tends to create small clusters.

Instead of constructing connected dominating sets, Lin and Gerla [12] used node ID numbers to build clusters of nodes that are reachable by two-hop paths. The distributed clustering algorithm is initiated by all nodes that have the lowest ID numbers among their neighbors. If all the lower ID neighbors sent their decisions and none declared itself as a cluster initiator, the node decides to create its own cluster and broadcasts its own ID as the cluster ID. Otherwise, it chooses a neighboring cluster with the lowest ID, and broadcasts such decision.

Similar to [12], Basagni [13] proposed to use nodes' weights instead of lowest ID or node degrees in clusterhead decisions. Weight is defined by mobility related parameters, such as speed. Basagni [14] further generalized the scheme by allowing each clusterhead to have at most k neighboring clusterheads and described an algorithm for finding a maximal weighted independent set in wireless networks.

One of the first protocols that use clustering for network longevity is the Low-Energy Adaptive Clustering Hierarchy (LEACH) protocol [15]. In LEACH, a node elects to become a clusterhead randomly according to a target number of clusterheads in the network and its own residual energy, and the energy load get evenly distributed among the sensors in the network. A limitation of this scheme is that it requires all current clusterheads to be able to transmit directly to the sink. Improvements to the basic LEACH algorithms include multi-layer LEACH-based clustering and the optimal determination of the number of clusterheads that minimizes the energy consumption throughout the network.

3 Modified Distributed Efficient Clustering Approach

Let the clustering duration Tc be the time interval taken by the clustering protocol to cluster the network. Let the network operation interval To be the time needed to execute the intended tasks. In many applications, $To >> Tc$. In general, nodes that travel rapidly in the network may degrade the cluster quality because they alter the node distribution in their clusters and make the clusters unstable, possibly long before the end of To. In this paper we have approached the problem from a different view point by taking into consideration the mobility of the nodes which leads to resilient clustering formation against mobility.

3.1 Assumptions

1. Each and every node v in set V must be mapped into exactly one cluster.
2. Each ordinary node in the cluster must be able to directly communicate to its clusterhead.
3. The nodes are distributed randomly in the play field.
4. The nodes are mobile.
5. The base station is static.
6. The clustering protocol must be completely distributed meaning that each node independently makes its decisions based only on local information.

3.2 Modified DECA Clustering Algorithm

In DECA, each node periodically transmits a Hello message to identify itself, and based on such Hello messages, each node maintains a neighbor list. In our modified version if DECA we define a score function at each node as :

$$score = w1B + w2C + w3P + w4M \qquad (1)$$

where B stands for battery power left,

C stands for node connectivity,

Let p be probability of failure and $P=1-p$. Probability of failure takes into account unfavorable & hostile environments in which certain nodes are placed.

M stands for mobility of the nodes. Lesser mobile the nodes greater is the value of M.

and weights follow$\sum_{i=1}^{4} w_i = 1$.

The scheme is divided into three phases.

Phase I. Cluster Head Selection

The computed score is used to compute the delay for a node to announce itself as the clusterhead. The higher the score, the sooner the node will transmit a message called clustering message. This message contains the sender's ID, the cluster ID i.e ID of the cluster head on which the sender node belong, and score of the clusterhead.

Sender's ID	Clusterhead's ID	Score of the clusterhead

Clustering message

The computed delay is normalized between 0 and a certain upper bound $Dmax$ which is a key parameter that needs to be carefully selected in practice. We choose $Dmax=$ 10 ms. After the clustering starts, the procedure will terminate after time $Tstop$ which is another key parameter whose selection needs to take node computation capability and mobility into consideration. We choose $Tstop=$ 1 s.

Phase II. Cluster Formation

The distributed clustering algorithm at each node is illustrated in the pseudo code fragments. Essentially, clustering is done periodically and at each clustering epoch, each node either immediately announces itself as a potential clusterhead or it holds for some delay time. Upon receiving clustering messages, a node needs to check whether the node ID and the cluster ID embedded in the received message are the same; same node and cluster ID means that the message has been transmitted from a clusterhead. Further, if the receiving node does not belong to any cluster, and the received score is better than its own, the node can mark down the advertised cluster and wait until its scheduled announcement to send its message.

Phase III: Cluster Conversion

There may be a case when an already declared cluster head finds a neighbor that has a better score than its own in its vicinity. If that happens we need to convert the cluster head from the current one to the newly found one. The message should be broadcasted to every member of the cluster currently under consideration.

Algorithm: The modified DECA clustering algorithm is presented below:

I. Start-Clustering-Algorithm()

/* calculating the score*/
1 myScore = w1B + w2C + w3P + w4M;
/* standardizing the delay value metric*/
2 delay = (1000 - myScore)/100;
/*if no delay then broadcast it immediately*/
3 **if** (delay < 0)
/* id is its own id,Cid is the clusterhead id and score is its own score*/
4   **then** bcastClstr (myId, myCid, myScore);
/*if delay then incur some delay before broadcasting its message*/
5 **else** delayAnnouncement ();
6 Schedule clustering termination.

II. Receive-Clustering-message(id, cid, score)

/*we are constructing only 2 hop clustering, so we need to not check the messages from any other node except the clusterhead, and if id==cid then the message is broadcasted by the clusterhead itself*/
1 **if** (id == cid)
/* if the receiving node has no clusterhead then assign it to some cluster*/
2   **then if** (myCid == NULL)
/* if the score of the clusterhead is better than the current node then the current node is assigned to the cluster*/
3   **then if** (score > myScore)
4   myCid = cid;
/*if the current node is already assigned to some cluster then if the broadcasted clustrhead has better score than the already assigned clusterhead then the current node must br converted from the previous cluster to the new cluster*/
5   **elseif** (score > myScore)
6   **then if** (myId == myCid)
7   needConvert = true;
/* else best cluster*/
8   **else** markBestCluster();

III. Finalize-Clustering-Algorithm()

1 **if** (needConvert)
2   **then if** (!amIHeadforAnyOtherNode ())
3   **then** convtToNewClst ();
4 **if** (myCid == NULL)
5   **then** myCid = cid;
6 bcastClstr (myId, myCid, score);

3.3 Correctness and Complexity

The protocol described above is completely distributed. To show the correctness and efficiency of the algorithm, we have the following results.

- Eventually MDECA terminates.
- At the end of Phase III, every node can determine its cluster and only one cluster.
- When clustering finishes, any two nodes in a cluster are at most two hops away.
- In MDECA, each node transmits only one message during the operation.
- The time complexity of the algorithm is $O(|V|)$.

4 Simulation Result

To evaluate the performance of MDECA, extensive simulations were carried out on several random 100 node networks in a 50m*50m field. Simulations performed in GCC compiler shows that it outperforms HEED and MDECA and this readily implies the efficiency of our model. The base station was located at (25m , 150m) and energy per node was varied.

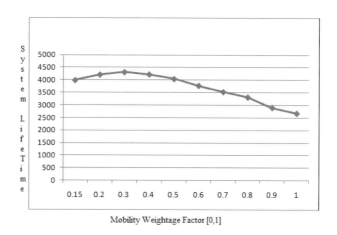

Fig. 1. Effect of mobility weightage on the network lifetime of WSN in MDECA

In the above simulation we have varied the mobility factors of the nodes and check the network's lifetime. According to Fig. 1 it is clear that the network performance will degrade if the mobility of the node increases.

From Fig. 2 it is clear that network become inefficient when 80% of the total nodes are dead therefore degrades the network performance. In our simulations, we can see that for a set of nodes in the network, the selection of clusterheads are done appropriately according to our clustering algorithm MDECA.

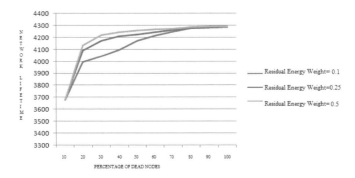

Fig. 2. Performance analysis of MDECA with different weightage for residual energy with Energy/node 1J

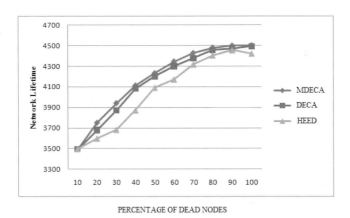

PERCENTAGE OF DEAD NODES

Fig. 3. Performance analysis of different protocols with Energy/ node 1J and Base Station at(25m,150m)

5   Conclusion

Clustering is one of the ways of attaining energy efficiency in wireless ad hoc sensor networks and thus extending the life time of the nodes. Various parameters have been taken into account to make the network more reliable, efficient and dependable. Sensor networks have widespread application in various fields. These include target tracking, security, environmental monitoring, system control, etc.

References

[1] Warneke, B., Last, M., Liebowitz, B., Pister, K.S.J.: Smart Dust: Communicating with a Cubic-Millimeter Computer. Computer Magazine 34(1), 44–51 (2001)
[2] Kahn, J.M., Katz, R.H., Pister, K.S.J.: Next Century Challenges: Mobile Networking for Smart Dust. In: The 5th Annual ACM/IEEE International Conference on Mobile Computing and Networking (MobiCom 1999), pp. 271–278 (August 1999)

[3] Hsu, V., Kahn, J.M., Pister, K.S.J.: Wireless Communications for Smart Dust. Electronics Research Laboratory Technical Memorandum M98/2 (February 1998)

[4] Pottie, G.J., Kaiser, W.J.: Wireless Integrated Network Sensors. Communications of the ACM 43(5), 51–58 (2000)

[5] http://www.janet.ucla.edu/WINS/wins_intro.htm

[6] Kahn, J.M., Katz, R.H., Pister, K.S.J.: Next Century Challenges: Mobile Networking for Smart Dust. In: The Proceedings of 5th Annual ACM/IEEE International Conference on Mobile Computing and Networking (MobiCom 1999), pp. 271–278 (August 1999)

[7] Li, J.H., Bhattacharjee, B., Yu, M., Levy, R.: A scalable key management and clustering scheme for wireless ad hoc and sensor networks. Future Generation Computer Systems 24, 860–869 (2008)

[8] Sivakumar, R., Das, B., Bharghavan, V.: The clade vertebrata: Spines and routing in ad hoc networks. In: Proc. of the IEEE Symposium on Computer Communications, ISCC 1998 (1998)

[9] Sivakumar, R., Das, B.: Spine-based routing in ad hoc networks. ACM/Baltzer Cluster Computing Journal 1, 237–248 (1998)

[10] Sivakumar, R., Sinha, P., Bharghavan, V.: CEDAR: A core-extraction distributed ad hoc routing algorithm. IEEE Journal on Selected Areas in Communications 17(8), 1454–1465 (1999)

[11] Wu, J., Li, H.: On calculating connected dominating sets for efficient routing in ad hoc wireless networks. Telecommunication Systems 18(1/3), 13–36 (2001)

[12] Lin, C.R., Gerla, M.: Adaptive clustering for mobile wireless networks. Journal on Selected Areas in Communications 15(7), 1265–1275 (1997)

[13] Basagni, S.: Distributed clustering for ad hoc networks. In: Proc. of the 1999 International Symposium on Parallel Architectures, Algorithms, and Networks (1999)

[14] Basagni, S., Turgut, D., Das, S.K.: Mobility-adaptive protocols for managing large ad hoc networks. In: Proc. of the ICC 2001, pp. 1539–1543 (2001)

[15] Heinzelman, W.R., Chandrakasan, A., Balakrishnan, H.: Energy efficient communication protocol for wireless microsensor networks. In: Proc. of the 3rd Hawaii International Conference on System Sciences, pp. 3005–3014 (2000)

[16] Krishna, P., Vaidya, N.N., Chatterjee, M., Pradhan, D.K.: A cluster-based approach for routing in dynamic networks. ACM SIGCOMM Computer Communication Review 49, 49–64 (1997)

[17] Younis, O., Fahmy, S.: HEED: A hybrid, energy-efficient, distributed clustering approach for ad hoc sensor networks. IEEE Transactions on Mobile Computing 3(4) (2004)

[18] Elson, L., Girod, L., Estrin, D.: Fine-grained network time synchronization using reference broadcasts. ACM SIGOPS Operating System Review 36, 147–163 (2002)

ERBR: Enhanced and Improved Delay for Requirement Based Routing in Delay Tolerant Networks

Mohammad Arif, Kavita Satija, and Sachin Chaudhary

Department of CSE, GSMVNIET, Palwal, Haryana, India
arif_mohd2k@yahoo.com, kavita.satija@gmail.com,
sachinrohal@gmail.com

Abstract. The highly successful architecture and protocols of today's Internet may operate poorly in environments characterized by very long delay paths and frequent network partitions. Delay Tolerant Networks (DTNs) are emerging solutions to networks that experience frequent network partitions and large end-to-end delays. In this paper, we study how to provide high-performance routing technique in DTNs. We develop a multicasting mechanism based on requirement of path discovery and overall situation awareness of link availability to address the challenges of opportunistic link connectivity in DTNs. Simulation results show that this method can achieve a better message delivery ratio than existing approaches, e.g. DTBR (a dynamic tree-based routing), with similar delay performance. ERBR approach also achieves better efficiency performance when the probability of link unavailability is high and the duration of link downtime is large.

Keywords: Delay tolerant networks, multicasting, Ad-hoc Networks, Intermittent Connectivity, Routing Protocols.

1 Introduction

In delay tolerant networks, end-to-end path between a source and destination does not exist. So it is a big challenge to study the data communication in such network scenarios where a links between nodes may be opportunistic or predictably/periodically connected. There is ongoing research [12, 10, 7, and 2] on delay tolerant networks (DTNs) that addresses such challenges. DTNs have a broad range of potential applications such as military battlefields [4], deep-space communications [6], habitat monitoring [14], and Internet access in rural areas [8]. Many DTN applications need multicast service. For example, in military battlefields, it is vital to quickly and reliably transmit orders from a command center to a group of field commanders. It is also helpful to share information of surrounding environments among different squads of soldiers. However, traditional multicast methods proposed for the Internet (e.g., MOSPF [3] and DVMRP [9]) or mobile adhoc networks (e.g., AMRoute [11] and ODMRP [13]) are not suitable for DTNs, due to the challenge of frequent network partitions. Firstly, it is difficult to maintain the connectivity of a source-rooted multicast tree (or mesh) during the lifetime of a multicast session.

N. Meghanathan et al. (Eds.): CCSIT 2011, Part II, CCIS 132, pp. 223–232, 2011.

Secondly, data transmissions suffer from large end-to-end delays along the tree because of the repeated disruptions caused by periodically broken branches. Thirdly, the traditional approaches may fail to deliver a message when the possibility of link unavailability becomes high (e.g. ~80%). In this paper, we address these issues and focus on studying how to provide high-performance multicasting in DTNs in terms of high delivery ratio and short delay. We investigate three multicasting methods for DTNs, which employ unicast-based, static tree-based and dynamic tree-based strategies respectively. We propose an enhanced requirement based approach (ERBR), which is a new dynamic tree-based method that integrates DTN multicasting with the situation discovery by the underlying network layer. DTBR [12] is another dynamic tree-based multicasting approach for DTNs. Simulation results show that ERBR can achieve smaller delays and better message delivery ratios than DTBR. This approach also achieves higher efficiency when the probability of link unavailability is high and the duration of link downtime is large.

The rest of the paper is organized as follows. Section 2 presents descriptions of the network model and multicast model of DTNs. Section 3 explains the basic DTN multicast approaches and the ERBR algorithm. Performance evaluations are illustrated in Section 4. Section 5 summarizes our contributions.

2   System Model

2.1   System Model

The architecture of delay tolerant network is based on the asynchronous message (called bundle) forwarding paradigm presented in [5]. Only those nodes that implement the DTN functionalities to send and receive bundles are DTN nodes, while the others are denoted as normal nodes. A DTN link may contain several underlying links in multiple hops. Fig. 1 depicts a simple example. In the DTN layer, bundles are transmitted in a hop-by-hop store-and-forward manner. Each DTN node has finite-size buffers for bundle acceptance and bundle custody. The details of custodian transfer are discussed in [7]. They are out of the scope of this study. Normally, the underlying network layer provides unicast routing capability to forward a bundle from one DTN node to another. The multicast service discussed in this research is only implemented in the DTN overlay. More details about our DTN architecture can be found in [2].

2.2   Multicasting Model

Multicast in DTNs is defined as the one-to-many or many to many bundle transmissions among a group of DTN nodes. Each DTN node is associated with a DTN *name* that potentially permits late binding to its underlying network address. The address translation between the DTN *name* and underlying network address is done by DTN routing agent. A multicast source uses a group name or an explicit list of the names of DTN receivers as the destination address for transferring bundles. The details of multicast membership management are discussed in Section 3.

3 Multicast Routing Approaches and Algorithms

3.1 Knowledge of Situation

As we know that DTNs suffer from frequent network partitions. This dynamic change of link state and due to which the maintenance of the multicast tree becomes challenging. The performance of different multicast approaches depends on the knowledge of network conditions discovered in DTN nodes.

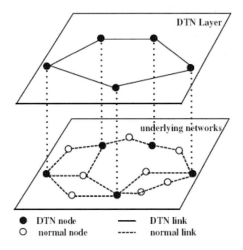

Fig. 1. An example DTN networks

Therefore, situational awareness can be applied to help DTN nodes control the message forwarding behavior and discover different message delivery paths, based on the policies and network conditions at different times. Situational awareness is achieved by making the multicast implementation collaborate with the routing methods in the underlying networks. We assume that before the DTN overlay starts, the underlying network has already been operating for a relatively long time. A DTN routing agent will send *req* message periodically to trigger its underlying routing agent to collect the current network conditions, such as the presently available outgoing links and the discovered paths from the current DTN node to the destinations. This requirement could be fulfilled by some source routing approaches such as DSR [1]. The routing agent then answers through *resp* message with all the detected information back to the DTN routing agent. Thus, a knowledge base of the link state and network topology is constructed in each DTN node. Both *req* and *resp* messages are system messages transmitted inside a node. [15]

3.2 Types of Multicast Approaches

Figure 2 shows three types of approaches for multicast communications in a DTN.

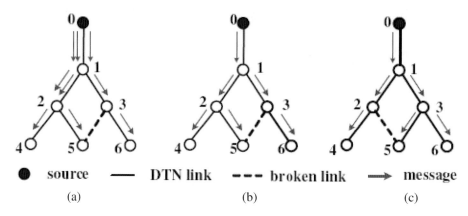

Fig. 2. Different Multicast approaches in DTN. (a) U-multicast (b) ST-multicast. (c) ERBR: when link 2→5 is unavailable and link 3→5 becomes available, node 3 will take advantage of the current available link immediately.

3.2.1   U-Multicast (Unicast-Based Multicast)

In this approach multicast service is implemented by using multiple source-to-destination unicast data transfer. In U-multicast, the source always tries to set up an end-to-end path to each destination and sends a copy of the bundle along the currently available shortest path. If there is no such path for a destination due to a network partition, the source will hold the bundle in its buffer and retransmit it once the destination is connected.

3.2.2   ST-Multicast (Static Tree-Based Multicast)

In ST-multicast, a source-rooted multicast tree is constructed at initialization by querying the shortest paths to reach each destination from its knowledge base. Then the source keeps sending bundles along this static tree and requires the intermediate DTN nodes with multiple downstream neighbors to duplicate the messages. Compare to U-multicast, each bundle is pushed to the DTN nodes that are nearest to the destinations using the available links, even if the end-to-end paths in the static tree are unavailable. Once the broken downstream links become available, the buffered messages will be forwarded further.

3.2.3   DTBR

DTBR [12] is another dynamic tree-based multicasting algorithm designed for DTNs. Similar to ERBR, DTBR also requires the intermediate DTN nodes to re-build a multicast tree. However, in each step of the bundle transmission, the upstream node will assign the receiver list for its downstream neighbors based on its local view of the network conditions. The downstream nodes are required to forward bundles only to the receivers in the list, even if a new path to another receiver (not in the list) is discovered. Fig. 3 depicts this issue.

This issue is solved in ERBR because each intermediate node has an equal chance to decide the receiver list. If a link towards a receiver becomes available, the DTN nodes which detect that will immediately take advantage of this new opportunity. We

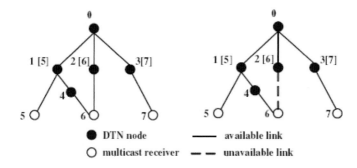

Fig. 3. (a) At time t0, the source (node 0) computes the multicast tree and decides that the receiver list for node 1 is {5}, for node 2 is {6}, and for node 3 is {7}. (b) At time t1 > t0, link 2→6 is down. Node 1 cannot forward the bundle to node 6 even if there is an available path 1→4→6 just because node 6 is not in its receiver list. Before the source detects this problem, it will keep sending bundles to node 2 and ignore the other better opportunity. [15]

call this greedy nature of ERBR as the *first availability property*. This property guarantees that the bundle will be delivered to the receivers as soon as possible and the opportunistic links will be utilized. DTBR assumes that each node has complete knowledge or the summary of the link states in the network.

3.3   ERBR Algorithm

In this section, we introduce the details of the proposed dynamic tree-based ERBR algorithm. We have an undirected graph G, at the start time t_0, end time T, source node s and the event list Events. The algorithm calculates the earliest time in which a message originated at s can reach to any other node of G within the time T if possible.

We first apply the breadth-first search initially to discover the nodes reachable immediately from s. We assume that all nodes reachable during the initial search are discovered at time t_0 and are marked. Now we process each event in the list Events. We always update the list Events when ever any edge is added or deleted. An edge can be added at any time which means that a new node has been discovered. In such case we will apply the breadth first search on the newly discovered node as the new source node. All new nodes discovered during the search are marked with the time of the event t_e, that led to their discovery. Whenever an ADD event takes place, it discovers the new node due to which the route is extended. If a DELETE takes place, it means that only topology has changed, length of route may or may not shorten.

We apply the standard breadth first search algorithm and we store the distance in the terms of number of hops from the source node. As per notation we use WHITE to denote nodes which are not yet discovered, and GRAY nodes represent the discovered nodes which are being explored. BLACK, for nodes discovered and explored. At the end of the execution of the breadth first search algorithm, all nodes are colored BLACK. To enforce storage constraint, we implement a drop policy on each node. Using the route found by Traversal algorithm, a message as it is being transmitted could be dropped due to storage constraint along the path. For a drop policy, we propose that the message with the longest life time in a queue would be dropped when there is no available storage.

3.3.1 Group Management

Every time source wants to send data to some destination, it will apply the algorithm to find the path for that specific node and then to join a multicast group, it registers with its membership period by explicitly sending a *JOIN_MEMB* message. For example, node *i* wants to join the multicast service during the period [*tsi, tei*], with the start-time *tsi* and the end-time *tei* of its membership. When the multicasting source is informed by the *JOIN_MEMB* message, it puts the membership information into a list, denoted as *LM* in each bundle. For every bundle received, generated or retransmitted at time *t*, a DTN node will check the validity of each receiver in *LM*. If the membership of a receiver has expired ($t > tei$) or was not activated ($t < tsi$), then it will not forward the bundle to that receiver. A receiver is called a valid receiver only if it owns valid membership for that bundle. This membership management method conforms to the TM semantic model proposed in [12] with an explicit receiver list known at the source.

3.3.2 Storage of Bundles

There is a specific storage amount locally at each DTN node. A received bundle will be saved in the buffer until eliminated due to buffer overflow or successfully forwarded toward all valid receivers based on the bundle acceptance policy. For example, when the buffer is full, the bundle at the head of the buffer will be dumped first with the arrival of a new bundle.

3.3.3 Maintenance of Forwarding State

Every bundle associates a forwarding state along with it. Two lists are maintained. One list is upstream list (called *LU*) which is maintained in the bundle and the other one is a pending list (called *LP*) which is maintained by node. When a bundle arrives, a node creates *LP* for that bundle by copying *LM* information from the bundle. *LP* is periodically checked to remove information corresponding to those receivers whose memberships have expired. When node *A* wants to forward the bundle to a downstream node *B* to reach a valid receiver *C*, it first checks if $B \in LU$ to avoid the redundancy. Then it removes *C* from *LP*. Once *LP* is empty, the bundle is then removed from the local buffer of node *A*.

3.3.4 Forwarding of Messages

After the generation of a bundle, the source queries its knowledge base to retrieve all the discovered paths to the receivers. The static mesh is formed by combining the source to the multicast mesh that covers all the valid receivers. The source then filters this mesh by deleting those currently unavailable outgoing links reported by the underlying routing agent. This is denoted by dynamic mesh. Based on the dynamic mesh, a source-rooted shortest path multicast tree is built and the source forwards the bundle to all its available downstream DTN neighbors, carrying the static mesh information in the bundle. Upon receiving a bundle, a node X will first query its knowledge base to find all the possible paths to the receivers. Then it combines the static mesh in the bundle with the query results to be a new static-mesh. A dynamic mesh is then constructed in the same way as what the source has done. Then the node X re-computes the shortest-path multicast tree by taking itself as the root to all the receivers and applying the breadth first search. The new static mesh is put into the bundle again and forwarded further to downstream neighbors. With the knowledge propagation and the dynamic decision made by each intermediate DTN node, eventually the bundle will arrive at those receivers in *LM*. Note that the same bundle will not be forwarded at each node more than once to avoid introducing redundant traffic into the networks.

3.3.5 Retransmission of Bundles

A node periodically checks its local storage to see if there is any opportunity to forward the buffered bundles further. It uses the current dynamic mesh to find out if there is a chance to forward the bundle to a receiver in *LP*. If so, the bundle is forwarded using this available forwarding opportunity and the covered receiver is removed from *LP*. To reduce the overhead of the ERBR, there is an upper bound *Rupper* to limit the maximum retransmission times for each receiver. If the retransmission to receiver *D* fails more than *Rupper* times, *D* would be removed from *LP*. Once *LP* is empty, the bundle will be deleted from the local buffer.

However, this is hard to be satisfied in most practical applications. In our design of ERBR, we use situational awareness with the help of underlying routing methods to collect the information of network conditions, such as the currently available outgoing links and the possible paths to destinations.

4 Performance Evaluation

In this study, we implemented U-multicast, ST-multicast, ERBR and DTBR in the *ns2* simulator to evaluate the performance of different multicast algorithms. Table 1 shows the simulation parameters used in the simulations. The performance metrics that are used to compare different multicast routing approaches are as follows.

Message Deliver Ratio: It is defined as the number of successful transfers which successfully arrive at all the receivers over the total number of messages which are expected to be received. Because of the long link disconnections, many transfers will still be in progress within the network at the end of simulation time. We do not count those in our calculation of delivery ratio.

Delivery ratio = $S / (S + N + D)$

Number of successful transfers (S): this metric defines the number of complete transfers with storage on intermediate nodes.

Number of No Routes (N): this metric defines the number of transfers that result in incomplete paths to the destination because the BFS algorithm fails to find a path within the given LAT.

Number of message drops (D): this metric defines the number of transfers failing to complete because of storage unavailability at intermediate nodes.

Average Message Delay: It is defined as the average of the end to end bundle transmission latencies for each algorithm. To make our comparison fair, we only calculate the delay of those bundles received by both multicasting methods because each method has different delivery capability.

Data Efficiency: It is defined as the ratio between the packets received successfully by the receivers and the total data traffic (i.e. data packets and the control packets) generated in the networks.

We have used DSR as the routing approach for the underlying ad hoc networks. And situational awareness is achieved by the communication between DTN multicasting agent and the DSR routing agent. The MAC layer is IEEE 802.11 with radio transmission range of 250 meters.

We study one multicast session in the DTN overlay. Node 0 is fixed to be the source and 5 DTN nodes are randomly chosen to be the receivers. The message sending rate is 1 bundle per 2 seconds with the bundle size of 512 bytes. Each DTN node can maximally keep 100 bundles in its local buffer. At every 5 seconds, each DTN node will query the underlying routing agent to find if there is any available opportunistic link to forward the buffered bundle to the destinations. If so a copy of the bundle will be forwarded. We study the performance of different multicasting algorithms by varying the percentage of link unavailability of each link from 10% to 90%. Fig. 3 shows the result of the message delivery ratios of U-multicast, ST-multicast, ERBR and DTBR. We observe that *i*) the delivery ratio decreases for all the algorithms when the downtime of links becomes large, i.e., the network is more easily partitioned; *ii*) ERBR can always achieve the best performance among all the algorithms; and *iii*) U-multicast performs better than ST-multicast when the downtime is small because it basically tries to forward bundles in a multicast mesh than a tree. For each bundle transmitted by each intermediate DTN node, ERBR tries to utilize multiple paths to the receivers and take advantage of the currently available opportunistic links to push the data closer to the destinations.

Table 1. Simulation Parameters

Simulation parameters	Values
No. of nodes	25
Simulation time	500 Sec
Look-ahead-time (LAT)	200 Sec
Message size	15KB
Storage amount on each node	5, 10, 15MB
Simulation Area	1000x1000

Link down time percentage	Message Delivery Ratio			
	U-multicast	ST-multicast	DTBR	ERBR
0.1	0.86	0.92	0.96	0.97
0.3	0.71	0.74	0.79	0.94
0.5	0.41	0.54	0.59	0.87
0.7	0.18	0.43	0.28	0.83
0.9	0.08	0.21	0.19	0.38

Fig. 4. Message delivery ratios of different multicasting algorithms

The above simulation is conducted by uniformly dividing the downtime of each link into 10 small periods. To better show the performance of ERBR, we also test the message delivery ratio performance by dividing the total downtime into 30 periods, i.e., making the link states vary more often and increasing the occurrences of opportunistic links. The result is illustrated in Fig. 4. It is obvious that *i*) all the methods deliver fewer bundles with more frequent link changes, and *ii*) ERBR outperforms the other approaches more than the result shown in Fig. 3. This demonstrates that ERBR is able to utilize the opportunistic links more effectively.

Link down time percentage	End to End Delay	
	DTBR	ERBR
0.1	3.1	2.4
0.3	7.9	4.4
0.5	23.8	9.6
0.7	37.7	23.6
0.9	46.4	32.7

Fig. 5. Average message delays between OS-multicast and DTBR

The following simulations are all carried out by dividing the downtime of each link into 10 periods. Fig. 5 depicts the median message delay of two dynamic-tree based multicasting approaches: ERBR and DTBR. ERBR has smaller delays than DTBR due to the issues illustrated in Fig. 5. In DTBR, each node only forwards bundles to the downstream nodes to reach the receivers in its receiver list. However, this receiver list is decided by the upstream node based on its snapshot of the network conditions. In this way, some opportunistic links to the receivers that are not in the list are missed. In contrast, the ERBR method always uses all the chances to forward bundles to the destinations. Note that results in [12] already show that DTBR achieves slightly better delay performance than ST-multicast.

Link down time percentage	Efficiency			
	U-multicast	ST-multicast	DTBR	ERBR
0.1	0.391	0.357	0.373	0.061
0.3	0.354	0.355	0.315	0.073
0.5	0.296	0.344	0.283	0.091
0.7	0.213	0.248	0.236	0.103
0.9	0.117	0.203	0.157	0.129

Fig. 6. Multicast efficiency of different algorithms

We also evaluate the efficiency of various multicasting approaches and illustrate the result in Fig. 6. It shows that although ERBR has the highest delivery ratio it has the worst efficiency when the link downtime is small. The reason is that a lot of redundant traffic has been introduced by ERBR due to its nature of utilizing multiple currently available links. However, when the link downtime percentage is larger than 80% of the total simulation time, its efficiency increases because the chance of redundancy decreases and it is still able to achieve the relatively high delivery ratio as shown in Fig.3. The efficiencies of the other three algorithms decrease while the network connectivity becomes worse.

5 Conclusion

We have developed an ERBR algorithm, which is able to dynamically adjust multicast routing decisions based on the current network conditions. We compare its performance with those achieved by DTBR, ST-multicast, and U-multicast. Simulation results ERBR can achieve better message delivery ratio than existing approaches with similar delay performance. When network connectivity becomes worse due to the high link unavailability, ERBR also has better efficiency. We are currently investigating on an improved version of our ERBR scheme that can achieve higher efficiency at low/medium link availability.

References

[1] Johnson, D.B., Maltz, D.A.: Dynamic source routing in ad hoc wireless networks. In: Imielinski, T., Korth, H. (eds.) Mobile Computing. ch. 5, pp. 153–181. Kluwer Academic Publishers, Dordrecht (1996)

[2] Chuah, M., Cheng, L., Davison, B.: Enhanced disruption and fault tolerant network architecture for bundle delivery (EDIFY). To appear at Globecom (2005)

[3] Moy, J.: Multicast extensions to OSPF. IETF RFC 1584 (1994)

[4] Malladi, R., Agrawal, D.P.: Current and future applications of mobile and wireless networks. Communications of the ACM 45, 144–146 (2002)

[5] Fall, K.: A delay-tolerant network architecture for challenged Internets. In: Proceedings of SIGCOMM 2003 (August 2003)

[6] Burleigh, S., Hooke, A., Torgerson, L., Fall, K., Cerf, V., Durst, B., Scott, K., Weiss, H.: Delay-tolerant networking - an approach to interplanetary internet. IEEE Communications Magazine (June 2003)

[7] Fall, K.: Messaging in difficult environments. Intel Research Berkeley, IRB-TR-04-019, December 27 (2004)

[8] Jain, S., Fall, K., Patra, R.: Routing in a delay tolerant networking. In: The Proceedings of SIGCOMM 2004 (August/September 2004)

[9] Waitzman, D., Partridge, C., Deering, S.: Distance vector multicast routing protocol (DVMRP). IETF RFC 1075 (1988)

[10] DARPA Disruption Tolerant Networks program, http://www.darpa.mil/ato/solicit/dtn/ (accessed on August 3, 2005)

[11] Xie, J., Talpade, R.R., Mcauley, A., Liu, M.Y.: AMRoute: ad hoc multicast routing protocol. Mobile Networks and Applications 7(6), 429–439 (2002)

[12] Zhao, W., Ammar, M., Zegura, E.: Multicasting in delay tolerant networks: semantic models and routing algorithms. In: The Proceeding of SIGCOMM Workshop in DTN (August 2005)

[13] Bae, S.H., Lee, S.-J., Su, W., Gerla, M.: The design, implementation, and performance evaluation of the on-demand multicast routing protocol in multihop wireless networks. IEEE Network, 70–77 (January 2000)

[14] Cerpa, A., Elson, J., Estrin, D., Girod, L., Hamilton, M., Zhao, J.: Habitat monitoring: application driver for wireless communications technology. In: The Proceeding of ACM SIGCOMM Workshop on Data Communications (April 2001)

[15] Ye, Q., Cheng, L., Chuah, M.C., Devison, B.D.: OS-Multicast: On-Deamand Situation Aware Multicasting in Disruption tolerant network. In: The Proceeding of IEEE VTC (Spring 2007)

Deterministic Approach for the Elimination of MED Oscillations and Inconsistent Routing in BGP

Berlin Hency[1], Vasudha Venkatesh[2], and Raghavendran Nedunchezhian[2]

[1] Department of Information Technology, MIT, Anna University, Chennai, India
hencyjoseph@annauniv.edu
[2] India Development Center, Oracle Corporation, Bangalore, India
{vasu18,raghavan291}@gmail.com

Abstract. Border gateway protocol is divided into two sub groups namely external BGP (eBGP) and internal BGP (iBGP). The latter is responsible for distributing the reachability information obtained through eBGP into its corresponding autonomous systems (ASes), which could be a very large system or an Internet service provider (ISP) on a smaller level. The multi exit discriminator (MED) attribute plays a pivotal role in selecting the best path to traverse into the ISP. Currently, MED cannot be compared across ISPs in different AS. Each AS has its own set of rules for MED. This introduces nondeterminism in the BGP protocol, which makes traffic engineering difficult. It also results in inconsistent routing and route oscillations. This paper analyzes the shortcomings of the current non-deterministic model and proposes a solution to make it deterministic as well as prevent route oscillations using an efficient computation of MED attribute that can be compared across ISPs on different ASes.

Keywords: BGP, MED attribute, routing, traffic engineering.

1 Introduction

The Internet is an interconnection of computer networks, which use Internet Protocol (IP) for transmission of data using packet switching technology. It is a "network of networks" that encompasses several small networks such as business; university networks and carries several services like chat, mail, video conferencing and document sharing.

The Internet is often viewed as a single network, centrally managed and operated, much like a typical centralized grid when in fact it is the contrary. It is a collection of independent networks that are managed and operated autonomously. These independent networks are called autonomous systems (ASes) [1]. The Internet currently consists of more than 18000 autonomous systems.

An autonomous system (AS) is a collection of IP networks and routers under the control of one entity (or sometimes more) that presents a common routing policy to the Internet [2].

Each of the AS in turn need not be just a single network. It can be a composition of many other networks, but managed by a single authority. An AS could be anything ranging from a small university network to an ISP itself.

N. Meghanathan et al. (Eds.): CCSIT 2011, Part II, CCIS 132, pp. 233–242, 2011.
© Springer-Verlag Berlin Heidelberg 2011

Internet routing protocols are needed for routing among the ASes. However, they pose some unique issues that need holistic solution. The Internet protocols are highly dependent on configuration values and there are far more configurable parameters in the Internet protocols than any other protocol. Consistent behavior of routing depends on coherent synchronization of each configurable parameter [4]. However, the gargantuan size of Internet coupled with dependencies across routers in various networks can give rise to conflicts in parameter settings and lead to unpredictable behavior. The conflict is exacerbated by the fact that each AS has its own set of policies, which are framed independent of other ASes [11]. Thus, routing conflicts tend to occur affecting the routing decisions considerably, which may in the worst-case lead to severe packet loss. An optimized Internet protocol not only considers the best path for routing, but also takes into account the tightly coupled interaction among the routers, the policy constraints within the AS as well as its effects outside the AS [5].

The current routing protocol on the Internet is the Border Gateway Protocol (BGP). ASes establish connectivity with other ASes by means of BGP sessions at border routers (also called egress points of border routers). Each of these AS have several routers with each router having a routing table containing the route for the destination. The routers choose the best route to the destination. It essentially selects the next hop to forward the packet and it need not be the final destination. The router at the intermediary point will select the next hop based on the best route selected from its own routing table [3].

2   BGP Decision Process

The BGP decision process is a sequence of steps used for selecting the routes that are going to be advertised to the neighbors [6].

When an Intra-BGP (I-BGP) speaker obtains advertisement from other peers, the following method is used to select the best route to go forward:

- The degree of preference for each route that gets advertised to the router is estimated. This value is calculated using either policy-based decisions or using Intra-AS decision parameters. While advertising routes, the ones with the highest degree of preference are advertised.

If the network we are dealing with is very small then the routes to be advertised are determined without ambiguity using only the above step. However, the scale of Internet demands further filtering. There could be multiple routes with the same degree of preference. This is when the BGP decision process introduces tie-breaking mechanism with a major role played by the MED attribute, to find out the exact route to send the packet through.

3   Tie Breaking and MED Attribute

The tie breaking process could be elaborated as follows [6]:

- The route with the highest "degree of preference" is selected for advertisement.
- For routes with the same degree of preference, the route with the minimum AS-PATH length is chosen.

- If there are several eligible routes from the previous step, then choose the routes with least Multi exit discriminator (MED) value within an AS. This is only for comparison inside a particular AS. MED is not compared across ASes.

(Note that if there are multiple neighboring ASes, there could be routes with minimal MED values corresponding to each AS.) If there is exactly one such route, this route is chosen.

- Prefer the route learned from E-BGP over the routes learned from I-BGP.
- For multiple I-BGP routes, choose the one with lowest IGP cost value.
- Form the above 5 steps, if there still exist multiple routes, then arbitrarily select the route with the lowest BGP identifier value.

However, the localization of MED attribute to a particular AS introduces nondeterminism in the flow.

Since MED is only compared between routes from the same AS, it is possible that an additional path could be selected as the best path. This may cause inconsistent routing if all routers in the forwarding path of the affected routers do not have the additional paths. In a simple topology, it may be possible to anticipate these scenarios and avoid inconsistent routing while still enabling appropriate applications.

4   Route Oscillations from MED Attribute in BGP

The route oscillations in BGP due to the MED attribute can be illustrated with the following scenario from the configuration in [6].

Consider a system shown in Fig. 1 with route reflectors (RR1 and RR2) with each route reflectors sending route information to its clients. Here, C1 and C2 are clients of RR1. C3 is a client of RR2. This configuration belongs to AS1, which has AS2 and AS3 as its neighbors. AS3 has 2 egress routers having MED value of 6 and 2 respectively. D is the destination. Node RR1 selects path P2 over path P1 due to its low IGP path value and node RR2 selects path P3 (assuming that it has not received advertisements from the other ASes and has only P3 in its router table). On receiving update from node RR2, node RR1 learns about path P3 also and it selects path P1 as its best path (This time it checks for the MED value between the egress routers in AS and eliminates path 2. Between P1 and P3 it selects P1). On receiving an update from node RR1, node RR2 learns about path P1 and it selects path P1 as its best path over P3 and as soon as this is done it withdraws its previous best path P3. When path P3 is withdrawn by node RR2, node RR1 selects path P2 over path P1 and withdraws its previous best path P1. When path P1 is withdrawn by node RR1, node RR2 selects path P3 over path P2 and the cycle repeats. This could be prevented if MED can be compared across all ASes.

The logic behind proposing a solution to make MED attribute comparable across all ASes is that, when route advertisements are received dynamically, the route selection becomes dynamic too. This will remain deterministic only as long as the parameters on which the best path is selected are fixed. The parameters should be quantifiable and configurable independent of the structure of the network. But currently in BGP MED attribute brings in an additional nondeterministic parameter, which is the structure of the network. Thus, a seemingly best route (a route that gets an edge over

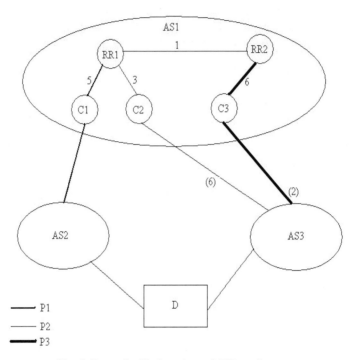

Fig. 1. Route Oscillations due to MED attribute

others only due to its presence in the same AS as the other route with which it is compared) may get eliminated during the later parts of the cycle based on other criteria, resulting in an endless cycle as shown in the scenario depicted by Fig 1.

However, the Multi Exit Discriminator attribute in its current form cannot be compared among all ASes, since each one deploys different intra gateway protocols such as OSPF, Djikstra etc. This prevents the universal comparison of MED across various ASes introducing nondeterminism and oscillations into the system [7]. BGP Model could be made deterministic if the comparison of MED across various ASes is possible. Hence, the proposed solution uses an Intra Optimal Aware algorithm for intra optimization, which uses a cost function to estimate the minimum cost path [5]. The minimum cost value obtained is set as the MED value in the decision process of the Border Gateway Protocol. This change introduced provides better convergence and optimized traffic flow in a network.

5   Intra Optimal Aware Heuristic Algorithm

The intra optimal aware algorithm is used to find the best path within an AS [8]. Since the best path is influenced by a plethora of factors, the minimum cost path is estimated with help from cost functions. This algorithm takes into consideration the following factors:

- Total traffic matrix
- Optimal routing algorithm, which calculates optimal paths and loads.

This makes sure that the output of the Intra Optimal Aware Heuristic algorithm contains the best path to traverse within an AS. There exists a close link between the Intra-AS routing and Inter-AS routing. If this connection is leveraged for BGP protocol, then the best path advertised by the protocol will not only be the best path from the egress routers perspective, but also the best path inside an AS.

The Intra optimal awareness algorithm is implemented in two phases. In the first phase, a virtual topology is constructed with all the link capacities set to their traffic capacity. The traffic capacity of each node is intuitively determined based on several practical factors. This is considered to be the ideal topology, where the traffic between each node is ideal and the link does not get over-utilized or under-utilized. In the second phase, best path routing is performed based on greedy algorithm. Here, greedy algorithm is used to make sure that each link is traversed while maintaining the ideal traffic capacity values set during the first phase (Exact conformance to the ideal values is not possible, but most of the time the result is close to the traffic capacities). Thus, the routing is done on paths consuming minimum costs with an optimal traffic capacity for each link.

A strict adherence to traffic capacity values is not possible in the practical sense. So, a deviation factor of Δ is allowed while routing traffic. The traffic is routed along a path if the capacity of any link along that path does not exceed $1+\Delta$.

However, Δ may not always accommodate the vagaries in the link loads. Hence, a considerable amount of paths may be left out from the first iteration or the first phase. Hence, the second level of iteration is mainly done to perform routing on the nodes that were left out from the first level of iteration. This is accomplished by minimum delay algorithm, this time not with the virtual link capacities but with the actual link capacities.

5.1 Cost Function

The cost of link (i, j) is given by Φ (f(i,j) ;c(i,j)), which is a piecewise linear function [9]. Cost is directly proportional to the traffic on the link. The more the practical traffic flowing through a link, greater is its rate of growth. This is done with the motive of accommodating any inadvertent increase in traffic flow along a link in the future. The priority of a link is dynamically updated using this method.

Notations used:

i,j-   links in the AS
f(i,j)-   the total flow on the link
c(i,j)-   the capacity of the link
U(i,j)-   the cost ratio
Φ(i,j)-   the cost function
G(V,ε)-the routing domain is represented by the graph 'G' with 'V' vertexes and 'ε' edges.
R= {r:r=(s,t) s,t $\in$ V}- 's' and 't' are the source and destination.
r represents the node pair s,t.
S(s,t) is the set of streams for every node pair 'r'.
Sk(s,t) is the kth stream in the node pair s,t.
bk(s,t) is the average intensity of the stream.
X(i,j) is the traffic allocation vector for the node pair 'r'.
Minimum cost path p(s,t,k) between nodes s and t for stream Sk(s,t) .

Cost Ratio

$$U(i,j)=f(i,j)/c(i,j) \text{ where } (i,j) \in \varepsilon \tag{1}$$

Piece wise linear function is defined by:

$$Q(i,j)=U(i,j) , U(i,j)<=1/3 \tag{2}$$

The network wide cost is defined to be the sum of the costs of each link, that is,

$$\Phi =\Sigma_{i,j \in \varepsilon} \Phi_{(i,j)}(f_{(i,j)} ,c_{(i,j)}) \tag{3}$$

Effectively, the flow and capacity values are used to calculate cost ratio and cost function as illustrated in this Fig 2.

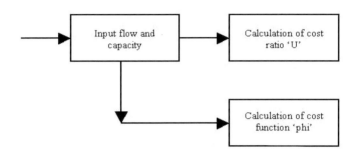

Fig. 2. Calculation of cost ratio and cost function

5.2 Algorithm

Notations used:
R – Set of all nodes

```
{ Phase 1:}


For all r ∈ R do

Construct the virtual topology  Gʳ   :  where (i,j)  ∈
ε, c(i , j) = X(i ,j) and  f1(i.j)=0

Let S(r) sorted based on f be S1(r).

While S1(r)!= 0 do

 Sk(s,t) be the first element of S1(r)

Identify the minimum cost path p(s,k,t)∈ P(s,t) between
nodes s and t

            p(s,t,k)= min(Σ(i,j)∈p (f1(i,j)+
bk(s,t),C(i,j)))

If f1(i,j)+ bk(s,t) <= C(i,j)(1+∆), where (i,j)∈
p(s,t,k) then
```

```
feasible path p(s,t,r) is identified.
f1(i,j)= f1(i,j)+ bk(s,t), V(i,j)Є p(s,t,k)
S1(r)= S1(r)- {Sk(s,t)}
  Else
No feasible path was identified.
  S1(r)= S1(r)- {Sk(s,t)}
  S2= S2 U {Sk(s,t)}
  End if
  End for
  End while


{Phase 2:}
```

1. Construct residual graph G1= (V, ε1) where {(i,j): (i,j)Єε}

2. Call procedure greedy heuristic on S2,G1,f.

6 Greedy Heuristic Algorithm

The "Greedy Heuristic", is a method that takes as input a set of streams, sorts them according to a specific order and performs the greedy algorithm [8,10]. It is greedy heuristic in the sense that every time it routes it makes sure that the path selected has the lowest cost according to the cost function used.

The greedy logic performed on the sorted list of streams S1 is shown below:

S sorted based on function f is S1 (f will be one of the choices f_{dec} or f_{inc}).

```
While S1!=0 do

Let Sk(s,t) be the first element of S1.

Compute minimum cost path p(s,t,k) between nodes s and
t for stream Sk(s,t) for the current network link loads

              p(s,t,k)= min(Σ(i,j)Єp (f(i,j)+
bk(s,t),C(i,j)))

f(i,j)= f(i,j)+ bk(s,t), where (i,j)Є p(s,t,k)

S1=S1 | {Sk(s,t))

End while
```

The convergence is determined using the following flow as shown in Fig. 3

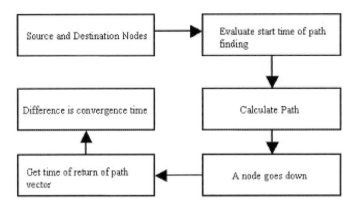

Fig. 3. Calculation of convergence time

The modified BGP decision process with the incorporation of the Intra AS optimization algorithm output for MED value is depicted below:

- The route with the highest "degree of preference" is selected for advertisement.
- For routes with the same degree of preference, the route with the minimum AS-PATH length is chosen.
- For the remaining routes, apply the intra optimal algorithm and set the corresponding cost values determined to be the MED for all the egress routers in each AS.
- For each eligible route from the second step, choose the routes with least Multi exit discriminator (MED) value with the routes compared across all ASes (Note that if there are multiple neighboring ASes, there could be routes with minimal MED values corresponding to each AS.) If there is exactly one such route, this route is chosen.
- Prefer the route learned from E-BGP to the routes learned from I-BGP.
- For multiple I-BGP routes, choose the one with lowest IGP cost value.
- Form the above 5 steps, if there still exist multiple routes, then arbitrarily select the route with the lowest BGP identifier value.

7   Simulation on a Network

The BGP decision process was simulated on a local network and the efficiency of the cost function and the convergence graphs were plotted. The convergence of BGP protocol is important because, with the addition of nodes in the future, it should not result in infinite loops. The convergence of the algorithm was tested by increasing the number of nodes and calculating the convergence time. Fig. 4 and Fig 5 shows the graph outputs for cost function and convergence when the algorithm was simulated on a network.

The cost function graph obtained in Fig. 4 is a marginal cost function curve that takes into account the additional cost incurred at each stage. This is especially important in the case of intra-optimization because, for a network whose traffic changes dynamically, the cost incurred at each step has to relate to the cost of change in the previous step.

The proposed algorithm was simulated on the local network of the campus. This was done to plot the convergence time of the algorithm in an environment with dynamically changing traffic. The scope of coverage was gradually increased to increase the node count. The algorithm always converged and the convergence time did not increase drastically at any point. The results of the convergence time analysis are as shown in Fig. 5.

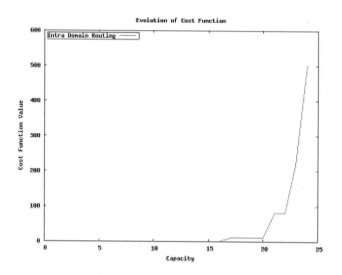

Fig. 4. Graph of cost function

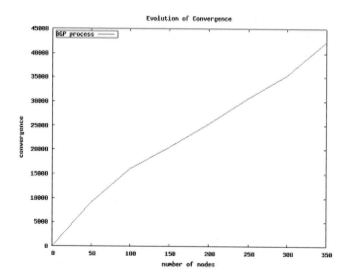

Fig. 5. Graph of convergence of algorithm

8 Conclusion

The value in the MED is advertised to other domains and is used to inform other do-mains of the optimal entry point into the current domain. Current practice is to take the IS-IS metric and insert it as the MED value.

This tends to cause external traffic to enter the domain at the point closest to the exit router. Note that the receiving domain may, based upon policy, choose to ignore the MED that is advertised. However, current practice is to distribute the IGP metric in this way in order to optimize routing wherever possible. This is possible in current networks that only are a single area, but becomes problematic if hierarchy is to be in-stalled into the network. This is again because the loss of end-to-end metric informa-tion means that the MED value will not reflect the true distance across the advertising domain.

Comparing the MED values is not logically correct in the current scenario among the autonomous systems.

This calls for the usage of an optimal flow that takes into account the fact that in-tra- and inter- AS routing are closely coupled and leveraging the joint algorithm to make BGP protocol deterministic. This was shown in this paper, by proposing changes in the MED attribute.

References

1. KalayDjieva, I.: The Border Gateway Protocol and its Convergence Properties. Technical University Munich (2003)
2. http://www.bgp4.as/autonomous-system-numbers
3. Feamster, N., Winick, J., Rexford, J.: A model of BGP routing for network engineering. In: SIGMETRICS (June 2004)
4. Feamster, N., Balakrishnan, H.: Detecting BGP Configuration Faults with Static Analysis. In: Proc. 2nd Symposium on Networked Systems Design and Implementation (NSDI), Boston, MA, pp. 43–56 (May 2005)
5. Ho, K.-H., Howarth, M., Wang, N., Eavlou, D., Georgoulas, S.: Joint Optimization of In-tra- and Inter-Autonomous System Traffic Engineering. Centre for Communication Sys-tems Research, University of Surrey (2006)
6. Griffin, T.G., Wilfong, G.: Analysis of the MED Oscillation Problem in BGP. In: Proc. In-ternational Conference on Network Protocols, pp. 90–99 (2002)
7. Basu, A., Rasala, A., Ong, C.L., Wilfong, G., Shepherd, B.: Route Oscillations in I-BGP with route reflection. In: Proc. SIGCOMM, vol. 32, pp. 235–247 (2002)
8. Sridharan, A., Guerin, R.: The Impact of Traffic Granularity on robustness of Traffic Aware Routing, Technical Report, Multimedia and Networking Lab, University of Penn-sylvanians, U.S. (April 2004)
9. Sridharan, A., et al.: Achieving Near-Optimal Traffic Engineering Solutions for Current OSPF/IS-IS Networks. IEEE ToN 13(2) (2005)
10. Chou, C.T.: Traffic Engineering for MPLS-based Virtual Private Networks. International Journal of Computer and Telecommunication Networking 44, 319–333 (2004)
11. Griffin, T.G., Shepherd, F.B., Wilfong, G.: The stable paths problem and interdomain rout-ing. ToN 10, 232–243 (2002)

Context Aware Mobile Initiated Handoff for Performance Improvement in IEEE 802.11 Networks

Abhijit Sarma, Shantanu Joshi, and Sukumar Nandi

Department of CSE, Indian Institute of Technology, Guwahati, India
abhijit_gu@yahoo.com,
{s.joshi,sukumar}@iitg.ac.in

Abstract. IEEE 802.11 is a widely used wireless LAN standard which offers a good bandwidth at low cost In an ESS, multiple APs can co-exist with overlapping coverage area. A mobile node connects to the AP from which it receives the best signal. Changes in traffic to and from different MNs occur over time. Load imbalance may develop on different APs. Throughput and delay of the different flows passing through the APs, where the load has increased beyond certain limit, may degrade. Different MNs associated to the overloaded APs will experience performance degradation. Overall performance of the ESS will also drop. In this paper we propose a scheme where MNs experiencing degraded performance will initiate action and with assistance from the associate AP perform handoff to less loaded AP within its range to improve performance.

Keywords: Load Balancing, Context Aware Handoff, IEEE 802.11.

1 Introduction

IEEE 802.11 [1] is the most popular standard wireless local area network (WLAN) in which a mobile user can connect to a local area network (LAN) through a wireless connection. Due to low cost and ease of deployment it is gaining popularity day by day Multiple access points (AP) may co-exists with overlapping coverage area. To increase the total available bandwidth and to allow more mobile nodes (MN) to connect, deployment of more than one interconnected AP with overlapping coverage area is usual. A 802.11 WLAN with interconnected APs forms an Extended Service Set (ESS). In an ESS, a MN will connect to the AP from which the MN receives the best signal disregard of the existing load on the different APs within its range. This may lead to an imbalance in the load on the different APs in the ESS. Decrease in performance of the different flows will occur when some APs gets overloaded even if some other APs within the same ESS have spare bandwidth. The applications in the MNs associated to such overloaded APs will experience reduced quality of service (QoS) in terms of throughput, delay and packet loss. The overall throughput of the ESS also suffers. As the load offered to an AP may change dynamically even when there is

N. Meghanathan et al. (Eds.): CCSIT 2011, Part II, CCIS 132, pp. 243–253, 2011.

no change in the number of MNs associated, admission control is not effective in solving this problem. The QoS of the suffering APs and the overall throughput of the ESS may be increased if some load of the overloaded APs can be transfered to the less loaded APs by handing off some of the associated MNs from the overloaded APs to the less loaded APs. In this paper we propose a scheme where the mobile nodes experiencing QoS degradation tries, with the assistance of its associated AP, to handoff to some alternate APs. The MNs experiencing performance loss tries to find alternate APs for handoff. As the MN does not know the load conditions on these APs it does not handoff to such an AP immediately but sends the list of such APs along with its own load information to the associated AP. The associated AP exchanges messages with the given APs to know the load on those APs and based on that, it selects a list of APs to which the MN can handoff and communicates the same to the MN. The MN chooses one of such APs and performs handoff. In this way, loads move from overloaded APs to the less loaded APs. Due to this, the bandwidth is better shared among the APs within an ESS and the overall throughput of the ESS increases.

1.1   Our Contribution

Our main contribution is to increase throughput to meet the offered traffic in an ESS with minimal load adjustment. The following are the salient features of our scheme : -

- Load adjusted only when MNs suffers
- MNs provide the list of APs which are reachable from the MN.
- AP offers alternatives to MN based on load on the MN and load on other APs as provided by MN.
- MN takes the final decision to shift association based on alternatives offered by AP.
- Minimal numbers of MNs changing association.
- APs communicated via infrastructure, MNs and wireless channels are not involved.
- Very low scanning overhead to locate alternate APs.
- Perfect balance is not tried. Balancing only enough to maximize throughput.

The rest of the paper is organized as follows. Section II introduces the IEEE 802.11 ESS. In section III we have a brief introduction to earlier works targeted to performance improvement in IEEE 802.11 WLAN by distributing load among APs. In section IV we describe our scheme. The simulation results are provided in section V. In section VI we conclude.

2   The IEEE 802.11 Extended Service Set

The basic service set (BSS) is a set of 802.11 nodes that can communicate with each other. There are two types of BSSs, namely, independent BSS (IBSS) and infrastructure BSS. An IBSS is an ad-hoc network that contains no access points and as such they can not connect to any other BSS. In an infrastructure BSS there is one access point and some mobile nodes. All communication to and from the MNs must go through the AP. MNs in an infrastructure BSS can communicate with other MNs in its own BSS and other BSSs as well as wired nodes through the AP. Two or more BSS may be interconnected by connecting the APs of each BSS by a distribution system. An ESS is a set of one or more interconnected BSSs. An ESS increases both the coverage area and bandwidth available within the area covered. The distribution system may be connected to other networks so that the stations in the ESS may communicate with other networks connected this way. To avoid disruption of communication to MNs, different APs should have overlapped coverage area. There can be up to fourteen different channels in the 2.4 GHz Industrial, Scientific and Medical (ISM) band in which a 802.11 WLAN may operate. Due to restrictions imposed, not all channels are available in all countries. Channels one to eleven are available in most of the countries. Each channel is of 22 MHz bandwidth but spaced only 5 MHz apart. As such there can be only three non overlapping channels in the eleven channels. Although the APs may operate on overlapping channels, it is not desirable to use overlapping channels in adjacent APs with overlapping coverage area due to interference and resulting performance loss. To increase the available bandwidth in an ESS the APs in an ESS should operate in different non overlapping channels.

3   Related Works

Most of the existing works target to performance improvement in terms of delay and throughput in 802.11 multi AP networks are centered around balancing load in the different APs. There are several such works. Gilbert Sawma et. el. presented a scheme in [2] where the loads in the APs are adjusted dynamically whenever a new MN tries to associate to an AP and the AP is already overloaded. In their scheme, several MNs are directed to change AP to balance the load. In their scheme, balancing is done only when a new MN is associated to the WLAN but if load changes due to increase in load from already associated AP no balancing is done. Moreover, the decision to switch APs is made solely by the AP based on the load condition of APs only. In the scheme presented in [3] a periodic probing is used in each MN which requires about 300 ms per probe. This recurring disruption in communication is unacceptable for real time traffic. The scheme also takes only AP load into account. In [4] also the load of only AP is considered. In [5] the authors are considering RSSI only for load balancing. However, RSSI can not be a good indicator of load. In [6] the AP decides which MNs should handoff. Also, the nearby access points are found by the AP. In [7] a static assignment of channels an placement of AP is done. It does not cater for the dynamic changes in the load pattern. In [8], [9] and [10] the decision is taken centrally and MNs are directed to move all at once. In [11] The decision is solely based on MN. AP broadcasts its load information through beacons. In [9] cell breathing technique as used in cellular mobiles is used. In this technique, the MNs are forced to handoff irrespective of their load condition and desire. In [12] a decision is taken centrally in an AP. In this scheme the throughput per AP is used as a metric for load.

4   The Scheme

The existing load balancing scheme in 802.11 infrastructure networks are found inadequate. In this paper we propose a scheme where load in an ESS having different APs with overlapped coverage area are adjusted by changing the association of MNs which experience degradation of performance. The adjustment is aimed at improving the throughput and delay of the suffering MNs and hence the ESS as a whole.

4.1   Assumptions

The following assumptions are made: -

- APs are connected through a backbone and form an ESS.
- APs have overlapping coverage area.
- Overlapping BSSs operate in non overlapping channels.

4.2   Details of the Scheme

Whenever a MN senses a degradation of performance, it scans the different channels to find suitable APs to which it can perform handoff. The degradation of performance is detected using the methods which are presented in subsection 4.3

To avoid the long scanning latency, the MN scans using interleaved scanning technique which is a modified version of the scanning technique used in [13]. This scanning technique is explained later. The MN thus collects a list of APs with which it can associate if needed. Let the list of such APs be called $APList$. The MN then informs its associated AP, say AP_a about its desire to disassociate from AP_a and re associate with another AP where a better performance may be expected. To do this, the MN sends a $MoveRequest$ message containing the $APList$ and its desired throughput to AP_a. The MN keeps updating the exponentially weighted moving average (EWMA) [14] of the queue length and sends the $MoveRequest$ message repeatedly at a fixed interval of t_{repeat}, for upto n_{repeat} times or until it gets a response from AP_a. Whenever AP_a receives a $MoveRequest$ message from a MN, it sends a $LoadRequest$ message to all the APs in the $APList$ through the backbone. The APs receiving the $LoadRequest$ message, replies with a $LoadResponse$ message through the backbone containing its current load status. AP_a receives the $LoadReesponse$ messages within a given time and based on the replies it receives and the $APList$ it received from the MN, selects zero or more APs to which the MN can handoff. AP_a keeps the list of such APs in $HCList$.

Let AP_i be the ith AP in the ESS. Let the concerned MN be associated to the jth AP. Let L_a be the traffic passing through the jth AP. Let L_i be the traffic passing through the ith AP and M is the load on the MN. Let also the set of APs in the $HCList$ be HC. Then: -

$$HC = \{AP_i | i \neq j \text{ and } L_i - M - L_a > \phi\} \tag{1}$$

Where L_i , M, L_a and ϕ are traffic volume in bits per second. ϕ is a small fraction of the maximum throughput. The value of ϕ is chosen considering the fact that, if it is too small, the MN that performed handoff to get better performance will tend to handoff again and too many handoffs may occur unnecessarily. If it is too large, potential opportunity to increase performance may be lost.

AP_a sends the $HCList$ in its reply message, $HTMsg$, to the MN. The MN, based on the RSSI, selects one of the APs in this list and performs handoff to that AP. The MN selects the AP from which it receives the strongest RSSI. It is likely that more than one MN sends $MoveRequest$ messages to AP_a. If all such MNs are allowed to handoff to another AP, a severe imbalance in load may result. To prevent it, whenever AP_a processes a $MoveRequest$ message, it drops all further $MoveRequest$ from any MN for some fixed period of time T_{ignore}.

4.3   Detection of Performance Degradation

The degradation of performance is sensed in two different ways. In the first method, the packet drop rate is used to sense the degradation of performance. A moving average of the number of packet dropped within a time window is kept. In this whenever the average increases above some threshold, the MN tries to find an alternate AP for association. It is observed that, when the traffic in the ESS increases gradually, packets gets delayed considerably even when the throughput does not get effected significantly. So, changing the association of MNs when degradation of performance is sensed this way will result in improvement of performance in terms of throughput but there may be still degradation of performance in terms of delay. In the second method the degradation of performance is sensed by observing the interface queue length. To smooth out the variations in the interface queue length the EWMA of the queue length is calculated every t units of time. Let E_t be the EWMA of the queue length at time t. Let E_{t-1} be the EWMA of the queue length at time $t-1$ and let Y_{t-1} be the actual queue length at time $t-1$. Then we calculate E_t as

$$E_t = \alpha \times Y_{t-1} + (1 - \alpha) \times E_{t-1} \ , \ 0 < \alpha \leq 1 \ , \ t \geq 3 \tag{2}$$

The value of α decides how fast the MN forgets the old values of Y. Whenever E_t crosses a threshold, the MN tries to find an alternate AP for association.

4.4   Interleaved Scanning

In the proposed scheme the scanning and data communication is interleaved in time. The MN keeps the information of different APs found during scanning in a list. Let the list be $APList$. When the MN senses degradation of performance, it prepares a circular list of channel numbers to scan. These are the channels that contains all the 802.11 channels except the current channel and the channels that overlaps with the current channel. It initializes a variable *NextChannel* to the channel number of the first channel in the list. It empties *APList*. It also starts a timer. We shall refer this timer as *ScanTimer*. Let the time out value of this timer be T. At the expiry of time T when the timer event is triggered the MN does the following in order: -

- it stops communicating in the channel in which it is communicating with the associated AP.
- it deletes all entries from *APList* where the channel number of the AP equals *NextChannel*.
- it changes channel to *NextChannel*.
- it sends a probe request and waits for a time period of t_1.
- if any probe response or beacon is found or the channel is busy during t_1 time period it extends the waiting time by another period of t_2.
- if any probe response or beacon is found within the waiting time, the AP information obtained are put into *APList*.
- it changes channel to the channel in which it was communicating with its associated AP.
- it updates *NextChannel* to the entry which is cyclically next to the current value of *NextChannel* in the channel list.
- it starts *ScanTimer* again and starts normal communication.

As the *ScanTimer* is restarted, it will be triggered again and the whole process will repeat again. Till that time normal communication continues. The timer is canceled when all the channels in the circular list of channels are scanned.

4.5   Choice of Load Metric

Load metric is an important aspect of a load balancing system. There may be several choices for measuring the load. Global System for Mobile Communications (GSM) uses number of calls to measure load. In GSM each call takes equal amount of bit rate and so number of call is a good metric in GSM. In WLAN, different flows require different bit rates. In [15] the authors show that metric based on measured traffic is a good metric for load balancing in WLAN. In [16], Number of competing stations is used as metric for load. In [10] the authors use wireless medium busy time (MBT) as the metric. In [17], the authors define client utilization estimate (CUE) as the fraction of time per time unit needed to transmit the flow over the network. CUE is an indicator of network resource usage. CUE is also used in [2] as load metric. In our scheme, we use traffic as load metric. However, for the initiation of the load adjustment process, in the MNs, we use packet drop and EWMA of the interface queue length to sense degradation of performance. Packet drop and EWMA of queue length gives an early indication of performance degradation.

5   Simulation Results

The proposed handoff scheme is simulated using ns-3 (version 3.8) [18] network simulator. We have modified ns-3 to implement the proposed scheme. In this section we present simulation results to demonstrate the performance of our scheme. Using the experiment, the initialization process and performance of the ESS with respect to throughput and delay are verified. The AP selection procedure is not verified.

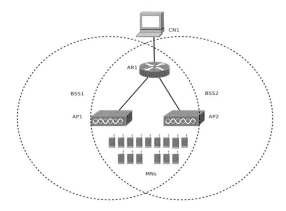

Fig. 1. Experiment Setup

5.1   Experiment Setup

As shown in Fig. 1, two BSSs, namely BSS1 and BSS2 are setup. Access points AP1 and AP2 are placed in BSS1 and BSS2 respectively. Fifteen MNs are placed in such a way that it falls in the coverage area of both BSS1 and BSS2. The dotted circles centered at the APs are the coverage area of the respective APs. AP1 and AP2 and a correspondent node CN1 are connected to the access router AR1 through point to point links each having a bandwidth of 100Mbps and delay 2 ms. The BSSs operate at different non overlapping channels in the 2.4 GHz ISM band and operate using the IEEE 802.11b standard. All the MNs initially operate in the channel of BSS1 and are associated to AP1. Constant bit rate (CBR) traffic are setup to flow from each MN to CN1. We kept the the default RTS-CTS threshold of ns3 which is set at 1500. Each MN sends packets of size 1500 bytes every 20 ms. The ith MN starts its traffic at the ith second. The initiation of the load adjustment is done by MNs based on rise in packet drop and rise in queue length. Three cases are studied. In case I, whenever the packet drop rate increases beyond 1% the MNs starts the process to handoff to another AP. In case II and case III, whenever the MN finds a rise in queue length beyond certain limit, say $qlength$, it starts the process of handoff. In case II $qlength$ is set at 10 and in case III it is set at a very low value of 1.3. The value of α as in Equation (2) is set to 0.1. The threshold ϕ as in Equation (1) is set at 250

250   A. Sarma, S. Joshi, and S. Nandi

kbps. T_{ignore} is set to 1 second. t_{repeat} is set to 200 ms and n_{repeat} is set to 4. Throughputs of each AP are measured at each second. The packet delay, that is the time the packet takes from transmission of the packet by the UDP client generating the CBR traffic, to the reception of the packet by the UDP server at the destination, is also measured for observing the performance of the scheme.

5.2   Results and Discussions

The results of our experiments are presented from Fig. 2 to Fig. 7. Fig. 2, Fig. 3, and Fig. 4 gives the load vs throughput for AP1, AP2 and the whole ESS for the cases I, II and III respectively. Fig. 5, Fig. 6 and Fig. 7 gives the delay incurred by different packets in AP1 for case I, case II and case III respectively. The total ESS throughput without using our scheme is put in each of Fig. 2 to Fig. 4 for ease of comparison. From the results we observe that when packet drop is used to sense performance degradation, the detection occurs late and when adjustment of load is done, the delay remains quite high. The throughput of the ESS drops a little and it takes some time for the throughput to recover. The detection occurs early when EWMA of queue length is used to detect performance degradation. An early adjustment avoids the loss of throughput. In all the cases, the network capacity increases when our scheme is used.

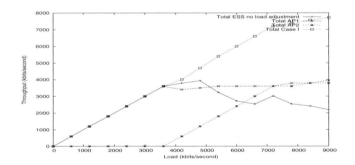

Fig. 2. Throughput vs load :Case I

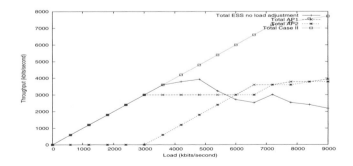

Fig. 3. Throughput vs load :Case II

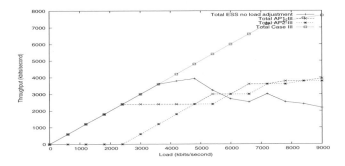

Fig. 4. Throughput vs load :Case III

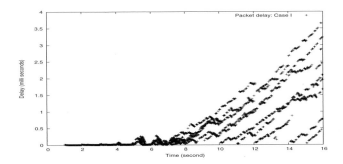

Fig. 5. Delay characteristics :Case I

The delay is high when adjustment is done late as in case I and case II. For significant improvement in delay, sensing should be very early as in case III. The sensing should be such that it detects a very small rise in the EWMA value of the queue length an adjustment in load is done. The possible explanation for this is, if the EWMA of queue length rises considerably, the queue length is already high and even after the time the load is adjusted, packets take some significant time to pass through the queue. If the load is not excessively high, the queue length eventually decays. At high load, which is higher than the case if detection and adjustment is earlier like case III, the queue length decays slowly and the delay remains high during this period. In case II, the threshold value of EWMA of queue length is set at 10 and no significant reduction in delay is observed. In case III, the threshold is set at a low value of 1.3 and the detection and adjustment is sufficiently early and there is significant improvement in delay.

The best throughputs are observed when number of MNs per AP is within six. The lowest delays are observed when number of MNs per APs are within five. When total number of MNs increases beyond twelve, throughput and delay of the whole ESS suffers as the ESS can no longer take the load without loss of performance. The handoff latency in all cases are observed to be within 50 ms.

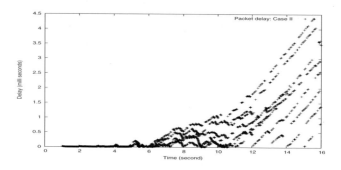

Fig. 6. Delay characteristics :Case II

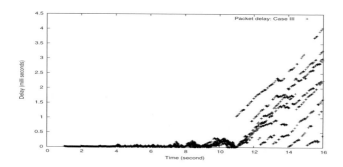

Fig. 7. Delay characteristics :Case III

6   Conclusion

In this paper we have proposed a scheme to adjust the load of APs in a WLAN whenever the MNs in some APs suffer from degradation of performance while other APs have spare capacity. By so adjusting the load, the performance as seen from the MNs as well as the overall performance of the WLAN increase. This performance increase occurs in terms of both throughput and delay. Instead of a complete load balancing, performance improvement is done only by adjusting association of one MN at a time. The proposed scheme is tested by simulation. The results show clear performance improvement of an ESS in terms of throughput and delay.

References

1. IEEE Std 802.11-1999, Part 11: Wireless LAN Medium Access Control (MAC) and Physical Layer (PHY) Specifications, IEEE, Édition (1999)
2. Sawma, G., Aib, I., Ben-El-Kezadri, R., Pujolle, G.: ALBA: An autonomic load balancing algorithm for IEEE 802.11 wireless networks. In: IEEE/IFIP Network Operations and Management Symposium (NOMS), pp. 891–894 (2008)

3. Gong, H., Kim, J.: Dynamic load balancing through association control of mobile users in WiFi networks. IEEE Transactions on Consumer Electronics 54(2), 342–348 (2008)
4. Ong, E.H., Khan, J.Y.: An integrated load balancing scheme for future wireless networks. In: Proceedings of the 4th International Conference on Wireless Pervasive Computing, ISWPC 2009, pp. 103–108 (2009)
5. Sheu, S., Wu, C.: Dynamic load balance algorithm (DLBA) for IEEE 802.11 wireless LAN, tamkang. Journal of Science and Engineering 2 (1999)
6. IEEE Std 802.11k-2008, Part 11: Wireless LAN Medium Access Control (MAC) and Physical Layer (PHY) Specifications Amendment 1: Radio Resource Measurement of Wireless LANs, IEEE, Édition (2008)
7. Lee, Y., Kim, K., Choi, Y.: Optimization of AP placement and channel assignment in wireless LANs. In: Proceedings of the 27th Annual IEEE Conference on Local Computer Networks, LCN 2002, pp. 831–836 (2002)
8. Bejerano, Y., Han, S., Li, L.: Fairness and load balancing in wireless LANs using association control. In: Proceedings of the 10th Annual International Conference on Mobile Computing and Networking, MobiCom 2004, pp. 315–329 (2004)
9. Bejerano, Y., Han, S.: Cell breathing techniques for load balancing in wireless LANs. IEEE Transactions on Mobile Computing 8(6), 735–749 (2009)
10. Daher, R., Tavangarian, D.: Resource reservation and admission control in IEEE 802.11 WLANs. In: Proceedings of the 3rd International Conference on Quality of Service in Heterogeneous Wired/Wireless Networks, QShine 2006, article 4 (2006)
11. Du, L., Jeong, M.R., Yamada, A., Bai, Y., Chen, L.: QoS aware access point selection for pre-load-balancing in multi-BSSs WLAN. In: IEEE Wireless Communications and Networking Conference (WCNC), pp. 1634–1638 (2008)
12. Velayos, H., Aleo, V., Karlsson, G.: Load balancing in overlapping wireless LAN cells. In: Proceedings IEEE International Conference on Communications, vol. 7, pp. 3833–3836 (2004)
13. Sarma, A., Gupta, R.K., Nandi, S.: A zone based interleaved scanning technique for fast handoff in IEEE 802.11 wireless networks. In: Proceedings of the 10th International Symposium on Pervasive Systems, Algorithms, and Networks, ISPAN 2009, pp. 232–237 (2009)
14. Engineering Statistics Handbook, Single Exponential Smoothing, http://www.itl.nist.gov/div898/handbook/pmc/section4/pmc431.htm
15. Bianchi, G., Tinnirello, I.: Improving load balancing mechanisms in wireless packet networks. In: IEEE International Conference on Communications, pp. 891–895 (2002)
16. Tinnirello, I., Sgora, A.: A kalman filter approach for distinguishing channel and collision errors in IEEE 802.11 networks. In: Global Telecommunications Conference (GLOBECOM), pp. 5329–5333 (2008)
17. Garg, S., Kappes, M.: Admission control for VoIP traffic in IEEE 802.11 networks. In: Global Telecommunications Conference (GLOBECOM), vol. 6, pp. 3514–3518. IEEE, Los Alamitos (2003)
18. The Network Simulator - ns-3, http://www.nsnam.org

Safety Information Gathering and Dissemination in Vehicular Ad hoc Networks: Cognitive Agent Based Approach

M.S. Kakkasageri[1] and S.S. Manvi[2]

[1] Department of Electronics and Communication Engg.
Basaveshwar Engineering College, Bagalkot-587102, India
[2] Department of Electronics and Communication Engg.
Reva Institute of Technology and Management, Bangalore-560064, India
mahabalesh@becbgk.edu, sunil.manvi@revainstitution.org

Abstract. Today's vehicles have capability of sensing, computing, and communicating capabilities. Different embedded components in a vehicle constantly exchange available information among them as well as with other vehicles on the road for cooperative, driving safety and comfort known as Vehicular Ad hoc Network (VANET). In VANET, critical information like navigation, cooperative collision avoidance, lane-changing, speed limit, accident, obstacle or road condition warnings, etc. play a significant role for safety-related applications. Such kind of critical information gathering and dissemination is challenging, because of their delay-sensitive nature. In this position paper, we propose a cognitive agent based framework (using Belief Desire Intention model) that consists of heavy-weight static and light-weight mobile agents. Proposed framework executes push (gather/store and disseminate) and pull (gather/store) operations on information gathered based on information relevance and importance. We provide a model to explore the gathering and dissemination capacity of the cognitive agent framework.

Keywords: Vehicular ad hoc networks, Cognitive agents, BDI architecture, Bayesian network learning.

1 Introduction

Vehicular ad hoc networks (VANETs) have recently attracted the attention of researchers, automotive industry, and governments for their potential of improving safety of the surrounding environment through either infrastructureless, vehicle-to-vehicle (V2V) or infrastructure based wireless communications. VANETs vision include applications such as route planning, road safety, e-commerce, entertainment in vehicles, cooperative driver assistance, sharing traffic and road conditions, user interactions, information services, etc. [1]-[6].

Major driving factor for investigation and deployment of the VANET is safety. Safety applications coexist with non-safety applications such as traffic information systems, commercial services, messaging (beaconing), etc. Although a separate control channel is used in DSRC (Dedicated Short Range Communications)

N. Meghanathan et al. (Eds.): CCSIT 2011, Part II, CCIS 132, pp. 254–264, 2011.
© Springer-Verlag Berlin Heidelberg 2011

for safety-related applications [7], applications still have to contend for the channel. Safety applications must rely on very accurate and up to date information about surrounding environment, which in turn requires the use of positioning systems and communication protocols for exchanging information. Communication protocols should guarantee fast and reliable delivery of information to all vehicles in which communication medium is shared, highly unreliable, and has limited bandwidth.

Cognitive software agents based applications is an emerging discipline which can be applied to provide flexible, adaptable, and intelligent services in VANETs. Software agents are autonomous and intelligent programs that execute tasks on behalf of a process or a user [8]-[10]. A cognitive agent provides reasoning like humans for decision making. A common approach to model cognitive agents is a BDI (belief, desire, intention) architecture. BDI-based framework acts as an assistant to a human user by performing tasks on user behalf or a process. BDI model has become predominant architecture for the design of cognitive agents [11].

The BDI model provides an explicit, declarative representation of three key mental structures of an agent: informational attitudes about the world (beliefs), motivational attitudes on what to do (desires) and deliberative commitments to act (intentions). BDI architecture basically rests on two main processes: deliberation and means-end reasoning. Deliberation is process by which an agent generates its intentions on basis of its beliefs and desires, while means-end reasoning consists in planning a sequence of actions to execute as an attempt at satisfying its intentions.

The problem addressed in the paper is critical information gathering and dissemination using software cognitive agents by considering the criticalness of information. Vehicles autonomously collect, classify and disseminate critical information using cognitive agents.

1.1 Proposed Work

This paper proposes cognitive agent based critical information gathering and dissemination in VANETs, which uses a set of static and mobile agents. Static agent is an autonomous program which executes on a host. Mobile agent is an itinerant agent consisting of program, data and execution state information which migrates from one host to another host in a heterogeneous network and executes at a remote host until it completes a given task. Agents require an agent platform at host vehicle. Agent platform provides services like communication, navigation, agent creation, security, persistence, deliberation, cooperation, collaboration, etc.

Three types of agents are used in scheme: Vehicle Manager Agent (VMA), Critical Information Push Agent (CIPSA) and Critical Information Pull Agent (CIPLA). All agents are located in an information agency of a vehicle. VMA is a static cognitive agent whereas CIPSA and CIPLA are mobile agents. VMA uses BDI (Belief-Desire-Intention) model to employ cognition.

In this work, push and pull approach are used for critical information dissemination and gathering respectively. In push, vehicles automatically and immediately broadcast critical event without waiting for the explicit time as well store the event. In contrast, a pull approach only stores the event in vehicle since event information is less critical and may be later accessed by vehicles in network, i.e., information is distributed on demand basis to the other vehicles in network.

The scheme operates in following steps. (1) Periodically sensed values from the environment through vehicle sensors are considered as belief sets of VMA. (2) Belief sets lead to the generation of beliefs for VMA. (3) VMA develops desire as push or pull. (4) If belief and desire are completely matched, intention is executed. (5) Otherwise modified desire is generated for an event. (6) This desire decides the intention to be executed (either push or pull). (7) Once intention is finalized, either CIPSA (for push) or CIPLA (for pull) is triggered.

1.2   Our Contributions

More specifically our contributions includes the following.

1. Design of cognitive agents based dynamic push-pull algorithm for critical information gathering and dissemination which optimizes overall delay of push and pull information.
2. Belief-Desire-Intention based approach for detection of an event as push or pull.
3. Elimination of unnecessary transmission of all the generated /received events of a vehicle saves the bandwidth significantly.
4. Usage of cognitive agents for delivering critical information either in push or pull mode provides reliability in delivering critical/noncritical information.

Rest of the paper is organized as follows. Cognitive agent based framework for critical information gathering and dissemination is given in section 2. Section 3 concludes paper and explains future work.

2   Cognitive Agent Based Critical Information Gathering and Dissemination

In this section, we describe network environment and cognitive agency for critical information gathering/dissemination in VANETs.

2.1   Network Environment

In this section, we introduce network environment used in the analysis of scheme for critical information gathering and dissemination in VANETs. We consider a VANET in which N number of vehicles are separated by the safety distance (between consecutive vehicles) S_d. Proposed VANET is purely based on vehicle-to-vehicle (V2V) architecture, where both the collection and the restitution of information are done within the VANET. We assume that vehicles move in an urban road scenario as shown in figure 1. All vehicles are equipped with

General Positioning Systems (GPS) and on-board communication devices for communication. Each vehicle is loaded with location digital map and is concerned about road information ahead of it on its direction. Each vehicle communicates with other vehicle within its communication range R. If the neighbor vehicle is not within communication range R, the vehicle delivers critical data to the data center "D", which may be associated with traffic light at cross junction.

All vehicles are assumed to have several sensors. Safety information in vehicle is determined by particular set of sensors. For example, tyre pressure and vehicle speed sensors are responsible for safety speed driving. Traffic density sensor, accident sensor (body pressure sensor) and vehicle speed sensor together sense the occurrence of accident, which will be disseminated for further decisions for driving.

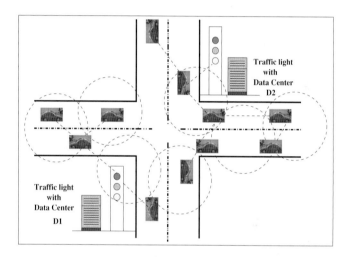

Fig. 1. Network environment

2.2 Cognitive Agency

Proposed agent framework for critical information gathering and dissemination is based on push-pull concept. For critical events, proposed scheme takes appropriate decisions (push or pull) as and when required. Using push approach, we can efficiently use bandwidth by broadcasting only the critical events that are detected (like accidents, heavy rain, fog, etc.) to the vehicles in VANET. In pull approach, non-critical applications (like road conditions, vehicle speed, etc.,) can be stored within vehicle itself.

The framework comprises of cognitive information agency. Components of agency and their interactions are depicted in figure 2. Agency consists of knowledge base (consists of critical information details and running application(s) details), static agents and mobile agents. Static agent is Vehicle Manager Agent (VMA). Mobile agents are Critical Information Push Agent (CIPSA) and Critical Information Pull Agent (CIPLA).

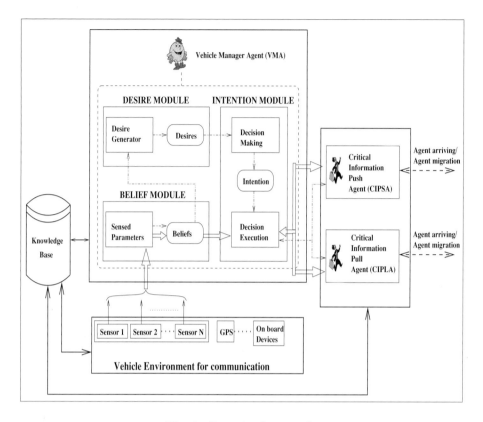

Fig. 2. Cognitive framework

Knowledge Base (KB): It comprises of information of node ID, neighbors list, available bandwidth for communication, node status (connected/disconnected to network), total number of critical information available, information status (old/new) and push/pull event of past and present critical information. KB is read or updated by VMA, CIPSA and CIPLA.

Vehicle Manager Agent: It is a static cognitive agent based on BDI model that runs in a node, creates agents and knowledge base, controls and coordinates activities of cognitive agency. This agent triggers CIPSA for pushing critical information, and CIPLA for delivering pulled information to vehicles in network. Belief set, desire and intention generation are part of VMA functions which are given as follows.

Belief set (μ) generation: VMA updates its beliefs according to sensed values from sensors and action taken in its knowledge base. Sensed parameters in knowledge base are shown in Table 1. We assumed that sensor has two states: LOW and HIGH. If sensor reading is greater than or equal to threshold value (assuming that threshold value is decided by VMA), then sensor state is treated as HIGH, otherwise it is LOW.

Table 1. Vehicle sensors and corresponding safety applications

Safety applications	Examples	Sensors	Sensor states	Action
Pre crash sensing	Approaching Emergency vehicle warning, Highway merge warning, etc.	Image sensor	LOW/HIGH	Push/Pull
		Speed sensor	LOW/HIGH	
		Engine pressure sensor	LOW/HIGH	
		Body pressure sensor	LOW/HIGH	
		Resettable crash sensor	LOW/HIGH	
		Tyre pressure sensor	LOW/HIGH	
Post crash sensing	Accident happened, Transmission of accident images to hospital, etc.	Speed sensor	LOW/HIGH	Push/Pull
		Engine pressure sensor	LOW/HIGH	
		Body pressure sensor	LOW/HIGH	
		Resettable crash sensor	LOW/HIGH	
		Tyre pressure sensor	LOW/HIGH	
Dangerous road and environmental conditions	Blind curve warning, Narrow/low bridge warning, Heavy rain situation Heavy fog situation	Wiper speed sensor	LOW/HIGH	Push/Pull
		Image sensor	LOW/HIGH	
		Rain sensor	LOW/HIGH	
		Rain light sensor	LOW/HIGH	
		Tyre pressure sensor	LOW/HIGH	
Driving assistance applications	Vehicle detection and registration, Visibility enhancing, Breakdown warning, Stolen down tracking	Break sensor	LOW/HIGH	Push/Pull
		Vehicle detection and registration sensor	LOW/HIGH	
		Image sensor	LOW/HIGH	

Generation of belief sets from the Table 1 is as follows. VMA observes individual sensor states for a fixed time window T (where T represents time duration from t_x to $t_{x'}$ where $t_{x'} > t_x$). During this time window, out of total transitions (T_{lh}), VMA counts number of LOW transitions $((T_l))$ and HIGH transitions $((T_h))$. Finally, VMA computes sensor state as either HIGH or LOW.

For example, probability of occurrence of HIGH state, $P(H)$ is given by equation (1).

$$P(H) = T_h/T_{lh} \tag{1}$$

If $P(H) \geq 0.5$, then sensor state is predicted as HIGH, otherwise the state is LOW. In this way for a fixed time window, all sensor states are predicted as either LOW or HIGH and leads to sensor status set σ. For example, pre crash sensing application sensor status set (σ) may be $\{\sigma = L, H, L, L, H, L\}$. Each sensor status set is associated with an action p (either push or pull). p may take the value of 0 or 1, i.e., "$p = 0$" means push and "$p = 1$" means pull.

For different time intervals (m), σ is generated as $\{\sigma_1, \sigma_2 .... \sigma_m\}$. Based on the sensor status set and the corresponding action, event belief set μ is generated. At time interval t_1, event belief set is $\mu_1 = \{\sigma_1, p\}$. For m^{th} time interval, event belief set is $\mu_m = \{\sigma_m, p\}$.

Belief ξ is generated by using event belief sets. For a particular time window, belief may be expressed as $\xi = \{\mu_1, \mu_2 ...\}$. For different time windows, $beliefs = \{\xi_1, \xi_2, ... \xi_n\}$, where n is the number of different time windows.

Desire (p) and Intention (ζ) generation: Desire and intention generation for an event is core part of cognition capabilities of VMA. A determined desire p (either push or pull) for current captured sensor status set σ_{cap} is generated using belief, if and only if all conditions leading to its generation are satisfied i.e., σ_{cap} is matching with either σ_1 or σ_2, ... or σ_n of belief ξ initially stored in knowledge base of cognitive agency. If σ is matching neither to σ_1 or σ_2, ...or σ_n, a desire (p') is generated. Generation of desire (p') is explained in following sequence.

1. **Extraction of nearest matching event belief sets**
   Let $\{\sigma_{cap} = L, H, L, L, H, L\}$ be event that has happened, which is having ambiguity to match with contents in the belief ξ. For this σ_{cap}, extract nearest matching event belief sets from belief ξ. Extraction of nearest matching event belief sets is done by comparing sensor states of σ_{cap} with sensor states of σ_1 to σ_n. If matching factor, $\kappa \geq \Theta$, then event belief set is nearest match for σ_{cap}. Matching factor κ is defined as ratio of total number of matching sensed parameters (C) to total number of available sensed parameters (K) in an event belief set. i.e., $\kappa = C/K$. Θ is in range of '0' to '1' and is decided by VMA.

2. **Segregation of matched belief sets**
   From extracted event belief sets, segregate them based on actions with $p = push$ or $p = pull$. From knowledge base, reorganize segregated event belief sets from sequence number 1 to x and 1 to y for push and pull actions, respectively. Matching sensor status sets for $p = push$ is $\sigma_{push} = \{\sigma_1, \sigma_2, ... \sigma_x\}$ and for $p = pull$ is $\sigma_{pull} = \{\sigma_1, \sigma_2, ... \sigma_y\}$, where $(x + y) < n$.

3. **Computation of joint density function for push and pull**
   Joint density function for σ_{push} is given by equation (2)

   $$f(\sigma_1, ... \sigma_x \mid push) = f(\sigma_1 \mid push) \cdot \cdot f(\sigma_x \mid push) \qquad (2)$$

   Using maximum likelihood,
   $L(push \mid \sigma_1, \sigma_2, ... \sigma_x) = \Pi_{i=1}^{x} f(\sigma_i \mid push)$.
   Using log-likelihood,

$\hat{l}(push \mid \sigma_1, \sigma_2, ...\sigma_x) = (1/x) \cdot ln \cdot L$
$= (1/x) \sum_{i=1}^{x} ln(\sigma_i \mid push)$
Maximum likelihood estimator (MLE) of 'push' is,
$\hat{push}_{mle} = arg_{(\sigma \epsilon \xi)} \ max \ \hat{l}(push \mid \sigma_1, \sigma_2, ...\sigma_x)$

Joint density function for σ_{pull} is given by equation (3)

$$f(\sigma_1, ...\sigma_y \mid pull) = f(\sigma_1 \mid pull) \cdot \cdot f(\sigma_y \mid pull) \qquad (3)$$

Using maximum likelihood,
$L(pull \mid \sigma_1, \sigma_2, ...\sigma_y) = \Pi_{i=1}^{y} f(\sigma_i \mid pull).$
Using log-likelihood,
$\hat{l}(pull \mid \sigma_1, \sigma_2, ...\sigma_y) = (1/y) \cdot ln \cdot L$
$= (1/y) \sum_{i=1}^{y} ln(\sigma_i \mid pull)$
MLE of 'pull' is given by
$\hat{pull}_{mle} = arg_{(\sigma \epsilon \xi)} \ max \ \hat{l}(pull \mid \sigma_1, \sigma_2, ...\sigma_y)$

4. **Desire selection:** Based on $\hat{push}_{mle}$ and $\hat{pull}_{mle}$, generated desire p' is selected as follows.
   $p' = max(\hat{push}_{mle}, \hat{pull}_{mle})$
5. Beliefs and desire are updated with σ and p' respectively.

Intention ζ of VMA is value associated with p_i of one of belief set i if γ matches with belief set i in beliefs ξ, otherwise p'. Functioning of VMA is depicted in algorithm 1 in an informal way.

Algorithm 1. Functioning of VMA
Function: Senses and takes decisions.

1. : Begin
2. : Sense parameters from sensors;
3. : Generate belief sets and beliefs;
4. : On occurrence of an event, check in beliefs for its
       presence;
5. :   IF {event is found in beliefs}
6. :   THEN {Desire = push/pull associated with event;
                  Intention = Desire};
7. :   ELSE {generate desire; update beliefs with event
               and desire};
8. :   Execute intention based on generated desire;
9. : End

Critical Information Push Agent (CIPSA): It is a mobile agent, employed to push critical information to other vehicles in network. It is triggered by VMA that travels around network by creating its clones (a clone is a similar copy of agent with different destination addresses) and disseminates critical information. For each visited vehicle, it updates KB in coordination with VMA of vehicle.

It is assumed that all vehicles have GPS facility and loaded with digital road map. VMA in each vehicle has knowledge of road length, road width, number of lanes and current position of the vehicle. Operation sequence of CIPSA are as follows.

1. Whenever critical information is detected source vehicle VMA identifies it's location based on the GPS.
2. VMA classifies the critical information dissemination area into four quadrants. First quadrant θ_1 covers 0^0 to 90^0, second quadrant θ_2 covers 90^0 to 180^0, third quadrant θ_3 covers 180^0 to 270^0 and fourth quadrant θ_4 covers 270^0 to 360^0.
3. VMA considers dissemination area as a pair of quadrant, considering source vehicle position and direction of travel. Pair of quadrant may be either θ_2 and θ_4 or θ_1 and θ_3. This helps to find the affecting area in VANET, i.e., vehicles moving towards to source vehicle.
4. VMA triggers CIPSA to move in any one of the quadrant (dissemination area).
5. CIPSA delivers critical information to all vehicles in the dissemination area. While delivering critical information to a vehicle, CIPSA also encapsulates available critical information in visited vehicle for delivery to other vehicles.
6. Encapsulated critical information is delivered to all vehicles on the way.
7. Once the CIPSA finds boundary vehicle of dissemination area (assuming vehicle has a mechanism to detect boundary of VANET based on GPS coordinates with respect to source vehicle), CIPSA queries for data centers. Data centers are usually attached with traffic lights, mobile towers, etc.
8. CIPSA pours critical information to data centers and destroys itself.

Usage of mobile agent CIPSA exhibits following advantages compared to traditional dissemination schemes.

- Reliability of information dissemination is better.
- Disseminating critical information in particular area helps to minimize congestion.
- CIPSA identifies beneficial vehicles with help of GPS. This helps to minimize information saturation time.
- While delivering critical information, CIPSA also encapsulates observed information for possible delivery to all the vehicles. This helps to use available bandwidth efficiently.
- CIPSA also identifies data centers by interacting with VMA. This helps to maximize critical information dissemination without much effort.

Critical Information Pull Agent (CIPLA): VMA triggers CIPLA when vehicle is interested to retrieve latest information like fog, weather condition, etc. available in other vehicles of a network. VMA knows relative positions of neighbor vehicles using stored road maps, by mapping vehicle's latitude and longitude coordinates to points on road in which vehicle is driving. Operation sequence of CIPLA are as follows.

1. VMA triggers CIPLA by mentioning required information and destination.
2. With the help of GPS, VMA gives its upfront neighbors list to CIPLA (source vehicle is interested in information available in forward direction).
3. From source vehicle, CIPLA moves in forward direction towards its required destination hopping from one vehicle to another.
4. At each visited vehicle, CIPLA interacts with VMA.
5. If required information or nearest matching information is available in visited vehicle, CIPLA sends back information to source vehicle. Otherwise, it updates itself and moves forward by using vehicle positioning information (based on GPS) till it reaches destination (based on GPS and Road maps). In this way CIPLA roams around network.
6. Once CIPLA reaches a vehicle at destination, it traces back to source with information picked at visited vehicles.
7. If CIPLA does not find a vehicle to reach vehicles at destination, it sends available information to source and keeps waiting for certain duration around place until it finds a vehicle moving towards required destination. Similarly, it performs waiting operation when moving towards source.

Usage of mobile agent CIPLA exhibits following advantages compared to traditional request/reply mechanism.

- Reliability of getting requested information is better.
- CIPLA querying for required information in forward direction helps in identifying relevant information for source vehicle.
- CIPLA has capability (by having some parameters related to required information) of identifying nearest matching information at visited vehicle.

3   Conclusion and Future Work

Vehicular ad hoc networks provide an exciting area of research at intersection of a number of disciplines and technologies. There is a good future for applications of VANET, ranging from diagnostic, safety tools, information services and traffic monitoring and management to in-car digital entertainment and business services. However, for these applications to become everyday reality an array of technological challenges need to be addressed. In this paper, we have developed a cognitive agent framework (BDI based) integrating mobile agents and norm-aware agents to deliver a rapid response with rational deliberation about critical information messages. This position paper addressed use of emerging cognitive agent technology in VANETs. It can be assumed that cognitive agent systems have a great potential to influence design of future VANET and their services. Cognitive agent systems should be regarded as an "add on" to existing service platforms, providing more flexibility, adaptability and personalization for realization of services within next generation VANET environments. We are planning to simulate proposed work by using NS-2 programming to evaluate performance of system interms of control overhead, push/pull decision latency, decision reliability, information saturation time and pull latency.

Acknowledgments

We thank Visvesvaraya Technological University (VTU), Belgaum, Karnataka, INDIA, for funding the part of the project under VTU Research Scheme (Grant No. VTU/Aca./2009-10/A-9/11624, Dated: 4 January 2010).

References

1. Caliskan, M., Mauve, M., Rech, B., Luebke, A.: Collection of Dedicated Information in Vehicular Ad Hoc Networks. In: Proc. 12th World Congress on Intelligent Transport Systems 2005, San Francisco, U.S.A. (November 2005)
2. Fubler, H., Torrent-Moreno, M., Transier, M., Krger, R., Hartenstein, H., Effelsberg, W.: Studying Vehicle Movements on Highways and their Impact on Ad-Hoc Connectivity. In: Proc. ACM MobiCom 2005, Cologne, Germany (August 2005)
3. Schnaufer, S., Fubler, H., Transier, M., Effelsberg, W.: Vehicular Ad-Hoc Networks: Single-Hop Broadcast is not enough. In: Proc. 3rd International Workshop on Intelligent Transportation (WIT 2006), Hamburg, Germany, pp. 49–54 (March 2006)
4. Nadeem, T., Dashtinezhad, S., Liao, C., Iftode, L.: TrafficView: Traffic Data Dissemination using Car-to-Car Communication. ACM Mobile Computing and Communications Review (MC2R) 8(3), 6–19 (2004)
5. Manvi, S.S., Kakkasageri, M.S., Pitt, J., Rathmell, A.: Multi Agent Systems as a Platform for VANETs. In: Proc. Autonomous Agents and Multi Agent Systems (AAMAS), ATT, Hakodate, Japan, pp. 35–42 (May 2006)
6. Manvi, S.S., Kakkasageri, M.S., Pitt, J.: Multiagent based information dissemination in vehicular ad hoc networks. In: Mobile Information Systems, vol. 5(4), pp. 363–389. IOS Press, Amsterdam (2009)
7. Rosi, U.T., Hyder, C.S., Kim, T.: A Novel Approach for Infrastructure Deployment for VANET. In: Proc. Second International Conference on Future Generation Communication and Networking (FGCN 2008), vol. 1, pp. 234–238 (December 2008)
8. Jansen, W., Karygiannis, T.: Mobile Agent Security, http://csrc.nist.gov/publications/nistpubs/800-19/sp800-19.pdf
9. Jansen, W.A.: Countermeasures for Mobile Agent Security, http://citeseerx.ist.psu.edu/...pdf
10. Manvi, S.S., Venkataram, P.: Applications of agent technology in communications: A review. Computer Communications 27, 1493–1508 (2004)
11. Rao, A.S., Georgeff, M.P.: Modeling agents within a BDI-architecture. In: Proc. of KR 1991, pp. 473–484 (1991)

Enhanced AODV Routing Protocol for
Mobile Adhoc Networks

K.R. Shobha and K. Rajanikanth

M.S. Ramaiah Institute of Technology,
Bangalore -560054, Karnataka, India
shobha_shankar@yahoo.com, principal@msrit.edu

Abstract. Enhancing route request broadcasting efficiency in protocols constitutes a substantial part of research in mobile adhoc network (MANET) routing. We suggest a novel approach to constrain route request broadcast based on node mobility. This technique is best suited for networks where the nodes move in the network with different mobility. Intuition behind this technique is that the nodes moving with higher mobility rates will have better recent routes compared to slow moving nodes which may not be aware of the drastic changes happening in the network. In this approach we select the neighborhood nodes for broadcasting route requests based on their mobility rate and recent involvement in routing so that blind flooding of the route request in the network can be avoided.

Our contributions include: (i) a new enhancement technique to reduce route request broadcast for reactive ad hoc routing protocols; (ii) implementation of Enhanced Ad-hoc On-demand Distance Vector routing (EAODV); (iii) an extensive simulation study of EAODV using Glomosim showing significant improvement in overhead, packet delivery ratio and the end-to-end delay; written using the abstract environment.

Keywords: MANET, reactive routing, AODV, flooding, mobility, network simulation.

1 Introduction

Mobile Adhoc Networks (MANETs) have recently been the subject of active research because of their unique advantages. MANETs [3][11][12] are self-creating, self-organizing, self-administrating and do not require deployment of any kind of fixed infrastructure. They offer special benefits and versatility for wide range of applications in military (e.g., battlefields, sensor networks etc.), commercial (e.g., distributed mobile computing, disaster discovery systems, etc.), and educational environments (e.g., conferences, conventions, etc.), where fixed infrastructure is not easily acquired. With the absence of pre-established infrastructure (e.g., no router, no access point, etc.), two nodes communicate with one another in a peer-to-peer fashion. Two nodes communicate directly if they are within the transmission range of each other. Otherwise, the nodes communicate via a multihop route. To find such a

N. Meghanathan et al. (Eds.): CCSIT 2011, Part II, CCIS 132, pp. 265–276, 2011.
© Springer-Verlag Berlin Heidelberg 2011

multi-hop route, MANETs commonly employ on demand routing algorithms that use flooding or broadcast messages. Many ad hoc routing protocols [14] [20] [21], multicast schemes [18], or service discovery programs depend on massive flooding. In flooding, a node transmits a message to all of its neighbours. The neighbours in turn relay to their neighbours and so on until the message has been propagated to the entire network. In this paper, we will refer to such flooding as blind flooding. As one can easily see, the performance of blind flooding is closely related to the average number of neighbours (neighbour degree) in the Carrier Sense Multiple Access/Collision Avoidance network. As the neighbour degree gets higher, blind flooding suffers from the increase of (1) redundant and superfluous packets, (2) probability of collision, and (3) congestion of wireless medium [1]. Performance of blind flooding is severely impaired especially in large and dense networks [2][30]. When topology or neighbourhood information is available, only subsets of neighbours are required to participate in flooding to guarantee the complete flooding. We call such flooding as efficient flooding. The characteristics of MANETs (e.g., node mobility, the limited bandwidth and resource), however, make the periodic collection of topology information difficult and costly (in terms of overhead). For that reason many on-demand ad hoc routing schemes and service discovery protocols simply use blind flooding [14] [18]. In contrast with on-demand routing methods, the proactive ad hoc routing schemes by virtue of periodic route table exchange, can gather topological information without much extra overhead. Thus, the leading MANET proactive ad hoc routing schemes use route aggregation methods to forward routing packets through only a subset of the neighbours [21].

In Ad-hoc On-demand Distance Vector routing (AODV) [20] which is a reactive routing algorithm, every intermediate node decides where the routed packet should be forwarded next. AODV uses periodic neighbor detection packets in its routing mechanism. At each node, AODV maintains a routing table. The routing table entry for a destination contains three essential fields: a next hop node, a sequence number and a hop count. All packets destined to the destination are sent to the next hop node. The sequence number acts as a form of time-stamping, and is a measure of the freshness of a route. The hop count represents the current distance to the destination node. On the contrary, Dynamic Source Routing (DSR) uses the source routing in which each packet contains the route to the destination in its own header and each node maintains multiple routes in its cache. In case of less stressed situation (i.e. smaller number of nodes and lower load and/or mobility), DSR outperforms AODV in delay and throughput but when mobility and traffic increase, AODV outperforms DSR [5]. However, DSR consistently experiences less routing overhead than AODV.

In this paper, we focus on on-demand reactive routing protocol AODV and propose a method for efficient flooding by selecting a few of the neighbouring nodes for forwarding the route requests based on their mobility and recent usage of the nodes for forwarding the data. We have tried to reduce flooding in a dynamic network where the nodes move in random directions with random mobilities. This technique does not create too much of extra overhead for routing, as the other techniques that are existing for reducing flooding like caching[31] [32] [22],clustering [10] [16] [19],node caching [32], single copy routing[23] etc.

The remainder of the article is organized as follows: In section 2 we discuss the various methods available for achieving efficient flooding. Section 3 gives an explanation about the algorithm AODV-NC and the algorithm we have proposed for achieving efficient flooding. Section 4 discusses the simulation parameters and results. The main conclusions from this paper are summarized in section 5.

2 Related Work

Several papers [1] [6] [7] [8] have addressed the limitations of blind flooding and have proposed solutions to provide efficient flooding. However, because of the problem of finding a subset of dominant forwarding nodes in MANETs, all the work about efficient flooding has been directed to the development of efficient heuristics that select a sub-optimal dominant set with low forwarding overhead.

In [1] [6], the authors propose several heuristics to reduce rebroadcasts. More specifically, upon receiving a flood packet, a node decides whether to relay it or not based on one of the following heuristics: (1) rebroadcast with given probability; (2) rebroadcast if the number of received duplicate packets is less than a threshold; (3) distance-based scheme where the relative distance between hosts determines the rebroadcast decision; (4) location-based scheme where the decision is based on pre-acquired neighbour location information; (5) cluster-based scheme where only pre computed cluster heads and gateways rebroadcast.

Another approach to efficient flooding is to exploit topological information [6] [7] [8] [24]. In the absence of pre-existing infrastructure, all the above schemes use a periodic hello message exchange method to collect topological information. The authors of [8] suggest two schemes called self-pruning and dominant pruning. Self pruning is similar to the neighbour-coverage scheme in [6]. With self-pruning scheme, each forwarding node piggybacks the list of its neighbours on outgoing packet. A node rebroadcasts (becomes a forwarding node) only when it has neighbours that are not covered by its forwarding nodes. While the self-pruning heuristic utilizes information of directly connected neighbours only, the dominant-pruning heuristic extends the propagation of neighbour information two-hop away. The dominant pruning scheme is actually similar to Multipoint Relay scheme (MPR) [7].

In Multipoint Relay scheme, a node periodically exchanges the list of adjacent nodes with its neighbours so that each node can collect the information of two-hop away neighbours. Each node, based on the gathered information, selects the minimal subset of forwarding neighbours, which cover all nodes within two-hops. Each sender piggybacks its chosen Multipoint Relay forwarding Nodes (MPRNs) on the outgoing broadcast packet.

Along the similar lines, several other schemes have proposed the selection of a dominant set based on topology [25] [26]. All of these schemes, however, again depend on periodic hello messages to collect topological information.

The extra hello messages, however, consume resources and drop the network throughput in MANETs [27]. The extra traffic brings about congestion and collision as geographic density increases [1]. Fig 1 [16] depicts the collision probability of hello messages in a single hop and a two hop network as the number of neighbour's increases. This result clearly shows that the neighbour degree causes the broadcast

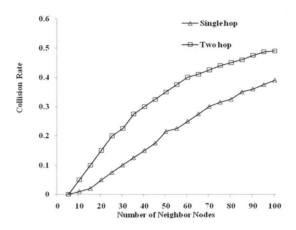

Fig. 1. The collision rate of broadcast

collision probability to increase (note, the collision probability is more than 0.1 with more than 15 neighbours). Moreover, the hidden terminal condition aggravates collisions in the two hop network. Note that Fig 1 assumes no data traffic -only hello messages.

With user-data packets, the collision probability of hello messages will dramatically increase. Thus, it will be hard to collect complete neighbour topology information using hello messages. As a consequence, the aforementioned schemes (e.g., neighbour coverage, MPR, etc.) are not scalable to offered load and number of neighbours.

A novel approach to constrain route request broadcast based on node caching was proposed in [32]. This approach assumes that the nodes involved in recent data packet forwarding have more reliable information about its neighbors and have better locations (e.g., on the intersection of several data routes) than other MANET nodes. The nodes which are recently involved in data packet forwarding are cached, and only they are used to forward route requests.

Lastly, we consider clustering. Clustering can be described as grouping of nodes. A representative of each group (cluster) is dynamically elected to the role of cluster head based on some criterion (e.g., lowest ID). Nodes within one hop of a cluster head become associated to its cluster. A node belonging to two or more clusters at the same time is called a gateway. Other members are called ordinary nodes. Various distributed computation techniques can be used to dynamically create clusters. In an active clustering lowest ID technique [15] each node attempts to become cluster head by broadcasting its ID to neighbours. It will give up only if it hears from a lower ID neighbour. Based on the above definition, any two nodes in a cluster are at most 2 hops away [9]. With the clustering scheme, the dominant forwarding nodes are the cluster heads and the gateways.

Clustering in ad hoc networks has been extensively studied for hierarchical routing schemes [9] [5],and for approaches like the master election algorithms [4], power control [17] [26], reliable broadcast [28], efficient broadcast [29] and efficient flooding [16][19]. Some clustering schemes are based on the complete knowledge of neighbours. However, the complete knowledge of neighbour information in ad hoc networks is hard to collect and introduces substantial control overhead caused by periodic exchange of hello messages. Passive clustering [16] [19] is an "on demand" protocol, it constructs and maintains the cluster architecture only when there are on-going data packets that piggyback "cluster related information". Each node collects neighbour information through promiscuous packet receptions. Passive clustering, therefore, eliminates setup latency and major control overhead of clustering protocols.

Passive clustering has two innovative mechanisms for the cluster formation: First Declaration Wins rule and Gateway Selection Heuristic. With the First Declaration Wins rule, a node that first claims to be a cluster head "rules" the rest of nodes in its clustered area (radio coverage). There is no waiting period (to make sure all the neighbours have been checked) unlike for all the weight-driven clustering mechanism [5]. Also, the Gateway Selection Heuristic provides a procedure to elect the minimal number of gateways (including distributed gateways) required to maintain the connectivity in a distributed manner.

Passive clustering scheme [16][19] requires neither the deployment of GPS like systems nor explicit periodic control messages to identify the subset of forwarding neighbours. This scheme makes the following contributions compared with previous efficient flooding schemes (such as multipoint relay, neighbour coverage, etc): (1) It does not need any periodic messages. Instead, it exploits existing data packets by attaching few more extra fields. (2) It is very resource-efficient regardless of the degree of neighbour nodes or the size of network. This scheme provides scalability and practicality for choosing the minimal number of forwarding nodes in the presence of dynamic topology changes; (3) It does not introduce any start-up latency; (4) It saves energy if there is no traffic; (5) It easily adapts to topology and available resource changes.

In this paper we propose a method for efficient flooding by selecting a few of the neighbouring nodes for forwarding the route requests based on their mobility and recent usage of the nodes for forwarding the data. This technique does not group the nodes in the network into clusters. We have used the mobility of the nodes as the criteria for selecting the nodes to forward the Route requests so that unnecessary flooding can be avoided. We have tested the implementation on AODV Routing protocol.

3 Proposed Technique

Node caching AODV(AODV-NC) technique[32] caches the nodes which have recently forwarded the data packets and uses only these selected neighbors for forwarding the Route request packets. Route request uses a fixed threshold parameter H. The first route request is sent with the small threshold H. When a node N receives the route request, it compares the current time T with the time T(N) when the last data packet through N has been forwarded. If T - H > T (N), then N does not belong to the current node cache and, therefore, N will not propagate the route request. Otherwise, if T - H ≤ T (N), then N is in the node cache and the route request is propagated as usual. Of course, the node cache cannot guarantee existence of paths between all source-destination pairs, therefore, if the route request with the small threshold H fails to find a route to destination, then a standard route request (which is not constrained by cache) is generated at the source.

In the default settings of AODV, if the route to the destination is broken, obsolete or unestablished, the route request originated from the source is propagated through the entire MANET. If the route reply is not received by source in a certain period of time, then the route request is periodically repeated. If all these Route Requests happened to be unsuccessful, several more requests with increasing time gaps are sent. In AODV-NC, modifications are restricted solely to the Route Request and its initiation.

Route Request in AODV-NC (H)
1) If a requested route is not available, then send an H restricted route request with the threshold H, i.e., for each route request recipient N
    ➤ if the destination is the known neighbor of N, then N forwards the route request to the destination
    ➤ if no more than H seconds are gone from the last time a data packet has been forwarded by N, then N rebroadcasts the route request to all its neighbors
2) Repeat H-restricted route request 2 times if route reply is not received during time 0.3 sec after route request
3) If no route reply received, then send unconstrained (standard AODV) route request with the standard repetition pattern

Best initial values for H are suggested to be between 0.1sec and 1 sec. So we have chosen it to be 0.5sec in our simulation.

We have modified this algorithm as listed below by adding the mobility factor to the existing criterion to select the neighborhood node for efficient flooding.

- The mobility of all the one hop neighbours are learnt and compared with the mobility of the current node.
- Only if the mobility of the neighbouring node is greater than the mobility of the current node the Route Request is sent to the neighbouring node. A threshold M_{th} is set in all the nodes. If M is the mobility of the current node, M_n is the mobility of neighbour node then Route Request is sent to the neighbouring node only if $(M_n - M) > M_{th}$. We limit the number of Route requests by using the mobility criterion and prevent the route request being flooded to the entire network.

So our algorithm selects a node for efficient flooding of route requests only if the node was recently used and also meets the mobility criterion mentioned above. We have named the AODV after incorporating this modification as EAODV (Enhanced AODV).

4   Simulation Results

The simulations were performed using Glomosim [13]. The mobility scenarios were randomly generated using modified Random Waypoint Model. We used Distributed Coordination Function (DCF) of IEEE 802.11 for wireless LANs as the MAC layer protocol.

In our simulation, 20 to 60 nodes were allowed to move in a 1000x1000 meter rectangular region for 900 seconds simulation time. Initial locations of the nodes are obtained using a uniform distribution. We assumed that each node moves independently with a random speed later. With the Random Waypoint Mobility model, a node randomly selects a destination from the physical terrain and moves in the direction of the destination with a uniform speed chosen between the minimal and maximal speed. After it reaches its destination, the node stays there for a pause time and then moves again. In our simulation, we have modified the random waypoint mobility model so that the node moves in random direction with random mobility and then stays there for the selected pause time till next random movement. This modification was done so that the movement matches the real world scenario. The pause time was varied from 0 to 30 seconds. The simulated traffic was Constant Bit Rate (CBR).

We have analyzed the performance of the proposed algorithm by varying the number of nodes in the network keeping the pause time of the nodes constant. This scenario helps us in knowing whether the algorithm supports scalability of the network as well as dynamic traffic conditions in the network. Fig 2 shows that the overhead generated by EAODV is less compared to AODV and AODV-NC; Fig 4 shows that the packet delivery ratio of EODV is higher than AODV and AODV-NC and Fig 6 shows that end to end delay time is less for EODV compared to AODV and AODV-NC. All these three graphs show that the performance of AODV is effectively enhanced by EAODV.

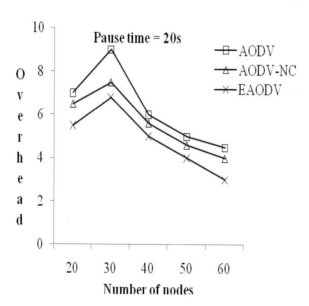

Fig. 2. Number of nodes v/s overhead

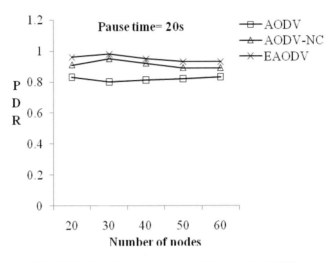

Fig. 3. Number of nodes v/s packet delivery ratio (PDR)

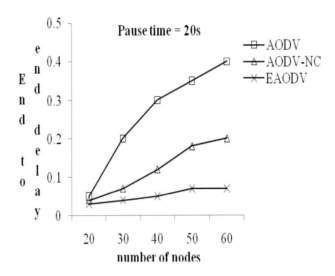

Fig. 4. Number of nodes v/s end-end delay

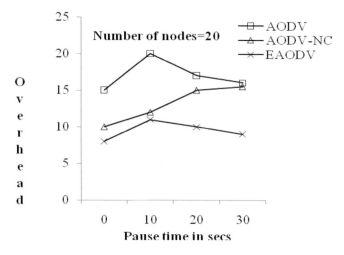

Fig. 5. Pause time v/s overhead

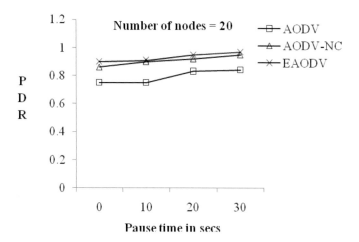

Fig. 6. Pause time v/s Packet delivery ratio

We have also tried to analyze the behavior of the protocol when the number of nodes in the network is kept constant and the time period for which they remain static are varied. This scenario helps us in analyzing the performance of the protocol when the number of users is fixed, traffic is fixed and they move in the simulation terrain with different mobilities.

We have analyzed the network keeping the number of users fixed at 20.Fig 5, 6 and 7 shows the same sort of improvement in the performance of EAODV as shown by Fig 2, 3 and 4 respectively. This shows that the EODV not only supports scalability of the network, dynamic traffic conditions in the network but also reduces the flooding of Route requests when the route to the destination is not known effectively.

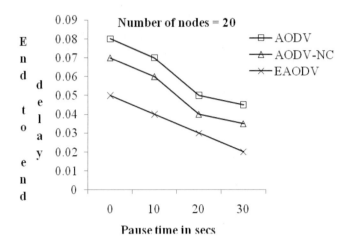

Fig. 7. Pause time v/s end - end delay

5 Conclusion

For carrying out this work we have investigated the problem of flooding based on topological information. To collect neighbour topology the network incurs a heavy overhead penalty- it is very costly to collect accurate topology information with node mobility and dynamically changing resources. The aforementioned topology based schemes, in consequence, are limiting in scalability and performance. Flooding scheme based on passive clustering removes such limitations but has some overhead and delay in transmission; it is also complex for implementation.

Our implementation has shown that EAODV is a very simple technique and require substantially less knowledge of the network. Results have shown that, it is suitable for highly scalable and dynamic networks as it has drastically reduced the amount of overhead, improved PDR and reduced end to end delay in the popular reactive routing protocol AODV. This algorithm can also be implemented and tested on the other reactive routing protocol like Dynamic Source Routing protocol (DSR), the On-Demand Multicast Routing Protocol (ODMRP) etc.

References

1. Ni, S.-Y., Tseng, Y.-C., Chen, Y.-S., Sheu, J.-P.: The broadcast storm problem in a mobile ad hoc network. In: MobiCom (1999)
2. Li, J., Blake, C., De Couto, D.S.J., Lee, H.I., Morris, R.: Capacity of Ad Hoc Wireless Networks. In: Mobicom (2001)
3. Carsom, S., Macker, J.: Mobile Ad hoc Networking (MANET): Routing Protocol Performance Issues and Evaluation Considerations. Internet Draft (January 1999), http://www.ietf.org/rfc/rfc2501.txt
4. Baker, D.J., Ephremides, A.: The Architectural organization of a mobile radio network via a distributed algorithm. IEEE Transaction on Communications 27 (November 1981)

5. Gerla, M., Tasi, J.: A Multicluster, mobile, multimedia radio network. ACM-Baltzer Journal of Wireless Networks 1 (1995)
6. Tseng, Y.-C., Ni, S.-Y., Shih, E.-Y.: Adaptive Approaches to Relieving Broadcast Storms in a Wireless Multihop Mobile Ad Hoc Network. In: Infocom (2001)
7. Qayyum, A., Viennot, L., Laouiti, A.: Multipoint relaying: An efficient technique for flooding in mobile wireless networks. INRIA report (March 2000)
8. Lim, H., Kim, C.: Flooding in wireless ad hoc networks. IEEE Computer Communications (2000)
9. Krishna, P., Vaidya, N.H., Chatterjee, M., Pradhan, D.K.: A clusterbased approach for routing in dynamic networks. Computer Communication Review 25 (April 1997)
10. Lin, C.R., Gerla, M.: Adaptive Clustering for Mobile Wireless Networks. IEEE Journal on Selected Areas in Communications 15, 1265–1275 (1997)
11. Nasipuri, A.: Mobile Adhoc networks. In: Department of Electrical & Computer Engineering, The University of North Carolina at Charlotte,
    http://www.ece.uncc.edu/~anasipur/pubs/adhoc.pdf
12. Perkins, C.E.: Ad Hoc Networking. Addison-Wesley, Reading (2001)
13. UCLA, Glomosim: A scalable simulation environment for Wireless and Wired Network systems, http://pcl.cs.ucla.edu/projects/glomosim
14. Johnson, D., Hu, Y., Maltz, D.: The Dynamic Source Routing Protocol (DSR) for Mobile Ad Hoc Networks for IPv4 (February 2007),
    http://www.ietf.org/rfc/rfc4726.txt
15. Parsec: A parallel simulation environment for complex systems. Computer 29(10), 77–85 (October 1998)
16. Yi, Y., Gerla, M., Kwon, T.-J.: Efficient flooding in adhoc networks using on-demand (passive) cluster formation. university of California, Part of MINUTEMAN Project Under Contract N00014 - 01 - C - 0016
17. Chen, B., Jamieson, K.H., Morris, R.: An energy-efficient coordination algorithm for topology maintenance in Ad Hoc wireless networks. In: Mobicom (2001)
18. Lee, S.-J., Su, W., Gerla, M.: On-Demand Multicast Routing Protocol (ODMRP) for Ad Hoc Networks. Internet Draft, draft-ietf-manetodmrp-02.txt (January 2000)
19. Yi, Y., Kwon, T.J., Gerla, M.: Passive Clustering (PC) in Ad Hoc Networks. Internet Draft, draft-ietf-yi-manet-pac-00.txt (November 2001)
20. Perkins, C., Das, S.: Ad Hoc On Demand Distance Vector (AODV). Routing IETF, Internet Draft, draft-ietf-manet-aodv-13, RFC 3561
21. Ogier, R.G., Templin, F.L., Bellur, B., Lewis, M.G.: Topology Broadcast Based on Reverse-Path Forwarding (TBRPF). Internet Draft, draft-ietf-manet-tbrpf-03.txt (November 2001)
22. Spyropoulos, T., Psounis, K., Raghavendra, C.S.: Efficient Routing in Intermittently Connected Mobile Networks: The Multiple-Copy Case. IEEE/ACM Transactions on Networking 16 (February 2008)
23. Chou, C.-C., Wei, D.S.L., Jay Kuo, C.-C., Naik, K.: An Efficient Anonymous Communication Protocol for Peer-to-Peer Applications over Mobile Ad-hoc Networks. IEEE Journal on Selected Areas in Communications 25 (January 2007)
24. Seddigh, M., Solano, J., Stojmenovic, I.: Internal nodes based broadcasting algorithms in wireless networks. In: Proc. HICSS 2001 (2001)
25. Wu, J., Li, H.: On calculating connected dominating set for efficient routing in ad hoc networks. In: Dial, M. (ed.) Adhoc and Sensor Networks, vol. 2. Nova Science Publishers, Inc., Bombay (1999)

26. Chen, B., Jamieson, K.H., Morris, R.: An energy-efficient coordination algorithm for topology maintenance in Ad Hoc wireless networks. In: Mobicom 2001 (2001)
27. Bianchi, G.: Performance analysis of the IEEE 802.11 distributed coordination function. IEEE Journal on Selected Areas in Communications 18 (March 2000)
28. Pagani, E., Rossi, G.P.: Reliable broadcast in mobile multihop packet networks. In: Mobicom 1997 (1997)
29. Jiang, M., Li, J., Tay, Y.C.: Cluster based routing protocol (CBR) functional specification. IETF Draft (1998)
30. Neely, M., Modiano, E.: Capacity and delay tradeoffs for ad hoc mobile networks. IEEE Trans. Inf. Theory 51, 1917–1937 (2005)
31. Ting, Y.-W., Chang, Y.-K.: A Novel Cooperative Caching Scheme for Wireless Ad Hoc Networks: GroupCaching. In: International Conference on Networking Architecture and Storage, NAS 2007 (2007)
32. Jung, S., Hundewale, N., Zelikovsky, A.: Node Caching Enhancement of Reactive Ad Hoc Routing Protocols. In: IEEE Wireless Communications and Networking Conference (2005)

A Comparative Study of Feedforward Neural Network and Simplified Fuzzy ARTMAP in the Context of Face Recognition

Antu Annam Thomas and M. Wilscy

Dept. of Computer Science, University of Kerala, Karyavattom Campus, Trivandrum, Kerala
antuannam@gmail.com, wilsyphilipose@gmail.com

Abstract. Face recognition has become one of the most active research areas of pattern recognition since the early 1990s. In this paper, a comparative study of two face recognition methods is discussed. One method is based on PCA (Principal Component Analysis), LDA (Linear Discriminant Analysis) and Feedforward Neural Network (FFNN) and the second method is based on PCA, LDA and Simplified Fuzzy ARTMAP(SFAM). Combination of PCA and LDA is used for improving the capability of LDA and PCA when used alone. Neural classifier (FFNN or SFAM) is used to reduce the number of misclassifications. Experiment is conducted on ORL database and results demonstrate SFAM as more efficient recognizer, both in terms of recognition rate and time complexity, when compared to FFNN. SFAM has the added advantage that the network is adaptive, that is, during testing phase if the network comes across a new face that it is not trained for; the network identifies this to be a new face and also learns this new face. Thus SFAM can be used in applications where database needs to be updated frequently.

Keywords: Face recognition, Principal Component Analysis, Linear Discriminant Analysis, Feedforward Neural Network, Simplified Fuzzy ARTMAP.

1 Introduction

Face recognition [1] is an important and a challenging research problem spanning numerous fields and disciplines. Face recognition is attention seeking because, in addition to having numerous practical applications such as bankcard identification, access control, security monitoring, and surveillance system, is a fundamental human behavior that is essential for effective communications and interactions among people. Two categories of methods can be employed for face recognition one is *global approach* or *appearance-based approach* and *second one is feature-based* or *component-based approach*. Among these two categories of solutions to the problem [2] the most successful seems to be appearance-based approaches [3], which generally operate directly on images or appearances of face objects and process the image as two dimensional patterns. These methods extract features to optimally represent faces belonging to a class and to separate faces from different classes. Ideally, it is desirable to use only features having high separability power while ignoring the rest [3].Most of

N. Meghanathan et al. (Eds.): CCSIT 2011, Part II, CCIS 132, pp. 277–289, 2011.
© Springer-Verlag Berlin Heidelberg 2011

the effort have been used to develop powerful methods for feature extraction [4]-[8] and to employ classifiers like Support Vector Machine (SVM) [9], Hidden Markov Models (HMMs) [10], Neural Networks [11]-[15] for efficient classification.

The main trend in feature extraction has been representing the data in a lower dimensional space. Principal Component Analysis (PCA) [16],[17], [5]-[6] and Linear Discriminant analysis (LDA) [7] are two main techniques used for data reduction and feature extraction in the appearance-based approaches. PCA maximizes the total scatter while LDA maximizes the between class scatter and minimizes the within class scatter. PCA might outperform LDA when the number of samples per class is small [18]. In the case of training set with a large number of samples, LDA outperform PCA [18]. A study in [17] demonstrated that; compared to the PCA method, the computation of the LDA is much higher and PCA is less sensitive to different training data sets. However, simulations reported in [17] demonstrated an improved performance using the LDA method compared to the PCA approach. But when dimensionality of face images is high, LDA is not applicable and therefore LDA is deprived from its advantage to find effective features for class separability. To resolve this problem PCA and LDA methods are combined [3], PCA is applied to preprocessed face images to get low dimensionality images which are ready for applying LDA. Finally to decrease the error rate, instead of Euclidean distance criteria which was used in [19], we implement a neural network, FFNN or SFAM, to classify face images based on its computed LDA features.

2   Feature Extraction Algorithm

Two powerful tools used for dimensionality reduction and feature extraction in most of pattern recognition applications are PCA and LDA. A brief review on fundamentals of PCA and LDA is given in the following sessions.

2.1   Principal Component Analysis (PCA)

Principal component analysis or karhunen-loeve transformation [20] is the method for reducing the dimensionality of a dataset, while retaining the majority of variation, present in the dataset. Thus PCA can be effectively be used for data reduction and feature extraction [21]. As the pattern often contains redundant information, mapping it to a feature vector can get rid of this redundancy and yet preserve most of the intrinsic information content of the pattern. These extracted features have great role in distinguishing input patterns.

A face image in 2-dimension with size $N \times N$ can also be considered as one dimensional vector of dimension N^2 [22]. For example, face image from ORL (Olivetti Research Labs) database with size 112×92 can be considered as a vector of dimension 10,304, or equivalently a point in a 10,304 dimensional space. An ensemble of images maps to a collection of points in this huge space. Images of faces, being similar in overall configuration, will not be randomly distributed in this huge image space and thus can be described by a relatively low dimensional subspace. The main idea of the principle component is to find the vectors that best account for the distribution of face images within the entire image space. These vectors define the subspace of face images, which we call "face space". Each of these vectors is of length N^2, describes an $N \times N$ image, and is a linear combination of the original face images.

Let the training set of face images be Γ_1, Γ_2, Γ_3, ...,Γ_M then the average of the set is defined by

$$\psi = \frac{1}{M}\sum_{n=1}^{M}\Gamma_n \tag{1}$$

Each face differs from the average by the vector

$$\Phi i = \Gamma i - \Psi \tag{2}$$

This set of very large vectors is then subject to principal component analysis, which seeks a set of M orthonormal vectors, U_m, which best describes the distribution of the data. The kth vector, U_k, is chosen such that

$$\lambda_k = \frac{1}{M}\sum_{n=1}^{M}\left(U_k^T \phi_n\right)^2 \tag{3}$$

is a maximum, subject to

$$U_I^T U_k = \delta_{IK} = \left\{ \begin{matrix} 1, if\ I=k \\ 0, otherwise \end{matrix} \right\} \tag{4}$$

The vectors U_k and scalars λ_k are the eigenvectors and eigenvalues, respectively of the covariance matrix

$$C = \frac{1}{M}\sum_{n=1}^{M}\phi_n\phi_n^T = AA^T \tag{5}$$

where the matrix A $=[\Phi_1, \Phi_2,......,\Phi_M]$. The covariance matrix C, however is $N^2 \times N^2$ real symmetric matrix, and calculating the N^2 eigenvectors and eigenvalues is an intractable task for typical image sizes. We need a computationally feasible method to find these eigenvectors.

Consider the eigenvectors v_i of $A^T A$ such that

$$A^T A v_i = \mu_i v_i \tag{6}$$

Premultiplying both sides by A, we have

$$A A^T A v_i = \mu_i A v_i \tag{7}$$

where we see that Av_i are the eigenvectors and μ_i are the eigenvalues of $C = AA^T$. Following these analysis, we construct the $M \times M$ matrix $L = A^T A$, where $L_{mn} = \Phi_m^T \Phi_n$, and find the M eigenvectors, v_i, of L. These vectors determine linear combinations of the M training set face images to form the eigenfaces U_I.

$$U_I = \sum_{k=1}^{M} v_{Ik}\phi_k, I = 1,....., M \tag{8}$$

With this analysis, the calculations are greatly reduced, from the order of the number of pixels in the images (N^2) to the order of the number of images in the training set (M). In practice, the training set of face images will be relatively small ($M \ll N^2$), and the calculations become quite manageable. The associated eigenvalues allow us to rank the eigenvectors according to their usefulness in characterizing the variation among the images. Because these vectors are the eigenvectors of the covariance matrix corresponding to the original face images, and because they are face-like in appearance, we refer to them as "eigenfaces". The eigenface images calculated from the eigenvectors of L span a basis set that can be used to describe face images. In practice, a smaller M' can be sufficient for identification, since accurate reconstruction of the image is not a requirement. In the framework of face recognition, the operation is a pattern recognition task rather than image reconstruction. The eigenfaces span an M' dimensional subspace of the original N^2 image space and hence, the M' significant eigenvectors of the L matrix with the largest associated eigenvalues, are sufficient for reliable representation of the faces in the face space characterized by the eigenfaces. Examples of ORL face database is given in Fig.1. Fig.2. shows examples of eigenfaces.

Fig. 1. Samples face images from the ORL database

Fig. 2. First 8 eigenfaces with highest eigenvalues

A new face image (Γ) is transformed into its eigenface components (projected onto "face space") by a simple operation,

$$w_k = U_k^T \left(\Gamma - \Psi \right) \qquad (9)$$

for $k = 1,...,M'$.

The weights form a projection vector,

$$\Omega^T = [w_1, w_2, \ldots\ldots\ldots, w_{M'}] \qquad (10)$$

describing the contribution of each eigenface in representing the input face image, treating the eigenfaces as a basis set for face images. The projection vector is then used in a standard pattern recognition algorithm to identify which of a number of predefined face classes, if any, best describes the face. Classification is performed by comparing the projection vectors of the training face images with the projection vector of the input face image. This comparison is based on the Euclidean Distance between the face classes and the input face image. This is given in Eq. (11). The idea is to find the face class k that minimizes the Euclidean Distance.

$$\varepsilon_k = \left\| \left(\Omega - \Omega_k \right) \right\|$$

(11)

Where, Ωk is a vector describing the kth faces class.

The PCA is advantageous because it removes the redundant data and gives an optimal representation of data but the main handicap of PCA is that by applying PCA to a dataset not only interclass scatter, but also intraclass scatter is maximized.

2.2 Linear Discriminant Analysis (LDA)

Linear Discriminant analysis or Fisherfaces method overcomes the limitations of eigenfaces method by applying the Fisher's linear discriminant criterion. This criterion tries to maximize the ratio of the determinant of the between-class scatter matrix of the projected samples to the determinant of the within-class scatter matrix of the projected samples. Fisher discriminants group images of the same class and separates images of different classes. Fisher discriminants find the line that best separates the points. As with eigenspace projection, training images are projected into a subspace. The test images are projected into the same subspace and identified using a similarity measure. What differs is how the subspace is calculated [22].

Unlike PCA which is a method that extracts features to best represent face images, the LDA method tries to find the subspace that best discriminates different face classes. The within-class scatter matrix, also called intra-personal, represents variations in appearance of the same individual due to different lighting and face expression, while the between-class scatter matrix, also called the extra-personal, represents variations in appearance due to a difference in identity. By applying this method, we find the projection directions that on one hand maximize the between-class scatter matrix S_b, while minimize the within-class scatter matrix S_w in the projective subspace [22].

The within-class scatter matrix S_w and the between-class scatter matrix S_b are defined as

$$S_w = \sum_{j=1}^{C} \sum_{i=1}^{N_j} \left(\Gamma_i^j - \mu_j \right)\left(\Gamma_i^j - \mu_j \right)^T$$

(12)

Where Γ_i^j is the ith sample of class j, μ_j is the mean of class j, C is the number of classes, N_j is the number of samples in class j

$$S_b = \sum_{j=1}^{C} \left(\mu_j - \mu \right)\left(\mu_j - \mu \right)^T$$

(13)

Where, μ represents the mean of all classes. The subspace for LDA is spanned by a set of vectors $W = [W_1, W_2, \dots, W_d]$, satisfying

$$W = \arg \max = \frac{\left| W^T S_b W \right|}{\left| W^T S_w W \right|}$$

(14)

When face images are projected into the discriminant vectors W, face images should be distributed closely within classes and should be separated between classes, as much as possible. That is, these discriminant vectors minimize the denominator and maximize the numerator in Equation (14). W can therefore be constructed by the eigenvectors of $S_w^{-1} S_b$. Fig. 3 shows the first 8 eigenvectors with highest associated eigenvalues of $S_w^{-1} S_b$. These eigenvectors are also referred to as the fisherfaces.

Fig. 3. First 8 Fisherfaces with highest eigenvalues

$$S = S_w + S_b \qquad (15)$$

Alternatively, can be used for LDA, because both $S_w^{-1} S_b$ and $S_w^{-1} S$ have the same eigenvector matrices

The test images are projected into the same subspace and identified using a similarity measure. The face which has the minimum distance with the test face image is labeled with the identity of that image. The minimum distance can be calculated using the Euclidian distance method as given earlier in Equation (11).

3   Neural Network as Classifiers

Neural networks, with massive parallelism in its structure and high computation rates, provide a great alternative to other conventional classifiers and decision making systems.

3.1   Feedforward Neural Network(FFNN)

FFNN is a suitable structure for nonlinear separable input data. In FFNN model the neurons are organized in the form of layers. The neurons in a layer get input from the previous layer and feed their output to the next layer. In this type of networks connections to the neurons in the same or previous layers are not permitted. Fig. 4 shows the architecture of the system for face classification. Simple Back propagation algorithm is employed for training the network.

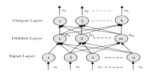

Fig. 4. Architecture of FFNN for classification

3.2 Simplified Fuzzy ARTMAP (SFAM)

SFAM comprises of two layers an input and an output layer (see Fig. 5) [24]. The input to the network flows through the complement coder. Here the input string is stretched to double the size by adding its complement also. The complement coded input then flows into the input layer and remains there. Weights (W) from each of the output category nodes flows down to the input layer. The category layer just holds the names of the M number of categories that the network has to learn. The match tracking and vigilance parameter of the network architecture are primarily for network training.

ρ, the vigilance parameter ranges from 0 to 1 and it controls the granularity of the output node encoding. Thus, high vigilance values make the output node much fussier during pattern encoding and low vigilance allows relaxed matching criteria for the output node.

The "match tracking" allows the network to adjust its vigilance during learning from some base level, in response to errors in classification during the training phase. It is through match tracking that the network adjusts its own learning parameter to decide when to create new output nodes or reshape its decision regions. During training, match tracking is evoked when the selected output node does not represent the same output category corresponding to the input vectors given [23].

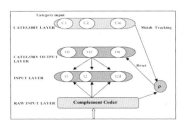

Fig. 5. Architecture of SFAM network

4 Face Recognition System

Fig. 6a shows the structure of the face recognition system using FFNN and Fig.6b shows the structure of the face recognition system using SFAM. System consists of two phases testing phase and training phase. In the next sections, role of each part is described.

Face recognition method is applied on ORL face dataset for separation of twenty classes. 340 sample faces are there out of which 140 are used for training and 200 used for testing. Fig. 7 shows examples of sample images used.

4.1 Preprocessing

In this phase first we resize the images to 40*40 sizes. After that we histogram equalize all input images in order to spread energy of all pixels inside the image. As a next step, we subtract mean images from face images to mean center all of them.

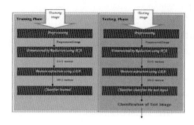 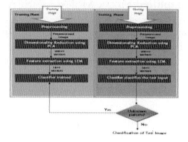

Fig. 6a. Structure of Face Recognition System using FFNN

Fig. 6b. Structure of Face Recognition System using SFAM

Fig. 7. Examples of Sample Face images used

Fig. 8. Examples of preprocessed images

Finally all preprocessed face images change to a vector (1600 ×1vector) and go to the next step. Fig. 8 shows example of preprocessed images.

4.2 Dimensionality Reduction

Every input image is cropped to 40×40 image in the preprocessing step; as a result the input of this stage is a preprocessed 1600×1 vector. These vectors are used to estimate the covariance matrix. After estimation of the covariance matrix, significant eigenvectors of the covariance matrix are computed. Number of eigen-vector depends on the accuracy that the application demands. Large number of eigen-vectors will obviously improve the accuracy of the method but computational complexity will increase in this step and next step. Thus considering accuracy and computational complexity 100 eigen vectors are selected as principal eigen vectors.

The preprocessed faces are now projected on to the space with 100 eigenfaces as base vectors to get 140, 100×1 vectors. Thus dimensionality reduction phase converts 1600×1 vectors to 100×1 vectors.

4.3 LDA Feature Extraction

Outputs of dimension reduction part are 100×1 vectors which are used to construct within class scatter matrix and covariance matrix. Significant eigen vectors of

$S_w^{-1} S$ (mentioned in Section 2.2) is used for seperability of classes. Using 100×1 vectors, $S_w^{-1} S$ is computed and then eigenvectors related to the greater eigenvalues are selected. Eigenvectors(Fisherafces) corresponding to 18 greater non-zero eigenvalues are selected in this case.

The preprocessed face images projected on to the eigen space, is now, projected onto the fisher space and thus results in 140, 18×1 vectors which are used as input of neural network.

4.4 Classification

4.4.1 Feedforward Neural Network (FFNN)

Three layered FFNN with 30 neurons in the first hidden layer, 25 neurons in the second hidden layer and 20 neurons in the output layer is used for the classification of input data. A simple back propagation algorithm is used to update weights according to desired values. FFNN will train using 140, 18×1 training face images and at its output layer, it produces a 20×1 vector. The output vector is such that elements of that vector is a number between zero and one representing similarity of input face images to each of twenty classes. Training face image enter the neural network and according to their class, a back propagation error, spread on the network and correct the weights toward the right values. The input face image will classified to the class which has the greatest similarity to it. For example if for a test input face image, row 12 of network's output be greater than other rows, that test face images will classified to class 12. Fig. 9 demonstrates classification process using three layer neural network.

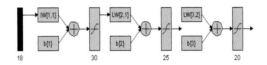

Fig. 9. Structure of Neural Network used

4.4.2 Simplified Fuzzy ARTMAP

For the direct application of SFAM to the face recognition problem, the architecture is trained using the 140, 18×1 vectors got from the feature extraction stage. The vigilance parameter is selected so that the number of categories to which the network settles is same as the number of classes in the training data.

The network took only 2 epochs for completing its learning or training phase. The time that it took for learning is negligible (0.125 seconds) and thus can be labeled as very efficient in terms of time complexity. Thus SFAM proves itself to be a classifier that learns very fast when compared to Feedforward Neural Network that takes more than 20 minutes to converge when trained for the same input.Once the training is over and the top-down weight matrices have been obtained, the testing can be carried out using the matrix equivalent of the test input image.

The most important point to note about the network in the classification stage is that it remains open to adaptation in the event of new information being applied to the network. If an unknown pattern is applied to the network SFAM will always attempt to assign a new class in the category output layer by assigning the unknown input to a node. But, Feedforward Neural Network is not able to learn new information on top of old thus can't be used as an adaptive network.

5   Performance Analysis and Discussions

Table 1 shows the result of the experiment conducted. Results show that SFAM exhibits a very good performance, both in terms of recognition rate and time required to train the net, when compared to FFNN.

SFAM took only 2 epochs for completing its learning or training phase. The time that SFAM took for learning is negligible (0.125 seconds in the first case) and thus can be labeled as very efficient in terms of time complexity. Thus SFAM proves itself to be a classifier that learns very fast when compared to Feedforward Neural Network that takes more than 20 minutes (in all the three cases) to converge when trained for the same input.

Table 1. Results of the Experiment

PCA+LDA					
Elapsed time is 32.500000 seconds					
No: of Training Images Used for Each Subject	No: of Testing Images Used for Each Subject	Name of the Classifier	No :of Epochs	Elapsed Time	Recognition rate
7	3	FFNN	100	20minutes 55.03 seconds	95.5%
		SFAM	2	0.125seconds	98.5%
6	4	FFNN	100	20minutes 50seconds	94%
		SFAM	2	0.115seconds	98%
5	5	FFNN	100	20minutes 53 seconds	93%
		SFAM	2	0.120seconds	97%

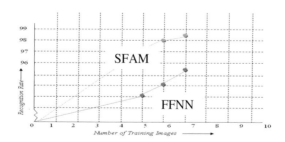

Fig. 10. Graph showing the result of the experiment conducted on ORL database

Table 1 along with Fig. 10. shows that the recognition rate increases when the number of training images increases and that the recognition rate of SFAM is much higher than FFNN.

The most important point to note about SFAM in the classification stage is that it remains open to adaptation in the event of new information being applied to the network. If the system encounters a face image that SFAM is not trained for, it will conclude that it is a face that it is seeing for the first time and it learns the new pattern, but, in case of FFNN the network will converge to a best fit.

Fig. 11. Test Image belonging to the class, network is not trained for

When the face recognition system using FFNN as the classifier is given input image(Fig.12), that belongs to a class for which system is not trained for, it will converge to the conclusion that it belongs to one of the class for which it is trained.

Fig. 12. Classification that FFNN yields

But, SFAM will conclude that this is a pattern for which it is not trained and it then learns the new pattern.

Since SFAM can adaptively be trained, this can be employed in the cases, like student record maintenance at institutions, attendance keeping at organizations and so on, where addition to database needs to be made frequently.

Fig. 13 shows the face image inputs where FFNN failed and SFAM recognized and Fig. 15 shows the cases where both systems failed. But, there is no test case where SFAM failed and FFNN recognized. Thus it is clear that the recognition rate of SFAM is much higher.

Fig. 14. Test cases where FFNN failed and SFAM recognized

Fig. 15. Test cases where both method failed

6 Conclusion

In this paper a two face recognition methods were compared. Experiment was conducted on ORL Database. SFAM was found to be a better recognizer when compared to FFNN. SFAM was efficient in terms of time complexity and recognition rate. Thus recognition system using SFAM can perform efficiently, when compared to FFNN, as a recognizer in cases where a speedy, secure and adaptive system is required. Future works include employing Fast SFAM a variation of SFAM for recognition.

References

1. Jain, A.K., Bolle, R., Pankanti, S.: BIOMETRIC – Personal Identification in Networked Society. Kluwer Academic Publishers, Boston (1999)
2. Solar, J.R., Navarreto, P.: Eigen space-based face recognition: a comparative study of different approaches. IEEE Tran. Systems man And Cybernetics- part c: Applications 35(3) (2005)
3. Sahoolizadeh, H., Ghassabeh, Y.A.: Face recognition using eigen-faces, fisher-faces and neural networks. In: 7th IEEE International Conference on Cybernetic Intelligent Systems, CIS 2008, September 9-10, pp. 1–6 (2008), doi:10.1109/UKRICIS.2008.4798953
4. Turk, M., Pentland, A.: Eigen faces for face recognition. Journal Cognitive Neuroscience 3(1) (1991)
5. Zhao, W., Chellappa, R., Krishnaswamy, A.: Discriminant analysis of principal component for face recognition. IEEE Trans. Pattern Anal. Machine Intel. 8 (1997)
6. Deniz, O., Castrill_on, M., Hern_andez, M.: Face recognition using independent component analysis and support vector machines. Pattern Recognition Letters 24, 2153–2157 (2003)
7. Wright, J., Yang, A.Y., Ganesh, A., Shankar Sastry, S., Ma, Y.: Robust Face Recognition via Sparse Representation. IEEE Trans. on Pattern Analysis and Machine Intelligence 31(2), 210–225 (2008)
8. Pham, T.V., Smeulders, A.W.M.: Sparse Representation for Fine and Coarse Object Recognition. IEEE Transactions on Pattern Analysis and Machine Intelligence 28(4), 555–567 (2006)
9. Lee, K., Chung, Y., Byun, H.: SVM based face verification with feature set of small size. Electronic Letters 38(15), 787–789 (2002)
10. Othman, H., Aboulnasr, T.: A separable low complexity 2D HMM with application to face recognition. IEEE Trans. Pattern Anal. Machine Intell. 25(10), 1229–1238 (2003)
11. Er, M., Wu, S., Lu, J., Toh, L.H.: Face recognition with radial basis function (RBF) neural networks. IEEE Trans. Neural Networks 13(3), 697–710
12. Er, M.J., Chen, W., Wu, S.: High speed face recognition based on discrete cosine transform and RBF neural network. IEEE Trans. on Neural Network 16(3), 679–691 (2005)
13. Pan, Z., Rust, A.G., Bolouri, H.: Image redundancy reduction for neural network classification using discrete cosine transform. In: Proc. Int. Conf. on Neural Network, Italy, vol. 3, pp. 149–154 (2000)
14. Nazeer, S.A., Omar, N., Khalid, M.: Face Recognition System using Artificial Neural Networks Approach. In: International Conference on Signal Processing, Communications and Networking, pp. 420–425. IEEE, Chennai (2007)

15. Gu, M., Zhou, J.-Z., Li, J.-Z.: Online face recognition algorithm based on fuzzy ART. In: International Conference on Machine Learning and Cybernetics, July 12-15, vol. 1, pp. 556–560 (2008)
16. Turk, M.A., Pentland, A.P.: Face Recognition Using Eigenfaces. In: Proceedings of the IEEE Conference on Computer Vision and Pattern Recognition, Maui, Hawaii, USA, June 3-6, pp. 586–591 (1991)
17. Swets, D.L., Weng, J.J.: Using Discriminant Eigen features for image retrieval. IEEE Trans. Pattern Anal. Machine Intel. 18, 831–836 (1996)
18. Martinez, A.M., Kak, A.C.: PCA versus LDA. IEEE Trans. Pattern Anal. Machine Intell. 23, 228–233 (2004)
19. Belhumeur, P.N., Hespanha, J.P., Kriegman, D.J.: Eigen faces vs. Fisher faces: Recognition using class specific linear projection. IEEE Trans. Pattern Anal. Machine Intel. 19, 711–720 (1997)
20. Papoulis, A., Pillai, U.: Probability, random variables, and Stochastic Processes. McGraw-Hill, New York (2002) 0073660116
21. Haykin, S.: Neural Networks: A comprehensive foundation. Prentice Hall, New Jersey (1999) 0-13-273350-1
22. Eleyan, A., Demirel, H.O.: PCA and LDA Based Face Recognition Using Feedforward Neural Network Classifier. In: Gunsel, B., Jain, A.K., Tekalp, A.M., Sankur, B. (eds.) MRCS 2006. LNCS, vol. 4105, pp. 199–206. Springer, Heidelberg (2006)
23. Rajasekaran, S., Vijayalakshmi Pai, G.A.: Image Recognition Using Simplified Fuzzy ARTMAP Augmented with a Moment based Feature Extractor. International Journal of Pattern Recognition and Artificial Intelligence 14(8), 1081–1095 (2000)
24. Rajasekaran, S., Vijayalakshmi Pai, G.A.: Neural Networks, Fuzzy Logic, and Genetic Algorithms. Prentice-Hall of India, New Delhi (2003)
25. Beale, R., Jackson, T.: Neural Computing. Institute of Physics Publishing, Bristol (2001)

A Multicast-Based Data Dissemination to Maintain Cache Consistency in Mobile Environment

Kahkashan Tabassum[1] and A. Damodaram[2]

[1] Associate Professor, CSED, Muffakham Jah College of Engineering & Technology,
Banjara Hills, Hyderabad – 500155, India
[2] Professor, CSED, Jawaharlal Nehru Technological University, Kukatpally,
Hyderabad - 500 085, India
kahkashan@mjcollege.ac.in, adamodaram@jntuh.ac.in

Abstract. Managing of complexities and challenges associated with vital and limited resources like battery power, wireless channel bandwidth, frequent disconnections and various other problems of the wired system such as variations in data size, time critical data updates and data access latency are the parameters that have given rise to the requirement for efficient cache management strategies. A heuristic approach based on different parameters that improve caching performance called Heuristic-based Cache Replacement Policy for selecting the page to be evicted is proposed in this paper. The proposed policy improves the data availability and reduce the local cache miss ratio on the client side in location-dependent environment and then perform multicast data dissemination to maintain cache consistency on the wireless network since it is based on factors that affect performance of cache such as the distance between the requester and data source, frequency of data access, data size and finally coherence.

Keywords: Cache Replacement Policy (CRP), Dynamic transmitting Agent (DTA), Protocol Independent Multicasting (PIM), Multicast-based data dissemination (MDD).

1 Introduction

In this paper we propose a cache replacement policy by studying the replacement problem for client data caching and perform data dissemination using multicasting instead of on-demand broadcasts. We use a cache replacement policy that evaluates the affect of retrieval delays; data access probability and update frequencies along with data item sizes. Multicasting can be proved to be a better technique for data dissemination since it is secure when compared to broadcasting. It is an acknowledged data dissemination strategy that is reliable (no packet loss guarantee) and allows coordination as well as sharing of cached data among different clients. It is a potential technique to improve the data access performance and availability in wireless networks. The typical problems associated with client's mobility make cache management a challenge such as different data sizes, frequent data updates, insufficient wireless bandwidth and limited client resources. A series of experiments are carried out to show the performance of multicasting in mobile environment. The work given in

N. Meghanathan et al. (Eds.): CCSIT 2011, Part II, CCIS 132, pp. 290–301, 2011.

this paper is based on a new concept wherein the data objects update is done by forming a special communicating node in the mobile network while multicasting data called Dynamic Transmitting Agent (DTA) to maintain cache consistency. Certain rules are to be satisfied by DTA in multicast data dissemination - DTA is periodically selected based on parameters such as access rate of the mobile node, stability of the mobile node acting as DTA node, life-time of the mobile node based on its level of energy, network distance (considers distance in networks not in plane).If the replicated data on a wireless network is to be sent to a group of the mobile clients with the help of a single source then multicasting is a reliable and effective data distribution mechanism that can provide not only scalability but also timely content delivery on the mobile network. Since it is a wireless network the mobile nodes will enter and leave the multicast group and this problem is best encountered and adjusted by the DTA node whose selection parameters are given above. In this paper we use multicasting instead of push/pull in broadcast environment to study the performance of HCRP with multicast data dissemination and associated issues. For this purpose in the scenario all the peer nodes implement a multicasting protocol (PIM). The anticipation in this strategy is that although as a single node it may not be possible to work that effectively when compared to in a group. Multicasting is best suited for this scenario where the multicast group maintains a dynamic node that is labeled as a DTA for the multicast group. Since the nodes in the group are mobile the DTA is dynamically elected based on the selection criteria of rules given above. There is a tradeoff between the overhead of maintaining the dynamic node (DTA) and the advantages of multicasting such as scalability, reliability, security issues better addressed in multicasting when compared to unicasting and broadcasting. This paper gives the performance details at various layers of communication when a novel policy based on the benefits of cooperative cache management strategy in wireless multicast environment called Dynamic Data Transmission is employed that uses HCRP on every mobile node as replacement policy.

The proposed HCRP considers several characteristics of mobile distributed systems, such as disconnection, mobility, handoff, data item update and request patterns from a user to achieve appreciable savings of energy in mobile devices. The results of simulation carried out have shown that the eviction policy used for wireless data dissemination when cache consistency must be enforced before a cached item is used performs better than LRU-CRP in multicast environment without any packet loss. The performance of HCRP over the other schemes becomes more effective when the cache validation delay is more.

The rest of the paper is formed in the following manner - Section 2 describes the related works in this area. Section 3 details the multicast-based data dissemination policy used, Section 4 discusses the proposed system, Section 5 outlines the System Architecture, Section 6 describes the performance metric that has been used in MDD and gives the simulation details of the model for performance evaluation. Section 7 concludes the paper.

2   Related Work

Satellite Systems and Cellular Systems in mobile computing has become a necessity for day to day life due to the challenges faced by wireless systems such as limited bandwidth and resources. Client side caching is famous policy for dealing with the complexities of data dissemination in mobile environment.[1] highlights the cache replacement policies for wireless data dissemination namely PIX where the cached data item having the least value of data access probability and same broadcast frequency gets evicted from the cache. A policy with optimal updates on memory that minimizes latency over the cache objects have been studied for a specified schedule of broadcast. All these studies are based on the assumption that the data objects existed with the same size without considering their updates and the possible disconnections. *SAIU*-CRP [2] was proposed for on-demand broadcast in mobile environment that was based on factors like data size, retrieval delay access probability, update frequency that are responsible for affecting cache performance but at the same time it did not consider the requirement of cache consistency. In this paper, we propose a cache replacement policy called HCRP in location-dependent mobile environment that ensures cache consistency during the communication among the mobile nodes in a multicast environment as crucial applications like financial transactions should effectively handle cache validation delays due to CRP. Another policy Min-SAUD uses a gain function based on retrieval delay, update frequency, access probability and data size to perform the page replacement [2]. The performance of the *Min-SAUD* policy is evaluated in on-demand broadcast scenario. The objects that are delay sensitive are addressed in [3]. Many Cache replacement policies have been studied in [4] that are based on assumptions like no updates, no disconnections and fixed data sizes which made the implementation impractical. The traditional CRPs assumed same size for the blocks of replacement. Due to this Cache miss penalties are the same and the cache hit ratio is dependent on the access latency. The shorter the access latency, the higher is the hit ratio. So Cache hit ratio is used as a measure for evaluating CRPs. But it cannot be used as the metric of evaluation when the size of blocks is variable. In some works byte hit ratio is used as evaluation performance metric. In the on-demand broadcast environment [1] access latency and stretch [3] is used as metric.

A caching strategy is used to minimize access latencies and increase data availability. Broadcast schedules are also affected by usage of caching method. Since they minimize the user requests to the server and change the access patterns of users. Also broadcast scheduling algorithms play important role in selection of caching strategies because they result in different retrieval delays for the request of similar data types. Therefore selection of the broadcast scheduling algorithm is vital to increase system performance. Many Algorithms like Longest Wait First (LWF), Longest Total Stretch first (LTSF) have been studied in [1].

Periodic propagation of Invalidation Report (IR) is an efficient strategy to maintain cache consistency [5, 6]. Server history of updates of w-broadcast intervals is specified in IR. An IR notifies every mobile user about the latest updates of data items. Each client listens the broadcast channel to invalidate cache data using these IRs. A mobile user should have updated data in its local cache to answer a query effectively. This is possible if the system uses IR-based Cache invalidation approaches [5].

In this paper a cache replacement policy H-CRP is proposed and data is disseminated using multicast strategy instead of on-demand broadcasts.

3   Multicast-Based Data Dissemination in Infra Structure Based Wireless Network

The data communication and propagation on a network is usually done using broadcasting and multicasting. A number of clients may be interested in accessing different sites to get. Stock exchange information, news or any location-dependent information and these requests use multicasting of the hot data objects to the interested users. Multicasting is used due to its reliable and secure data dissemination mechanisms. Some issues that arise when using Multicasting are:

- Scheduling objects using an appropriate dissemination method
- The frequency and order in which the objects will be multicoated.
- System support for maintaining consistency among objects
- System support for concurrent access of data objects.
- Managing Cache Replacement of objects on client-side caches
- Minimizing the waiting time of the clients by using methods such as indexing and synchronizing them

A middleware support can be used to efficiently address the issues illustrated above. For this purpose in the scenario (figure 5) all the clients (mobile nodes) in the wireless network implement a multicasting protocol (PIM). One of the nodes is designated as Dynamic Transmitting Agent (DTA) based on the parameters given in section 1. The mobile nodes can efficiently carry out data transmission given the resource constraints stated earlier. In our paper a proposal is made as follows - a new strategy of communication is employed that takes into consideration the coordination of nodes of a particular network with the anticipation that although as a single node it may not be possible to work that effectively when compared to in a group. Multicasting is best suited for this scenario where the multicast group maintains a dynamic node that is labeled as a transmitting agent for the multicast group. Since the nodes in the group are mobile the TA is dynamically elected based on the selection criteria of rules given in the section above. Thus there exists a tradeoff between the maintenance of the dynamic transmitting node (DTA) over the benefits of multicasting that offers scalability, reliability, security issues as compared to unicasting and broadcasting. Infrastructure-based wireless networks exist in a fixed topology that uses mobile users, base stations and a set of switches as their components. The different multicast routing protocols used are Open Shortest Path First (MOSPF), Distance Vector Multicast Routing Protocol (DVMRP) and Protocol Independent Multicast (PIM). PIM can be used in sparse and dense modes whereas DVMRP is unreliable since it has a tendency to drop multicast packets that are passed between mobile users and MOSPF is prone to inefficient routing of packets in multicast environment. PIM is the suitable protocol for multicasting data where the mobile users get the flexibility to enter the multicast group from any point but still provide correct and efficient multicast routing. A sparse mode PIM (PIM-SM) and Core- Based Tree (CBT) permits the mobile nodes to send multicast packets from any point over the wireless network and can enroute datagrams based only on destination. Multicasting is an efficient method of group communication since it is capable of transmitting and routing packets to multiple destinations than other strategies like unicasting and broadcasting. The dynamically improving capabilities of mobile devices combined with vast deployment of wireless networks, the content and service providers are mostly interested in supporting multicast communications over the sophisticated worldwide mobile work force.

4   Proposed System

An efficient cache replacement policy is the required key that controls the operation of cache management in location-dependent wireless environment. Existing Cache Replacement policies such as LRU are not suitable for use in location-dependent environments since it is based on caching objects that are of same size thus giving rise to same penalty of miss rates. Thus LRU do not perform well in wireless location-dependent data dissemination. In this section a novel heuristic-based cache replacement policy (H-CRP) and its performance in multicast-based location dependent wireless data dissemination environment is given. The important issue for cache replacement is to determine a victim set $Victim_k$ when the free space in the client cache is insufficient to accommodate the incoming kth data item.

Cache replacement policy selects the data items with high update rate, small retrieval delay, lower access probability, large size of data object and the cost of cache validation. Consider the following parameters for data object k:

S_{cache} represents the size of client cache
A_k represents the mean arrival rate for accessing k.
U_k represents the mean arrival rate for updating k.
$N_k = U_k / A_k$
F_k represents the frequency of accessing k.
S_k represents the size of k.
L_k represents the cache validation latency of an invalidation report.
V_k represents the victim page (page selected for eviction)

The cache miss penalty in multicast environment can be computed as follows:

$L_k = W + X + Y + Z$

where   W = coefficient of the stability of a DTA
          X = delay associated for designating DTA
          Y = time taken by DTA to multicast the latest update to the nodes
          Z = network distance (distance between networks not in plane)

Since it is a location-dependent environment the updates are frequent in this scenario multicasting is a better suited in comparison with on-demand broadcasting. The DTA constantly updates the cache in the multicast group until it is likely to leave the specific network or its energy level falls low.

Heuristic-based Replacement Algorithm for client cache: For an access to every segment S corresponding to a block B:

1.   Increment the location counter of each block B in set S for recording movements in affined locations: B.loc_cntr = B.loc_cntr + 1
2.   If the access is a hit, reset B's counter after recording the current entry:

B.cur_mv = maximum(B.exist_mv, B.prev_mv) and B.loc_cntr = 0.

When the access to an object is a miss (no value found in cache) $Victim_k$ is selected as follows:

3. The expired blocks are identified in all blocks of set S, An expired block B is selected based on the following:

    B.loc_cntr > B.cur_mv and B.loc_cntr > B.prev_mv

4. A replacement block V_k is determined based on the heuristic having:

    a) least value for U_k, L_k, cost validation and
    b) high value for F_k, A_k, S_k.

5. After making the selection mark this block for eviction. Replace $Victim_k$ and update the cache with by placing block B in the cache

5 System Architecture

In this section, we give a brief description of the existing system architecture for data dissemination in mobile environment.

5.1 A DTA Architecture for Cache Coherence in Mobile Environment

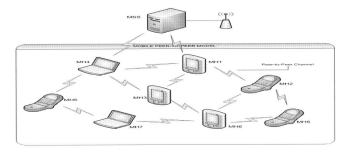

Fig. 1. A DTA Architecture for Cache Coherence in Mobile Environment

5.2 On-Demand Broadcast for Cache Coherence in Mobile Environment

Fig.2 outlines the On-Demand broadcast data dissemination strategy in which the clients send pull requests to the server through the uplink channel. In response, the server disseminates the requested data items to the clients through the broadcast channel based on a scheduling algorithm [2]. The clients retrieve the items of their interest off the air by monitoring the broadcast channel. Push-based broadcast is a common alternative to on demand broadcast for wireless data dissemination [1]. In push-based broadcast, a fixed set of data is periodically broadcast based on precompiled data access patterns. In fact, push-based broadcast can be seen as a data access patterns. In fact, push-based broadcast can be seen as a special case of on-demand broadcast, where uplink cost is zero and data scheduling is based on the aggregate access patterns. Consequently, the result presented in this paper can also be applied to push-based broadcast. As illustrated, there is a cache management

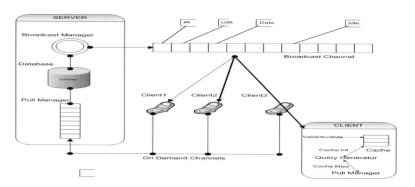

Fig. 2. System Architecture for On-Demand Broadcast

mechanism in a client. Whenever an application issues a query, the local cache manager first checks whether the desired data item is in the cache. If it is a cache hit, the cache manager still needs to validate the consistency of the cache-hit item with the master copy at the server. Thus, it retrieves the next invalidation report (see below for details) from the broadcast channel to validate the item. If the item is verified as being up-to-date, it is returned to the application immediately. If it is a cache hit but the value is obsolete or it is a cache miss, the cache manager sends a pull request to the server in order to schedule broadcast of the desired data. When the requested data item arrives in the wireless channel, the cache manager keeps it in the cache and answers the query. The issue of cache replacement arises when the free cache space is insufficient to accommodate a data item to be cached. Techniques based on Invalidation Report (IR) have been proposed to address the cache consistency issues [3, 6]. Interleaved with the broadcast data, IR's are periodically disseminated on the broadcast channel. An IR consists of the server's updating history up to w (constant or variable)broadcast intervals. Every mobile client maintains the timestamp T1 of the last cache validation. Thus, upon reception of an IR, a client checks to see whether it's Tl is within the coverage of the IR received. If yes, the client starts the invalidation process. Otherwise, it drops the cache contents entirely (w is a constant) [3] or ignores the IR and sends its Tl to the server in order to enlarge w of the next IR (w is a variable) [6]. Stretch [2] the ratio of the access latency of a request to its service time, where service time is defined as the ratio of the requested item's size to the broadcast bandwidth. Compared with access latency, which does not count the difference in data size/service time, the stretch is a more reasonable metric for items with variable sizes.

6   Simulation Model

The simulation model used for experimental evaluation is given in figure 4 and the details are outlined in section 3. It is implemented using QualNet Simulator. A single cell environment is considered. The model consists of a single server and number of clients. Multicast is employed for wireless data dissemination. The default system parameter settings are specified in Table 1 and 2 corresponding to the parameter settings made for different components on the network.

6.1 Multicast-Based Data Dissemination to Maintain Cache Consistency in Location Dependent Mobile Environment

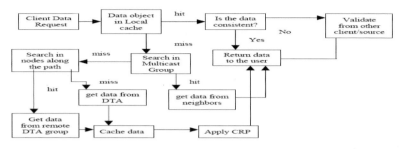

Fig. 3. Flowchart of service of a request of client using DTA-strategy

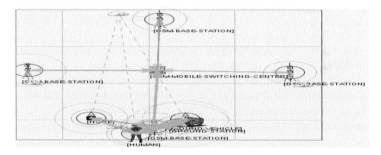

Fig. 4. A Scenario depicting Multicast data dissemination in Wireless Environment

Table 1. Parameter Settings for Base Station & Ground Station (BS&GS) (Server), Switch Center (SC)

Parameter	GS & BS Settings	SC Settings
IP Queue Scheduler	Strict Priority	Strict Priority
Maximum Segment Size	512	512
Send Buffer Size	16384	16384
Receive Buffer Size	16384	16384
Routing policy	--	Dynamic
Enable Multicast?	NO	NO
Mobility	FALSE	FALSE
Channel Frequency	2.4GHz	2.4GHz
Data Rate	2Mbps	2Mbps

6.2 Client Model

Each client is simulated by a mobile node that implements HCRP Algorithm given in section 4. It generates a set of queries and data by using Constant Bit Rate (CBR). After the data exchange occurs, the mobile client waits for a specific period of time. During this time if it moves outside the cell, it hands off the data to Server. Instead we use a multicast scenario wherein one node is designated as DTA that is responsible for making the multicast when it leaves a particular range. There is a probability p for the client to enter the disconnected state and when it happens then it is updated by the

Table 2. Parameter Settings for Mobile DTA (MDTA) and Stationary DTA (SDTA) (client)

Parameter	MDTA Settings	SDTA Settings
IPQueueScheduler	Strict Priority	Strict Priority
Max Segment Size	512	512
Send Buffer Size	16384	16384
ReceiveBuffer Size	16384	16384
Enable Multicast?	YES	YES
Multicast Protocol	PIM	PIM
GMP	IGMP	IGMP
Router List	MN1-{7,8,9,10},MN2-{11,12,13,14}, MN3-{15,16,17,18}	In n/w1-{7,8,9,10},n/w2-11,12,13,14} n/w3-15,16,17,18}
Mobility	TRUE	FALSE
Data Rate	2.4GHz	2.4GHz
ChannelFrequency	2Mbps	2Mbps

other nodes about the new DTA and it can then resume into the thinking state (the state when a node is idle not transmitting data but can receive data). The disconnected state of the client reflects an exponential distribution with a mean time. Each client has a cache of defined by S_{cache} specified in section 4. An assumption that the different caching strategies, includes space needed for storing data object along with its attributes and that the client access pattern follows a Zipf distribution[2]. The data objects are sorted such that the object 0 is the most frequently used and the last object is assumed to be least frequently used. The access probability of any data object within a specified region is uniform (assuming the Zipf distribution to these regions). The default client (stationary DTA) parameter settings are given in Table 2. A summary of client activities is provided in fig 3 and fig 5.

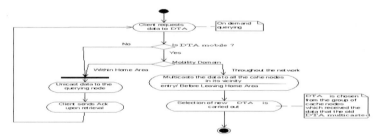

Fig. 5. Client activities for multicast-based data dissemination

6.3 Server Model

Table 1 gives the server (base station) parameter settings. The requests from the clients are buffered at the server using an IP Queue Scheduler that employs first come first serve scheduling algorithm (FCFS) and the buffer size is assumed to be unlimited. In FCFS the server selects the request from one end of the buffer then broadcasts it then the next one and so on. The overhead due to scheduling and request processing are assumed to be negligible at the server when compared to the data transmission delay and are not considered in the multicast-based data dissemination strategy. Data updates follow an exponentially distributed inter-arrival time for the updates at the server side.

The broadcasts are done periodically from server and also all the nodes in the network form a multicast group with DTA as the group head following the parameter criteria specified in section 3 and then re-nominated as the different clients move from one location to another. The server activities are summarized in the flowchart given Fig 6:

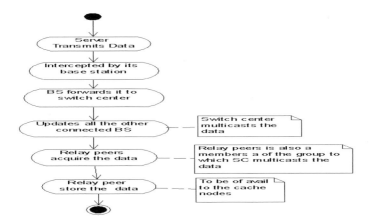

Fig. 6. Server activities for multicast-based data dissemination

6.4   Experimental Results

The following section gives the performance details of multicasting (comparison with broadcasting could not be depicted for space constraints) at the different levels of OSI layers such as Network Layer, Transport layer, Application layer and Physical Layer. Fig 7 (a),(b)specifies node number on X-axis and number of Hello packets sent and received on Y-Axis (node numbers - 7,8,11,12,15,16).(c) Current no: of neighbors are 7,8,11,15 & 16.

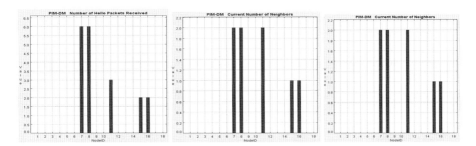

Fig. 7. NETWORK LAYER Packets exchanges in MDD using PIM-DM: (a) Number of Hello packets sent and (b) received (c) Current number of neighbors

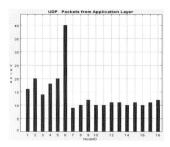
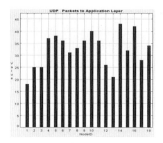

Fig. 8. TRANSPORT LAYER (a) UDP packets from application layer (b) UDP packets to application layer

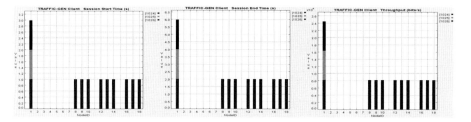

Fig. 9. APPLICATION LAYER (a), (b) Client in terms of session start time and end time (c) Client Throughput details in bits/s

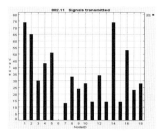
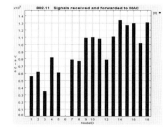

Fig. 10. PHYSICAL LAYER (a) Signals Transmitted (b) Signals received and forwarded

7 Conclusions

This paper proposes a heuristic cache replacement policy namely HCRP based on factors that affect various issues of cache management and we have investigated its performance in multicast-based mobile environment different from the previous works. A series of simulation experiments have been carried out to understand and evaluate the benefits of MDD over on-demand broadcasts. The final results demonstrate that the multicast-based data dissemination is better than the well known broadcasting strategy under different workloads and for clients favoring access to a definite set of data objects of any size. This strategy is also scalable. Thus multicast-based data dissemination is that uses HCRP could be practically used instead of On-demand broadcasts. In future study we are interested in giving the design of an optimal cache policy with a strong data consistency requirement in multicast scenario by using prefetching techniques.

References

1. Xu, J., Hu, Q.L., Lee, W.-C., Lee, D.L.: An optimal cache replacement policy for wireless data dissemination under cache consistency. Technical Report, Hong Kong University of Science and Technology (January 2001)
2. Xu, J., Hu, Q.L., Lee, W.-C., Lee, D.L.: SAIU: An efficient cache replacement policy for wireless on-demand broadcasts. In: Proceedings of the 9th ACM International Conference on Information and Knowledge Management (CIKM), McLean, VA, USA, pp. 46–53 (2000)
3. Abrams, M., Standridge, C., Abdulla, G., Williams, S., Fox, E.: Caching proxies: Limitations and Potentials. In: Proceedings of 4th International International Conference on WWW, p. 6 (2002)
4. Chen, H.: Update-based cache replacement policies in wireless environment. Broadband Networks (2005)
5. Wang, Z., Das, S., Che, H., Kumar, M.: SACCS: Scalable Asynchronous Cache Consistency Scheme for Mobile Environments, Center for Research in Wireless Mobility and Networking. In: Proceedings of the 23rd International Conference on Distributed Computing Systems Workshops, ICDCSW 2003 (2003)
6. Kahol, A., Khurana, S., Gupta, S.K.S., Srimani, P.K.: A strategy to manage cache consistency in a distributed mobile wireless environment. IEEE Trans. on Parallel and Distributed System 12(7), 686–700 (2001)

Quantitative Analysis of Dependability and Performability in Voice and Data Networks

Almir P. Guimarães[1,2], Paulo R.M. Maciel[2], and Rivalino Matias Jr.[3]

[1] Campus Arapiraca, Federal University of Alagoas, Arapiraca, AL, Brazil
almir@arapiraca.ufal.br
[2] Center of Informatics, Federal University of Pernambuco, Recife, PE, Brazil
apg2,prmm@cin.ufpe.br
[3] Computing School, Federal University of Uberlândia, Uberlândia, MG, Brazil
rivalino@facom.ufu.br

Abstract. In this paper, we investigate the performance and dependability modeling of voice and data services in computer networks. We use Stochastic Petri Net as an enabling modeling approach for analytical evaluation of complex scenarios. We apply our proposed modeling approach in a case study to evaluate the dependability and performability of an enterprise network in differents scenarios. The performability will be analyzed by considering the influence of network topologies.

Keywords: Dependability; Performability; Performance Evaluation; Stochastic Petri Net; VoIP; Queuing Policies.

1 Introduction

Over the last few years, the use of voice and data networks has significantly increased. This considerable growth is somewhat related to the interoperability offered by voice and data services and their low costs. These services should be continuously provided even when unexpected hardware or software failures happen. The design, deployment and management of communication network infrastructure ought to meet such requirements.

In the last few years, much has been done to deal with issues relating to performance and dependability of real-time applications, such as Voice over Internet Protocol (VoIP) services. Researchers have used different approaches to deal with these problems.

[7] proposes a realistic distribution model for VoIP traffic from different applications, based on real traffic traces. In particular, this model captures the features of the inter-packet time of VoIP traffic. Additionally, an algorithm for resource allocation in TDMA networks was proposed. Similarly, [9] conducts controlled experiments considering VoIP traffic with different parameters (e.g., codec type and packet size). [7] and [9] rely on traffic characterization and measurement, which are obtained directly from controlled sources for performance analysis.

N. Meghanathan et al. (Eds.): CCSIT 2011, Part II, CCIS 132, pp. 302–312, 2011.

In turn, [6] presents a systematic approach for quantifying the reliability of enterprise VoIP networks. [6] provides an enhanced method and procedure of reliability calculation, using a network matrix representation and RBD (Reliability Block Diagram). [11] discusses algorithmic methods to obtain network availability values in a given topology and presents two tools for computation of network availability in large and complex networks. [8] discusses different issues related to network availability. First, the paper presents some of the elements that impact the availability of a solution. Then, it discusses how network designers can calculate the exact availability of their solution and provides means to determine the optimal level of availability.

In this paper we focus on performance, including dependability aspects, of voice and data services. Several scenarios are evaluated through Stochastic Petri Net (SPN) models [4]. The model parameters used were obtained from a system through performance measurement. We also used values provided by manufactures of network elements. We identify traffic thresholds to avoid performance degradation in the investigated network. Regarding dependability, we evaluate the impact over the voice and data traffics when faults occur in network components.

The rest of the paper is organized as follows: Section 2 presents concepts of dependability for voice and data networks. Section 3 describes the proposed performance models along with the dependability models. Section 4 presents the evaluation of performance, dependability and performability metrics for a range of voice and data traffic patterns. Finally, Section 5 discusses the results of this study and introduces further ideas for future research.

2   Dependability Requirements for Voice and Data Networks

Standard IP applications traffic is characterized by burstiness. However, such applications are not highly sensitive to delay and jitter. On the other hand, voice applications run continuously and steady, they could thus be strongly affected by long delays and jitter.

Critical services as VoIP have strict QoS requirements for both performance tolerance and service dependability. Dependability of a computer system must be understood as the ability to avoid service failures that are more frequent and more severe than is acceptable [1]. Dependability requirements encompass the concepts of availability, reliability, safety, integrity and maintainability [1].

Inputs to dependability include component Mean Times to Failure (MTTF) models and Mean Times To Repair (MTTR). The hardware component MTTFs are supplied by the manufacturer and represent the mean time for a component failure. The MTTRs are tightly related to the maintenance policy adopted.

3   Proposed Models

The models can be evaluated using the TimeNet tool (http://www.tu-ilmenau.de). Our work is based on a system that was built in order to obtain performance,

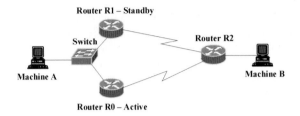

Fig. 1. Test Bed

dependability and performability results that can be considered similar to those obtained in small and medium enterprise networks scenarios. The test bed is composed of two machines, a switch and three routers. We used the MyPhone (myphone.sourceforge.net) tool as VoIP workload generator. For data traffic, TFGEN traffic generator (www.st.rim.or.jp/yumo/pub/tfgen.html) is used. Data and voice traffics vary according to the scenarios. WireShark (www.wireshark.org) is used for network analysis. Also, a probe machine collects data from the router interfaces in a 300s-time window by monitoring internal counters from routers' operating system. The queuing policy evaluated is the Custom Queuing (CQ) [10].

3.1 Abstract Performance Model

This section presents the proposed SPN abstract model (see Figure 2). The places, Pv and Pd, represent application processes located at machine A that

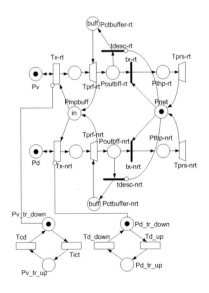

Fig. 2. Proposed Abstract Model

generate the voice and data traffics. Regarding voice traffic, the Tx-rt exponential timed transition represents the inter-packet time in accordance with voice codec. Place Pv_tr_up represents the voice transmission (#Pv_tr_up=1). During an idle period (#Pv_tr_down=1), there is no voice transmission (inhibitor arc from place Pv_tr_down to transition Tx-rt). Exponential timed transitions Tiat and Tcd represent respectively the call inter-arrival time and the call duration.

Moreover, regarding data traffic, the Tx-nrt exponential timed transition represents the inter-packet time. Place Pd_tr_up represents the data transmission (#Pd_tr_up=1). During an idle period (#Pd_tr_down=1), there is no data transmission (inhibitor arc from place Pd_tr_down to transition Tx-nrt). Exponential timed transitions Td_down, Td_up represent respectively transmission and idle periods.

In turn, the generic stochastic transitions, Tprf-rt, Tprf-nrt, Tprs-rt, and Tprs-nrt, represent the processing time of each packet in router interfaces. Tprf-rt and Tprf-nrt represent the processing time in input interface of the Router R0. In addition, Tprs-rt and Tprs-nrt represent the processing time in output interface of the Router R0. The timing associated to these transitions is obtained by analyzing the packet size (in bits), and the total transmission rate (voice and data) in bps. Variables vf, df, vs, and ds represent this timing.

Regarding router R0, the input buffer is represented by place P$inpbuff$ and its size (in packets) is represented by the variable in (see Figure 2). Moreover, the place P$ctbuffer$ represents the access control to the output buffer. The corresponding variable $buff$ (in packets - see Figure 2) is set to an upper bound value so as to obtain a bounded model.

To represent the queuing management policy in output buffer of the router R0, the *Weights* represented by the variables $w1$ and $w2$ indicate the firing probability of simultaneously enabled immediate transitions (tx-rt and tx-nrt) within an Extended Conflict Set (ECS). In case of the number of tokens in places P$outbff$-rt and P$outbff$-nrt is greater than the queues size standard (variables $n1$ and $n2$), then the immediate transitions t$desc$-rt and t$desc$-nrt fire. This is modeled by the enabling function assigned to these transitions (#P$outbff$-rt> $n1$ and #P$outbff$-nrt> $n2$).

In turn, regarding output rate in the router R2, in packets per second (pps), variables *VOR* (Voice Output Rate) and *DOR* (Data Output Rate) are calculated through the reciprocal of the Tprs-rt and Tprs-nrt generic stochastic transitions, namely $1/vs$ and $1/ds$, multiplied by the probability that the places Pthp-rt and Pthp-nrt have a number of tokens greater than zero (P{#Pthp-rt>0}*(1/vs) and P{#Pthp-nrt>0}*(1/ds)).

SPN Refined Model. A variant of the model presented in Section 3.1 considers the refinement of transitions in order to cover first and second moments. For an adequate representation of activities modeled by generic stochastic transitions Tprf-rt, Tprf-nrt, Tprs-rt, and Tprs-nrt there should be a replacement of these transitions by *hypoexponential* s-transitions, according to the mean, standard deviation and Coefficient of Variation (CV) of each transmission rate (voice and

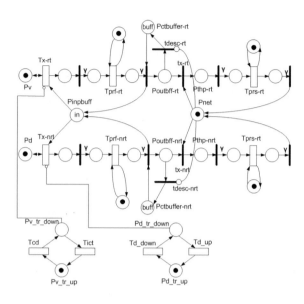

Fig. 3. Refined Model

data). However, as the number of phases increased to a high value for all the transitions, we faced the state space explosion problem [3]. Assuming that an Erlangian model is a particular case of a hypoexponential model, where each individual phase rate has the same value, we adopt a small number of stages as Erlangian s-transitions, with results very close to those obtained directly in the system. Furthermore, it adopted a phase number of four (value of γ in Figure 3). Hence, a refined version of the abstract performance model is obtained by replacement of abstract model transitions Tprf-rt, Tprf-nrt, Tprs-rt and Tprs-nrt by Erlangian s-transitions.

Performance Model Validation. It is important to note that the validation process is accomplished by comparing the obtained results, through numerical simulation, to measures collected directly from the system under test using the Mean-Matched Pairs method [5]. This method shows that the zero (0) is part of the estimates' confidence interval. It indicates the impossibility of refuting the equivalence between the system and model values. Several data transmission rates (40 *Kbps*, 50 *Kbps*, 60 *Kbps*, 70 *Kbps*, and 80 *Kbps*) are applied. With respect to data and voice traffics, it was considered a permanent transmission and constant input rate. Regarding queuing policy, we used 0.75 and 0.25 values for the variables *w1* and *w2* plus the value of 20 for the variables *n1* and *n2*. With respect to *in* and *buff* variables, we used the values 75 and 20,000. Figure 4 shows the change in total output rate (voice and data) due to different DIR (Data Input Rate, in Kbps).

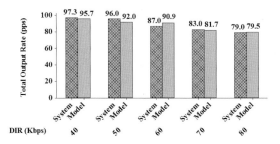

Fig. 4. Total Output Rate

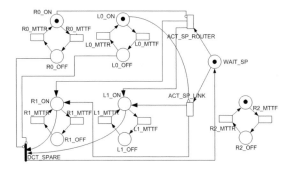

Fig. 5. Dependability Model

3.2   Dependability Model

The dependability model (see Figure 5) represents aspects of fault-tolerance based on the so-called *cold-standby* redundancy approach. The model includes ten relevant places, which are R0_ON, R0_OFF, with corresponding places of R1, R2, L0 and L1 components. Places R0_ON and R0_OFF, along with their corresponding pairs, model component's activity and inactivity states, respectively. These components have two parameters, namely MTTF and MTTR, which represent delays associated to corresponding exponential transitions X_MTTF and X_MTTR (Label "X" must be instantiated according to the component name). Exponential transitions ACT_SP_ROUTER and ACT_SP_LINK represent the spare components starting operation. This time period (delay), in hours, is named Mean Time to Activate (MTA). As the main components fail, the transitions ACT_SP_ROUTER or ACT_SP_LINK are fired. These transitions firing represents the spare component taking over the failed one. In turn, immediate transition DCT_SP represents the return to normal operation.

This model can compute the availability of the system through *SA* (*System Availability*) variable ($SA = $ P{(((#R0_ON=1 AND #Link0_ON=1) OR (#R1_ON=1 AND #Link1_ON=1)) AND #R2_ON=1}). This expression represents the probability that the system is up.

A variation of the model presented above (see Figure 6) consider a system that can only have redundancy at the link level (#Link0_ON=2).

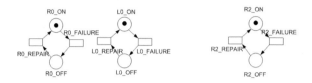

Fig. 6. Model without Redundancy of Network Elements

Moreover, most modelers kept performance and dependability models separated. Thus, it is essential that methods for the combined evaluation of performance and dependability be developed, allowing the performability evaluation. [2] defines performability as a measure to assess the system's ability to perform when performance degrades as a consequence of faults. Section 4 shows the use of performance and dependability models for obtaining system performability.

4   Case Study

We consider the studied system as an enterprise network. Our goal is to compute the network performance, dependability and performability using the proposed models. The components MTTF and Total Cost of Ownership (TCA) used in this work are respectively: Component 1, 131,000 hours and US$ 8,390; Component 2, 105,000 hours and US$ 895; Component 3, 68,000 hours and US$ 1,095.

Different redundancy schemes lead to different levels of availability. The higher redundancy, will lead to higher availability. However, within a specified redundancy scheme there may be distinct values of availability with different devices.

Initially, we calculate the corresponding TCA, availability and downtime to a period of one year, according to various scenarios. Each evaluated scenario assumes different topologies and devices. The value of MTTR of twelve hours and a link availability of 0.99 are used. For MTA, a value of 0.0027 hours is used.

A non-redundant scenario, R0 (Component 1) router in series along with R2 (Component 2) router, shows a downtime of 89.38 hours and its TCA of $ 9,285. Regarding redundant scenarios (see Figure 7), it is worth observing scenario 7, where it has a TCA of $2,685 and an availability of 0.9998 and scenario 4, that has a TCA of $17,875 and an availability of 0.9997. On the other hand, for the same availability, scenarios 1, 2, 6 and 7 show the lower TCA. In particular, scenario 7 presents the lowest TCA. These scenarios have values very close to downtime, so they are similar scenarios in relation to availability. In practical terms, the redundant scenarios have less downtime in relation to the non-redundant scenario. This fact is directly related to the parallelism of the R0 and R1 routers.

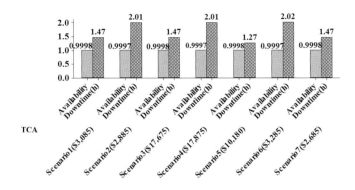

Fig. 7. Availability and Downtime for different TCAs

Also, as the router failures occur much less frequently than link failures, the link availability is an important point for the whole system availability. Figure 9 shows the system availability as a function of the link availability.

Figure 8 shows the system availability in different scenarios (Scenario 1, 2 and 3). Scenario 1 (see Figure 5) is based on the *warm-standby* redundancy approach. Scenario 2 considers a system that have redundancy at the link level. Scenario 3 shows network elements with no redundancy mechanism. Scenario 3 shows the lowest values of system availability. However, a greater link availability will lead to a system availability closer to the three scenarios.

Another important aspect of system availability refers to the MTTR. It is an important factor in system availability since it will affect the downtime of network elements. For a redundant topology, Figure 10 shows the system availability as a function of the MTTR.

Finally, we analyze combined performance and dependability. The performance considering the traffic variation is analyzed. This variation occurs in terms of transitions T*iat*, T*cd*, T*d_up* and Td_down. Weights of 0.75 and 0.25 to the tx-rt and tx-nrt immediate transitions (variables *w1* and *w2*) and a system availability of 0.9897 were considered, corresponding a downtime of 89.38 hours, with a non-redundant topology.

Regarding voice, we based on samples of Call Detail Records (CDR), obtained from a real Brazilian Telco operator database. For call duration (hold time) we consider 90 seconds (Transition T*cd*) , and 101 seconds for call inter-arrival time (Transition T*iat*). Scenario 1 will adopt a G.711 codec [14]. Scenario 2 will use a G.729 codec [13]. Finally, scenario 3 will use a G.726 [12] codec (see Table 1).

Table 1. Total Fine Cost in different Scenarios (Non-Redundant Topology)

Scenario	Codec	Tp_Voice(pps)	Tp_Data(pps)	VPNT	TFC $
1	G.711	29.65	0.54	795,035.1	39,751.75
2	G.729	15.39	0.57	412,667.5	20,633.37
3	G.726	89.11	0.54	2,389,395.5	119,469.77

Table 2. Performability in different Scenarios (Non-Redundant Topology)

Scenario	Tp_Voice(pps)	Tp_Data(pps)	Downtime(h)
1	29.34	0.53	89.38
2	15.23	0.56	89.38
3	88.19	0.53	89.38

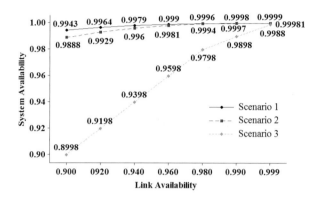

Fig. 8. System Availability according to Link Availability for differents scenarios

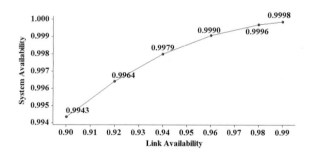

Fig. 9. System Availability according to Link Availability

Regarding data traffic, the purpose is to show the behavior of SNMP (Simple Network Management Protocol) [15]. Real scenarios were created with periodic update of 15 seconds. Transition Td_down represents the transmission period (0.09 seconds) and transition Td_up represents the idle period ((14.91 seconds).

In order to assess the financial impact of outages to a period of one month, suppose that a WAN services provider pays a fine of \$50.00 per each group of 1,000 Voice Packets not Transmitted (VPNT) over WAN networks. In accordance with voice codec, the Total Fine Cost (TFC) will vary (see Table 1). Scenario 3 presents the lowest fine. This result is due to the lower transmission rate of G.729 codec (17 pps). We must observe that different results can be obtained by varying the call duration and the call inter-arrival time.

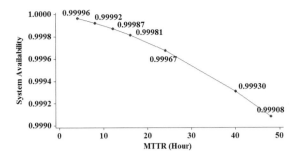

Fig. 10. System Availability according to MTTR

Moreover, Table 2 shows the resulting performance (performability) considering a non-redundant topology and a system availability of 0.9897. According to the results, the performance is slightly affected. This is directly related to the redundancy of routers (R0 and R1 in parallel). Thus, different levels of performability can be achieved through different topologies.

5   Conclusion

In this paper, we propose SPN models to evaluate several dependability and performability aspects of voice and data networks. The results, obtained through analysis and simulations, are statistically equivalent to the results obtained by measurements from the system under test. They also support the analysis of system availability based on different topologies and network elements. Regarding system availability in terms of TCA, it was seen that you can get similar values with different costs.

For future work, we plan to extend these models to include network availability with redundant topology, software failures, different recovery strategies as well as taking into account different failure dependent rates.

References

[1]   Avizienis, A., Laprie, J.C., Randell, B., Landwehr, C.: Basic concepts and taxonomy of dependable and secure computing. IEEE Transactions on Dependable and Secure Computing 1(1), 11–33 (2004)

[2]   Meye, J.F.: On Evaluating the Performability of Degradable Computing Systems. IEEE Trans. Comput. 29(8), 720–731 (1980)

[3]   Antti, V.: The State Explosion Problem. In: Lectures on Petri Nets I: Basic Models, Advances in Petri Nets, the Volumes are Based on the Advanced Course on Petri Nets, pp. 429–528. Springer, London (1998)

[4]   Bolch, G., Greiner, S., De Meer, H., Trivedi, K.S.: Queuing Networks and Markov Chains: Modelling and Performance Evaluation with Computer Science Applications, 2nd edn. John Wiley & Sons, Wiley-Interscience, New York, NY, USA (1998) ISBN 0-471-19366-6

[5]   Tukey, J.W.: Exploratory Data Analysis. Princeton University, Addison-Wesley (1977)

[6]   Chu, C.H.K., Pant, H., Richman, S.H., Wu, P.: Enterprise VoIP Reliability. In: 12th International Telecommunications Network Strategy and Planning Symposium, NETWORKS 2006, pp. 1–6 (2007)

[7]   Haghani, E., De, S., Ansari, N.: On Modeling VoIP Traffic in Broadband Networks. In: Global Telecommunications Conference GLOBECOM, pp. 1922–1926. IEEE, Los Alamitos (2007)

[8]   Semaan, G.: Designing Networks with the Optimal Availability. In: National Fiber Optic Engineers Conference, OSA Technical Digest (CD), Optical Society of America, Paper JWA124 (2008)

[9]   Cruz, H.T., Roman, D.T.: Traffic Analysis for IP Telephony. In: Proc. 2nd International Conference on Electrical and Electronics Engineering (ICEEE), pp. 136–139 (2005)

[10] Chen, X., Wang, C., Xuan, D., Li, Z., Min, Y., Zhao, W.: Survey on QoS management of VoIP. In: Proc. International Conference on Computer Networks and Mobile Computing, ICCNMC, p. 69 (2003)

[11] Zou, W., Janic, M., Kooij, R., Kuipers, F.: On the availability of networks. In: BroadBand Europe 2007, Antwerp, Belgium, December 3-6 (2007)

[12] Recommendation G.726, 40, 32, 24, 16 kbit/s : Adaptive Differential Pulse Code Modulation (ADPCM), ITU (December 1990)

[13] Annex to Recommendation G.729, Coding of Speech at 8 kbit/s using Conjugate Structure Algebraic-Code-Excited Linear-Prediction (CSACELP), Annex A: Reduced Complexity 8 kbit/s CS-ACELP Speech Codec, ITU (November 1996)

[14] Recommendation G.711 : Pulse Code Modulation (PCM) of Voice Frequencies, ITU (November 1988)

[15] Case, J., Fedor, M., Schoffstalll, M., Davin, J.: A Simple Network Management Protocol (SNMP), IETF - RFC 1157 (May 1990)

Rain Fade Calculation and Power Compensation for Ka-Band Spot Beam Satellite Communication in India

Jayadev Jena and Prasanna Kumar Sahu

Electrical Engineering Department
National Institute of Technology
Rourkela, India
jjaydev1@gmail.com,
pksahu@nitrkl.ac.in

Abstract. The growing wireless and satellite communications market makes it more and more difficult to assign frequency resources in the commonly used C and Ku- frequency bands. Thus, frequency bands above 20 GHz i.e., the available Ka-band is of increasing interest for future satellite communication links. But propagation impairments impose a limitation on the use of the20/30-GHz frequency band for these applications. The attenuation due to rain can drastically reduce the received power level, requiring appropriate system design and fade countermeasures. This paper proposes a model of beam locations to implement TDM spot beams using steerable phased array antenna for Ka-band satellite communication over Indian sub-continent taking the statistical data of socio-economic market, geographical variation and rain rate distribution strategy. A comparison of attenuation levels using global crane, ITU-R and Moupfouma rain attenuation models in Indian region is simulated using daily collected data. The variation in instantaneous rain fall rate and corresponding attenuation data can be utilised to compensate power levels so that a reliable satellite link is available at user end for all time. It is found that a power variation of 20-30 dB occurs during 8-10 hrs in a year which need enhancement of power to attend minimum level for detection of signal with accuracy. The on-board data management, uplink and on-board downlink system power enhancement methodology can provide a useful receive signal service to rain affected spots by dynamically varying the allocation of power and bandwidth on-demand.

Keywords: Ka-band satellite communication, phased array, rain rate, power compensation.

1 Introduction

This The tremendous growth worldwide in the use of Internet and multimedia services prompted the ambitious planning [7] and evolution of commercial, broadband satellite communication systems. The proposed systems must provide two-way, interactive services to support aggregate data rates in the range from 1 to 20 Gbps per satellite. With the lower allocations for C and Ku-band already congested,

N. Meghanathan et al. (Eds.): CCSIT 2011, Part II, CCIS 132, pp. 313–320, 2011.

the ITU has granted licenses to satellite organizations to operate broadband satellite systems in the Ka-band spectrum, which is often referred to as 30/20 GHz. This paper assesses the future role of satellite communications in providing mobile or fixed Internet users with broadband Internet connections in India. It analyzes Ka-band satellite communications link availability in various geographical separated spot beams in India. It is based on global rain models [1][3][6] integrated with the link budget. The models developed allow us to examine major system design issues encountered in Ka-band (or higher) satellite communications that are susceptible to propagation impairments.

1.1 Ka-Band and Proposed Features

Worldwide, there have been considerable experimental Ka-band Satellites to solve the problem of saturation of the available orbital slots at C and Ku-band and to provide new service for the information age [4]. Ka-band system is recognized as a new generation of communications satellites that encompasses a number of innovative technologies such as on board processing (OBP) for multimedia applications and switching to provide full two way services to and from small ground terminals. To do this efficiently multiple pencils like spot beams are used.

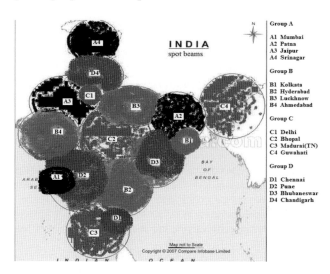

Fig. 1. Outline of proposed spot-beam locations and grouping of disjoint beams for frequency re-use

Ka-band is having raw bandwidth of around 13 GHz (27-40 GHz) and some additional 9 GHz of K-band typically used for Ka-band satellite downlinks and range from 18-27 GHz, compares well with the 6 GHz of Ku-band(12-18 GHz.).The advantage of Ka-band over other forms of internet via satellite is that is only requires a 65cms×75cms dish. Additionally Ka-band uses spot beams for internet via satellite, which make better use of the available bandwidth than a C or Ku-band satellite, i.e. more users can get higher level of services.

This paper proposes 16 spot-beam locations to cover Indian main land. The on board processing and switching (effectively the provision of the equivalent of a sophisticated telephone switch board on a satellite) are already employed in satellites providing mobile communications to handheld receivers in some western part of world.

1.2 Ka-Band Propagation Impairments and Analysis

At Ka-band the propagation impairment strongly limits the quality & availability of satellite communications. Attenuation due to rain plays a significant role in (tropical regions) India as a great diversity of climatic condition exists [2]. Tropospheric scintillation also increases with frequency, creating fast amplitude variations and additional phase noise in the transmission Scintillation is one of the many effects the Earth's atmosphere may have on a propagating microwave signal. Both the amplitude and the phase of a signal can be affected by these rapid temporal fluctuations. Scintillation occurs as the wave travels through regions of the atmosphere exhibiting slight spatial and temporal variations in the dielectric parameters affecting propagation. These variations cause an alternating focusing and scattering of the transmitted wave which is perceived by the receiver as scintillation. Currently in Indian region C and Ku-band frequencies are being used for commercial satellite communications. In future Ka-band will be used for wideband applications. Propagation studies are essential for estimation of attenuation so that Ka-band satellite links operating in different parts of Indian region can be registered appropriately.

Table 1. ITU-R Annual rain rate cumulative distributions for region K and N (ITU-R)

Percentage of time rain rate exceeded (mm/hr)	10	0.3	0.1	0.03	0.01	0.003	0.001
Region K	1.5	4.2	12	23	42	70	100
Region N	5	15	35	65	95	140	180

Attenuation by atmospheric gases depends on frequency, elevation angle, and altitude above sea level and water vapour density. It is relatively small compared to rain attenuation. Frequency below 10GHz it may normally be neglected, however it is significant above 10GHz, especially for low elevation angles. Water vapour is the main contributor to gaseous attenuation in the frequency range below 30GHz with a maximum occurring at 22.275GHz, which is the resonance frequency of water particles with RF [8]. The attenuation due to oxygen absorption exhibits an almost constant behavior for different climatic conditions, whereas the attenuation due to water vapour varies with temperature and absolute humidity.

Rain fade is the signal degradation due to interference of rainfall or clouds with radio waves (RF). Attenuation due to rain is a dominant factor for determining link availability at frequencies above 10 GHz. It depends on temperature, drop size distribution, terminal velocity and the shape of the raindrops. Also Ka-band is affected by cloud in the path [8].

Table 2. ITU-R Annual average rain rate in 16 spot beam areas of interest   (0.01% of time)

Name of the spot beam	Rain rate exceeded (mm/hr)
Mumbai	99.7
Patna	77.7
Jaipur	56.8
Srinagar	37.9
Kolkata	99.6
Hyderabad	60.0
Luck now	75.3
Ahmedabad	51.2
Delhi	69.1
Bhopal	64.8
Madurai	91.6
Gawhati	86.6
Chennai	81.1
Pune	79.9
Bhubaneswar	82.8
Chandigarh	69.8

Resource allocation and Concept of Data Flow to Spot-beams Here, we are given a set of queues, each queue representing the traffic destined for a downlink cell, and a set of servers which the downlink antennas are serving the bursts arriving from those queues. We want to allocate the downlink queues, or buffers (whose number is much larger than the number of antennas), to the antennas, with the primary objective of maximizing the aggregate priority of packets transmitted by the antennas in a given time, while ensuring fairness in the allocation policy at the burst level.

NOC- Network operating center (Hub)

Bursts are formed by a fixed number of packets, while packets belong to various flows. As every queue carries packets from different flows, each flow having one of four different priorities, our scheduler aims at providing fairness (of resources allocated) among queues with varying priorities or weights (or profits).The queues are known to be FIFO and are filled with packets. Each packet has a priority, which is the priority of the flow to which the packet belongs. There are four   priority levels, as described in the following section.

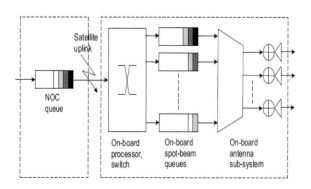

Fig. 2. Conceptual view of on-board satellite and spot beam queue

$$\text{Antenna arrays} = \begin{bmatrix} A1 & A2 & A3 & A4 \\ B1 & B2 & B3 & B4 \\ C1 & C2 & C3 & C4 \\ D1 & D2 & D3 & D4 \end{bmatrix} \quad \dots (1)$$

$$\text{Time slot1} = \begin{bmatrix} A1 & - & - & - \\ - & B2 & - & - \\ - & - & C3 & - \\ - & - & - & D4 \end{bmatrix} \quad \dots (2)$$

$$P_{\text{Total}} = A1 + B2 + C3 + D4 \qquad \dots (3)$$

$$\text{Time slot2} = \begin{bmatrix} - & A2 & - & - \\ - & - & B3 & - \\ - & - & - & C4 \\ D1 & - & - & - \end{bmatrix} \quad \dots (4)$$

$$P_{\text{Total}} = A2 + B3 + C4 + D1 \qquad \dots (5)$$

$$\text{Time slot} = \begin{bmatrix} - & - & A3 & - \\ - & - & - & B4 \\ C1 & - & - & - \\ - & D2 & - & - \end{bmatrix} \quad \dots (6)$$

$$P_{\text{Total}} = A3 + B4 + C1 + D2 \qquad \dots (7)$$

$$\text{Time slot4} = \begin{bmatrix} - & - & - & A4 \\ B1 & - & - & - \\ - & C2 & - & - \\ - & - & D3 & - \end{bmatrix} \quad \dots (8)$$

$$P_{\text{Total}} = A4 + B1 + C2 + D3 \qquad \dots (9)$$

So, at any moment the sum of power of all antennas is constant.

2 Power Distribution Strategy:

On the basis of two driving parameters i.e., Channel condition and Number of users in the spot beam area [5]. The power distribution can be made as following strategy.

2.1 Equal Antenna Share (EAS)

$$P_{A_K} = P_{B_K} = P_{C_K} = P_{D_K} = P_{Total} / 4, \quad \dots (10)$$

$$\text{for, } K=1, 2, 3, 4.$$

And all antennas shared with same power.

2.2 Balanced Antenna Share (BAS)

The antennas with different power subject to a minimum threshold power (P_{min})

$$\text{So, } P_{Total} - 4P_{min} = P_s, \quad \dots (11)$$

For P_s is the extra power which can be shared unequally among all or some of the beams.

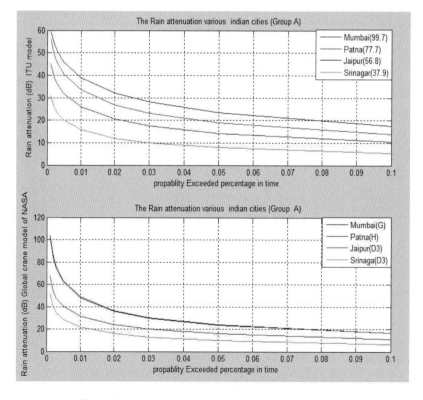

Fig. 3. Rain attenuation in group-A Spot-beam locations

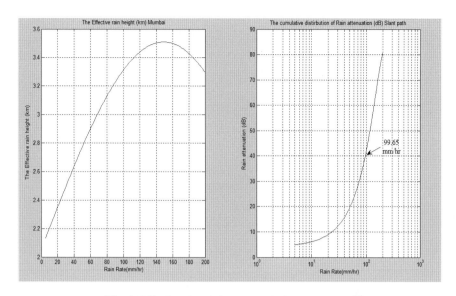

Fig. 4. Effective slant height and rain fade(Mumbai)

3 Conclusions

This analyses the terrestrial and slant path variation of rain heights and calculates different rain attenuations using mumbai geographical and ITU parameters. It is found from the result that there is about 15 dB for the duration less than 0.1 (about 87 hrs) time and 30-55 dB rain attenuation occurs for less than 0.01% (about 8 hrs) over an average year. So 15 dB can be taken as the standard ateenuation level and it can be varied upto 50 dB statistically taking different attenuation level and demand of users in 16 spot-beams. The Moufaouma model calculation and ITU model attenuation are having close approximation with ITU model but, the Crane model shows a large variation.In this paper possible rain fade and power allocation system to compensate the service during rain attenuation specifically in Indian cities, at 16 spot-beam locations is focused.

References

1. Crane, Robert, K.: Prediction of attenuation by rain. IEEE Transaction Communications, 28, 1717–1733 (1980)
2. Madgum, D.: Application of propagation models to design Geo-stationary satellite link operating in ka-band over Indian rain zones. In: CSSTEAP-UN, SAC, ISRO, Ahmedabad (2005)
3. Moufouma, F.: Improvement of rain attenuation prediction method for terrestrial microwave links. IEEE, France (1984)
4. Gargione, F., Iida, T., Valdoni, F., Vatalaro, F.: Services, Technologies, and Systems at Ka Band and Beyond—A Survey. IEEE Journal on Selected Areas in Communications 17(2) (February 1999)

5. Akkor, G.: Multicast communication support over satellite networks. University of Maryland (2005); ITU-R Recommendations. Specific Attenuation Model for Rain for Use in Prediction Methods, pp. 838-1 (1999); ITU-R Recommendations. Rain Height Model for Prediction Methods, pp. 839-2 (1999)
6. Bandyopadhyaya, K.: GSAT-4, A step towards Indian advanced communication satellite. In: IIT Kharagpur, IWSSC (October 2008)
7. Pratt, T., Bostian, C., Alnutt, J.: Satellite communications, 2nd edn. Wiley and sons, Chichester (2007)

Generalized N X N Network Concept for Location and Mobility Management

C. Ashok Baburaj[1] and K. Alagarsamy[2]

[1] Assistant Professor, Dept. of MCA,
KLN College of Engineering, Sivagangai District
ashokbaburaj@yahoo.com
[2] Associate Professor, Computer Centre
Madurai Kamaraj University, Madurai
alagarsamymku@gmail.com

Abstract. Recent Technological trends in the miniaturization of computing devices and the availability of inexpensive wireless communication have led to an expansion of effort in Mobile Computing. Therefore Location cum Mobility Management is a very important and complex problem in today's Mobile computing environments. There is a need to develop algorithms to capture this complexity. In this paper, a Generalized N X N Network concept has been introduced to minimize the total cost and to balance the Registration (Location Update) and Search (Paging) operation by maintaining the mobility history. A Genetic Algorithm technique is a biologically inspired optimization and search technique which has been implemented to solve the reporting cells planning problem for various networks. This technique shows that the total cost is less when compared with the existing cost based updating and paging scheme. This concept has been extended to prove for N X N Network.

Keywords: Location Management, Genetic Algorithm, Mobility Management.

1 Introduction

The challenges faced in today's mobile computing are the tracking of the current location of users- the area of Location Management. In order to route incoming calls to appropriate mobile terminals, the network must from time to time keep track of the location of each mobile terminals. The goal of mobility tracking or location management is to balance the registration and search operation, to minimize the cost of mobile terminal location tracking. Two simple location management strategies known are the always-update strategy and the never- update strategies. In the always-update strategy each mobile terminal performs a location update whenever it enters a new cell. However no search operation could be required for incoming calls. On the other hand in the never-update strategy, no location update is ever performed. Instead, when a call comes in, a search operation is conducted to find the intended user.One of the common location management strategy used in existing systems today is the location area scheme. [7], [8], [9]. In this scheme, the network is partitioned into

N. Meghanathan et al. (Eds.): CCSIT 2011, Part II, CCIS 132, pp. 321–328, 2011.
© Springer-Verlag Berlin Heidelberg 2011

Fig. 1. Regions representing Location area (LA) and individual cells in this figure there are four LAs each consisting of 16 cells

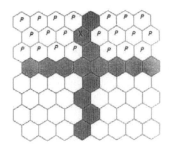

Fig. 2. Network with (shaded areas represent reporting cells)

regions or location areas (LA), with each region consisting of one or more cells (figure.1). For example, in Figure 1, if a call arrives for user X, search is confined to the 16 cells of that Location Area.

Another Location Management scheme similar to the LA scheme is suggested in [10].In this strategy a subset of cells in the network is designated as the reporting cell (Figure 2), it represents the network with reporting cells (shaded areas represent reporting cell). Regions representing Location Areas (LA) and individual cells (in this figure there are four LAs each consisting of 16 cells). Another location management scheme is a subset of cells in the network is designated as the reporting cells (figure.2).

1.1 Location Management Cost

The total cost of the two cost components (location update and cell paging) over a period of time T, as determined by simulation can be averaged to give the average cost of a location management strategy. The following simple equation can be used to calculate the total cost of a location management strategy [3].

$$\text{Total Cost} = \text{C.NLU} + \text{NP}$$

Where   NLU   - the number of location updates performed during time T

NP- the number of paging performed during time T and C is a constant representing the cost ratio of location update and paging. It is recognized that the cost of a location update is usually much higher than the cost of paging- several times higher. [11]

1.2 Network Structure

Most of today's wireless network consists of cells. Each cell contains a base station, which is wired to a fixed wire network. These cells are usually represented as hexagonal cells. Resulting in six possible neighbors for each cell. The Data set for N X N Network in Cell planning problem are movement weight, Call arrival weight, Vicinity, Vicinity value of a cell. When calls arrive for a user, the user has to be located. Some cells in the network, however, may not need to be searched at all, if there is no path from the last location of the user to that cell, without entering a new reporting cell (a reporting cell i.e. not the last reporting cell the user reported in). That is, the reporting cells form a "solid line" barrier, which means a user will have to enter one of these reporting cells to get to the other side.

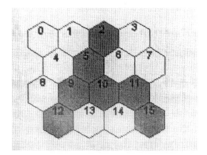

Fig. 3. Network with reporting cells (Shaded areas represent reporting cells)

For example in Figure. 3, a user moving from cell 4 to cell 6 would have to enter a reporting cell. As such, for location management cost evaluation purposes, the cells that are in bounded areas are first identified, and the maximum area to be searched for each cell is calculated which is described below.

We can define the vicinity of reporting cell i as the collection of all the cells that are reachable from a reporting cell i without entering another reporting cell as the vicinity of reporting cell i. We can define the vicinity value of reporting cell i that as the number of cells in the vicinity of a reporting cell i is the maximum number of cells to be searched, when a call arrives for a user whose last location is known to be cell i.

As an example, in figure.4, the vicinity of reporting cell 9 includes the cells 0, 1,4,8,13,14 and cell 9 itself .The vicinity value is then 7, as there are seven cells in the vicinity. Each non reporting cell can also be assigned a vicinity value. For example, in figure. 4, a cell 4 belongs to the vicinity of reporting cells 2, 5, 9 and 12, with vicinity values 8, 8, 7 and 7 respectively.

Another two parameters associated with each cell i movement weight and call arrival weight, denoted Wmi and Wcj respectively. The movement weight represents the frequency or total number of movement into a, cell while the call arrival weight represents the frequency or total number or total number of call arrivals within a cell. Clearly, if a cell i is a reporting cell, then the number of location updates occurring in that cell would be dependent on the movement weight of that cell.

Further, because call arrivals result in a search/paging operation, the total number of paging performed would be directly related to the call arrival weight of the cells in the network. As such the formula for the total number of location updates and paging performed during a certain time period T is

$$N_{lu}= \sum_{i \in S} W_{mi} \qquad (1)$$

$$N_P= \sum_{j=0}^{N-1} (W_{cj} * v(j)) \qquad (2)$$

Where,

Nlu denotes the number of locations updates during time t , NP denotes the number of paging performed during time t , Wmi denotes the movement weight associated with cell I Wcj denotes the call arrival weight associated with cell j , N denotes the total number of cells in the network , S denotes the set of reporting cells in the network.

By using (1) and (2) we get the formula to calculate the location management cost of a particular reporting cells configuration.

$$\text{Total cost} = C. \sum_{i \in S} W_{mi} + \sum_{j=0}^{N-1} (W_{cj} * v(j))$$

2 Mobility Management System

In the proposed scheme, a technique is being introduced which maintains history or mobility pattern (of size h) of the last visited reporting cell. The updating does not take place when the user roams within the reporting cells of his mobility pattern. That is the location information is updated when the enters to a new reporting cell, which is not in his user history. As a result, the updating cost is proportionately reduced with the value of h (no. of entries in the history). When we increase the number of reporting cells in the history, the location update cost is proportionately reduced. Hence the cost equation can be modified as follows:

$$N_{LU} = \sum_{i \in s} NW_{mi}$$

Where NW_{mi} - the new movement weight.

$$NW_{mi} = W_{mi} * \frac{(S-h)}{(S-1)}$$

Where h - the number of reporting cells maintained in the history.

Here if we keep h=1, the NWmi tends to Wmi. By increasing h value the NWmi will be reduced, as a result the updating cost is reduced. Consequently, the paging cost gets increased proportionately to the h value. But it can be kept under control by using the following technique. Whenever the user enters into the reporting cells of his previous history, the mobility pattern in the mobile is modified and does not leads to the location update.

The new paging cost equation is obtained from the new call arrival weight

$$NW_{cj}= \quad W_{cj} \quad * NW_{mi}$$
$$W_{mi}$$

Search Cost for the Location updated users: N-1

$$NP_1= \sum_{j=0} (NW_{cj}) * v(j)$$

Search Cost for the non-updated users from the same reporting cell:

$$NP_2= \sum_{j=0}^{N-1} (W_{cj} - NW_{cj}) * v(j) * 1/S$$

Search Cost for non-updated users from different reporting cell: (first call)

$$NP_3 = \sum_{j=0}^{N-1} (W_{cj} - NW_{cj})*(S-1)/S*v(j)*h/2 \quad \text{Call factor}$$

(Subsequent calls)

$$NP_4 = \sum_{J=0}^{N-1} (W_{cj} - NW_{cj})* (S-1)/S * (1- 1/\text{Call factor}) * v(j)$$

The call factor can be calculated as follows, if (Wcj / Wmi) < 1   then call factor =1 else call factor = (Wcj / Wmi).

Total Paging Cost :

$$Np' = N_{p1} + N_{p2} + N_{p3} + N_{p4}$$

Total Cost = $C.N_{LU'} + N_{P'}$

The total paging cost is divided into four sub components and except the third component (Np3) the other component costs are similar to the old method. As a result the increase in the paging cost is under control; it improves the total cost for the reporting cell configuration. The cost function described above shows that by varying the size of the mobility pattern (h), the total cost can be reduced to some extent. If h=1 then this cost is equivalent to the old cost. So in the worst case it behaves like the old scheme and in best case, we can introduce h value so that the entire cost is reduced.

The problem of marking the cells in the network as reporting cells and deciding the value of h can be seen and solved using one of the artificial life cycle Techniques like Genetic Algorithm. By generating the number of generations and history value the hidden information that has been derived for various data sets are the total cost (updates cost and search cost).

3 Genetic Algorithm

A Genetic algorithm (GA) [22], [32] is biologically inspired optimization and search technique. Its behavior mimics the evolution of simple, single celled organism. It is particularly useful in situations where the solution space to search is huge, making sequential search computationally expensive and time consuming. Each binary gene, represents a cell in the network, can have a value of either "0", representing a non reporting cell, and a "1" represents a reporting cell.

Each binary gene, which represents a cell in the network, can have a value of either "0", representing a non reporting cell, and a "1", representing a reporting cell. Thus, high-fitness (``good'') individuals stand a better chance of ``reproducing'', while low-fitness ones are more likely to disappear.

> Begin G:=0 (generation counter) Initialize population P(g) while not done do
> Evaluate population P(g) Compute Objective function Compute Expected
> Count Reproduce P(g)
> Crossover P(g) Mutate P(g) g:=g+1;
> end while end GA

Table 1. Input Data Set for 6 x 6 Network

CELL	WCI	WMJ	CELL	WCI	WMJ
0	514	839	8	346	1629
1	100	1276	9	121	96
2	214	162	10	656	593
3	439	242	11	852	117
4	219	852	12	138	307
5	132	1702	13	764	403
6	294	244	14	589	1279
7	610	903	15	257	556

This table illustrates the Data Set for 6 x 6 network that is totally for 36 Cells. But for illustration the Input Data set for 15 cells are given where WCI represents the call arrival weight associated with cell I. WMJ represents the movement weight associated with cell J.

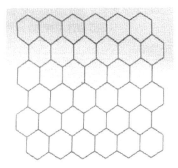

Fig. 4. Network of Size 6 X 6 Cells

Table 2. Result for Data Set 6 x 6 Network Number of Generations = 500

HISTORY VALUE	DATA SET 1	DATA SET 2	DATA SET 3	DATA SET 4
1	15422.4	18076.2	21500.4	25230.4
2	14928.1	17364.0	20830.6	24449.6
3	16368.3	19064.7	22904.4	26924.4
4	17524.8	20475.7	24597.5	28913.0
5	18526.3	21672.6	26146.3	30768.7

The Table 2 gives the Result for Data Set 6 x 6 network that is number of Iterations(Generations) are 500 . For History value one the results for various data sets are generated. Similarly for other history values from 2 to 5 the results for various data sets are generated and given in the Table 2.

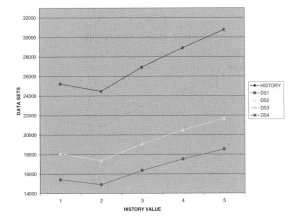

Fig. 5. Graph for Data Set 6 x 6 Network Number of Generations = 500

4   Conclusion

This paper Generalized N X N Network concept for Location and Mobility management suggests a modification in the existing location management scheme by maintaining a history of the user mobility pattern. The solution to the reporting cell planning problem can be improved by using the user mobility pattern and this concept is proved by implementing through Genetic Algorithm. This program works for any N X N Network like 4 x 4 , 6 x 6 , 8 x 8 Network.

References

1. Subrara, R., Zomaya, A.Y.: A comparison of three artificial life techniques for reporting cell planning in mobile computing. IEEE Trans. on Parallel and Distributed Systems 14(2) (February 2003)
2. Gondim, R.L.: Genetic Algorithms and the location area partitioning problem in cellular networks. In: Proc. IEEE 46th Vehicular Technology Conf. (1996)
3. Subrara, R., Zomaya, A.Y.: Location Management in mobile computing. In: Proc. ACI/IEEE Int'l Conf. Computer Systems and Applications (2001)
4. Schiller, J.: Mobile Communications. Addison - Wesley publications, Reading
5. Lee, W.C.Y.: Mobile Cellular Telecommunications, 2nd edn. MC graw hill International, New York
6. Goldberg, D.E.: Genetic Algorithms in Search, Optimization, and Machine Learning. Addison-Wesley, Mass (1989)
7. Okasaka, S., Onoe, S., Yasuda, S., Maebara, A.: A New Location Updating Method for Digital Cellular Systems. In: Proc. 41st IEEE Vehicular Technology Conference (1991)
8. Plassmann, D.: Location Management Strategies for Mobile Cellular Networks fo 3rd Generation. In: Proc. IEEE 44th Vehicular Technology Conf. (1991)
9. Yeung, K.L., Yum, T.S.P.: A Comparative Study on Location Tracking Strategies in Cellular Mobile Radio Systems. In: Proc. IEEE Global Telecomm. Conf. (1995)
10. Bar, N.A., Kessler, I.: Tracking Mobile Users in Wireless Communications Networks. IEEE Trans. Information Theory 39, 1877–1886 (1993)
11. Imielinski, T., Badrinath, B.R.: Querying Locations in Wireless Environments. In: Proc. Wireless Comm. Future Directions (1992)
12. Goldberg, D.E.: Genetic Algorithms in Search, Optimization and Machine Learning. Addison-Wesley, Reading (1989)
13. Michalewicz, Z.: Genetic Algorithms + Data Structures = Evolution Programs. Springer, Berlin (1994)
14. Histrory based location and mobility management, M.Phil dissertation
15. Effective and Efficient Mining of Data in Mobile Computing. IAENG IJCS 32(4), IJCS_32_4_5

A Weight Based Double Star Embedded Clustering of Homogeneous Mobile Ad Hoc Networks Using Graph Theory

T.N. Janakiraman and Senthil Thilak A.

Department of Mathematics, National Institute of Technology,
Tiruchirapalli - 620015, Tamil Nadu, India
janaki@nitt.edu, asthilak23@gmail.com

Abstract. In this paper, we propose a new multi-parameter weight based double star embedded clustering algorithm for MANETs. The weight of a node is a linear combination of six different graph theoretic parameters which deal with the communication capability of a node both in terms of quality and quantity, the relative closeness relationship between a node and the other nodes in the network, the maximum number of hops a node has to take in order to communicate with the other nodes. This paper deals with the description of the algorithm and an analysis of the algorithm in situations which lead to topology changes.

Keywords: MANET, Double Star, Hops, Relative Closeness Relationship.

1   Introduction

MANET also called as multi-hop/peer-to-peer network is a network formed by integrating a series of autonomous mobile nodes by means of wireless links. They communicate with each other by means of radio signals. Each node initiates a handshake by broadcasting a "Hello" message containing information like its position, id etc. Each node has its own transmission power. Those nodes within the transmission range of the broadcasting node alone can respond to the broadcast message. The most challenging issues in a MANET are the mobile nature of the devices, scalability and constraints on resources like bandwidth, battery power, etc. Scalability refers to the network's capability to facilitate efficient communication even in the presence of a large number of network nodes. Clustering is the process of partitioning the network nodes into different groups to perform an efficient and cost effective communication by providing a hierarchical network organization. Based on this organization, routing can be performed efficiently by incurring less overhead and resolving the scalability issue [15]. The hierarchical organization also enables one to concentrate more only on a fraction of the network nodes rather than the entire network. This is accomplished by dividing the sharing of information among the nodes into two, such as inter-cluster and intra-cluster sharing. Generally, clustering involves two phases, namely, cluster formation and cluster maintenance. Initially, the nodes are grouped together based on some principle to form clusters. Then, as the

N. Meghanathan et al. (Eds.): CCSIT 2011, Part II, CCIS 132, pp. 329–339, 2011.

nodes move continuously in different directions with different speeds, the existing links between the nodes get changed and hence, the initial cluster structure cannot be retained for a longer period. So, it is necessary to go for the next phase, namely, cluster maintenance phase. Maintenance includes the procedure for modifying the cluster structure based on the movement of a cluster member outside an existing cluster boundary, battery drainage of cluster-heads, link failure, new link establishments, addition of a new node, node failure and so on.

Several procedures are proposed for clustering of MANETs and a survey of these are available in [1], [9], [11], [14], [16-18]. This paper gives another different approach for clustering of such networks.

2   Definitions and Terminologies

2.1   Graph Preliminaries

A graph G is defined as an ordered pair (V, E), where V is a non-empty set of vertices/nodes and E is the set of edges/links between different pairs of nodes in V. Communication networks can in general be modeled using graphs. The set of all nodes in the network is taken as the vertex (or node) set V where two nodes are made adjacent (connected by a link) in G, if the corresponding two nodes can communicate with each other and the graph so obtained is called the underlying graph or network graph. The transmission range of each node may be either uniform or non-uniform. Based on this and the network architecture, the networks can be classified as homogeneous (of similar nature) and heterogeneous (of dissimilar nature) networks. The network considered in this paper is a homogeneous network. So, henceforth, by a network we mean a homogeneous mobile ad hoc network and also underlying graph will be an undirected graph.

For any two nodes u and v, $d(u, v)$ denotes the *Hop-distance* between u and v, i.e., the least number of hops to move from u to v and vice versa and $ed(u,v)$ denotes the Euclidean distance between u and v. Thus, in a homogeneous network, for a given transmission range r, two nodes u and v can communicate with each other only if $ed(u, v) \leq r$. Graph theoretically, two nodes u and v are joined by a link $e=(u,v)$ or made adjacent in the network graph if $ed(u, v) \leq r$. Nodes u and v are called the *end nodes* of the link e. The set of those nodes which are within the transmission range of u, i.e, the set of those nodes which are 1-hop away from u is defined as the neighbor set of u, denoted by $N(u)$ and the cardinality of $N(u)$ is called *degree* of u, denoted by $deg(u)$. The hop-distance between u and its farthest node is called the *eccentricity of u*, denoted by $ecc(u)$. i.e., $ecc(u) = \max_{v \in V(G)} \{d(u,v)\}$. The average of the Hop-distances between u and each of the other nodes is called *the mean-hop-distance of u*, denoted by $MHD(u)$, i.e., $MHD(u) = \frac{1}{|V|} \left[\sum_{v \in V(G)} d(u,v) \right]$. The average of the Euclidean distances between u and each of the other nodes is defined to be *the mean Euclidean distance of u*, denoted by $MED(u)$ i.e., $MED(u) = \frac{1}{|V|} \left[\sum_{v \in V(G)} ed(u,v) \right]$. The graph rooted at a vertex, say v, having n nodes, $v_1, v_2 \ldots v_n$, adjacent to v is referred to as *Star graph* and is denoted by $K_{1,\,n}$ (Fig. 1(a) shows an example). A *double star,* otherwise called as *(n, m)-bi-star* is the graph formed by joining the root vertices of the stars $K_{1,\,n}$ and $K_{1,\,m}$ by means of an edge as shown in Fig. 1(b).

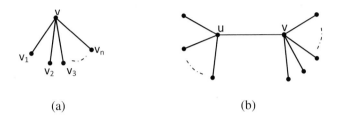

(a)   (b)

Fig. 1. (a) *Star graph* $K_{1,\,n}$, (b) *(n, m)-bi-Star*

2.2 Node Closeness Index

For a given pair of nodes (u, v) in a graph G, if $c(u/\,v)$ denotes the number of nodes closer to u than to v and $f(u, v) = c(u\,/\,v) - c(v\,/\,u)$, then the node closeness index of u, denoted by $g(u)$ is defined as in (1).

$$g(u) = \sum_{v \in V(G)-u} f(u,v). \tag{1}$$

For example, consider the graph shown in Fig. 2. The node closeness index of node 1 is calculated as below.

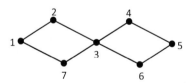

Fig. 2. An example network graph

$$g(1) = \sum_{i \in V(G)-\{1\}} f(1,i) = f(1,2) + f(1,3) + f(1,4) + f(1,5) + f(1,6) + f(1,7)$$
$$= (-3) + (-1) + (0) + (-1) + (-3) + (-3) = (-11).$$

If $g(u)$ is positive, then it indicates the positive relative closeness relationship, in the sense that, if for a node u, $g(u)$ is positive maximum, then it is more closer to all the nodes in the network compared to the other nodes. If $g(u)$ is negative maximum, then it indicates that the node u is highly deviated from all the other nodes in the network compared to others. It gives a measure of the negative relative closeness relationship.

2.3 Categorization of Neighbors of a Node

Depending on the Euclidean distance between the nodes, their signal strength varies. For a given node u, the nodes closer to u receive stronger signals and those far apart from u get weaker signals. Based on this notion, we classify the neighbors of a node into three categories. A node v is said to be a *strong neighbor* of a node u, if $0 \leq ed(u,v) \leq r/2$. A node v is said to be *medium neighbor* of u, if $r/2 < ed(u, v) \leq 3r/4$ and a *weak neighbor* of u, if $3r/4 < ed(u, v) \leq r$.

2.4 Neighbor Strength Value of a Node

For any node u, the neighbor strength value of u, denoted by $NS(u)$ is defined by (2).

$$NS(u) = (m_1 + m_2/2 + m_3/4)K. \tag{2}$$

Here K is any constant (a fixed threshold value) and m_1, m_2, m_3 denote respectively the number of strong, medium and weak neighbors of u. For a node u with greater connectivity, its greater value is due to the contribution of all strong, weak and medium neighbors of u. But, if there exists another node v such that $deg(u) > deg(v)$ and $m_1(u) < m_1(v)$, $m_2(u) > m_2(v)$, $m_3(u) > m_3(v)$, then as per the strategies used in most of the existing algorithms having node degree as an important parameter, it is obvious that node u will be elected as cluster-head because of having greater connectivity value. However, its weak neighbors have greater tendency to move away from u. This affects the stability of u and hence the corresponding cluster, if u is chosen as a master/proxy. Hence, we use the parameter $NS(u)$ to determine the quality of the neighbors of a node and hence the quality of the links.

2.5 Calculation of Node Weight

For any node u, the node weight of u is denoted by W(u) and is calculated using (3).

$$W(u) = \alpha_1 \deg(u) + \alpha_2 g(u) + \alpha_3 \left(\frac{1}{ecc(u)} \right) + \alpha_4 \left(\frac{1}{MHD(u)} \right) + \alpha_5 \left(\frac{1}{MED(u)} \right) + \alpha_6 NS(u) \tag{3}$$

Here, the constants $\alpha_1, \alpha_2, \alpha_3, \alpha_4, \alpha_5$ and α_6 are the weighing factors of the parameters which may be chosen according to the application requirements. In the proposed algorithm, in order to give equal weightage to all the parameters, we choose all the weighing factors as $(1/n)$, where n denotes the number of parameters. Here, $n = 6$.

2.6 Status of the Nodes in a Network Graph

In the proposed algorithm, each node in the network is assigned one of the following status:

1. **Master** – A node which is responsible for coordinating network activities and also responsible for inter and intra cluster communication.
2. **Proxy** – A node adjacent to a master node which plays the role of a master in case of any failure of the master.
3. **Slaves** – Neighbors of Master nodes and/or Proxy nodes.
4. **Type I Hidden Master** – A neighbor node of a Proxy having greater weight than proxy.
5. **Type II Hidden Master** – A node with greater weight and eligible for Master/Proxy selection, but not included in cluster formation because of not satisfying distance property and also not adjacent to any Proxy node.
6. **A node which is neither a slave nor a Master/Proxy.**

3   Prior Work

In each of the existing clustering procedures, the clusters are formed based on different criteria and the algorithms are classified accordingly. Based on whether a special node with specific features is required or not, they are classified as cluster-head based and non-cluster-head based algorithms [9], [18]. Based on the hop distance between different pair of nodes in a cluster, they are classified as 1-hop and multi-hop clustering procedures [9], [18]. Similarly, there exists a classification based on the objective of clustering, as Dominating set based clustering, low maintenance clustering, mobility-aware clustering, energy efficient clustering, load-balancing clustering, combined-metrics based/weight based clustering [18]. The proposed algorithm is a multi-hop cum combined-metrics based clustering algorithm. Hence, we give an overview of some of the algorithms coming under the two categories.

LID Heuristic. This is a cluster-head based, 1-hop, weight based clustering algorithm proposed by Baker and Ephremides [2], [3]. This chooses the nodes with lowest id among their neighbors as cluster-heads and their neighbors as cluster members. However, as it is biased to choose nodes with smaller ids as cluster-heads, such nodes suffer from battery drainage resulting in shorter life span. Also, because of having lowest id, a highly mobile node may be elected as a cluster-head, disturbing the stability of the network.

HD Heuristic. The highest degree (HD) heuristic proposed by Gerla et al. [10], [13], is again a cluster-head based, weight based, 1-hop clustering algorithm. This is similar to LID, except that node degree is used instead of node id. Node Ids are used to break ties in election. This algorithm doesn't restrict the number of nodes ideally handled by a cluster-head, leading to shorter life span. Also, this requires frequent re-clustering as the nodes are always under mobility.

Least cluster change clustering (LCC) [7]. This is an enhancement of LID and HD heuristics. To avoid frequent re-clustering occurring in LID & HD, the procedure is divided into two phases as in the proposed algorithm. The initial cluster formation is done based on lowest ids as in LID. Re-clustering is invoked only at instants where any two cluster-heads become adjacent or when a cluster member moves out of the reach of its cluster-head. Thus, LCC significantly improved stability but the second case for re-clustering shows that even the movement of a single node (a frequent happening in mobile networks) outside its cluster boundary will cause re-clustering.

3-hop between adjacent clusterheads (3hBAC). The 3hBAC clustering algorithm [19] is a 1-hop clustering algorithm which generates non-overlapping clusters. It assigns a new status, by name, cluster-guest for the network nodes apart from cluster-head and cluster member. Initially, the algorithm starts from the neighborhood of a node having lowest id. Then, the node possessing highest degree in the closed neighbor set of the above lowest id is elected as the initial cluster-head and its 1-hop neighbors are assigned the status of cluster members. After this, the subsequent cluster formation process runs parallely and election process is similar to HD heuristic. The cluster-guests are used to reduce the frequency of re-clustering in the maintenance phase.

Weight-based clustering algorithms. Several weight-based clustering algorithms are available in the literature [4-6], [8], [12], [19], [20]. All these work similar to the above discussed 1-hop algorithms, except that each node is initially assigned a weight and the cluster-heads are elected based on these weights. The definition of node weight in each algorithm varies. Some are distributed algorithms [4], [5], [8] and some are non-distributed [6], [20], [19]. Each has its own merits and demerits.

4 Basis of Our Algorithm

In all cluster-head based algorithms, a special node called a cluster-head plays the key role in communication and controlling operations. These cluster-heads are chosen based on different criteria like mobility, battery power, connectivity and so on. Though, a special care is taken in these algorithms to ensure that the cluster-heads are less dynamic, the excessive battery drainage of a cluster-head or the movement of a cluster-head away from its cluster members require scattering of the nodes in the cluster structure and re-affiliation of all the nodes in that cluster. To overcome this problem, in the proposed algorithm, in addition to the cluster-heads (referred to as Masters in our algorithm), we choose another node called Proxy, to act as a substitute for the cluster-head/master when the master gives up its role and also to share the load of a master. In our algorithm, each node is assigned a weight which is a linear combination of six different graph theoretic parameters. The advantage of considering more parameters is that the (Master, Proxy) pairs can be chosen more precisely without giving bias to mobile nodes having certain specific combinations. The algorithm concentrates on maximum weighted node, where the weight will be maximum if the parameters $deg(u)$, $g(u)$, $NS(u)$ are maximum and $ecc(u)$, $MHD(u)$ and $MED(u)$ are all minimum. The following characteristics are considered while choosing the parameters.

1. The factor $deg(u)$ denotes the number of nodes that can interact with u or linked to u, which is otherwise stated as the connectivity of the node. By choosing a node u with deg(u) to be maximum, we are trying to choose a node having higher connectivity. This will minimize the number of clusters generated.
2. The metric, neighbor strength value, gives the quality of the links existing between a node and its neighbors. By choosing $deg(u)$ and $NS(u)$ to be simultaneously maximum, we prefer a node having good quantity and quality of neighbors/links.
3. The parameter $g(u)$ gives a measure of the relative closeness relationship between u and the other nodes in the network. By choosing $g(u)$ to be maximum, we concentrate on the node having greater affinity towards the network.
4. By choosing a node with minimum eccentricity, we look at a node capable of communicating with all the other nodes in least number of hops compared to others.
5. By selecting a node with minimum MHD and MED, we choose a node for which the average time taken to successfully transmit the messages (measured both in terms of number of hops and Euclidean distance) among/to the nodes in the network is much lesser.

5 Proposed Algorithm - Double Star Embedded Clustering Algorithm (DSECA)

The algorithm proposed herein is an extension of the 3hBAC clustering algorithm [19] and the weight-based clustering algorithms [4-8], [20]. As in LCC, 3hBAC and other clustering algorithms, the proposed clustering procedure also involves two phases, namely, cluster set up phase and cluster maintenance phase.

5.1 Cluster Set Up Phase

DSEC(*G*). In the cluster set up phase, initially, all the nodes are grouped into some clusters.

Initial (Master, Proxy) election. Among all the nodes in the network, choose a node having maximum weight. It is designated as a Master. Next, among all its neighbors, the one with greater weight is chosen and it is designated as a Proxy. Then the initial cluster is formed with the chosen Master, Proxy and their neighbors. Since this structure will embed in itself a double star, the algorithm is referred to as a double star embedded clustering algorithm.

Second and subsequent (Master, Proxy) election. For the subsequent (Master, Proxy) election, we impose an additional condition on the hop distance between different (Master, Proxy) pairs to generate non-overlapping clusters. Here, as in 3hBAC, we impose the condition that all the (Master, Proxy) pairs should be atleast 3 hops away from each other. Nodes which are already grouped into some clusters are excluded in the future cluster formation processes. Among the remaining pool of nodes, choose the one with higher weight. Next,

(i) Check whether the newly chosen node is exactly 3-hop away from atleast one of the previously elected Masters (or Proxies) and atleast 3-hop from the corresponding Proxy (or Master)
(ii) The newly elected node should be at distance atleast 3-hop from rest of the (Master, Proxy) pairs.

If the above chosen higher weight node satisfies these two conditions, it can be designated as a Master.

To choose the corresponding Proxy, among the neighbors of above chosen Master, find the one with higher weight and at distance atleast 3-hop from each of the previously elected (Master, Proxy) pairs. Then, obtain a new cluster with this chosen (Master, Proxy) pair and their neighbors. Repeat this procedure until all the nodes are exhausted. The nodes which are not grouped into any cluster and all Type I Hidden Masters are collected separately and are termed as "Critical nodes". The set of all nodes grouped into clusters is denoted by S and the set of critical nodes is denoted by C. Hence, after the cluster set up phase, the sets S and C are obtained as output.

5.2 Cluster Maintenance Phase - Treatment of Critical Nodes Generated by DSECA

Nature of Critical Nodes. A node in the critical node set C generated after implementing DSECA may be any one of the following categories:

(i)   A Hidden Master of type I.
(ii) A Hidden Master of type II.
(iii) A Node neglected in cluster formation because of lesser weight.

Neighbors of Critical Nodes. Let u be a critical node and v be a neighbor of u. Then the following cases may arise:

Case i: v is another critical node. Here, if v is a Hidden Master of type I, then v will have an adjacent Proxy node such that w(v) is greater than that of the proxy node.

Define N''(v)=Set of those neighbors of v which are not proxy nodes and also having lesser weight than that of v and N''(v) will be used to form adjusted double-star embedded clusters. In other cases, we simply consider all the neighbors of v for the required adjusted cluster formation.

Case ii: v is a slave node (an existing cluster member). In this case, v will be used for adjusted cluster formation provided v is not adjacent to any existing Master. In such a case, we consider all the neighbors of v having lesser weight than v except the neighbors which are Proxy nodes.

Formation of adjusted Double star embedded clusters. In the formation of adjusted clusters, we try to form clusters of these critical nodes either among themselves or by extracting nodes from existing clusters and regroup them with critical nodes to form better clusters. The below adjusted clustering procedure is invoked to minimize the number of critical nodes.

adjusted_DSECA(S, C)
From C, extract a node with maximum weight. Let it be c. Then any one of the following cases arises:

Case i: c may be a Hidden Master of type I. Then, c will have an adjacent Proxy, say P. From N(c)\{P}, choose a node, say c', having greater weight.
Subcase i: c' is another critical node. If c' is a Hidden Master of type I, then find N''(c') and form the new adjusted double star embedded cluster with {c, c'} ∪ (N(c)\P) ∪ N''(c'). The node c acts as the Master and c' as the Proxy of the new adjusted cluster. Otherwise, the set {c, c'} ∪ (N(c)\P) ∪ N(c') will form the new adjusted double star embedded cluster with c as Master and c' as Proxy.
Subcase ii: c' is a slave node. In this case, c' may be adjacent to some Proxy of existing clusters. So, obtain a new cluster with c, c', N(c)\P and the neighbors of c' having lesser weight than c' excluding the adjacent Proxy nodes. Here, c acts as the Master and c' as the Proxy of the new adjusted cluster.
Case ii: c is not a Hidden Master of type I. In this case, from N(c), choose a node, say c' having greater weight, then form a new adjusted cluster, with c, c', N(c) and the neighbors of c' which are not adjacent to any master and having lesser weight than c'.

Repeat this procedure until either all the nodes are exhausted or no such selection can be performed further. If there is any node left uncovered after completing this procedure, it will become a Master on its own. Further, as the position of nodes may change frequently due to mobility, each (Master, Proxy) pair should periodically update its neighbor list so that if any slave node moves outside its cluster boundary, it can attach itself to its neighboring cluster by passing find_CH messages to (Master, Proxy) pairs. If it receives an acknowledgment from some Master/Proxy, it will join that cluster. In case getting an acknowledgement from two or more nodes, the slave chooses the one with higher weight.

5.3 An Illustration

Consider the network graph given in Figure 3 consisting of 23 nodes. The figure depicts the node ids and the weight values of the 23 nodes. Fig. 4 shows the clusters obtained after implementing the procedures given in sections 5.1 and 5.2. The critical nodes obtained in Fig. 4(b), are taken as individual Masters.

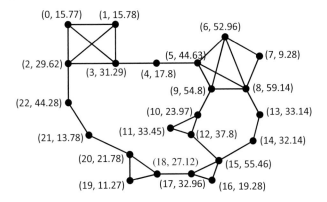

Fig. 3. Network Graph with weights

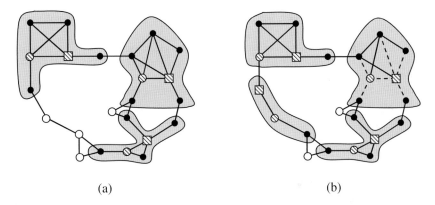

(a)   (b)

Fig. 4. (a) Clusters generated after executing DSEC(*G*), **(b)** Adjusted Clusters formed after executing adjusted_DSECA *(Here, the Striped circles denote Masters, Striped squares denote Proxies, Shaded circles denote slaves and blank circles denote Critical nodes)*

Remark: It is to be noted that each node in a cluster will be atmost two hops away from the Master/Proxy nodes. Further, it can be seen that each cluster embeds in itself a double star structure (shown in dotted lines in Fig. 4(b), for instance) and hence the algorithm is referred to as a double star embedded clustering algorithm.

6 Categorization of DSE Clustering

Any clustering which yields no critical nodes after initial cluster formation is said to be a *perfect clustering*. The one which yields some critical nodes but the number is reduced to zero after executing adjusted procedure is said to be a *fairly-perfect clustering* scheme and the one in which the number of critical nodes cannot be reduced to zero even after implementing adjusted procedure is said to be an *imperfect clustering*.

7 Conclusion

The algorithm yields a cluster structure, where the clusters are managed by Master nodes. In case of any failure of Master nodes, the cluster is not disturbed and the functions are handed over to an alternative which behaves in a similar way to Master nodes (Perhaps with less efficiency than Masters but better than other slaves). This enables us to increase the life time of the network. Further, since the clusters are managed by the Masters as well as by the Proxy nodes at times of necessity, the load is well balanced. The event of re-clustering can be avoided as long as possible.

References

1. Abbasi, A.A., Buhari, M.I., Badhusha, M.A.: Clustering Heuristics in Wireless Networks: A survey. In: Proc. 20th European Conference on Modelling and Simulation (2006)
2. Baker, D.J., Ephremides, A.: A distributed algorithm for organizing mobile radio telecommunication networks. In: 2nd International Conference on Distributed Computer Systems, pp. 476–483. IEEE Press, France (1981)
3. Baker, D.J., Ephremides, A.: The architectural organization of a mobile radio networks via a distributed algorithm. IEEE Transactions on Communications COM-29(11), 1694–1701 (1981)
4. Basu, P., Khan, N., Little, T.D.C.: A mobility based metric for clustering in mobile ad hoc networks. In: Proc. of IEEE ICDCS, Phoenix, Arizona, USA, pp. 413–418 (2001)
5. Chatterjee, M., Das, S.K., Turgut, D.: A Weight Based Distributed Clustering Algorithm for MANET. In: Prasanna, V.K., Vajapeyam, S., Valero, M. (eds.) HiPC 2000. LNCS, vol. 1970, pp. 511–521. Springer, Heidelberg (2000)
6. Chatterjee, M., Das, S.K., Turgut, D.: WCA: A Weighted Clustering Algorithm for Mobile Ad Hoc Networks. In: Cluster Computing, vol. 5, pp. 193–204. Kluwer Academic Publishers, The Netherlands (2002)
7. Chiang, C.: Routing in clustered multihop, mobile wireless networks with fading channel. In: Proc. of IEEE SICON 1997 (1997)
8. Choi, W., Woo, M.: A Distributed Weighted Clustering Algorithm for Mobile Ad hoc Networks. In: Proc. of AICT/ICIW 2006. IEEE, Los Alamitos (2006)
9. Francis, S.J., Rajsingh, E.B.: Performance Analysis of Clustering Protocols in Mobile Ad Hoc Networks. J. Computer Science 4(3), 192–204 (2008)
10. Gerla, M., Tsai, J.T.C.: Multi-cluster, mobile, multimedia radio network. Wireless Networks 1(3), 255–265 (1995)
11. Hincapié, R.C., Correa, B.A., Ospina, L.: Survey on clustering Techniques for mobile ad hoc networks. IEEE, Los Alamitos (2006)
12. Inn Inn, E.R., Seah, W.K.G.: Performance Analysis of Mobility-based d-Hop (MobDHop) Clustering Algorithm for Mobile Ad Hoc Networks. Elsevier Comput. Networks 50, 3339–3375 (2006)
13. Parekh, A.K.: Selecting routers in ad-hoc wireless networks. In: Proc. SB/IEEE International Telecommunications Symposium. IEEE, Los Alamitos (1994)
14. Agarwal, R., Motwani, M.: Survey of clustering algorithms for MANET. Int. J. on Computer Science and Engineering 1(2), 98–104 (2009)
15. Al-Omari, S.A.K., Sumari, P.: An overview of mobile ad hoc networks for the existing protocols and applications. Int. J. App. of Graph Theory in Wireless Ad Hoc Networks and Sensor Networks (Graph-Hoc) 2(1) (2010)

16. Gajurel, S.: Multi-Criteria Clustering (2006)
17. Xing, Z., Gruenwald, L., Phang, K.K.: A Robust Clustering Algorithm for Mobile Ad Hoc Networks. Handbook of Research on Next Generation Networks and Ubiquitous Computing (2008)
18. Yu, J.Y., Chong, P.H.J.: A Survey of Clustering Schemes for Mobile Ad Hoc Networks. IEEE Communications Surveys and Tutorials, First Quarter 7(1), 32–47 (2005)
19. Yu, J.Y., Chong, P.H.J.: 3hBAC (3-hop Between Adjacent cluster heads: a Novel non-overlapping clustering algorithm for mobile ad hoc networks. In: Proc. IEEE Pacrim 2003, vol. 1, pp. 318–321 (2003)
20. Yang, W., Zhang, G.: A Weight-based clustering algorithm for mobile Ad hoc networks. In: Proc. 3rd Int. Conf. on Wireless and Mobile Communications (2007)

An Enhanced Secured Communication of MANET

J. Thangakumar and M. Robert Masillamani

School of Computer Science and Engineering,
Hindustan Institute of Technology and Science,
Chennai, Tamilnadu, India
{thang.kumar,rmasillamani}@gmail.com
http://www.hindustanuniv.ac.in

Abstract. The communication between the mobile nodes in the Mobile Ad hoc networks are not secure due to inside attacks and outside attacks in the hostile environment. We refer to any protected and authenticated nodes resulting in disruption of the routing service such as drop packets, modify packets and miss-route packets, error packets and to such an adversary as a Byzantine adversary. Nodes may exhibit Byzantine behavior, either alone or colliding with other nodes. Several routing protocols were proposed to cope with insider attacks, outsider attacks and selective data forwarding attacks. To mitigate these vulnerabilities of routing protocols in wireless ad hoc networks, we propose a new Reactive Secure Routing Protocol for mobile ad hoc networks provides resilience against Byzantine attacks. The proposed protocol provides security for inside attacks, outside attacks and selective data forwarding attacks in mobile ad hoc networks. Simulation results demonstrate that effectively mitigates the identified attacks while providing better delivery ratio, and also more resistant against node capture attacks.

Keywords: Byzantine attacks, MANETs, Reactive Secure Routing Protocol, Hop Count.

1 Introduction

Wireless ad-hoc network is a computer network that uses wireless communication links. In wireless ad hoc networks each node is willing to forward data for other nodes. This is in contrast to wired network technologies in which the task of forwarding the data is performed using some designated nodes, usually with custom hardware and variously known as routers, switches, hubs, and firewalls. In addition, it is in contrast to managed wireless networks in which a special node known as an access point manages communication among other nodes is used.

Routing protocols for ad hoc networks generally can be divided in to two main categories: *periodic* protocols and *reactive* protocols. In a periodic (or proactive) routing protocol, nodes periodically exchange routing information with other nodes in an attempt to have each node always know a current route to all destinations. In an reactive protocol, on the other hand, nodes exchange routing information only when needed, with a node attempting to discover a route to some destination only when it has a packet to send to that destination[13].The proposed protocol is an reactive protocol that provides resilience against Byzantine attacks.

N. Meghanathan et al. (Eds.): CCSIT 2011, Part II, CCIS 132, pp. 340–348, 2011.

1.1 Vulnerabilities in MANET

In order to provide protected communication between mobile nodes in a hostile environment security has become a primary concern [1]. In contrast to the wire line networks, a number of nontrivial challenges are posed to security design by the unique characteristics of mobile ad hoc networks, for instance open peer-to-peer network architecture, shared wireless medium, stringent resource constraints, and highly dynamic network topology. The research activities about security in MANETs are still at their beginning, while the routing aspects of MANETs are already well understood. In addition to the problems of regular networks, a number of new security problems are also faced by MANETs [2].some of the vulnerabilities are as follows.

MANET nodes would not be any safe. The node could be compromised and thus would act as a hostile node. Easy theft might also lead to node tampering. Tampered node might disrupt network operations or release critical information. Securing such a protocol in the presence of hostile nodes presents a challenge.

Without appropriate protection, the malicious nodes can readily function as routers and prevent the network from correctly delivering the packets. For example, the malicious nodes can announce incorrect routing updates which are then propagated in the network, or drop all the packets passing through them. Thus security issue in ad hoc networks, namely the protection of their network-layer operations from malicious attacks is very important.

1.2 Requirements in Ad Hoc Networks

All Secure ad hoc routing protocols must satisfy the following requirements to ensure that path discovery from source to destination functions correctly in the presence of malicious adversaries [12].

The network topology must not be exposed neither to adversaries nor to authorized nodes by the routing messages. Exposure of the network Topology may be an advantage for adversaries trying to destroy or capture nodes.

Significant work focused on the security of uni-cast wireless routing protocols. Several secure routing protocols resilient to outside attacks such as authentication were proposed in the last few years such as Ariadne [8], SEAD [13], and ARAN [12]. Several routing protocols were proposed to cope with insider attacks such as dropping packets, modifying packets [8] – [11]. Methods proposed to address insider threats in routing include monitoring [9], multi-path routing [8], [10] and acknowledgment-based feedback [5].

1.3 Byzantine Attacks

Not forwarding packets, injecting, modifying or replaying packets, rushing packets or creating wormholes are some examples of such Byzantine behavior.

1. A Byzantine adversary can drop the request and/or response, or can influence the route selection by using wireless specific attacks such as wormhole and flood rushing to prevent a route from being established.
2. In addition, the packets carrying the route selection metric such as hop count or node identifiers can be modified by a Byzantine adversary.
3. Termination of routes due to unpredicted movement of the node in the network can drop the request or response [19].

We propose a new Reactive Secure Routing Protocol (RSRP) that provides resilience against Byzantine attacks to mitigate these vulnerabilities of routing protocols in wireless ad hoc networks.

2 Related Work

A mechanism of detecting node misbehavior in terms of selfishness was presented by Tarag Fahad and Robert Ask with. The working of their algorithm has been illustrated with two scenarios. Their algorithm PCMA detected selfish nodes which perform full/partial packets attack in a successful manner [3].

A credit-based Secure Incentive Protocol (SIP) that simulates cooperation in packet forwarding for infrastructure less MANETs was proposed by Yanchao Zhang. SIP was cautiously designed to be a secure yet lightweight charging [4].

The routing misbehavior in MANETs was studied by Kejun Liu. The 2ACK scheme that serves as an add-on technique for routing schemes to detect routing misbehavior and to mitigate their adverse effect was presented. [5].

A proof-of-concept implementation of a secure routing protocol(SRP) based on AODV over IPv6, further reinforced by a routing protocol-independent Intrusion Detection and Response system for ad-hoc networks was presented by Anand Patwardhan. [6].

Li Zhao and José G. Delgado-Frias have proposed and evaluated a Multipath Routing Single path transmission (MARS) scheme to detect misbehavior on data and mitigate adverse effects. [7].

Attacks against routing in ad hoc networks were presented by YihChun H. In addition, the design of Ariadne, a new secure reactive adhoc network routing protocol was presented and its performance was evaluated. In addition, it prevents a large number of types of Denial-of-Service attacks [8].

Two techniques that improve throughput in an ad hoc network in the presence of nodes that agree to forward packets but fail to do so are presented by Sergio Marti. They have proposed categorizing nodes based upon their dynamically measure behavior to mitigate this problem. [9].

The SMT and SSP protocols for secure data communication in ad hoc networks were presented and analyzed by Panagiotis Papadimitratos and Zygmunt J. Haas. Owing to the fact that the two protocols provide lightweight end-to-end security services and operate without knowledge of the trustworthiness of individual network nodes, they are applied extensively [10].

An routing protocol for ad hoc wireless networks that provides resilience to byzantine failures caused by individual or colluding nodes was presented by Baruch Awerbuchl. After log n faults have occurred (where n is the length of the path), a malicious link is detected by their adaptive probing technique. [11].

The notion of a tunneling attack, in which collaborating malicious nodes can encapsulate messages between them to subvert routing metrics, was introduced by Kimaya Sanzgiri, et al. A solution for secured routing in the managed-open environment was provided by their protocol [12].

The design and evaluation of SEAD, a secure ad hoc network routing protocol using distance vector routing was presented by Yih-Chun Hu, et. al. They used efficient one-way hash functions against Denial-of-Service (DoS) [13].

Gergely Acs [14] have argued that flaws in ad hoc routing protocols can be very subtle, and they advocated a more systematic way of analysis. They have proposed a mathematical framework in which security can be precisely defined and routing protocols for mobile ad hoc networks can be proved to be secure in a rigorous manner.

Syed Rehan Afzal et al. [15] have explored the security problems and attacks in existing routing protocols and then they have presented the design and analysis of secure routing protocol, called SRP. The proposed (SRP) secure routing protocol was based on DSR, which uses a broadcast authentication scheme.

3   AODV Protocol Overview

The AODV [17, 18] routing protocol is a reactive routing Protocol; therefore, routes are determined only when needed. The message exchanges of the AODV protocol is given below.

Hello messages may be used to detect and monitor links to neighbors. If Hello messages are used, each active node Periodically broadcasts a Hello message that all its neighbors receive. Because nodes periodically send Hello messages, if a node fails to receive several Hello messages from a neighbour, a link break is detected.

When a source has data to transmit to an unknown destination, it broadcasts a Route Request (RREQ) for that destination. At each intermediate node, when a RREQ is received a route to the source is created. If the receiving node has not received this RREQ before, is not the destination and does not have a current route to the destination, it rebroadcasts the RREQ. If the receiving node is the destination or has a current route to the destination, it generates a Route Reply (RREP). The RREP is uni-cast in a hop-by hop fashion to the source. As the RREP propagates, each intermediate node creates a route to the destination. When the source receives the RREP, it records the route to the destination and can begin sending data. If multiple RREPs are received by the source, the route with the shortest hop count is chosen.

As data flows from the source to the destination, each node along the route updates the timers associated with the routes to the source and destination, maintaining the routes in the routing table. If a route is not used for some period of time, a node cannot be sure whether the route is still valid; consequently, the node removes the route from its routing table.

If data is flowing and a link break is detected, a Route Error (RERR) is sent to the source of the data in a hop-by hop fashion. As the RERR propagates towards the source, each intermediate node invalidates routes to any unreachable destinations. When the source of the data receives the RERR, it invalidates the route and reinitiates route discovery if necessary. This process will be repeated again and again.

4   Reactive Secure Routing Protocol (RSRP)

In this section we describe our proposed protocol named Reactive Secure Routing Protocol.

4.1   Overview of the Protocol

We employ an authentication framework which eradicates a large class of outside attacks by ensuring that only authorized nodes can perform certain operations. Every node authorized to take part in the routing and data transmission is presented with a pair of public/private keys and a node certificate that connects public key of the node to its IP address. The token used to authenticate the nodes to be communicated in the network is periodically refreshed and disseminated by a special node, authorizer. Consequently, only the nodes that are currently participating in the routing or data forwarding operations will possess a valid tree token.

Both route request and route reply are flooded by the protocol which guarantees that a path is established even if route activation messages are dropped to mitigate inside attacks that try to prevent a node from establishing a route to the destination by employing a timeout based mechanism. If an adversarial-free route subsists, the protocol ensures the reaction of a route.

In order to provide resilience to selective data forwarding attacks, a reliability metric containing a list of link weights where high weights correspond to low reliability to capture adversarial behavior, is employed. Every node maintains its own weight list and includes it in each route request to ensure that a new route to the tree avoids adversarial links. The link's reliability is determined by the number of packets successfully delivered on that link. The destination node monitors the rate of receiving data packets and it is compared with the transmission rate specified by the source. If the variation amid the perceived transmission rate and the rate specified by the source on a link falls below a threshold value, the weight of that link is enhanced. Subsequently, the discovery of a new route is initiated.

4.1.1 Network Model and Authentication Framework

We consider a multi- hop wireless network where nodes participate in the data forwarding process for other nodes. We assume that the wireless channel is symmetric. All nodes have the same transmitting power and consequently the same transmission range. The receiving range of a node is identical to its transmission range. Also, nodes are not required to be tamper resistant: If an attacker compromises a node, it can extract all key material, data or code stored on that node.

We assume that nodes have a method to determine the source authenticity of the received data. The framework prevents unauthorized nodes to be part of the network or of the routing path. Each authorized node of the network has a pair of public/private keys and a node certificate that binds its public key to its IP address.

4.1.2 Token Distribution

The source node employs the pair-wise shared keys established between the neighbors to periodically refresh and broadcast the token used to authenticate all the nodes along the routing path. Hence, a valid token will be possessed by the nodes that are at present on the routing path. The source utilizes a one-way hash function F to periodically broadcast a token authenticator in the whole network. Nodes can apply the function F to the route token and compare it with the last received token authenticator to authenticate it.

4.1.3 Hop Count

Some malicious nodes will claim that they are at shorter hop distance from the source, though it is large. To prevent such nodes, a technique based on a hash chain similar to [6] is proposed. Let f be a one-way hash function and let dm be the maximum hop-distance of a path from a node to the source.

The source node S calculates the hop count index

$$HI = f^{dm}(X)$$

where X is a random number selected by S. A node along the routing path receives the following information from its parent:

$$[X, d, dm, f^{dm}(X)]$$

Where d is the parent's hop distance to the source and $f^{dm}(x)$ is the hop count index.

4.3 Mitigating Inside Attacks During Route Discovery

A modified route request/route reply procedure utilized by the reactive routing protocols is employed by the protocol. The route request (RREQ) message created by the source node and signed using its private key includes the node id, its weight list, and a request sequence number in a concatenated format.

Only if the total weight is less than any previously forwarded RREP message with same response sequence number, the hop count authentication and all the signatures collected on the response are considered to be valid. After the validation of the message, the node adds its id to the message and updates the hop count authentication information. Subsequently, the node signs the entire message and rebroadcasts it. While the RREP message propagates across the network, the nodes set pointers to the node from which the RREP was received in order to establish the forward route.

The procedure followed by the intermediate nodes during the RREP propagation when it receives a RREP is also performed by the source. Besides, the source verifies the validity of the route token included in the RREP message.

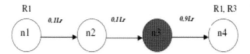

Fig. 1. Selective Data Forwording Attack

The source periodically broadcasts the data transmission rate R in a message (TR_MSG) after signing it. Nodes which receive this message, add their estimated transmission rate to the message and stores the copy of the last received TR_MSG.

5 Performance Evaluation

We use NS2 to simulate our proposed algorithm. In our simulation, the channel capacity of mobile hosts is set to the same value: 2 Mbps. We use the distributed coordination function (DCF) of IEEE 802.11 for wireless LANs as the MAC layer protocol. It has the functionality to notify the network layer about link breakage.

Our simulation settings and parameters are summarized in table 1.

Table 1. Parametes for our Simulation

No. of Nodes	25
Area Size	500 X 500
Mac	802.11
Radio Range	250m
Simulation Time	50 sec
Traffic Source	CBR
Packet Size	512 KB/s
Speed	5m/s t 10m/s
Misbehaving Nodes	5,10,15 and 20

6   Results

Average Packet Delivery Ratio: This is the fraction of the data packets generated by the sources that are delivered to the destination. This evaluates the ability of the protocol to discover routes [12]

Average end-to-end delay: The end-to-end-delay is the average time taken by data packets to reach from the sources to the destinations. This includes all the delays caused during route acquisition, buffering and processing at intermediate nodes, retransmission delays at the MAC layer, etc.

Node Reliability: The node reliability is calculated by the packet delivery ratio of that particular node. If the ratio is high means reliability is also high.

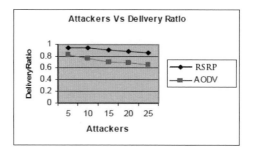

Fig. 2. Attackers Vs Delivery Ratio for 25 Nodes

Fig. 2 shows the results of delivery ratio for the misbehaving nodes 5,10,....25 for 50 nodes scenario. Clearly our RSRP scheme achieves more delivery ratio than the AODV scheme since it has better reliability compared with AODV.

7   Conclusion

In mobile ad hoc networks, the Byzantine behavior of authenticated nodes results in route disruption actions. To mitigate these vulnerabilities of routing protocols in wireless ad hoc networks, we propose a new Reactive Secure Routing Protocol (RSRP) that provides resilience against Byzantine attacks. Since existing routing protocols provide solutions separately for insider attacks, outsider attacks and selective forwarding attacks, our proposed protocol provides total protection against all these attacks. Through simulation results, we have demonstrated that RSRP effectively mitigates the identified attacks with stronger resistance against node capture by providing better delivery ratio. As a future work, we will try to reduce the overhead and delay of the proposed protocol by maintaining much more resistance against the identified attacks.

References

1. Yang, H., Luo, H.Y., Ye, F., Lu, S.W., Zhang, L.: Security in mobile ad hoc networks: Challenges and solutions. IEEE Proceedings on Wireless Communications 11(1), 38–47 (2004), doi:10.1109/MWC.2004.1269716
2. Khan, O.A.: A Survey of Secure Routing Techniques for MANET, Course Survey Report (Fall 2003)
3. Fahad, T., Askwith, R.: A Node Misbehaviour Detection Mechanism for Mobile Ad-hoc Networks
4. Zhang, Y., Louy, W., Liu, W., Fang, Y.: A Secure Incentive Protocol for Mobile Ad Hoc Networks. Proc. of Journal on Wireless Networks 13(5), 569–582 (2007)
5. Liu, K., Deng, J., Varshney, P.K., Balakrishnan, K.: An Acknowledgment-based Approach for the Detection of Routing Misbehavior in MANETs. IEEE Transactions on Mobile Computing 6(5), 536–550 (2007)
6. Patwardhan, A., Parker, J., Joshi, A.: Secure Routing and Intrusion Detection in Ad Hoc Networks. In: Proc. of 3rd International Conference on Prevasive Computing and Communications, March 8 (2005)
7. Zhao, L., Delgado-Frias, J.G.: MARS: Misbehavior Detection in Ad Hoc Networks. In: Proc. of IEEE Conference on Global Telecommunications, November 26-30, pp. 941–945 (2007), doi:10.1109/GLOCOM.2007.181
8. Hu, Y., Perrig, A., Johnson, D.B.: Ariadne: A Secure ReactiveRouting Protocol for Ad Hoc Networks. In: Wireless Networks (WINET), vol. 11(1-2), pp. 21–38. ACM, Springer (January 2005)
9. Marti, S., Giuli, T.J., Lai, K., Baker, M.: Mitigating Routing Misbehavior in Mobile Ad Hoc Networks. In: Proc. of 6th Annual International Conference on Mobile Computing and Networking, pp. 255–265 (2000)
10. Papadimitratos, P., Haas, Z.J.: Secure Data Communication in Mobile Ad Hoc Networks. Proceedings of IEEE Journal on Selected Areas in Communications 24(2) (February 2006)
11. Awerbuch, B., Holmer, D., NitaRotaru, C., Rubens, H.: An On Demand Secure Routing Protocol Resilient to Byzantine Failures. In: Proc. of 1st ACM Workshop on Wireless Security, pp. 21–30 (2002)
12. Sanzgiri, K., Dahill, B., Levine, B.N., Shields, C., Belding-Royer, E.M.: A Secure Routing Protocol for Ad Hoc Networks. In: Proc. of 10th International Conference on Network Protocols, November 12-15, pp. 78–87 (2002)
13. Hu, Y.-C., Johnson, D.B., Perrig, A.: SEAD: Secure Efficient Distance Vector Routing for Mobile Wireless Ad Hoc Networks. In: Proc. of 4th IEEE Workshop on Mobile Computing Systems and Applications, pp. 3–13 (2002), doi:10.1109/MCSA.2002.1017480

14. Acs, G., Buttyan, L., Vajda, I.: Provably Secure ReactiveSource Routingin Mobile Ad Hoc Networks. IEEE Transactions on Mobile Computing 5(11) (November 2006)
15. Afzal, S.R., Biswas, S., Koh, J.-b., Raza, T., Lee, G., Kim, D.-k.: RSRP: A Robust Secure Routing Protocol for Mobile Ad hoc Networks. In: Proc. of IEEE Conference on Wireless Communication and Networking, Las Vegas, NV, March 31- April 3, pp. 2313–2318 (2008), doi:10.1109/WCNC.2008.408
16. Perrig, A., Stankovic, J., Wagner, D.: Security in Wireless Sensor Networks. In: The Proceedings of Communications of the ACM, vol. 47(6), pp. 53–57 (June 2004)
17. Perkins, C.E., Belding-Royer, E.M., Das, S.: Ad hoc On- Demand Distance Vector (AODV) Routing. RFC 3561 (July 2003)
18. Perkins, C.E., Royer, E.M.: The Ad hoc Reactive Distance Vector Protocol. In: Perkins, C.E. (ed.) Ad Hoc Networking, pp. 173–219. Addison-Wesley, Reading (2000)
19. Masillamani, M.R., Jamalipour, A.: Intelligent MANET. Hindustan Journal 3, 73–80 (2010)

Dr. M Roberts Masillamani received his B.E. degree in Electrical and Electronics Engineering from RECT in 1974. He obtained his Masters from IIT Madras and Doctorate from the faculty of Information and Communication Engineering, Anna University, Chennai. He is an alumni of REC Trichy, IIT Madras, Anna University, SRM University, University of Sydney, and Haggai Institute USA. Dr. Roberts has 36 years of Industrial, Administration, Academic and Research experience. He has to his credit quite a few papers in refereed International journals and Conferences. He is member of ISTE, IE, ITEEA, AACE, CSI and IEEE as well. He is now the Dean, Computing Sciences at the Hindustan Institute of Technology & Science, Chennai, Tamilnadu, India.

J. Thangakumar received his B.E Degree in Electrical & Electronics Engineering from Dr.Sivanthi Aditanar College of Engineering, Tamilnadu in 2003, He obtained his M.tech in Computer Science & Engineering, SRM University, Chennai. He is presently working as Assistant professor in Hindustan Institute of Technology & Science, Chennai, Tamilnadu, India. He has six years of industrial, academic and research Experience. He is a Member of IEEE & CSI. His area of Interests is Mobile Ad hoc Networks, Cryptography & Network Security, Data mining & software Engineering.

MIMO-OFDM Based Cognitive Radio for Modulation Recognition

R. Deepa[1] and K. Baskaran[2]

[1] Assistant Professor, ECE, Amrita Vishwa Vidhyapeetham, Coimbatore
[2] Assistant Professor, CSE, Government College of Technology, Coimbatore
r_deepa@cb.amrita.edu

Abstract. This paper describes the design of a MIMO-OFDM based Cognitive Radio for a fixed WLAN scenario. While OFDM is utilized to realize the goal of transmit/receive spectrum shaping, multiple antennas help exploit the inherent orthogonality of severe multipath channels to realize spatial multiplexing, thereby enhancing the effective throughput of the system. The availability of multiple antennas also introduces the possibility of varying the data rates by employing antenna selection schemes based on the channel state information (CSI) that is available at the receiver and/or transmitter. The proposed system simultaneously utilizes the various degrees of freedom – space, time and frequency to realize the goal of a cognitive radio. A modulation recognition scheme is demonstrated to enable the radio to move between different networks and therefore recognize and work with different modulation schemes.

Keywords: Antenna-Selection, Cognitive Radio, MIMO, OFDM, Spatial Multiplexing, VBLAST/VLST, Modulation Recognition.

1   Introduction

Achieving high throughput while maintain robustness is one of the biggest challenges in wireless communications. In general practical systems sacrifice the crucial diversity that is required for high performance in exchange of high data rates. MIMO systems provide high data rate and improved quality of wireless transmission [1], [2]. Recently MIMO has been adopted by the IEEE 802.11n WLAN and IEEE 802.16e WiMAX standard. OFDM has been identified as a promising interface solution for broadband wireless networks and 802.11a for its excellence performance over frequency selective channels [3], [4] OFDM has an important property of spectrum utilization that distributes each tone, which is orthogonal with every tone. The combination of OFDM with MIMO improves the transmission performance by properly allocating the resources among different users. Good QoS is often a result of effective management and distribution of resources and effective mitigation of interference and other channel impairments. Studies conducted by the FCC over the previous decade have shown that despite the allocation of large amounts of spectra at very high prices, overcrowding of frequency bands is a common phenomenon [5]-[6]. Much has been blamed on the inefficient utilization of the spectral resources and ineffective protocols and standards, which has led to the crowding of certain bands.

N. Meghanathan et al. (Eds.): CCSIT 2011, Part II, CCIS 132, pp. 349–356, 2011.
© Springer-Verlag Berlin Heidelberg 2011

Recent works have proposed the concept of Dynamic Resource Allocation (DRA) and specifically Dynamic Spectrum Allocation (DSA) to allow the unlicensed SU's to temporarily access unused licensed bands, after ensuring LU's are not present.[6]-[10]. Most of this work is based on the idea of spectrum sharing and spectrum pooling [10] that allows a group of SU's to acquire part of the spectrum as required. A Cognitive Radio (CR) [5], [6] is defined by the virtue of its ability to continuously remain aware of the resources that are available to it (Temporal, Spectral and Spatial), and to adapt its internal parameters, such as the transmit/receive spectrum, data-rates and modulation schemes, based upon the requirements, in real time. In this work, a MIMO-based cognitive radio has been designed with the prime objective of enabling secondary users (SU) to tune into un-utilized spectra (spectrum holes) belonging to licensed users (LU) that own the spectra under concern. This helps mitigate the problem of under-utilization of spectrum by LUs, caused mainly due to excessive crowding in certain bands [7]. The designed system combines the spatial multiplexing (SM) and frequency multiplexing gains of MIMO (Multiple Input Multiple Output) [6] and OFDM to effectively exploit the three degrees of freedom, using a VBLAST-ML decoding scheme in the receiver using Vertical Layered Space Time Coding (VLST/VBLAST) using an ML (Maximum Likelihood) decoder. The paper is organized as follows. The model of the system is discussed in Section 2 and Section 3 discusses the various receiver architectures. In Section 4 a detailed procedure on modulation recognition schemes and the simulation procedure are discussed in Section 5. Results and discussions are presented in Section 6 and the conclusions are outlined in Section 7.

2 System Model

The proposed model for the Secondary User (SU) is depicted in Fig.1. Spatial Multiplexing (SM) refers to the ability of multi-antenna systems to exploit the rich scattering nature of the channel to transmit more information in parallel spatial streams without much mutual interference. Spatial Multiplexing is combined with OFDM at each transmitting antenna. The received signals are estimated using an optimal ML decoding technique, albeit its complexity.

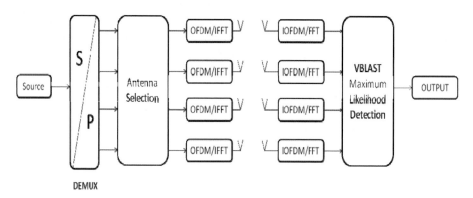

Fig. 1. The MIMO-OFDM Spatial Multiplexing Cognitive Radio

2.1 The Transmitter (Vertically Layered Transmission)

The MIMO system utilizes multiple transmit (N_t) and receive (N_r) antennas to exploit the spatial multiplexing gain provided by inherent orthogonality severe multipath-channels. The transmission sequence is modulated using Binary Phase Shift Keying (BPSK) and demultiplexed (serial-to-parallel conversion) into N_t independent parallel streams, each of which is assigned to each transmit-antenna. Such a scheme results in a vertically-layered sequence of data, that is to be interpreted at the receiver. The transmission at the kth OFDM symbol-period is analytically represented as

$$r_k = H_k c_k + n_k \qquad (1)$$

where c denotes the $N_t \times 1$ transmitted vector $c = [c_1,c_2,...,c_{Nt}]^T$, r denotes the $N_r \times 1$ received vector $r = [r_1,r_2,...,r_{Nr}]^T$, n denotes $N_r \times 1$ additive white gaussian noise (AWGN) vector ($N(0,1)$) and H denotes the $N_r \times N_t$ channel matrix $[h_{ij}]_{Nr \times Nt}$, assumed to represent an i.i.d. Rayleigh quasi-static (constant during one OFDM symbol) and flat-fading channel, each element of which is a circularly symmetric zero-mean unit-variance Gaussian random variable representing the complex gain between the respective transmit and receive antennas.

2.2 Orthogonal Frequency Division Multiplexing

OFDM is performed on each transmit-antenna branch. The block divides the incoming symbol-stream into blocks of size N, denoting the number of subcarriers in the OFDM symbol, and modulates each subcarrier with each symbol using an N-point IFFT operation, Fig.2. This is followed by a parallel-to-serial conversion of the data, addition of a cyclic prefix and transmission. OFDM has multiple advantages in the cognitive radio context – once the spectrum holes are determined, unwanted sub-carriers in the OFDM symbols generated by the SU can be removed by nulling the corresponding inputs at the IFFT block [8]. Also, the transmission of independent data using orthogonally separated carriers further enhances the multiplexing gain provided by the MIMO system. This creates a system, wherein, even in wideband situations (frequency – selective channels), the OFDM separates the frequency selective channels into independent and parallel narrowband (flat fading) channels. This means that the MIMO-OFDM system can be interpreted as N separate spatial multiplexing systems, where for the pth tone (subcarrier)

$$r_p = H_p c_p + n_p \qquad (2)$$

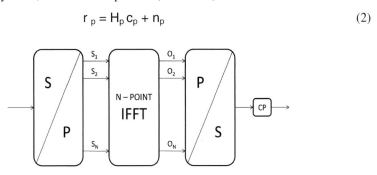

Fig. 2. The OFDM module

3 Linear Receiver Architectures

The receiver consists of N_r antennas, a subset (using antenna - selection), or all could be used to receive a combination of the symbols from all transmit-antennas. Each sub-stream is applied to an N-point FFT module to demodulate the OFDM symbols, Fig. 3. In Maximum likelihood detection each resultant $N_r \times 1$ vector $g = [g_1, g_2, ..., g_{Nr}]^T$ is applied to an ML decoder, that estimates the transmitted vector $\hat{c}_{est}$, by using a decision metric that minimizes the Frobenius norm $\| g - H \hat{c} \|$, where $\hat{c}$ chosen from the alphabet consisting all possible vectors formed using the constellation elements for BPSK.

$$\hat{c}_{est} = \arg \min_{\hat{c} = \{c1, c2, ...c2^N\}} \| g - H \hat{c} \|^2 \tag{3}$$

VLST/VBLAST - ML - decoding provides an optimal decoding algorithm, giving lower error-rates when compared with other receiver schemes. The complexity of ML decoding increases exponentially with the number of antennas. ML decoding allows for a receive-diversity of N_r as each antenna at the receiver receives all transmitted symbols. The spatial multiplexing gain is min $\{N_t, N_r\}$.

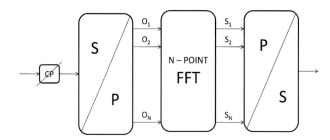

Fig. 3. The Inverse OFDM Module

4 Modulation Recognition

MR is the method for recognizing modulation schemes of received signals without any prior knowledge. [27-28] provide an exhaustive survey and description of all MR schemes proposed up to date. Modulation Recognition schemes can be classified into Likelihood based and feature based recognition. Feature based technique rely on extracting features from the received signals and estimating the modulation schemes after observing certain statistical data. Likelihood based scheme offer better recognition probability. In this paper, MR schemes have been implemented as part of the CR-based SU that helps classify between BPSK, QPSK and 16 QAM. The two algorithms are described below:

4.1 Algorithm 1 – Plug in Classifier

This classifier is suitable for detection even in fading channels. Assume that the set of symbols c is chosen from a constellation $c_i = \{c_1, c_2 ..... c_m\}$ having m symbols. Assume that there are a set of constellation (modulation schemes) to choose from {m1,m2...mc}. If eqn,(1) is used to describe the system, the modulation scheme mi that maximizes l (y.m) is

Assign Cest to l (y,mi) ≥ l (y,mj) for all j= 1 to c

Where $l(y,mj) = \sum_{k=1}^{Ns} \ln \{\frac{1}{M} \sum_{i=1}^{M} exp(\frac{-1}{\sigma^2}) / yk - ci/^2\}$

Essentially 'l' is determined for each modulation scheme and the largest 'l' value is chosen as the modulation scheme. This algorithm requires CSI at the receiver.

4.2 Algorithm 2- QHLRT

The following algorithm helps classify the digital modulation scheme in slow fading channels. This method does not require the knowledge of CSI at the receiver and can be applied to MIMO-SM system after the separation of spatial data streams. This helps to approximate the MIMO system as a SISO system with the channel providing complex gain. This method chooses the modulation scheme that maximizes a likelihood function $LF^{(i)}(y)$

$$I = arg\ max\ LF^{(i)}(y) \tag{4}$$

where *LF is calculated as* $LF^{(i)}(r) = E_{\{ck^{(i)}\}\ K=1}{}^{K}\ \{f(y,u^{(i)})\}$

and $f(y,u^{(i)}) = \frac{1}{(\pi N)k} exp^{\{-\frac{1}{N}(r - \alpha e\ j\Phi c(i))\}2}$

Both Modulation techniques have been implemented as a part of the system. If both provide the same answer (modulation technique), then the choice is unanimous. Otherwise the choice depends on the first choice.

5 Simulation Methodology

Monte Carlo Simulations are employed to determine the error rate performance of the system. The Cognitive Radio employs a 4 × 4 MIMO system, along with a 64-subcarrier OFDM symbol. 64-point IFFT and FFT blocks are considered. In the first scenario, the data is BPSK modulated, before being split into four parallel streams and supplied to the OFDM block (one for each antenna). At the receiver each stream is applied to a 64-point IFFT block followed by ML detection. None of the sub-carriers are removed and the primary user (LU) is assumed to be absent.In the second scenario, the LU is assumed to use the same OFDM technique as the SU. Three simulations are run with the PU assumed to use the first 20, 22 and 24 sub-channels of the 64-subcarrier OFDM symbol. The SU system uses subcarriers 25 to 64 to generate the OFDM symbols. Thus, to the SU-CR, the LU appears as noise. This is done to demonstrate the ability of the SU-CR employing OFDM to effective steer away from the frequencies used by the LU (spectrum shaping). The Bit Error Rate (BER) is calculated at the receiving-end with respect to the transmission sequence, for a range of values for the signal-to-noise (SNR) ratio.

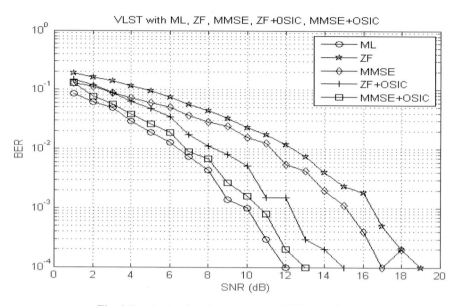

Fig. 4. Result showing the superiority of ML decoding

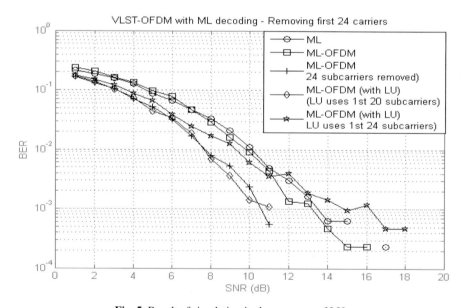

Fig. 5. Result of simulation in the presence of LU

6 Results and Discussions

The results of the simulations are shown in Fig. 5. It is clearly noted that in the absence of LU, the performance of SM-ML system is close to that of MIMO-OFDM with all subcarriers allotted to the SU-CR. When the LU uses 20 or 22 subcarriers, the performance of the system does not degrade much, as OFDM helps the SU-CR to clearly steer off the frequencies used by the LU. When the LU uses 24 subcarriers, the symbols of the LU interfere with that of SU-CR (some subcarriers), resulting in a significant degradation of performance. It can be clearly understood that MIMO-OFDM systems are suitable for implementing CR's and could be a suitable candidate for implementing SA schemes due to its good frequency localization properties. Two modulation recognition schemes have also been included to recognize most M-PSK systems and MQAM modulation techniques. The probability of error in recognition is very low due to the use of both schemes, even at low SNR's.

7 Conclusion

Based on the simulations, it is seen that the combination of MIMO and OFDM techniques help realize a robust Cognitive Radio even in the absence of coding. The spatial multiplexing gain provided by the MIMO system is easily enhanced by the OFDM block that effectively diversifies the MIMO – CR to N different MIMO – CRs separated by the orthogonality in the frequency domain. Antenna selection schemes can be applied to vary the data-rates by increasing or decreasing the number of antennas used at the transmitter and/or receiver. This work can be extended by employing adaptive modulation schemes at CR transceivers. Also, antenna recognition schemes can be utilized, when different modulation schemes are used at different antennas at the transmitter. This way the degree of configuration of the CR can be increased and diversified.

References

[1] Foschini, G., Gans, M.J.: On limits of wireless communications in a fading environment when using multiple antennas. Wireless Personal Communicaitons 6(3), 311–335 (1998)
[2] Murch, R.D., Letaief, K.B.: Antenna systems for broadband wireless access. IEEE Communication Magazine 40(4), 76–83 (2002)
[3] Berzdivin, R., Breinig, R., Raytheon, R.T.: Next generation wireless communications, concepts and technologies. IEEE Communication Magazine 40(3), 108–116 (2002)
[4] Keller, T., Hanzo, L.: Adaptive multicarrier modulation: a convenient framework for time, frequency processing in wireless communications. IEEE Proceedings 88, 611–640 (2000)
[5] FCC Spectrum Policy task Force, Report of the spectrum efficiency working group (November 2002)
[6] Hatfield, D., Weiser, P.: Property rights in spectrum: taking the next step. In: Proc. 1st IEEE Symp. New Frontiers Dynamic Spectrum Access Networks, pp. 420–444 (2005)
[7] Lehr, W., Crowcrft, J.: Managing shared access to a spectrum commons. In: Proc. 1st IEEE Symp. New Frontiers Dynamic Spectrum Access Networks, pp. 420–444 (2005)
[8] Etkin, R., Parekh, A., Tse, D.: Spectrum sharing for unlicenced bands. In: Proc. 1st IEEE Symp. New Frontiers Dynamic Spectrum Access Networks, pp. 251–258 (2005)

[9] Huang, J., Berry, R., Honing, M.: Spectrum sharing with distributed interference compensation. In: Proc. 1st IEEE Symp. New Frontiers Dynamic Spectrum Access Networks, pp. 88–93 (2005)

[10] Weiss, T.A., Jondral, F.K.: Spectrum Pooling: An Innovative Strategy for the Enhancement of Spectral Efficiency. IEEE Commn. Mag. 42, S8–S14 (2004)

[11] Zhao, Q., Sadler, B.M.: A survey of Dynamic Spectrum Access: Signal Processing, Networking and regulatory policy. IEEE Communication Magazine, 79–89 (May 2007)

Mutual Authentication of RFID Tag with Multiple Readers

Selwyn Piramuthu

RFID European Lab, Paris, France &
Information Systems and Operations Management, University of Florida
Gainesville, Florida 32611-7169, USA
selwyn@ufl.edu

Abstract. Mutual authentication is critical in scenarios where impersonation of RFID tag and/or reader by an adversary could result in nontrivial consequences. Several extant authentication protocols address this
issue considering mutual authentication between an individual tag and
reader. However, a majority of these protocols have been shown to be
vulnerable to attacks by an active or passive adversary. We consider mutual authentication between a tag and a reader through the addition
of an auxiliary reader that reinforces the process. We present a mutual
authentication protocol for this scenario.

Keywords: RFID, mutual authentication.

1 Introduction

As RFID tags gain popularity, there is a need to strengthen authentication
protocols used to maintain security/privacy of the tagged object. Authentication
protocols are necessary to prevent unintended entities from interfering with the
normal day-to-day processes as related to RFID tags and associated systems. In
a majority of situations, it is enough to authenticate just one or a few of the
interacting entities simply because of the absence of need to authenticate the
other entities. For example, while inside a public transportation the need for
the ticketed passenger to authenticate the conductor is minimal to non-existent
when private information about the passenger are not revealed. However, there
are situations where mutual authentication is necessary. For example, in the
same public transportation scenario the passenger may want to authenticate the
conductor when sensitive or private information such as credit card number, date
of birth, etc. are involved.

Mutual authentication is the process by which two or more entities authenticate one another to confirm that each of the entities are whom they claim to be.
From an RFID systems perspective, several cryptographic protocols have been
developed over the years for mutual authentication of a tag and a reader (e.g.,
[2], [4], [6], [8]). However, a majority of existing mutual authentication protocols have been shown to be vulnerable to attacks from a resourceful adversary
(e.g., [9]). While the identification of vulnerabilities in existing mutual authentication protocols and means to avoid such attacks or at least alleviate deleterious

N. Meghanathan et al. (Eds.): CCSIT 2011, Part II, CCIS 132, pp. 357–361, 2011.
© Springer-Verlag Berlin Heidelberg 2011

effects arising from such attacks help improve the overall security and privacy of tagged object in the long run, there is a need to develop stronger protocols that can resist such attacks. We utilize the presence of a second (auxiliary) reader to develop a mutual authentication protocol. The premise here is that it is more difficult to simultaneously impersonate or otherwise (cryptographically) compromise the mutual authentication process between a tag and a reader when two readers are present.

This paper is organized as follows: The proposed mutual authentication protocol is presented in the next section. The last section concludes the paper with a brief discussion.

2   Proposed Mutual-authentication Protocol

The following notations are used throughout the paper:

- t, r_1, r_2: random m-bit nonce
- s, s_a: tag's shared (with readers) keys
- r_a: shared key between readers
- f_k: keyed (with key k) encryption function

The proposed protocol (Figure 1) can be used for mutual authentication of a tag and a reader with the help from an auxiliary reader (Reader$_a$ in Figure 1). We assume the presence of a secure channel between the two readers. The over-the-air channel between the readers and tag are not assumed to be secure. At least three entities are required to execute this protocol including a tag and at least two readers. When there are more than two readers, the protocol can be modified to accommodate the authentication process. The primary and auxiliary reader can be switched depending on the situation. These readers may or may not be located in close physical proximity to each other. However, during mutual authentication, the tag should simultaneously be within the field of both the readers.

The protocol includes several shared secret keys between pairs of entities. The shared key between Reader and Reader$_a$ is r_a and those between Reader and Tag and Reader$_a$ and Tag are s and s_a respectively. The messages in the protocol form four loops: the first is the loop between Reader and Tag, the second is the loop between Reader and Reader$_a$, the third is the loop between Reader$_a$ and Tag, and the fourth is the loop between Reader and Tag. The protocol begins when the Reader generates a random nonce (r_1) and encrypts it using its shared key with the Tag and sends the message to the Tag ($f_s(r_1)$). In response, the tag generates a random nonce (t) and encrypts its message to the Reader (i.e., $f_s(t||r_1)$). The Reader waits for a pre-specified amount of time to receive this message from the Tag. When this fails (i.e., the Reader does not receive message from the Tag during this time), it generates another random nonce (i.e., r_1) and repeats its message to the Tag. This process continues until the Tag's message

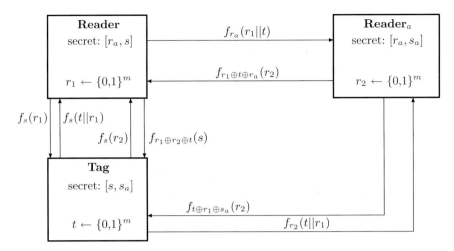

Fig. 1. Tag-Readers mutual authentication protocol

is successfully received and validated along with the decryption and retrieval of t sent by the Tag. This completes the first loop in the protocol. The purpose of this loop is to authenticate the Tag by the Reader.

The following two loops are used by the Tag to authenticate the Reader and the Reader to reconfirm authentication of Tag using auxiliary Reader$_a$. The second loop is initiated by the Reader when it sends $f_{r_a}(r_1||t)$ to Reader$_a$, which decrypts this message using their shared key (r_a) to retrieve r_1 and t. Reader$_a$ then generates its own random nonce (r_2) and sends an encrypted message $(f_{t\oplus r_1\oplus s_a}(r_2))$ to the Tag. Since low-cost RFID tags do not have an on-board clock, these tags do not have the capability to measure the time taken between messages. However, this is not of concern in this protocol. After sending its message to the Tag, Reader$_a$ waits for a reply from Tag for a pre-specified amount of time and repeats the message with a freshly generated random nonce when it fails to receive a valid response from Tag. The Tag decrypts the message to retrieve r_2 and sends $f_{r_2}(t||r_1)$ to Reader$_a$. Reader$_a$ now validates the tag and sends $f_{r_1\oplus t\oplus r_a}(r_2)$ to Reader, which decrypts and retrieves r_2 from this message. The Reader then sends $f_{r_1\oplus r_2\oplus t}(s)$ to Tag, which authenticates the reader. The Tag then replies with $f_s(r_2)$. The Reader waits for a pre-specified amount of time for the final reply from the Tag, and repeats its message until it successfully receives and validates the last message from Tag. The first, third, and fourth loops are timed while the second loop (between Reader and Reader$_a$) is not timed.

Security Analysis

We briefly consider a few security violations that can arise in a mutual authentication context and evaluate the proposed protocol.

- *Denial of Service (DoS) / desynchronization attack*: Denial of Service (DoS) attacks can arise due to several reasons including desynchronization between tag and reader and can lead to disconnect between tag and reader. When this occurs, the tag (or, reader) will not be able to communicate with the reader (or, tag). In the proposed protocol, there is very little chance for desynchronization to occur since the shared keys are not updated and there really is no need for synchronization of shared data among entities. I.e., the protocol assumes that all shared data (e.g., keys) are set at time zero and never modified from that point onward.

- *Forward Security*: Forward security is necessary to maintain the integrity of the system and is especially critical in systems where messages are exchanged over the air. Forward security implies that even if an adversary copies every message that has been exchanged between two entities, the adversary cannot decipher any of them even though the secret keys at a later point in time are known to the adversary. This protocol does not guarantee forward security since none of the messages are encrypted using a hashing function and the keys are not updated over time. It is possible to address this issue through the use of hashed functions to encrypt messages throughout the protocol. However, that could lead to increased computational load on the entities, especially the tag which is bound by extreme resource constraints.

- *Replay attack*: Replay attack occurs when an adversary passively observes communication among entities and copies those messages for later use. At some later point in time, the adversary strategically replays some of these messages, which are accepted as valid by the receiving entity. Since most messages that could be replayed in the proposed protocol include freshly generated random nonce, replaying any of these will not work (i.e., will not be validated by the receiving entity).

- *Impersonation attack*: Impersonation attack occurs when an adversary is able to completely impersonate an entity to all other entities that participate in the protocol. In the proposed protocol, an adversary cannot impersonate either of the readers to the other since communication between the readers occur through a secure channel. As for impersonating the tag to both the readers, it is not likely due to the use of freshly generated random nonce in each of the first three loops. It is also difficult for an adversary to obtain the shared secrets (i.e., s, s_a).

3   Discussion

Mutual authentication is critical in environments where the authenticity of either or both the parties (here, RFID tag and RFID tag reader) may be suspect. Several researchers have proposed protocols that purport to address this issue. However, a majority of extant protocols have been shown to be vulnerable to attacks from an active or even a passive adversary. We proposed a mutual authentication protocol where the tag and primary reader mutually authenticate each other with the help of an auxiliary reader. The presence of the auxiliary reader renders it difficult for an adversary to impersonate the primary reader since in addition to the need to identify vulnerabilities in the open-air communication between tag and reader for attack, the adversary has to identify vulnerabilities between the two readers. The latter is relatively difficult since communication between the two readers occurs through a secure channel. We considered mutual authentication between a tag and a reader. There are situations that dictate mutual authentication among more than two entities. We are in the process of developing authentication protocol that address this scenario.

While it is possible, in principle, to develop secure mutual authentication protocols, it is difficult to ensure protection from relay attacks. Relay attacks occur when adversaries simply relay messages between a honest reader and a honest tag with or without the knowledge of either party (e.g., [1], [3], [5], [7]). The difficulty with relay attacks lies in the absence of cryptographic manipulations by the adversary. We are in the process of developing mutual authentication algorithms that address relay attacks.

References

1. Brands, S., Chaum, D.: Distance Bounding Protocols. In: Helleseth, T. (ed.) EUROCRYPT 1993. LNCS, vol. 765, pp. 344–359. Springer, Heidelberg (1994)
2. Chen, C.-L., Deng, Y.-Y.: Conformation of EPC Class 1 and Generation 2 Standards RFID System with Mutual Authentication and Privacy Protection. In: Engineering Applications of Artificial Intelligence (2009)
3. Desmedt, Y.: Major Security Problems with the 'Unforgeable' (Feige)-Fiat-Shamir Proofs of Identity and How to Overcome Them. In: Proceedings of the Securicom 1988, 6th Worldwide Congress on Computer and Communications Security and Protection, pp. 147–159 (1988)
4. Han, S., Potdar, V., Chang, E.: Mutual Authentication Protocol for RFID Tags Based on Synchronized Secret Information with Monitor. In: Gervasi, O., Gavrilova, M.L. (eds.) ICCSA 2007, Part III. LNCS, vol. 4707, pp. 227–238. Springer, Heidelberg (2007)
5. Hering, J.: The BlueSniper 'rifle'. Presented at 12th DEFCON, Las Vegas (2004)
6. Kang, S.-Y., Lee, I.-Y.: A Study on Low-Cost RFID System Management with Mutual Authentication Scheme in Ubiquitous. In: Ata, S., Hong, C.S. (eds.) APNOMS 2007. LNCS, vol. 4773, pp. 492–502. Springer, Heidelberg (2007)
7. Kfir, Z., Wool, A.: Picking Virtual Pockets using Relay Attacks on Contactless Smartcard Systems. In: Proceedings of the 1st International Conference on Security and Privacy for Emerging Areas in Communication Networks (SecureComm), pp. 47–58 (2005)
8. Luo, Z., Chan, T., Li, J.S.: A Lightweight Mutual Authentication Protocol for RFID Networks. In: Proceedings of the IEEE International Conference on e-Business Engineering (ICEBE 2005), pp. 620–625 (2005)
9. Piramuthu, S.: RFID Mutual Authentication Protocols. Decision Support Systems (2010)

Design Space Exploration of Power Efficient Cache Design Techniques

Ashish Kapania[1] and H.V. Ravish Aradhya[2]

[1] Student, Electronics & Communication Engineering,
RV College of Engineering, Bangalore, India
ashish.ec06@rvce.edu.in
[2] Assistance Professor, Electronics & Communication Engineering
RV College of Engineering, Bangalore, India
ravisharadhya@rvce.edu.in

Abstract. Optimal power is an essential design goal for both compute environments and embedded systems as it helps preserve the environment. Caches, as major power consumer within embedded systems are a viable candidate for energy optimization. We perform design space exploration to benchmark power, performance, area and size across multiple cache design choices and propose an energy optimal design that reduces unnecessary internal activities thereby reducing dynamic switching power.

Keywords: Design space exploration, cache design, low power design, architecture modeling, and power modeling.

1 Importance of Cache Power Reduction

On-chip caches present in most embedded systems have been found to account for nearly 30-60% of processor energy. Instruction and data cache together, account for 44% of total power consumed in ARM920T [1]. This suggests that caches are an attractive target for power efficiency. We will briefly examine various low power design strategies for cache and select the most optimal one based on our analysis.

2 Low Power Design Techniques

Different low power design techniques are applicable across different design abstraction layers within computer systems as depicted in Table 1 [2].

Table 1. Techniques applicable for low power design

Design abstraction layer	Available techniques for low power design
System/Application	Algorithm Design
Software	Amount of concurrency
Architecture	Parallel vs. Pipelined, Generic vs. application specific etc.
Register transistor logic	Logic family, standard cell vs. custom cell
Circuit	Sizing, supply, thresholds
Technology	Bulk vs. SOI

N. Meghanathan et al. (Eds.): CCSIT 2011, Part II, CCIS 132, pp. 362–371, 2011.
© Springer-Verlag Berlin Heidelberg 2011

It has also been observed that quantum of benefits realized from power optimization efforts tends to be higher at higher layers of design [2]. We have therefore chosen to focus on the architecture layer for cache power optimization. Further, there are two categories of power consumption i.e. dynamic and static, both of which can be optimized at design time and / or at runtime. As of now, we will target reduction in dynamic power via design time optimizations.

3 Selecting Optimal Baseline Cache Design

To start with, we will review some of the prevalent cache design alternatives to select optimal cache architecture as our initial baseline. Subsequently we will optimize this selected design by applying low power techniques at the architecture layer.

3.1 Set Associative Cache Is a Power Optimal Choice

A set-associative cache [3] employs a combination of mapping function based search and a fully associative tag search as shown in Fig. 1. On receiving an access request from the CPU, set associative cache decodes the index bits during the first stage, to determine the set that contains the cache way containing the desired data block. After the cache set is decoded, the request address' tag is compared concurrently with the tags stored in each of the cache ways present in the decoded set whose valid bit, V, is set. A match implies cache hit, and the corresponding data block is sent to the sense amplifier (SA), else it is a cache miss and the data request moves to the next lower

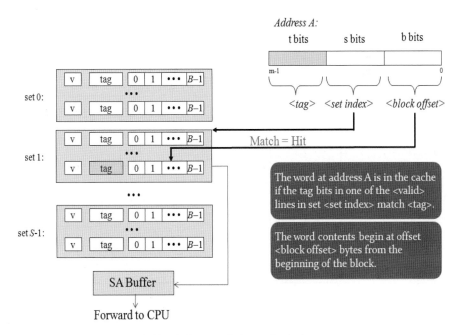

Fig. 1. Set associative cache design

level memory. In case of hit, offset bits are used to hash the desired byte from the data block in the SA and returned to CPU. Set-associative caches have better hit ratio which optimizes power used and makes them suitable design choice.

3.2   LRU Cache Replacement Policy Offers Best Temporal locality

When CPU requests data (D-cache) or instructions (I-cache) from the cache, the request either leads to a hit or a miss in the cache. A cache replacement policy is applied in response to a cache miss. The simplest cache replacement policy will be random replacement which randomly chooses any one block to replace with new data and evict old data. This policy will be very inefficient. A more refined replacement such as the least-recently-used (LRU) policy will evict that old data which was least-recently used by the processor. This policy will maximize temporal locality and outperform other strategies such as random and not most-recently used.

3.3   Proposed N-Way Cache Micro-architecture

Our baseline cache uses n-way set associative cache. Fig. 2 depicts micro-architecture for this design. As shown, memory address for each data access is divided into three sub-fields, namely, tag, set index and offset bits. The set index bits of the desired address are loaded into the decoder to determine the set that may contain the desired data item. One of the decoder output lines becomes high, and is strengthened by a word line driver, consisting of a pair of cascaded inverters, thus activating a particular cache set and its corresponding n cache lines. The tag and data arrays, corresponding to the n cache lines, are read out through the sense amplifiers into their respective buffers. In parallel, n comparators simultaneously compare the requested address tag

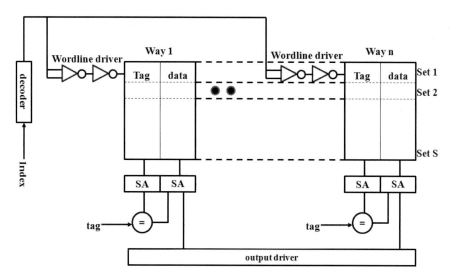

Fig. 2. N-way cache micro-architecture

with the tags read from the cache tag array. The data from the hit way is then sent back to the processor through a MUX and output driver.

3.4 Processing Algorithm Used in N-Way Cache

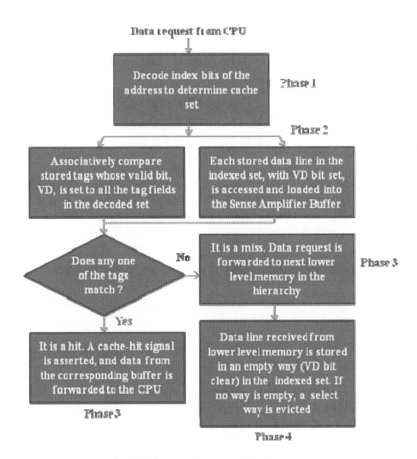

Fig. 3. N-way cache processing algorithm

4   Energy Optimized Cache Design

We will now discuss the design changes that have been made to the baseline architecture defined in section 3 in order to achieve energy optimization.

4.1   Way Predicting Cache Micro-architecture

In way-predicting n-way set associative cache [4], LSB m bits of each tag are stored in a separate sub-tag array in addition to the main tag array as depicted in Fig. 4

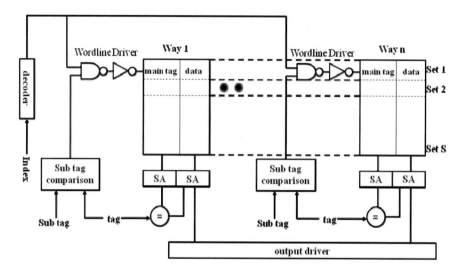

Fig. 4. Micro-arechitecture for way predicting cache

above. The major architectural changes in this cache over baseline cache design are the bifurcation of tag array into a sub-tag array and main tag-array. Comparison circuitry is also added for comparing the stored sub tags with the desired sub tag. A sub tag valid bit, SV, is added to the control field of the tag array. Idea of comparing lower order tag bits instead of whole tag was first suggested by Efthymiou et.al. [5] Key characteristics of way predicting cache design are as follows:

- Tag array is divided into sub tag array and main tag array
- All tags in sub tag array are checked in parallel with address index decoding. Sub tags which match, set their corresponding sub tag valid bit, SV.
- Parity of main tag is computed in parallel with address index decoding.
- Decoded index activates the main tag array and data arrays of ways that have their SV bit set, and whose parity bit, P, matches the computed parity bit.
- Mismatches is predetermined sub tag or parity bit result in a cache miss and prevent unnecessary overhead of data and tag array access.

Way-predicting cache also makes use of an even parity generator to compute parity of main tag array. An additional parity bit, P, is stored as part of control bit field and is used for comparing parity of stored main tag with that of the main tag for request address. A request address received from CPU is interpreted as containing four subfields: the set-index bits, main tag array bits, sub tag array bits and the offset bits.

4.2 Way Predicting Cache Algorithm

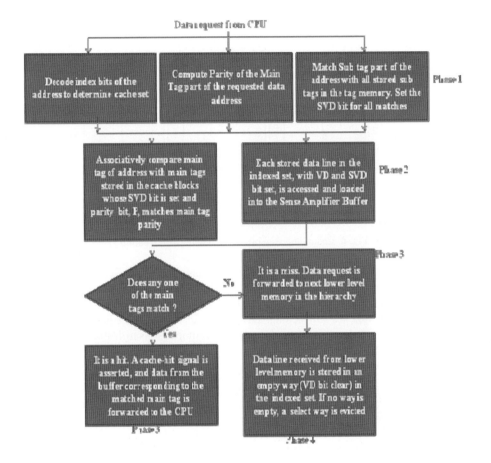

Fig. 5. Algorithm used in way-predicting cache design

4.3 Sub-tag Overhead Reduction Using Banking

A major drawback of way-predicting cache is the large number of sub tag comparisons that need to be carried out. Since request address' sub tag is compared with all sub tags stored in the tag memory whose valid bit, VD, is set, the total number of comparisons is very large, thus, contributing towards an unwanted increase in dynamic switching power. This sub tag comparison power overhead alleviates the benefits of way-prediction by resulting in unwanted dynamic power dissipation. In order to overcome this, we have introduced banking in our design.

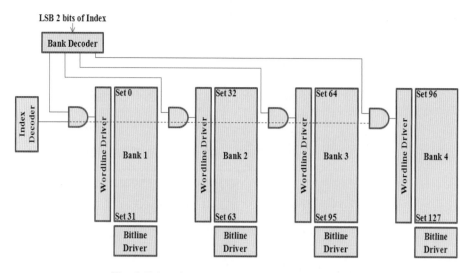

Fig. 6. Enhancing way predicting cache with banking

Fig. 6 illustrates a four way associative cache having 128 sets which implements four banks resulting in 32 sets per bank. The LSB two index bits are decoded in parallel with the regular set-index bit decoding in order to determine the cache bank to which the decoded set will belong. Dividing total cache into 4 banks effectively reduces scope of search and hence reduces sub tag comparisons to 1/4th.

4.4   Choosing Sub-tag Size

In order to make an optimal sub tag size choice, we have benchmarked baseline cache architecture and way-predicting caches having different sub tag sizes as shown in Fig. 7. Data line access activity is lower for both 8 bits and 4 bits sub tags. We will select 4 bits over 8 bits as the circuitry required to compare 8 bits can potentially introduce more gate delays compared to what is required for 4 bit comparison.

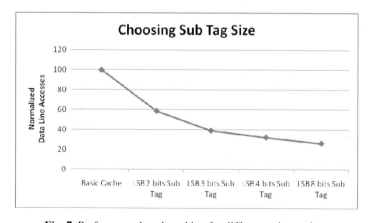

Fig. 7. Performance benchmarking for different sub-tag sizes

5 Benchmarking Analysis of Energy Optimized Design Choices

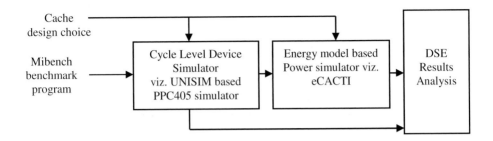

Fig. 8. Benchmarking flow implemented using UNISIM and eCACTI

Design space exploration (DSE) tools can assist with power optimization at design time [6]. We have selected combination of UNISIM architectural simulator [7] and eCACTI power modeler [8] as our DSE tools. As shown in Fig. 8, eCACTI is used to calculate unit power cost for cache access which is multiplied with access count obtained from UNISIM PowerPC 405 (PPC405) simulator against each cache design.

5.1 Cache Miss Analysis for Selecting Optimal Cache Configuration

After a review of cache miss analysis of different cache configurations shown in Fig. 9, following cache configuration has been selected : Cache of 16384 bytes size, 4-way set-associative with 128 sets , 512 cache lines, 32 bytes block size, 48 bit virtually addressed with tag size = 36 bits, index = 7 bits, offset = 5 bits.

This selected cache configuration has been implemented using three candidate cache architectures which are modeled on PPC405 device and analyzed using UNISIM and eCACTI modeling tools. Selected benchmarks from MiBench suite [9] have been used for comparing the dynamic power consumption of three designs.

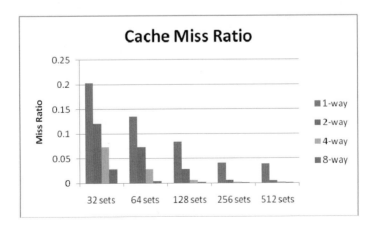

Fig. 9. Cache miss analysis across different cache configurations

5.2 Comparison of Performance / Area / Power Estimates

We obtained following access times using UNISIM for all the cache designs.

Table 2. Performance / access time estimates for three cache designs

Access time (ns)	Baseline cache design	Way prediction cache with parity	Way prediction cache with parity/ banking
Data side	0.483114	0.470843	0.4653
Tag Side	0.677504	0.63016	0.624623

We also obtained following area and size metrics for three designs using eCACTI.

Table 3. Area estimates for cache designs

Size / Area	Baseline Cache	Way prediction cache with parity
Aspect Ratio (Hit/Width)	1.48615	1.520087
Area of 1 sub array (mm^2)	0.3304	0.3614
Data array area (mm^2)	0.2773	0.2773
Tag array area (mm^2)	0.044	0.0753

As seen above, area increase associated with way predicting cache architecture is negligibly small. There are however mild performance gains from use of both way-predicting cache architecture choices.

We also executed MiBench benchmarks in order to estimate power consumption for the three alternatives. Table 4 lists the power consumption metrics for Read Hits / Misses and Write Hits / Misses across the three choices.

Table 4. Normalized Power estimates for MiBench suite against three cache designs

Benchmark Name/ Power Component	Baseline cache design	Way prediction cache with parity	Way prediction cache with parity/ banking
Bitcount / Read Hits	19.23	14.55	11.11
bzip2 / Read Hits	84.88	100.00	58.55
Fft / Read Hits	94.28	81.66	56.31
ss.large / Read Hits	27.32	33.63	20.35
Bitcount / Read Misses	0.64	0.47	0.40
bzip2 / Read Misses	98.59	100.00	69.41
Fft / Read Misses	1.18	0.96	0.76
ss.large / Read Misses	7.15	7.57	5.36
Bitcount / Write Hits	6.16	6.40	4.87
bzip2 / Write Hits	29.21	48.46	27.76
Fft / Write Hits	83.21	100.00	68.15
ss.large / Write Hits	31.63	53.60	31.23
Bitcount / Write Misses	0.57	0.54	0.42
bzip2 / Write Misses	66.8	100	59.28
Fft / Write Misses	1.41	1.55	1.09
ss.large / Write Misses	4.89	7.51	4.53

On reviewing above power consumption metrics, we can conclude that way predicting cache with parity check reduces the number of unnecessary tag and data accesses which helps reduce power. Sub tag array comparisons required to implement way predicting cache however contribute to overhead, thus nullifying the power gains. By introducing banking we could reduce these sub tag comparisons and therefore achieve reduction in the overhead power.

6 Conclusions

We have demonstrated the benefits of using DSE tools such as UNISIM and eCACTI for architecture analysis based on metrics driven evaluation of cache architectural choices. This analysis has helped us arrive at way prediction cache with parity check and banking as the most efficient cache design choice for optimal dynamic power consumption. During next phase, we propose to optimize static power leakage in cache design as that is likely to assume much greater significance at higher process technology nodes during the coming years.

References

1. Segars, S.: Low power design techniques for microprocessors. In: International Solid-State Circuits Conference Tutorial (2001)
2. Rabaey, J.: Low Power Design Essentials. Series on Integrated Circuits and Systems. Springer Science & Business Media, LLC (2009)
3. Megalingam, R.K., Deepu, K.B., Joseph, I.P., Vikram, V.: Phased set associative cache design for reduced power consumption. In: 2nd IEEE International Conference on Computer Science and Information Technology, ICCSIT, pp. 551–556 (2009)
4. Powell, M., et al.: Reducing set-associative cache energy via way-prediction and selective direct-mapping. In: Proc. of the Intl. Symp. On Microarchitecture (2001)
5. Efthymiou, Garside: An adaptive serial-parallel CAM architecture for low-power cache designs. In: International Symposium on Low Power Electronics and Design (2002)
6. Holzer, M.: Design Space Exploration for the Development of Embedded Systems, PhD thesis, Institut für Nachrichten- und Hochfrequenztechnik, Vienna University of Technology (2008)
7. August, D., et al.: UNISIM: An Open Simulation Environment and Library for Complex Architecture Design and Collaborative Development. IEEE Comp. Arch. Letters (August 2007)
8. Mamidipaka, M., Dutt, N.: eCACTI: An Enhanced Power Estimation Model for On-Chip Caches, http://www.ics.uci.edu/~maheshmn/eCACTI/main.htm
9. Guthaus, M.R., Ringenberg, J.S., Ernst, D., Austin, T.M., Mudge, T., Brown, R.B.: MiBench: A free, commercially representative embedded benchmark suite. In: IEEE 4th Annual Workshop on Workload Characterization, Austin, TX (December 2001)

Secured WiMAX Communication at
60 GHz Millimeter-Wave for Road-Safety

Bera Rabindranath[1], Sarkar Subir Kumar[2], Sharma Bikash[1],
Sur Samarendra Nath[1], Bhaskar Debasish[1], and Bera Soumyasree[1]

[1] Sikkim Manipal Institute of Technology, Sikkim Manipal University, Majitar,
Rangpo, East Sikkim, 737132
[2] Jadavpur University, Kolkata 700 032
{rbera50,samar.sur,debasishbhaskar,soumyasree.bera}@gmail.com

Abstract. With the successful worldwide deployment of 3rd generation mobile communication, security aspects are ensured partly. Researchers are now looking for 4G mobile for its deployment with high data rate, enhanced security and reliability so that world should look for CALM, Continuous Air interface for Long and Medium range communication. This CALM will be a reliable high data rate secured mobile communication to be deployed for car to car communication (C2C) for safety application. This paper reviewed the WiMAX ,& 60 GHz RF carrier for C2C. The system is tested at SMIT laboratory with multimedia transmission and reception. Technical expertise are developed towards Simulink programming, methods of poring to VSG, IF and millimeter wave hardware, RTSA use, Data Acquisition and DSP. With proper deployment of this 60 GHz system on vehicles, the existing commercial products for 802.11P will be required to be replaced or updated soon.

Keywords: C2C, CALM, WiMAX, WiFi, VSG, RTSA.

1 Introduction

Safety and security are very important in car-to-car communication. It is even more important when wireless systems are used because it is generally perceived that wireless systems are easier to attack than wireline systems. In search of best, secured and reliable communication technology towards next generation e-car safety application, IEEE 802.16, an emerging wireless technology for deploying broadband wireless metropolitan area network (WMAN), is one the most promising wireless technology for the next-generation ubiquitous network. Though IEEE802.11P WiFi based products are commercially available for same functionality. But, disadvantages incurred in the Wi-Fi security have been addressed into the IEEE 802.16 standard and also flexibility parameters are also addressed in WiMAX. WiMAX is designed to deliver next-generation, high-speed mobile voice and data services and wireless "last-mile" backhaul connections [1].

The University of Texas at Austin. IEEE 802.16e (Mobile WiMax) deals with the Data Link Layer security. The Data-Link Layer authentication and authorization makes sure that the network is only accessed by permitted users while the encryption ensures privacy and protects traffic data from hacking or spying by unauthorized

N. Meghanathan et al. (Eds.): CCSIT 2011, Part II, CCIS 132, pp. 372–382, 2011.
© Springer-Verlag Berlin Heidelberg 2011

users. The WiMAX 802.16e provides number of advanced security protections including: strong traffic encryption, mutual device/user authentication, flexible key management protocol, control/ management message protection, and security protocol optimizations for fast handovers when users switch between different networks. Fig.1 shows a WiMAX architectural components.

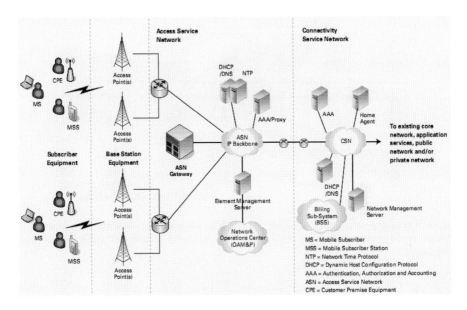

Fig. 1. WiMAX architectural components [2]

Commercial products of vehicular networks exists viz. DENSO's Wireless Safety Unit (WSU), Hitachi-Renesas.

DENSO's Wireless Safety Unit (WSU) is the follow up development to DENSO's first generation 802.11p communication module, the Wave Radio Module (WRM). The WSU is a feasibility test platform for communication protocol evaluation and application prototyping. It is specifically designed for automotive environments (temperatures, shock, vibration) and has its primary focus on safety related applications. [4]

Fig. 2. DENSO's Wireless Safety Unit (WSU)

During normal driving, the equipped vehicles anonymously share relevant information such as position, speed and heading.

In a C2C environment message authorization is vital. The possibility to certify attributes and bind those to certain vehicles is particularly important for public safety. [5]

Fig. 3. Shows a possible attack in a typical Car2Car environment. Assuming no security, his attacker could generate valid messages for and consequently disturb the whole transportation system.

While unlicensed spectrum around 2.5 GHz and 5 GHz is also available internationally, the amount of available 60G bandwidth is much higher than that around 2.5GHz and 5GHz [3]. Unlicensed spectrum surrounding the 60 GHz carrier frequency has the ability to accommodate high-throughput wireless communications. It is highly directive and can be used for long and directed link. 60GHz system enjoys the size reduction and cost reduction advantages. Additionally, due to availability of 5GHz bandwidth the data-rate for communication is more interesting. Many commercial products have been developed facing these challenges.

Thus ,exploring the WiMAX 802.16e for its security, reliability and high throughput features, exploring 60 GHz millimeter wave as carrier for its size and cost reduction, wide bandwidth and highest throughput , the Car2Car communication system is required to be developed for the next generation Car for safety applications. The development of 60 GHz C2C communication system comprised of two step procedure discussed below. The MATLAB/SIMULINK is used for the design verification and simulation at the 1st stage. The final simulation result in the form of *.mdl file is ported to the ARB unit of one R&S VSG for the realization of the base band hardware. The transmit IF at 1 GHz and transmit RF at 60 GHz are realized through RF block of R&S VSG and separate 60 GHz transmit module respectively as shown in figure 10 and 11 respectively. The signal reception is developed using 60 GHz RF front end, RF Tuner and RTSA (Tektronix real Time spectrum analyzer). in Laptop, Data is retrieved at the Laptop using data acquisition and digital signal processing.

The above system development efforts are discussed below. Section II will discuss all about WiMAX simulation at the base band level. The successful development of section 2 will produce one *.mdl file which is ported to the VSG for base band hardware realization. Section III will discuss the efforts pertaining to hardware development.

2   WiMax Simulation at Baseband Level

The full WiMAX simulation is shown in the Fig 4.

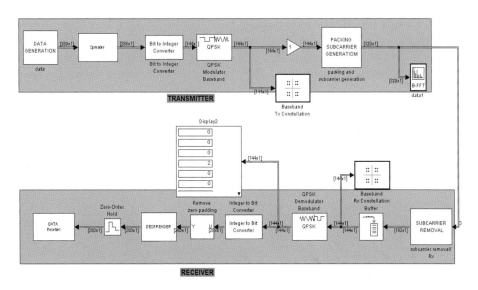

Fig. 4. The Simulink model of WiMAX transmitter and receiver

The descriptions of some important blocks are as follows:

(1) Data generator [MAC PDU] block under 'data' block:

The 802.16 standard is designed with the network and communication security keeping in considerations. Over the wireless link the robust security aspects are to be considered as the most important to control the confidentiality during data communication. In 802.16 standards, the security keys and encryption techniques are involved as shown in the Fig. 5. It has the similarity in concepts of adopting the security parameters as of IPsec. After the authorization from Security Association, the X.509 certificate, consists of an authorization key (AK), a key encryption key (KEK), and a hash message authentication code (HMAC) key, which are used for authorization, authentication, and key management [6] Here in the following model, we have 10 blocks utilized for message authentication and security management. From the top to bottom, those blocks are: (i) HT: Header

Type, (ii) EC: Encryption Control, (iii) Type: Payload Type, (iv) RSV: Reserved, (v) CI: CRC Identifier, (vi) EKS: Encryption Key Sequence, (vii) RSV: Reserved, (viii) LEN: Length of Packet, (ix) CID: Connection Identifier and (x) HCS: Header Check Sequence.

In terms of message authentication, there are some important shortcomings in IEEE 802.16 standard implemented at the MAC Layer. To avoid the serious threats arise from its authentication schemes, the WiMAX involves a two-way sequential transactions for controlling, authorization and authentication. During the basic and primary connection, MAC management messages are sent in plain text format which is not a robust type of authentication and so can be easily hijacked over the Air and this can be done by the attacker once again. So, as per the X.509 Certificate, the Public Key Infrastructure (PKI) defines a valid connection path to identify a genuine Security Systems. It uses RSA Encryption with SHA1 hashing. The certificate, as pre-configured by the specific manufacturer and embedded within the system must be kept secret so that it can not be stolen by other users/vendors. A Security System that is certificated by a particular manufacturer is implemented in a Base Station (BS) and the particular BS can not know the internal standards priorly.

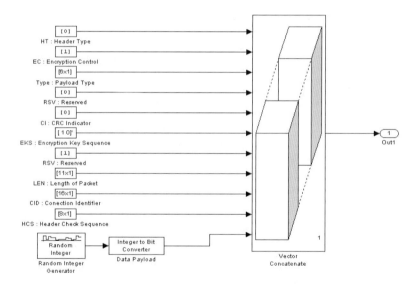

Fig. 5. The MAC PDU generator including header scheme and payload

Since, mutual authentication verifies the genuineness of a BS, it should be present in any wireless communication as it is virtually open to all. Extensible Authentication Protocol (EAP) is mostly utilized in any WiMAX Base Stations as to protect IEEE 802.16 / WiMAX against masquerading parties.

The Mac PDU was modeled according to the packing standards specified in 802.16d. The header design is shown below.

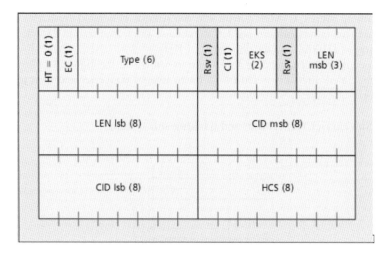

Fig. 6. Mac PDU

The spectrum of the base band just after the Mac PDU packing is shown in Fig.7.

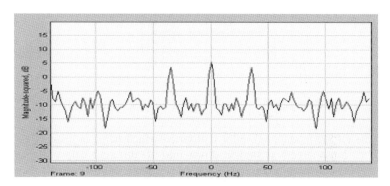

Fig. 7. Base band spectrum

(2) The PN spreading block

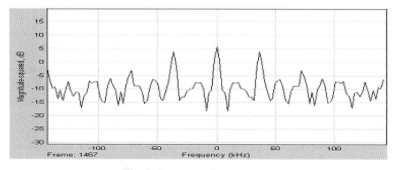

Fig. 8. Spectrum after spreading

The incoming signal is XOR'd with the bit pattern generated by a PN Sequence Generator. This is further zero padded to increase the frame size to 288×1. The Chip sample time is 1/1000 S, so the chip rate is 1 KHz.

The spectrum after spreading looks like as shown in the figure 8 below: The bit pattern generated after this is fed into a bit to integer converter and then to a QPSK modulator.

(3) The Sub carrier Generation and packing sub system:

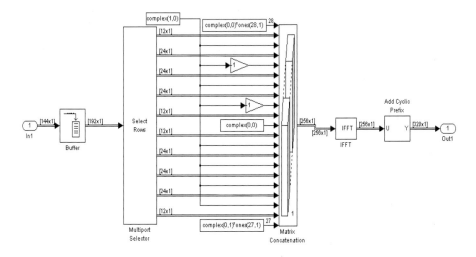

Fig. 9. Input packing before IFFT transformation and cyclic prefixing

After the QPSK modulation, pilot is inserted which helps in channel estimation. Here 192×1 input stream is broken down into 10 different data pipes and pilots inserted in between them according to the above figure. All the rows of the resulting data are combined before feeding it to the IFFT block for sub carrier generation in time domain and then cyclic prefixing to add guard time. The final Tx blocks looks like as depicted in Fig.9.

3   Hardware Implementation of the 60 GHz System

3.1   Description of Transmitter Section

The prototype model of the 60 GHz transmitter is shown in Fig.10 and its block schematic diagram is shown in Fig.11.The Tx section consists of several parts as shown in Fig.11. The PC is used to programme the VSG using Matlab/ Simulink for the generation of two orthogonal basis functions. In the base band section we programmed the ARB section of the VSG to generate the base band WiMAX signal and it is then up converted to IF level of 1 GHz and fed to the 60 GHz varactor tuned Gunn oscillator, which is supplied with 4.7-volt dc voltage obtained from a combination of regulated power supply and precision regulator. The basic block diagram is shown in the Fig.11.

The varactor terminal is connected with the signal to be transmitted so that the desired signal is up converted to millimeter wave by this process. The Gunn oscillator is followed by 60 GHz attenuator and frequency meter for the control and frequency measurement of 60 GHz transmitted signal respectively [7]. The 2 feet parabolic disc antenna is connected at the output for radiation of 60 GHz signal.

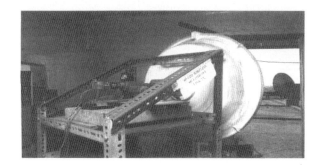

Fig. 10. The 60 GHz Transmitter

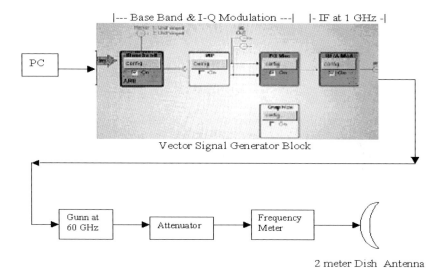

Fig. 11. Block diagram of the WiMAx Transmitter

3.2   Description of Receiver Section

The prototype model of the 60 GHz receiver is shown in Fig.12. The block schematic diagram is shown in Fig.13 where the receiver consists of a front end, which receives signal through a horn antenna. There is another Gunn oscillator generating 61GHz frequency. These two frequencies are fed to a mixer and produces 1GHz signal at the output. This signal is further amplified by two IF amplifiers and is fed to input of the

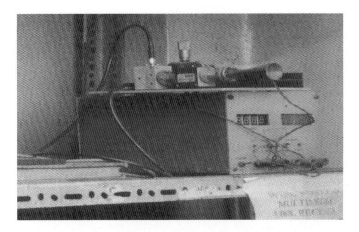

Fig. 12. The 60 GHz Received RF Front End

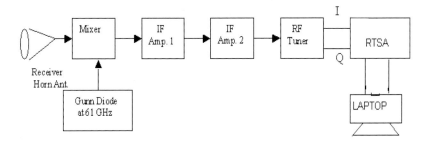

Fig. 13. Block diagram of the 60 GHz WiMAX receiver

DVB satellite receiver tuner. The I-Q signal from the receiver tuner is connected to the RTSA as shown in Fig.13. We store the received I-Q data in RTSA for further analysis, as shown in Fig.16.

The Rx spectrum at IF level is shown in Fig.15.

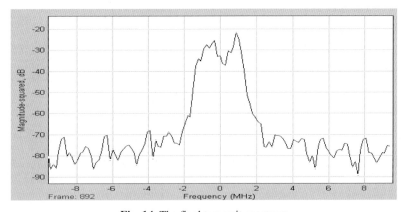

Fig. 14. The final transmit spectrum

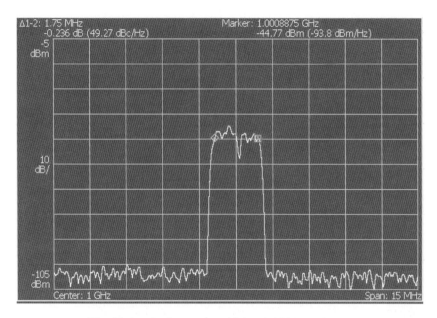

Fig. 15. Received spectrum with bandwidth is 1.75 MHz

The Received In-Phase and Quadrature-Phase Signals in Real Time Spectrum Analyzer is shown in figure 16.

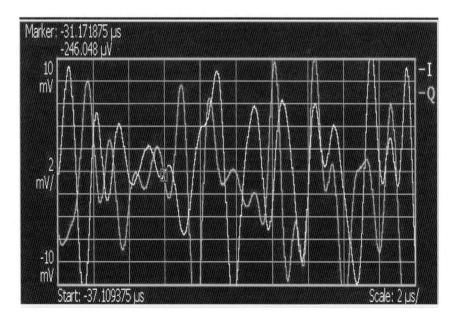

Fig. 16. Received I, Q Signals in RTSA

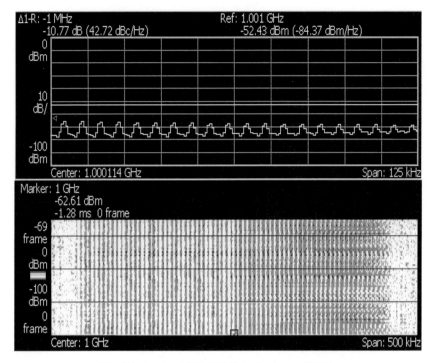

Fig. 17. Received WiMAX Sub-Carriers in RTSA

4 Conclusion

Lots of efforts are imparted for the development of the 60 GHz C2C link. The system is tested at SMIT laboratory with multimedia transmission and reception. Technical expertise are developed towards Simulink programming, methods of poring to VSG, IF and millimeter wave hardware, RTSA use, Data Acquisition and DSP. The system is operational at SMIT laboratory but yet to be tested after mounting on the vehicles. This successful development encourages the active groups at the laboratory. With proper deployment of this 60 GHz system on vehicles, the existing commercial products for 802.11P will be required to be replaced or updated soon and we look forward for the improved society with intelligent vehicles.

References

1. Daniels, R.C., Heath Jr., R.W.: 60GHz Wireless Communications: Emerging Requirements and Design Recommendations
2. WiMAX Security for Real-World Network Service Provider Deployments
3. White paper Airspan Mobile WiMax Security
4. DENSO's WSU Unit Car-to-Car Communication Consortium
5. C2C-CC Security Baselines, Car2car communication consortium, http://www.car-to-car.org
6. IEEE 802.16/WiMax Security Hyung-Joon Kim Dept. of Electrical and Computer Engineering Stevens Institute of Technology, Hoboken, New Jersey
7. Honma, S., Uehara, N.: Millimeter-Wave Radar Technology for Automotive Application

A Light-Weight Protocol for Data Integrity and Authentication in Wireless Sensor Networks

Jibi Abraham[1], Nagasimha M P[2], Mohnish Bhatt[2], and Chaitanya Naik[2]

[1] Dept. of Computer Engg.
College of Engineering
Pune - 5, India
jibia.comp@coep.ac.in
[2] Dept. of Computer Science & Engg.
M.S. Ramaiah Institute of Technology,
Bangalore – 560054, India
{nagasimha.mp,mohnishmb,chaitanyanaikcs021}@gmail.com

Abstract. In a wireless sensor network, pre-distribution of secret keys is possibly the most practical approach to protect network communications. To meet the stringent resource constraints of the sensor nodes, such as limited storage capability, low computation capability, and limited battery life, key pre-distribution schemes should be highly efficient, namely requiring as little storage space as possible, and at the same time, maintain a strong security strength, i.e., high resilience against node capture. In this paper, a new approach for random key pre-distribution is proposed to achieve both efficiency and security goals. The novelty of this approach lies in that, instead of using a key pool consisting of random keys, a random key generation technique is carefully designed such that a large number of random keys can be represented by a small number of key generation keys. Then, instead of storing a big number of random keys, each sensor node stores a small number of key-generation keys while computes the shared secret key during the bootstrapping phase on-the-fly using efficient hash operations.

1   Introduction

A wireless sensor network (WSN) consists of a large number of tiny sensor nodes with limited computation capacity, storage space and power resource. Typically, WSNs are deployed at high density in regions requiring surveillance and monitoring. In military applications, sensor nodes may be deployed in unattended or hostile environments such as battlefields. WSNs are, therefore, vulnerable to various kinds of malicious attacks like eavesdropping, masquerading, traffic analysis, etc. Hence, it is important to protect communications among sensor nodes to maintain message confidentiality, authenticity and integrity. Symmetric secret key pre-distribution is possibly the only practical approach for establishing secure channels among sensor nodes since the low-power sensor nodes have very limited computational capacity which excludes the applicability of computation-intensive public key cryptographic algorithms.

N. Meghanathan et al. (Eds.): CCSIT 2011, Part II, CCIS 132, pp. 383–390, 2011.

384 J. Abraham et al.

In this paper, we focus on the random key pre-distribution scheme without network pre-deployment knowledge. The drawback of most of the random key pre-distribution schemes [3], [4] is that they are not suitable for large scale sensor networks as they require each node to be loaded with a large number of keys. For instance, implementation of random key distribution schemes in [3], [4] results in a storage overhead of at least 200 keys at each sensor node for a WSN of size 10,000, which is almost half of the available memory (assume 64-bit keys and less than 4KB [2] of data memory). The problem becomes even worse when the network size is larger. This fact makes the previous proposed random key distribution schemes less practical for large-scale WSNs. Identifying these limitations, we propose a highly efficient random key pre-distribution scheme in this paper, which combines the random key pre-distribution technique and the hash chain technique. The novelty of our scheme is that, instead of requiring the sensor nodes store all the chosen keys, the majority of the keys are represented and stored in term of key-generation key sets with a very small size by carefully designing the key pool, and therefore, significantly reduces storage overhead while holding the same security strength. The performance of the proposed scheme is justified by our thorough analysis and simulation.

2 The Proposed Scheme

A. Terms and Notation

In this paper we use the following terms and notation for the convenience of description.

- **Key Pool:** A *key pool* K is a pool of random symmetric keys, from which each sensor node is independently assigned a subset, namely, a key chain in the key pre-distribution scheme for a WSN. The cardinality of K equals to K.

- **Key Chain:** A *key chain* C is a subset of K, and L equal-sized key chains in total form a complete key pool. Therefore, we have C = K / L. Each key chain Ci is independently generated via a unique generation key, namely, gi and a publicly known seed, namely, seed, by applying a keyed hash algorithm repeatedly. The value of the publicly known seed is the same for every key chain. The illustration of key pool and key chain is shown in figure 1.

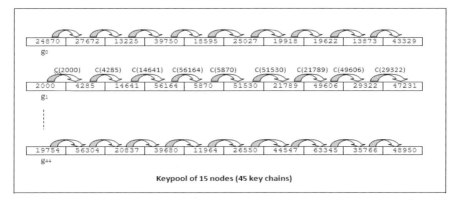

Fig. 1. A sample key chain and key pool

A cryptographically secure one-way hash function H in $y = H(x; k)$ has the following properties: 1) given x, it is computationally infeasible to find y without knowing the value of k; 2) given y and k, it is computationally infeasible to find x. A keyed hash algorithm like CBCMAC is probably secure and can be easily constructed on top of any secure one-way hash algorithms like SHA-1 [13]. However, a general purpose hash algorithm like SHA-1 is not suitable for sensor nodes, because 1) it is too complicated for an 8-bit micro-processor; 2) its message block length is at least 512-bit, which might be too large for sensor nodes and thus is not energy efficient.

The proposed key pre-distribution scheme takes n as its input parameter, where n is the network size. The proposed scheme then generates the key pool from which each sensor node is chosen its own 2-element tuple r0 and r1. The computation of the values of these parameters will be discussed later.

B. Random Key Pre-distribution Scheme:

The proposed key pre-distribution scheme consists of two phases: key assignment phase and shared-key discovery and path-key establishment phase. The details of the proposed schemes are described below:

1. Key Assignment Phase:

- **Key pool generation:** Key pool K is determined by the following two parameters: key pool size |K| and the number of key chains L. Therefore, a key pool K consists of L different key chains:

$$K = \cup C_i (i = 0 \dots L - 1)$$

and $C_i \cap C_j = \emptyset$ $(i \neq j)$. Each key chain C_i is generated via a unique generation key gi and the publicly known seed by applying a keyed hash algorithm repeatedly. Thereby, the ith key of key chain C_i is conceptually computed as

$$K_{C_i,L} = H^L_{(seed,gi)}$$

where $H^L_{(seed,gi)} = H(H^{L-1}_{(seed,gi)}, gi)$ and so on. We use the pair (C_i, L) to index the corresponding key.

- **Assignment of r0 and r1:** In this step, each node is loaded with two parts, r0 and r1, where r0 is the generation knowledge of the number of key chains and r1 is a set of random keys. The assigning rules are as follows. First, node i is assigned with r0 randomly selected key chains. However, instead of storing all the K / L keys in each key chain, node i only stores the corresponding key chain generation keys (one key per key chain). From these r0 key-generation keys, r0 * (K / L) random keys can be calculated effectively. Second, node i is additionally assigned with r1 randomly selected keys each from a different key chain.

2. Shared-key discovery and path-key establishment phase:

During the network bootstrapping phase, each sensor node is required to broadcast the key index information of its key ring i.e., r1, to expose its key information to the neighbor nodes. Hence, each node will know which keys its neighbors have. Each node then examines the key index information of its own key ring to find or calculate the keys it shares with the neighbor nodes. Each node compares its r0 and r1 index information with the received information to find the keys shared. If there are more than one shared key, the final pair wise key is simply computed as the XOR of the shared keys. If there are no keys shared, then the path key is establishment ie. XNOR operation on the r1 information received from the neighbor is performed.

3   Performance Evaluation

• *Varying the r_0 and r_1 values*

A performance analysis was done by varying the r0 and r1 values, for a sensor network containing ten and fifteen nodes respectively. The results of the same are as shown in figures 2 and 3 respectively. The tabular representations of the same are shown in Tables 1 and 2.

➢ Number of nodes = 10

Table 1. Avg no. of keys shared for varying r_0 AND r_1 values for ten nodes

	$r_0 = 3$	$r_0 = 4$
r_1	Avg no. of keys shared	
1	0.31	0.333
2	2	2
3	3.2	2.7
4	3.1	3.8
5	4.4	4.4
6	5.6	4.6

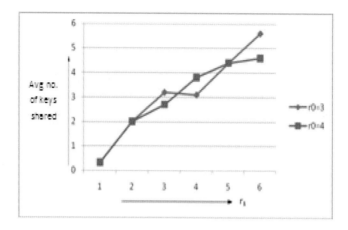

Fig. 2. Graphical Representation of Table 1

➢ Number of nodes = 15

Table 2. Avg no. of keys shared for varying r_0 AND r_1 values for fifteen nodes

r_1	$r_0 = 3$	$r_0 = 4$
	Avg no. of keys shared	
1	0.31	0.333
2	1.2	1.066
3	1.933	2
4	2.133	2.333
5	2.8	3.133
6	3.333	3.866

From the figures 2 and 3, it can be concluded that as the number of nodes in the network increases, the average number of keys shared between neighboring nodes decreases. Hence the probability of a key being shared between two neighboring nodes decreases.

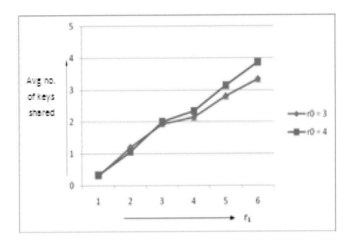

Fig. 3. Graphical Representation of Table 2

4   Security Analysis

In the proposed scheme, each node actually has the knowledge of $(r_0K \,/\, L + r_1)$ keys, where K is the size of the key pool, L is the number of key chains. Then the probability that a given key does not belong to a node is hence $1 - (r0 \,/\, L + r1 \,/\, K)$. Therefore, if there are m compromised nodes, the probability that a given key is not compromised should be $(1 - (r_0/L + r_1/K))^m$. The expected fraction of total keys compromised is thus $1 - (1 - (r_0/L + r_1 \,/\, K))^m$. If the communication link between two nodes has its link key computed from s ($s \geq 1$) shared keys (before XOR-ing), the probability of that link being compromised is then $(1 - (1 - (r_0 \,/\, L + r_1 \,/\, K))^m)^s$ and hence, in the worst case the compromising probability is $P = (1 - (1 - (r_0 \,/\, L + r_1 \,/\, K))^m)^s$.

Therefore, the average compromising probability is calculated which also represents the fraction of additional communications that an adversary can compromise based on the key index information retrieved from m captured nodes in the worst case.

A security analysis was done and the number of keys shared (s) by each node with its neighbors was observed. Worst case compromising probability for each node was calculated by using the above equation and the results were tabulated as given in Table 3, where $K = 300$, $L = 10$, $r_0 = 3$, $m = 3$, $r_1 = 6$.

From the graph in figure 4, it can be concluded that the worst case compromising probability is inversely related to the number of keys shared between any two neighboring nodes. It is proved by nodes 4 and 10 which had the least number of keys shared with their neighboring nodes, and the highest numerical value for the worst case probability. The reverse was found in the case of nodes 6 and 8.

Table 3. Worst case compromising probability for each node

Node	No. of shared keys (s)	Worst case compromising Probability(P)
1	4	0.221
2	7	0.071
3	7	0.071
4	2	0.470
5	7	0.071
6	8	0.049
7	7	0.071
8	4	0.221
9	8	0.049
10	2	0.470

The graphical representation of the above result is shown in figure 4.

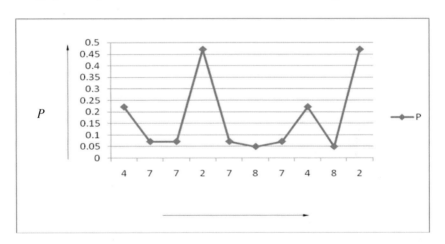

Fig. 4. Graphical Representation of Table 3

5   Conclusion

In this paper, we have proposed a new approach for random key pre-distribution in WSNs. The novelty of this approach is that, instead of requiring the sensor nodes store all the assigned keys, the majority of the keys are represented and stored in terms of key generation sets with a very small size by carefully designing the key pool, which significantly reduces storage space while holding the same security strength. The proposed scheme is hence, highly scalable to the larger network sizes. As such, for our proposed protocol, the base station is assumed to have infinite capacity in terms of its computational power, storage etc. Also, the system is designed to incorporate direct information transfer from a normal sensor node to its one - hop distant neighbour only. The results obtained when the scheme was tested in different scenarios confirm to the fact that the proposed scheme is light-weight and provides for data integrity and authentication during data transmission in a wireless sensor network.

References

[1] Ren, K., Zeng, K., Lou, W.: On Efficient Key Pre Distribution in Large Scale Wireless Sensor Networks. In: Military Communications Conference, IEEE MILCOM, Atlantic City, NJ, October 17-20 (2005)

[2] Perrig, A., Szewczyk, R., Wen, V., Culler, D., Tygar, J.: SPINS: Security Protocols for Sensor Networks. In: Proceedings of MOBICOM, Rome, Italy (July 2001)

[3] Eschenauer, L., Gligor, V.: A Key-management Scheme for Distributed Sensor Networks. In: Proceedings of ACM CCS 2002, Washington, DC (2002)

[4] Chan, H., Perrig, A., Song, D.: Random Key Predistribution Schemes for Sensor Networks. In: Proceedings of IEEE Symposium on Research in Security and Privacy (2003)

[5] Liu, D., Ning, P.: Location-Based Pairwise Key Establishments for Relatively Static Sensor Networks. In: SASN 2003 (2003)

[6] Liu, D., Ning, P.: Establishing Pairwise Keys in Distributed Sensor Networks. In: Proceedings of ACM CCS 2003 (2003)

[7] Du, W., Deng, J., Han, Y., Varshney, P.: A Pairwise Key Predistribution Scheme for Wireless Sensor Networks. In: Proceedings of ACM CCS 2003 (2003)

[8] Du, W., Deng, J., Han, Y., Chen, S., Varshney, P.: A Key Management Scheme for Wireless Sensor Networks Using Deployment Knowledge. In: IEEE INFOCOM 2004, Hongkong (2004)

[9] Zhu, S., Xu, S., Setia, S., Jajodia, S.: Establishing Pair-wise Keys for Secure Communication in Ad Hoc Networks: A Probabilistic Approach. In: Proceedings of ICNP 2003 (2003)

[10] Yuksel, K., Kaps, J., Sunar, B.: Universal Hash Functions for Emerging Ultra-Low-Power Networks. In: Proceedings of CNDS 2004 (2004)

[11] Huang, D., Mehta, M., Medhi, D., Harn, L.: Location-aware Key Management Scheme for Wireless Sensor Networks. In: SASN 2004 (2004)

[12] Erdos, Renyi: On Random Graphs. I. Publ. Math. Debrecen 6, 290–297 (1959)

[13] Krawczyk, H., Bellare, M., Canetti, R.: HMAC: Keyed-Hashing for Message Authentication. IETF INTERNET RFC 2104 (1997)

Intrusion Detection Using Flow-Based Analysis of Network Traffic

Jisa David[1] and Ciza Thomas[2]

[1] Dept. of Electronics and Communication
Rajagiri School of Engineering and Technology
Rajagiri Valley, Kochi, India
jisadavid@yahoo.com
[2] Dept. of Electronics and Communication
College of Engineering, Trivandrum
Trivandrum, India
ciza_thomas@yahoo.com

Abstract. Security threats for computer systems have increased immensely with viruses, denial of service, vulnerability break-in, etc in the recent past. While many security mechanisms have been introduced to undermine these threats, none of the reported techniques could completely prevent these attacks. This work presents an appreciable improvement in intrusion detection using flowbased analysis of network traffic to detect DoS and DDoS attacks. The aggregation of packets that belong to identical flow reduces processing overhead in systems. This method is based on anomaly detection and uses adaptive threshold values in the detection unit. For illustrative purpose, DARPA 1999 data set is made use of.

Keywords: Intrusion detection System; Change point detection.

1 Introduction

The operation of a computer network is a challenging task, especially if the network is connected to, or is a part of the Internet. Security threats for computer system have increased immensely in the recent past. An Intrusion Detection System (IDS) generally detects unwanted manipulations to systems. The manipulations may take the form of attacks by skilled malicious hackers or script kiddies using automated tools. An IDS is required to detect all types of malicious network traffic and computer usage that cannot be detected by a conventional firewall.

Flooding-based Denial-of-Service (DoS) or Distributed Denial of Service (DDoS) attacks present a very serious threat to the stability of the Internet. Identifying, diagnosing and treating anomalies in a timely fashion are a fundamental part of day-to-day network operations. However, modeling the traffic at the packet level has proven to be very difficult since traffic on a high-speed link is the result of a high level of aggregation of numerous flows.

N. Meghanathan et al. (Eds.): CCSIT 2011, Part II, CCIS 132, pp. 391–399, 2011.
© Springer-Verlag Berlin Heidelberg 2011

Flow aggregation techniques are used to aggregate flows (packets) into a single flow with a larger granularity of classification (e.g., from port number to IP address). Aggregated flows have a larger number of packets and longer flow duration that dramatically reduces the amount of monitoring data and handles high amount of statistics and packet data. Therefore, Internet traffic flow profiling has become a useful technique in the passive measurement and analysis field. The integration of this feature has enabled the 'flow' concept to become a valuable method.

A flow is defined as an unidirectional stream of IP packets that share a set of common properties; with, the five-tuple of protocol, source IP address, destination IP address, source port and destination port. The exported flow data comprises the statistics about the observed flows, such as the number of octets and packets measured within a given time interval. One well known representative of this technique is the Netflow technology developed by Cisco [1].

The different kinds of DoS attacks and DDoS attacks are described in the work of Stephen M.Specht, Ruby B.Lee [2]. In the work of Tao Peng, Christopher Leckie [5], detection of DDoS attacks is by checking the volume of traffic or the number of new source IP addresses. These methods may have low overhead, but can result in false alarms. Sequential change-point detection technique is developed to detect the start of flooding DDoS attack. In the work of Petar Cisar [3] a static threshold algorithm for detecting flooding attacks is presented. The network activities and user's behavior could alter over time by various changes. To overcome this limitation, IDS must be capable of adapting to these changing conditions typical an intrusion detection environment [6].

In the proposed work, detection of DoS and DDoS attacks gets the main focus. This detection method uses flowbased analysis which reduces processing overhead and increase speed of analysis. The work is based on adaptive threshold algorithm for various network conditions which improve the detection accuracy.

The organization of this paper is as follows. Section 2 describes detection of DoS attacks and adaptive threshold algorithm. Section 3 describes detection of DDoS attacks. In section 4 present the results investigating the performance algorithm. Conclusion is given in section 5.

2   Detection of DoS Attacks

DoS attack is an attack with the purpose of preventing legitimate users from using a specified network resource such as a website, web service, or computer system. Figure 1 shows an example of DoS attack.

In flooding attack, the user sends several authentication requests to the server, filling it up. All requests may have false return addresses, so the server can't find the user when it tries to send the authentication approval. The server waits, sometimes more than a minute, before closing the connection. When it does close the connection, the attacker sends a new batch of forged requests, and the process begins again-tying up the service indefinitely.

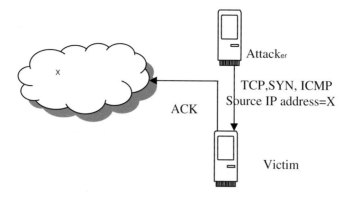

Fig. 1. Example of DoS Attack

The detection module receives flow information from monitoring systems. On detecting abnormal traffic, an alert is generated. As illustrated in Figure 2 overall process contains flow header detection. The flow header detection takes part in checking the fields of the flow header. It detects logic and flooding attacks.

Figure 3 classifies attacks by the field values of the flow header. It can detect logic attacks or other attacks with a specific header such as broadcast destination or specific port number. The flow count refers to the number of packets that belongs to the flow.

If the transport protocol is ICMP and its type is echo request and destination is broadcast, then this flow is determined to be a smurf attack. The reason is that the attack mainly sends spoofed source IP packets to the destinations of broadcast.

In TCP transport protocol, if the pair of source IP, source port is identical with the pair of destination IP, destination port for the purpose of detecting a land attack.

In UDP flows, Fraggle and Ping-Pong attacks use UDP reflecting services. Therefore, the port numbers of source and destination port are validated. If both destination and source ports are reflecting port numbers, then this flow is used for the Ping-Pong attack. If the destination port is a reflecting port and the destination IP is a broadcast address, the flow is supposed to be a Fraggle attack, similar to the Smurf attack.

In each transport protocol, the flow header detection part searches flows with a large packet count and flow size in order to identify flooding flows.

Since the behavior of network changes over time, the proposed method uses adaptive threshold value for various network conditions. Here the IDS must be capable of adapting to these changes and threshold value must be updated at regular intervals in order to improve the detection accuracy.

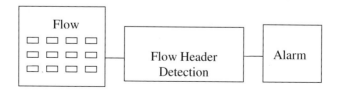

Fig. 2. Detection Process

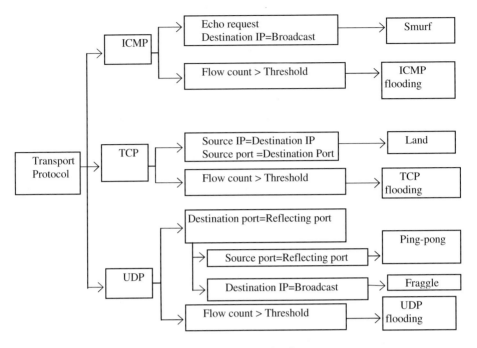

Fig. 3. Flow Header Detection Sequence

2.1 Adaptive Threshold Algorithm

In this work, the anomaly detection algorithm applies for detecting flooding attacks. This algorithm detects anomalies based on the violations of a threshold that is adaptively set based on recent traffic measurements. The algorithm exhibits satisfactory performance for some type of attacks such as high intensity attacks without necessarily being complex or costly to implement because of the adaptive threshold.

The algorithm relies on testing whether the number of flows for a particular connection over a given interval exceeds a set threshold. The value of the threshold is changed adaptively based on an estimate of mean number of flows, which is computed from recent traffic measurements.

If $X_{m, n}$ is the number of flows in the mth connection and n^{th} time interval, and $\mu_{m, n-1}$ is the mean rate estimated from measurements prior to n, then the alarm condition is

$$X_{m,n} \geq (\alpha + 1)\mu_{m,n-1} \qquad (1)$$

If equation 1 is satisfied then alarm signaled at time n, where $0 \leq \alpha < 1$ is a parameter that indicates the percentage above the mean value. We consider this to be an indication of anomalous behavior. The mean $\mu_{m,n}$ can be computed over some past time window or using an exponentially weighted moving average (EWMA) of previous measurements.

$$\mu_{m,n} = \beta\mu_{m,n-1} + (1-\beta)X_{m,n} \qquad (2)$$

Where β is the EWMA factor.

Direct application of the above algorithm would yield a high number of false alarms. A simple modification that can improve its performance is to signal an alarm after a minimum number of consecutive violations of the threshold. In this case the alarm condition is given by

$$\sum_{i=n-k+1}^{n} 1_{\{X_{m,i} \geq (\alpha+1)\mu_{m,i-1}\}} \geq k \tag{3}$$

If equation 3 is satisfied, then alarm at time n where k > 1 is a parameter that indicates the number of consecutive intervals, the threshold must be violated for an alarm to be raised.

The tuning parameters of the above algorithm are the amplitude factor α for computing the alarm threshold, the number of successive threshold violations k before signaling an alarm, the EWMA factor β, and the length of the time interval over which traffic measurements are taken.

3   Detection of DDoS Attacks

A DDoS attack deploys multiple attacking entities to deny legitimate application from obtaining a service. The DDoS attacks overwhelm the target host and associated network links with extraordinary huge amount of packets that the victims are incapable of handling.

As shown in Figure 4, the attacker simply exploits the huge resource asymmetry between the Internet and the victim. The magnitude of the increased traffic is large enough to crash the victim machine by resource exhaustion, or jam its connection by bandwidth exhaustion, or both. Therefore, DDoS attacks can effectively take the victim off the Internet.

To avoid being caught by trace back techniques, attackers launch attacks using spoofed IP addresses from innocent victims.

Routers monitor all flows at each interface and count the incoming and outgoing packet number per time slot. If there is abnormal increase of incoming rate on a flow, the router will check the pattern of change propagation. The Deviation From the Average (DFA) is used to differentiate abnormal short-term behavior from normal long-term behavior.

For a given flow, let X(t, i) be the number of packets during time slot t coming in by port i and μ(t, i) be the average number of packets, then the DFA and the historical average is computed by:

$$DFA_{in} = X(t,i)/\mu(t,i) \tag{4}$$

$$\mu(t,i) = (1-\alpha)\mu(t-1,i) + \alpha X(t,i) \tag{5}$$

where $0 < \alpha < 1$. This shows how sensitive the long-term average is to current variations. DFA_{in} is defined as abnormality in incoming packet number. While a DDoS flooding attacks start, the current deviation should be noticeably larger than normal random fluctuations. If the abnormality level exceeds a threshold, it is considered suspicious. Similarly, the DFA of outgoing traffic is calculated by:

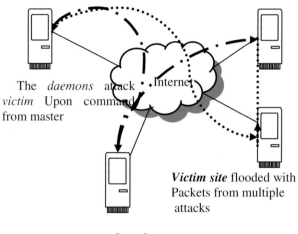

The *daemons* attack *victim* Upon command from master

Victim site flooded with Packets from multiple attacks

Intruder

Fig. 4. Traffic pattern of typical DDoS attack

$$DFA_{out} = Y(t,i)/\mu_1(t,i) \qquad (6)$$

$$\mu_1(t,i) = (1-\alpha)\mu_1(t-1,i) + \alpha Y(t,i) \qquad (7)$$

where $Y(t, i)$ be the number of packets in time slot t leaving by interface i and $\mu_1(t, i)$ be the long-term average number of packets. DFA_{out} is defined as abnormality level of outgoing packet number. With routing table, routers know which port the flow goes. Therefore, once a DFA_{in} at port i_{in} is considered suspicious, the outgoing port i_{out} is easily identified.

Attack pattern is characterized by the Deviation Ratio (DR) and Offset Ratio (OR) between the DFAs at the input and output ports of each router. DR specifies the deviation from the average of a flow at input port i_{in} and output port i_{out}. OR describes the ratio of absolute volume of abnormal changes passed through the router from i_{in} to i_{out}

$$DR(in, out) = DFA_{out}(i_{out})/DFA_{in}(i_{in}) \qquad (8)$$

$$OR(in, out) = \frac{Y(t,i_{out}) - \mu_1(t,i)}{X(t,i_{in}) - \mu(t,i)} \qquad (9)$$

Different combinations of DR and OR indicate different patterns of anomaly propagation and aggregations.

a) DR ≈ 1 and OR ≈ 1: The flow cuts through the router. The router essentially forwards all increased traffic.

b) DR < 1 and OR ≈ 1: The outgoing flow merges multiple incoming flows, but not all incoming flows contain abnormally increased packets. As all of them are forwarded out through port i_{out}, this is a partial aggregation pattern.

c) DR $\approx$ 1 OR > 1: The outgoing flow merges multiple incoming flows, each incoming flow contains abnormal increase with the same deviation rate and they aim at the same destination. The router is a merge point on the attacking path and it is a full aggregation pattern.

d) DR < 1 and OR < 1: The changes are scattered, so it is not part of a DDoS attack.

Scenarios a, b, and c indicate possible starting of a DDoS flooding attack. Similar works are carried out in parallel for other flows.

4   Experimental Results

Experiments are carried out on a subset of DARPA dataset used in intrusion detection evaluation program [6]. DARPA 1999 dataset contains 4 gigabytes of compressed tcpdump data of five weeks of network traffic. This data can be processed into about 5 million connection records of about 100 bytes each. The dataset contains the entire content of every packet transmitted between hosts inside and outside a simulated military base. The data contains four main categories of attacks: DoS, R2L, U2R, and probe.

R2L: Attacker having no account gains a legal user account on the victim machine by sending packets over the network.

U2R: Successful execution of attacks results in normal user getting root privileges. Probing Attack: Attacks that can automatically scan a network of computers to gather information or find known vulnerabilities.

4.1   Header Separation

The proposed method is based on flow based analysis which requires only packet header information. DARPA dataset contains data in the form of tcpdump file. This tcpdump file was converted to ASCII file and header information was extracted for flow aggregation.

In header separation, the result was obtained in the following form "Timestamp SourceIP Source_Port DestinationIP Destination_Port Packet_size". The result obtained is as shown in Table 1.

Table 1. Header Information

Sl.No:	Header Information
1	20: 33: 44.609196 194.7.248.153.1024 172.16.112.194.21591 24
2	20:33:44.609574 194.7.248.153.1024 172.16.112.194.21591 0
3	18:31:01.217699 172.16.114.169.1028 197.182.91.233.smtp 0
4	18:31:35.711732 194.7.248.153.1028 172.16.112.194.smtp 32

4.2   Flow Aggregation

In flow Aggregation, the header information was aggregated in a particular time interval, which belongs to identical 5 tuple (Source IP address, Destination IP address,

Source port, Destination port, Protocol Number). The time interval in the proposed work is one hour. By flow aggregation, processing overhead was reduced and speed of analysis was increased. The result was obtained as shown in Table 2.

Table 2. Flow Aggregation

SourceIP Address	Destination IP Address	Source Port	Destination Port	Protocol	Flow
194.7.248.153	172.16.112.194	1029	21591	TCP	10
172.16.112.194	194.7.248.153	21591	1029	TCP	11
172.16.115.234	172.16.112.100	1024	32776	UDP	3
172.16.112.100	172.16.112.10	1081	32804	TCP	5

4.3 Detection of DoS/DDoS Attacks

Table 3 shows detection of different kinds of attacks. Fig. 5 shows an indication of various types of attacks that appear on the test data at various instance of time.

Table 3. Detection of DoS/DDoS Attacks

Sl.No	SourceIP Address	DestinationIP Address	Timestamp	Attacks
1	172.16.112.194	172.16.112.194	18:13:17.781940	Land Attack
2	172.16.112.194	194.7.248.153	21:13:19.785180	Ping Pong Attack
3	172.16.115.234	172.16.112.100	22:04:30.410683	Smurf Attack
4	172.16.112.100	172.16.112.10	00:05:37.510024	Flood Attack

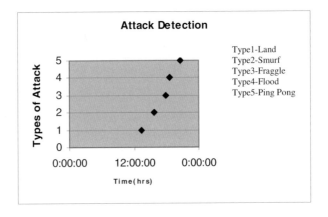

Fig. 5. Detection of different attacks

5   Conclusion

The paper presents an algorithm for improving the intrusion detection systems. The algorithm uses flow based analysis which reduces processing overhead and thereby increasing the speed of analysis. The approach to detect DoS and DDoS attacks uses an adaptive threshold for varying network conditions. The results demonstrate the improved performance of the Intrusion Detection System in detecting DoS and DDoS attacks.

References

1. Claise, B.: Cisco Systems NetFlow Services Export Version 9, RFC 3954 (Informational) (October 2004), http://www.ietf.org/rfc/rfc3954.txt
2. Specht, S.M., Lee, R.B.: Distributed Denial of Service: Taxonomies of Attacks, Tools and Countermeasures. In: Proceedings of the International Conferences on Parallel and Disributed System, pp. 543–550 (September 2004)
3. Cisar, P.: A Flow based algorithm for Statistical Anomaly Detection. In: Proceedings of the 7th International Symposium of Hungarian Researches on Computational Intelligence
4. Peng, T., Leckie, C., Ramamohanarao, K.: Proactively detecting distributed denial of service attacks using source IP address monitoring. In: Mitrou, N.M., Kontovasilis, K., Rouskas, G.N., Iliadis, I., Merakos, L. (eds.) NETWORKING 2004. LNCS, vol. 3042, pp. 771–782. Springer, Heidelberg (2004)
5. Hossain, M., Bridges, S.M.: A Framework for an Adaptive Intrusion Detection System with Data Mining. In: Proceedings of the 1999 IEEE Symposium on Security and Privacy (1999)
6. http://www.ll.mit.edu/darpa/
7. Northcutt, S., Novak, J.: Network Intrusion Detection, 3rd edn. Pearson Education, London
8. Song, S., Ling, L., Manikopoulo, C.N.: Flow-based Statistical Aggregation Schemes for Network Anomaly Detection. In: Proceedings of the 2006 IEEE International Conference on Networking, Sencing and Control (2006)

A Threshold Cryptography Based Authentication Scheme for Mobile Ad-hoc Network

Haimabati Dey and Raja Datta

Dept. of Electronics & ECE,
Indian Institute of Technology Kharagpur,
Kharagpur, India
haima.dey@gmail.com, rajadatta@ece.iitkgp.ernet.in

Abstract. Mobile ad hoc network (MANET) requires high security to exchange information for its usage in environments like military deployment, disaster management and rescue operations. But due to the vulnerabilities of wireless domain, and the lack of any infrastructure in most of the deployment cases, establishing a secure MANET system is a non trivial matter. Many secure routing and cryptographic protocols that are related to packet forwarding, key management and authentication among nodes have been suggested in the literature. As MANET nodes are mobile and have constrained resources, the proposed cryptographic techniques in most cases are not suitable for practical purposes due to high communication and computation overhead. Our work aims to establish a distributed certification authority that is based on threshold secret sharing trust establishment keeping in mind the above constraints.

Keywords: MANET, security, threshold cryptography, trust.

1 Introduction

Mobile Ad hoc networks (MANET) are formed in a region using a group of independent self-organized wireless nodes that can perform various network operations like routing, forwarding, mobility management etc. These operations are done independently by the network without depending on any pre existing infrastructure. With the advancement in mobile computing and portable communication devices, MANET is supposed to be an important network technology in the next generation wireless domain. The scope of application includes military domain, rescue operations, disaster management, and also tactical networks. However, in spite of many advantages, the implementation of MANET still faces many challenges due to vulnerability of wireless link to passive attacks like eavesdropping, sniffing etc. and active attacks like message replay or message forging.

Key establishment, maintenance and authentication among nodes in MANET are more difficult than in wired domain due to the dynamic network topology and lack of infrastructure. Most of the cryptographic operations demand high power for calculation and communication purpose. MANET nodes are required to be highly portable and have limited access to resources like, memory, processing capacity, energy and bandwidth. So establishment of a secure authentication scheme in MANET requires much effort.

N. Meghanathan et al. (Eds.): CCSIT 2011, Part II, CCIS 132, pp. 400–409, 2011.

2   Related Work

The existed techniques can be broadly divided in two categories:

1) Models based on a centralized Trusted Third Party where a single server or a group of servers act as the main controller of authentication purposes. Public Key Infrastructure is widely used in this type of systems. Several proposals can be found in [1], [11]. Here user nodes have lower administration burden for key distribution and maintenance. But these types of systems correspond to single point of failure for complete dependency on the centralized server. Also, for large number of nodes, the system overhead and delay time increases.

2) Models based on distributed Authority among participating nodes. Here the responsibility of authentication is distributed among several nodes and servers using threshold cryptography. Some approaches use cluster based architecture with distribution of authority among a set of selected cluster heads or local controllers [4]. User' private/public key pairs are generated by users themselves and authentication certificates are created using the relation of public key certificated with trust graphs implying a chain of public key certificates obtained from other t nodes[2],[3]. These systems eliminate dependency of all nodes on a single entity, thus removing single point failure problem. Service response delay is reduced. If the total number of compromised nodes in the network is less than t, they cannot authenticate invalid users or obtain the system's private key. So the system is more robust against attacks generated by internal malicious nodes. However, for these models, inter node communication to change/update the shares periodically throughout the region is very important which may congest the network consuming high BW and power.

Our scheme is based on the second approach where we propose a partially distributed trust-graph for authentication among the network nodes. Similar to the model proposed in [3] we use the threshold cryptographic approach for trust exchange among the various nodes in the network. We also add a new feature named *Session Leader Election* to eliminate the problem of finding t servers by a new node and to provide a temporary infrastructure and centralized information maintenance among the server nodes inside the system architecture. The *session leader* acts as a delegate node for any new node joining the system. It also maintains the session information. In our proposed scheme we also assume that some of the nodes in the system have more battery power and computational capability. These nodes may be chosen as *Authenticator* nodes and maintain a multicast group among themselves. These special set of *Authenticators* are chosen by the authority that is responsible for deploying the MANET. Use of multicasting among these authenticator nodes to save network resources is another added feature in our proposal.

3   Threshold Cryptography: A Background

A (k, n) threshold scheme $(k \leq n)$ is a cryptographic technique that can be used to hide a secret in n different shares in such a way that at least k shares are required to recover the original secret. Shamir's secret sharing scheme [5] is a well-known threshold scheme based on polynomial interpolation answer where an univariate polynomial of degree $k - 1$ is uniquely defined by distinct k points in (x_i, y_i). The initial set up steps of threshold cryptography is as given below:

Set up: 1. A trusted third party, T, chooses a secret integer $S \geq 0$ that it wants to share among n number of users.
2. At first T selects a prime $p > Max (S, n)$ and defines $F (0) = a_0 = S$
3. Next T selects random coefficients $a_1, a_2,...,a_{k-1}$ having value less than p-1 and greater than zero. These coefficients define an unique polynomial F(x) over Z_p as

$$F(x) = \sum_{j=0}^{k-1}(a_j x^j) .$$

(1)

4. Lastly, the third party T computes $S_i = F(i) mod\ p, \ 1 \leq i \leq n.$

(2)

and securely transfers the share S_i to user P_i along with public index i.

Recovering the secret: To recover the initial secret S, a subgroup of at least k user must exchange their shares. After that exchange has taken place each user of the subgroup will get k distinct points (i, S_i) of polynomial $F(X)$.These k points allow to calculate the coefficient of polynomial $F(x)$ using Lagrange Interpolation as follows:

$$F(x) = \sum_{i=1}^{k} S_i \times \Pi_{1 \leq j \leq k; j \neq i} \frac{x-j}{i-j} .$$

(3)

Since $F(0)=S$, the shared secret can be expressed as

$$S = \sum_{i=1}^{k}(c_i S_i) \quad where \ c_i = \Pi_{1 \leq j \leq k; j \neq i} \frac{j}{j-i} .$$

(4)

4   System Model

In our system, we assume the existence of an offline authority that is responsible for deploying the MANET. During deployment the offline authority divides the working nodes into two categories: (a) *Ordinary nodes*, (b) *Authenticator nodes*. All the nodes have certificates signed with system's private key. The *authenticator* nodes are few in number and have higher battery back-ups, procession capacity, memory storage, and can transmit at higher transmission range than the *ordinary* nodes. The authenticator nodes also hold a secret share of system's private key. It is assumed that initially the nodes are distributed in the region in such a manner that the authenticator nodes have almost an equal number of ordinary nodes in their neighborhoods. This is assumed to maintain the balance in workloads for the authenticators.

In addition to the above, our system also holds the following property as is done in some of the earlier system models [2], [3], [10]:

1) Each of the user nodes, irrespective of their types, creates their own private/public key pair.
2) An ordinary node gets partial authentication certificates from at least k nodes out of m authenticator nodes in the network in order to get full authentication. On the other hand, an authenticator node needs $k - 1$ partial certificate as it holds its own share of

secret. The system model is partially distributed where the authenticator nodes can authenticate themselves after getting $k–1$ shares from its peer authenticator nodes that have joined the network earlier.

5 Our Proposed Scheme

In the existing schemes when a new node wants to authenticate itself, it has to contact all the authenticator nodes of the network. For a dense network, where large number of authenticator nodes is present, it is indeed time as well as bandwidth consuming for the new node to contact all the authenticator nodes and obtain partial shares from at least k of them. In our work a new node is required to contact only the session leader which is selected based on trust values described later in this section.

The following are the key features in our scheme:

1. In the network each node holds a unique Identification number (*ID*). Both the authenticators and the ordinary nodes have *ID*s of same bit length. The *ID*s apparently seem to be random in nature. But the ID of an ordinary node can be distinguished from that of an authenticator node using a *Verification Algorithm*. The *Verification Algorithm* takes the *ID* as an input and gives either of the following output:
(a)ID for an authenticator;(b)ID for an ordinary node;(c)Invalid ID.
The *Verification Algorithm* is installed in each user machine, but users cannot access the underlying code of the algorithm. This property enables all nodes to check other node's validity in the network without revealing the basic underlying principle of the *Verification Algorithm*.
2. Each of the authenticator nodes belongs to a common multicast group. Therefore they all have groups' secret key.
3. Here a new node does not know the identity of the authenticator nodes. This property helps in maintaining better secrecy of the network from its adversaries.
4. All the authenticator nodes periodically monitor other authenticators and they send each other a list of newly joined nodes that they have just authenticated.
5. All nodes in the system will eventually generate a weighted trust graph periodically. In the graph a directed edge from a node A to a node B exists if B has got an authentication share form node A.
6. The weight of the edges in the trust graph is given by all nodes to the authenticator nodes using the procedure GENERATE_WEIGHT_TRUST_() as has been described in section 5.2.

There are mainly 4 phases in our scheme:

1. Initialization Phase; 2. Trust Weight Generation and Session Leader Selection; 3. New node joining; 4. Partial Certificate exchange.

Now we present the operations involved with each of these phases in detail.

5.1 Initialization Phase

Step 1: Prior to the network deployment the offline authority (i.e. the Trusted third Party *T* as described in section II) selects a System's Private / Public Key pair. Thereafter it chooses a Polynomial $F(X)$ (described in section II) as follows:

$$F(x) = \sum_{r=1}^{k-1} \alpha_r x^r + S_0. \tag{5}$$

Where S_0=System's Private Key.

Next, the value $F(i)$ is computed and secretly given to the ith authenticator. The value of i lies between 1 and the total number of authenticators.

Step 2: All of the ordinary and the authenticator nodes form the network after they get a certificate signed by the offline authority with the system's private key. Each of the authenticator nodes additionally posses a private secret share as described in step 1.

It is assumed that the nodes that have joined the network at the *Initial phase* know each other with a prior trust. They also know each others public key. Using these public keys, they collect and share information with each other for a time span T_{SPREAD}.

Step 3: Within the time T_{SPREAD} the nodes that are initially present at the starting of the network need to collect complete authentication certificate. This can be achieved by collecting k shares of the secret shares mentioned in earlier phase. Authenticator nodes have their own share. So they need other k -1 shares. On the other hand, ordinary nodes need to collect k secret shares from k authenticators.

After T_{SPREAD} the *Initial phase* gets completed, the nodes start the next phase *Trust Weight Generation and Session Leader Selection* in the network. *Initial phase* occurs only once in the network life time. The other 3 phases occur periodically.

5.2 Trust Weight Generation and Session Leader Selection

At the starting of each period, the nodes use the information they have gathered during the earlier phase or period about other nodes behavior and performances. Based on that the nodes generate weighted trust graphs as follows:

Step 1: All ordinary nodes are authenticated by at least k authenticators. So in their graph, each node has edges with arrows directed form the k authenticator nodes to that node.

Step 2: The ordinary nodes calculate final trust weight of the k authenticators using *GENERATE_WEIGHT_TRUST ( )* as described in *table 1*.

Step 3: Similar to *step 1* and 2 each of the authenticator nodes also generate trust graphs for the *k-1* authenticators from whom it has collected partial authentication certificates.

Table 1. Procedure **GENERATE_WEIGHT_TRUST()** run by each node for i^{th} authenticator node

---

Positive_Trust= $C1 \times SNRi + 2 \times Pi + C3 \times (1/Ti) + C4 \times (MinVi/MaxVi)$
Where $C1+C2+C3+C4=1$;Ci s are weights assigned to each parameters.
SNRi=Signal to Noise ratio of received signal at receiver end from i^{th} node.
Pi=Power remained in node i as notified to the receiver. **Ti**= Service response delay between node i and receiver; **MaxVi**=Maximum Velocity of node i.;
MinVi=Minimum velocity of node i
Negative_Trust= $D1 \times IMi + D2 \times ICi$
where D1+D2 =1 where Di s are weight assigned to each parameter.
IMi=Number of irrelevant messages send by node i to receiver; *ICi*=Number of invalid certificates received from node i.
[Final trust weight]i=*Postive_Trust – Negative_Trust*

Step 4: Each of the ordinary nodes sends its trust graphs to two authenticators. One authenticator is the elected Session Leader from earlier Period (or a random authenticator in case of the first periodic operation of the algorithm where a *Session Leader* is yet to be selected). The second authenticator is the one who has highest trust weight to that ordinary node.

Step 5: The authenticator nodes merge its own trust graph with the incoming trust graphs of the node i where parameter *Final trust weight* $_i[j]$ denotes Trust weight of authenticator *j* by node *i*.

Step 6: The authenticator nodes then multicast their merged trust graphs with *Final trust weight* $_i[j]$ parameter.

Step 7: On receiving *Final trust weight* $_i[j]$ for all *i, j*. all nodes then compute the *Final trust weight[j]*.The authenticator having highest *Final trust weight* is selected as *Session Leader*.

Step 8: If it is found that the trust weight of an authenticator is below a threshold level, it will be suspended from its authentication duty.

Similar to this trust weights, a *performance weight* can also be maintained for each of the ordinary node by other nodes. But this will involve high communication and computational complexity.

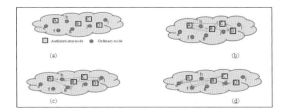

Fig. 1. Authentication among nodes in a network for n=10.m=4,k=3:(a):Initial Network; (b): Authentication among Authenticators; (c) and (d): Authentication of ordinary nodes (Arrows shows the authentication certification exchange)

Here in Figure 1, a network of 10 nodes, with 4 authenticators *(A,B,C,D)* and 6 ordinary nodes *(e,f,g,h,i,j)* are shown. The value of the threshold *k* is set as 3. So the ordinary nodes collect their certificate from 3 authenticators and each of the authenticators collects their shares from 2 other authenticators. The corresponding calculation for final trust weight is shown in table 2.

Table 2. Table for trust weight Calculation

	TW_A	TW_B	TW_C	TW_D
By node e	W_eA	W_eB	W_eC	
By node f	W_fA	W_fB	W_fC	
By node g	W_gA	W_gB	W_gC	
By node h		W_hB	W_hC	W_hD
By node i		W_iB	W_iC	W_iD
By node j		W_jB	W_jC	W_jD
By node A		W_AB	W_AC	
By node B	W_BA		W_BC	
By node C		W_CB		W_BD
By node D		W_DB	W_DC	
Total Trust Weight	Total TW_A	Total TW_B	Total TW_C	Total TW_D

TW_(NODE ID): Total Trust weight of node;
W_ID1_ID2: Weight assigned to nodeID1 by node ID2 following
Generate Weight Trust Algorithm by each authenticated node in the network

5.3 New Node Joining

When a new node wants to join in the network, it cannot distinguish between an authenticator node and an ordinary node. The joining of a new node includes the following steps:

Step 1: Before a new node joins the network, the off line Authority has to select an authenticator from all the authenticators that are already in operation in the network. This authenticator node is called the *Introducer*. The offline Authority then gives the new node the ID of this *Introducer*.

Step 2: The new node, after coming in the region where MANET has been formed, sends the *Introducer* a *JOIN_REQ* message, along with its public key.

Step 3: On receiving the *JOIN_REQ*, the introducer node runs the *Verification Algorithm* as described earlier. If the result is satisfactory (i.e. the output is not equal to *Invalid ID*), it sends the request to *Session Leader* and replies to the new requesting node with *Session Leader*'s *ID* encrypted with the new node's public key.

Step 4: The new node contacts the *Session Leader*. The *Session Leader* uses some *zero knowledge proof protocol* [12] with the new node and if the result is satisfactory, generates a secret polynomial *p(x)* of degree *k–1*(as described in equation No. 6) to produce a shuffling factor. The *Session Leader* there after sends the polynomial along with the JOIN_REQ of the requesting node to other authenticators using multicasting.

$$p(x) = p_0 + \sum_{r=1}^{k-2} p_r x^r \tag{6}$$

Step 5: The authenticators, who are willing to give shares to the new node, generate their own shuffling factors after receiving *p(x)* and JOIN_REQ. The ith receiver authenticator calculates own share as:

$$S_i = F(i)I_k(i) + p(i)I_{k-1}(i) \tag{7}$$

Where *F(i)*=Secret share given to the ith node by offline trusted third party *T*. *p(i)*=calculate value of the polynomial *p(x)* putting *x = i*. $I_k(i)$ = Lagrange Interpolation

$$I_k(i) = \Pi_{1 \le j \le k; j \ne i} \frac{j}{j - i} \tag{8}$$

The authenticator then sends its own calculated S_i to the new node.

Step 6: The *Session Leader* calculate its own share as

$$Share_{SessionLeader} = F(SessionLeader)I_k(SessionLeader) - p_0 \tag{9}$$

Where p_0 is the constant term of the polynomial *p(x)* from *eqn. 6*.

Step 7: The new node, after getting shares from at least *k–1* authenticators, add those *k–1* shares with the share sent by the *Session Leader* and get the final secret S_0 of the network and can generate the full authentication certificate.

This procedure reduces the communication required in other proposals [3], [4] where a new node floods its requests to CAs (which increases message complexity) and may not get reply from many CAs.

- New node--------(Join_REQ, Certificate)------------→Introducer node
- New node←----Zero knowledge Proof-----→Introducer node
- Introducer node---(if Certificate is valid & result of ZKP is true, forwards the message)--->Session Leader
- Session Leader--(if Certificate is valid, send requesting node's Id, & Join_REQ, with a polynomial to generate shuffling factors)-→ to other authenticators(using secure multicasting)
- Willing authenticators----(generate shuffling shares, sends it with own secret share)--------→new node.
- New Requesting node----combining all shares get the final system private key to get authorized threshold signature.

Fig. 2. Steps performed in the network during the Joining of a new node

The addition of the shuffling factor eliminates chance of recovery of a node's own secret by a requesting node.

5.4 Partial Certificate Exchange and Public Key Authentication

The partial certificate exchange protocol is quiet similar to the [2], [4]. It is performed periodically where authenticator nodes issue partial certificate for ordinary nodes and other authenticators. For one authenticator node j, if it believes that another node i in the network have public key K_i it would create a public key partial certificate in which the public key of i (K_i) is bound to user id i ,and signs it using its private share+last shuffling factor given by session leader. This is represented by a directed edge from the respective authenticator node to the ordinary node.

6 Security and Performance Analysis

Our system is resistant to external attacks for the following reasons:

1. To join a network, a node needs to hold a valid *Verification ID*.
2. Unless a node produces its authenticity to the session leader or the first introducer authenticator, it cannot access the ID s of other authenticator nodes.
3. If an external node pretends to be an authenticator, it has to sign partial certificates for other nodes using a valid private share. It also needs to hold an ID that will result in an authenticator's ID as output of the *Verification Algorithm*.

Our system is resistant to internal attacks for the following reasons:

1. An internal malicious node acting as an authenticator may issue a false certificate to a legitimate user by delaying its joining. If one authenticator gives false certificate share to a legitimate user, the user can still get valid shares from other willing authenticators without waiting unlike the schemes described in [4], [2].
2. If an internal malicious authenticator issues a valid certificate to an invalid user, the invalid user cannot be part of the network unless it has a valid ID according to the *Verification Algorithm*. In addition, an invalid user has to collect shares from at least other $k-1$ authenticators.

Performance evaluation of Authenticators:
The authenticator nodes hold the main responsibility of distributed authentication in the MANET. During their operation within the lifetime of a MANET they are supposed to keep their *Final trust weight* above a threshold level (defined by the offline authority). In case it is not done, they will be taken off from their authentication duty. Hence it can be seen that, using our proposed scheme, both secure authentication among nodes and performance monitoring of the authenticators can be done simultaneously.

Ease of network operation: For an emergency situation, the operation (joining of new nodes etc.) of a MANET needs to be fast and easy. In our proposal, a new node only needs to send two request messages initially. The willing authenticators directly send their shares to the new node thereby saving time, bandwidth and battery power of the new node. The *Session Leader* controls the joining operation making it centralized and faster.

Communication and Message Passing Required:

1. For Partial authentication at the initial state of the network, it is assumed that authenticators have prior trust relationships, so they just need to answer each other's Zero knowledge proof question or can use the *Verification Algorithm* as required. But the ordinary nodes have to prove their authenticity to at least k authenticators. So total massage generation= $(n-m)*k$ for this case.

2. For trust graph creation and exchange, each of the authenticators and ordinary nodes need to change trust weight, thus generation of at least k such messages for k authenticators. The formation of trust graph and Session Leader election can is performed together reducing further consumption of communication resources.

3. When a new node joins in the network, it does not need to flood its request unlike other proposals [2], [3]. It only needs to selectively send the request message to the Introducer and then the Session leader. Here the willing authenticators themselves send the shares to the new node. So there is no scope of wasting the request messages from the new node to the authenticator nodes who do not want to give shares to the new node. So the required message passing is minimized with respect to other protocols.

Table 3. Table for trust weight Calculation

Network Operation	Protocol By [3]	The Proposed Protocol
Network setup/Initialization	O(n*r) where r lies between k and n	O((n-m)*k) where m is total number of authenticators
Trust Graph Creation and Election Procedure Performed in the Network	O(n*k)+O(n)+O(n*n/2)	O((n-m)*k) +O(m*k)
New Node Joining	O(r) where r lies between k and n	O(k)

Calculus Requirement:
Both our protocol and Protocol by Omar use Shamir's secret sharing scheme. So, the Calculation required for that purpose is same. But the generation of shuffling factor is

different. In Omar's protocol [3], each node requires to do k exponentiations and k summations for each authenticator. It also requires sharing of some pair wise secret number Sjr beforehand between nodes r and j through side channels using each others public key pair. This increases communication messages. However, in our system the nodes do not need to share a secret beforehand. The Session Leader multicasts a single message including the Shuffling Generator Polynomial $p(x)$. Thus use of multicasting reduces communication overhead in this case.

7 Conclusion

In this paper we have focused on trust establishment among nodes and their performance in a mobile ad hoc network. We have proposed a public key management system based on partially distributed trust model. Our proposal achieves the advantages of both centralized and fully distributed certification authorities with minimum transmission requirement. Use of multicasting for communication among authenticators saves network resources. Use of threshold cryptography, trust weight and session leader selection makes this proposal highly robust against both internal and external attacks. Detection of false certificate through threshold scheme, evaluation of performance using trust weight are the key features that make this proposal a promising solution to establish a secure mobile ad hoc network.

References

1. Zhou, L., Hass, Z.J.: Securing Ad-hoc networks. IEEE Networks 13(6), 24–30 (1999)
2. Capkun, S., Buttyan, L., Hubaux, J.-P.: Self-Organized Public Key Management for Mobile Ad-hoc Networks. IEEE Transaction on Mobile Computing 2(1), 52–64 (2003)
3. Omar, M., Challal, Y., Bouabdallah, A.: Reliable and Fully Distributed Trust Model for Mobile Ad hoc Networks. Computer & Security (28), 199–214 (2009)
4. Dong, Y., Yiu, S.A.-F., Li, S.M., Victor, O.K., Hui, L.C.K.: Providing Distributed Certificate Authority Services in Cluster Based Mobile Ad hoc Networks. Computer Communication (30), 2442–2452 (2007)
5. Shamir, A.: How to share a secret. Communication of the ACM 22(11), 612 (1979)
6. Vergadose, D.D., Stergiou, G.: An Authentication Scheme for Ad hoc Networks using Threshold Secret Sharing. Wireless Press Communication (43), 1767–1780 (2007)
7. Stinson, D.R.: Cryptography, Theory and Practice, 2nd edn., p. 176. Chapman & Hall/CRC, Boca Raton (2002)
8. Lazos, L., Poovendram, R.: Energy aware secure multicast communication in Ad-hoc networks using Geographical Location Information. In: IEEE International Conference on Acoustics Speech and Signal Processing, pp. 201–204 (2003)
9. Abdulrahman, A.: The PGP trust model. J. Electron Commerce (1997)
10. Capkun, S., Buttyan, L., Hubaux, J.: Small worlds in security systems: an analysis of the PGP certificate graph. I. In: New Security Paradigms Workshop (2002)
11. Kohl, J., Neuman, B.: The Kerberos network authentication service version 5. RFC-1510 (1991)
12. Quisquater, J.J., Guillou, L.C., Berson, T.A.: How to Explain Zero-Knowledge Protocols to Your Children. In: Brassard, G. (ed.) CRYPTO 1989. LNCS, vol. 435, pp. 628–631. Springer, Heidelberg (1990)

Formal Verification of a Secure Mobile Banking Protocol

Huy Hoang Ngo, Osama Dandash, Phu Dung Le,
Bala Srinivasan, and Campbell Wilson

Faculty of Information Technology, Monash University, Melbourne, Australia
{Harry.Ngo,Osama.Dandash,Phu.Dung.Le,Bala.Srinivasan,
Cambell.Wilson}@monash.edu

Abstract. Current mobile banking protocols simply are not as well guarded as their Internet counterparts during the transactions between a mobile device and a financial institution. Recently, many mobile banking protocols using public-key cryptography have been proposed. However, they are designed to provide a basic protection for traditional flow of payment data as they only rely on basic identification and verification mechanisms, which is vulnerable to attack and increase the user's risk. In this paper we propose a new secure mobile banking protocol that provides strong authentication mechanisms. These mechanisms rely on highly usable advanced multifactor authentication technologies i.e. (biometrics and smart cards). The proposed mobile banking protocol not only achieves a completely secure protection for the involved parties and their financial transactions but also minimizes the computational operations and the communication passes between them. An analysis and a proof of the proposed protocol security properties will be provided within this paper.

Keywords: Internet banking; authentication; smart card; biometric; security.

1 Introduction

Mobile banking is a new banking technology which brings new security implications and threats. The growing number of banking users has led to exploring on more convenient methods for those users to perform their financial transactions. As a result the mobile banking technology was introduced to enable its users to access their bank accounts and conduct all their financial activities through their mobile devices. The security architecture for its network is proven to be not entirely secure where different security loopholes and possible attacks have been discovered as described in GSM [1] or UTMS [2].

Therefore, consumers are increasingly getting concerned from their banking information being sent insecurely across open mobile phone network. On the other side, banks are required to enhance their security measures to address all the serious security issues that mobile banking users are concerned about.

Several security approaches have been proposed to secure mobile banking payments. Arabo [3] has proposed a mobile cash withdrawing protocol that relies on

N. Meghanathan et al. (Eds.): CCSIT 2011, Part II, CCIS 132, pp. 410–421, 2011.
© Springer-Verlag Berlin Heidelberg 2011

biometrics features and password. However, the biometrics data is considered an unchangeable identity, which makes it vulnerable while transferring over wireless networks.

Narendiran et al. [4] has also proposed a framework for mobile banking using X.509. But the proposed framework could not resist man-in-the-middle attacks using replay messages. In [5], Espelid et al. presented an attack on a Norwegian online banking protocol, BankID. In conclusion, none of the above approaches provide a strong secure solution for mobile banking services. In addition, their design schemes are not concerned about the users' confidentiality issues. The user identity and transaction details are revealed not only to merchant but also to the payment gateway and the banks.

The aim of this paper is to propose a secure mobile banking protocol that relies on advanced authentication technology to provide strong authentication mechanisms. The integration of smart card and bio feature as two-factor authentication will enhance the client's authentication procedure as no transaction will take place without matching the right keys that are stored on the smart card.

The paper is organized as follows: Section 2 presents an overview of the basic scenario of the proposed mobile banking protocol without applying the advanced authentication technologies. Section 3 presents the proposed mobile banking protocol using Smart Card and Biometric. Section 4 describes the security analysis of our proposed protocol. Section 5 concludes our work.

2 Basic Scenario for Mobile Banking

In the mobile banking scenario, there are two basic elements, a mobile user using mobile devices (client) and a banking service. The following assumptions are made.

2.1 Notation

Table 1. Notation used in the basic banking protocol

C	A mobile client
U	A human (client's owner)
B	The bank service
K_B^+	The bank's public key
K_B^-	The bank's private key
K_{BC}	Shared secret key between B and C
SK	A session key
req	A user's transaction request
res	The result of transaction performed by the bank service
N_{B1}, N_{C1}, N_{C2}	Nonces (random numbers) using as challenges
$h(X)$	A one way hash function of message X
$\oplus$	The exclusive-OR operation

2.2 Assumptions

When a user U subscribes to a mobile banking service B, s/he will be provided with a mobile client C. during the registration, C will be provided with a shared secret key K_{BC} with the banking service B. The secret key K_{BC} can be derived from hashing user's password. It is used to authenticate C with B. At the same time, C also stores the banking service's public key K_B^+. The following assumptions can be made:

1. C knows B's public key K_B^+
2. Only B knows its private key K_B^-
3. Only C and B know the shared secret key K_{BC}.

2.3 The Basic Mobile Banking Protocol

The basic mobile banking protocol contains two steps: authentication and transaction request-response. The mutual authentication between C and B must be made to prevent both unauthorized access and phishing attacks. The result of the authentication is a secure communication channel between B and C. Messages of the transaction request-response are secured by the established communication channel between B and C. The two steps are conducted in four following phases:

1. C generates a random number N_C to challenge B and sends it with its identity to B.
2. In turn, B generates another random number N_{B1} to challenge C during authentication. It generates a session key SK to secure communication channel if C is able to authenticate its identity successfully. B encrypts the SK with the authentication shared key K_{BC}. Before sending the SK to C, B encrypts both the SK and the nonce N_C using its private key K_B^-.
3. C uses B's public key K_B^+ to decrypt the response. C verifies the challenge N_C, and uses K_{BC} to decrypt the response and obtains SK. A message authentication code is attached into the third message to protect the integrity of the transaction request.
4. B validates the response N_B and performs the request. Upon the completion of the request, B sends the request response (result) back to C. Similar to the previous phase, a message authentication code is attached into the forth message to protect the integrity of the transaction response.

The four phases are formalized as four following messages:

1. $C \rightarrow B : C, N_{C1}$
2. $B \rightarrow C : N_{B1}, \{N_{C1}, \{SK\}K_{BC}\}K_B^-$
3. $C \rightarrow B : \{req, N_{B1}\}SK, N_{C2}, h(req \oplus SK)$
4. $B \rightarrow C : \{res, N_{C2}\}SK, h(res \oplus SK)$

After completing the authentication, all messages related to the transaction are signed with *SK* to protect their integrity. In the above protocol, the transaction request and response are signed with the *SK* before being hashed to be message authentication code. When receiving these messages, either *B* or *C* can validate the messages using the message authentication code.

The protocol is extended to adapt to multiple factor authentication as following:

3   An Extension Protocol Using Smart Card and Biometric

The main idea of using smart cards and biometrics are supporting multiple factors authentication for transactions. Smart cards are embedded integrated circuits to be able to perform encryptions. The use of encryption in authentication is an extra challenge-response mechanism besides traditional challenge-response method. Smart card responses the challenge of the bank by encrypting the nonce (random number) created by the bank. However, stolen smart cards may lead to unauthorized access. Therefore, biometric authentication is usually combined with smart card to reduce the risk.

Authentication using biometric can be conducted at either the client side (user's mobile devices) or the server side (bank service). While the biometric data (such as a fingerprint, retina, iris, hand, face or voice) is obtained from hardware of the mobile devices, the validation can be either performed at the mobile devices or remotely at the bank services. Usually because the biometric identity is usually static, a compromising of a sample of biometric identity may incur high costs. Therefore, authentication usually prefers validating biometric authentication at clients'.

3.1   Notation

Table 2. Notation used in the extended mobile banking protocol

SC	A smart card
Biometric	The *U*'s biometric identity
response$_{bio}$	The result of biometric authentication
K_{BC}	The user secret key derived from the biometric data
K_{SC}	The smartcard 's secret symmetric key
N_{B2}	A nonce (random number) using as a challenge
MAC(X)	The message authentication code of message X

3.2   Assumptions

In the basic protocol, the user *U* has subscribed to the bank and received his/her mobile client *C*, which shares K_{BC} with *B*. in this assumption, the subscribed *U* will be provided a smart card *SC*, which will be sharing another secret key K_{SC} with *B*.

Both two secret keys, K_{BC} and K_{SC}, are used to authenticate the identities of *C* and *SC*. The following assumptions are summarized as follows:

1. C knows B's public key K_B^+

2. Only B knows its private key K_B^-

3. Only C and B know the share secret key K_{BC}

The mobile banking protocol using smart card and biometric contains eight steps:

1. User U authenticates his/her biometric identity with the client C.
2. Client C locally validates the biometric identity and returns the result $reponse_{bio}$.
3. After user U authenticates with C, C sends to B a request to access U's internet banking account; the message is similar to message 1 in the basic protocol.
4. Similar to step 2 in the basic protocol, B creates a SK and sends it back to C encrypted with both K_{BC} and its private key K_B^-. B also challenges C's two-factor authentication with two nonce N_{B1} and N_{B2}.
5. C receives and extracts the SK using B's public key K_B^+, and K_{BC}. The two-factor authentication includes U's authentication (via K_{BC}) and SC authentication (via K_{SC}). However, C does not have K_{SC}, it requests U to use SC to encrypt the nonce N_{B2}.
6. SC encrypts N_{B2} using its K_{SC} and return it to C.
7. C combines a request with the response from the SC and N_{B1} encrypted with SK and sends it to B. The request also has a message authentication code (hash value of request exclusive-OR with SK).
8. B decrypts, extracts and validates the responses from the SC ($\{N_{B2}\}K_{SC}$), and from C ($\{N_{B1}\}SK$). After validating the authentication from both two factors, B validates the request and the message authentication code. It processes the request and returns a response to C as in step 4 in the basic protocol.

The protocol is formalized as follows:

3.3   The Extended Mobile Banking Protocol

1. $U \rightarrow C$: *Biometric*
2. $C \rightarrow U$: *Response$_{bio}$*
3. $C \rightarrow B$: C, N_{C1}
4. $B \rightarrow C$: $N_{B1}, N_{B2}, \{N_{C1}, \{SK\}K_{BC}\}K_B^-$
5. $C \rightarrow SC$: N_{B2}
6. $SC \rightarrow C$: $\{N_{B2}\}K_{SC}$
7. $C \rightarrow B$: $\{req, N_{B1}, \{N_{B2}\}K_{SC}\}SK, N_{C2}, h(req \oplus SK)$
8. $B \rightarrow C$: $\{res, N_{C2}\}SK, h(res \oplus SK)$

The message flow in the eight steps of the authentication protocol is described in Fig. 1.

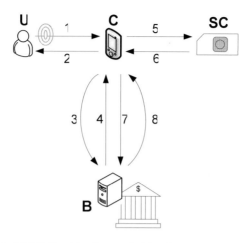

Fig. 1. The Mobile Banking Protocol Using Smart Card and Biometric

4   Analysis

The security of the basic authentication protocol is analyzed using SVO [6] logic. There are sixteen desired following goals for the protocols specified as follows:

Authentication Goals for *B*

    G1. B believes C says X

    G2. B believes $(C$ says $F(X,N_{BI}) \wedge \text{fresh}(N_{BI}))$

    G3. B believes $B \xleftrightarrow{SK} C$

    G4. B believes $\text{fresh}(SK)$

    G5. B believes C says $B \xleftrightarrow{SK} C$

    G6. B believes $(B \xleftrightarrow{SK} C \wedge C$ says $F(SK))$

    G7. B believes C says $(F(req, N_{BI}) \wedge \text{fresh}(N_{BI}))$

    G8. B believes C says $(F(req, MAC(req))$

G1 to **G6** are six authentication goals derived from SVO for *B*. *B* also has two desired transaction goals.

    G7 named as "recent transaction request goal" explains that *B* wants to know the transaction request from *C* has information relevant to the present conversion. Let N_{BI} be fresh information to *B*. The recent transaction request goal requires *C* to have recently sent a message $F(req, N_{BI})$ that describes that *C* has seen N_{BI} and processed it. The goal G7 is used to prevent replay attacks for the protocol.

    G8 named as "message authentication goal" explains that *B* wants to know the transaction request from *C* is genuine. The goal uses message authentication code MAC(req) writing as $h(req \oplus SK)$ so that *B* is able to verify the message integrity of the transaction request.

Authentication Goals for *C*

G9. *C* believes *B* says X

G10. *C* believes (*B* says F(X,N_{C1})∧fresh(N_{C1}))

G11. *C* believes $B \xleftarrow{\;SK\;} C$

G12. *C* believes fresh(*SK*)

G13. *C* believes *B* says $B \xleftarrow{\;SK\;} C$

G14. *C* believes ($B \xleftarrow{\;SK\;} C$ ∧ B says F(SK))

G15. *C* believes *C* says (F(*res*, N_{C2}) ∧ fresh(N_{C2}))

G16. *C* believes *B* says (F(*res*, MAC(*res*⊕*SK*))∧ $B \xleftarrow{\;SK\;} C$

Six messages **G9** to **G14** are authentication goals for *C*. Besides these six authentication goals, *C* also has two following transaction goals.

Similar to **G7**, **G15** named as "recent transaction response goal" explains that *C* wants to know the transaction response from *C* has information relevant to the present conversion. The goal **G15** is used to prevent replay attacks for the protocol.

The **G16**, "response message authentication goal" explains that *C* wants to know the transaction response from *C* is genuine. It uses message authentication code (MAC) writing as *h*(*res*⊕*SK*) to validate message integrity of the transaction response.

4.1 Security Analysis for the Basic Protocol

Initial State Assumptions

P1. *C* believes fresh(N_{C1})

P2. *C* believes fresh(N_{C2})

P3. *B* believes fresh(N_{B1})

P4. *C* believes $B \xleftarrow{\;K_{BC}\;} C$

P5. *B* believes $B \xleftarrow{\;K_{BC}\;} C$

P6. *C* believes PK_ψ(B, K_B^-)

P7. *B* has K_B^-

P8. *C* believes *B* controls $B \xleftarrow{\;SK\;} C$

P9. *C* believes *B* controls fresh(*SK*)

P10. *B* believes $B \xleftarrow{\;SK\;} C$

P11. *B* believes fresh(*SK*)

Received Message Assumptions

From 4 messages of the basic protocol, we have:

P12. *B* received (*C*, N_{C1})

P13. *C* received $N_{B1}, \{N_{C1}, \{SK\}K_{BC}\}K_B^-$

P14. B received $\{req, N_{B1}\}SK, N_{C2}, h(req \oplus SK)$

P15. C received $\{res, N_{C2}\}SK, h(res \oplus SK)$

Comprehension Assumptions

P16. B believes B received $(C, \langle N_{C1}\rangle_{*B})$

P17. C believes C received $\langle N_{B1}\rangle_{*C}, \{N_{C1}, \{\langle SK\rangle_{*C}\}K_{BC}\}K_B^-$

P18. B believes B received $\{\langle req\rangle_{*B}, N_{B1}\}SK, \langle N_{C2}\rangle_{*B}, h(req \oplus SK)$

P19. C believes C received $\{\langle res\rangle_{*C}, N_{C2}\}SK, h(res \oplus SK)$

Interpretation Assumptions

P20. C believes C received $\langle N_{B1}\rangle_{*C}, \{N_{C1}, \{\langle SK\rangle_{*C}\}K_{BC}\}K_B^- \rightarrow C$ believes C

received $\langle N_{B1}\rangle_{*C}, \{N_{C1}, \{B\xleftarrow{\langle SK\rangle_{*C}} C\}, fresh(\langle SK\rangle_{*C})\}K_{BC}\}K_B^-$

Derivation for B

1. B believes C said $\{\langle req\rangle_{*B}, N_{B1}\}SK, \langle N_{C2}\rangle_{*B}, h(req \oplus SK)$ by Source Association Axiom, P18, P10 and Belief Axioms.

2. B believes C says $\{\langle req\rangle_{*B}, N_{B1}\}SK, \langle N_{C2}\rangle_{*B}, h(req \oplus SK)$ by Freshness, Nonce Verification, 1, P3 and Belief Axioms.

3. B believes C says $(\langle req\rangle_{*B}, B\xleftarrow{SK} C, \langle N_{C2}\rangle_{*B})$ by Freshness, Nonce Verification, 2 and Belief Axioms.

4. B believes $(\langle req\rangle_{*B}, B\xleftarrow{SK} C, \langle N_{C2}\rangle_{*B})$ by Saying, 3 and Belief Axioms.

5. B believes C says $(\langle req\rangle_{*B}, MAC(req))$ by Freshness, Nonce Verification, 2 and Belief Axioms.

G1 and **G2** are derived from 2. **G3** and **G4** are found in P9 and P10. **G5**, and **G7** are found in 3. **G6** is found in 4. **G8** is found in 5.

Derivation for C

1. C believes C received $\langle N_{B1}\rangle_{*C}, \{N_{C1}, \{B\xleftarrow{\langle SK\rangle_{*C}} C\}, fresh(\langle SK\rangle_{*C})\}$

$K_{BC}\}K_B^-$ by Modus Ponens using P20 and P17.

2. C believes B said $\langle N_{B1}\rangle_{*C}, \{N_{C1}, \{B\xleftarrow{\langle SK\rangle_{*C}} C\}, fresh(\langle SK\rangle_{*C})\}K_{BC}\}K_B^-$ by Source Association Axiom, 1, P4, P6 and Belief Axioms.

3. C believes B say $\langle N_{B1}\rangle_{*C}, \{N_{C1}, \{B\xleftarrow{\langle SK\rangle_{*C}} C\}, fresh(\langle SK\rangle_{*C})\}K_{BC}\}K_B^-$ by Freshness, Nonce Verification, 2, P1 and Belief Axioms.

4. C believes $B \xleftarrow{\langle SK \rangle_{\cdot C}} C$ by Saying, Jurisdiction, 3, P8 and Belief Axioms.

5. C believes $\mathit{fresh}(\langle SK \rangle_{\cdot C})$ by Saying, Jurisdiction, 3, P9 and Belief Axioms.

6. C believes B said $(\langle res \rangle_{\cdot C}, N_{C2}, B \xleftarrow{SK} C, h(res \oplus SK))$ by Source Association, P19, 4 and Belief Axioms.

7. C believes B says $(\langle res \rangle_{\cdot C}, B \xleftarrow{SK} C, h(res \oplus SK))$ by Freshness, None verification, P19, 5, 6, P2 and Belief Axioms.

8. C believes $(\langle res \rangle_{\cdot C}, B \xleftarrow{SK} C, h(res \oplus SK))$ by Saying Axioms, 7 and Belief Axioms.

G9 is found in 3. **G10** is derived from 3 and P1. **G11** is found in 4. **G12** is found in 5. **G13**, **G15** and **G16** are found in 7. **G14** is found in 8.

4.2 Security Analysis for the Extended Mobile Banking Protocol

Besides the sixteen goals derived from the analysis of the basic mobile banking protocol, the analysis for the extended mobile banking protocol has five extra authentication goals (G17-G21) expressing the belief in authenticity of the smart card.

G17. B believes SC says X

G18. B believes (SC says $F(X, N_{B2}) \wedge \mathit{fresh}(N_{B2})$)

G19. B believes $B \xleftarrow{K_{SC}} SC$

G20. B believes SC says $B \xleftarrow{K_{SC}} SC$

G21. B believes ($B \xleftarrow{K_{SC}} SC \wedge C$ says $F(K_{SC})$)

Because the Internet banking protocol using smart card and biometric is similar to the basic protocol, the derivation of sixteen goals, **G1** to **G16**, are similar to the above derivation. The following analysis aims to derive **G17** to **G21**.

P1. B believes $\mathit{fresh}(N_{B2})$

P2. C believes $B \xleftarrow{K_{SC}} SC$

P3. B believes $B \xleftarrow{K_{SC}} SC$

Received Message 4 to 7 Assumptions

P4. C believes C received $N_{B1}, N_{B2}, \{N_{C1}, \{SK\}K_{BC}\}K_{B}^{-}$

P5. SC believes SC received N_{B2}

P6. C believes C received $\{N_{B2}\}K_{SC}$

P7. B believes B received $\{req, N_{B1}, \{N_{B2}\}K_{SC}\}SK, N_{C2}, h(req \oplus SK)$

Comprehensive Assumptions

P8. C believes C received $\langle N_{B1}\rangle_{*C},\langle N_{B2}\rangle_{*C},\{N_{C1},\{\langle SK\rangle_{*C}\}K_{BC}\}K_{B}^{-}$

P9. SC believes SC received $\langle N_{B2}\rangle_{*SC}$

P10. C believes C received $\langle\{N_{B2}\}K_{SC}\rangle_{*C}$

P11. B believes B received $\{\langle req\rangle_{*B},N_{B1},\{N_{B2}\}K_{SC}\}SK,\langle N_{C2}\rangle_{*B},$ $\langle h(req\oplus SK)\rangle_{*B}$

Interpretation Assumptions

P12. C believes C received $\langle N_{B1}\rangle_{*C},\langle N_{B2}\rangle_{*C},\{N_{C1},\{\langle SK\rangle_{*C}\}K_{BC}\}K_{B}^{-}\to C$

believes C received $\langle N_{B1}\rangle_{*C},\langle N_{B2}\rangle_{*C},\{N_{C1},\{B\xleftarrow{\langle SK\rangle_{*C}}C\},fresh(\langle SK\rangle_{*C})\}$ $K_{BC}\}K_{B}^{-}.$

P13. B believes B received $\{\langle req\rangle_{*B},N_{B1},\{N_{B2}\}K_{SC}\}SK,\langle N_{C2}\rangle_{*B},$ $\langle h(req\oplus SK)\rangle_{*B}\to$ B believes B received $\{\langle req\rangle_{*B},N_{B1},\{N_{B2}\}K_{SC},$ $B\xleftarrow{K_{SC}}SC\}SK,\langle N_{C2}\rangle_{*B},\langle h(req\oplus SK)\rangle_{*B}$

Derivation for B

1. B believes SC said $\{N_{B2}\}$ K_{SC} by Source Association Axiom, P13, P3, and Belief Axioms.
2. B believes SC says $\{N_{B2}\}K_{SC}$ by Freshness, Nonce Verification, 1, P1 and Belief Axioms.

G17, G18 is found in 2, **G19** is found in P2, **G20** is derived from 1 and P2. Finally **G21** is derived 2 and P2. The analysis shows that the bank B trust on the authentication from both client C and the smart card SC.

5 Analysis

In the section, we examine the two banking protocols under security attacks: replay attacks, man-in-the-middle attacks, phishing attacks and risks from stolen devices and/or smart cards.

5.1 Replay Attacks

Replay attacks in [7] are efforts of using messages captured from previous communication transaction in order to perform unauthorised operation while internal replay attacks repeat a message (or part of a message) of the current communication to perform unauthorised operations or to obtain unauthorised access. The SVO formal verification in section 4 confirms that the four nonces, N_{B1}, N_{B2}, N_{C1}, and N_{C2} can be used to resist replay attacks for both mobile banking protocols. N_{B1}, N_{B2} and N_{C1} are used in detecting replay attacks in the authentication stage. N_{B1} and N_{C2} secure the protocols from replay attacks in the transaction request stage.

5.2 Man in the Middle Attacks

Murdoch et al. [8] described "man-in-the-middle attack" as a common attack method of intercepting communications in banking protocols. The attackers are able to read, insert, and modify messages in the intercepted communication. The attack method targets the integrity of the protocol.

To resist the man in the middle attack method, the mobile banking protocols utilize message authentication code (MAC). MAC is a hash value of transaction request (or transaction response) exclusive-ORs with the session key SK. MAC is attached with the message so that receiver can validate integrity of the transaction. Without knowledge of the session key SK, attackers are not able to produce the valid MAC. Thus, the mobile banking protocols are able to resist man-in-the-middle attacks.

5.3 Phishing Attacks

Phishing attack is a very common attack method in Internet banking. It refers to attempts to criminally and fraudulently obtain authentication keys or passwords. Attackers usually divert victims to counterfeit internet banking websites masquerading as legitimate in order to capture authentication data. The vulnerability is minimized if a mutual authentication is conducted. With mutual authentication, users are able to validate the authentication of banking services. Both mobile banking protocols offers mutual authentication in the first steps before starting the authentication to the bank service, (the bank service has to sign the session key with its private key K_B^-). Therefore, the protocols have minimum risks under phishing attacks.

5.4 Risks from Stolen Devices and/or Smart Cards

We examine the risks via three following cases:

    a.   Attacker has a stolen/lost smart card;
    b.   Attacker has a stolen/lost mobile device; and
    c.   Attacker has both a stolen device and its smart card

All three cases above create minimum risks for attackers. In case (a), the attacker is not able to perform authentication without the mobile device having the authentication key K_{BC}. In cases (b) and (c), the attacker cannot activate the authentication module at the client without a valid biometric identity. Hence, the attacker cannot perform a valid authentication to mobile banking system.

6 Conclusion

Mobile banking protocols need to be able to provide strong authentication mechanisms that protect the transmitted information between engaged parties. In this paper, we have proposed a novel protocol and its extension that uses advanced authentication technologies approach such as bio features and smart cards. Both protocols are able to protect the financial transactions between the clients' mobile devices and the mobile bank server. So, users can securely access their bank accounts and conduct their financial activities. The proposed protocols also satisfy the convenience and ease of use that are required by mobile users. They are also adaptable with future improvements of the mobile network technologies. The future work will concentrate on improving the identification and verification solution by applying a new dynamic key scheme that strengthens mobile users' authentication and authorization for mobile payment transactions.

References

1. Maximov, A., Johansson, T., Babbage, S.: An improved correlation attack on A5/1. In: Handschuh, H., Hasan, M.A. (eds.) SAC 2004. LNCS, vol. 3357, pp. 1–18. Springer, Heidelberg (2004)
2. Ahmadian, Z., Salimi, S., Salahi, A.: New attacks on UMTS network access. In: Conference on Wireless Telecommunications Symposium, pp. 291–296 (2009)
3. Arabo, A.: Secure Cash Withdrawal through Mobile Phone/Device. In: International Conference on Computer and Communication Engineering, pp. 818–822 (2008)
4. Narendiran, C., Rabara, S.A., Rajendran, N.: Performance evaluation on end-to-end security architecture for mobile banking system. In: 1st IFIP Wireless Days, pp. 1–5 (2008)
5. Espelid, Y., Netland, L.-H., Klingsheim, A.N., Hole, K.J.: A proof of concept attack against norwegian internet banking systems. In: Tsudik, G. (ed.) FC 2008. LNCS, vol. 5143, pp. 197–201. Springer, Heidelberg (2008)
6. Syverson, P., Cervesato, I.: The logic of authentication protocols. In: Focardi, R., Gorrieri, R. (eds.) FOSAD 2000. LNCS, vol. 2171, pp. 63–136. Springer, Heidelberg (2001)
7. Syverson, P.: A Taxonomy of Replay Attacks. In: 7th IEEE Computer Security Foundations Workshop, pp. 187–191 (1994)
8. Murdoch, S.J., Drimer, S., Anderson, R., Bond, M.: Chip and PIN is Broken. In: IEEE Symposium on Security and Privacy, pp. 433–446 (2010)

A Novel Highly Secured Session Based Data Encryption Technique Using Robust Fingerprint Based Authentication

Tanmay Bhattacharya[1], Sirshendu Hore[2],
Ayan Mukherjee[3], and S.R. Bhadra Chaudhuri[4]

[1] Sr. Lecturer, Dept. of IT, JIS College of Engineering, Kalyani,
West Bengal, India
tanmay_bhattacharya@yahoo.co.in
[2] Lecturer, Dept. of CSE, Hooghly Engineering & Technology College,
Pipulpati, Hooghly, West Bengal, India
shirshendu_hore@yahoo.com
[3] Lecturer, Dept. of CSE, Institute of Science & Technology,
Chandrakona Town, Paschim Mednapur, West Bengal, India
ayanmca@gmail.com
[4] Professor, Dept. E&TC, Bengal Engineering & Science University,
Shibpur, Howrah, West Bengal, India
prof.jisce@gmail.com

Abstract. Fingerprint based authentication does not give a foolproof security because fingerprint image can be scanned and can be used later on for the purpose of authentication. In this paper we proposed another level of security by using Session based password in addition to the features of the fingerprint for authentication. The proposed approach shows significant promise and potential for improvement, compared with the other conventional authentication techniques with regard to efficiency of the process.

Keywords: ANN; Minutiae; Sessionbased; Training; MD5.

1 Introduction

Fingerprints have long been used in the identification of individuals because of a well-known fact that each person has a unique fingerprint. Classification is usually performed by noting certain features. The lines that flow in various patterns across fingerprints are called ridges and the spaces between ridges are valleys. The three basic patterns of fingerprint ridges are Arch, Loop, and Whorl. Minutiae are local discontinuities in the fingerprint pattern. A total of 150 different minutiae types have been identified. In practice only ridge ending and ridge bifurcation minutiae types are used in fingerprint identification. All popular AFIS are minutiae-based [2] [4] [5] [6]. Usually each minutiae is described by the position in the coordinate, the direction it flows and the type, whether it is ridge ending or bifurcation. [7] [8] [9] [10] [12]. Figure 1 illustrates the structure of Minutiae.

N. Meghanathan et al. (Eds.): CCSIT 2011, Part II, CCIS 132, pp. 422–431, 2011.

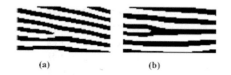

(a)   (b)

Fig. 1. Minutiae (a) Ridge ending (b) Bifurcation

Artificial Neural Network: Artificial neural networks are constituted of artificial neurons. An ANN is a system consisting of processing elements (PE) with links between them. A certain arrangement of the PEs and links produce a certain ANN model, suitable for certain tasks [1] [3]. A Multi-Layer Perceptron (MLP) is a kind of feed-forward ANN model consisting of three adjacent layers; the input, hidden and output layers [1]. Each layer has several PEs. Figure 2 illustrates the structure of a MLP.

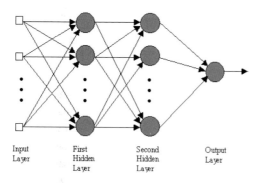

Input   First   Second   Output
Layer   Hidden   Hidden   Layer
             Layer   Layer

Fig. 2. A schematic diagram of a MLP neural network

2 Proposed Algorithm

Following are the main steps of proposed algorithm.

   A. Biometric Key Generation

      Step 1   Image Acquisition
      Step 2   Enhancement of the Image
      Step 3   Feature extraction
      Step 4   Training with different sample images using ANN
      Step 5   Template Finger print is obtained
      Step 6   Biometric Key of 128 bit is generated from the given template.

   B. Session Key generation
   C. Combined Key generation
   D. Encryption of data using Combined Key
   E. Decryption of data is done using the combined key after fingerprint is match with the template.

The sequence of steps for complete authentication process is given in the schematic diagram. Figure 3 illustrates the scheme.

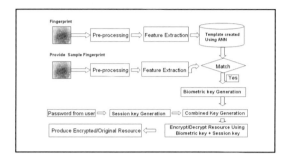

Fig. 3. Schematic diagram of fingerprint authentication process

3 Explanation of Algorithm

Following are the steps involved in the Biometric Key generation

Step 1:   In the initial phase the Fingerprint image is obtained using Bio-sensor scanner which is a flatbed scanner with 600 DPI.

Step 2:   Then the image is preprocessed to remove the noise using various preprocessing techniques like segmentation, Normalization, Orientation, Ridge frequency estimation and, Gabor filtering. Figure 4 illustrate the Image enhancement process.

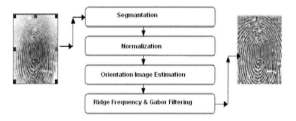

Fig. 4. A schematic diagram of an Image Enhancement

Step 3:   Enhanced image is then binaries and thinning operation is performed to make the ridges single pixel width. Try to find the location of "1" in the thinned image. The number "1" basically represent the ridges. Taking a '3*3' window mask with 1 as a starting point finding the absolute difference between the center pixel and neighborhoods pixel. If the value is 1(ridge ending) or 3 (bifurcation) then find the angel at which the ridge is moving. Store the coordinates, angles and the calculated values. Figure 5 illustrate enhanced image, Thinned image and image with minutiae points.

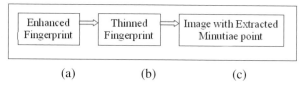

(a)   (b)   (c)

Fig. 5. A schematic diagram of (a) Enhanced image, (b) Thinned Image and (c) Minutiae Point

Step 4:   Before the ANN training the data was divided into three datasets; the training, validation and test. Here data are Minutiae points (ridge ending and bifurcation) which are extracted from a set of fingerprint images. The training set was used to train the MLP, the validation set was used for early-stopping of the training process and the test set was used to evaluate the MLP performance after completion of the training process. The training data set consist of different sample images.

Steps involved:

Forward propagation: The output of each node in the successive layers is calculated

$$O \ (output \ of \ a \ node) = 1/ \ (1 + exp \ (-\Sigma W_{ij} \ x_i)) \qquad (a)$$

The Error E (Im) of an image pattern Im is calculated with respect to Target (T)

$$E \ (Im) = 1/2(\Sigma T \ (Im) - O \ (Im)) \ 2 \qquad (b)$$

Reverse Propagation: The error δ for the nodes in the output layer is calculated

$$\delta(output \ layer) = o(T) - o(\ Im) \qquad (c)$$

The new weights between output layer and hidden layer are updated

$$W \ (n+1) = W \ (n) + \acute{\eta} \ \delta(output \ layer) \qquad (d)$$

The training of the network is stopped when the desired mean square error (MSE) is achieved

$$E \ (MSE) = \Sigma E \ (Im) \qquad (e)$$

Step 5:   A Template is created using the training sets .The implementation and simulation were carried out with the aid of neural networks built in function using Matlab (MATLAB 7.5.0 (R2007 b)).

Step 6:   A biometric key of length 128 bit is generated using MD5 hash algorithm. With MD5 a variable-length message is converted into a fixed-length output of 128 bits. The input message is broken up into chunks of 512-bit blocks (sixteen 32-bit little endian integers); the message is padded so that its length is divisible by 512. The padding works as follows: first a single bit, 1, is appended to the end of the message. This is followed by as many zeros as are required to bring the length of the message up to 64 bits less than a multiple of 512. The remaining bits are filled up with a 64-bit integer representing the length of the original message; after initialization of MD5 buffer with a four-word buffer (A,B,C,D), compute the message digest and finally process message in 16-word blocks to get the output. Figure 6 illustrates the Biometric key generation process.

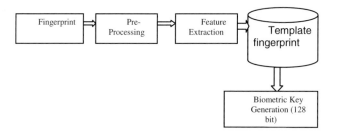

Fig. 6. A schematic diagram of Biometric key Generation

Step 7: Taking a season based password from the user generate a session key of length 128 bit using MD5 key generation algorithm using step 3. Figure 7 illustrates the Session key generation process.

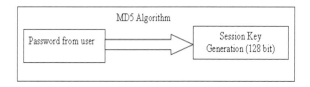

Fig. 7. A Session key of length 128 bit is generated

Step 8: A combined key of length 256 bit is generated combining the session key of length 128 bit with Biometric key of length 128 bit. Open Session Key file and Encryption Key file. Insert Session Key at the Mod 2 position of the Encryption Key file to create the Combined Key and store it in a text file Figure 8 illustrates the Combined Key generation process.

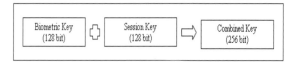

Fig. 8. A combined key of length 256 bit is generated

Step 9:   Taking the File from the user encrypts the data using the combined Key. After taking the file from the user store it in a temporary array after converting the character of the file into their corresponding binary format. Stored the binary values in the 8x8 matrix which is filled up row wise where each row corresponds to a single character. Perform columnar transposition on the matrix. Finally perform the bitwise AND operation on the data using combined key .Given file is now encrypted.

Step 10:   Taking the Sample fingerprint from the user extract the feature and compare it with the template to find whether the matching score is within the threshold. If it is within the range then generate the Biometric key (128 bit) from the template. A session key (128 bit) is created after accepting the password from the user. The combined key (256) is generated using the biometric key and session key. Decrypt the encrypted file using the Combined key.

4   Results and Discussions

In this section, we have presented the experimental results of the proposed approach, which is implemented in Matlab (Matlab7.5.0 (R2007b)) we have tested the proposed approach with different sets of input images. Initially Fingerprints are scanned using standard Bio-sensor scanner with required resolution. As there can be some imperfection in the capture of fingerprint due to lighting condition as well as dirt in the fingerprint enhancement has been done followed by binarization and thinning. Minutiae points are than extracted from the fingerprint. Figure 9 illustrate the different stage of the fingerprint image.

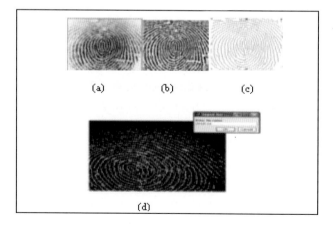

Fig. 9. (a) Raw Image, (b) Enhanced Image, (c) Thinned Image and (d) Image with Minutiae points

428   T. Bhattacharya et al.

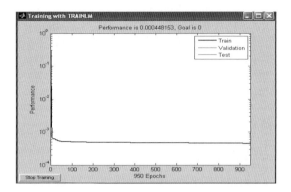

Fig. 10. Learning Performance vs. Epoch in ANN Training process

The figure 10 illustrates the schematic diagram of training process using ANN based on extracted Minutiae points.

Figure 11 and 13 shows the data that are not match with the template data while figure 12, 14 shows data that are closely matched with the template. Figure 15 shows Biometric key generated from template while figure 16 shows session key and figure 17 shows combined key generation process.

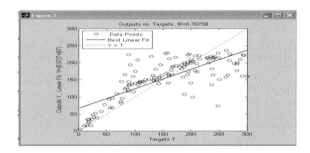

Fig. 11. Target output vs. Computed output on Test data

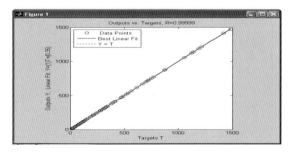

Fig. 12. Target output vs. Computed output on Test data

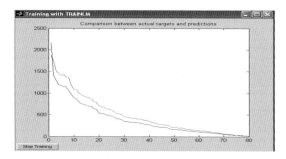

Fig. 13. Epoch vs. Actual data (up) and Epoch vs. Predicted data (down)

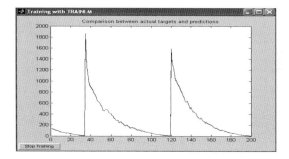

Fig. 14. Epoch vs. Actual data (up) and Epoch vs. Predicted data (down)

Fig. 15. Biometric key generated from template

Fig. 16. Session Key after accepting password from the user

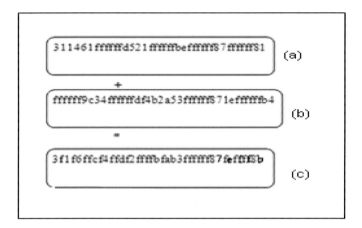

Fig. 17. Combined Key generation. (a) Biometric Key (b) Session key (c) Combined key.

5 Conclusions

The reliability of any authentication technique based on finger print as well as session based techniques relies on the precision obtained in the minutiae extraction process. This research has combined many methods to make the sensitive data as secured as possible also the experimental results shows significant promise and potential for improvement, compared with the other traditional authentication techniques with regard to efficiency of the process. Therefore the finding suggests that using the proposed approach data can be made more secure than before. The proposed approach may be further extended using more reliable biometric features like retina, iris, palm print etc.

References

1. Jayaraman, B., Puttamadappa, C., Anbalagan, E., Mohan, E., Madane, S.: Fingerprint Authentication using Back-propagation Algorithm. International Journal of Soft Computing 3(4), 282–287 (2008) ISSN:1816-9503
2. Mohamad-Saleh, J., Hoyle, B.S.: Improved Neural Network Performance Using Principal Component Analysis on Matlab. International Journal of The Computer, the Internet and Management 16(2), 1–8 (2008)
3. Gil, Y., Ahn, D., Pan, S., Chung, Y.: Access Control System with High Level Security Using Fingerprints. In: Proceedings of the 32nd Applied Imagery Pattern Recognition Workshop (AIPR 2003). IEEE, Los Alamitos (2003), 0-7695-2029-4/03 $ 17.00 © 2003
4. Tanghui, Z., Jie, T., Yuliang, H., Xin, Y.: A Combined Fingerprint Matching Algorithm Based on Similarity Histogram. Chinese Journal of Computers 28(10), 1728–1733 (2005)
5. Jain, A., Ross, A.: Fingerprint Matching Using Minutiae and Texture Features. In: ICIP, pp. 282–285 (2001)
6. Kovocs-Vajna, Z.M.: A Fingerprint Verification System Based on Triangular Matching and Dynamic Time Warping. IEEE Tran's. on PAMI 22(11), 1266–1276 (2000)

7. Jain, A.K., Prabhakar, S., Hong, L., Pankanti, S.: Filterbankbased Fingerprint Matching. IEEE Trans. on Image Precessing 9(5), 846–859 (2000)
8. Jain, A.K., Prabhakar, S., Chen, S.: Combining Multiple Matchers for A High Security Fingerprint Verification System. Pattern Recognition Letters 20(11-13), 1371–1379 (1999)
9. Jain, A.K., Hong, L., Pantanki, S., Bolle, R.: An Identity Authentication System Using Fingerprints. Proc. of the IEEE 85(9), 1365–1388 (1997)
10. Hong, L., Wan, Y., Jain, A.K.: Fingerprint Image Enhancement: Algorithm and performance Evaluation. IEEE Trans. PAMI 20(8), 777–789 (1998)
11. Jain, A., Hong, L., Bolle, R.: On-line Fingerprint Verification. IEEE Trans. on Pattern Analysis and Machine Intelligence 19(4), 302–313 (1997)
12. Jain, A.K., Prabhakar, S., Hong, L.: A Multichannel Approach to Fingerprint Classification. IEEE Trans. on PAMI 21(4), 348–359 (1999)

An Active Host-Based Detection Mechanism for ARP-Related Attacks

F.A. Barbhuiya, S. Roopa, R. Ratti, N. Hubballi,
S. Biswas, A. Sur, S. Nandi*, and V. Ramachandran

Department of Computer Science and Engineering
Indian Institute of Technology Guwahati, India - 781039
{ferdous,roopa.s,r.ratti,neminath,santosh_biswas,
arijit,sukumar}@iitg.ernet.in, vivek.securitywizard@gmail.com
http://www.iitg.ernet.in

Abstract. Most of the LAN based-attacks involves the spoofing of the victim host with falsified IP-MAC pairs. MAC Spoofing is possible because of the stateless nature of the Address Resolution Protocol (ARP), which is responsible for resolving IP Addresses to MAC Addresses. Several mechanisms have been proposed to detect and mitigate ARP spoofing attempts both at the network level and at the host level, but each of them have their own drawback. In this paper we propose a Host-based Intrusion Detection system for LAN attacks which work without any extra constraint like static IP-MAC, modifying ARP etc. The scheme is successfully validated in a test bed with various attack scenarios and the results show the effectiveness of the proposed technique.

1 Introduction

In Local Area network (LAN), when a host wants to communicate with another, it needs to know the MAC address of the destination host. If the MAC address is not known, it sends an ARP request to the broadcast domain asking for the MAC address corresponding to the destination host's IP address. The destination host identifies that the ARP request is meant for its IP address and hence, sends back its MAC address in a unicast ARP reply packet. Most of the LAN based attacks are launched by sending falsified IP-MAC pairs to a host being targeted. The victim host assumes the MAC address in the forged ARP packet as the genuine MAC address associated with the IP. Now when the victim host wants to communicate with the system having the given IP, it is forced to send all packets to the false MAC address (i.e., to a different host the attack wants the victim to send). Attacks based on falsified IP-MAC pairs are feasible because host updates its ARP cache without verifying the genuineness of the IP-MAC pair of the source [1]. Also, the hosts cache all the ARP replies sent to them even if they had not sent an explicit ARP request for them. In other words, ARP spoofing is possible because of the stateless nature of the ARP.

* The work reported in this paper is a part of the project "Design, Development and Verification of Network Specific IDS using Failure Detection and Diagnosis of DES", Sponsored by Department of Information Technology, New Delhi, INDIA.

N. Meghanathan et al. (Eds.): CCSIT 2011, Part II, CCIS 132, pp. 432–443, 2011.

Various mechanisms have been proposed to detect and mitigate these ARP attacks at both the host-level and network-level. In [2], a literature review on network based IDS for detecting ARP spoofing attacks with their drawbacks have been discussed. The authors also present a new network based IDS to detect such spoofing attacks and highlights how many of the drawbacks are eliminated. The present paper is focussed towards development of an host based IDS for ARP spoofing based attacks. So, all discussions regarding existing techniques for ARP attack detection are confined to host-based ones; the techniques can be broadly classified as:

Static ARP [3]: ARP related attacks can be avoided completely by manually assigning static IP addresses to all the systems in the network [3]. The ARP cache of the host has the static mapping of IP-MAC pairings of all other hosts inside the network. Since these entries are immutable, any spoofed packets will be blindly ignored by the kernel. However, this solution is not applicable to large networks because of the problem of scalability and management especially in a dynamic environment.

Stateful ARP [4,5]: The technique is based on extending the existing the standard ARP protocol by modifying the ARP cache from a stateless to a stateful one. Here, the host has a state ARP cache which holds the states of the previous requests and verifies the replies with it. Two queues requestedQ and respondedQ are used to store the state information of cache. Now the incoming responses are matched from corresponding requestedQ and enters into responded queue till timeout.

A major problem in the Stateful ARP based approach is that Gratuitous request/reply, is not supported. Moreover, the modification of stateless cache to stateful cache requires the extension of the protocol specification thereby making it more complex. ARP is basically designed to keep the protocol simple and so, modification to standard ARP is not desirable.

Cryptographic Solutions [6,7]: Another solution is to utilize the cryptographic techniques to prevent the ARP attacks. The limitation of such techniques is that each host has to maintain the public key for every other hosts in network. Also, all the hosts inside the network must be configured to understand the new protocol which requires the upgradation of the network stacks of all the systems involved. Moreover, lots of processing overhead for the signature generation, verification and key management is involved.

Signature based IDS [8]: Signature based IDS like Snort [8] can be used to detect ARP attacks, but the main problem here is the generation of a large number of false alarms. Furthermore, the ability of IDSs to detect all forms of ARP related attacks is limited [9].

Software based Solutions [10,11,12]: Many software solutions are commercially available such as, ARPWATCH, Arp-Guard, X-ARP etc. These softwares basically maintain a table with IP-MAC associations and any change in the association is immediately reported to the system administrator. The problem with this approach is, if the first sent packet itself is having a spoofed MAC address then the whole system fails. Further, any genuine change in IP-MAC pair will be discarded (e.g., when notified by Gratuitous request and reply).

Active techniques for detecting ARP attacks: In active detection based techniques, probe packets are sent across the network to get the information of the suspected host for which the IP-MAC pair has been changed. Several active techniques for detecting ARP attacks have been reported; they are briefly discussed below.

In [13], a database of known IP-MAC pairs is maintained and on detection of a change the new pair is actively verified by sending a TCP SYN packet as the probe. Also, any new pair of IP-MAC is first verified by the probing technique before entering it in the database. On receiving the probe, the genuine system will respond with SYN/ACK or RST depending upon whether the port is open or not. This scheme is able to detect ARP spoofing attacks but it violates the network layering architecture.

Another means to confirm the authenticity of the receiving ARP response packet is by crafting a RARP request packet [14], which seeks the IP address corresponding to the given MAC address. By comparing the IP addresses of the responses, MAC cloning might be detected. However, a single MAC address may genuinely correspond to a number of IP addresses, in which case, a lot of false positives could be generated. In a similar scheme proposed in [15], ARP probe packets (instead of RARP request packet) are used for IP-MAC validation of the source host from which an ARP packet is received. Unicast ARP probe packets are send to the host (identified by the MAC) for verification. If a mismatch occurs in the IP addresses of the probe reply compared to the ARP packet being verified, spoofing is notified. The scheme follows the network layering concepts but fails if the attacker is spoofing some IP with its own MAC address. This is because the unicast ARP probe generated by the IDS will go only to the attacker (identified by the MAC) and it would reply back with the same spoofed IP associated with its MAC.

Hence, from the review it may be stated that an ARP attack prevention/detection scheme needs to have the following features

- Should not modify the standard ARP or violate layering architecture of network
- Should generate minimal extra traffic in the network
- Should detect a large set of LAN based attacks
- Hardware cost of the scheme should not be high

In this paper, we propose an active host based IDS (HIDS) to detect a large set of ARP related attacks namely, malformed packets, response spoofing, request spoofing and denial of service. This technique does not require changes in the standard ARP and does not violate the principles of layering structure.

Rest of the paper is organized as follows. In Section 2 we present the proposed approach. In Section 3 we discuss the test bed and experimental results. Finally we conclude in Section 4.

2   Proposed Scheme

In this section we discuss the proposed host-based active intrusion detection scheme for ARP related attacks. The following assumption is made regarding the LAN

- Non-compromised (i.e., genuine) hosts will send a response to an ARP request within a specific interval T_{req}.

2.1 Data Tables for the Scheme

The proposed IDS running in a host ensures the genuineness of the IP-MAC pairing (of any ARP packet it receives) by an active verification mechanism. The IDS sends verification messages termed as probe requests upon receiving ARP requests and ARP replies. To assist in the probing and separating the genuine IP-MAC pairs with that of spoofed ones, we maintain some information obtained along with the probe requests, ARP requests and ARP replies in some data tables. The information and the data tables used are enumerated below. Henceforth in the discussion, we use the following short notations: IPS - Source IP Address, IPD - Destination IP Address, $MACS$ - Source MAC Address, $MACD$ - Destination MAC Address. Fields of any table would be represented by $\langle TableName \rangle_{\langle field \rangle}$; e.g., RQT_{IPS} represents the source IP filed of "Request-sent table". Also, $\langle TableName \rangle_{MAX}$ represents the maximum elements in the table at a given time.

1. Every time an ARP request is sent from the host querying some MAC address, an entry is created in the "Request-sent table" (denoted as RQT) with the destination IP(RQT_{IPD}) of the ARP packet. Also the time τ when the request was sent is recorded in the table as RQT_τ. Its entries timeout after T_{req} seconds. The value of T_{req} will depend on the ARP request-reply round trip time, which can be fixed after a series of experiments on the network. According to [15], the approximate ARP request-reply round trip time in a LAN is about 1.2 ms - 4.8 ms.
2. Every time an ARP reply packet is received by the host from any other system in the network, an entry is created in the "Response-received table" (denoted as RST) with its source IP (RST_{IPS}) and source MAC (RST_{MACS}). Also the time when the response was received is recorded in the table. Its entries timeout after T_{resp} seconds. The T_{resp} value can be determined based on the ARP cache timeout value of the host.
3. When some IP-MAC pair is to be verified, an ARP probe is sent and response is verified. The probe is initiated by the HIDS, upon receiving either a Request or a Response. The source IP address and the source MAC address from the Request/ Response packets used for verification are stored in "Verification table" (denoted as $VRFT$). The entries in this table are source IP ($VRFT_{IPS}$) and source MAC ($VRFT_{MACS}$).
4. Every time any IP-MAC pair is verified and found to be correct, an entry is created for the pair in the "Authenticated bindings table" (denoted as $AUTHT$). There are two fields in this table, IP address ($AUTHT_{IP}$) and MAC address ($AUTHT_{MAC}$).

2.2 Algorithms of the IDS

The proposed HIDS algorithm has two main modules namely, ARP REQUEST-HANDLER() and ARP RESPONSE-HANDLER() to handle incoming and outgoing ARP packets respectively. The modules are discussed below

Algorithm 1 processes all the ARP request packets received by the host. For any ARP request packet RQP received, the HIDS first checks if it is malformed (i.e., is there any change in the immutable fields of the ARP packer header or different MAC addresses in the MAC and ARP header field) or unicast; if so, a status flag is set accordingly and stops further processing of this packet.

The HIDS next finds whether the packet received is a Gratuitous ARP request and the status flag is set accordingly. Gratuitous ARP request can be determined if $RQP_{IPS} ==$ RQP_{IPD}. For such Gratuitous ARP request, ARP probe is sent for checking the correctness of the IP-MAC pair. Hence, the VERIFY IP-MAC() module is called for RQP along with τ (the time information when RQP was received).

If neither of the above cases match, then RQP_{IPS} is searched in the Authenticated bindings table. If a match is found as $AUTHT_{IPS}[i]$(where i is the ith entry in the $AUTHT$) and the corresponding MAC address $AUTHT_{MACS}[i]$ in the table is same as RQP_{MACS}, the packet has genuine IP-MAC pair which is already recorded in the Authenticated bindings table. In case of a mismatch in the MAC address (i.e., $RQP_{MACS} \neq AUTHT_{MACS}[i]$) the packet is spoofed with a wrong MAC address and hence the status flag is set as spoofed. It may be noted that this checking of spoofing could be done without ARP probe thereby reducing ARP traffic for verification.

Also, it may be the case that IP-MAC pair given in RQP_{IPS} is not verified as yet and no entry can be found in Authenticated bindings table corresponding to RQP_{IPS}. In such a case, an ARP probe is to be sent by the HIDS to RQP_{IPS} and RQP_{MACS} for verifying the correctness of the RQP_{IPS}-RQP_{MACS} pair. This is handled by the VERIFY IP-MAC() module with RQP and τ as parameters.

Algorithm 1. ARP REQUEST HANDLER

Input : RQP - ARP request packet, τ - time at which RQP was received, Request-sent table, Verification table, Authenticated bindings table
Output: Updated Request-sent table, Status

```
 1: if (RQP is malformed) then
 2:     Status=malformed
 3: else if (RQP is Unicast) then
 4:     Status=Unicast
 5: else
 6:     if (RQP_IPS == RQP_IPD) then
 7:         Status=Gratutious Packet
 8:         VERIFY IP-MAC(RQP, τ)
 9:     else
10:         if (RQP_IPS == AUTHT_IPS[i] (for some i, 1 ≤ i ≤ AUTHT_MAX) then
11:             if (RQP_MACS == AUTHT_MACS[i]) then
12:                 Status= Genuine
13:             else
14:                 Status=Spoofed
15:             end if
16:         else
17:             VERIFY IP-MAC(RQP, τ)
18:         end if
19:     end if
20: end if
```

Algorithm 2. ARP RESPONSE HANDLER

Input : RSP - ARP response packet, τ - time at which RSP was received, Request-sent table, Verification table, Authenticated bindings table
Output: Updated Response-received table, Status

```
 1:  if RSP is malformed then
 2:      Status= malformed
 3:  else
 4:      Add RSP_IPS, RSP_MACS and τ to Response-received table
 5:      if (RSP_IPS == RSP_IPD) then
 6:          Status= Gratuitous
 7:          VERIFY IP-MAC(RSP, τ)
 8:      else
 9:          if ((RSP_IPD == IP(HIDS) && RSP_MACD == MAC(HIDS)) &&
               (RSP_IPS == VRFT_IPS[k]))(for some k, 1 ≤ k ≤ VRFT_MAX)) then
10:              EXIT
11:          else
12:              if (RSP_IPS == RQT_IPD[i] (for some i, 1 ≤ i ≤ RQ_MAX)) then
13:                  if (RSP_IPS == AUTHT_IPS[j] (for some j, 1 ≤ j ≤ AUTHT_MAX))
                     then
14:                      if (RSP_MACS == AUTHT_MACS[j]) then
15:                          Status= Genuine
16:                      else
17:                          Status=Spoofed
18:                      end if
19:                  else
20:                      VERIFY IP-MAC(RSP, τ)
21:                  end if
22:              else
23:                  UNSOLICITED-RESPONSE-HANDLER( τ)
24:              end if
25:          end if
26:      end if
27:  end if
```

Algorithm 2 is an ARP response handler. For every ARP response packet RSP received by the host, the HIDS determines whether the reply is malformed; if malformed, a status flag is set accordingly and the next packet is processed. Otherwise, the source IP (RSP_{IPS}), source MAC (RSP_{MACS}), and timestamp τ of the received packet are recorded in the Response-received table. Next, it verifies whether the packet is a Gratuitous ARP reply by checking if $RSP_{IPS} == RSP_{IPD}$. For such a Gratuitous ARP reply, an ARP probe is sent to check the correctness of the IP-MAC pair. Hence, the VERIFY IP-MAC() module is called.

If the reply packet is not Gratuitous, next it verifies if it is a reply for any ARP probe sent by the VERIFY IP-MAC() module (i.e., ARP probe by the HIDS). The response for the ARP probe can be determined if $RSP_{IPD} == IP(HIDS)$ and RSP_{MACD} $== MAC_{HIDS}$ and RSP_{IPS} has an entry in the Verification table. For such response packets, Algorithm 2 calls SPOOF-DETECROR() module.

If none of the above cases holds, the reply packet is then matched for a corresponding request in the Request-sent table, using its source IP RSP_{IPS}. If a match is found (i.e., $RSP_{IPS}== RQT_{IPD}[i]$), the RSP_{IPS} is searched in the Authenticated bindings table. If a match is found and the corresponding MAC address in the table is same as RSP_{MACS}, the packet has genuine IP-MAC pair (which is already recorded in the Authenticated bindings table). In case of a mismatch in the MAC address (i.e., $RSP_{MACS} \neq AUTHT_{MACS}[j]$) the packet may be spoofed with a wrong MAC address and hence the status flag is set as spoofed. If the RSP_{IPS} is not present in the Authenticated bindings table, then an ARP probe is sent for verification by the VERIFY IP-MAC() module. If there was no corresponding request for the response packet in the Request-sent table, then it is an unsolicited response packet. Hence, the UNSOLICITED-RESPONSE-HANDLER() is called with the time at which such a response is received τ.

The main modules discussed in Algorithms1 and Algorithm 2 are assisted by three sub-modules namely, VERIFY IP-MAC(), SPOOF-DETECTOR() and UNSOLICITED-RESPONSE-HANDLER(). Now, we discuss these sub-modules in detail.

Algorithm 3. VERIFY IP-MAC

Input : RP- ARP request/reply packet, τ - time of arrival of RSP, Verification table
Output: Updated Verification table, Status

```
 1: if (RP_IPS ∈ VRFT_IPS[i]) (for some i, 0 ≤ i ≤ VRFT_MAX) then
 2:    if (RP_MACS == VRFT_MACS[i]) then
 3:       EXIT
 4:    else
 5:       Status=Spoofed
 6:    end if
 7: else
 8:    Send ARP Probe Request to RP_IPS
 9:    Add RP_IPS and RP_MACS to the Verification table
10:    SPOOF-DETECTOR(RP, τ)
11: end if
```

VERIFY IP-MAC() (Algorithm 3) sends ARP probes to verify the correctness of the IP-MAC pair given in the source of the request packet RQP or response packet RSP. Every time a probe is sent, its record is inserted in Verification table. Before, sending the ARP probe request, we need to verify if there is already such a request made by the HIDS and response is awaited. This can be verified by checking IP and MAC in the Verification table; if a match pair is found the module is exited. A spoofing may be attempted if IP matches the entry in the Verification table but MAC does not; in this case, the status is set as spoofed. This checking in the Verification table (before sending probe) limits the number of ARP probes to be sent for any known falsified IP-MAC address, thereby lowering extra ARP traffic. If the corresponding IP address is not found in the Verification table, a probe request is sent and the algorithm adds the IP and the MAC into the Verification table. At the same time SPOOF-DETECTOR() module is called which waits for a round trip time and then analyzes all the entries in the Response-received table collected within this period (for analyzing the probe responses).

SPOOF-DETECTOR() (Algorithm 4) is called from VERIFY IP-MAC() after sending the ARP $Probe\ Request$ to source IP of the packet to be checked for spoofing (RP_{IPS}). As discussed, it is assumed that all replies to the ARP probe will be sent within T_{req} time. So, SPOOF-DETECTOR() waits for T_{req} interval of time, thereby collecting all probe responses in the Response-received table. As it is assumed that non-comprised hosts will always respond to a probe, at least one response to the probe will arrive. In other words, in one of the replies to the probe, genuine MAC for the IP RP_{IPS} would be present. Following that, Response-received table will be searched to find IP-MAC (source) pairs having IP of RP_{IPS}. If all IP-MAC pairs searched have same MAC, packet under question is not spoofed. In case of the packet being spoofed, more than one reply will arrive for the probe, one with genuine MAC and the other with spoofed MAC. The reason for assuming more than one replies in case of spoofing is explained as follows. Let a packet be spoofed as IP(of B)-MAC(of D). Now for the ARP probe to B, B will reply with IP(of B)-MAC(of B) leading to tracking the attacker (MAC (of D)). To avoid self identification, attacker D has to reply to all queries asking for B with spoofed IP-MAC pair IP(B)-MAC(D). The IDS has no clue whether IP(B)-MAC(D) or IP(B)-MAC(D) is genuine; only possibility of spoofing is detected.

If a spoofing attempt is determined the status is returned as spoofed and it is exited. If the packet is found genuine, Authenticated bindings table is updated with its source IP (RP_{IPS}) and the corresponding MAC.

Algorithm 4. SPOOF-DETECTOR

Input : RP- ARP request/reply packet, T_{req} - Time required for arrival of all responses to an ARP probe (ARP request-reply round trip time), Response-received table
Output: Updated Authenticated bindings table, Status

1: Wait for T_{req} time interval
2: **if** (RP_{IPS} == $RST_{IPS}[i]$) & & ($RP_{MACS} \neq RST_{MACS}[i]$)(for some i, $1 \leq i \leq RST_{MAX}$) **then**
3:    Status=$Spoofed$
4:    EXIT
5: **end if**
6: Update Authenticated bindings table with RP_{IPS}, RP_{MACS}

UNSOLICITED-RESPONSE-HANDLER() (Algorithm 5) is invoked whenever an unsolicited ARP reply packet is received (i.e., ARP reply packet did not find a matching ARP request in the Request-sent table) and is used for detection of denial of service (DoS) attacks. In general, ARP replies are received corresponding to the ARP requests. If more than a certain number of unsolicited responses are are sent to a host within a time window, it implies an attempt of DoS attack on the given host. Algorithm 5 maintains an "Unsolicited response counter (denoted as $URSP_{counter}$) for storing the number of unsolicited responses received by the host within a specified time interval (δ) and declares DoS attack if the number of unsolicited ARP replies within a time interval (δ) exceeds a preset threshold DoS_{Th}.

Algorithm 5. UNSOLICITED-RESPONSE-HANDLER

Input : τ - Time when RSP is received, δ- Time window, DoS_{Th}- DoS Threshold, Unsolicited response table
Output: Status

```
1:  if (τ − URSP_τ < δ) then
2:      URSP_counter++
3:      URSP_τ = τ
4:      if (URSPT_counter > DoS_Th) then
5:          Status=DoS
6:          EXIT
7:      end if
8:  else
9:      URSP_counter=1
10:     URSP_τ = τ
11: end if
```

2.3   An Example

In this sub-section we illustrate ARP response verification in normal and spoofed cases.

Consider a network with four hosts - A, B, C, D and host D is the attacker. HIDS be installed on all the hosts which need to be secure.

Figure 1 shows the sequence of packets (indicated with packet sequence numbers) injected in the LAN when (i) host B is sending a genuine reply to B with IP(B)-MAC(B) followed by ARP probe based verification (of the reply) by the HIDS at host A, (ii) attacker D is sending a spoofed reply as "IP(C)-MAC(D) " to host A and its verification by the HIDS at host A. The sequences of packets as recorded in Request-sent

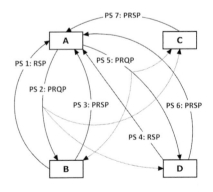

Fig. 1. Example of a Normal and Spoofed Reply

table, Response-received table, Verification table and Authenticated bindings table in the HIDS running in host A are shown in Table 1 - Table 4.

Genuine reply from B to A and its verification
- Packet Sequence (PS) 1: Reply is sent by B to A for informing its MAC address (to B). Assume this reply packet to be a gratuitous reply or a response to a request sent by A, so that it is not considered unsolicited. Response-received table is updated with a new entry IP(B)-MAC(B) .
- Packet Sequence 2: Since there is no entry for IP-MAC of B in Authenticated bindings table, the HIDS A will send an ARP Probe to verify its correctness and hence an entry is made in the Verification table.
- Packet Sequence 3: Following PS 2, SPOOF-DETECTOR() starts. Within T_{req} only B will respond to this ARP Probe request and Authenticated bindings table is updated with the valid entry of IP-MAC of B.

Spoofed reply from D to A and its verification
- Packet Sequence 4: Let D respond to A with IP of C and its own MAC (D), which is recorded in the Response table. As in the above case, we consider this reply packet to be solicited
- Packet Sequence 5: Since there is no entry for IP-MAC of C in Authenticated bindings table, the HIDS A will send an ARP probe to know C's MAC. Hence, IP (C)-MAC(D) is entered in the Verification table.
- Packet Sequence 6 and 7: SPOOF-DETECTOR() is executed. Within T_{req}, both C and attacker D will respond to the ARP Probe request (sent to know MAC of B) with their own MACs. These responses are recorded in the Response table.
  There are two entries in Response table for IP(C), one is MAC of C and the other is MAC of D. So response spoofing is detected by the HIDS running at A.

Table 1. Request-sent table

PS	DST IP
-	-

Table 2. Response-received table

PS	SRC IP	SRC MAC
1	IP B	MAC B
3	IP B	MAC B
4	IP C	MAC D
6	IP C	MAC D
7	IP C	MAC C

Table 3. Verification table

PS	IP	MAC
2	IP B	MAC B
5	IP C	MAC D

Table 4. Authenticated bindings table

PS	MAC
IP B	MAC B

3   Experimentation

The test bed created for our experiments consists of 5 machines running different operating systems. We name the machines with alphabets ranging from A-D. Machines

A-D are running the following OSs: Ubuntu 9.04, Windows XP, Windows 2000 and Backtrack 4, respectively. The machine D with Backtrack 4 is acting as the attacker machine. HIDS is installed in all genuine machines.

The tables mentioned above are created in mysql database. The algorithms are implemented using C language. The HIDS has two major modules namely, Packet grabber and Packet injector. Packet grabber sniffs the packets from the host's network interface card (NIC), filters the ARP packets and invokes either the Algorithm 1 or Algorithm 2 depending upon the packet type - request or response. The Packet injector module generates the ARP probes necessary for the verification of IP-MAC pairs. Attack generation tools Ettercap, Cain and Abel were deployed in machine D and several scenarios of spoofing MAC addresses were attempted.

Table 5. Comparison of ARP Attack Detection Mechanisms

ATTACKS	PROPOSED	ACTIVE [13]	X-ARP [12]	ARPWATCH [10]	ARPGUARD [11]
ARP spoofing	Y	Y	Y	Y	Y
ARP DoS	Y	N	N	N	N
Malformed Packets	Y	Y	Y	N	N

In our experiments we tested our proposed scheme with several variants of LAN attack scenarios (including the one discussed in the example above). Table 5 presents the types of LAN attacks generated and detected successfully by the proposed scheme. Also, in the table we report the capabilities of other LAN attack detecting tools for these attacks.

Figure 2 shows the amount of ARP traffic generated in the experimentation in 4 cases. The first case is of normal operation in the absence of the IDS. Second case is when the IDS is running and there are no attacks generated in the network. Third case is when we injected 100 spoofed IP-MAC pairs into the LAN and IDS is not running. Fourth case is when we injected 100 spoofed IP-MAC pairs into the LAN with IDS running. We notice almost same amount of ARP traffic under normal situation with and without IDS running. Once genuine IP-MAC pairs are identified (by probing) they are stored in Authenticated bindings table. Following that no probes are required to be sent for any ARP request/reply from these IP-MAC pairs. In case of attack, a little extra

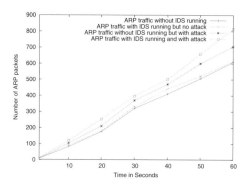

Fig. 2. ARP traffic

traffic is generated by our IDS for the probes. With each spoofed ARP packet, our IDS sends a probe request and expects at least two replies (one from normal and the other from the attacker), thereby adding only three ARP packets for each spoofed packet.

4 Conclusion

In this paper, we have presented an HIDS for detecting some of the LAN specific attacks. The scheme uses an active probing mechanism and does not violate the principles of network layering architecture. This being a software based approach does not require any additional hardware to operate.

At present the scheme can only detect the attacks. In other words, in case of spoofing it can only determine the conflicting IP-MAC pairs without differentiating the spoofed IP-MAC and genuine IP-MAC pair. If to some extent diagnosis capability can be provided in the scheme, some remedial action against the attacker can be taken.

References

1. Held, G.: Ethernet Networks: Design, Implementation, Operation, Management, 1st edn. John Wiley & Sons, Ltd., Chichester (2003)
2. Hubballi, N., Roopa, S., Ratti, R., Barburiya, F., Biswas, S., Nandi, S., Sur, A., Ramachandran, V.: An active intrusion detection system for lan specific attacks. In: The 4th International Conference on Information Security and Assurance (2010) (in press)
3. Kozierok, C.M.: TCP/IP Guide, 1st edn. No Starch Press (October 2005)
4. Tripunitara, M.V., Dutta, P.: A middleware approach to asynchronous and backward compatible detection and prevention of arp cache poisoning. In: Proceedings of the 15th Annual Computer Security Applications Conference, ACSAC 1999, Washington, DC, USA, p. 303. IEEE Computer Society, Los Alamitos (1999)
5. Zhenqi Wang, Y.Z.: Monitoring arp attack using responding time and state arp cache. In: The Sixth International Symposium on Neural Networks (ISNN 2009), pp. 701–709 (2009)
6. Gouda, M.G., Huang, C.T.: A secure address resolution protocol. Comput. Networks 41(1), 57–71 (2003)
7. Lootah, W., Enck, W., McDaniel, P.: Tarp: Ticket-based address resolution protocol, pp. 106–116. IEEE Computer Society, Los Alamitos (2005)
8. Zhao, S.L.: Weight intrusion detection, http://www.snort.org
9. Abad, C.L., Bonilla, R.I.: An analysis on the schemes for detecting and preventing arp cache poisoning attacks. In: Proceedings of the 27th International Conference on Distributed Computing Systems Workshops, ICDCSW 2007, Washington, DC, USA, pp. 60–67. IEEE Computer Society, Los Alamitos (2007)
10. arpwatch, http://www.arpalert.org
11. arpguard, https://www.arp-guard.com
12. xarp, http://www.chrismc.de/
13. Ramachandran, V., Nandi, S.: Detecting arp spoofing: An active technique. In: Jajodia, S., Mazumdar, C. (eds.) ICISS 2005. LNCS, vol. 3803, pp. 239–250. Springer, Heidelberg (2005)
14. Whalen, S.: An Introduction to ARP Spoofing (April 2001)
15. Sisaat, K., Miyamoto, D.: Source address validation support for network forensics. In: Yoshiura, H., Sakurai, K., Rannenberg, K., Murayama, Y., Kawamura, S.-i. (eds.) IWSEC 2006. LNCS, vol. 4266, pp. 387–401. Springer, Heidelberg (2006)

Privacy-Preserving Naïve Bayes Classification Using Trusted Third Party Computation over Vertically Partitioned Distributed Progressive Sequential Data Streams

Keshavamurthy B.N. and Durga Toshniwal

Department of Electronics & Computer Engineering,
Indian Institute of Technology Roorkee,
Uttarakhand, India
{kesavdec,durgafec}@iitr.ernet.in

Abstract. Privacy preservation in distributed progressive data stream is an active area of research in the present time. In a typical scenario, multiple parties may be wishing to collaborate to extract interesting global information such as class labels without breaching privacy. This may be particularly useful in applications such as customer retention, medical research etc. In the present work, we aim to develop a global classification model based on the Naïve Bayes classification scheme. The Naïve Bayes classification has been used because of its applicability in case of customer retention application such as car evaluation dataset. For privacy preservation of the data, the concept of trusted third party has been used. We have proposed algorithms and tested car evaluation dataset for vertical partitioned progressive sequential data streams.

Keywords: Privacy preservation, Naïve Bayes classification, progressive sequential data streams, offset computation, vertical partition.

1 Introduction

In recent years, due to the advancement of computing and storage technology, digital data can be easily collected. It is very difficult to analyze the entire data manually. Thus a lot of work is going on for mining and analyzing such data.

Of the various techniques of data mining analysis, progressive databases analysis is one of the active areas of research work. Progressive data mining discover the results in a defined period of interest or focus. The Progressive databases have posed new challenges because of the following inherent characteristics such as it should not only add new items to the period of interest but also removes the obsolete items from the period of interest. It is thus a great interest to find results that are up to date in progressive databases.

In many real world applications such as hospitals, retail-shops, design-firms and universities databases, data is distributed across different sources. The distributed database is comprised of horizontal, vertical or arbitrary fragments. In case of horizontal fragmentation, each site has the complete information on a distinct set of

N. Meghanathan et al. (Eds.): CCSIT 2011, Part II, CCIS 132, pp. 444–452, 2011.

entities. An integrated dataset consists of the union of these datasets. In case of vertical fragments each site has partial information on the same set of entities. An integrated dataset would be produced by joining the data from the sites. Arbitrary fragmentation is a hybrid of previous two.

The key goal for privacy preserving data mining is to allow computation of aggregate statistics over an entire data set without compromising the privacy of private data of the participating data sources. The key methods such as secure multiparty computation use some transformation on the data in order to perform the privacy preservation. One of the methods in distributed computing environment which uses the secure sum multi party computation technique of privacy preservation is Naïve Bayes classification.

The mining of Naiye Bayes classification for static database and distributed databases has been studied extensively. However progressive distributed data streams are a new area of research.

This paper addresses the key issue of effective usage of secure multi-party computation using trusted third party computation and it also addresses the privacy preservation Naïve Bayes classification for progressive sequential distributed data streams.

The rest of the paper is organized as follows: Section 2 briefs about related research work. Section 3 presents privacy preservation Naïve Bayes classification using trusted third party computation over distributed progressive databases. Section 4 gives experimental results. Section 5 includes conclusion.

2 Preliminaries

2.1 Problem Definition

There are many research papers which have discussed the progressive data streams but the existing proposals do not extract the important knowledge such as the Naïve Bayes classification values for a progressive sequential data streams. The proposed work of this paper addresses this issue effectively by using the concept of sliding window and secure multi-party concept with trusted third party computation.

2.2 Related Research

Sequential Pattern Mining
There are many researches about mining sequential patterns in a static database. It was first addressed by Agarwal and Srikant [1]. In general sequential pattern mining algorithms can be classically categorized into three classes. (i) Apriori based horizontal partitioning methods such as Generalized Sequential Pattern mining [2], which adopts multiple-pass candidate generation and test approach in sequential pattern mining. (ii) Apriori based vertical partitioning methods such as Sequential Pattern Discovery using Equivalent classes [3], utilizes combinatorial properties to decompose the original problem into smaller sub-problems that can be independently solved in main memory using efficient lattice search and simple join operations. (iii) Projection based pattern growth algorithms such as prefix-projected sequential pattern mining algorithms [4], which represents the pattern growth methodology and finds the

frequent items after scanning database once. In addition to the traditional algorithms there are many which include closed sequential pattern mining [5], maximal sequential pattern mining [6] and constraint sequential pattern mining [7].

Incremental Sequential Pattern Mining

The incremental sequential pattern mining algorithms resolve major drawback of the sequential pattern mining algorithms such as mining the patternsfrom up-to-date database without deleting the obsolete. The key algorithms of incremental sequential pattern mining are: incremental mining algorithm ISM by maintaining a sequence lattice of an old database [8]. Sequence lattice includes all the frequent sequences and all the sequences in the negative border. Incremental algorithm ISE for incremental mining of sequential patterns when new transactions are added to the database [9], this algorithm adopts candidate generation and test approach. Incspan algorithm mines sequential patterns over an incremental database [10]. The limitation of these algorithms is its inability to delete the obsolete data.

Progressive Sequential Pattern Mining

Progressive sequential pattern mining is a generalized pattern mining methodology that brings out the most recent frequent sequential patterns. This algorithm works both static as well as dynamic changing databases and is unaffected by the presence of obsolete data. The patterns are not affected by the old data. This algorithm uses the sliding window to progressively update sequences in the database and accumulate the frequencies of candidate sequential patterns as time progresses. The sliding window called period of interest determines the time stamp over which the algorithm is currently working.

Definition 1: Period of Interest (*POI*) is a sliding window. The length of the *POI* is a user specified time interval. The sequences having elements whose timestamps fall into this period *POI*, contribute to / *DB* / for sequential patterns generated at that timestamp. On the other hand, the sequences having elements with timestamps older than those in the *POI* are pruned away from the sequence database immediately and do not contribute to the / *DB* / thereafter.

There are few proposals on progressive sequential pattern mining. The initial study on progressive sequential pattern mining was proposed by Jen W. Huang et al. [11], it gives the complete details of progressive tree concept to capture the dynamic nature of data over a period of interest.

Privacy Preservation

Initially, for privacy preserving data mining randomization method were used, the randomization method has been traditionally used in the context of distorting data by probability distribution [12]. In [13], it was discussed about privacy protection and knowledge preservation approach for classification by using the method of ananymization, it anonymizes data by randomly breaking links among attribute values in records by data randomization.

A number of other techniques which includes for the privacy preservation which works on different classifiers such as in [14] combine the two strategies of data transform and data hiding to propose a new randomization method, Randomized Response with Partial Hiding (RRPH), for distorting the original data. Then, an effective Naive Bayes classifier is presented to predict the class labels for unknown samples according to the distorted data by RRPH.The work in [15] describes the methods of improving the effectiveness of classification such as in it proposes a method which eliminates the privacy breach and increase utility of the released database.

In case of distributed environment, the most widely used technique in privacy preservation mining is secure sum computation [16]. Here when there are n data sources $DS_0, DS_1, ... D_{n-1}$ such that each DS_i has a private data item $d_i, i = 0,1,...,n-1$ the parties want to compute $\sum_{i=0}^{n-1} d_i$ privately, without revealing their private data d_i to each other. The following method was presented:

We assume that $\sum_{i=0}^{n-1} d_i$ is in the range $[0, m-1]$ and DS_j is the protocol initiator.

Following steps were followed:

1. At the beginning DS_j chooses a uniform random number r within $[0, m-1]$.

2. Then DS_j sends the sum $d_i + r \pmod{m}$ to the data source $DS_j + 1 \pmod{n}$.

3. Each remaining data sources DS_i do the following: upon receiving a value x the data source DS_i sends the sum $d_i + x \pmod{m}$ to the data source $DS_i + 1 \pmod{n}$.

4. Finally, when party DS_j receives a value from the data source $DS_{n-1} - 1 \pmod{n}$), it will be equal to the total sum $r + \sum_{i=0}^{n-1} d_i$. Since r is only known to DS_j it can find the sum $\sum_{i=0}^{n-1} d_i$ and distribute to other parties.

The Naïve Bayes classification scheme applies to learning tasks where each instance x is described by a conjunction of attribute values and the target function f (x) can take on any value from some finite set C. A set of training examples of the target function is provided, and a new instance is presented, described by the tuple of attribute values $a_1, a_2, ... a_n$. The learner is asked to predict the target value, or classification, for this new instance. The Bayesian approach to classifying the new instance is to assign the most probable target value, C_{MAP}, given the attribute values $a_1, a_2, ... a_n$ that describe the instance.

$$C_{MAP} = \arg_{\max} \ P(c_j / a_1, a_2, ... a_n) \ . \tag{1}$$

Using Bayes theorem,

$$C_{MAP} = \arg_{\max} \ P(a_1, a_2, ... a_n / c_j) P(c_j) / P(a_1, a_2, ... a_n) \ .$$

$$= \arg_{\max} \ (P(a_1, a_2, ... a_n / c_j) \, P(c_j)) \ . \tag{2}$$

The Naïve Bayes classifier makes the further simplifying assumption that the attribute values are conditionally independent given the target value. Therefore,

$$C_{NB} = \arg_{\max} \ (P(c_j)) \cap P(a_i / c_j). \tag{3}$$

Where C_{NB} denotes the target value output by the Naïve Bayes classifier.

The conditional probabilities $P(a_i / c_j)$ need to be estimated from the training set. The prior probabilities $P(C_j)$ also need to decide by some heuristics. Probabilities are computed differently for nominal and numerical attributes.

For a nominal attribute in a horizontally partitioned data, the conditional probability $P(C = c / \ A = a)$ that an instance belongs to class c given that the instance has an attribute value $A = a$, is given by

$$P(C = c \cap A = a) = \frac{P(C = c \cap A = a)}{P(A = a)} = \frac{n_{ac}}{n_a} \ . \tag{4}$$

Here n_{ac} is the number of instances in the (global) training set that have the class value c and an attribute value of a, while n_a is the number of instances in the global training set which simply have an attribute value of a. The necessary parameters are simply the counts of instances n_{ac} and n_a. Due to horizontal partitioning of data, each party has partial information about every attribute. Each party can locally compute the local count of instances. The global count is given by the sum of the local counts. Secure computing a global count is straightforward. Assuming that the total number of instances is public, the required probability can be computed by dividing the appropriate global sums where the local number of instances will not be revealed.

For an attribute with l different attribute values and a total of r distinct classes, l.r different counts need to be computed for each combination of attribute value and class value. For each attribute value a total instance count also to be computed, this gives l additional counts [17].

3 Progressive Naïve Bayes Classification Using Trusted Third Party Computation over Vertically Distributed Data Streams

In nominal attributes, each party calculates their local instances of n_{ac} and n_a, of the attribute values they have. As each party have different attributes, so no parties have same value of instance of attribute and class. Hence there is no need to calculate the sum of values. At a particulate timestamp, we calculate the local values of n_{ac} and n_a, and send them to the trusted third party. The corresponding algorithm will be given in Fig.1.

---

void UpdateValues (List c^i_{yz}, List n^i_y)

{ For transaction at $t = t_{current}$

{   For all class values y do

For all z, Party P_i locally computes c^i_{yz}Party P_i

locally computes n^i_y

End For }

c^i_{yz} (new) = c^i_{yz} (previous) + c^i_{yz} (transaction at $t = t_{current}$)

n^i_y (new) = n^i_y (previous) + n^i_y (transaction at $t = t_{current}$)

If (($t_{current}$ -POI)>0)

{   For transaction at $t = (t_{current}$ -POI)

{   For all class values y do

For all z, Party P_i locally computes c^i_{yz}

Party Pi locally computes n^i_y

End For }

c^i_{yz} (new) = c^i_{yz} (current) - c^i_{yz} (transaction at $t = t_{current}$ - POI)

n^i_y (new) = n^i_y (current) - n^i_y (transaction at $t = t_{current}$ }   }

Fig. 1. Naïve bayes algorithm for vertical partition

The Update Value function of vertical scenario shown in Fig.2 will be described as follows: As in the progressive database, the new data is keep on arriving at every timestamp and data become obsolete to keep database up to data, so we also have to modify n_{ac} and n_a at every timestamp. In the algorithm, we keep on updating n_{ac} and n_a, until $t_{current}$ is less than POI, as no data become obsolete so we keep adding number of instances in both n_{ac} and n_a.

As $t_{current}$ exceeds POI then we also have to remove the instances which are no more in the required period of interest. At every timestamp, we store the records which will be obsolete in next time stamp, as these records have the values which have to be reduced to update n_{ac} and n_a. As the time increases new data will come and also we have n_{ac} obsolete data. We update n_{ac} and n_a by adding the values of n_{ac} and n_a of new data, and by removing values of n_{ac} and n_a by the obsolete data as shown in updateValue function.

Assumption: n parties, r class values, z attribute values, j^{th} attribute contain l_j different values, S– supervisor, P– parties, $C_{l,r}^i$ = no of instances with party P_i having classes r and attribute values l, N_r^i = no of instances with party P_i having classes r.

At P:
Algorithm getData(POI)
{   While (new data is arriving on the site)
      For (each n parties having specific attributes)
      updateValues(c_{yz}^i, n_y^i);
      Encrypt the values and send to trusted third party;
}
At S:
Receive values and decrypt them;

From all parties, we can get all possible $C_{l,r}^1$ and N_r^1

Parties calculate the required probabilities from $C_{l,r}^1$ and N_r^1, on that basis will predict the class.

Fig. 2. One Update value function

4 Results

The dataset used for the purpose of experimentation is car-evaluation [18]. The aggregate analysis results of vertically partitioned distributed progressive data streams at different specific period of interest are given in as follows Table 1 and the classification accuracy is in percentage:

Table 1. Vertical partition classification analysis

Sl. No.	Description	Number of parties	Total number of attributes	Total number of records	% Accuracy
1	Classification of data is at single party (No distribution)	1	7	1728	85
2	Classification of data distributed in vertical partition with trusted third party	3	Party1:2 attributes Party2:2 attributes Party3:3 attributes	1728	85

5 Conclusion

In our proposed work, we have proposed algorithms for classifying data using Naïve Bayes from a group of collaborating parties without breaching privacy. The non distributed scenario and the vertical distributed progressive sequential scenario are compared and their accuracy is calculated on the data. The accuracy comes out to be the same showing that the algorithm is giving best case results. Privacy is also preserved using privacy preserving technique such as offset computation and encryption. The trusted third party concept also introduced to calculate the global classification results with privacy preservation. The algorithm can also be extended for distributed progressive sequential arbitrary partition in future work. Also the algorithm can be modified for numeric data to widen its scope.

References

1. Agarwal, R., Srikanth, R.: Mining Sequential Patterns. In: 11th Int'l Conf. Data Eng. (ICD 1995), pp. 3–14 (1995)
2. Srikant, R., Agrawal, R.: Mining Sequential Patterns: Generalization and Performance Improvements. In: 5th Int'l Conf. on Extending Database Technology, Avignon, France, pp. 3–17 (1996)
3. Zaki, M.J.: SPADE: An Efficient Algorithm for Mining Frequent Sequences. Journal of Machine Learning 42, 31–60 (2001)
4. Pei, J., Han, J., Pinto, H., Chen, Q., Dayal, U., Hsu, M.C.: PrefixSpan: Mining Sequential Patterns Efficiently by Prefix- Projected pattern Growth. In: 12th Int'l Conf. on Data Eng., Germany, pp. 215–224 (2001)
5. Cong, S., Han, J., Pandu, D.: Parallel Mining of Closed sequential Patterns. In: 11th ACM SIGKDD Int'l Conf. Knowledge Discovery and Data Mining (KDD 2005), pp. 562–567 (2005)
6. Luo, C., Chung, S.M.: Efficient mining of maximal sequential patterns using multiple samples. In: 5th SIAM Int'l Conf. Data Mining (SDM) (2005)

7. Hirate, Y., Yamana, H.: Sequential pattern mining with time intervals. In: Ng, W.-K., Kitsuregawa, M., Li, J., Chang, K. (eds.) PAKDD 2006. LNCS (LNAI), vol. 3918, pp. 775–779. Springer, Heidelberg (2006)
8. Parthasarathy, S., Zaki, M., Ogihara, M., Dwarakada, S.: Incremental and Interactive Sequence Mining. In: 8th Int'l Conf. on Information and Knowledge Management (CIK 1999) (1999)
9. Masseglia, F., Poncelet, P., Teissere, M.: Incremental Mining of Sequential Pattern in Large Database. Journal of Data Knowledge Eng. 46(1), 97–121 (2003)
10. Cheng, H., Yan, X., Han, J.: INCPAN: Incremental mining of Sequential Patterns in Large Database. In: 10th ACM SIGKDD Int'l Conf. Knowledge Discovery and Data Mining (KDD 2004), pp. 527–532 (2004)
11. Huang, J.W., Tseng, C.Y., Ou, J.C., Chen, M.S.: A general Model for Sequential Pattern Mining with a Progressive Databases. Int'l Journal of Knowledge and Data Eng. 20, 1153–1167 (2008)
12. Leew, C.K., Choi, U.J., Liew, C.J.: A data distortion by probability distribution. ACM TODS, 395–411 (1985)
13. Agarwal, R., Srikanth, R.: Privacy–preserving data mining. In: Proceedings of the ACM SIGMOD Conference (2005)
14. Zhang, P., Tong, Y., Tang, D.: Privacy–Preserving Naïve Bayes Classifier. In: Li, X., Wang, S., Dong, Z.Y. (eds.) ADMA 2005. LNCS (LNAI), vol. 3584, pp. 744–752. Springer, Heidelberg (2005)
15. Poovammal, E., Poonavaikko, M.: An improved method for privacy preserving data mining. In: IEEE IACC Conference, Patiala, India, pp. 1453–1458 (2009)
16. Yao, A.C.: Protocol for secure sum computations. In: Proc. IEEE Foundations of Computer Science, pp. 160–164 (1986)
17. Vaidya, J., Kantarcıoğlu, M., Clifton, C.: Privacy-Preserving Naïve Bayes Classification. International Journal on Very Large Data Bases 17, 879–898 (2008)
18. Bohanec, M., Zupan, B.: UCI Machine Learning Repository (1997), http://archive.ics.uci.edu/ml/datasets/Car+Evaluation

Copyright Protection in Digital Multimedia

Santosh Kumar, Sumit Kumar, and Sukumar Nandi

Deaprtment of Computer Science and Engineering,
Indian Institute of Technology Guwahati, India
{santosh.kr,sumit.kr,sukumar}@iitg.ernet.in

Abstract. Copyright protection has become a need in today's world. We have analyzed various spatial domain watermarking techniques and after having a good understanding of the same we have proposed a novel algorithm named as Stage Staffing Algorithm that generates results with high effectiveness. We have implemented the algorithm and results of the simulations are shown. The various factors affecting spatial domain watermarking are also discussed.

Keywords: Copyright Protection, Stage staffing watermarking, Digital Multimedia, Encryption and Decryption algorithm for watermarking.

1 Introduction

The enforcement of distribution policies for sensitive intelligence documents is important but difficult. Sensitive documents may be found left behind in conference rooms, common areas, printing rooms, or public folders. Access control based on cryptography alone cannot address this problem. Once after obtaining access to a sensitive document may a person make redundant copies or handle it without care. A major challenge in the reinforcement of sharing policies for sensitive documents is the support of non-repudiation in the primary process so that unauthorized copies of intellect documents can be identified and traced back to their users [1]. The reinforcement should also be appropriate to both hard copies and soft copies of the documents. Conventional cryptographic schemes that cover only soft copies are insufficient to handle this constraint.

Digital watermarking is a promising technology employed by various digital rights management (DRM) systems to achieve rights management [2]. It supports copyright information (such as the owner's identity, transaction dates, and serial numbers) to be embedded as unperceivable signals into digital contents. The signals embedded can be perceivable or insignificant to humans.

2 Categories and Performance Evaluation of Digital Watermarking

2.1 Categories of Digital Watermarking

Visible and invisible watermarking are two categories of digital watermarking. The concept of the visible watermark is very simple; it is analogous to stamping a mark on

N. Meghanathan et al. (Eds.): CCSIT 2011, Part II, CCIS 132, pp. 453–463, 2011.

paper. The data is said to be digitally stamped. An example of visible watermarking is seen in television channels when their logo is visibly superimposed in the corner of the screen. Invisible watermarking, on the other hand, is a far more complex concept. It is most often used to identify copyright data such as author, distributor, etc. This paper focuses on this category, and the word "watermark" will mean, by default, the invisible watermark.

In addition, robust watermarking techniques have been designed to oppose tampering and support later extraction and detection of these watermark signals. These signals recover the rights information originally embedded in the document. In this paper we introduce an advanced stage staffing watermarking algorithm, which enables the watermark signal to affectively encrypt into the host image and generate back the watermark. The main idea of algorithm is that there must be a very large difference between the size of host image and the watermark signal. This affects the cyclic behavior and redundancy in the pixels.

2.2   Performance Evaluation of Digital Watermarking

The performance of a watermarking mechanism is evaluated according to: robustness, capacity and imperceptibility. An effective image watermarking algorithm must have the following features:

a) **Imperceptibility:** The watermark must be imperceptible, i.e. the perceived quality of the watermarked image should not be noticeable

b) **Robustness:** The watermark should be difficult, rather impossible, to remove or to degrade, intentionally or unintentionally, by image processing attacks.

c) **Low computational complexity:** The watermarking algorithm should not be computationally complex for embedding as well as extracting the watermark, especially for real time applications

3   Principle and Application of Watermarking Schemes

In this section we present the basic principle of watermarking scheme and describe its practical application. Over the last two decades, digital watermarking has been addressed as an effective solution to safeguard copyright laws and an extensive effort has been made to design robust watermarking algorithms [3].

The two major applications for watermarking are protecting copyrights and authenticating photographs. The main reason for protecting copyrights is to prevent image piracy when the provider distributes the image on the Internet [4]. One way to achieve this goal is by embedding a digital watermark that automatically adjusts itself during image modification [4]. The practice of using images as evidence against crimes, for example, assumes that the images are reliable. Ensuring this requires image authentication [4]. Ensuring the authenticity of an image, i.e., that it has not been tampered with is needed by many organizations, such as hospitals, insurance companies, etc. Many methods are used to authenticate physical images, but this is not the case for digital images. Digital images must be authenticated by digital means.

One method authenticates digital images by embedding a digital watermark that breaks or changes as the image is tampered with. This informs the authenticator that the image has been manipulated. In the case of images captured by a digital camera, this can be accomplished by a special chip in the camera, which encrypts a watermark into captured images. This method can also be useful to video and audio formats as well.

3.1 Watermarking Insertion Scheme

Digital watermarking describes the process of embedding additional information into a digital media, without compromising the media's value. In this process the embed data called watermark into a media such that watermark can be detected or extracted later to make an assertion about the media [5], [6], [7]. Here input watermark refers to watermark insertion and extract the information is referring as watermark detection. Fig.1. shows the processes for watermark insertion, in which, suppose we have a digital document X, a watermark W, and a permutation function σ. A watermark insertion scheme I inserts a watermark W to the document X, where $X' = I(X, W, \sigma)$ [7].

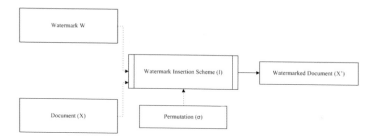

Fig. 1. Process of Watermarking Insertion

For illustration, let us explain the principle of the insertion scheme based on a popular secure spread-spectrum watermarking technique proposed by Cox et al. [8]. In spread spectrum communications, one transmits a narrowband signal over a much larger bandwidth such that the signal energy present in any single frequency is undetectable. Similarly, the watermark is spread over very many frequency bins so that the energy in any one bin is very small and definitely undetectable. To insert a watermark in the frequency domain of an image we should first apply DCT (Discrete Cosine Transformation). This is a usual way to represent an image in frequency domain.

3.2 Watermarking Detection Scheme

Corresponding to the watermark insertion scheme I, there is a watermark detection scheme D, which returns a confidence measure of the existence of a watermark W exists in a piece of document X'.

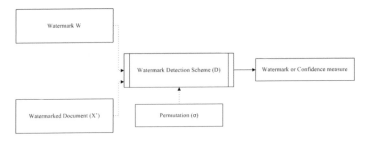

Fig. 2. Process of Watermarking Detection

Fig.2. Shows the processes for the watermarking detection in which watermark detection scheme D, which returns a confidence measure of the existence of a watermark W exists in a piece of document X'. A watermarking technique is referred to as non-blind watermarking when its detection scheme D requires the knowledge of the original document X, i.e., $D(X, X', W, \sigma) = false$ if W does not exist in X' or $D(X, X', W, \sigma) = true$ if W exists in X' [7].

3.3 The Spread-Spectrum Technique of Watermarking

The spread-spectrum technique assumes:

a) The document is a vector of "features", i.e., $X = \{x_1, x_2, ..., x_n\}$ where n is the number of features in a document.

b) The watermark signal is a vector of "watermark elements", i.e., $W = \{w_1, w_2, ..., x_m\}$ where m is the number of component in a watermark signal, with $n \geq m$.

In which the number of features in a document must be much greater than the number of components in a watermark signal. So that the signal is unperceivable in the watermarked document X'. The permutation function σ is a bijection that shuffles the watermark elements before inserting them to the document X. As such, the shuffled watermark is a vector of $\sigma(W) = \{w_1, w_2, ..., x_m\}$ where $w_i = \sigma(w_j)$ with $i, j \leq m$. The permutation function is used for protecting the secrecy of the watermark to be inserted to the document X. The shuffled watermark elements are then inserted to the document X by means of a linear insertion operation $\oplus$ (XOR), such that X' in the insertion scheme I is given by:

$$X \oplus \sigma(W) = \{X_1 \oplus W_1', X_2 \oplus W_2', ..., X_n \oplus W_n'\} \tag{1}$$

4 Proposed Watermarking Technique

The watermarking used is visually meaningful binary image rather than a randomly generated sequence of bit. Thus human eyes can easily identify the extracted watermark. In fact, embedding a watermark is the least significant bits of pixels are less sensitive to human eyes. However the watermark will be destroyed if some common image operations such as low-pass filtering are applied to the watermarked image. Therefore, to make the embedded watermark more resistant to any attack, the watermark must be embedded in the more significant bits. This will introduce more distortion to the host image and conflicts with the invisible requirement. To meet both invisible and robust requirement, we will adaptively modify the intensities of some selected pixels as large as possible and this modification is not noticeable to human eyes.

4.1 Encryption to Watermark Signal

The watermark image is first converted into the signal form. This can be done in many ways. As converting the signal from binary to ASCII initially, then some sort of encryption is performed. There are many encryption algorithms that completely chaos the watermark signals [8], [9]. We may use 1-D Logistic Map to generate a random sequence. In this, the initial condition and parameters of chaotic map are kept as the secret key; next, the encoded watermark bits are encrypted by chaotic sequence. Therefore, a number of uncorrelated, random like and reproducible encrypted watermarking signals are generated. A commonly used chaotic map is the Logistic map, which is described by equation (2).

$$Z_n + 1 = \mu Z_n \left(1 - Z_n\right) \tag{2}$$

Where Z_n belongs to $(0,1)$, when $\mu > 3.5699456$, the sequence iterated with an initial value is chaotic, different sequences will be generated with different initial values. The encryption formula is as follows in equation (3).

$$w_{en} = w \oplus c_n \tag{3}$$

Where, w_{en} is the nth encrypted watermark signal, w is the original watermark signal and c_n is the chaotic sequence. The randomizing sequence will give random numbers such that it will be most chaos. But we have assumed a simple DES encryption algorithm to be used as encrypted watermark. This will lead to a sequence of many encrypted watermark signals. Then each sequence is embedded into the Host Image, the image to which copyright protection is needed. The Simple DES Algorithm also provides a good randomness in the watermark signal. This is preferred since, it's easy to implement.

4.2 Encryption to the Host Image through Encrypted Watermark Signal

Embedding the watermark signal into the host image is very important task. There are many things to be taken care of while doing this.

a) This must be done in random fashion such that, it is equivalently spread all over.
b) The density of the watermark signal in the host image should be intermediate since, the more the watermarks will be, the more there will be the distortions.

A technique 2-D Arnold Cat Map.[9] is used to implement this. The 2-D Arnold Cat Map is described by equation (4).

$$\left.\begin{aligned} x_{n+1} &= (x_n + y_n) \\ y_{n+1} &= (x_n + 2y_n) \end{aligned}\right\} \mod 1 \tag{4}$$

Where, notation "$x \mod 1$" denotes the fractional parts of a real number x by adding or subtracting an appropriate integer. Therefore, (x_n, y_n) is confined in a unit square of $[0,1] \times [0,1]$ we write equation (4) in matrix form to get equation (5).

$$\begin{pmatrix} x_{n+1} \\ y_{n+1} \end{pmatrix} = \begin{pmatrix} 1 & 1 \\ 1 & 2 \end{pmatrix} \begin{pmatrix} x_n \\ y_n \end{pmatrix} = A \begin{pmatrix} x_n \\ y_n \end{pmatrix} \mod 1 \tag{5}$$

A unit square is first stretched by linear transformation and then folded by modulo operation, so the cat map is area preserving, the determinant of its linear transformation matrix |A| is equal to 1. The map is known to be chaotic. In addition, it is one to one map; each point of the unit square is uniquely mapped onto another point in the unit square. Hence, the watermark pixel of different positions will get a different embedding position. The cat map above can be extended as follows: firstly, the phase space is generalized to $[0,1,2,......,N-1] \times [0,1,2,.......,N-1]$, i.e., only the positive integers from 0 to $N-1$ are taken; and then equation (5) is generalized to give equation (6), 2-D invertible chaotic map.

$$\begin{pmatrix} x_{n+1} \\ y_{n+1} \end{pmatrix} = \begin{pmatrix} a & b \\ c & d \end{pmatrix} \begin{pmatrix} x_n \\ y_n \end{pmatrix} = A \begin{pmatrix} x_n \\ y_n \end{pmatrix} \mod N \tag{6}$$

Where, a, b, c and d are positive integers, and $|A| = ad - bc = 1$, therefore, only three among the four parameters of a, b, c and d are independent under this condition. The generalized cat map formula is also of chaotic characteristics. By using the generalized cat map, we can obtain the embedding position of watermark pixels, i.e., the coordinate (i, j) of watermark pixel is served as the initial value, three independent parameters and iteration times n are served as the secret key, after n rounds of iterations, the iterating result (x_n, y_n) will be served as the embedding position of watermark pixel of (i, j). When the iteration time's n is big enough, two arbitrary adjacent watermark pixels will separate apart largely in host image; different watermark pixels will get different embedding positions.

But, there is a drawback in this scheme, i.e. if the Watermark image and the host image are of relatively same size then there exists many cycles within the new pixel generation [10]. This is shown in the implementation part. These cycles can't be omitted. Thus, we implement the same as with **Stage Staffing watermarking scheme**.

4.3 Proposed Stage Staffing Scheme for Watermarking

In this scheme, we create an initial distance such that the watermarked signal equally spreads in the image. Then this distance is iteratively decreased in the quadratic manner and again the encrypted watermark signal is inserted in the image. The number of depth increases the detection of the watermark within the image and comes resistive from the low pass filtering, high pass filtering, median pass filtering attacks etc. The brief algorithm explained by Fig.3.

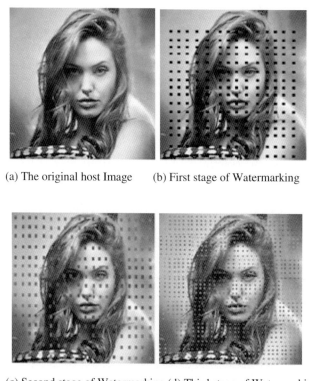

(a) The original host Image   (b) First stage of Watermarking

(c) Second stage of Watermarking (d) Third stage of Watermarking

Fig. 3. Stages of Stage Staffing scheme for Watermarking

From the above four images, the first image is the original image without any watermark signal embedded into it. The second is the one level watermarking in which the complete image is having one watermark signal with equal distribution. Likewise the third image contains 16 watermark signals. These may be two signals or more than two. The final, the third level is showing the densest watermark in the image. Thus the image consists of 1 + 16 + 64 watermark signals. This gives image high resistivity.

The other important part of this is the place where to embed the watermark signal bit. As we know that for a colored image consists of 24 bits RGB format we can substitute 1 bit in any of these 24 bits. For this, some random number generator algorithm should be used. The bit selected is substituted to 1 if watermark signal is 1 else substituted as 0. If the bit is same previously then no change is made.

Encryption Steps:

1. Generate a watermark signal from the Watermark image.
2. Encrypt this signal to become chaotic. The initial signal and the keys for encryption will be used as secret keys.
3. Embed the encrypt signal in the image in the three stages. i.e., from stage1 to stage3. Usually different bits will be used to store the watermark signal value in the host image.

Extraction Steps:

1. Extract the watermark signals from the image from stage3 to stage1.
2. Decrypt all watermark signals with their respective keys.
3. Average the outcome to give the watermark image.

5   Simulation Results

The algorithm enables the watermark signal to affectively encrypt into the host image and generate back the watermark. From the simulation results, we have observed that there must be a very large difference between the size of host image and the watermark signal. This affects the cyclic behavior and redundancy in the pixels.

Further, the algorithm can resist through low pass filtering, median pass filtering and high pass filtering. Restriction being that the size of window, used for the filtering must not be large. The regenerated watermark is lost if the window size is taken large. The stages help to detect watermark in robust conditions. Since it may resist through some noise signals to some extent.

Fig.4. shows various image outputs from the simulation. Description of each is given as follows.

a) The original image used in simulation.
b) The watermark image used for simulation.
c) Image, signal where the watermark is embedded.
d) Regenerated watermark, through extraction procedure.
e) Applying LPF to Watermarked image.
f) Regenerated watermark for LPF.
g) Applying MPF to Watermarked image.
h) Regenerated watermark for MPF.
i) Applying HPF to Watermarked image.
j) Regenerated watermark for HPF.
k) Regenerated watermark signal if the window size is taken large, this is not resistive for this

We are giving here various output of image from simulation result of proposed algorithm.

(a). Original Image   (b). Watermarked Image

(c). Encrypted Image   (d). Watermark Regenerated

(e). Image after LPF   (f). Watermark Regenerated

(g). Image after MPF   (h). Watermark Regenerated

(i). Image after HPF   (j). Watermark Regenerated

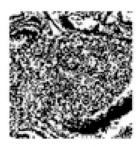

(k). Watermark Regenerated

Fig. 4. Enhanced Image and Regenerated Watermark after applying different Image Enhancements

6 Conclusions

In this paper, a novel watermarking algorithm proposed to address the problem. Proposed algorithm is able to resist attacks of filtering, robustness. A robust watermark scheme based on a block probability for color image is presented, which operates in spatial domain by embedding the watermark image four times in different positions in order to be robust for cropping attack. The experimental results shows that our scheme is highly robust against various of image processing operations such as, filtering, cropping, scaling, compression, rotation, randomly removal of some rows and columns lines, self-similarity and salt and paper noise. But it is not resistive for several compressions like jpeg etc.

References

1. Miller, I.J., Roberto, M.L., Bloom, V.C.: A technology for copyright of valuable digital contests: Security issues in digital watermarking. In: Digital Watermarking. Academic Press, New York (2002)
2. Russ, A.: Digital Rights Management Overview. In: Security Essentials v1.2e, Bethesda, Maryland, pp. 181–189 (2001)
3. Pan, J.S., Huang, H.C., Jain, L.C.: Intelligent Watermarking Techniques, p. 852. World Scientific Publishing Co. Pte. Ltd., Singapore (2004) ISBN: 978-981-238-757-8

4. Lin, C.-Y., Change, S.F.: Multimedia authentication. In: International Conference in Security and Watermarking of Multimedia Contents, pp. 206–216. IEEE, Los Alamitos (2005)
5. Voyatzis, G., Pitas, I.: The Use of Watermarks in the Protection of Digital Multimedia Products. In: Privacy Principles for Digital Watermarking, Greece, vol. 87, pp. 1197–1207. IEEE, Los Alamitos (2008)
6. Cheung, S.C., Chiu, D.K.W.: A watermarking infrastructure for enterprise document management. In: Proceedings of the 36th Hawaii International Conference on System Sciences (HICSS-36), CDROM, Big Island, Hawaii, pp. 675–685. IEEE Press, Los Alamitos (2003)
7. Lee, C.H., Lee, Y.K.: An Adaptive Digital Image Watermarking Technique for Copyright Protection. In: IEEE, Taiwan, vol. 45, pp. 1005–1015 (1999)
8. Cox, I., Kilian, J., Leighton, T., Shamoon, G.: Secure spread spectrum watermarking for multimedia. In: Proceedings of the IEEE International Conference on Image Processing, vol. 6, pp. 1673–1687 (1997)
9. Wu, X., Guan, Z.-H., Wu, Z.: A Chaos Based Robust Spatial Domain Watermarking Algorithm. In: Liu, D., Fei, S., Hou, Z., Zhang, H., Sun, C. (eds.) ISNN 2007. LNCS, vol. 4492, pp. 113–119. Springer, Heidelberg (2007)
10. Zhang, J.S., Tian, L.H.: A New Watermarking Method Based on Chaotic Maps. In: IEEE International Conference on Multimedia and Expo., China, pp. 342–352 (2006)

Trust as a Standard for E-Commerce Infrastructure

Shabana[1] and Mohammad Arif[2]

[1] Department of Management Studies, LFMVNIET, Palwal, Haryana, India
ershabana@yahoo.co.in
[2] Department of CSE, GSMVNIET, Palwal, Haryana, India
arif_mohd2k@yahoo.com

Abstract. As consumers settle into the realities of a world where the Internet has changed many aspects of how they live their lives, they are starting to question more and more how much they should trust Web content. Electronic commerce (e-commerce) has grown exponentially over the past few years. The success of web based business depends essentially on their consumers trust. This survey paper outlines essential issues that affect customers trust on Internet or vendors. It also discusses key elements that are used to improve the visitor's sense of trustworthiness on websites. Factors affecting the intention of purchasing online have been investigated for many years. On the other hand, the question of what keeps online customers repurchasing through the Internet has rarely been examined. This survey sheds the light on the means of enhancing customer loyalty to promote online purchasing.

Keywords: Online repurchasing, Customer loyalty, Perceived trust, Perceived risk, Trust, B2C, Expectation Confirmation Theory (ECT), Theory of Acceptance Model (TAM).

1 Introduction

Trust is a fundamental principle of every business relationship. There is no oversight group that can objectively anoint a web site as being completely trustworthy. Trust is a subjective judgment that must be made by every user for any site, because individual goals vary and definitions of trust are unlikely to be consistent. The merchants face the difficult task of selling themselves to the users on the web site interface and on the advertising of the brand. Commerce sites must convince potential customers to trust the site; commerce sites have two critical messages for users, buy from us and trust us. Without the users trust, the merchant can't sell. Tan and Thoen (2002) proposed that e-commerce could only become a success if the general public trusted the virtual environment. By investigating inter-organizational relationships and trust in e-commerce, we will be able to identify factors leading to successful e-commerce participation (adoption and integration). Drawing on theories such as trust in business relationships, inter-organizational relationship, transaction cost economics, and resource dependency theory, a conceptual model can be developed to examine the impact of trust of trading partner in e-commerce participation. Despite the acknowledged importance of trust, only a limited amount of research exists that examines the role of trust in these relationships.

N. Meghanathan et al. (Eds.): CCSIT 2011, Part II, CCIS 132, pp. 464–471, 2011.

Therefore, the importance of initiating, building, and maintaining trust in e-commerce is increasingly being recognized. This article is structured as follows: Section 2 presents some definitions of trust and a basic model for Internet commerce. In section 3, we outline the most common risks, customers face when accomplishing transactions on the Internet. In section 4, we describe what security measures, a customer may adopt for online purchasing. Section 5 reviews some repurchasing concept. Lastly, we present some concluding remarks in Section 6.

2   Trust and E-Commerce

In e-commerce, there are several entities (buyers, sellers, and third parties) that are involved in accomplishing a transaction. The Internet has become an essential business platform for trading, distributing and selling products between organizations, among organizations & consumers, and even between consumers. One important concept in the relationship-marketing paradigm related to the development of this B2C e-commerce is trust. As Quelch and Klein [1] noted, trust is a critical factor in stimulating purchases over the Internet. Keen [2] argues that the most significant long-term barrier for realizing the potential of Internet marketing is the lack of consumer trust, both in the merchant's honesty and in the merchant's competence to fill Internet orders. Trust has a vital influence on consumer activities and thereby on e-commerce success. Ganesan [3] builds the notion of trust leading to a causal function: trust is responsible for creating consumer activity. Jarvenpaa et. al. [4] argues that online retailers might increase consumer trust and thereby increase willingness of prospective customers to shop on Internet.

In accomplishing transactions on the Internet, visitors are usually required to provide some personal data, such as snail mail/email addresses, product preferences, telephone numbers, and credit card information. Because of lack of familiarity with the websites and with the people behind them compared to the materiality of bricks-and-mortar retail stores, many users hesitate to reveal information. Most consumers lack trust over what web merchants could do with their data afterwards, such as selling them or sharing them with third parties without their permission [5, 6].

2.1   A Simplified View of Internet Commerce

In a very straightforward approach, Business to-Customer (B2C) Internet commerce may be regarded as an electronic-based marketplace where a customer willing to acquire a product, service, or property interacts with a vendor through a website on the Internet. In some cases the consumer is not necessarily be aware of the need beforehand; he identifies it during navigation. The merchant, on the other hand, has a set of products or services available for sale, rent, or exchange on a web page. There can also be third parties that participate in the transaction such as banking institutions, recommended systems, technology providers, and so on [6]. The customer may bring with him some knowledge (previous information about the vendor and/or the product or service) as well as some preferences, such as his willingness to buy, a maximum acceptable price, a deadline for delivery, a given set of characteristics for the product/service he wants to get, and so on. The merchant uses a technical platform such as servers, information systems, databases, security/ privacy/ payment mechanisms, to convince the customer, as well as a set of business practices and strategies.

Some basic services such as product/ service display, order processing, and maybe customer support (before, during, and/or after the purchase) should be provided on websites. Several models of Internet Commerce have been defined in the literature, such as, B2B, C2C, Web Presence, Brokerage, and so on. For the purpose of this article, we will limit our scope to B2C. Although some of the practices described here are also applicable to other Internet Commerce models.

2.2 Egger's Initial Model of Trust for E-Commerce (MoTEC)

According to Bhattacherjee [7], Eggers initial model of trust for e-commerce was developed in 1998. Eggers research on his model included a comprehensive review of trust from different perspectives, namely psychology, marketing, management and human computer interaction (HCI). After a number of empirical tests the initial model was revised and in 2000, the revised model was published. As can be seen from Figure 1, the components making up the MoTEC are: pre-interactional filters, interface properties, informational content and relationship management. Pre-interactional filters contain a number of individual model components. The first component is the general propensity to trust that differs from individual to individual. Individuals also have different expectations with respect to a certain company or industry. These expectations can be influenced by the reputation of the company's brand name, previous experience of interactions with the company. Interface properties are often influenced by the first impression of a commercial system. Appeal refers to the graphical design and layout of the system. Overview refers to the overview of organization. The terms such as System reliability, ease of use and familiarity etc. refer to the usability aspect of the system. Informational content stresses that information on the products and services should be complete, relevant and well structured. The company component should provide information of the company, including history, values and commitments. Information of financial risk and guarantees are covered by security. The privacy policies should be transparent to the customer. Relationship management refers to the management of the relationship between the vendor and the customer. The relationship can become more long-term if and only if the customer has enough trust in the vendor through positive experiences of post purchase communication and customer service. Communication refers to frequent and personalized vendor-customer interactions in order to maintain trust.

2.3 Trust in Internet Commerce

A definition of trust may encompass several aspects, depending on the application domain. In a very general sense, trust may be defined as assured reliance on the character, ability, strength, or truth of someone or something. It can also be defined as the confidence or reliance on some quality or attribute of a person or thing. Some views consider it as a personal response, others just as a rational assessment of reliability. B. J. Fogg and H. Tseng point out that trust indicates a positive belief about the perceived reliability, dependability, and confidence in a person, object, or process.

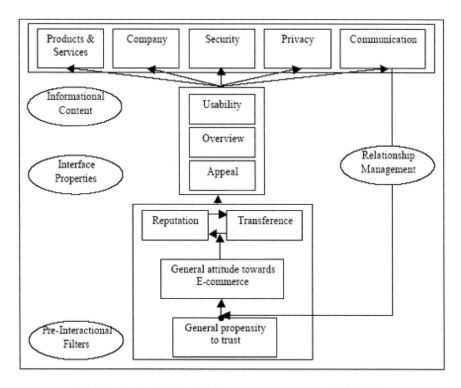

Fig. 1. Egger's initial model of trust for e-commerce (MoTECH)

Bhattacharji [7] proposed following 12 hypotheses as shown in figure 2, for the relationship between market orientation and trust:

H1:   Perceived market orientation is positively related to the level of customer's trust perception.

H2:   Perceived market orientation is positively related to the level of customer's e-commerce participation.

H3:   Perceived technology trustworthiness is positively related to level of perceived trust.

H4:   Perceived technology trustworthiness is negatively related to the level of perceived risk.

H5:   User's web experience is positively related to e-commerce participation.

H6:   User's web experience is positively related to the degree of perceived trust.

H7:   User's web experience is negatively related to the degree of perceived risk.

H8:   Perceived site quality is positively related to trust.

H9:   Perceived site quality is positively related to marketing orientation.

H10:   Perceived site quality is positively related to technology trustworthiness.

H11:   Level of perceived risk is negatively related to the level of customer's trust perception.

H12:   Customer's trust encourages him to participate in e-commerce.

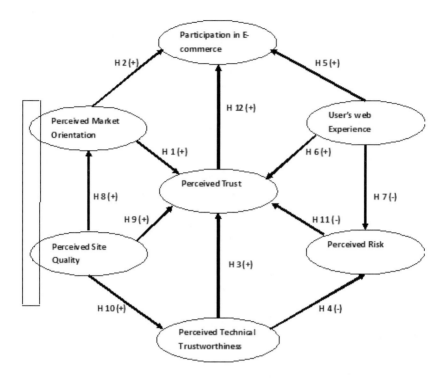

Fig. 2. Trust in Internet Commerce (Proposed by Bhattacharji [7])

3 Risks in E-Commerce

During a commerce transaction on the Internet, a customer navigates through the Web site of a vendor. In this process, one may face several uncertainties, due to the inherent characteristics of the interaction medium (a Web browser). According to Tucker [8] and Hart [9] these uncertainties may be classified as follows:

Pre-purchase uncertainties: Customers in a website are unable to have a direct contact with the vendor. Pictures and a description of the merchandize may be available, but not the real items. The customer may have access to a catalog with all the products or services, but one cannot walk along the corridors to see and compare all the available options.

Post-purchase uncertainties: Frequently, customers have to supply personal information (such as names, addresses, and credit card information) in order to be able to accomplish a transaction, unlike the anonymity granted by cash. Once this information is provided to the Web site of a merchant, there is no way to take it away from the vendor, even if the transaction is cancelled.

3.1 Technology-Related Risks

There are some risks faced by customers derived from the use of Web-based technology platforms on Internet commerce sites:

Security: The underlying technology of a Web site may require a large amount of information protection. Additionally, without appropriate firewalls and other security practices, private consumer information residing on a vendor's servers could be stolen by hackers or insiders.

Privacy: Consumers' card numbers may be intercepted and stolen during transmission. Information about a user such as his login name or his personal preferences may be collected and used to profile him through cookies, creating serious privacy concerns.

Integrity: Records of electronic transactions may be easily lost, modified, duplicated, or incorrectly processed.

3.2 Business-Related Risks

Websites may keep records of the history of goods and services demanded by specific customers. This information may be used for illegitimate data mining (e.g. demographic or product preferences analysis) and also may be provided to (or exchanged with) unauthorized third parties.

Incorrect fulfillment of transactions: Once a product or service has been purchased or rented, the provider may decide not to carry out the order as claimed, or charge an incorrect amount for it.

4 Security Measures

An electronic commerce site requires the appropriate security mechanisms to protect both the customer and the merchant. As the data are being transmitted over the Internet, outsiders may access, modify, or delete critical information, either during transmission or at the vendor's servers. The terms of every accomplished transaction must be guaranteed. In order to achieve this, methods such as passwords, encryption mechanisms, electronic signatures and firewalls are being widely used. According to Ratnasingham et al. [10] and Stalling [11], following security measures are necessary.

Privacy and Confidentiality: Privacy means that the owner of information can control it. Conversely, confidentiality means secrecy that is only the intended recipients of a message should read it. On any transaction on the Internet, consumer's information (such as purchases and personal data) should only be accessed by authorized parties. Encryption is the basis for several methods to secure both permanent data (such as a customer's profile on a web server disk) and temporary data (such as a cookie in a user's computer or a log file on a web server disk). There are several schemes to secure transactions such as cryptography, Secure Socket Layer (SSL) and Transaction Layer Security (TLS). All are designed to support credential exchange during client and server authentication.

Availability: Availability means to keep a system up and running. On a commerce website, availability refers to the availability of information whenever it is required without any disruptions of service. This may be accomplished with both hardware (redundant servers/disks, high bandwidth connections to the Internet, parallel processors) and software (fault-tolerant and scalable applications).

Integrity: Integrity means that the data arrived at a recipient location should be exactly the same as that was sent. Information that is stored on a Web server, or on a cookie in a customers computer should not be altered by unauthorized entities.

Authentication: All the participants in a business transaction on the Internet (merchants, costumers, and third parties) need to be confident of the identities of one other. The use of digital certificates is a method widely applied for authentication. Vendors and customers may generate these certificates through the bilateral use of secret keys that authenticate the legitimacy of each party involved in a transaction.

Non-repudiation: For any transaction, the parties should be accountable for it. He should not be able to deny his participation on it. Conversely, as entities should not be able to deny their participation, they should also be able to prove their non-participation in an exchange where they have not actually been involved.

5   Purchasing and Repurchasing

To keep the customer repurchases the product/ service is essential to maintain the profitability of the business. Despite this need to succeed in business [12], the factors affecting the repeat purchasing on the Internet have rarely been explored. The synthesis of the strength of the base model and the potential customer loyalty factor composes the research model of this study. The behavior relationship model can be represented and evaluated in the form of a factor network that consists of constructs and links between them. Jarvenpaa et al. [4] used six constructs – Repurchase intention (R), Satisfaction (S), Confirmation (C), Perceived Usefulness (PU), Perceived Incentives (PI), and customer Loyalty (L) and investigated the hypotheses:

H1:   A customer's satisfaction with Internet shopping positively affects his or her intention to repurchase through Internet shopping $(S \rightarrow R)$.

H2:   A customer's confirmation level positively affects his or her satisfaction with Internet shopping $(C \rightarrow S)$.

H3:   A customer's perceived usefulness of Internet shopping positively affects his or her intention to repurchase through Internet shopping $(PU \rightarrow R)$.

H4:   A customer's confirmation level positively affects his or her perceived usefulness of Internet shopping $(C \rightarrow PU)$.

H5:   A customer's perceived incentives positively affect his or her intention to repurchase through Internet shopping $(PI \rightarrow R)$.

H6:   A customer's loyalty positively affects his or her intention to repurchase through the Internet shopping $(L \rightarrow R)$.

H7:   A customer's satisfaction with Internet shopping positively affects his or her customer loyalty $(S \rightarrow L)$.

The above seven constructs were measured using multi-item scales. Each construct contains several items measured by the fully anchored, 5-point Likert scale ranging from 1(i.e. strongly agree) to 5 (i.e. strongly disagree). The items were generated from previous research projects and were modified to fit the context of Internet shopping when necessary.

6 Conclusion

All five factors, i.e., satisfaction, confirmation, perceived usefulness, customer loyalty and perceived incentives, keep the online customer repurchasing through the Internet. Specifically, we found that perceived incentives had a significant effect on the intention to repurchase, which is contrast to the finding of Bhattacherjee. Therefore, it deserves to study what kind of incentives and which incentive tools are useful for the promotion of online repurchasing. Our study shows that customer loyalty is nearly as important as perceived usefulness in influencing the repurchase intention. This implies that not only perceived usefulness but also customer loyalty are strong indicators of customers intention to repurchase through the Internet. Therefore, it is one of the factors affecting online repurchasing. It would be interesting to determine if customer loyalty by itself has any effect on the intention to repurchase. The differences between online customer nationalities regarding their perceptions about repurchasing through the Internet will yield insights that can help Internet shops better retain customers in different world market segments.

References

[1] Quelch, J.A., Klein, L.R.: The Internet and international marketing. Sloan Management Review 37(3), 60–75 (1996)
[2] Keen, P.G.W.: Are you ready for: trust economy. Computer World 31(16), 80 (1997)
[3] Ganesan, S.: Determinants of longterm orientation in buyer seller relationships. Journal of Marketing 58, 1–19 (1994)
[4] Jarvenpaa, S.L., Tractinsky, N., Vitale, M.: Consumer trust in an Internet store. Information Technology and Management, 45–71 (2000)
[5] Barnes, S.J., Vidgen, R.T.: An integrative approach to the assessment of e-commerce quality. Working Paper (2000)
[6] Berners-Lee, T.: Weaving the Web. Orion Business, New York (1999)
[7] Bhattacherjee, A.: An empirical analysis of the antecedents of electronic commerce service continuance. Decision Support Systems 32, 201–214 (2000)
[8] Tucker, J.M.: EDI and the net: a profitable partnering. Datamations, 62–69 (1997)
[9] Hart, P., Saunders, C.: Power and trust: critical factors in the adoptions and use of electronic data interchange. Organizational Science 8(1), 23–42 (1997)
[10] Ratnasingham, P., Kumar, K.: Trading Partner Trust in Electronis Commerce Participation. In: Proceedings of the Twenty First International Conference on Information Systems, ICIS 2000 (December 2000)
[11] Stalling, W.: Business Data Communications. Macmillan, London (1990)
[12] Atchariyachanvanich, K., Okada, H., Sonehara, N.: What Keeps Online Customers Repurchasing through the Internet? ACM SIGecom Exchanges 6(2), 47–57 (2006)

A Scalable Rekeying Scheme for Secure Multicast in IEEE 802.16 Network

Sandip Chakraborty, Soumyadip Majumder,
Ferdous A. Barbhuiya, and Sukumar Nandi

Department of Computer Science and Engineering
Indian Institute of Technology Guwahati, India - 781039
{c.sandip,s.majumder,ferdous,sukumar}@iitg.ernet.in

Abstract. IEEE 802.16e is the next generation wireless metropolitan area network (WMAN) that provides wide coverage and higher bandwidth than conventional wireless networks. Multicast or group communication is an efficient scheme to communicate with several users simultaneously. IEEE 802.16e introduces Multicast and Broadcast Rekeying algorithm (MBRA) for secure group communication in WiMAX network. But it has been shown in different literatures that MBRA lacks scalability as well as forward and backward secrecy. So different types of multicast security protocols have been proposed in several literatures where best known performance (in terms of scalability, security and simplicity) is achieved with ELAPSE that works in $O(log\ n)$ message complexity. But this is also a scalability issue with large value of n. In this paper we propose a scalable algorithm for secure multicast in WiMAX, based on a hybrid group rekeying protocol with a trade-off between collusion resistance and scalability.

1 Introduction

IEEE 802.16e, *"Air Interface for Fixed and Mobile Broadband Wireless Access Systems"*, also known as *"WiMAX"*, is the next generation Wireless Metropolitan Area Network, that offers wide coverage and higher bandwidth than the traditional wireless network. Multicast enables efficient large scale data distribution over the network and has become popular for applications such as pay-TV and other one way streaming media applications. IEEE 802.16 also supports multicast applications like pay-TV, videoconferencing and other one way media streaming applications. For secure multicast over IEEE 802.16 networks, the standard [1] defines Privacy and Key Management Protocol (PKM) and Multicast and Broadcast Re keying Algorithm (MBRA) which operates at security sublayer of IEEE 802.16 protocol stack.

The challenge of a secure multicast service is to provide an efficient access control method for the group members. In a dynamic group the rekeying algorithm is used to guarantee that the newly joined members can not get previous messages, called the *backward secrecy*, and also the members who left the group can not read any future messages, known as *forward secrecy*. Another important

N. Meghanathan et al. (Eds.): CCSIT 2011, Part II, CCIS 132, pp. 472–481, 2011.

issue of group communication is collusion resistance, which can be described as, "two or more users should not obtain some secrets which they are not allowed to know by exchanging their own secret". A good group communication security algorithm should ensure these four properties - group confidentiality, forward secrecy, backward secrecy and collusion resistance.

For secure multicast communication,as defined in IEEE 802.16 standard [1], the MBRA uses a Group Key Encryption Key (GKEK) and Group Traffic Encryption Key(GTEK). The GKEK is used to encrypt GTEK and the GTEK is used to encrypt multicast traffics. Both the key are used to ensure the forward abd backward secrecy based on their lifetime. But in [4], [5] and [6] the authors have shown that the MBRA fails to ensure forward and backward secrecy. Also the MBRA is not scalable for large group as the message complexity is $O(n)$.

In this paper we propose a multicast scheme based on the hybrid of Logical Key Hierarchy(LKH), as mentioned by Weiler *et al.* [10] and Wong *et al.* [11], and the Linear Ordering of Receivers (LORE) proposed by Fan *et al.* [9]. The hybrid scheme is also known as Hybrid Structuring of Receivers (HySOR) proposed by Fan *et al.* [9]. Our protocol is based on HySOR scheme that requires much less message passing than ELAPSE and ELAPSE+ proposed by Huang *et al.* [8], based on LKH scheme. The proposed scheme is also computationally efficient than the scheme described by Sun *et al.* [7], based on LORE and uses the properties of one way hash function and modular squaring, a computationally complex affairs.

2   Related Works

The 802.16e-2005 version of the standard [1] introduces the Multicast and Broadcast Rekeying Algorithm (MBRA) for multicast traffic confidentiality and handling forward and backward secrecy. The project report by J. Y. Kuo [3] introduces a reply attack on MBRA. But it does not cover forward and backward secrecy which is an important consideration for secure group communication. In [4] and [5], the authors identify the lack of forward and backward secrecy in MBRA architecture. They also discuss the scalability issues in MBRA. MBRA requires $O(n)$ message transmissions for each time rekeying. The security of forward and backward secrecy in MBRA is highly dependable on the lifetime of Group Traffic Encryption Key (GTEK) and Group Key Encryption Key (GKEK), which is vulnerable for dynamic groups, where users join and leave frequently.

In [8], Huang *et al.* introduces an approach that handles backward and forward secrecy, *Efficient sub-Linear rekeying Algorithm with Perfect Secrecy (ELAPSE)*, and a cross-layer approach for an improved version of ELAPSE, namely ELAPSE+. Both ELAPSE and ELAPSE+ are based on Logical Key Hierarchy(LKH), as described in [10] and [11], that works in $O(\log n)$ message complexity. The ELAPSE and ELAPSE+ can handle forward and backward secrecy with a set of KEKs and Sub Group Key Encryption Keys (SGKEK), and works in $O(\log n)$ as like LKH. But this is still a problem with large number of n. Typically, applications like pay-TV uses a large value of n for one-to-many group communication. In [7], Sun *et al.* introduces a new rekeying algorithm for multicast and broadcast in IEEE 802.16 network, that works in $O(1)$ constant time complexity. Their scheme is based on LORE, as proposed in [9], a linear ordering key distribution algorithm that can handle forward and backward secrecy, but does not provide collusion resistance, which can be an important consideration for extreme secure information multicasting. To handle collusion resistance, they have modified the basic LORE algorithm with the use of one way hash function and modular square property of public key cryptography, which is computationally inefficient for large n. If the key distribution center(KDC) uses simple Pseudo-Random Generator (PRNG) for forward and backward key construction in case of LORE, then it becomes computationally efficient, and the keys need not to be stored by the KDC because of the regeneration property of the PRNG. Again the security of the protocol described by Sun *et al.* depends on the prime factoring of a large number.

In [9], Fan *et al.* introduces a hybrid scheme for key distribution, Hybrid Structuring of Receivers (HySOR), which is a hybrid scheme between the LKH and LORE. This scheme is the main motivation behind our work. The HySOR scheme is a trade off between the message complexity and collusion resistance. In practice, collusion attack is very rare, and so strong collusion resistance is not always required. In stead, a weak collusion resistance scheme with small message complexity is desirable in practice. If fact, it has also been shown that the best message complexity one can achieve if strict non-member confidentiality and non-collusion are required is $\Omega(log\ n)$, as demonstrated in [12] and [13]. In [9], the authors have shown that LKH has a message complexity of $O(log\ n)$ whereas it provides strong collusion resistance. But LORE works in $O(1)$ message complexity, but insecure in collusion attack. The HySOR scheme uses a subgrouping scheme in LKH, where the members in each subgroup uses LORE. They have shown that HySOR provides a fair collusion resistance and the message complexity is less than LKH scheme.

3   Background of 802.16 Multicast Security

3.1   IEEE 802.16 Multicast and Broadcast Rekeying Algorithm(MBRA)

The MBRA algorithm can be represented as follows;
  1) Message 1: BS $\rightarrow$ SSes : $\{GKEK\}_{KEK}$
  2) Message 2: BS $\Rightarrow$ SS : $\{GTEK\}_{GKEK}$
Here $\rightarrow$ is used for unicast and $\Rightarrow$ is used for multicast or broadcast message transmission.Both the key GTEK and GKEK is required for maintaining the forward and backward secrecy based on their lifetime.

Clearly the scheme requires $O(n)$ message transmissions, and hence not scalable. The forward and backward secrecy also depends on the lifetime of GTEK, which is 30 minutes minimum, 12 hours by default and 7 days maximum according to IEEE 802.16e standard [1]. So the scheme is vulnerable for dynamic group changes, where join and leave operations occur frequently.

3.2 ELAPSE

The ELAPSE scheme as described by Huang *et al.*[8] is an important improvement over standard IEEE 802.16 MBRA protocol.ELAPSE uses a logical key hierarchy structure as shown in figure 1. The multicast group is divided in subgroups. Each subgroup maintains a hierarchy of Sub-Group KEKs (SGKEK) instead of a single GKEK. According to a binary tree hierarchy, each SS within a subgroup will store k SGKEKs, where k is the hight of the tree. For example, according to figure 1, the nodes in subgroup 3 will store the three keys $SGKEK_3, SGKEK_{34}$ and $SGKEK_{1234}$. Here $SGKEK_{1234}$, that is the key at root, will function as the traditional GKEK in MBRA. The ELAPSE scheme works as follows:

Case 1: Normal Case:
$$BS \Rightarrow SS : \{GTEK\}_{GKEK_{1234}}$$
Case 2: Node joins in Subgroup 2:
$$BS \rightarrow SS_{SG2}:\{SGKEK_{1234}, SGKEK_{12}, SGKEK_2\}_{KEK}$$
$$BS \Rightarrow SS_{SG3}, SS_{SG4} : \{SGKEK_{1234}\}_{SGKEK_{34}}$$
$$BS \Rightarrow SS_{SG1} : \{SGKEK_{1234}, SGKEK_{12}\}_{SGKEK_1}$$
$$BS \Rightarrow SS : \{GTEK\}_{SGKEK_{1234}}$$
Case 3: Node leaves from Subgroup 2:
$$BS \rightarrow SS_{SG2}:\{SGKEK_{1234}, SGKEK_{12}, SGKEK_2, GTEK\}_{KEK}$$
$$BS \Rightarrow SS_{SG3}, SS_{SG4}:\{SGKEK_{1234}, GTEK\}_{SGKEK_{34}}$$
$$BS \Rightarrow SS_{SG1} :\{SGKEK_{1234}, SGKEK_{12}, GTEK\}_{SGKEK_1}$$

In case of join operation, the GTEK is delayed to support multiple join at the same time. But in case of node leave, there is no benefit to delay the GTEK multicast. Clearly, the algorithm supports forward and backward secrecy and runs in $O(log\ n)$ message complexity. But this is also not scalable for large value of n. We need a more scalable approach than ELAPSE, also considering the forward

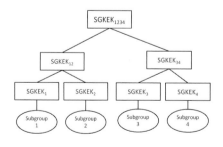

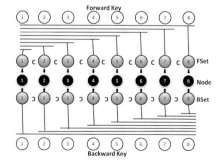

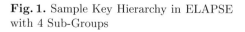

Fig. 1. Sample Key Hierarchy in ELAPSE with 4 Sub-Groups

Fig. 2. The Forward and Backward Key set assignment for LORE

and backward secrecy methods used. At the same time ELAPSE provides strong collusion resistance just like LKH method for rekeying in group communication.

4   Review of LORE and HySOR

These schemes are proposed by Fan *et al.* [9].HySOR is a hybrid scheme based on LKH and LORE. The LORE is based on linear ordering of receiver nodes. The nodes are ordered based on their IDs or some other ordering parameters. Each node has two set of keys - one *Forward Key Set (FSet)* and one *Backward Key Set (BSet)*. The assignment of these key sets are shown in figure 2 using an example of eight nodes.

For example, Node 3 has FSet={1,2,3} and BSet={3,4,5,6,7,8}. If f_i denotes the forward key i, b_i denotes the backward key i, KC is Key distribution center and GK and $\widehat{GK}$ denote the old and updated Group Key respectively,then the LORE scheme works as follows:

1) Node U_i joins Group G:

$$KC \Rightarrow G : \{\widehat{GK}\}_{GK}$$
$$KC \rightarrow U_i : \{\widehat{GK}\}_{SK_i}$$

2) Node U_i leaves Group G:

$$KC \Rightarrow G : \{\widehat{GK}_{f_{i+1}}\}_{GK} \text{ if i < n;}$$
$$KC \Rightarrow G : \{\widehat{GK}_{b_{i-1}}\}_{GK} \text{ if i > 1;}$$

Here SK_i is the session key between the KC and U_i that is established during the authentication time. The interesting part of above scheme is the handling of leave operation. Clearly after leaving the multicast group G, node U_i can not decrypt the updated key $\widehat{GK}$, because it does not have the forward key f_{i+1} and backward key b_{i-1}. All the other nodes can successfully decrypt the message using either the forward key f_{i+1} or the backward key b_{i-1}. After the end of the current communication the forward and backward key set can be recalculated in offline, and that does not create any delay at the time of communication. During the communication, any join or leave operation takes *O(1)* message passing to re-establish the group key. One assumption in this case is that no node is allowed to join the current session unless it is authenticated and received is FSet and BSet prior to the session establishment.

As described by Fan *et al.* [9], LORE is vulnerable in collusion attack. So they combined LORE with LKH and come up with a solution that provides sufficient collusion resistance and works in much less message complexity than LKH. The combined scheme is known as Hybrid Ordering of Receivers (HySOR). The basic concept behind HySOR is to use the leaves of LKH tree as a group of receivers, and the receivers themselves use LORE. Thus the strong collusion resistance property of LKH boils down, but provides much better collusion resistance than LORE which is more practical. Whereas, the message complexity of HySOR is much less than LKH because there is no unicast messages used for rekeying. The HySOR scheme is mainly for normal wired multicast applications that does not consider the properties of BS to SSes multicast in wireless channel, such as the

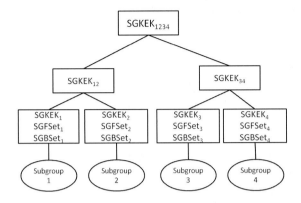

Fig. 3. Sample Key Hierarchy in the Proposed Scheme with 4 Sub-Groups

re-grouping capability of BS in IEEE 802.16 PMP network. This scheme can be modified to suit for IEEE 802.16 BS to SSes multicast security. We use this concept for further improvement of ELAPSE scheme to make it more scalable, and suitable for large practical multicast applications for IEEE 802.16 networks.

5   The Proposed Scheme

In our scheme, we use the architecture of LORE in a subgroup of ELAPSE. When a node authenticates and registers with the BS, the BS allocates it in a subgroup and provides it with a Subgroup Forward Key Set (SGFSet) and Subgroup Backward Key Set (SGBSet). These key sets are constructed using PRNG and maintaining the ordering of nodes inside a subgroup just like LORE. For example lets there are k nodes in a subgroup. So, there are total k numbers of Subgroup Forward Key (SGFK) and k numbers of Subgroup Backward Key (SGBK). So, for node i,

SGFSet $= \{SGFK_m | 1 \leq m \leq i\}$; and
SGBSet $= \{SGBK_m | i \leq m \leq k\}$

The modified ELAPSE tree structure is shown in figure 3. For example, each node i in subgroup $SG2$ has three keys $SGKEK_{1234}$, $SGKEK_{12}$, $SGKEK_2$, and two key sets $SGFSet_2^i$ and $SGBSet_2^i$. The key sets $SGFSet_2^i$ and $SGBSet_2^i$ are generated during the registration phase and prior to multicast session establishment and remain unchanged during the entire multicast session. In a multicast session node can join if it is already registered itself prior to the session establishment. During the multicast session, node join and leave lead to the rekeying that changes the SGKEKs and GTEK, but no change in SGFSet and SGBSet. Each multicast session remains active for a predefined time T, and after that it should be renewed with new set of SGKEKs as well as SGFset and SGBSet. This is a normal requirement in each secure group communication. During this time the BS can follow the standard MBRA protocol to unicast the keys to each

SS. After that, the newly registered SSes can join in the particular multicast services for which it is registered.Our proposed scheme works as follows:

1) Normal Case:
   i) $BS \Rightarrow SS : \{\widehat{GTEK}\}_{GKEK_{1234}}$
2) Node U_i joins at Subgroup 2 with KEK as KEK_{U_i}:
   i) $BS \Rightarrow SS_{SG2}\text{:}\{\widehat{SGKEK}_{1234}, \widehat{SGKEK}_{12}, \widehat{SGKEK}_2\}_{SGKEK_2}$
   ii) $BS \rightarrow U_i\text{:}\{\widehat{SGKEK}_{1234}, \widehat{SGKEK}_{12}, \widehat{SGKEK}_2\}_{KEK_{U_i}}$
   iii) $BS \Rightarrow SS_{SG3}, SS_{SG4} : \{\widehat{SGKEK}_{1234}\}_{SGKEK_{34}}$
   iv) $BS \Rightarrow SS_{SG1} : \{\widehat{SGKEK}_{1234}, \widehat{SGKEK}_{12}\}_{SGKEK_1}$
   v) $BS \Rightarrow SS : \{\widehat{GTEK}\}_{\widehat{SGKEK}_{1234}}$
3) Node U_i leaves from Subgroup 2:
   i) $BS \Rightarrow SS_{SG2}\text{:}\{\{\widehat{SGKEK}_{1234}, \widehat{SGKEK}_{12},$
      $\widehat{SGKEK}_2, \widehat{GTEK}\}_{SGFK_{i+1}^2}\}_{SGKEK_2}$
   ii) $BS \Rightarrow SS_{SG2}\text{:}\{\{\widehat{SGKEK}_{1234}, \widehat{SGKEK}_{12},$
      $\widehat{SGKEK}_2, \widehat{GTEK}\}_{SGBK_{i-1}^2}\}_{SGKEK_2}$
   iii) $BS \Rightarrow SS_{SG3}, SS_{SG4} \text{:}\{\widehat{SGKEK}_{1234}, \widehat{GTEK}\}_{SGKEK_{34}}$
   iv) $BS \Rightarrow SS_{SG1} \text{:}\{\widehat{SGKEK}_{1234}, \widehat{SGKEK}_{12}, \widehat{GTEK}\}_{SGKEK_1}$

Here (⌢) denotes the updated keys. In case of join the message for SG2 is encrypted with the old $SGKEK_2$, which ensures that all the members except the new one can decrypt the message. So another message is sent via unicast to the new member. Similarly in case of leave, the message is encrypted twice using forward and backward key such that the member that leaves the group can not decrypt the message. It should noted that in case of member leaving, the messages are further encrypted using the old SGKEK ($SGKEK_2$ in case of given example) to ensure that the members who have left the group before can not decrypt the message. Only the current members including the one that left the group last can decrypt the outer encryption using the old SGEK, and then all the members except the one that left the group last can decrypt the inner encryption.

6   Analysis of Proposed Scheme

6.1   Security Analysis

As described in previous sections, the main four requirements for secure group communication are - Group Confidentiality, Forward Secrecy, Backward Secrecy and Collusion Resistance. Here we review all these four requirements and how much they are applicable in our proposed scheme.

1. Group Confidentiality: From the structure of the rekeying algorithm, it is obvious that group confidentiality is satisfied, because only group members can have the decryption key.

2. Forward Secrecy: This property is also satisfied in our scheme. When a node leaves a multicast group, the rekeying algorithm sends the updated key to each member of the group except the one that left the group. The new GTEK is used to encrypt further traffics.

3. Backward Secrecy: The backard secrecy is handled in our proposed scheme using the rekeying of group keys after a node joins in a multicast group. It should be noted that prior to join in a multicast group, a node must authenticate itself, and obtain the Subgroup Forward Key Set and Subgroup Backward Key Set.

4. Collusion Resistance: As like HySOR, our scheme also uses a weak collusion resistance.In fact, it has also been shown that the best message complexity one can achieve if strict non-member confidentiality and non-collusion are required is $\Omega(log\ n)$, as demonstrated in [12] and [13]. In practice strong collusion resistance is only required in highly confidential data transmission. Collusion attack requires someone to share its own secrets with others which may be treated as a rare event in practice. In our proposed scheme collusion attack is only possible when two parties in same subgroup share their secret keys. If the BS generates subgroups randomly, and a fresh subgroup is created after the end of each multicast session and the expiration of lifetime of keys, then the collusion attack is rare in our case, as two parties should be in same subgroup to fire collusion attack.

6.2   Performance Analysis

In this section we analyze the performance of our proposed scheme and compare it with existing scheme like MBRA and ELAPSE.

Node Join: In case of node join, total number of $log(n)+1$ multicast is needed. We need one more unicast to the newly joined node. So we need a total of $log(n)+1$ multicast and 1 unicast. In case of ELAPSE it needs $log(n)+1$ multicast and $\frac{n}{D}$ number of unicasts where D is the number of subgroups. So our scheme requires less number of unicast in case of node join. Figure 4 shows a comparative anaylisys of number of messages required . NEW8 denotes our proposed scheme with 8 subgroups. The graph clearly shows that our scheme requires less messages than ELAPSE.

Node Leave: In case of node leave we required a total of $log(n)+2$ multicasts . Here we need no unicast. On the other hand ELAPSE requires $log(n)+1$ number of multicasts and $\frac{n}{D}$ number of unicasts to handle node leaving. Figure 5 shows a comperative analisys of message complexity for different schemes in case of node leaving. From the graph, it is clear that our scheme performs better in this case also. Infact we need no unicast message to handle node leaving.

Comperative Analysis: The table in Figure 6 shows a comperative analysis of different schemes proposed for secure multicast and group communication in IEEE 802.16 network. The comparison table shows that though our scheme

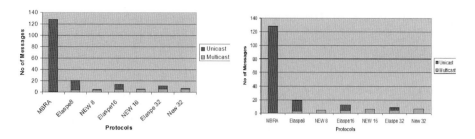

Fig. 4. Message Required for Node Join

Fig. 5. Message Required for Node Leave

Scheme	Node Join		Node Leave		Forward Secrecy	Backward Secrecy	Collusion Resistance
	Unicast	Multicast	Unicast	Multicast			
MBRA	O(n)	O(1)	O(n)	O(1)	No	No	No
ELAPSE	n/D	O(log n) + 1	n/D	O(log n) +1	Yes	Yes	Strong
Proposed Scheme	1	O(log n) + 1	0	O(log n) +2	Yes	Yes	Weak/ Moderate

Fig. 6. Comparative Analysis of Several Schemes

supports weak collusion resistence but it performs better than other existing schemes in terms of unicast message transmissions.

7   Conclusion and Future Works

In this paper we have analyzed the performance and drawbacks of the standard MBRA protocol for secure group communication in IEEE 802.16 network and also the existing modifications over the standard MBRA protocol. We have studied the ELAPSE scheme which is an alternate to the standard MBRA, and then based on the HySOR architecture, we have improved the performance of ELAPSE with the cost of collusion resistance. Though our protocol does not support strong collusion resistance, it can provide a sufficient amount of resiatance against the collusion attack based on the random ordering and sub-grouping of SSes by the BS. Our proposed scheme also reduces the number of unicast messages required for rekeying in group communication.

References

1. IEEE std. 802.16e-2005, IEEE standard for local and metropolitan area networks, part 16, Air Interface for Fixed and Mobile Broadband Wireless Access Systems. Technical Report 802.16e. IEEE Press, Piscataway, NJ (2005)

2. Xu, S., Huang, C.T.: Security Issues in privacy and Key Management Protocols of IEEE 802.16. In: Proceedings of the 3rd International Symposium on Wireless Communication Systems (September 2006)
3. Kuo, J.Y.: Analysis of 802.16e Multicast/Broadcast Group Privacy Re keying Protocol, CS259 Final Project Report, Stanford University, Tech. Rep. (2006)
4. Xu, S., Huang, C.-T., Matthews, M.M.: Secure Multicast in WiMAX. Journal of Networks 3(2) (February 2008)
5. Deininger, A., Kiyomoto, S., Kurihara, J., Tanaka, T.: Security Vulnerabilities and Solutions in Mobile WiMAX. International Journal of Computer Science and Network Security (IJCSNS) 7(11) (November 2007)
6. Xu, S., Huang, C.-T., Matthews, M.: Secure Multicast in Various Scenarios of WirelessMAN. In: The Proccedings of IEEE SoutheastCon. (March 2007)
7. Sun, H.-M., Chang, S.-Y., Chen, S.-M., Chiu, C.-C.: An Efficient Re keying Scheme for Multicast and Broadcast (M&B) in Mobile WiMAX. In: The Proccedings of Asia-Pacific Services Computing Conference (December 2008)
8. Huang, C.-T., Matthews, M., Ginley, M., Zheng, X., Chen, C., Chang, M.: Efficient and Secure Multicast in WirelessMAN: A Cross-Layer Design. Journal of Communications Software and Systems 3(3), 199–206 (2007)
9. Fan, J., Judge, P., Ammar, M.: HySOR: Group Key Management with Collusion-Scalability Trade offs Using a Hybrid Structuring of Receivers. In: Proceedings of Eleventh International Conference on Computer Communications and Networks, pp. 196–201 (2002)
10. Weiler, N.: SEMSOMM-A scalable multicast encryption scheme for one-to-many multicast. In: Proceedings of the 10th IEEE International WETICE Enterprise Security Workshop (2001)
11. Wong, C.K., Gouda, M.G., Lam, S.S.: Secure Group Communication using Key Graphs. IEEE/ACM Transaction on Networking 8(1), 16–30 (2000)
12. Snoeyink, J., Suri, S., Varghese, G.: A lower bound for multicast key distribution. In: Proceedings of the Conference on Computer Communications, Anchorage (April 2001)
13. Yang, Y.R., Lam, S.S.: A secure group keym anagement communication lower bound, Tech. Rep., Department of Computer Sciences, UT Austin (2000)

Secure Data Aggregation in Wireless Sensor Networks Using Privacy Homomorphism

M.K. Sandhya[1] and K. Murugan[2]

[1] Research Scholar, Ramanujan Computing Centre, Anna University Chennai, Chennai-25
mksans@gmail.com
[2] Assistant Professor, Ramanujan Computing Centre, Anna University Chennai, Chennai-25
murugan@annauniv.edu

Abstract. Data aggregation is a complex task in wireless sensor networks because of its limited power and computing capabilities. Due to large scale deployment of sensor nodes for various applications, multiple nodes are required to aggregate the relevant information from huge data sets. This data aggregation process is vulnerable to many security threats due to loss of cryptographic keys, node compromise etc. This eventually leads to breach of confidentiality. In this paper we propose a scheme called Secure Data Aggregation using Privacy Homomorphism (SDAPH) which offers high degree of confidentiality through encrypted data processing. It has lesser computing overhead as it uses additive privacy homomorphism which is a symmetric key homomorphic encryption technique.

Keywords: Wireless Sensor Networks, Data Aggregation, Security, Confidentiality, Additive Privacy Homomorphism.

1 Introduction

Wireless Sensor Networks comprise of numerous sensor nodes having constraints in terms of energy, computing ability, or network bandwidth. Initially the development of wireless sensor networks was motivated by military applications such as battlefield surveillance. Now they are used in many industrial and civilian application areas, like industrial process monitoring and control, environment and habitat monitoring, healthcare applications, home automation, and traffic control. Fig 1 represents the multi-hop wireless sensor networks. It shows how the sensor nodes interact with the base station through the gateway sensor node.

Data aggregation is an important and complex task in wireless sensor networks. There are different types of nodes for performing data aggregation. They are the normal sensor nodes, the aggregator nodes and the querying nodes. The aggregator nodes collect data from a subset of the network, aggregate the data using a suitable aggregation function and then transmit the aggregated result to the next aggregator. A few nodes called the querying nodes process the received sensor data and derive meaningful information reflecting the events in the target field. The base station interacts with the network through the gateway sensor node to get the aggregated information.

N. Meghanathan et al. (Eds.): CCSIT 2011, Part II, CCIS 132, pp. 482–490, 2011.
© Springer-Verlag Berlin Heidelberg 2011

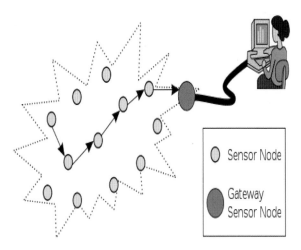

Fig. 1. Multi-hop Wireless Sensor Networks

In this process of data aggregation, security is a serious issue as it is vulnerable to many attacks or threats due to node compromise, loss of cryptographic keys etc. A node is compromised when an attacker gains control over a node in the network after deployment. After gaining control, the attacker can listen to the information in the network, inject malicious or false data, cause Denial of Service, black hole, or launch other attacks. This leads to breach of security in the network. Generally confidentiality is viewed as a secondary concern in the context of data aggregation in wireless sensor networks. In this paper, a scheme is proposed to provide data confidentiality in wireless sensor networks through encrypted data processing.

2 Preliminaries

Privacy homomorphism or homomorphic encryption is a special class of encryption functions which allow the encrypted data to be operated on directly without requiring any knowledge about the decryption function.

Definition 1. Suppose $E_K (\cdot)$ is an encryption function with key K and $D_K (\cdot)$ is the corresponding decryption function, then $E_K (\cdot)$ is homomorphic with the operator $\circ$, if there is an efficient algorithm Alg such that: Alg $(E_K(x), E_K(y)) = E_K(x \circ y)$

For example, RSA algorithm is a multiplicative homomorphic encryption, that is, $\circ$ is multiplication. Although RSA gives a good demonstration of privacy homomorphism, it cannot support addition which is the frequently used operation in most of the applications. A practical homomorphic encryption scheme needs to support two basic types of encrypted data processing, namely addition and scalar multiplication.

Addition: Given $E_K(x)$ and $E_K(y)$, there exists a computationally efficient algorithm Add such that: $E_K(x + y) = $ Add $(E_K(x), E_K(y))$. This implies that $E_K(x + y)$ can be found easily from $E_K(x)$ and $E_K(y)$ without knowing the values for x and y.

Scalar Multiplication: Given $E_K(x)$ and t, there exists a computationally efficient algorithm sMulti such that: $E_K(t \cdot x) = sMulti(E_K(x), t)$. This implies that $E_K (t \cdot x)$ can be found easily from t and $E_K(x)$ without knowing the value of x. When a scheme supports addition, it will also support scalar multiplication because $E_K (t \cdot x)$ can be achieved by summing $E_K(x)$ successively t times.

3   Related Work

In wireless sensor networks, a lot of research is carried out to provide secure data aggregation. In [1], the security mechanism detects node misbehavior such as dropping or forging messages and transmitting false data. In [2], random sampling mechanisms and interactive proofs are used to check the correctness of the aggregated data at the base station. In [3], witness nodes aggregate data and compute MAC to verify the correctness of the aggregators' data at the base station. Because data validation is performed at the base station, the transmission of false data and MAC up to the base station adversely affects the utilization of sensor network resources. In [4], sensor nodes use the cryptographic algorithms only when a cheating activity is detected. Topological constraints are introduced to build a Secure Aggregation Tree (SAT) that facilitates the monitoring of data aggregators. In [5], a Secure hop-by-hop Data Aggregation Protocol (SDAP) is proposed. In this protocol more trust is placed on the high-level nodes (i.e., nodes closer to the root) compared to low level sensor nodes during the aggregation process. Privacy homomorphism was introduced by Rivest et al. [6]. For example, Rivest's asymmetric key algorithm RSA is multiplicatively homomorphic. Due to its high computational overhead it is not feasible for sensor networks. The privacy homomorphic encryption algorithm introduced by Domingo-Ferrer [7] is a symmetric key based scheme. However, in order to hierarchically aggregate the data in the network, the proposed scheme must use a secret key known to all sensor nodes which leads to the following attack. If a sensor node is compromised, it can decrypt the data of any sensor node which is encrypted by the secret key. Girao et al. [8] presents a scheme for data confidentiality in networks with a cluster of aggregators based on Domingo-Ferrer's [7] additive and multiplicative homomorphism.

4   SDAPH Scheme

In this section we propose the Secure Data Aggregation using Privacy Homomorphism (SDAPH) scheme for wireless sensor networks. Fig 2 shows the process of data aggregation. The aggregator node gathers data from the sensor nodes and sends the aggregated data to the sink.

Due to large scale deployment of sensor nodes, a single aggregator node is not sufficient to collect and aggregate the data. Hence multiple aggregator nodes are required for the process of data aggregation. The aggregators are selected periodically from the normal sensors in the network and they aggregate the relevant information from the sensor nodes. The periodical selection of aggregator nodes from the normal sensors helps to make a balance for resource utilization and energy drain. The sensor

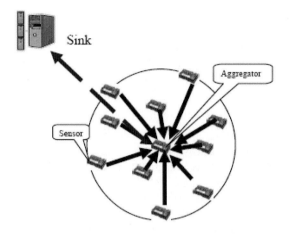

Fig. 2. Process of Data Aggregation

nodes transmit encrypted data to the aggregators. Hence the aggregators must be capable of performing encrypted data processing. This encrypted data processing avoids confidentiality breaches that occur in the process of aggregation. It ensures that the aggregated data is accessed only by authorized entities.

For encrypted data processing we make use of Modified Rivest Scheme (MRS) [9]. This scheme demonstrates additive privacy homomorphism. The scheme is described below:

Key Generation

- Two large prime numbers p and q are chosen
- Compute $n = p.q$
- Secret key K is of the form: $(p, q, r_1, r_2...r_l, s_1, s_2...s_l)$ where $1 \leq i \leq l$.

Encryption Process

- Split the message m into l arbitrary values as $m_1, m_2, . . . , m_l$ such that: $m = \Sigma m_i \bmod n$ where $i=1$ to l
- Randomly choose $r_i < p$ and $s_i < q$, for all $i \in [1, l]$ which are kept secret.
- $E_K(m) = ((m_1r_1 \bmod p, m_1s_1 \bmod q),(m_2r_2 \bmod p, m_2s_2 \bmod q), ... , (m_lr_l \bmod p, m_ls_l \bmod q)) = ((x_1, y_1), (x_2, y_2), . . . , (x_l, y_l))$

Decryption Process

To decrypt the given cipher text $c = ((x_1, y_1), (x_2, y_2). . . (x_l, y_l))$
- Multiply the components with the corresponding r_i^{-1} and s_i^{-1} in mod p and mod q respectively.
- Use CRT to find $m_1, m_2, m_l \pmod{n}$.
- Sum up all m_i's to get m.

Homomorphism

Consider the following:

- $E_K(a)=((x_1,y_1), \ldots , (x_l,y_l))$
- $E_K(b)=((u_1,v_1), \ldots , (u_l,v_l))$
- $t \in Zn$ is a constant

Then the cipher text $E_K(a+b)$ can be viewed as a l-tuple of 2-component vectors. Addition and scalar multiplication of the cipher texts are then just component-wise vector addition and scalar multiplication of the corresponding l-tuples.

Addition: $E_k(a + b) = (((x_1 + u_1), (y_1 + v_1)), \ldots , ((x_l + u_l), (y_l + v_l))) \bmod n$
Scalar multiplication: $E_k(ta) = ((tx_1, ty_1), \ldots , (tx_l, ty_l)) \bmod n$

5 Performance Evaluation

In this section we analyze the properties of SDAPH scheme and compare its performance with the asymmetric key based encrypted data processing scheme.

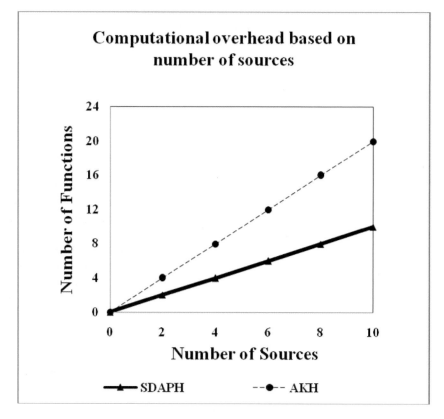

Fig. 3. Computational overhead based on the number of sources for aggregation

5.1 Analysis of SDAPH Scheme

This scheme has the following properties suitable for the scenario in wireless sensor networks.

a) Secure to Cipher text-only Attacks: Given only the cipher text $E_K(x)$, it is hard for an adversary or an attacker to find the encryption key K or the corresponding plain text x.

b) Additive: $E_K(x+y)$ can be found easily from $E_K(x)$ and $E_K(y)$ without knowing the values for x or y.

c) Scalar Multiplicative: $E_K(t \cdot x)$ can be found easily from t and $E_K(x)$ without knowing the value for x.

d) Randomized Zero Encryption: Suppose $x_1 + y_1 = 0$ and $x_2 + y_2 = 0$ (in modular arithmetic, say in Zn), then

- $Add(E_K(x_1),E_K(y_1)) = Add(E_K(x_2),E_K(y_2))$ If and only if $x_1 = x_2, y_1 = y_2$
- $D_K(Add(E_K(x_1),E_K(y_1)))=D_K(Add(E_K(x_2), E_K(y_2)))=0.$

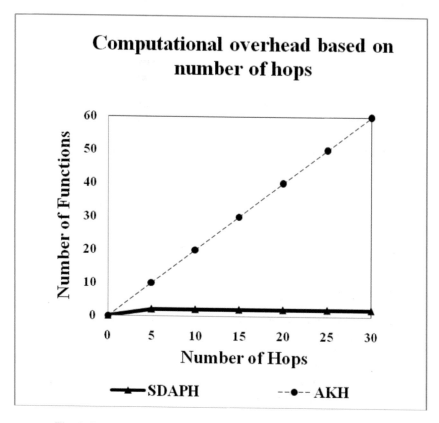

Fig. 4. Computational overhead based on the number of hops in a route

The additive and scalar multiplication properties are necessary for most of the applications that require encrypted data processing. $E_K(0)$ has different representations, depending on the processing of the encrypted data that results in it. But all these representations are decrypted back to 0. This implies that $D_K(.)$ is a many-to-one mapping. The randomized zero encryption property precludes any test for encrypted zero which is a basic requirement needed for problems like secure set intersection computation. In order to reduce the temporary key storage overhead, set $s_i=r_i=c$, for all i.

5.2 Performance Comparison

The SDAPH scheme is compared with the Asymmetric Key Homomorphic (AKH) scheme in terms of the number of functions required for encryption and decryption. The functions represent the computational overhead involved in the data processing. The performance comparison is made based on the sources for data aggregation, the number of hops and the total number of nodes in the sensor network. We also analyze the probability of confidentiality achieved by this scheme.

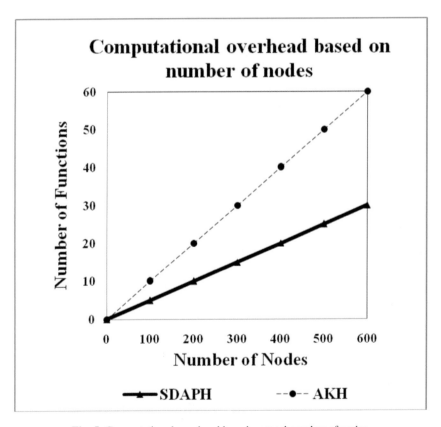

Fig. 5. Computational overhead based on total number of nodes

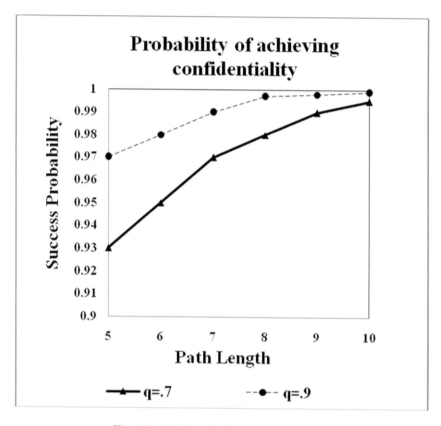

Fig. 6. Probability of achieving confidentiality

First we analyze the computational overhead based on the number of sources for data aggregation in the network model proposed. It is found that the number of functions required in AKH scheme is almost twice the number of the functions required in SDAPH scheme (refer Fig 3). This is because the asymmetric key based homomorphic encryptions are expensive in terms of computing.

Next we compare the computational overhead in terms of the number of functions associated with the number of hops in a route to the base station. In SDAPH scheme end to end encryption is followed between the aggregators. The decryption takes places only at aggregator nodes and the base station. Therefore the number of encryption and decryption functions required is a constant. In case of AKH the number of functions is not a constant. It is evident from Fig 4. It is because AKH functions require decryptions at the intermediate hops for endorsing the messages. This leads to an increase in the number of functions.

From Fig 5, we analyze the computational overhead based on the total number of nodes present in the network. The entire process of aggregation involves an additional computational overhead at each aggregator or even at the sensor nodes. As the number of nodes in the network increases, the number of aggregators increases which in turn increases the overhead of the number of functions.

Now we analyze the probability that this SDAPH scheme offers confidentiality. This probability is represented as $P\{Y>0\}$ and can be computed as:

$$P\{Y>0\} = 1 - P\{Y=0\} \tag{1}$$

The value of $P\{Y=0\}$ is calculated based on the equations (2) and (3).

$$P\{Y=0\} = \sum P\{\Omega_0=0\}^m \, (^L C_m) q^m (1-q)^{L-m} \tag{2}$$

$$P\{\Omega_0=0\} = \{N - E_\pi(X)\}/N \tag{3}$$

Here N is the number of nodes, L is the path length, q is the coin flip probability and m varies 1 to L.   Based on the equations (1), (2) and (3), the values are computed and graph is plotted as shown in Fig 6. It shows the probability of achieving confidentiality under different values of path length and coin flip probability. The values chosen for q=0.7 and 0.9 and L is chosen as 5 to 10. It is seen that the probability of achieving confidentiality increases as the path length increases.

6 Conclusion

The SDAPH scheme offers better security to the process of data aggregation in wireless sensor networks by avoiding breach of confidentiality. The probability of achieving confidentiality is higher as the path length increases. This is evident from the analysis of security. This scheme makes use of MRS which is an additive privacy homomorphism technique to provide encrypted data processing among the aggregator nodes. This scheme does not involve much computing overhead as it uses additive homomorphic encryption which is a symmetric key processing technique.

References

1. Hu, L., Evans, D.: Secure aggregation for wireless networks. In: Proc. of Workshop on Security and Assurance in Ad hoc Networks (2003)
2. Przydatek, B., Song, D., Perrig, A.: SIA: Secure information aggregation in sensor networks. In: Proc. of SenSys 2003, pp. 255–265 (2003)
3. Du, W., Deng, J., Han, Y.S., Varshney, P.K.: A Witness-Based Approach for Data Fusion Assurance in Wireless Sensor Networks. In: Proc. GLOBECOM 2003, pp. 1435–1439 (2003)
4. Wu, K., Dreef, D., Sun, B., Xiao, Y.: Secure data aggregation without persistent cryptographic operations in wireless sensor networks. Ad Hoc Networks 5(1), 100–111 (2007)
5. Yang, Y., Wang, X., Zhu, S., Cao, G.: SDAP: A Secure Hop-by-Hop Data Aggregation Protocol for Sensor Networks. In: Proc. of ACM MOBIHOC 2006 (2006)
6. Rivest, R.L., Adleman, L., Dertouzos, M.L.: On Data Banks and Privacy Homomorphisms. Foundations of Secure Computation, 169–179 (1978)
7. Domingo-Ferrer, J.: A provably secure additive and multiplicative privacy homomorphism. In: Chan, A.H., Gligor, V.D. (eds.) ISC 2002. LNCS, vol. 2433, pp. 471–483. Springer, Heidelberg (2002)
8. Girao, J., Schneider, M., Westhoff, D.: CDA: Concealed data aggregation in wireless sensor networks. In: Proc. of the ACM Workshop on Wireless Security (2004)
9. Chan, A.C.-F.: Symmetric-Key Homomorphic Encryption for Encrypted Data Processing. In: Proc. IEEE ICC (2009)

Deniable Encryption in Replacement of Untappable Channel to Prevent Coercion

Jaydeep Howlader[1], Vivek Nair[1], and Saikat Basu[2]

[1] Department of Information Technology
National Institute of Technology, Durgapur, India
jaydeep.howlader@it.nitdgp.ac.in
[2] National Institute of Technology, Durgapur, India
Department of Computer Science and Engineering

Abstract. The incoerciblety to prevent rigging in e-voting and e-auction have been studied in different literatures. It is realized that the notion of a *virtual booth* and *untappable channel* are required to prevent coerciveness. *Virtual booth* protects the candidates to cast their private values without being observed by the adversary/coercer. However the adversary can influence the candidates after their casting. Adversary used to acquire the encrypted votes/bids either from the colluded authorities (voting server, auctioneer) or by eavesdropping the communicating channel. The adversary then coerces the candidates to disclose their private values with their private keys and verifies whether the ciphers are the encryption of the private values. In the prior literatures of e-voting and e-auctioning, threshold-encryption and receipt-free mechanism are used to prevent the coercion and collusion respectively. But they assumed untappable channel to restrict eavesdropping. However, untappable channel is difficult to achieve. It should be a dedicated trusted link or continuous fiber link to implement untappable channel. In this paper we present an alternative of untappable channel using deniable encryption. Deniable encryption does not restrict the adversary to eavesdrop, but if the candidates are coerced, they are able to find a different value v_f and can convince the adversary that the ciphers are the encryption of v_f, without reveling the true private value v_r. Therefore, eavesdropping does not help the coercer, as he may be plausible denied by the candidates. Our scheme is based on public key probabilistic encryption mechanism. We assume that the sender side (candidate) coercion is only possible, that is, the coercer can not coerce the receivers (authorities).

1 Introduction

The notions of uncoercibilety and receipt-freeness were first introduced by Benaloh and Tuinstra [1] to deal with *vote-selling* and *coercing* in electronic voting systems. They pointed out that, all the prior cryptographic electronic voting schemes were suffering from one common deficiency: the voters were allowed to encrypt their votes, but at the same time they were allowed to carry the *receipt* of their vote cast, which could be exploit to prove to a third party that a particular vote had been caste. This simple defect enables some serious

N. Meghanathan et al. (Eds.): CCSIT 2011, Part II, CCIS 132, pp. 491–501, 2011.
© Springer-Verlag Berlin Heidelberg 2011

problems like vote selling and coercing. The problem was further studied in different electronic election literatures [2,3,14] and also in electronic sealed-bid auction literatures [4,5,13,14,16]. In this paper auction means sealed bid auction. The problem of vote-selling or bid-selling occurs when the voters/bidders are the adversary. A group of voters/bidders make a conspiracy and commit to cast their vote/bid to a certain value as decided by the colluded voters/bidders. This type of collusion is called a *ring*. Generally privacy is maintained in any voting/auctioning system. Therefore the votes/bids are generally in encrypted form. The voters/bidders have to prove their cast/bid to the ring to convince the other colluded members that he has not broken the collusion. The traditional election system discourages vote selling because of the voting booth. The voter promises to the ring to cast his vote in favor to a particular party, but within the privacy of the voting booth, he may cast the opposite vote without bring afraid of any further consequence. As the voting process does not issue any receipt/acknowledgment of the vote cast; there is no question of proving the private value (caste vote) to any third party, even the voter wants to (e.g. for exchange of bride). Similar protection is there for sealed-bid auction, where the bids are submitted in the sealed envelop and no receipts are issued. On the other hand, coercing is the problem where the adversary influences/threatens the voters/bides to cast a particular value. This is known as rigging. Due to the physical existence of booth, coercer cannot able to control the voters during their vote casting. However, coercing can be done in the following manner:

- The adversary (coercer) acquires the encrypted ciphers either from the colluded authorities or by eavesdropping the communication and orders the voters/bidders to disclose their private values and private keys to check whether the encryption of the reviled private information result to the same ciphers or not.

To overcome the rigging, different approaches were proposed. Multiple authority model with threshold-encryption [4,5,16] was used to overcome the collusion of the authorities. Generally, the secret value of the cast/bid was shared among the authorities in such a way that a subsequent number of authorities can reconstruct the secret. It was assumed that the adversary can not collude the subsequent number of authorities. Whereas the problem of eavesdropping was overcame with the assumption of untappable channel. Untappable channel is a physical assumption, such that the adversary can not eavesdrop the communication. This can be achieve either by dedicated private link or by peer to peer fiber link, which may not be feasible for many applications.

The implementation of secure electronic election/auction is seemed to be difficult with the two physical assumptions: virtual booth and untappable channel. This paper presents an alternative of the untappable channel. We propose a deniable encryption scheme using the public key, which may be used as a replacement of untappable channel. Our technique is well suited for electronic election and auction system. Deniable encryption was introduced by Canetti *et.al.* [17]. Deniable encryption allows an encrypted message to be decrypted to different sensible plaintexts, depending on the key used, or otherwise makes it impossible to prove the existence of the real message without the proper encryption key. This allows the sender to have plausible deniability if compelled to give up his or her encryption key.

1.1 Related Works

The receipt-free incoercible protocols in [2,5,13,14,16] were based on two physical assumptions: bulletin/bidding booth and untappable channel. It is understood that with out the untappable channel, uncoercibilety can not be guaranteed. However, implementing the untappable channel might not be an easy task. In some literature [20,21] tamper resistant smartcard were used to overcome the sender side coercing. The smartcard was used to generate the random inputs independently to encrypt the candidates' private values. The candidates had no control over the randomness nor were they informed about the value of the randomness. Therefore, coercing at the sender side did non make any sense. However, the scheme is suitable for large scale election/auction mechanism and requires an infrastructure and deployment policy for smartcard distribution. The smartcard based systems restrict the unregistered candidates (those who were not having smartcards) to participate in the voting/auctioning. This may be applicable in large scale election, but not suitable for auctioning, where any bidder can participate in the process either per-registered or un-registered.

   This paper presents a deniable encryption scheme as an alternative of the untappable channel. The framework of deniable encryption was proposed by Canetti *et.al*, where they defined a *translucent* set $S \subset \{0,1\}^t$ for some large t and a trapdoor function d. The cardinality of *translucent* set S was relatively quite smaller then 2^t. It was easy to generate a random $x \in_R S$ without the trapdoor d, but difficult to determine the membership of a given random $x \in \{0,1\}^t$ without the trapdoor d. The sender-side deniable encryption scheme based on Quadratic Residuosity of Blum's composite modulus was proposed in [19]. The scheme is inefficient and difficult to fit in the election/auction protocol. In [22], a sender-side deniable encryption scheme was introduced, based on the intractability assumption of the Quadratic Residuosity Problem [18]. The scheme used one-time-padding technique to encrypt a message. The resultant cipher was two tuples (c, A), where c represented the padded message and A was a finite set of random elements $a \in \mathbb{Z}_n^*$ (n is the product of two distinct large primes) that represented a random string $r \subset \{0,1\}^*$ which was used in one-time-padding process. The receiver could reconstruct the string r with negligible error probability. In case of coercing, the sender could decode the random set A to some other string r_f and could conveniently disclose a different message m_f to prove that encryption of m_f and r_f resulted to the same cipher c.

   The following is organized as follows: Section II describes the general methodology used in electronic voting and auctioning system, the method of coercing and the general techniques used to overcome the coercion. Section III describes the requirement of untappable channel to achieve the uncoerciveness and how

deniable encryption can be used to replace the untappable channel. We present
the technique to use deniable encryption with the existing protocols used in
electronic voting and auctioning system.

2   Electronic Casting System and Coerciveness

The general electronic casting systems are consist of; a set of valid candidates, the
authorities of the system and adversary (coercer). The systems have a published
list of nominees/items and the defined *rule* of the game (e.g. single candidate
winning, the highest price winning auction). The systems have the essential three
phases:

- **Casting:** The candidates encrypt their private values with the authorities'
  public keys and the randomness to form conceal votes/bids and send to the
  authorities.
- **Opening:** The authorities co-operate to open the encrypted casts.
- **Tallying:** After opening, the result has to be declared. The election protocol
  determines the winning nominee, not discloses the votes of the individuals.
  Whereas, the auction protocol determines the winning price, not the winner.
  The winner has to claim his victory with sufficient proof.

The coercer is the adversary in the system who wants to find the private values
of some selected candidates. The coercer does the following to:

- coerce co-operates with the candidates before or after their casting. Ballot-
  ing/Bidding booth does not allow the coercing during the casting.
- eavesdrop the communication link between the candidates and the authorities.
- conspires with a set of colluded authorities. It is assumed that the coercer
  can not collude more then a certain number of authority.

The candidates must reveal any information if they are coerced. However, the
candidates may plausibly deny or produce false information (fake message), provided that the coercer cannot verify the deniability or falseness.

2.1   How to Get Uncoerciveness

Uncoerciveness can be achieved based on the three premises: *booth, untappable
channel, receipt-freeness*. The existence of booth allows the candidates to cast
their private values without being observed by the coercer [1,3]. This allows the
candidates to make promises to the adversary (coercer), buy within the privacy
of the *booth* they can break the promises without being identified.

As the coercer cannot control the candidates during their casting, he taps
the communication channel and acquires the encrypted values and coerces by
forcing the candidates to revile their randomnesses and plaintexts and verifies
whether the ciphers are the encryption of the plaintexts. All the prior electronic
election and auctioning schemes ensure uncoerciveness based on the assumption

of a physical untappable channel between the *booths* and the *authorities*. The untappable channel disallows the coercer to tap the communication and hence guaranties uncoerciveness.

The only way to coerce the candidates is to acquire the encrypted values from the colluded authorities. To overcome the problem of authorities collusion, receipt-free threshold encryption and anonymous voting/bidding scheme is used. Anonymous casting hides the candidates identity from their cast in such a way that the identity can be extracted in case of repudiation. Many protocols use mixnet [6,7,8,15] to get anonymous submission. With receipt-freeness the candidates should not be able to convince a third party of the values of their cast nor the coercer can demand the proof of the candidates' private cast values. A homomorphic public key encryption with randomness is used to get receipt-freeness [2,5,13,16,14]. The private key is shared among the authorities such that a certain number of authorities has to co-operate to decrypt ciphers [4,5,16]. Thus a threshold encryption [9,10,11] is used to overcome the collusion of the authorities.

3   Untappable Channel and Deniable Encryption

The existence of untappable channel is essential to get uncoerciveness in electronic election and auction systems. However, untappable channel is difficult to achieve. Here we present a deniable encryption scheme as an alternative of the untappable channel. Let $\mathbb{M}$ is message set and $\mathcal{M} \subset \mathbb{M}$ is the set of all sensible palintexts. Any $m \in \mathcal{M}$ is called valid message and $\mathcal{M}$ is the set of all valid messages. Generally the cardinality of the valid message set $|\mathcal{M}|$ is comparatively smaller then the cardinality of the message space $|\mathbb{M}|$. Let E is an probabilistic deniable encryption process that encrypts a message m with randomness r. If $c = E(m, r)$ is a cipher of a valid message $m \in \mathcal{M}$ and r is the randomness, then the plausible deniability allows the sender to find different plaintexts $m_f \in \mathcal{M}$ and different randomnesses r_f easily such that the encryption $E(m_f, r_f)$ results to the same cipher c. The m_f and r_f is called the fake message and fake randomness respectively. It is obvious that the fake message should be the member of the valid message set so that the sender can easily convince the third party with the fake message by concealing the true message m.

Thus deniable encryption does not restrict the coercer to eavesdrop the communication, but if the coercer enforces the candidates to reveal the plaintexts and the randomness for their corresponding ciphers, they can easily find fake messages and fake randomnesses whose encryption *looks like* the same ciphers. Thus the candidates can confidently make a lie to the coercer without being afraid of being caught. Hence, eavesdropping does not provide any advantage to the coercer.

3.1   A Deniable Encryption Scheme

In [22] a sender-side deniable encryption scheme was proposed. Let n is a product of two distinct large primes (p and q) of equal size. The receiver's public key is n

and the private key is (p, q). Let $d : \{0, 1\} \rightarrow \mathbb{J}_n^*$ is a random trap-door function that randomly maps the binary set to an element in the set $\mathbb{J}_n^*$ is defines as follows:

$$d(0) \quad = a \qquad \text{where } a \in_R \mathbb{J}_n^+$$
$$d(1) \quad = a \qquad \text{where } a \equiv x^2 \ mod \ n, x \in \mathbb{Z}_n^* \text{ and } a \in_R \mathbb{Q}_n$$

The set $\mathbb{J}_n^+ \subset \mathbb{Z}_n^*$ denotes the set of all elements for which Jacobi symbol with respect to modulo n is 1 and $\mathbb{Q}_n \subset \mathbb{Z}_n^*$ is the set of all quadratic residue set of modulo n. With the trap-door information (that is p and q) it is easy to compute the inverse mapping of d;

$$d^{-1}(a) \quad = 0 \qquad \text{where } \left(\frac{a}{p}\right) = \left(\frac{a}{q}\right) = -1$$
$$d^{-1}(a) \quad = 1 \qquad \text{where } \left(\frac{a}{p}\right) = \left(\frac{a}{q}\right) = 1$$

But without knowing the value of p and q it is *hard* to compute the inverse of d.

Deniable Encryption by Sender. One-time-padding is used as the encryption procedure. Let m is the message and r is a random string, the encrypted message is $c = m \oplus r$. The sender computes the cipher as a two tuple (c, A). The tuple A is a representation of r, such that, the receiver can decode the random string r from A with negligible error probability. Whereas, if the sender is coerced, sender can easily construct a different fake random string r_f for A and produce a fake message m_f to prove that the cipher c is the encryption of m_f and r_f. The tuple A is a $k \times t$ matrix of elements from $\mathbb{J}_n^+$ and constructed as follows: The ith row of the A matrix is

$$A[i][1 \ldots t] \quad = d(0) \qquad \text{if the } b_r^i = 0$$
$$A[i][1 \ldots t] \quad = d(1) \qquad \text{if the } b_r^i = 1$$

That is, if the ith bit of r (denoted as b_r^i) is 0, then the ith row of A contains t random elements computed by the function $d(0)$, otherwise, if $b_r^i = 1$, then the ith row of A contains t random elements computed by the function $d(1)$. Sender sends (c, A) to the receiver.

Receiver Decryption. Receiver first decodes A to the binary string r. The receiver's private key is (p, q). So receiver can easily compute the inverse of d. Receiver decodes the tuple A as follows:

$$b_r^i \quad = 0 \qquad \text{if } \exists j = \{1, 2, \ldots t\} \text{ where } d^{-1}(A[i][j]) = 0$$
$$b_r^i \quad = 1 \qquad \text{if } \forall j = \{1, 2, \ldots t\} \text{ where } d^{-1}(A[i][j]) = 1$$

After reconstructing r, the message is decrypted as $m = c \oplus r$. The probability of erroneous reconstruction of one 0 bit to 1 is $\left(\frac{1}{2}\right)^t$.

Dishonest Opening by the Sender. If the sender is coerced; he dishonestly opens the random string to some fake string r_f and computes the fake message m_f to satisfy that the encryption of r_f and m_f results to c. Now, neither the sender nor the coercer knows the trap-door information (p, q). So, they do not compute the inverse of d. To open the random string r, sender has to disclose the values of x for the function $d(1)$. The sender discloses r as follows:

$$b_r^i = 1 \qquad \text{when } x_{i,j} \in \mathbb{Z}_n^*, \text{ and } x_{i,j}^2 \equiv A[i][1 \ldots t] \bmod n$$
$$b_r^i = 0 \qquad \text{otherwise}$$

That is, to open the ith bit of r as 1, sender has to show the square roots of t elements of the ith row of A. As the square root computation in modulo n is *hard*, neither the coercer nor the sender can explicitly compute the square root of any element $a \in A$. Hence, the coercer has to believe upon the sender, as he opens the random string. The sender can flip any bit from 1 to 0 by concealing the t square roots of as in a particular row of A, but he cannot flip a 0 bit to 1.

3.2   A Valid Message Deniable Encryption Scheme

The scheme allows the sender to deny a true message m by producing the fake message m_f and the fake randomness r_f. But the fake message m_f is a function of the fake random string r_f, (that is, $m_f = c \oplus r_f$). As the valid message set $\mathcal{M}$ in electronic election and auction are comparatively very small related to the message space $\mathbb{M}$, the probability of $m_f \in \mathcal{M}$ is very less. That is, if the sender randomly flips some bits of r to form r_f, then there may be very less possibility that m_f will be a valid message. So the sender has to determine the possible fake messages beforehand and then generates the random string r in such a way that he can produce the corresponding fake random strings r_f easily for which the encryption of m_f and r_f results to the cipher c. To do this the sender computes the message difference $m_d = m \oplus m_f$. The 1 bits in m_d implies that, if we flip the bits of m at that positions the result will be m_f. The encryption process works as follows:

1. Sender computes m_d
2. Sender generates the random string r by changing some 0 to 1 in the m_d
3. Sender encrypts the true message as $c = m \oplus r$
4. Sender computes the matrix A for the random string r

The random string r must be between m_d and $[11 \ldots 1]$. If $r = m_d$ then the cipher c will be m_f and if $r = [11 \ldots 1]$ then the cipher c will be $\bar{m}$. During the dishonest opening, the sender flips only those positions of r where there are 1s in the m_d.

3.3   Implementation Constrains

Consider an election/auction protocol with the valid message set $\mathcal{M}$. Let $m_1, m_2 \in \mathcal{M}$ and m_1 is the true message and during dishonest opening, the sender would produce the fake message as m_2. Sender computes a random string r that contains the m_d (where $m_d = m_1 \oplus m_2$). In this scenario the following cases may happens:

$r = m_d$, then the cipher will equals to m_2.
$r = [11 \ldots 1]$, then the cipher will equals to $\bar{m}$.
$m_d \in r$, then cipher is a random string and deniability can be guaranteed.

But at the same time, according to the basic principle of the deniable encryption the string r must be a random string. So the sender can not compute a string r which does not seem to be random (the distribution of 0s and 1s must be random). To ensure the above, we define a random mapping $I : \mathcal{M} \to \mathcal{I}$, where I is called an indexing of the valid message m to an indexed message $\hat{m}$. The mapping I should follows the following properties:

1. All the indexed message $\hat{m} \in \mathcal{I}$ are *equal in size*
2. All the indexed messages must be *theoretically random*
3. For any two indexed messages $\hat{m}_1, \hat{m}_2 \in \mathcal{I}$, the message difference contain less numbers of 1s.

Now the sender computes the random string r properly. Sender generates a string r randomly and computes the randomness for one-time-padding as $r = r \vee m_d$, where m_d is the message difference of $I(m)$ and $I(m_f)$ (m is the true message and m_f is the fake message). As $I(m)$ and $I(m_f)$ are equal in size and their difference contains less number of 1s, the OR operation of r and m_d does not lose the randomness of r. After decryption or dishonestly opening the cipher, the receiver/sender has to compute the inverse index function to get back the message.

The above is also useful to overcome the multiple coercing problem. If there are multiple coercers, those can coerce a candidate individually, then the candidate has to dishonestly open the same cipher to different fake messages in front of the individual coercer. Let m is the true message and $m_{f1}, m_{f2}, \ldots m_{ft}$ are the fake messages that the candidate would open during coerced by the coercer $C_1, C_2, \ldots, C_t$ respectively. In that case, the candidate generates r randomly and computes the random string for one-time-padding as $r = r \vee m_{d1} \vee m_{d2} \vee \cdots \vee m_{dt}$, where $m_{di} = I(m) \oplus I(m_{fi})$. The mapping I ensures that m_{di}s do not contain many number of 1s. Therefore the successive OR operations with m_{di} lose less amount the randomness in r.

3.4 Existing Schemes without Untappable Channel

The existing election [2,3,14] and auction [5,13,16] schemes use encryption with randomness to secure the votes/bids form adversary. The encryption process produces the cipher which are random string over $\mathcal{C}$, called cipher space. The cipher space $\mathcal{C}$ is sufficiently big and the ciphers are generally equal in size. But the bit differences among any two ciphers is also a random element in $\mathcal{C}$. So, any

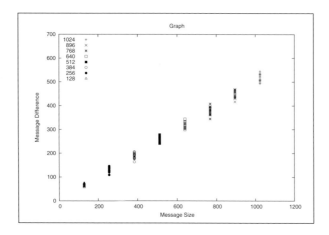

Fig. 1. Average Message Difference Between to Random Messages

pre-encryption mechanism results a random element over a sufficiently big set $\mathcal{C}$ which satisfy the first two properties of I function described in the previous section. However, the relaxation of the third property may not overcome the coercion by multiple coercions.

Fig 1 shows a simulation result for the estimation of the message difference string, where pre-encryption is used before the deniable encryption scheme. We vary the cipher space $\mathcal{C}$ from 128-bits to 1024-bits strings and calculate the number of 1s in the message-difference string for any randomly selected two ciphers from the cipher space $\mathcal{C}$. The result shows that the distribution of 1s in the message-difference string are random and the count of occurrence of 1s are approximately half of the size of the ciphers.

To plausibly deny a true message m, the candidate first determines the fake message m_f. Then he computes the pre-encryption of m and m_f. Let c and c_f be the corresponding ciphers of m and m_f. Then the candidate computes $c_d = c \oplus c_f$ and computes the random string r by flipping some 0 bit of c_d to 1 randomly. The deniable encryption of c is $\hat{c} = c \oplus r$. During dishonest opening, the candidate flips the bits 1 to 0 of r where there is 1 in the c_d and produces r_f and c_f to the coercer. The candidate also opens the fake message m_f and proves that pre-encryption of m_f results to c_f. Thus the candidate conceals the true message m and conveniently convince the coercer with the fake message. Fig.2 describes the model of deniable encryption.

However the ciphers of the deniable encryption are relatively bigger then the plaintexts. Generally the pre-encryption proposed in different literatures [2,3,14] and [5,13,16] are mapping from $\mathcal{M} \to \mathcal{C}$, where $\mathcal{C} = \mathbb{Z}_p$, p is large prime, then the plaintexts for the deniable encryption are $log_2 p$ bits. Deniable encryption encrypts each bits of the plaintext to t random number in $\mathbb{Z}_n^*$, where the A matrix in the cipher has t columns. So the number of bits in the cipher are $t \times log_2 p \times log_2 n$.

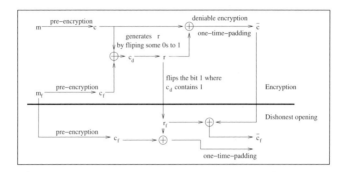

Fig. 2. Deniable Encryption Model

4   Conclusion

In this paper we have presented a technique that would replace the untappable channel used in election and auction protocol by deniable encryption. The adversary is allowed to tap the communication but is the adversary coerces the sender, then the sender can easily convince the coercer with a fake message that the cipher is the encryption of the fake message by concealing the true message. The deniable encryption scheme does not require any infrastructure and easy to deploy. The prior protocols which are based on public key cryptography and assume the existence of untappable channel are easily upgrade to a protocol without untappable channel without changing the basic encryption principle. However, deniable encryption has an expansion of the cipher size.

References

1. Benaloh, J., Tuinstra, D.: Receipt-Free Secter-Ballot Election (Extended Abstract). In: Proc. 26th ACM Symposium on the Theory of Computing (STOC), pp. 544–553. ACM, New York (1994)
2. Hirt, M., Sako, K.: Efficient Receipt-Free Voting Based on Homomorphic Encryption. In: Preneel, B. (ed.) EUROCRYPT 2000. LNCS, vol. 1807, pp. 539–556. Springer, Heidelberg (2000)
3. Okamoto, T.: Receipt-Free Electronic Voting Schemes for Large Scale Elections. In: Cluet, S., Hull, R. (eds.) DBPL 1997. LNCS, vol. 1369, pp. 25–35. Springer, Heidelberg (1998)
4. Franklin, M.L., Reiter, M.K.: The Design and Implementation of a Secure Auction Service. IEEE Trans. Software Engineering 2, 302–312 (1996)
5. Abe, M., Suzuki, K.: Receipt-Free Sealed-Bid Auction. In: Chan, A.H., Gligor, V.D. (eds.) ISC 2002. LNCS, vol. 2433, pp. 191–199. Springer, Heidelberg (2002)
6. Abe, M.: Universally Verifiable Mix-Net with Verification Work Independent of the Number of Mix-Servers. In: Nyberg, K. (ed.) EUROCRYPT 1998. LNCS, vol. 1403, pp. 437–447. Springer, Heidelberg (1998)
7. Markus, M., Patrick, H.: Some Remarks on a Receipt-Free and Universally Verifiable Mix-Type Voting Scheme. In: Kim, K.-c., Matsumoto, T. (eds.) ASIACRYPT 1996. LNCS, vol. 1163, pp. 125–132. Springer, Heidelberg (1996)

8. Baudron, O., Fouque, P.-A., Pointcheval, D., Stern, J., Poupard, G.: Practical Multi-Candidate Election System. In: Proc. PODC 2001, 20th Annual ACM Symposium on Principles of Distributed Computing, pp. 274–283. ACM, New York (2001)
9. Yvo, D.: Threshold Cryptography. Trans. on European Transaction on Telecommunications 5(4), 449–457
10. Shamir, A.: How to Share a Secret. Trans. on Commun. ACM 22(11), 612–613 (1979)
11. Pedersen, T.P.: A Threshold Cryptosystem without a Trusted Party (Extended Abstract). In: Davies, D.W. (ed.) EUROCRYPT 1991. LNCS, vol. 547, pp. 522–526. Springer, Heidelberg (1991)
12. Sako, K.: An Auction Protocol Which Hides Bids of Losers. In: Imai, H., Zheng, Y. (eds.) PKC 2000. LNCS, vol. 1751, pp. 422–432. Springer, Heidelberg (2000)
13. Chen, X., Lee, B., Kim, K.: Receipt-Free Electronic Auction Scheme using Homorphic Encryption. In: Lim, J.-I., Lee, D.-H. (eds.) ICISC 2003. LNCS, vol. 2971, pp. 259–273. Springer, Heidelberg (2004)
14. Burmester, M., Magkos, E., Chrissikopoulos, V.: Uncoercible e-Bidding Games. Trans. Electronic Commerce Research 4(1-2), 113–125 (2004)
15. Sako, K., Kilian, J.: Receipt-Free Mix-Type Voting Scheme - A Practical Solution to the Implementation of a Voting Booth. In: Guillou, L.C., Quisquater, J.-J. (eds.) EUROCRYPT 1995. LNCS, vol. 921, pp. 393–403. Springer, Heidelberg (1995)
16. Howlader, J., Ghosh, A., Roy, T.D.: Secure Receipt-Free Sealed-Bid Electronic Auction. In: Proc. IC3 2009. CCIS, vol. 40. Springer, Heidelberg (2009)
17. Canetti, R., Dwork, C., Naor, M., Ostrovsky, R.: Deniable Encryption. In: Kaliski Jr., B.S. (ed.) CRYPTO 1997. LNCS, vol. 1294, pp. 90–104. Springer, Heidelberg (1997)
18. Goldwasser, S., Micali, S.: Probabilistic Encryption. Trans. on Journal of Computer and System Sciences 28, 270–299 (1984)
19. Ibrahim, M.H.: A Method for Obtaining Deniable Public-Key Encryption. Trans. on International Journal of Network Security (IJNS) 8(1), 1–9 (2009)
20. Magkos, E., Burmester, M., Chrissikopoulos, V.: Receipt-Freeness in Large-Scale Elections without Untappable Channels. In: Proc. 1st IFIP Conference on E-Commerce, E-Business, E-Government 2001, IFIP Conference Proceedings, vol. 202, pp. 683–694 (2001)
21. Lee, B., Kim, K.: Receipt-Free Electronic Voting Scheme with a Tamper-Resistant Randomizer. In: Lee, P.J., Lim, C.H. (eds.) ICISC 2002. LNCS, vol. 2587, pp. 389–406. Springer, Heidelberg (2003)
22. Howlader, J., Basu, S.: Sender-Side Public Key Deniable Encryption Scheme. In: Proc. ARTCom 2009, pp. 9–13. IEEE, Los Alamitos (2009)
23. Menezes, A.J., van Oorschot, P.C., Vanstone, S.A.: Handbook of Applied Cryptography. CRC Press, Boca Raton (1996) ISBN 0849385237

Author Identification of Email Forensic in Service Oriented Architecture

Pushpendra Kumar Pateriya[1], Shivani Mishra[2], and Shefalika Ghosh Samaddar[3]

[1] Student, M.Tech. IV semester (Information Security)
[2] Research Scholar, Ph.D III Sem
[3] Assistant Professor, CSED
Motilal Nehru National Institute of Technology, Allahabad,
Uttar Pradesh, 211004, India
{pushpendra.mnnit,shivanialld,shefalika99}@gmail.com

Abstract. Author identification in e-mail usually follows stylometry based methodology. These methodologies are successful to a great extent. However, these methodologies do not provide any legal binding for the pieces of information collected from such e-mails and do not provide a proof of repudiation or non-repudiation. Typically author identification with the purpose of non-repudiation, privacy, integrity of the e-mail message, confidentiality of the message or a breach of contract using e-mails etc. come under the purview of e-mail forensic. E-mail forensic must achieve the goal of author identification in the domain of node identification, device identification and signature identification. All these functionalities may be made available in distributed system architecture or may be obtained in the form of services in a Service Oriented Architecture (SOA). In SOA, as service identification can be clearly obtained from Registry (UDDI) by way of publisher/vendor specification and subscriber/consumer identification. It is possible to legally identify an object in SOA. SOA provides the requisite legal binding by design. A Case Study has been considered to obtain the solution of author identification of a virus in SOA to prove the point of automatic legal binding in SOA.

Keywords: e-mail forensic, legal binding in UDDI, author identification in SOA, chain of custody, e-discovery.

1 Introduction

Legal fact finding of computer based attacks as Virus, Worms, Trojan horse are not very difficult to detect. To prove or disprove claim on accused, concrete evidence are necessary. For dealing issues like computer fraud, spreading virus worms containing malicious code through emails, authorship of code gives clue for successful establishment of computer based offense in courts of law.

Electronic communication has now become a base for running businesses at organizational and individual level. Frequently used electronic communication through

N. Meghanathan et al. (Eds.): CCSIT 2011, Part II, CCIS 132, pp. 502–515, 2011.

emails may contain virus, worms, Trojan horse, spyware and other malware as an attachment. Authors of this malicious program propagate them without caring of being identified.

This paper reviews the method of tracking of malicious program authors. A further analysis of the subject matter has been done based upon new paradigm, namely, web enabled application utilizing Service Oriented Architecture (SOA). A real life case study utilizing this method in email forensic science strengthens and establishes the authenticity of the method. The format of e-header is defined in RFC 822 [1] and RFC 2822 [2], that are used for information extraction from e-header.

Genesis of the problem

Threat mail, hate mail and spam are common now a days, Such mail may contain Virus, Worms, logic bombs and Trojan horse as an attachment. Authors of such programs have their own style of design and coding the vicious instruction. The author and transmitter (knowingly or unknowingly) of such executable programs can be identified on the basis of malignant code and by the means of style of communication. The focus should be on stylometric characteristic of the program. While focusing on the transmission part of the malicious code, if any modification in the suspect's code has not been observed but discovered as a mutated polymorphic code (polymorphism describes multiple possible states for a single property) though keeping the original algorithm intact it may be studied for further investigation. A polymorphic code characterized by date and time, is considered for investigation purpose for its various variants divulging stylometry.

Our contribution

Author identification happens to be the starting point of the probe taken up through stylometric characteristics. The results of the probe, both theoretical and implementational have been presented in this paper. It has been shown, that author identification gets facilitated if we move towards Service Oriented Architecture (SOA). Authorship detection through this technique includes pattern mining and then matching codes with previously known codes. This technique has imposed a limitation on identification of authors through stylometric technique. We propose a methodology to identify author and collect other relevant evidences at prima facie in web enabled email service based on Service Oriented Architecture (SOA).

2 Related Work

Andrew Gray et al has referred this field as software forensics which involves the areas of author Identification, discrimination, characterization and author intent determination.

The paper suggests source code analysis by reverse engineering techniques which trace back from executable to object code, to source code and then to analyze each type of data structure used, cyclometic complexity of control flow of the program, types of variable names, layout conventions etc by assuming that programmers tend to have coding styles that are distinct at least to some identifiable degree. Thus analyzing the code with reference for the:

1. Purpose of code written
2. Authorship of code
3. Locational identification in network
4. Intention/ (benign/purposeful).

Martinez Barco has suggested use of some stylometric tools to solve the problem of author identification. Farkhund Iqbal et. al. in his work determined the author of malicious email by data mining methods for refined results. Sir K.Calix has defined stylometry for email identification and authentication.

All the papers employ stylometric features to analyze the related facts. They took sample of code and filter some patterns. The patterns were matched with predefined patterns. If unusual patterns are found, the statistical techniques can be applied for more accurate results but this technique does not always reveal concrete and relevant results.

Digital forensics covers a wide area; E-mail forensics comes as a proper subset of digital forensic, but that does not make e-mail forensics any less important. E-mail forensics requires a sub set of techniques and tools from the pool of digital forensics. In e-mail forensics, concern of information extraction is somewhat different like generator information, time information, route information etc.In 2004, Marwan Al-Zarouni discussed about e-mail header tracing techniques and difficulties. He addressed both HTTP and SMTP initiated e-mails tracing. He also discussed different ways used by e-mails senders to evade tracing and workarounds investigators to track e-mails. He emphasized on message-id analysis and packet level analysis of emails. He did not suggest a model for e-mail forensics [3] to depict a desirable workflow.

In 2008, Satheesaan Pasupatheeswaran revealed the utility of email message-ids for forensic analysis. He analyzed message-id generation schemes for different versions of 'Sendmail' message transfer agent (MTA), especially for version 8.14 [4].He had shown the utility factor of such message ID generation schemes after analyzing the related metadata.

Legal Nomenclature related to e-mail Forensics

Following terms are having definitive legal implications in the case study undertaken:

E-discovery

Electronic discovery (also called e-discovery or ediscovery) refers to any process in which electronic data is sought, located, secured, and searched with the intent of using it as evidence in a civil or criminal legal case. E-discovery can be carried out offline on a particular computer or it can be done in a network too. Court-ordered or government sanctioned hacking for the purpose of obtaining critical evidence is also a type of e-discovery [5].

Chain of Custody

Chain of custody (CoC) refers to the chronological documentation or paper trail, showing the seizure, custody, control, transfer, analysis, and disposition of evidence, physical or electronic [6].

E-mail Disclaimer

Email disclaimers are statements that are either detached or appended to e-mails. These statements are usually of a legal character but can also be used for marketing purposes. A disclaimer can also be used on a website [7] for the whole or part of the information published.

Litigation that is commonly concerned with e-mail

E-mail related litigations may be one of the following types:

- The civil and criminal offenses of harassment under the Protection from Harassment Act involve a course of conduct that causes distress. The sending of emails may amount to a course of misconduct.
- A libel occurs when a person makes a statement to another about a third party. This causes others to consider of the third party inferior and thus the said third party gets defamed amount to harassment. Obviously, emails can be used to communicate such libelous statements.
- The Malicious Communication Act criminalizes the sending of 'hate mail'.
- A person can breach their duty of confidence in confidential e-mail through the sending of an e-mail to another person containing confidential matter.
- E-mail can be used to send infringing copies of copy protected materials.
- Unlawfully obtained personal data in emails is a criminal offense under the Data Protection Law.
- Using a computer without the permission of the authorized owner to gain access to e-mails is a hacking offense under the Information Technology Act, 2008 in India, and serve all other countries (as per their acts).
- Disclosing emails without the permission of the authorized owner or lawful authority can infringe a person's right to privacy under the Human Rights Act.
- Intercepting emails without lawful authority is a criminal offense under the Information Technology Act, 2008.
- Sending of Spam emails is unlawful. There can be many more ways to breach a contract. To secure the system and make a clear understanding of law to the common users, e-mail system should have an effective organizational policy.

3 Proposed Methodology

3.1 Introduction to SOA

Service-oriented architecture (SOA) is an evolution of distributed computing based on the request/reply design paradigm for synchronous and asynchronous applications. An application's business logic or individual functions are modularized and presented as services for consumer/client applications. The key to these services is their loosely coupled nature; i.e., the service interface is independent of the implementation. Application developers or system integrators can build applications by composing one or more services without knowing the services' underlying implementations [8]. Work flow management dictates the composability of the services to be composed.

Web services can be implemented in service oriented architecture. Web services make functional building-blocks accessible over standard Internet protocols independent of platforms and programming languages [9].

SOA building blocks are considered to be:

1. The service provider.

2. The UDDI registry (universal description discovery and integration).

3. The service consumer.

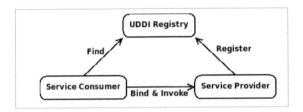

Fig. 1. Working of SOA building blocks

3.2 Proposed Model

In this section we propose a conceptual email service model. SOA can be depicted in layered architecture where collection of services are coordinated and assembled to form composite services. It is not necessary that all services should work simultaneously on a specific layer but may serve at different layer for some application at different point of time in the time frame of workflow of services.

In case of Email services, the proposed model emphasizes on Node authentication, User authentication and Device authentication to ensure authentication and hence identification.

To implement authentication service, common login authentication server is utilized which uses SAML (security assertion markup language). SAML is well known markup language for describing security information about a user in a standardized way. Before authentication SOAP messages are used for managing identity through identity request and response messages. JINI (java based infrastructure for handling service discovery) services makes Java object enabled for remote services. These objects are stored in the registry and copied to the service user's address space at run time. Thus the communication protocols local function calls are associated with services.

Information of end user is stored inside the object which is kept hidden from the service user. This gives clues to forensic evidence to be collected such as data, rules, services, configurable settings and other variations.

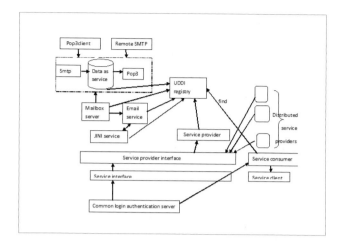

Fig. 2. Email services in SOA

Identity, authentication, and authorization management module as security services and its layered approach in our proposed SOA based modeling are the elements for the proposed framework consisting of layered email security services and their possible composition in SOA.

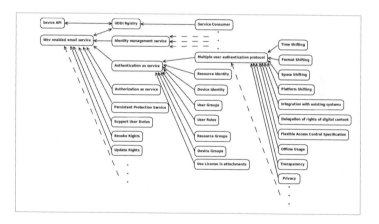

Fig. 3. Layered e-mail security services and their possible composition in SOA

We propose a functionally advanced framework for emailing in SOA. It provides the following:

1. Extendibility
2. Reusability
3. Flexibility
4. Availability

5. Pluggability
6. Interoperability
7. Evolvability

Each of the above stated elements may be captured by the attributes or properties they assume in course of time and the number of states they enter due to such change in attribute values.

The author identification should clearly be different from identification. We consider a case study in Section 3.3 to consider one of the flavours of such cases.

3.3 The Case

1. Professor John Doe a medical specialist and an Associate Professor had communications with researchers all over the world. Mr. Doe was working in a university 'A', but later left it, but still using yahoo email services to supplement the capacity of the email box provided by the university 'A' [10].
2. Professor Doe had no knowledge of developing computer programs. He was just using his computer as he was using telephone to support his day to day work.
3. Professor Doe received an email via the yahoo email with an attachment. He opened his email and continued to work as usual. After few days his computer was confiscated because he was found guilty prima facie for transmitting virus from his computer. His supervisors also claim that professor Doe has created virus program. The program was actually spreading political message.
4. Professor Doe was charged for violating US federal law for knowingly transmitting a program and as a result intentionally damaged the interest of the country without authorization.

Professor Doe was charged for writing malicious code and transmitting the code through email attachment.

4   Proposed Framework

Proposed framework is shown in Figure 4. There are some services shown like:

1. Message Formatting/Displaying Service:
It behaves like an interface between user and system. It provides support for formatting messages and support for displaying messages.

2. Authentication Service:
It is responsible for checking authentication of users, domains and devices.

3. SOA registry and repository is shown in figure 5. The major services are:

   a. Message Transfer Service:
      It is responsible for transferring messages. It helps to track the sender's IP address with composition of IP detection service.

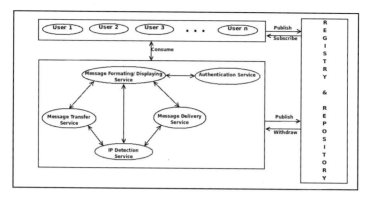

Fig. 4. Proposed Framework for e-mail in SOA

    b.   Message Delivery Service:

        It will be responsible for delivering messages. It also manages the IP trail with the composition of IP detection service.

    c.   IP Detection Service:

        This service is responsible for capturing the IP address of the user. It will generate a link for user to click on at the time of sending as well as receiving of any message.

Following Script in PHP shows the content in header field of email.

```php
<?php
        $ip=$_SERVER['REMOTE_ADDR'];
        $dt=date("Id S \of F Y h : i : s A");
        $file=fopen("iplog.txt","a");
        $data=$ip." $dt"."\n";
        fwrite($file,$data);
        fclose($file);
        header('URL to display in header field');
?>
```

- Save the script into a file with .php extension like IP.php
- Make a text file with .txt extension like IP log.txt
- Set permissions like 777 for IP log.txt
- Put these files into the root folder of the website.
- The link of IP.php file will be published every time a user wants to access the mail service.

    4. ID Masking Service:

   This service provides a protection against spamming. It will be responsible for generating a masking e-mail ID for an original e-mail ID, for a user specified time (Figure 5).

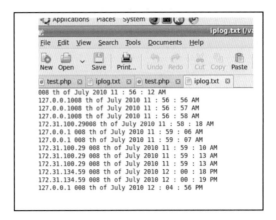

Fig. 5. Script PHP for displaying of content in head or field

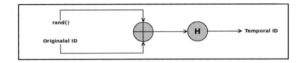

Fig. 6. Temporal ID generation

Table 1. Original to Temporal ID matching

Original ID	Temporal ID	Duration (In Hours)
pushpendra.mmnit@gmail.com	FDFA AGKDLEIWODL 4LK23@gmail.com 12	12
-	-	-

Standard SOA registry and repository in shown in Figure 8.

There are three layers defined in this framework according to their functionality

1. Application Layer
2. Security Layer
3. TCP/IP Layer

In fractured archiving system the problems of concurrency and duplicate message handling are countered in the proposed archiving system by invoking the security layer through a number of instances of the service depending upon the number of users.

A centralized archiving system is shown in Figure 7. Proposed e-mail archiving is shown in Figure 8.

It may be noted here that the presence of the secondary server is to provide a backup to the whole system and central management system to control all activities promoting interoperability and pluggability. The systems that are considered in SOA are mostly real time systems having temporal constraints the rigid temporal

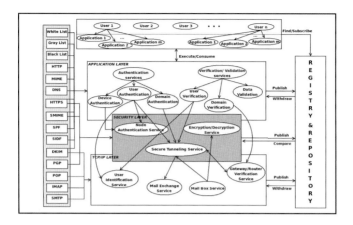

Fig. 7. Centralized Archive Store

constraints on the outcome of the services are employed for services composition. Email services, in particular may be combined with a number of other services like chat services, Video –on –demand, audio-on-demand etc. The services required to be composed with the email service may be third party services .The third party services require binding on the part of composite services.

E-mail Services in SOA

Web enabled SOA based email forensic system ensures to give traces of threat mail or mail containing malicious code as an attachment. The services are properly registered in UDDI. Adding proper identity verification of user or group through LDAP or any identity management solution ensures to give the detail as and when user was logging, on or off. The node and user authentication in SOA based system can provide most

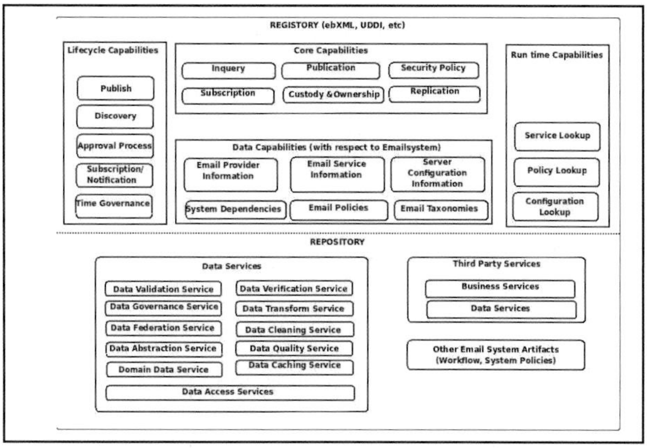

Fig. 8. SOA registry and repository with centralized archiving system

relevant evidence to prove or disprove the defendant, guilty or innocent. Further device authentication gives more concrete evidence when applying forensics techniques to acquire the evidence.

5   Validity of the Proposed Model

In order to prove the validity of the proposed model following scenarios are considered for mapping.

Scenario 1

Mapping the first scenario in service oriented architecture requires to prove that Professor Doe had communication with researchers all over the world. This can be depicted as email service through web service API where common login, identity and authentication service are available through registry. The above scenario in UML diagram may be presented as follows:

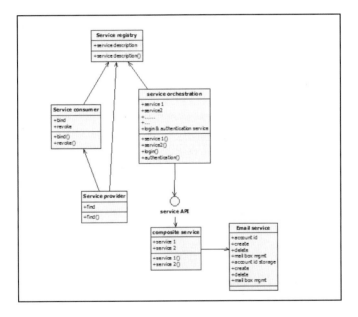

Fig. 9. UML Diagram for Scenario 1 for implementation of services

Scenario 2 and 3

Email attachments can be described through SOAP messages. There are three scenarios:

1.   In SOAP envelope when there is no element to provide a reference body and they are bound through WSDL in the soap body.

2.   When there is a reference to SOAP body.
3.   When there is No reference to SOAP body.

Malicious attachments can be found in first category of SOAP messages where they are attached to message and modeled through web service description language (WSDL).

SOA application using attachments actually convert data format of web service to the data format used by SOA. For such purpose java API, XML based with soap through http concept may be used (Figure 10).

During run time these attachments are imported and exported with a web service binding, thus service identifiers details can be found in figure 10. The process is service identifier capturing (figure 10).

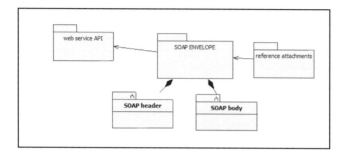

Fig. 10. Web Service Binding for Scenario 2

Scenario 3: The scenarios may actually be mapped through Use Case diagram, System Sequence diagram, Activity diagram, Collaboration diagram and Partial Domain Model or Class Diagram. Only few representative diagrams for each scenario in presented here for understanding (figure 11).

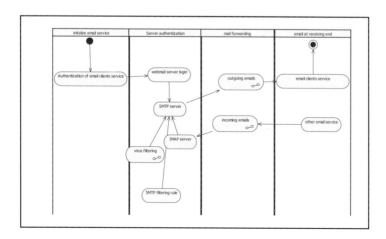

Fig. 11. Sequence Diagram for Scenario 3

Since all the details of further transmission of email (with attachment) can be revealed through mail server, email service with comparison of the date and time of some e-mails can give proper evidence.

Analyzing above mentioned case in service oriented architecture environment, we consider the detail of services in case of message related matters above mentioned entities give author identification, Subsequent investigation tends to establish a connection between the message and alleged author. Routed information or forwarded message information are contained in node authentication table which gives the reliable and admissible evidence, because these electronic data are stored in standard format (log file). The service identification from UDDI registry gives following details:

- service name,
- service description,
- Service version,
- Service location,
- Service contact name,
- Phone number, email etc.

We can make use of all these discrete data for node identification, device identification and finally for author identification.

To execute email services in SOA, proper identification details are stored in UDDI registry thus some concrete evidence can be revealed from above mentioned detailing.Attached executables details can be discovered from JINI services which actually store the end user and sender details.

A modeling attempt for various scenarios is presented in figure 10. The figures are self explanatory and provide a requirement of the e-mail forensic case in SOA.

Conclusion and Future Work

Proposed framework will provide a proactive scheme for e-mail forensic from header information. It also provides a masking service to avoid spamming. The framework provides an effective archiving scheme. It is easy to extend, flexible and robust framework. It provides easy E-discovery, Identification, and Acquisition of services within the framework.

Limitations of proposed framework are the following:

1. Overhead on central registry.
2. IP detection service will increase the access time for user.
3. It will provide limited spamming control.
4. Proposed centralized archiving server requires high performance speed and security.

Future Direction of Work

Some Advanced policies for spamming control may be included for efficiency in the framework level.

We could include some advanced e-mail ID detection Mechanism including device identification, node identification as stylometry algorithms in the software architecture of the framework.

References

[1] Internet Message Format, http://tools.ietf.org/html/rfc2822 (accessed on May 20, 2010)
[2] Standard for the Format of ARPA Internet Text Messages, http://tools.ietf.org/html/rfc822 (accessed on May 20, 2010)
[3] Pasupatheeswaran, S.: Email Message-IDs helpful for forensic analysis? In: School of Computer and Information Science, Edith Cowan University (June 2008)
[4] http://www.javaworld.com/javaworld/jw-06-2005/jw-0613-soa.html
[5] Electronic Discovery, http://searchfinancialsecurity.techtarget.com/sDefinition/0,,sid185_gci115017,00.html (accessed on May 16, 2010)
[6] Chain of Custody, http://en.wikipedia.org/wiki/Chain_of_custody (accessed on June 16, 2010)
[7] E-mail Disclaimers, http://www.emaildisclaimers.com/ (accessed on May 22, 2010)
[8] Al-Zarouni, M.: Tracing E-mail Headers. In: School of Computer and Information Science, Edith Cowan University (May 2004)
[9] http://en.wikipedia.org/wiki/Service-oriented_architecture
[10] http://ieeexplore.ieee.org/iel5/10612/33521/01592527.pdf?arnumber=1592527

A Chaos Based Approach for Improving Non Linearity in S Box Design of Symmetric Key Cryptosystems

Jeyamala Chandrasekaran[1], B. Subramanyan[1], and Raman Selvanayagam[2]

[1] Department of Information Technology, Thiagarajar College of Engineering, Madurai
[2] Department of Information Technology, KLN College of IT, Madurai

Abstract. In cryptography, an S-Box (Substitution-box) is a basic component of symmetric key algorithms which performs substitution and is typically used to obscure the relationship between the key and the cipher text. This paper proposes a new method for design of S boxes based on chaos theory. Chaotic equations are popularly known for its randomness, extreme sensitivity to initial conditions and ergodicity. The modified design has been tested with blowfish algorithm which has no effective crypt analysis reported against its design till date because of its salient design features including the key dependant s boxes and complex keys. However every new key requires pre-processing equivalent to encrypting about 4 kilobytes of text, which is very slow compared to other block ciphers and it prevents its usage in memory limited applications and embedded systems. The modified design of S boxes maintains the non linearity[2][4] and key dependency factors of S boxes with a major reduction in time complexity of generation of S boxes and P arrays. The algorithm has been implemented and the proposed design has been analyzed for size of key space, key sensitivity and Avalanche effect. Experimental results on text encryption show that the modified design of key generation continues to offer the same level of security as the original Blowfish cipher with a less computational overhead in key generation.

Keywords: S Box, Chaos, Non Linearity, Symmetric Cryptosystems, Blowfish.

1 Introduction

An S box can be thought of as a minature substitution cipher. The input to an s box could be a n bit word, but the output can be an m bit word where m and n are not necessarily the same. An S box can be keyed or keyless and linear or nonlinear. Shannon suggested that all block ciphers should have two important properties namely diffusion and confusion. The idea of diffusion is to hide the relation ship between the plain text and the cipher text which will frustrate the adversary who uses cipher text statistics to find the plain text. Diffusion implies that each symbol in the cipher text is dependant on some or all symbols in the plain text. The idea of confusion is to hide the relation ship between the cipher text and the key which will frustrate the adversary who uses cipher text to find the key. In other words, if a single bit in the key is changed, most or all bits in the cipher text will also be changed. Diffusion and confusion can be achieved using iterated product ciphers where each iteration is a combination of S boxes, P boxes and other components.

N. Meghanathan et al. (Eds.): CCSIT 2011, Part II, CCIS 132, pp. 516–522, 2011.

2 Blowfish – Algorithm Description

Blowfish has a 64-bit block size and a variable key length from 32 up to 448 bits. It is a 16-round Feistel cipher and uses large key-dependent S-boxes which is similar in structure to CAST-128, which uses fixed S-boxes. There is no effective cryptanalysis on the full-round version of Blowfish known publicly as of 2009. A sign extension bug in one publication of C code has been identified. In 1996, Serge Vaudenay[6] found a known-plaintext attack requiring 2^{8r+1} known plaintexts to break, where r is the number of rounds. Moreover, he also found a class of weak keys that can be detected and broken by the same attack with only 2^{4r+1} known plaintexts. This attack cannot be used against the regular Blowfish; it assumes knowledge of the key-dependent S-boxes. Vincent Rijmen, in his Ph.D. thesis, introduced a second-order differential attack that can break four rounds and no more. There remains no known way to break the full 16 rounds, apart from a brute-force search.

Blowfish is a variable-length key, 64-bit block cipher. The algorithm consists of two parts: a key-expansion part and a data- encryption part. Key expansion converts a key of at most 448 bits into several subkey arrays totaling 4168 bytes. Data encryption occurs via a 16-round Feistel network. Each round consists of a key-dependent permutation, and a key- and data-dependent substitution. All operations are XORs and additions on 32-bit words. The only additional operations are four indexed array data lookups per round.

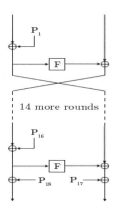

Fig. 1. Blowfish Schematic Diagram

2.1 Initialization

Blowfish uses a large number of subkeys.

1. The P-array consists of 18 32-bit subkeys:
P1, P2,..., P18.

2. There are four 32-bit S-boxes with 256 entries each:
S1,0, S1,1,..., S1,255;
S2,0, S2,1,..,, S2,255;
S3,0, S3,1,..., S3,255;
S4,0, S4,1,..., S4,255.

2.2 Generating the Subkeys

The subkeys are calculated using the Blowfish algorithm. The exact method is as follows:

1. Initialize first the P-array and then the four S-boxes, in order, with a fixed string. This string consists of the hexadecimal digits of pi (less the initial 3). For example:

P1 = 0x243f6a88
P2 = 0x85a308d3
P3 = 0x13198a2e
P4 = 0x03707344

2. XOR P1 with the first 32 bits of the key, XOR P2 with the second 32-bits of the key, and so on for all bits of the key (possibly up to P14). Repeatedly cycle through the key bits until the entire P-array has been XORed with key bits. (For every short key, there is at least one equivalent longer key; for example, if A is a 64-bit key, then AA, AAA, etc., are equivalent keys.)

3. Encrypt the all-zero string with the Blowfish algorithm, using the subkeys described in steps (1) and (2).

4. Replace P1 and P2 with the output of step (3).

5. Encrypt the output of step (3) using the Blowfish algorithm with the modified subkeys.

6. Replace P3 and P4 with the output of step (5).

7. Continue the process, replacing all entries of the P- array, and then all four S-boxes in order, with the output of the continuously-changing Blowfish algorithm.

In total, 521 iterations are required to generate all required subkeys. Applications can store the subkeys rather than execute this derivation process multiple times.

3.1 Encryption

Blowfish is a Feistel network consisting of 16 rounds (see Figure 1). The input is a 64-bit data element, x.

Divide x into two 32-bit halves: xL, xR
For i = 1 to 16:
xL = xL XOR Pi
xR = F(xL) XOR xR
Swap xL and xR
Next i
Swap xL and xR (Undo the last swap.)
xR = xR XOR P17
xL = xL XOR P18
Recombine xL and xR
Function F (see Figure 2):
Divide xL into four eight-bit quarters: a, b, c, and d
$F(xL) = ((S1,a + S2,b \bmod 2^{32}) \; XOR \; S3,c) + S4,d \bmod 2^{32}$

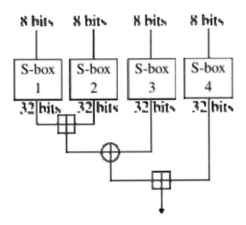

Fig. 2. One Step in Blowfish

Decryption is exactly the same as encryption, except that P1, P2,..., P18 are used in the reverse order.

Implementations of Blowfish that require the fastest speeds should unroll the loop and ensure that all sub keys are stored in cache.

3 Proposed Design

Blowfish algorithm [6] requires 521 encryptions of itself to generate the sub keys namely 18 entries in P arrays and 1024 entries in S boxes. The proposed design replaces the 521 encryptions by adapting chaos functions in order to generate highly non linear and key dependant P arrays and S boxes.

3.1 Chaos Functions

One of the simplest chaos functions is $f(x)=p*x*(1-x)$ which is bounded for the limits $0<p<4$. This function can be written in iterative form as $x_{n+1}=p*x_n*(1-x_n)$ with x_0 as the starting value. A thorough treatment and analysis of this function can be found in [3].

3.2 Initial Secret Parameter Exchange

For application of the above function for generating P arrays and S boxes in Blow fish algorithm, it is proposed that the values yielded by the chaos function are to be converted to appropriate key representations. For this, the following three factors have to be agreed upon by the users.

   i) The starting value for the iterations (x_0),

   ii) The number for decimal places of the mantissa that are to be supported by the calculating machine

   iii) The number of iterations after which the first value can be picked for generating keys.

   iv) The number of iterations to be maintained between two picked values thereafter.

3.3 Global Parameters

An indexed key table consisting of all possible keys for a desired key length is published globally. For example if a key of length 32 is required, all possibilities of the keys are generated, tabulated and indexed. The index identifies the key to be selected at any instant of time based on the chaotic value generated.

3.4 Key Generation

Using the above mentioned secret parameters, both the sender and receiver runs the chaotic equation

$$f(x+1) = 4*x*(1-x)$$

for required number of iterations. The value of every element in P array and S box is identified by the value of the chaotic equation generated during the agreed iteration count. The chaotic value generated will be converted to a suitable index within the range by the formula

$$z_j = (c_i - f_{min})* ((index_{max} - index_{min})/(f_{max} - f_{min})) + index_{min}$$

where, z_j is the index to be identified for generating the element in P array or S box, c_i is the chaotic value generated during i^{th} iteration, f_{max} and f_{min} are the maximum and minimum values generated by the chaotic equation, $index_{max}$ and $index_{min}$ are the maximum and minimum values of the indices in key index table

4 Experimental Results for Text Encryption

4.1 Text Encryption – Avalenche Effect Analysis

The resistance of any encryption algorithm offered against cryptanalysis is measured by its avalanche effect [5] i.e., For a small change even in one bit of plain text or key should produce significantly differing cipher texts by many number of bits. The modified Blowfish algorithm is experimentally found to exhibit good avalanche effect for plain texts differing by one bit. The results of every round has been tabulated below.

Table 1. Round ciphers for seed differing by order of 10^{-10}

Round	Seed1=0.3	Seed2=0.30000000001
0	9791280931051205	9791280931051205
1	40F6CB26BBE4776A	9BB99294B01BBD8E
2	2652FE3338F04A0B	218A90959BBB3291
3	43B1848AF40D9DC5	F06B6704DE8E5461
4	E46F1E6847AF2AA	FD8DABEB9D669997
5	62C6F5248A4A6BCC	7AB0BA1FD2EB559
6	15687B1D6E4C2941	173A04AF4BE303AF
...	...	...
16	776E8A9FB8F75872	4AA90ED7A7F496C6

4.2 Key Space Analysis

The strength of any cryptographic algorithm depends on the size of its key space to make brute force attack infeasible. The values of P arrays and S boxes depend on the initial seed and its related parameters associated with the chaotic equation. The number of initial seed can vary between 0.2 to 0.8 and hence the key space depend upon the number for decimal places of the mantissa that are to be supported by the calculating machine which is approximately infinitely large making brute force attack computationally infeasible. Even for the same initial seed with different skip value the P arrays and S boxes generated are completely different and non linear.

4.3 Key Sensitivity Analysis

The modified Blowfish algorithm is experimented with different seed values for the chaotic equation and the results demonstrate that a perfect non linear relation ship exists between the plain text and the seed thus providing high resistance towards differential crypt analysis.

Table 2. Key Sensitivity Analysis

Sample	Initial seed Value	Cipher
Seed 1	0.43728423	A8A81271EC3F92D0
Seed 2	0.43728423008	1F26570DBCEFC409
Seed 3	0.43728422999	1DEEDFBD12A21B26
Seed 4	0.4372846578	9F2E0B32FA1A1D5D

4.4 Sample Depicting the Non Linear Relationship between S Box Values for Random Seed Samples

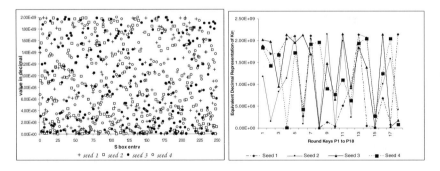

Fig. 3. Non Linear Relationship between S Box and Random Seed Samples

5   Conclusion

The proposed work explains a new way of generating the elements in and P arrays and S box. Experimental results clearly show that the algorithm generates highly non linear S boxes and P arrays while preserving the same level of security as in Blowfish.

The encryption quality for text has been measured by means of key sensitivity tests, key space analysis and Avalenche effect analysis. The algorithm produces good quality cipher texts by employing chaos theory for generation of P arrays and S boxes used in blowfish at a reduced time complexity.

References

1. Daemen, J., Govaerts, R., Vandewalle, J.: Correlation Matrices. In: Preneel, B. (ed.) FSE 1994. LNCS, vol. 1008, pp. 275–285. Springer, Heidelberg (1995)
2. Youssef, A., Tavares, S., Mister, S., Adams, C.: Linear Approximation of Injective S-boxes. IEE Electronics Letters 31(25), 2168–2169 (1995)
3. Jiri, F.: Symmetric ciphers based on two dimensional chaotic maps. Int. J. Bifurcat. Chaos 8(6), 1259–1284 (1998)
4. Youssef, A., Tavares, S.: Number of Nonlinear Regular S-boxes. IEE Electronics Letters 31(19), 1643–1644 (1995)
5. Zhang, X., Zheng, Y.: GAC – the Criterion for Global Avalanche Characteristics of Cryptographic Functions. Journal for Universal Computer Science 1(5), 316–333 (1995)
6. http://www.schneier.com/paper-blowfish-fse.html

Implementation of Invisible Digital Watermarking by Embedding Data in Arithmetically Compressed Form into Image Using Variable-Length Key

Samanta Sabyasachi[1] and Dutta Saurabh[2]

[1] Haldia Institute of Technology, Haldia, WB, India
sabyasachi.smnt@gmail.com
[2] Dr. B.C. Roy Engineering College Durgapur, WB, India
saurabh.dutta@bcrec.org

Abstract. In this paper, we have assigned a unique range for both, a number of characters and groups using the characters. Long textual message which have to encrypt, is subdivided into a number of groups with n characters. Then the group of characters is encrypted into two floating point numbers by using arithmetic coding, where they are automatically compressed. Depending on key, the data bits from text are placed to some suitable nonlinear pixel and bit positions about the image. In the proposed technique, the key characters are alphanumeric and key length is also variable. Using the symmetric key technique again they are decrypted into original text message from the watermarked image.

Keywords: pixel, invisible digital watermarking, arithmetic coding, symmetric key, nonlinear function.

1 Introduction

Digital Watermarking describes the way or technology by which anybody can hide information, for example a number or text, in digital media, such as images, video or audio. Arithmetic compression technique takes a stream of input symbols and replaces it with a single floating point number less than 1 and greater than or equal to 0. That single number can be uniquely decoded to exact the stream of symbols that went into its assembly. Most computers support floating point numbers of up to 80-bits or so. This means, it's better to finish encoding with 10 or 15 symbols. Also conversion of a floating point number to binary and reverse is maximum time erroneous. Arithmetic coding is best to accomplish using standard 16-bit and 32-bit integer mathematics [1] [8] [9] [10].

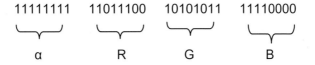

Fig. 1. Bit Representation of a 32-bit RGB Pixel

N. Meghanathan et al. (Eds.): CCSIT 2011, Part II, CCIS 132, pp. 523–534, 2011.
© Springer-Verlag Berlin Heidelberg 2011

A pixel with 32-bit color depth consists of α value, R (Red), G (Green) and B (Blue) value. α value is the value of opacity. If α is 00000000, the image will be fully transparent. Each of three(R, G & B) 8-bit blocks can range from 00000000 to 11111111(0 to 255) [11].

In this paper, we have proposed a technique, initially to encrypt the each and every character of message and from that to a compressed stream of bits. First, we have assembled a table (Table 1) taking a number of characters or symbols available in keyboard or the special symbols as per user's prerequisite. Each character (Ch) is assigned a range (r_c) indicated by high (H_c) and low (L_c) range between 0-1. Then taking a number of characters (maximum 10), a group (G) is defined. Each group is also assigned a range (r_g) indicated by high (H_g) and low (L_g) range. Hence, we can put maximum 100 characters in table, if we use unique probability range. Afterward the long message is broken into a number of small messages. Every short message(less than or equal to 9 characters) is converted into two floating point numbers using arithmetic coding technique. The first one is used for character range (i.e. taking r_c) and the next one is for group i.e. in which group (G) the character belongs (i.e. taking r_g). Then we have transformed each one to an unsigned long integer number (removing the floating point) and it to equivalent binary number. Here we have used the variable length key with the key length of 1 to 39 alphanumeric characters. The characters of the key must be defined with their individual range in Table 1. From that alphanumeric key we have generated a four digit key value (K_v). To get it we have applied the similar method as we have broken the long message into groups. From every group we get two floating point number and from that to two long integer number as before. Taking the first integer number we have generated a reminder by modulus division with 4-digit maximum number. Add that reminder with the second integer from that group. Again calculate modulo division and add reminder to the integer number of the next group, if any. Apply the same method repetitively for the number of groups calculated from the key. If the reminder of modulo division becomes zero finally then take the divisor as key value (K_v). Taking that key value (K_v) we have placed the data bits form the text message in some suitable nonlinear pixel and bit positions. We have positioned the data bits in any one bit of last four significant bit of each R, G & B taking the α value as 255 or as it is in the original image [4] [5] [6] [7].

Example: A text with 24 characters, will be encrypted to an array of 168 $(8+2*((2*30) + (1*20)))$ bits of stream. If we use ASCII-8 (American Standard Code for Information Interchange) to encode 192 bits are required. An image with 800 X 600 has 2, 40,000 pixels. In our work only we are altering any one bit of last four significant bit of each R, G & B. Here maximum 56 pixels will be affected by this process. If any bit generated from characters become same to the targeted bit of image, then there will be no change.

Section 2 represents the scheme followed in the encryption technique. Section 3 represents an implementation of the technique. Section 4 is an analytical discussion on the technique. Section 5 draws a conclusion.

2 The Scheme

This section represents a description of the actual scheme used during implementing "Implementation of Invisible Digital Watermarking by Embedding Data in Arithmetically Compressed Form into Image using Variable-Length Key" technique. Section 2.1 describes the encryption technique using four algorithms 2.1.1, 2.1.2, 2.1.3 and 2.1.4 while section 2.2 describes the decryption technique using two algorithms 2.2.1 and 2.2.2 [2] [3].

2.1 Encryption of Data Bits about the Image

2.1.1 Assignment of Range for Individual Characters and Groups
Step I: Take special characters/symbols or characters available in keyboard.
Step II: Count the number of characters (chlen) and calculate number of groups (nogp=chlen/10) and remaining characters (extch=chlen%10).
Step III: Assign range (r_c) to each characters/symbols indicated by high (H_c) and low (L_c) range between 0 to 1.
Step IV: Taking a set of characters (maximum 10 characters) define a group (G).Also assign a range (r_g) indicated by high (H_g) and low (L_g) range to each of these.
Step V: If extch =0 then repeat *Step II* to *Step IV* for i= *1* to *nogp*.
        Otherwise repeat *Step II* to *Step IV* for i= 1 to (nogp+1).
Step VI: Stop.

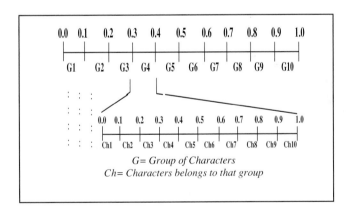

Fig. 2. Subdivision of Encoded Characters

2.1.2 Encode Message Using Arithmetic Coding and Store It to Encrypted Array as Binary Values
Step I: Take characters as input from keyboard or special characters (which must be in Table 1).
Step II: Calculate the string length (chlen) from input.
Step III: Convert the length (chlen) into its 8-bit binary equivalent. Store that data bits to earr[bit] as LSB (Least Significant Bit) to earr[1] and MSB (Most Significant Bit) to earr[8] respectively.

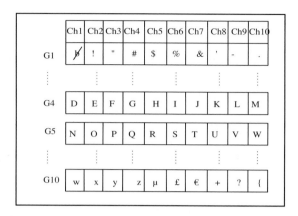

Fig. 3. Characters in Group

Table 1. Characters and Groups with Range

Characters	Range for Characters ($L_c \leq r_c < H_c$)	Range for Groups ($L_g \leq r_g < H_g$)
#	$0.3 \leq rc < 0.4$	$0.0 \leq rg < 0.1$
&	$0.6 \leq rc < 0.7$	$0.0 \leq rg < 0.1$
A	$0.7 \leq rc < 0.8$	$0.2 \leq rg < 0.3$
B	$0.8 \leq rc < 0.9$	$0.2 \leq rg < 0.3$
E	$0.1 \leq rc < .0.2$	$0.3 \leq rg < 0.4$
I	$0.5 \leq rc < .0.6$	$0.3 \leq rg < 0.4$
L	$0.8 \leq rc < .0.9$	$0.3 \leq rg < 0.4$
N	$0.0 \leq rc < .0.1$	$0.4 \leq rg < 0.5$
O	$0.1 \leq rc < 0.2$	$0.4 \leq rg < 0.5$
R	$0.4 \leq rc < 0.5$	$0.4 \leq rg < 0.5$
:	:	:

Step IV: Calculate number of broken messages n = chlen/9 and remaining characters r =chlen%9.

Step V: Taking the range from Table 1 apply arithmetic coding technique to encode the character set into a single floating point number in between 0 - 1.

Set low to 0.0

Set high to 1.0

While there are still input characters do

get an input character

code range = high - low.

high = low + range*high_ range

low = low + range*low_ range
End of While

Continue this process to get input (1 to 9) for first n times and (1to r) at (n+1)th time and stop. Output the low.

Step VI: From the Low value and High value convert Low value (low) to an unsigned long integer number removing the floating point.

Step VII: Convert that number into equivalent binary number. For n times if total number of 0 or 1 is less than 30 then left fill with 0's. For the case of r:

    a) If (r≥6 ‖ r=0) as in Step VII.

    b) If (r≥3 ‖ r<6) and if total number of 0 or 1 is less than 20 then left fill with 0's.

    c) If (r>0 ‖ r<3) and if total number of 0 or 1 is less than 10 then left fill with 0's.

Step VIII: Store the binary values, LSB to earr[9] and rest to earr[bit] respectively.

Step IX: Repeat *Step V* to *Step VIII*

    a)   If r=0 then for i= 1 to (2*n) times

    Otherwise for i= 1 to (2*(n+1)) times taking r_c and r_g from separately and respectively.

Step X: Stop.

2.1.3   Selection of the Nonlinear Pixel Positions from the Key

Step I: Take key (*K*) input from keyboard.

Step II: Repeat *Step II* to *Step VI* of *Algorithm 2.1.2* to get the floating point number.

Step III: Taking the number getting from character range (r_c) calculate the reminder (r) by modulus division with 4-digit maximum number.

Step IV: Add the reminder (r) with the integer number calculated from group range (r_g) and again calculate the reminder (r) by following *Step III*.

Step V: To calculate through all the group of characters runs through *Step IX* of *algorithm 2.1.2*.

Step VI: Store the final reminder as key value (K_v).

    a)   If the value of (K_v) is 0 the then takes the value of Kv as 9999.

Step VII: Take the value of *bit* from array e*arr[bit]* to calculate total number of pixels is required as three following data bit replaced in R, G & B of every pixel. So calculate number of pixel p= (ceil (bit /3)).

Step VIII: Take the key value (K_v) and calculate the value of function

    $F(x, y) = K_v{}^P$ [i.e. POW (K_v, p)].

Step IX: Store the exponential long double values into file one by one.

Step X: Repeat *Step III* to *Step IV* for i= (1 to p) and go to *Step VI*.

Step XI: Read the values as character up to "e" of the every line of the file and store it to another file with out taking the point [.].

Step XII: Modify the value as numeric and store it to an array *arrxyz[p]*

Step XIII: Take most three significant digit to *arrx[p]*, next three digits to array *arry[p]* and last significant digit to *arrz[p]*.

Step XIV: Repeat *Step VI* to *Step VIII* up to end of the file.

Step XV: Stop.

2.1.4 Replacement of the Array Elements with R, G & B Values of Pixels

Step I: Calculate the width (w) and height (h) of the image.

Step II: Set x=*arrx[p]* and y=*arry[p]*.

Step III: To select the pixel position into image, compare the value of x and y with the value of w and h (where addressable pixel position is (0, 0) to (w-1, h-1)).

   a)   If (x >(w-1)) or (y >(h-1)) then

  Set P (x, y) = P (0+(x % (w-1)), (0 +(y %(h-1)))

     Otherwise Set   P (x, y) = (x, y).

Step IV: To select the bit position (b) of selected pixel i.e. with which bit the array data will be replaced. Set *z =arrz[p]*.

     i)   If (z%4=0) then b=LSB

     ii) If (z%4=1) then b=2nd LSB

     iii) If (z%4=2) then b=3rd LSB

     Otherwise b=4th LSB of each R, G & B of a pixel.

Step V: Verify the pixel or bit positions which previously have used or not about the image.

   a)   If ((P(x, y)= (P(x, y)) ‖ P (x, y)= P (x++, y++)) && (b=b++])then

  Set P ((x, y), b) =P (0, h) and b as *Step IV*.

  Repeat *Step V (a) for j=1 to p;*

  Repeat *Step V (a) for k=j to p.*

  Go to *Step VI*.

Step VI: To replace the array elements with the selected bit position of selected pixel and to reform as a pixel

  a) After reading the values of R, G & B convert each to its equivalent 8-bit binary values.

  b) Replace subsequent element of earr[bit] by following *Step III to Step V*.

  c) Taking values of R, G & B switch it to the pixel value and place it to its position of the image (taking α value as before).

Step VII: For replacing the array element to pixels using the above mentioned process starting from the 0th element up to the end of the array.

     A) If bit%3 = 0

        Go to *Step VIII*.

     B) If bit%3 = 1

for 0th element to (bit-1)th element of the array repeat *Step VII (A)*.For (bit)th element to R, value for G and B will be remain same. And go to S*tep VIII*.

     C) If bit%3=2

for 0th element to (bit-2)th element of the array repeat *Step VII (A)*.For (bit-1)th element to R, (bit)th to G and B will be remain same. And go to S*tep VIII*.

Step VIII: Repeat *Step II to Step VII* for i=1 to p.

Step IX: Stop.

2.2 Decryption of the Data Bits from the Image

2.2.1 Retrieving the Replaced Bits from the Encrypted Image

Step I: Take the key (K) input as it was at the time of encryption.

Step II: To get the key value (K$_v$) go through *Step II* to *Step VI* of *algorithm 2.1.3*.

Step III: To get the pixel positions with in the image and bit position in R, G & B of selected pixels run through *Step VII* to *Step XIV* of *Algorithm 2.1.3* and *Step I to Step VIII* of *Algorithm 2.1.4.*

Step III: Retrieving the encrypted bits from the selected bit positions of delectated pixels store it to decrypted array from darr[1] to darr[bit] respectively.

Step IV: To get the length repeat *Step II to Step III* for i= 1 to 3 times (as every pixel contain three data bits).

Step V: Taking data bits of darr [1] as LSB and darr [8] as MSB calculate the length (chlen) of message.

Step VI: To find out the total number of bits in decoding array (i.e. value of *bit* in *darr[bit]*), calculate n=chlen/9 and r=chlen%9 (as in *Step IV Algorithm 2.1.2*).

Step VI: Taking the value of n and r calculate bit= (2*(30*n + rbit) +8).

Where *rbit* are calculated as

    a) If (r≥6) then *rbit =30*
    b) If(r≥3 ‖ r<6) then *rbit =20*
    c) If(r>0 ‖ r<3) then *rbit=10 (as in Step VII algorithm 2.1.2*).

Step VII: Now go through *Step VII to Step XIV of Algorithm 2.1.3* and *Step I to Step VIII of Algorithm 2.1.4 for i=4 to p.* Store the data's *darr[10]* to *darr[bit]* respectively.

Step VIII: Stop.

2.2.2 Decompress Array Elements to Text Using Decoding Algorithm

Step I: To translate the data bits to floating point number

    a) If n≠0, assign the value *darr[8+n*i]* to LSB and *darr[8+30*n]* to MSB respectively and covert it to equivalent decimal number.

        If the total number of digits of that decimal number is less than nine left filling with 0's translate it to nine digits floating point number.

    b) If r≠0, assign the value *darr[(8+30*n) +1]* to LSB and da*rr[(8+30*n)+1)+rbit]* to MSB respectively and covert it to equivalent decimal number.

        If the total number of digits of that decimal number is less than *r* left filling with 0's translate it to *r* digits floating point number.

Step II: Apply the decoding algorithm of arithmetic coding to convert it into individual range.

    Get encoded number

    Do

    Find range from the table

    Output the range

        Subtract symbol low value from encoded number

    Divide encoded number by range

    Until no more symbols or zero.

Step III: Comparing the ranges of first time iteration of *Step II* and second time iteration of *Step II* alongside (i.e. comparing the range r_c and the r_g at same time) from the table (Table 1) find out the encoded characters (Ch).

Step IV: Executing the work of *Step (a)* go to *Step (b)*

a) If n≠0 repeat *Step I (a)* to *Step III* for i= 1 to 2 times.
Repeat *Step IV for i=1* to *n* times.
b) If r≠0 repeat *Step I (b)* to *Step IV* for i=1 to 2 times. And Go to *Step VII*.
Step V: Finally put the characters one by one and assemble the original message.
Step VI: Stop.

3 An Implementation

Let the message to be encrypt is NONLINEAR.
So the length of the message
=09(Decimal equivalent)
=00001001(8 Bit Binary equivalent)
All the characters of the message are defined in the Table 1 with their distinct range.
Starting from the range 0.0 to 0.1 *Ch1's* (maximum10 characters from *G1* to *G10*) are
defined. In that range the first character N is also defined. Applying the technique
described in algorithm 2.1.2 we get the codeword for the r_c as,

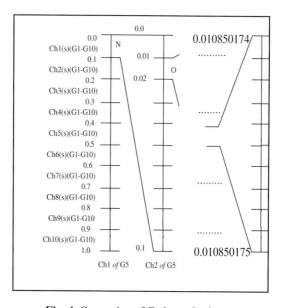

Fig. 4. Generation of Codeword using r_c

Hence we get the codeword for characters
0.010850174 ≤codeword_for_Ch< 0.01050175.
And for groups we get,
0.444334324≤codeword_for_group <0.444334325
Taking the low values for characters
Codeword
=0.010850174(floating point number)
=10850174(integer number removing floating   point)
=000000101001011000111101111110 (30 bit binary equivalent)

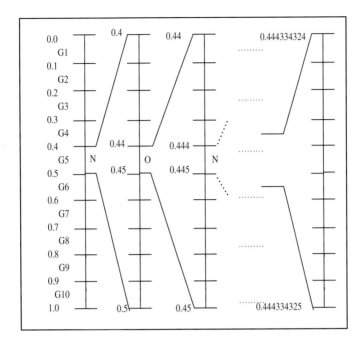

Fig. 5. Generation of Codeword using r_g

And taking low value for group we get codeword

       =0.444334324 (floating point number)

       =444334324 (integer number removing floating point)

       =011010011111000000000011110100(30 bit binary equivalent)

First store the bits form length to encrypted array earr[bit], then store bits of stream from code words respectively as,

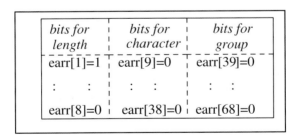

bits for length	bits for character	bits for group
earr[1]=1	earr[9]=0	earr[39]=0
: :	: :	: :
earr[8]=0	earr[38]=0	earr[68]=0

Fig. 6. Data bits in Encrypted Array

Let the key (K) =6M3U7NU9.

From Key (K), for r_c we get,

0.25933635(floating point number)

=25933635 (integer number removing floating point)

For r_g, we get,

0.24152452(floating point number)

=24152452 (integer number removing floating point)

Now the reminder (r) =mod (25933635, 9999) =6228.

Adding r with the second integer we get = (6228+24152452) = 24158680.

Again the reminder (r) = 1096.

As their only 8-alphanumeric characters in key (K) finally we get the key value (K_v) =1096.

The image size= 800 X 600(w x h).

Number of affected pixel (p) = [ceil (68/3)] =23.

In the Table-2 how the array data's are replaced with R, G & B values in selected nonlinear pixels of an image is described (as described in algorithm 2.1.3 and algorithm 2.1.4).

Table 2. Replacement of Data Bits about Image

Key(K),i	Value	Value of pixel P(x,y)	Bit position b= Z%4	Array data to replace
1096,1	1.096000 e+03	P(109,600)	1st LSB	earr[1] earr[2] earr[3]
⋮	⋮	⋮	⋮	⋮
1096,5	1.581440e+15	P(158,144)	1st LSB	earr[13] earr[14] earr[15]
⋮	⋮	⋮	⋮	⋮
1096,23	8.234605e+69	P(223,005)	2nd LSB	earr[79] earr[80] B as same

Table 3. Decode into Original Message

Codeword (Using r_c)	Codeword (Using r_g)	Character Range	Group Range	Character
0.010850174	0.444334325	$0.0 \leqslant r_c < 0.1$	$0.4 \leqslant r_g < 0.5$	N
0.10850174	0.44334325	$0.1 \leqslant r_c < 0.2$	$0.4 \leqslant r_g < 0.5$	O
0.0850174	0.4334325	$0.0 \leqslant r_c < 0.1$	$0.4 \leqslant r_g < 0.5$	N
0.850174	0.334325	$0.8 \leqslant r_c < 0.9$	$0.3 \leqslant r_g < 0.4$	L
0.50174	0.34325	$0.5 \leqslant r_c < 0.6$	$0.3 \leqslant r_g < 0.4$	I
0.0174	0.4325	$0.0 \leqslant r_c < 0.1$	$0.4 \leqslant r_g < 0.5$	N
0.174	0.325	$0.1 \leqslant r_c < 0.2$	$0.3 \leqslant r_g < 0.4$	E
0.74	0.25	$0.7 \leqslant r_c < 0.8$	$0.2 \leqslant r_g < 0.3$	A
0.4	0.5	$0.4 \leqslant r_c < 0.5$	$0.4 \leqslant r_g < 0.5$	R
0.0				

Thus we can transmit the encrypted watermarked image through any communication channel. Afterward applying the decryption technique as described in algorithm 2.2.1 and algorithm 2.2.2 we will be able to get back the encrypted message from that watermarked image in the decryption end. Taking character range and group range we get the encrypted characters which are defined in Table 3.

Finally, we get the encrypted message "NONLINEAR" after assembling the characters.

4 Analysis

By this process, we have taken a number of characters and grouped them with their distinct range of probabilities, which is unique to sender and receiver. Sender and receiver can change the order of occurrence and range of probabilities of both the characters and groups in Table 1. Here the key length may vary from 1 to 39 alphanumeric characters. As we have taken the key value (K_v) from the key as 4 digits maximum number. Using this method, only $^{95}C_1$ to $^{95}C_{39}$ number of key combinations is possible (taking input the characters of key only from keyboard). If anybody wants the value of K_v more than 4 digits, he or she may take more number of alphanumeric characters as key and then more number of key combinations will be possible (but *message_lenght* $\infty 1$ / *number_of_keydigit.*). Using single key we can only replace data bits of maximum 30 characters (as using 4 digits maximum numbers only 77 pixels is truly addressable). If anybody wants to encrypt long message using this technique, he or she can use subset of keys (using characters of key) from the key (K) and may assign them to different regions of image. Binary values generated form both textual information and message length are replaced in different nonlinear places in the image. As bits are placed in any one bit of lower four bits of each R, G & B, the change of color of the modified pixels are invisible to human eye. If size of the text is less, the number of pixels affected from the text will also be less. At that time it will be harder to differentiate the encrypted image from the original image. If the image size is large and number of pixels is less, it will also be harder to differentiate [2] [5].

5 Conclusion

We have formed a table (Table 1) with different ranges of probability for each and every character and group, which is totally unknown to the others i.e. except from sender and receiver. Here we have used the variable length key technique. By this technique a large number of key combinations are possible. Again we generated a key value (K_v) from key (K) by arithmetic coding and our proposed algorithm. Using key value (K_v) and nonlinear function technique we have selected both the pixel positions and bit position where the data will be hidden inside the image [4]. After all, it produces the similar image to see in necked eye at the time of watermarking. If the key becomes unknown to anybody who wants to attack the information, we think, it will be quite impossible to the attacker to find out the information from the watermarked image.

Acknowledgement

Let us express our heartiest gratitude to respective authority of Haldia Institute of Technology, Haldia, West Bengal, INDIA, for providing resources used during the entire development process.

References

1. Samanta, S., Kandar, S., Dutta, S.: Implementing Invisible Digital Watermarking on Image. The Bulletin of Engineering and Science 3(2), 79–82 (2008) ISSN: 0974 7176
2. Samanta, S., Dutta, S.: Implementation of Invisible Digital Watermarking on Image Nonlinearly of Arithmetically Compressed Data. IJCSNS International Journal of Computer Science and Network Security 10(4), 261–266 (2010) ISSN: 1738-7906
3. Samanta, S., Dutta, S.: Implementation of Invisible Digital Watermarking on Image Nonlinearly Encrypted with Galois Field (GF- 256). In: 2010 International Conference on Informatics, Cybernetics, and Computer Applications (ICICCA 2010), July 19-21, pp. 26–30 (2010)
4. Samanta, S., Dutta, S.: Implementation of Invisible Digital Watermarking on Image Nonlinearly. Accepted by International Conference on Computer Applications, 2010 (ICCA 2010), December 24-27 (2010)
5. Tyagi, V., Agarwal, J.P.: Digital Watermarking. In: Computer Society of India (26.09.2008)
6. Petitcolas, F.A.P., Anderson, R.J., Kuhn, M.G.: Information Hiding-A Survey by Fabien A. P. Proceedings of the IEEE, Special Issue on Protection of Multimedia Content 87(7), 1062–1078 (1999)
7. Owen, T., Hauck, S.: Arithmetic Compression on SPIHT Encoded Images. WEE Technical Report, Number UWEETR-2002- 0007 of 05/06/2002
8. Willen, I.H., Neal, R.M., Cleary, J.G.: Arithmetic coding for Data compression. Communications of the ACM 30(6), 520–540 (1987)
9. Howard, P.G., Vitter, J.S.: Practical Implementations of Arithmetic Coding. Department of Computer Science, Brown University Providence, R.I. 02912-1910
10. Petitcolas, F.A.P.: Watermarking schemes evaluation. Microsoft Research
11. Banerjee, A., Ghosh, A.M.: Multimedia Technology. TMH, New Delhi

Transmission Power Control in Virtual MIMO Wireless Sensor Network Using Game Theoretic Approach

R. Valli and P. Dananjayan

Department of Electronics and Communication Engineering,
Pondicherry Engineering College,
Pondicherry
pdananjayan@rediffmail.com, pdananjayan@pec.edu

Abstract. Power management is one of the vital issues in wireless sensor networks, where the lifetime of the network relies on battery powered nodes. Transmitting at high power reduces the lifetime of both the nodes and the network. One efficient way of power management is to control the power at which the nodes transmit. In this paper, a virtual multiple input multiple output wireless sensor network (VMIMO-WSN) communication architecture is considered and the power control of sensor nodes based on the approach of game theory is formulated. The use of game theory has proliferated, with a broad range of applications in wireless sensor networking. Approaches from game theory can be used to optimize node level as well as network wide performance. The game here is categorized as an incomplete information game, in which the nodes do not have complete information about the strategies taken by other nodes. For virtual multiple input multiple output wireless sensor network architecture considered the Nash equilibrium is used to decide the optimal power level at which a node needs to transmit, to maximize its utility. Outcome shows that the game theoretic approach considered for VMIMO-WSN architecture achieves the best utility, by consuming less power.

Keywords: Wireless sensor networks, Power control, Game theory.

1 Introduction

The birth of wireless sensor network (WSN) has brought out the practical aspects of pervasive computing and networking. Wireless sensor networks have been used in the context of high end applications, security applications and consumer applications. The sensors are responsible for data collection, sensing or monitoring a specific environment. Generally sensors are battery powered and have feeble data processing capability and short radio range [1].

Energy consumption is a major constraint in WSN as it determines the lifetime of a sensor and that of a sensor network. Battery capacity is limited and it is usually impossible to replace them. Data communication is the main consumer of energy in WSN. Hence transmission at optimal power level is very essential. An approach for

N. Meghanathan et al. (Eds.): CCSIT 2011, Part II, CCIS 132, pp. 535–545, 2011.

node energy conservation in sensor network is cooperative multi input-multi output transmission technique [2]. The best modulation and transmission strategy to minimize the total energy consumption required to send a given number of bits is analyzed in [3]. In this paper, a game theoretic approach to regulate the transmit power level of the nodes in a VMIMO-WSN is considered and investigated. The concept of game theory has been used in networks for designing mechanisms to induce desirable equilibria both by offering incentives and by punishing nodes [4-7].

The rest of the paper is organized as follows. Section 2 examines some related works in transmission power control and also analyses VMIMO. Section 3, deals with the system model of VMIMO-WSN. In Section 4, the basics of game theory and its application in sensor networks is discussed. A non-cooperative power control game is constructed and a utility function suitable for VMIMO-WSN is designed. Simulation results are given and discussed in section 5. Finally, conclusion of the work is given in Section 6.

2   Related Work

Transmission power control is an imperative process to improve the performance of the network. With shorter communication ranges, the probability of hidden terminals and the number of collisions is smaller, reducing energy consumption. However, it may split the whole network. Increased transmission power may bring interference and unnecessary energy cost. There have many power control algorithms for WSNs such as COMPOW (COMmon POWer), LEACH (Low Energy Adaptive Clustering Hierarchy). In COMPOW [8] a minimum common transmitting range needed to ensure network connectivity is adopted. The outcomes show that the value of the transmitting range has the beneficial effects of maximizing network capacity, reducing the contention to access the wireless channel and minimizing energy consumption. The LEACH [9] based algorithm lets some nodes to be cluster leader and uses higher transmission power to help the neighbour transmitting data to the sink. Channel fading and radio interference pose a big challenge for power control in wireless sensor networks. To reduce the fading effects in wireless channel, multi-input multi-output (MIMO) scheme is utilized for sensor network [2]. In the physical layer, multiple antenna techniques have been shown to be very effective in improving the performance of wireless systems in the form of diversity gain, array gain and multiplexing gain. Many schemes proposed in previous researches [2,3] have shown that diversity can influence in the physical, data link or network layer to provide reliable transmission with low power and can extend the network lifetime. But incorporating multiple antennas directly to sensor nodes is impractical. Cooperative MIMO schemes have been proposed [2] to improve the communication performance.

3   Virtual MIMO Wireless Sensor Network

Multiple-input-multiple-output (MIMO), or multiple antenna communication is one of the techniques that has received significant importance in wireless systems. However, a drawback of MIMO techniques is that they require intricate transceiver circuitry and huge sum of signal processing power ensuing in large power consumptions at the circuit level. This fact has prohibited the application of MIMO techniques to wireless sensor networks consisting of battery operated sensor nodes. And also nodes in a wireless sensor network may not be able to accommodate multiple antennas. Due to the circuit complexity and obscurity of integrating separate antenna, virtual MIMO concepts are applied in wireless sensor networks for energy efficient communication to hoard energy and enhance reliability. The optimum time management and power budget allocation for virtual MIMO is proposed [10] and the analysis of this shows that virtual MIMO functions like actual MIMO for low signal to noise ratio. The concept of VMIMO is explained in Fig. 1 which shows the scenario of using three transmitters and two receivers. The sender node, S, transmits a message to the destination node, D. First, S transmits the message to three transmitter nodes, t1, t2, and t3. These transmitter nodes transmit the message to the receiver nodes, r1 and r2. Then, the receiver nodes forward the message to the destination node, D.

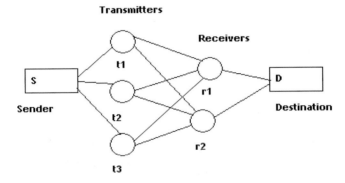

Fig. 1. Virtual MIMO scenario

The total power consumption along a signal path in a VMIMO can be alienated into two main components [2, 3]: the power consumption of all the power amplifiers P_{PA} and the power consumption of all other circuit blocks P_C.

The total power consumption of the power amplifiers can be approximated as

$$P_{PA} = (1 + \alpha) P_{out} \tag{1}$$

where P_{out} is the transmit power which depends on the Friss free space transmission, $\alpha = \xi/\eta - 1$ with η being the drain efficiency of the RF power amplifier and ξ being the peak-to-average ratio (PAR) that depends on the modulation scheme and the constellation size.

The total circuit power consumption for a VMIMO is estimated as

$$P_C \approx N_T \left(P_{DAC} + P_{mix} + P_{filt} \right) + 2P_{synth} + N_R \left(P_{LNA} + P_{mix} + P_{IFA} + P_{filr} + P_{ADC} \right) \tag{2}$$

where P_{DAC}, P_{mix}, P_{filt}, P_{synth}, P_{LNA}, P_{IFA}, P_{filr} and P_{ADC} are the power consumption values for the D/A converter (DAC), the mixer, the active filters at the transmitter side, the frequency synthesizer, the low noise amplifier (LNA), the intermediate frequency amplifier (IFA), the active filters at the receiver side and the A/D converter (ADC).

The total power consumption P_{total} is given by,

$$P_{total} = P_{PA} + P_C \tag{3}$$

If the transmission power of each sending node in a single input single output network is P_{total}, the transmission power of each sending node in $N_T \times N_R$ network will be $P_{total}/\min(N_T,N_R)$.

4 Game Theory for Sensor Networks

Game theory is a theory of decision making under conditions of uncertainty and interdependence. A strategic game consists of: a set of players, a set of actions for each player and preferences over the set of action profiles for each player. In any game utility represents the motivation of players. If there is a set of strategies with the property that no player can profit by changing his or her strategy while the other players keep their strategies unchanged, then that set of strategies and the corresponding payoffs constitute the Nash equilibrium. Energy harvesting technologies essential for independent sensor networks using a non cooperative game theoretic technique [11] is proposed and analyzed. Nash equilibrium was projected as the solution of this game to attain the optimal probabilities of sleep and wake up states that were used for energy conservation. The energy efficiency problem in wireless sensor networks as the maximum network lifetime routing problem [12] is looked upon. Here the transmit power levels is adjusted to just reach the anticipated next hop receiver such that the energy consumption rate per unit information transmission can be reduced.

Non Cooperative Power Control Game

The game is considered when node 'i' is transmitting to node 'j'. The existence of some strategy sets $p_1,p_2,...p_{N+1}$ for the nodes 1,2....N+1 is assumed. These sets consist of all possible power levels ranging from the minimum transmit power p_{min} to maximum transmit power p_{max}. In this game, if node 1 chooses its power level p_1, and node 2 chooses its power level p_2, and so on, then,

$$p = \{p_1, p_2 \cdots p_{N+1}\} \tag{4}$$

This vector of individual strategies is called a strategy profile. The set of all such strategy profiles is called the space of strategy profiles P'. The game is played by having all the nodes concurrently pick their individual strategies. This set of choices results in some strategy profile $p \in P'$, and is called as the outcome of the game. At the end of an action, each node $i \in I$ receives a utility value,

$$u_i(p) = u_i(p_i, p_{-i}) \tag{5}$$

p_{-i} is the strategy profile of all the nodes but for the ith node.

The utility to any one node depends on the entire strategy profile. During every game, the node decides whether to transmit or not, rise or lower its power level, and chooses a power level if it decides to transmit. The ith node has control over its own power level p_i only, and the utility if a node is transmitting is given as [13]

$$u_i(p_i,p_{-i}) = \frac{br}{Fp_i}(f(\gamma_j))$$ (6)

where
b   is the number of information bits in a packet of size F bits
r   is the transmission rate in bits/sec using strategy p_i
$f(\gamma_j)$ is the efficiency function which increases with expected signal to interference noise ratio (SINR) of the receiving node. The efficiency function, is defined as
$f(\gamma_j) = (1-2P_e)^F$
where P_e is the bit error rate (BER) and it is a function of SINR. With a noncoherent frequency shift keying (FSK) modulation scheme, $P_e = 0.5e^{\frac{-\gamma_j}{2}}$, with a differential phase shift keying (DPSK) modulation scheme $P_e = 0.5e^{-\gamma_j}$, and with a binary phase shift keying (BPSK) modulation scheme, $P_e = 0.5e^{\sqrt{\gamma_j}}$,where γ_j denotes the expected SINR of node j. It is assumed that the utility value obtained by a node when it decides not to transmit is 0.
For a VMIMO-WSN, the net utility is given by

$$u_i(p_i,p_{-i}) = \sum_{j=1}^{N_R} \frac{br_j}{F\sum_{i=1}^{min(N_T,N_R)} \frac{p_i}{min(N_T,N_R)}}(f(\gamma_j))$$ (7)

where N_T and N_R are the number of cooperative sensors which act as VMIMO transmitting and receiving antennas respectively.
With the utility defined, the net utility is obtained by considering the penalty incurred by a node. The penalty incurred accounts for the energy drained by the nodes with the usage of transmission power. If the strategy of the ith node is to transmit at signal power $p \in P'$, the cost incurred is a function of p_i, which is denoted as $A(p_i)$. p_i is a random variable denoting transmitting signal power of ith node.

$$A(p_i) = k \times p_i$$ (8)

where k is the scaling factor.
The net utility

$$u_i^{net} = \begin{cases} u_i(p_i,p_{-i})-A(p_i), & \text{if transmitting} \\ 0, & \text{if not transmitting} \end{cases}$$ (9)

A node cannot transmit at arbitrarily high power and must make a decision on a maximum threshold power p_t. Exceeding this threshold will bring in non beneficial net utility for the node. A node transmits at a power level p_i such that $0 < p_i \leq p_t$. As far as Nash equilibrium point is concerned, the expected net utility for transmitting and for being silent should be equal at the threshold, i.e., $p_i = p_t$.

$$p_s = 1 - (1 - p_e)^F \qquad (10)$$

where p_s is the probability of successful transmission of a packet containing F bits from node 'i' to node 'j'.

5   Results and Discussion

For performance evaluation, it is assumed that a source node is transmitting data to a destination node. The destination node not only hears from source but also from other neighbouring nodes if they are transmitting. If γ_j is the SINR alleged by destination, then the bit error probability for the link is given by some inverse function of γ_j. The bit corruption is assumed to be independently and identically distributed. The simulation was carried in MATLAB 7.8 and the simulation parameters are given in Table.1. The performance of the proposed VMIMO-WSN using game theoretic approach is evaluated in terms of net utility and power efficiency, for various power levels and varying channel conditions.

Table 1. Simulation Parameters

Simulation Parameter	Description
Transmission Power	1mW, 100mW
Signal to interference noise ratio (SINR)	-15dB to 15dB
Number of information bits per frame (b)	32 bits
Number of bits per frame (F)	40 bits
Modulation	BPSK, DPSK, FSK
Data Transmission rate	1 Mbps
Number of transmitting and receiving antennas (N_T, N_R)	2,2

5.1   Average Probability of Error

In the receiver side BER is affected by transmission channel noise, interference, distortion and fading. Fig. 2 shows the average probability of error for different values of SINR(dB) alleged by node j.

The result shows that with improvement in channel condition, the average bit error rate decreases. DPSK and FSK exhibit higher error rates compared to BPSK which makes BPSK appropriate for low-cost passive transmitters. This feature enables BPSK to be used as the modulation scheme in IEEE 802.15.4, 868–915 MHz frequency band.

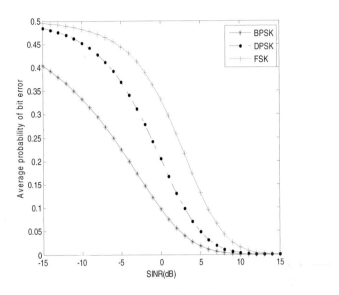

Fig. 2. Average probability of bit error

5.2 Probability of Successful Frame Transmission

The probability of successful frame transmission depends on the channel conditions and the probability of bit error. Fig.3 shows the frame success probability for different values of SINR(dB) perceived by node j. The results show that with increase in SINR, the average bit error rate decreases which in turn increases the probability of

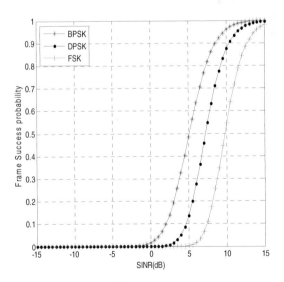

Fig. 3. Probabilty of successful transmission

successful transmission. DPSK and FSK incur a higher probability of bit error, which in turn leads to higher probability of frame error.

5.3 Power Efficiency

The performance of a modulation scheme is often measured in terms of its power efficiency. Power efficiency describes the ability of a modulation technique to preserve the fidelity of the digital message at low power levels. Figs. 4 and 5 show the

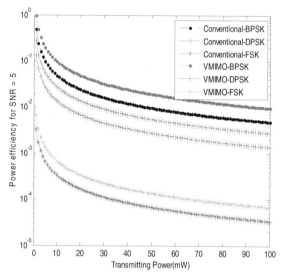

Fig. 4. Power efficiency for SINR=5dB

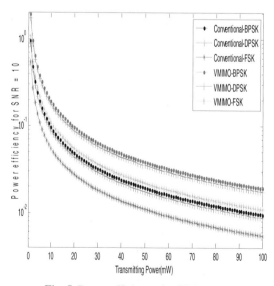

Fig. 5. Power efficiency for SINR=10dB

power efficiency attained both in the case of conventional and VMIMO scheme for different values of signal to interference noise ratio.

If SINR is low and transmitting power P is high, the power efficiency is almost zero. During worse channel conditions, a node should not transmit and this only increases the power consumption. The result indicates that the increase in power efficiency is due to the exploitation of multiple antennas used for transmission and reception. At high SINR, a node should transmit with low power to maximize its power efficiency. Here, increasing transmitting power unnecessarily will decrease the power efficiency below its maximum. When the interference from neighbouring nodes is less, then the SINR increases and in this case all the modulation schemes considered provide near equal performance.

5.4 Net Utility

Net utility is computed by considering the benefit received and the cost incurred $A(p_i)$ for transmissions as discussed in section 4. Fig.6 shows the disparity of the net utility with increasing transmitting power. It is perceptive that there will be an optimal value of p_i, beyond which the net utility will only decline. A subset of nodes is assumed to be active and operate with fixed strategies. In VMIMO the subset of nodes cooperate to transmit the data from source to destination.

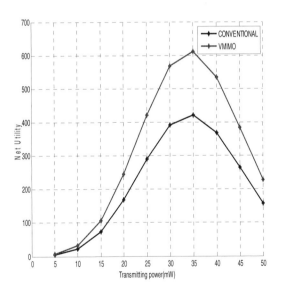

Fig. 6. Net utility for discrete power levels

When the transmitting power is 15mW, VMIMO provides an improvement of 5% in net utility as compared to the conventional scheme. As the transmitting power is increased further, at an optimal p_i, there is an increase in net utility by 27%. From this figure, it is intuitive that a transmitting power level of 35mW gives the best response for the node. As long as the transmitting power complies with the threshold the net utility increases. It is also evident from this figure that even if the node unilaterally changes its strategy and does not transmit with the optimum transmitting power level, the node will not get its best response and will not be able to reach Nash equilibrium. The Nash equilibrium point is the best operating point to increase the traditional utility function.

6 Conclusion

This paper provides a non cooperative game theoretic approach to solve the problem of power control found in wireless sensor networks. The nodes in the sensor network cooperate to transmit the data from source to destination. A utility function with an intrinsic property of power control was designed and power allocation to nodes was built into a non-cooperative game. The performance and existence of Nash equilibrium is analyzed. In the case of VMIMO-WSN the node transmits only when the channel conditions are good and its transmission power is below the threshold power level. Results show that the game theoretic approach used in VMIMO-WSN enhances the net utility by minimizing the power at which the nodes transmit. The outcome of the simulation results also shows the desired power level at which the nodes should transmit to maximize their utilities.

References

1. Akyildiz, F., Su, W., Sankarasubramaniam, Y., Cayirci, E.: A survey on sensor networks. IEEE Communications Magazine, 102–114 (2002)
2. Cui, S., Goldsmith, A.J., Bahai, A.: Energy-efficiency of MIMO and cooperative MIMO techniques in sensor networks. IEEE Journal on Selected Areas of Communications 22(6), 1089–1098 (2004)
3. Cui, S., Goldsmith, A.J., Bahai, A.: Energy constraint modulation optimization. IEEE Transactions on Wireless Communication 4(5), 2349–2360 (2005)
4. Buchegger, S., Le Boudec, J.: Performance analysis of the CONFIDANT protocol. In: 3rd ACM International Symposium on Mobile AdHoc Networking & Computing, pp. 226–236 (2002)
5. Buttyan, L., Hubaux, J.P.: Nuglets: A virtual currency to stimulate cooperation in selforganized mobile ad-hoc networks. Technical report, DSC/2001/001, Swiss Fed. Inst. Of Technology (2001)
6. Wang, W., Chatterjee, M., Kwiat, K.: Enforcing cooperation in ad-hoc networks with unreliable channel. In: 5th IEEE International Conference on Mobile Ad-Hoc and Sensor Systems (MASS), pp. 456–462 (2008)
7. Srinivasan, V., Nuggehalli, P., Chiasserini, C., Rao, R.: Cooperation in wireless ad-hoc networks. In: IEEE INFOCOM, vol. 2, pp. 808–817 (2003)
8. Narayanaswamy, S., Kawadia, V., Sreenivas, R., Kumar, P.: Power control in ad hoc networks: Theory, architecture, algorithm and implementation of the COMPOW protocol. In: European Conference on Wireless Communication, pp. 15–22 (2002)
9. Kejun, D., Xingshe, Z., Xinguo, Z., Zhigang, L.: HETCP: A Hierarchical energy efficient topology control protocol for wireless sensor networks. In: International Conference on Wireless Communication, Networking and Mobile Computing, Wuhan, pp. 1–4 (2006)

10. del Coso, A., Savazzi, S., Spagnolini, U., Ibars, C.: A simple transmit diversity technique for wireless communications. In: 40th Annual Conference on Information Sciences and Systems (2006)
11. Niyato, D., Hossain, E., Rashid, M., Bhargava, V.: Wireless sensor networks with energy harvesting technologies: A Game-theoretic approach to optimal energy management. IEEE Wireless Communication 14(4), 90–96 (2007)
12. Chang, J., Tassiulas, L.: Maximum lifetime routing in wireless sensor networks. IEEE/ACM Transactions on Networking 12(4), 609–619 (2004)
13. Xing, Y., Chandramouli, R.: Distributed discrete power control for bursty transmissions over wireless data networks. In: IEEE International Conference on Communication, vol. 1, pp. 139–143 (2004)

Protocols for Network and Data Link Layer in WSNs: A Review and Open Issues

Ankit Jain, Deepak Sharma, Mohit Goel, and A.K. Verma

Computer Science and Engineering Department,
Thapar University Patiala, Punjab, India
{jain.ank8,dee.rip01,mgoel9}@gmail.com,
akverma@thapar.edu

Abstract. Recent development in wireless sensor network (WSN) has shown the importance of routing protocols as they differ in application and networking architecture. The efficiency of WSNs strongly depends on the routing protocol used. In this paper, we have discussed some of the important protocols of network and data-link layer. Various issues such as energy efficiency, lifetime, scalability of network and mobility of nodes have been discussed here. The paper concludes with open research issues.

Keywords: Data link layer, network layer, protocols, wireless sensor networks.

1 Introduction

Recent advances in micro-electro-mechanical systems (MEMS) and low power and highly integrated digital electronics have led to the development of micro sensors [1]. Wireless Sensor Networks (WSNs) are composed of large number of sensor nodes which are deployed in the vicinity or inside the physical environment. Sensor nodes are provided with facility of computation and therefore, instead of transmitting raw data to the nodes responsible for fusion they transmit required data or partially processed data which saves energy. In WSNs, maximizing battery lifetime is a very important design criterion, because in many applications changing or recharging battery after deployment is not economical or feasible.

Routing in sensor networks is very challenging due to several characteristics that distinguish them from contemporary communication and wireless ad-hoc networks. First, it has limited resources i.e. power, processing capacity and storage capacity. Second, unique ID based system such as IP is not possible because they are deployed randomly in large numbers. Third, it has high data redundancy due to presence of large number sensor within the vicinity of event. Therefore, in order to meet these challenges we need different routing protocols other than the traditional wireless protocols. The paper is organized as follows. In section 2, we have discussed network layer. Section 3, discusses Data Link layer. Section 4 concludes the paper with comparative summary and open research area.

N. Meghanathan et al. (Eds.): CCSIT 2011, Part II, CCIS 132, pp. 546–555, 2011.

2 Network Layer

Our main aim in network layer is to develop energy efficient routing protocol and reliable transmission of data from nodes to sink. It can contribute in increasing lifetime of the network [1]. Network layer routing protocols are divided into four groups: (1) data–centric, (2) hierarchical, (3) location-based, and (4) QoS-based. Here we discuss some important data-centric and hierarchical protocols.

2.1 Data-Centric

Sensor nodes are deployed randomly in large number and therefore it is not feasible to assign unique IDs to each sensor node. The lack of unique ID and randomness make it difficult to collect data from a specific set of sensor modes. Therefore, data is usually transmitted from each sensor node which consumes a large amount of energy but since wireless sensor networks have energy constraints this approach is not feasible. The energy inefficiency in traditional routing method has led to consideration of different routing protocol, data-centric protocol. In data-centric routing, routing protocols route the data based on description of data [2].

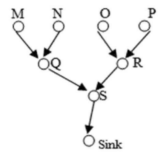

Fig. 1. Data aggregation

Since in data-centric approach we query from certain regions and not from individual node, we need attribute based naming. It is used to specify the properties of data. We are interested in sensing a specific region and not a specific node.

Data is aggregated from nodes M and N at Q and from O and P at R and this data is further aggregated at S as shown in Fig. 1. The main aim of the data aggregation is to reduce redundancy and save energy. Data aggregation is shown in Fig. 1.

Directed Diffusion. Directed Diffusion [3] is a very important data-centric routing protocol. In directed diffusion routing, task descriptor naming is used and this type of naming is based on attribute-value pairs. This type of naming is used for both type of data i.e. request data and response data. Interest, defined by task descriptor, is injected in a node called sink. The sink broadcasts this interest through its neighbours. Each interest has a requested data type, timestamp field i.e. the time when interest was entered or refreshed, interval between two responses, expire time of interest entry, geographical area, etc. Every node has an interest cache which maintains a list of interests. Interest entry also contains several gradient fields. A gradient is a response link established from a node which receives the interest to the node which sends the interest. It has data rate field and duration field. A gradient is removed after getting expired, but point is that all gradient entries will not expire simultaneously. In Fig. 2, interest propagation and initial gradient setup has been shown.

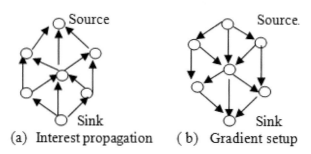

(a) Interest propagation   (b) Gradient setup

Fig. 2. Interest propagation and Gradient setup

When a node witnesses an event, it tries to match the data with entries in its interest cache. If a match exists, node sends the sensed data to all its outgoing gradients. Node that receives the data tries to match the received data with its interest entries. If no match exists, it gets discarded and if match exists then the data cache which keeps the record of recent data with each interest entry is checked. If received data has a match in data cache then this received data is discarded. Hence, we can stop looping. If all gradients of matching interest list is greater than or equal to incoming data events, the node will send the all events. But, if one of the gradients is having value less than incoming events then the number of events send will be downconvert [3] i.e. reduced according to gradient value. Reinforcement is implemented in directed diffusion by reinforcing those neighbours which are sending data at low in order to draw data at high rates.

In directed diffusion, each node has caching and aggregation facility which results in energy efficient communication. Path repair through reinforcement is also possible. Negative reinforcement is used to prune alternate paths because they deliver data with high latency and expend more energy. It is not good for those applications where continuous data delivery to sink is required since it is based on query-driven data delivery model.

Rumor Routing. Rumor routing [4] is an energy efficient data-centric routing protocol. In directed diffusion, a query is generally flooded in absence of geographic routing criteria which consumes a lot of energy. In directed diffusion, a query is flooded while in some cases event can also be flooded if number of queries is very less than number of events. Rumor routing is a compromise between query flooding and event flooding. Each node maintains a list of neighbours and events. Whenever a node detects an event it adds it into its list and probabilistically generates an agent.

Agent is a long lived packet used to propagate the event. Agent carries a list of events it has encountered along with the number of hops to that event. When an agent travels from one node to other nodes, it keeps updating their list with its own list. The agent tries to create straight paths by avoiding recent visited nodes and neighbour of current node. Whenever an agent crosses a path leading to another event, it starts to create an aggregate path to both events. The agent tries not to form loops by avoiding recent visited nodes and neighbour of current node. Query generated by a node is routed to event if path is known and if path is unknown it forwards it to its neighbour. If it is forwarded to random neighbour, it avoids looping by maintaining a list of visited nodes. Agents and queries both have time to live i.e. TTL after which they expire [1]. Rumor routing algorithm is shown in Fig. 3.

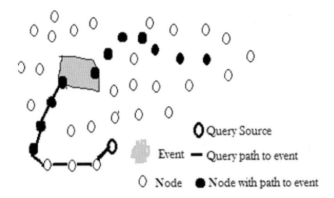

Fig. 3. Query is originated from the query source and searches for a path to the event. As soon as it finds a node on the path, it's routed directly to the event.

Simulation results have shown that performance of this algorithm does not vary significantly even this algorithm is based on random decisions. It is an effective algorithm when events cannot be located geographically. It maintains a single path between source and destination while Directed diffusion maintains multiple paths. It is able to handle node failure. It is much more energy efficient algorithm than event folding but number of events should be small. Another issue related to this algorithm is tuning the algorithm parameters such as TTL for agents and queries [1].

2.2 Hierarchical Protocols

Hierarchical Protocols have been developed to face the challenges imposed by scalability and energy consumption. In hierarchical architecture, sensors organize themselves into clusters and each cluster has a cluster head, which fuse and aggregate data to conserve energy. Some of the important hierarchical protocols are LEACH [5], PEGASIS [2], TEEN [2], APTEEN [2], etc. In this paper we have discussed the LEACH protocol.

LEACH: Low-Energy Adaptive Clustering Hierarchy. It is a very popular clustering protocol [5] in which nodes organize themselves into local clusters, having one node as cluster as cluster head. Cluster heads keep changing with time in order to maintain energy balance of all nodes. Optimal number of cluster heads is estimated to be 5% of the total number of nodes [1]. On the basis of energy left at the node, each node decides independently of the other nodes about whether to be cluster head or not. Node made this decision by choosing a random number between 0 and 1. The node becomes a cluster head for the current round if number is less than a threshold T (n):

$$T (n) = \begin{cases} P (1-P*[r \bmod (1/p)]) & \text{if n belongs to 0} \\ \\ 0 & \text{otherwise.} \end{cases} \quad (1)$$

where P = the desired Percentage of cluster heads (e.g. 0.05), r is = the current round, and G is the set of nodes that have not been cluster-heads in the last 1/p rounds.

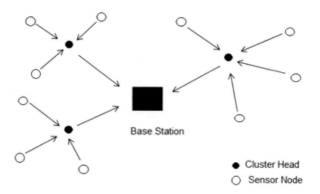

Fig. 4. Communication in leach protocol

Each selected cluster head advertises itself as a cluster head and then on the basis of received signal strength sensor nodes decide the cluster they want to belong. Afterwards, each node informs the cluster head that it will be the member of its cluster. Each cluster-heads assign the time on which the sensor nodes can send the data based to cluster head based on Time Division Multiple Access approach. After receiving all the data, the cluster head node performs signal processing functions to compress the data into a single signal. This compress signal is sent to the base station. Transmission from one cluster can interfere with another cluster and therefore to reduce this type of interference each cluster communicates using different CDMA codes.

LEACH is completely distributed, self-organized, and requires no global knowledge of network. It achieves over a factor of 7 reduction in energy dissipation compared to direct communication and a factor of 4-8 compared to the minimum transmission energy routing protocol. In this protocol, first node death occurs 8 times later and last node death occurs 3 times later than any other protocol i.e. nodes life increase significantly. However, it is not applicable to networks deployed in large region because it uses single-hop routing where each node can transmit directly to the cluster-head and the sink. It uses Time Division Multiple Access (TDMA) as a scheduling mechanism which makes it prone to long delays when applied to large sensor networks.

3 Data Link Layer

The main objectives of the data link layer are multiplexing/demultiplexing of data, data frame detection, medium access, and error control. Each sensor node shares the same physical wireless medium with other nodes inside their transmission region. Since the nodes communicate through a common wireless multiple access channels, the design of Medium Access Control (MAC) layer is of crucial importance.

The MAC protocols are divided it into two major categories:

1. Reservation-based Medium Access
2. Contention-based Medium Access

3.1 Reservation-Based Medium Access

Reservation based protocols have the advantage of collision-free communication since each node transmits data to a central agent during its reserved slot, hence these are time-division multiple access (TDMA)-based protocols. The main idea is to divide the network into clusters and each node communicates according to a specific super-frame structure. The super-frame structure generally consists of two main parts .The reservation period, which is used by the nodes to reserve their slots for communication through a central agent, i.e., cluster-head. The data period consists of multiple slots that are used by each sensor for transmitting information.

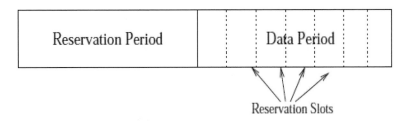

Fig. 5. General frame structure for TDMA-based MAC protocols

Lightweight MAC (LMAC). It has been adopted for RCX robots and for a different scenario where all nodes are mobile [6]. It divides a frame into 32 equal slots. Each slot can be assigned to only one node and this node has control over this time slot, so each node can use its own time slot to transfer data without having to content for the medium or deal with energy wasting collision of transmissions.

A slot consists of a 12 bytes traffic control section (Table 1) and a fixed-length data section. When a node wants to send a packet, it waits until its time-slot comes around, then broadcasts a message header in the control section detailing the destination and length, and then immediately proceeds with the transmitting of data. If a node which has already chosen a slot number starts moving, it may reach one-hop neighbourhood of another node with the same slot number, so they will collide as both start transmission in the same time (same slot number). Then they will be informed by other neighbours, and after waiting for a back off time, they will choose another free slot number.

Table 1. The Control Message used in LMAC

Description	Size (bytes)
Identification	2
Current Slot Number	1
Occupied Slots	4
Distance to Gateway	1
Collision in Slot	1
Destination ID	2
Data Size (bytes)	1
Total	**12**

Mobile-LMAC (M-LMAC). The main problem with LMAC is that, if the mobile node enters a crowded area, it may find no free slot number after one back off time, so the protocol fails to continue. Therefore, modify LMAC to M-LMAC [7]. Since mobility causes this problem, it can help to solve it, too. In other words, when some mobile nodes leave the crowded area, other nodes can find some free slot numbers and do their slot reselection easily. So, when there is no free slot number, the node is allowed to wait for more than one back off time until it succeeds to find a free slot number. However, during this time "waiting for reselection", when these nodes do not have any assigned slot numbers, they cannot send any packets which have been forwarded to them. Therefore, these packets may be delivered after a long waiting time which may not be acceptable. To prevent this case, we add a field to the control message that register the time in which this control frame has been sent. In this way, every node can periodically update its neighbour list. Therefore, in M-LMAC, when a mobile node reaches a crowded area and collides with another node, it gives up its slot number and goes to the "waiting for reselection" mode. Also, during this waiting time it will be removed from the neighbouring list of all its physical neighbours. As a result, no frames are routed to this node from its physical neighbours. The only case in which it needs to send a frame is when its own application layer generates a packet. In this case, the node should wait until it finds a free slot number and then waits for its turn to send the packet.

Overall, TDMA-based protocols provide collision-free communication in the WSN, achieving improved energy efficiency. However, such TDMA-based protocols require an infrastructure consisting of cluster heads which coordinate the time slots assigned to each node .In addition, TDMA-based protocols cause high latency due to the frame structure. Hence, TDMA-based MAC protocols may not be suitable for WSN applications where delay is important in estimating event features and the traffic has bursty nature.

3.2 Contention-Based Medium Access

The contention-based protocols generally do not require any infrastructure such as clusters since every node tries to access the channel based on carrier sense mechanism. These protocols provide robustness and scalability to the network. However, the probability of collision increases with the increase in node density.

Sensor-MAC (S-MAC). The primary goal of this protocol [8] is to reduce energy consumption. Besides, it has also achieved good scalability and collision avoidance by utilizing a combined scheduling and contention scheme.

It achieves efficient energy consumption by using a scheme of periodic listen and sleep which reduces energy consumption by avoiding idle listening. To maintain synchronization, for every a predefined number (which is usually ten) of cycles, each node broadcasts its schedule in a SYNC message, so that its neighbours can update that information in their schedule tables. To avoid two neighbour nodes never see each other, each node periodically follows the neighbour discovery scheme. For this scheme, the synchronization period (10 seconds) is repeated every 2 minutes. SMAC does not require all nodes in the entire network, but only in each virtual cluster to synchronize. This design increases latency, since sender must wait for the receiver to wake up before it can send out data. Hence a new technique, called Adaptive Listen which is able to greatly reduce such latency, in which S-MAC tries to coordinate and synchronize neighbour's sleep schedules to reduce latency and control overhead, is majorly used.

Mobility-Aware Sensor MAC (MS-MAC). The objective of this MAC [9] protocol in sensor networks is a protocol that can work energy-efficiently in both stationary scenarios as well as when there are mobile nodes. To achieve this objective, we take S-MAC as a starting point and extend the protocol to support mobile sensors. The mobility aware MAC protocol for sensor networks (MS-MAC) would work similar to S-MAC to conserve energy when nodes are stationary. At the other extreme, this medium access scheme may also switch to work similar to IEEE 802.11 for a mobile ad hoc scenario (MANET).

The SMAC protocol works well when the network is mainly stationary, in which the connection formations and brake-ups are not frequent. If a mobile node wants to set up a new connection with a new node in a different cluster, it has to wait for a new synchronization period (which is 10 seconds every 2 minutes), to be able to detect the SYNC message from the new node. During this connection setup time, the mobile node is disconnected from the rest of the network. This waiting period of up to 2 minutes could be far too long for some time critical applications.

To expedite connection setups, a new mechanism in MS-MAC has been introduced to handle mobility based on actual mobility status of nodes. Each node discovers the presence of mobility within its neighbourhood based on the received signal levels of

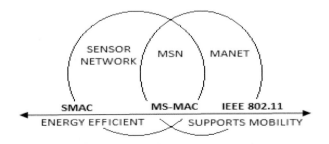

Fig. 6. MS-MAC duty cycle varies with level of mobility

periodical SYNC messages from its neighbours. If there is a change in a signal received from a neighbour, it presumes that the neighbour or it-self are moving. The level of change in the received signals also predicts the level of the mobile's speed. Instead of storing only information on the schedule of the sender node as for SMAC, the SYNC message in MS-MAC also includes information on the estimated speed of its mobile neighbour or mobility information. If there is more than one mobile neighbour, then the SYNC message only includes the maximum estimated speed among all neighbours. This mobility information is used by neighbours to create an active zone around a mobile node when it moves from one cluster to another cluster, so that the mobile node can expedite connection setup with new neighbours before it loses all its neighbours. In the active zone, nodes run the synchronization periods more often resulting in higher energy consumption, but the time it takes to create new connections is lower.

Low-Latency MAC (LL-MAC). This protocol [10] improves the problem of the conflict between energy efficiency and low-latency. This scheme uses asynchrony (ASYNC) message package to broadcast the schedule information between neighbour nodes instead of SYNC package in S-MAC, and brings in a stagger active schedule which derives from DMAC, it ensures the sender and the receiver node will be both active for one packet transmitting time, which avoids the data forwarding interruption problem and reduces the transmission latency.

4 Conclusion and Open Issues

Routing in sensor network has a lot of importance in order to face the challenges imposed by wireless sensor networks.

- Directed diffusion is not efficient when geographic routing criteria is not possible. However, rumor routing is efficient in this condition. LEACH has addressed the issue of scalability and energy efficiency of sensor nodes.
- SMAC protocol is energy efficient, but suffers performance degradation when nodes are mobile. MS-MAC adds mobility handling to S-MAC, but can only handle a single mobile node that collects data from stationary nodes. M-LMAC (Mobile LMAC) as a TDMA-based MAC protocol which can support continuous mobility in the wireless sensor networks.

Table 2. Comparison of Reservation and Contention Based Medium Access

Reservation based (using TDMA)	Contention based
Energy efficient	Less energy efficient
Minimal collisions	Greater collisions
Latency	Less latency
Requires overhead of clusters	No need for overhead on cluster head

Attribute-value based query might not be sufficient for complex queries. Cluster based routing has overhead of forming clusters as well as they have latency in data communication. Therefore, some of the important issues for research in future are:

- Developing efficient naming techniques for data-centric routing
- Developing efficient protocols for cluster creation in hierarchical routing that reduce the latency.
- Developing energy consumption and incorporating techniques such as cross layer integration and spatio-temporal correlation.

Hence, we believe that working on these open research issues can help us to lead to the ultimate goal of WSN phenomenon discussed in this paper.

References

1. Akkaya, K., Younis, M.: A Survey on Routing Protocols for Wireless Sensor Networks. Ad Hoc Networks 3(3), 325–349 (2005)
2. Akyildiz, I.F., Vuran, M.C., Akan, O.B., Su, W.: Wireless Sensor Networks: A Survey Revisited. Computer Networks Journal (2005)
3. Intanagonwiwat, C., Govindan, R., Estrin, D.: Directed diffusion: A scalable and robust communication paradigm for sensor networks. In: 6th Annual ACM/IEEE International Conference on Mobile Computing and Networking, Mobicom, Boston, USA, pp. 56–67 (August 2000)
4. Braginsky, D., Estrin, D.: Rumor Routing Algorithm for Sensor Networks. In: First Workshop on Sensor Networks and Applications, WSNA, Atlanta, GA, pp. 22–31 (October 2002)
5. Heinzelman, W., Chandrakasan, A., Balakrishna, H.: Energy-efficient communication protocol for wireless sensor networks. In: Hawaii International Conference System Sciences, Hawaii (January 2000)
6. van Hoesel, L., Havinga, P.: A lightweight medium access protocol (LMAC) for wireless sensor networks: reducing preamble transmissions and transceiver state switches. In: The International Conference on Networked Sensing Systems (INSS), SenSys, pp. 303–304 (2004)
7. Mank, S., Karnapke, R., Nolte, J.: An adaptive TDMA based MAC Protocol for Mobile Wireless Sensor Networks In: International Conference on Sensor Technologies and Applications, Spain (2007)
8. Ye, W., Heidemann, J., Estrin, D.: An Energy-Efficient MAC protocol for Wireless Sensor Networks. In: USI/ISI technical report ISI-TR-543 (September 2001)
9. LAN MAN Standards Committee of the IEEE Computer Society: Wireless LAN Medium Access Control (MAC) and Physical Layer (PHY) specifications. IEEE Std 802.11-1999, IEEE (1999)
10. Yu, Q.C., Tan, C., Zhou, H.: A Low-Latency MAC Protocol for Wireless Sensor Networks. In: International Conference on Wireless Communications, Networking and Mobile Computing, Shanghai. IEEE, Los Alamitos (2007)

Psychoacoustic Models for Heart Sounds

Kiran Kumari Patil[1,*], B.S. Nagabhushan[2], and B.P. Vijay Kumar[2]

[1] Research Scholar at Dr. MGR University, Chennai
[2] Reva Institute of Technology and Management,
Bangalore
kiran_b_patil@rediffmail.com,
nagabhushanab@kpitcummins.com,
vijaykbp@yahoo.co.in

Abstract. The phonocardiography (PCG) — the art and science of recording and interpreting of heart sounds using latest digital technology has significantly helped us to understand and interpret the complex heart sounds (normal, abnormal sounds including murmurs) and in particular valvular diseases. In general, the classification and interpretation of heart sounds and murmurs is based on a adjective 0-6/6 grade scale and described by using "faint", "soft", "loud", " high pitch", "clear", "thrill", "tremor", "musical" and others terms. The adjective scales vary among the doctors and difficult to derive a standard model for heart sound quality and correct clinical interpretation. In this work, we propose a novel framework based on psychoacoustic principles and derive psychoacoustic models for the heart sounds and murmurs. We discuss the theoretical foundations, psychoacoustic principles and derive the mathematical models for the psychoacoustic features such as loudness, sharpness, intensity, strength, roughness, tonality etc. for a set of heart sounds and murmurs. The proposed framework helps in deriving heart sound quality and also helps in Identifying heart defects.

Keywords: psychoacoustics principles, psychoacoustic models, heart sounds, auscultation, phonocardiography.

1 Introduction

Heart sounds and murmurs are acoustic phenomenon caused by the mechanical events of the heart. Auscultation or hearing of heart sounds using conventional stethoscope or electronic stethoscope is not purely a mechanical phenomenon of sound wave propagation, but also auditory, sensory, cognitive and perceptual event. Digital cardiac auscultation is an art and science of interpreting heart sounds and murmurs used for clinical diagnostics. Cognitive process therapy plays significant role in heart sound perception and clinical interpretation. The phonocardiography (PCG) — the art and science of recording and interpreting of heart sounds using latest digital technology has significantly helped to understand and interpret the complex heart sounds (normal, abnormal sounds including murmurs). The PCG is a display of the heart sound signal with respect to time (time domain) and frequency components or

---

* Corresponding author.

N. Meghanathan et al. (Eds.): CCSIT 2011, Part II, CCIS 132, pp. 556–563, 2011.
© Springer-Verlag Berlin Heidelberg 2011

spectral properties (frequency domain) and plotting the heart sounds and murmurs can provide useful information to the physician by complementing cardiac auscultation. The PCG is a display of the heart sound signal with respect to time (time domain) and frequency components or spectral properties (frequency domain) and plotting the heart sounds and murmurs can provide useful information to the physician by complementing cardiac auscultation.

Phonocardiography techniques are used for the effective clinical investigations and corrective diagnostic heart related diseases and in particular valvular heart diseases. When a heart valve is stenotic or damaged, the abnormal blood flow patterns produce a series of audible vibratory sounds known as murmurs [3]. Doctors and physicians detect these disorders by listening to heart sounds at different locations across the torso. Murmurs heard during routine physical examinations offer important clues to the presence of undetected and asymptomatic cardiac disease. The process of interpreting heart sounds is called cardiac auscultation. It is a simple, non-invasive technique helps in early detection of cardiac disorders. Different cardiac ailments produce a potentially overwhelming set of acoustic pathological events and correctly identifying a disorder requires discrimination of subtle variations in the timing characteristics and spectral properties of heart sounds. The analysis and interpretation is complicated by the natural variations in heart sounds introduced by factors such as the gender, age and dynamic state of the patients. Even in adults, anxiety, stress, fever, anemia etc. may also cause benign murmurs. Typically, these cases are distinguished by examining the intensity of sounds, in addition to their timing and frequency content. Sounds that are interesting from the perspective of auscultation are often short lived (less than 20 milliseconds) and separated from one another by less than 30 milliseconds. Pathological signals indicative of cardiac diseases are also often much quieter than other heart sounds and their audibility varies across successive heart beats. Even with extensive experience, physicians may often disagree about sounds, in particular with brief heart sounds. These inaccuracies are attributed to human auditory limitations which include insensitivity to frequencies, slow response to rapidly occurring changes in acoustic signals and an inability to unmask soft sounds in the proximity of loud ones. Murmurs are extra heart sounds that are produced as a result of turbulent blood flow which is sufficient to produce audible noise. Murmurs may be present in normal hearts without any heart diseases are called innocent murmurs. The murmurs due to valvular heart diseases are called pathologic murmurs and needs to evaluate by the cardiologists. In general, the murmurs [3, 4] can be classified by seven different physical characteristics: timing, shape, location, radiation, intensity, pitch and quality. It may also include psychoacoustic characteristics such as loudness, heart sound intensity, heart sound pressure, sharpness and fluctuations. Timing refers to whether the murmur is a systolic or diastolic murmur depending on the S1 and S2 sounds of a standard heart sound cycle and plays vital role in clinical decisions. Shape refers to the intensity of the heart sounds over time. We can derive the intensity contours and can be described in musical note such as "crescendo", "decrescendo", or "crescendo-decrescendo". Radiation refers to where the sound of the heart sounds and murmurs radiates and normally radiates in the direction of the blood flow. The radiated sound can be Captured and displayed as radiation patterns and helps in specific characterizations of murmurs. Intensity refers to the loudness of the murmur, and is graded on a scale from 0-6/6 adjective scale as shown in the following Table 1. The terms such as "soft", "faint"," loud", "blowing", "harsh", "rumbling" and others have a subjective meaning and needs to be modeled precisely.

The pitch of a murmur is low, medium or high and is determined by whether it can be auscultated best with the bell or diaphragm of a stethoscope. Pitch mainly refers to the fundamental frequency of the heart sounds and murmurs. From the above discussions, it clear that the physical characteristics such as timing, shape, pitch, loudness, radiation, sound intensity, sound pressure and other parameters are clinically important and described using a adjective scales. In order to address the above challenges, we derive psychoacoustics principles for the hearts sounds and murmurs in a novel way and specific contributions of the research work are: We propose and derive psychoacoustic models based on the psychoacoustics principles for heart sounds and murmurs. We derive psychoacoustic models and map them to the psychoacoustics features such as loudness, pitch, sound intensity, sharpness, etc. with mathematical equations. We also discuss the classification of murmurs and adjective scales and relate them into the psychoacoustic features. For example, the grade 4 murmur which is loud and thrill and derive the loudness contour and characterize the thrill by observing the contour of loudness pattern. We highlight the usage of psychoacoustic model for the heart sound qualities.

Table 1. Murmur Grade on 1-6/6 Adjective Scales

Grade	Description
Grade 1	Very faint
Grade 2	Soft
Grade 3	Heard clearly on Pericardium.
Grade 4	Loud with palpable thrill sound. May also be vibratory or tremor on palpitation.
Grade 5	Loud, clear with thrill.
Grade 6	Very loud with thrill.

1.1 Psychoacoustic Principles and Modles

A. Psychoacoustic Principles and Models

Psychoacoustics is the study of the subjective human perception of sounds [1]. Alternatively it can be described as the study of psychological correlates of the physical parameters of acoustics [1]. The field of psychoacoustic aims to model parameters of auditory sensation in terms of physical signal parameters and provide a framework and modeling capabilities for the acoustic sounds. The psychoacoustic models of sound perception exploiting the imperceptible sounds are used in the audio compression such as MP3 standards; non-linear response of the ear is exploited in the noise reduction systems and communication networks. The human ear can nominally hear sounds in the range 20 Hz to 20,000 Hz (20 kHz). Frequency resolution of the ear is 0.36 Hz within the octave of 1,000–2,000 Hz. That is, changes in pitch larger than 0.36 Hz can be perceived in a clinical setting. Other scales have been derived directly from experiments on human hearing perception, such as the Mel scale and Bark scale and these are approximately logarithmic in frequency at the high-frequency end, but nearly linear at the low-frequency end. Our ear drums are sensitive only to variations in the sound pressure, but can detect pressure changes as small as $2 \times 10_{-10}$.ATM and as great or greater than 1 ATM. The sound pressure level (SPL) is also measured logarithmically, with all pressures referenced to $1.97385 \times 10_{-10}$ ATM. The lower limit of audibility is therefore defined as 0 dB, but the upper limit is not as clearly defined. By measuring this minimum intensity for testing tones of various frequencies, a frequency dependent absolute threshold of hearing (ATH) curve may be derived. Typically, the ear shows a peak of sensitivity (i.e., its lowest ATH) between 1 kHz and 5 kHz, though the threshold changes with age, with older ears showing decreased sensitivity above 2 kHz. Equal-loudness contours indicate the sound pressure level (dB), over the range of audible frequencies, which are perceived as being of equal loudness and may be plotted. We use classical reference [5] which represents a set of algorithms for calculating auditory sensations including loudness, sharpness, roughness, softness, sound strength and intensity, and fluctuation strength and extend it for the heart sounds and murmurs.The classification of murmurs is characterized by using the psychoacoustic features and derives mathematical equations.

B.   Loudness of heart sound and murmurs

The loudness is modeled by the following equation, where N is loudness, N' is the loudness of a given critical band or also know as specific loudness, and dz is the increment in the critical band scale.

$$N = \int_0^{24} N' dz \tag{1}$$

The unit of loudness, the sone, is a ratio scale referenced against the sensation produced by a 1 kHz sine tone with a sound pressure level of 40 dB. The models draw on data gained from subjective testing and from a physiological understanding of the auditory periphery.

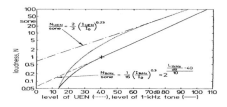

Fig. 1. Loudness function of a 1- kHz tone (solid) and of Uniform Exciting Noise (dotted), broken and dashed-dotted lines with corresponding equations (adopted from [5])

From psycho acoustically measured loudness of Uniform Exciting Noise, a function relating loudness and level in a single critical band can be deduced using equation 2.

$$N'(z) = N_0 \left(\frac{E_{THQ}(z)}{s(z)E_0}\right)^{0.23} \left[\left(1 - s(z) + s(z)\frac{E(z)}{E_{THQ}(z)}\right)^{0.23} - 1 \right]$$ (2)

where N' is the specific loudness in sone/Bark, E excitation (corresponds to the level in one critical band) and E_{THQ} excitation at hearing threshold. Total loudness is obtained by integrating specific loudness across all critical bands. The "loudness" property of heart sounds and murmurs helps in characterization, classification and discrimination of various murmurs in clinical investigations. We can plot the loudness contour using above equations and derive deep insight in the heart sound analysis and interpretations. The complexity of the loudness of complex heart sound needs to in-vestigated in multi- stages and becomes complicated for time varying sounds, dy-namical effects like forward masking and temporal loudness integration [2, 6, and 5] have to be considered. When the physician hears the heart sounds and murmurs, the loudness is a clinically significant feature and can be measured in sone and be mapped to the vertical axis of the Figure 1 in terms of the adjective scales of murmur classifications.

C.   Sharpness of heat sound and murmurs

Sharpness or brightness is one of the most prominent features of the timbre. Timbre is more complicated, being determined by the harmonic content of the signal. The hear-ing is based on the amplitude of the frequencies and is very insensitive to their phases. The shape of hearts sounds and murmurs in time domain waveform is only indirectly related to hearing and poses serious challenges in correct interpretation of heart sounds. The models are based on the centroid (signal spectrum or loudness pattern) of the heart sounds and murmurs. The sharpness is modeled as a weighted centroid of the specific loudness pattern. The unit is acum, referenced to a band of noise 1 critical band wide, centered 1 kHz at 60 dB. It is also referred to the perception that the sound is "sharp", "harsh" or "soft" when used in the context of heart sound perception and clinical interpretations. It is related to the proportion of high frequency energy present in the sound, weighted towards energy in the region above 3 kHz. For harmonic tones, sharpness can be controlled through distribution of the harmonic spectral envelope. The model used [5, 9, 7] for the calculating the sharpness of tones is summarized by the Equation 3, where the S is sharpness, N' is specific loudness, z is the bark scale of auditory filters and g(z) is a weighting function that emphasis z for the critical band rates. It was found that the sharpness of narrow band noises increases proportionally with the critical band rate for center frequencies below about 3 kHz. At higher fre-quencies, however, sharpness increases more strongly, an effect that has to be taken into account when the sharpness S is calculated using a formula that gives the weighted first momentum of the specific loudness pattern:

$$S = 0.11 \frac{\int\limits_{0}^{24\,Bark} N' g(z) z \, dz}{\int\limits_{0}^{24\,Bark} N' \, dz} \, acum \qquad (3)$$

In equation (3), the denominator gives the total loudness, while the upper integral is the weighted momentum mentioned. The psychoacoustic feature - sharpness can be used for the following murmurs. Early systolic ejection click murmur is a high frequency, early systolic sound occurring 0.03-0.07 second after S1 [4]. The sound is generated either by the sudden upward doming of an abnormal semi lunar valve (aortic or plutonic) and sharp click sounds. Opening Snap murmur is a high frequency, early diastolic sound that is associated with MS [3]. It occurs 0.04-0.12 second after S2 and may or may not be associated with a late peaking or rumbling diastolic murmur of varying sharpness with peaking at specific temporal patterns.

D. Pitch of heart and murmurs

A psycho acoustical pitch ratio scale is a difficult concept due to the complexity of pitch perception and cognition. Reference [6, 10] describes some of the complexity of pitch structures for harmonic tones (such as pitch height, octave equivalence and cycle of fifths) through multidimensional geometric figures. In addition to complex structures of pitch height, pitch has the dimension of pitch strength, also known as "tonal ness". The harmonic series is of great importance in pitch perception, and mainly pitched sounds in everyday experience exhibit harmonic spectra. In general, it is usually determined by the fundamental frequency as a pitch percept. A model of pitch perception is analyzed using template matching or autocorrelation techniques. Pitch is used to describe the tonal quality of the murmur be it high pitched or low pitched. For those of us not musically inclined, a simple way to distinguish pitch is to determine whether the sound is heard best with the diaphragm of the stethoscope, i.e., high pitched, or with the bell, i.e., low pitched. Murmurs of mitral or tricuspid stenosis are best heard with the bell. Some of other hearts sounds that can characterize the pitch are: S3 sound is a low frequency, mid diastolic sound occurring 0.14 -0.22 second after S2.The frequency components of low frequency heart sounds are difficult to hear and can be modeled and uniquely find pitch features of the heart sounds and murmurs [3]. S4 sound is also a low frequency, late diastolic sound occurring 0.08-0.20 second prior to S1. It is generated during pre systolic ventricular filling due to atrial contraction, hypertension and diastolic dysfunction. The sequencing and ordering with respect to the S1 and S2 in a standard cardiac cycle and obtain pitch pattern and frequency components using spectral techniques will assist the doctor for the better clinical decisions [3].

E. Fluctuation Strength of heart sounds and murmurs

These hearing sensations are correlated to the temporal variations of sounds. Fluctuation strength measured as a function of modulation frequency shows a maximum near 4 Hz, whereas roughness can be described by band pass characteristic at 70 Hz. This means that very slow variations (< 0.5 Hz) hardly affect these dynamic hearing sensations.

Another important fact is that roughness and fluctuation strength increase with increasing modulation depth up to about 30 dB, where saturation can be observed. Both roughness and fluctuation strength can be calculated from the specific loudness time pattern [5] and used in sound quality design. How much loudness, sharpness, roughness and fluctuation strength a specific sound needs, however, can not be answered generally, since this depends strongly on the sound properties of the sound under investigations? Using the equation 4, we derive the fluctuation strength a specific heart sounds and murmurs. The unit of fluctuation strength is the vacil, referenced to a 60 dB 1 kHz pure tone 100% amplitude modulated at 4 Hz.

$$F = \frac{0.008 \int_0^{24Bark} (\triangle L/dB\ Bark)dz}{(f_{mod}/4Hz) + (4Hz/f_{mod})}\ vacil \qquad (4)$$

For example, aortic stenosis (AS) may be congenital, rheumatic, or degenerative-calcify and this murmur is a crescendo-decrescendo (<>), mid to late peaking, harsh systolic murmur. It is heard best at the right base and often radiates to the right carotid. Intensity of the murmur varies with cycle length, typically becoming louder after a pause and may exhibit very high fluctuations.

F. Roughness of heart sounds and murmurs

Roughness is a sensation caused by quite rapid amplitude modulation within auditory filters. This modulation can be caused by beats between two pure tone components, or by a signal with amplitude or frequency modulation. Beating within an auditory filter channel has been used to explain the acoustic component of tonal dissonance and represent roughness of the heart sounds [5]. The unit of roughness is the as per, which is referenced to a 1 kHz tone at 60 dB with 100% amplitude modulation at 70 Hz. The model presented in [5, 8] by for calculating the roughness of modulated tones having a single modulation frequency, the roughness of the heart sound can be used for the modeling aortic insufficiency (AI) may be congenital rheumatic, and collagen vascular disease. The murmur is a high frequency (blowing) decrescendo murmur beginning in early cardiac cycle and uniquely radiates to the top of the head. The roughness of the murmurs can be uniquely characterized using the above equation and needs further investigations. Mitral regurgitation (MR) is associated with endocarditic and ischemic heart diseases [4]. The murmur is typically a high frequency, holo systolic, plateau murmur that is best heard at the apex. The murmur often radiates to the left axilla and back. There is no appreciable change in murmur intensity with cycle length (as with AS). MR may be associated with S3 in more severe cases. Here we have to use intensity, high frequency and radiation patterns in a consistent way and need further investigation and clinical validations.

2 Conclusions

The cardiac auscultation is an effective diagnostic technique used in the early detection of cardiac diseases in particular the valvular diseases, including the murmurs. It is argued that the most of the doctors and physicians depend on their experience and make subjective interpretations of heart diseases. In this paper, we proposed psychoacoustic models based on a psychoacoustic principles and mathematical foundations and discussed the psychoacoustic features (pitch, intensity, timbre, loudness, power, intensity and other clinically important psychoacoustic features) that can be modeled, analyzed and provide effective aid of clinical decisions related to heart diseases, and in particular murmurs. These models offer a reasoning framework for the subjective reasoning of heart sounds and derived psycho acoustical models. It is also used to model the quality of heart sounds for many standardization efforts and can be used as an effective teaching aid for the cardiac auscultations. Our preliminary investigations and experimental results on our psychoacoustic models are quite encouraging and provide a deeper insight into the perception and interpretation of cardiac auscultations. The visualization tools for the psychoacoustic models are in progress and will help in clinical decisions. Further investigations and validation of the proposed psychoacoustic models are planned for the future work.

Acknowledgment

We thank Prof. Dr. R.P Reddy, Principal, REVA College of Engineering Bangalore for his constant support and motivation for the research work. We thank Prof. Dr. Cyril Raj, MGR University, Chennai, for research discussions, for providing critical inputs and guidance for the research work.

References

[1] Christopher, J.P.: The Sense of Hearing, 2nd edn. Routledge, New York (2005)
[2] Katz, J., Burkard, R.F., Medwetsky, L.: Handbook of Clinical Audiology. Lippincott Williams and Wilkins, New York (2002)
[3] Stein, P.: A physical and physilogical basis for the interpreation of cardiac auscultation: evaluations based primarily on the second sound and ejection murmurs. Futura Publishing Company (1981)
[4] Shipton, B., Wahba, W.: Valvular heart disease: review and update. American Family Physician 63(11), 2201–2208 (2001)
[5] Zwicker, E., Fastl, H.: Psychoacoustics: Facts and Models. Springer, Berlin (1999)
[6] More, B.C.J., Glasberg, B.R., Baer, T.: A model for the prediction of thresholds, loudness and partial loudness. Journal of the Audio Engineering Society 45(4), 224–240 (1997)
[7] Glasberg, B.R., Moore, B.C.: Amodel of loudness applicable to time- varying sounds. Journal of the Audio Engineering Society 50(5), 331–342 (2002)
[8] Daniel, P., Weber, R.: Psychoacoustical roughness: implemantion of an optimized model. Acustica (83), 113–123 (1997)
[9] Bismark, G.V.: Sharpness as an attribute of the timbre of steady sounds. Acustica 30, 159–172 (1974)
[10] Stevens, S.S., Volkman, J., Newman, E.: A scale for the measurement of psychological magnitude of pitch. Journal of Acoustical Society of America 8, 185–190 (1937)

Location Based GSM Marketing

Sparsh Arora and Divya Bhatia

Symbiosis International University, Pune, India
{Sparsh.Arora,Bhatia.Divya}@gmail.com

Abstract. The recent fast growth of technology in telecom and IT domain has led to expansion of literature in terms of industry service. Location based or proximity marketing has been recently introduced in industry. The proximity marketing has been introduced with Bluetooth and Wi-Fi networks. Both these networks have higher privacy and limited range. These are hurdles for the promoters investing in these services.

History tells us that how much effective is the marketing with respect to sale of goods and services. Now a day the marketing and quality provides to competitive edge. Looking into this new option for marketing using GSM based proximity marketing technology our idea it to promote marketing to next level. More successful products are consistently associated with greater inputs of Marketing Intelligence; Proximity marketing can help adding more knowledge to this base.

Keywords: Marketing, GSM, Proximity, Trilateration, Triangulation, Assisted GPS, Advertising, Promotions.

1 Introduction

In last decade we have seen a great evolution in mobile service, device and technology. The market penetration of mobile phones, PDA and GPS navigator has reached level beyond imagination in just one decade. Nevertheless, the prevalent paradigm of information provision to mobile user is still requiring users to actively seek information, or at other extreme broadcast information to all users. Localized and profile based promotion though had been proposed to study in literature; it is only the beginning to find a way to market. Tourist information, news alerts, promotion and advertisements are some typical example of context aware promotion service.

User behavior towards mobile context based advertisements can be different from online advertisements. A user on move can take time out to read and follow promotions on his mobile phone. Bombardment of promotion or advertisements on a user's personal device can be irritating, user may completely ignore them. However, if the promotions or advertisements are contextual the user may actually find it very useful and will interest user with high probability. Looking at positive aspect; user in future may even pay for such helpful promotions. Therefore it is necessary to provide user a handful of beneficiary advertisements or promotions. Key point in this technique is detecting the location of the consumer on virtual map by identifying longitude and latitude coordinates of subscriber held device [1].

N. Meghanathan et al. (Eds.): CCSIT 2011, Part II, CCIS 132, pp. 564–572, 2011.
© Springer-Verlag Berlin Heidelberg 2011

The proximity is captured by Base Transmission Station (BTS) based on virtual Global Positioning System (GPS) techniques and can be shared with promoters. In this process based on the context which includes proximity and profiling of consumer the advertisement can be beneficial. Second is to capture movement behavior of consumer to understand his needs i.e. building the consumer profile. This can be done by tracking in account context information such as time, his location (work, home and shopping mall etc) and personal profile. This context information capture will act as another valuable feed to Marketing Information System (MIS) by not just acquiring information from marketing transaction or informal sources [2].

2 Problem Statement

This paper focuses on two problem areas; one from the view point of marketing and other from technical which includes shortcomings of Bluetooth and Wi-Fi based technology. Let us see separately what are two different problem scopes and later see how this proposal helps us in solving both.

2 1 Marketing Shortcomings[1]

Advertisements have characteristic to make an impression in the mind of consumer, so that the consumer comes to the product i.e. buys the product. This characteristic fades with time and location i.e. advertisement is more effective if done at right time and on right location [3].

This characteristic of advertisements is not addressed by broad casting mediums like Television, Radio and Newspapers etc. These mediums broadcast the information irrespective of the time and location.

The other key factor missed by these medium of promotion is the dynamism in advertisements. Advertisements are same for each and every consumer though market is not same. This may even de-advertise the product. It's very important to address right section of consumer while promoting or advertising a product or service.

2.2 Subscriber Tracking for MIS

The effective way to monitor subscriber shopping behavior is through transaction point data analysis [4]. By tracking exact purchase of quantity and item subscriber future need is judged by MIS. For example if a subscriber owns an I-Phone he might be interested in I-Phone accessories. Such information is very vital for marketers. However this information is very rarely integrated with other Point of Transactions. Two separate businesses may also not share their private sale information with one other.

Other problem with subscriber tracking in transaction point system is that the consumer information can also be redundant with same consumer i.e. same consumer can

---

[1] Marketing shortcoming mentioned here only focus on the problems related to media advertisements on television, internet and billboards. It does not focus on shortcomings of marketing as whole subject area.

be recognized by system as two if she purchases a product or make transaction at different point of time or places.

2.3 Bluetooth and Wi-Fi Shortcomings

Solutions provided by Bluetooth and Wi-Fi marketing have shortcomings in terms of range, subscriber information sharing, security etc [5]. These shortcomings are discussed in detail below:

- Consumer must be informed to turn on their Wi-Fi or Bluetooth on order to receive promotions or advertisements. As per consumer behavior there will be very less consumers willing to put some extra effort to receive advertisement.
- This is limited to a short span of area. Its range depends on the range of subscriber mobile radio i.e. it varies from five to fifty meters.
- It requires additional broadcasting instruments and servers to be installed, i.e. expanding scope can be very expensive to cover larger area.
- Device recognition is based on Heuristics, i.e. only new devices implement device ID profiles.
- In order to gather subscriber information from a mobile device a special agent has to be installed, which can be issue of platform compatibility, privacy and security.
- It can be used for Spamming as the promotion server is sole vendor proprietorship.
- Consumers are skeptical about spread of virus over Bluetooth and Wi-Fi.
- Many device manufactures do not support to receive free interactive content e.g. I-phone and Black Berry.

3   High Level Solution

The problems discussed here are very simply and logically solved by using the combination of GSM and Proximity Marketing techniques. Instead of using Bluetooth or Wi-Fi, promoting media through WAP push or SMS will be more effective as subscriber most likely turn off his GSM very less often in comparison to Bluetooth and Wi-Fi. Generally consumer goes offline in GSM when he/she wishes not to receive any call e.g. in Airplanes, Hospital or Radio Frequency restricted area and this happens very less often as compared to Bluetooth and Wi-Fi [6].

Subscriber location can be detected by triangulation, multi-alteration or any other combination of technologies discussed in section 4 of this document. This location in terms of Longitudinal and Latitudinal coordinates will be mapped on a matrix and used in proximity marketing. This data feed will be sent to a repository of MZ matrix i.e. market zone and matched with a business code in that MZ matrix. Along with Consumer ID, Business code and location information can be fed in a Marketing Information System to extract intelligent promotion to be sent to consumer on his device or digital billboard (Out of Home Media).

Other way round, this data of subscriber location and time spent in that location can be fed into Marketing Information System as an additional data to study and analyze consumer time spending behavior [4].

4 Solution Detail

4.1 Consumer Tracking

By using mobile phone tracking technique we can track subscriber even on the move. Phone emits radio waves to contact nearby BTS (Base Transceiver Station). This process even works when phone is not engaged in any call. Mobile phone location can be disclosed by longitudinal and latitudinal coordinates by telecom companies by using various techniques or combined techniques discussed in section 4.1.1.

4.1.1 Technology
By using mobile phone tracking technique we can track mobile device by measuring the strength of signal in mobile. Using antenna pattern and concept that mobile phone always communicates with the BTS, any communication or call is made to one which is nearest but mobile is connected to various BTS at a time.

System determines the location of the mobile based on the sector in which phone resides. This is done by interpolating the signals of the different antennas. A high quality service can produce accuracy up to 50 meters in urban areas [7]. The technique used by GSM is known as multi-alteration. This technology can be further divided into three categories, Network based, Handset Based and Hybrid.

Network Based
Network based technology uses architecture of network service provider. Service provider has to install hardware and software at their site. The advantage of this technology is that it does not require interference with subscriber device i.e. not software or hardware changes is required in subscriber's handset. This works on the method called triangulation.

Handset Based
Handset based technology uses software and hardware of handset itself to determine location. Handset uses more or less the same technique as used by Network Based to identify location and transmit it over network to the server. The main disadvantage of this is that it requires special software to determine location. It is quite difficult to produce software for different environments and distribute it over network. One solution can be providing software as embedded, but again it's very difficult to convince the manufacturer and the technology used may be different from service provider to service provider.

Hybrid
Hybrid technology works on both segments: Network as well as Handset. The best example would be AGPS which use network as well as GPS signal to find location. Hybrid technology provides more accuracy than any of the sole method discussed [8]. The various methods that can be implemented on Network as well as Hybrid technology are discussed below.

Trilateration: It determines the relevant position of object using the location information of at least three fixed reference points i.e. base station and signal strength from each station. It follows a simple concept that the lever of signal is indirectly proportional to the distance from base. As shown in figure below, the point at which three circle intersect can only be one, so at a fixed point on surface of earth, signal values from fixed base station will always be same.

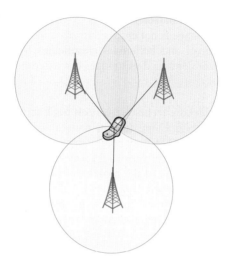

Fig. 1. Trilateration

By using more than three base stations we can get more accuracy. Use of more than three base signals is known as Multialteration [7].

Triangulation: Triangulation is the method of positioning a mobile by measuring angle of arrival in mobile and arriving point and sides of reference points. This technique is used with multiple towers at a time. Larger the number of towers higher is the accuracy of position. Many schemes are used for determining angle of arrival: Maximum output power, maximum likelihood estimation and subspace based approach.

Assisted GPS: Assisted GPS works in coagulation with information from GPS enabled device. The location from device received and location determined from base coagulate to provide even higher accuracy and help in avoiding common errors caused by interference.

All the techniques discussed can only be used to determine the location of subscriber. This is only one prospect of this paper. The main objective here is to use this information intelligently for marketing.

4.2 Dynamic Zonal Marketing

Marketing zone is defined as the area or zone for proximity based marketing, in other words we can say that marketing based on the location of subscriber.

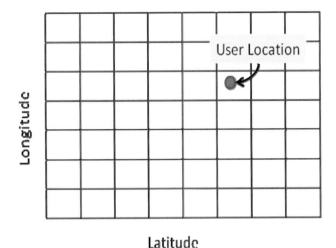

Fig. 2. Marketing Zone Matrix

Once the subscriber's location coordinates are tracked, the subscriber location, Unique Identification[2] and his mobile device profile can be sent by service provider to Position Organizer. Position organizer can map subscriber to virtual map and add parameters like location promotion, Kiosks or OOH id (if present in that particular location) and send this information to Marketing Intelligent System. The parameters add can depend upon service designs and usage. The parameter can be used to define:

- Type of promotion; MMS, SMS, Video, Video Call, Animation or Flash.
- Where to display promotion; on user device or billboard installed nearby?
- Whether to address user or not?
- Any other information helpful in building dynamic advertisement.

By using this information and by studying the consumer buying behavior pattern MIS can generate dynamically advertisement or promotion for subscriber. This promotion or advertisement can be pushed to consumer mobile device or can be displayed on nearby digital billboard. The promotion then is directed back to Mobile service provider or OOH service provider as shown in figure 3.

This technique opens a world for addressable advertisement where subscriber can be addressed by surname or his first name as a part of advertisement. MIS can generate advertisement on fly with consumer characteristics.

Example: a consumer is standing in front of an Adidas showroom. His location is identified by cellular service provider and forwarded to Position Organizer along with subscriber's Unique ID. Position organizer determines the promotion code on the coordinates specified. This promotion code will tell what type of media to be promoted, whether to include subscriber's personal information in media like his name, where vendor wants media to be displayed on Digital Billboard or consumer's cell

---

[2] Unique Identification can be any parameter of subscriber used to identify subscriber in mobile domain, it can either of the following: MSISDN, IMEI or IMSI number.

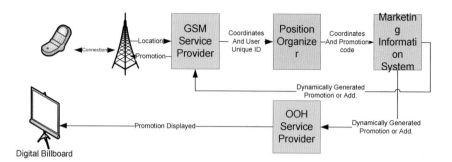

Fig. 3. System Diagram

phone, media ID etc. The MIS will study subscriber profile like if consumer is more interested in Golf so, a Golf promotion will be send to consumer.

4.3 Subscriber Roaming Analysis

As discussed in section 2.2 of this paper it is very hard to integrate used Transaction information among separate businesses and uniquely identify consumer.

One possible solution to this problem is by tracking subscriber location and time spending behavior. As defined in section 4.2 of this paper area of coverage is divided in Marketing Zones. Subscriber can be tracked to be present in a particular MZ for time duration. For example, if use is located in MZ with Pizza Hut, we can feed into MIS that subscriber likes pizza. Next time when he visits same MZ he can get promotion or advertisement.

One direct dilemma with this solution is that the presence does not ensure spending. However in particular MZ if user is present he is spending e.g. cinemas, baseball game etc.

5 Business Benefit

This will provide business in following areas:

- It will overcome the shortcomings of advertisements discussed in section 2.1.
- It will provide a greater consumer shopping experience.
- It will provide a medium for direct marketing, i.e. from marketers to consumer eyes.
- Promotion will be cheaper as it bypasses the broadcasting.
- It will make advertisements more useful and not a bombardment of promotions.
- Dynamically generated advertisements or promotion codes which will be consumer specific and not generic.
- It will increase the personal touch between vendor and consumer.

All the business benefit discussed will help in increasing sales and thus improving revenue.

6 Key Success Factors

Following are the success factors for successful implementation of the solution discussed.

- Handset and Network capability.
- GPRS availability (In case of multimedia promotion).
- Three way adaptation, Subscriber, Service Provider and Marketer.
- Security and Privacy Concerns.

7 Challenges

The solution discussed is not as easy to implement as explained in text. The technique has many challenges involved.

Consumer tracking techniques: Different techniques used with varied accuracy. The quality of service depends on service provider and technique used.

Consumer Privacy: This can be a legal issue to track location of a consumer without his pre-concern. Subscriber has full right not to be disturbed with campaigns or promotions. This is in fact the dilemma of benefits of proximity marketing with subscriber privacy.

Lack of standard: Though this is a very novel service, in order to expand, it demands some standard to be followed.

8 Future Scope

The technology discussed in the paper can be expanded into other service zones. It can be used in emergency service, road side assistance, news. It can also be expanded in parking services and tolling. It can be used for insurance purpose, medical aid, family tracking, employee movement, maintaining law and justice etc.

The basic idea is to implement location parameter in day to day service, not only marketing but it has its scope way beyond that.

9 Conclusion

Context based marketing is not a new concept; it has been there for a while. It has shortcomings, challenges and success factors. If applied in right business sense it can be a very powerful yet cheap marketing tool. It can be a very easy and expanding investment in the field of marketing.

Its integration with Marketing Information System makes it even more powerful by showing subscriber what he wants i.e. promoting the right product to right consumer at right time and location.

References

1. Liapis, D., Vassilaras, S., Yovanof, G.S.A.: Implementing a low-cost, personalized and location based service for delivering advertisements to mobile users. In: 3rd International
   Symposium on Wireless Pervasive Computing, ISWPC 2008, vol. 3, pp. 133–137 (2008),
   10.1109/ISWPC.2008.4556182
2. Marketing Information System,
   `http://www.businessdictionary.com`,
   `http://www.businessdictionary.com/definition/`
   `marketing-information-system.html` [Cited: June 6, 2010]
3. Kotler, P., Keller, K.L.: Marketing Management. Pearson Education Ltd., India (2006)
   ISBN 0-13-145757-8
4. Marketing Information Systems. FAO Corporate Document Repository. FAO,
   `http://www.fao.org/docrep/w3241e/w3241e0a.htm` [Cited: June 7, 2010]
5. Bluetooth Marketing. Marketing Minefield (2007),
   `http://www.marketingminefield.co.uk/unusual-ideas/`
   `bluetooth-marketing.html` [Cited: May 20, 2010]
6. Bennett, V., Capella, A.: Location-based services. IBM (March 1, 2002),
   `http://www.ibm.com`,
   `http://www.ibm.com/developerworks/ibm/library/i-lbs/`
   [Cited: June 2, 2010]
7. Wang, S., Min, J., Yi, B.K.: IEEE International Conference on Communication (ICC) (2008),
   `http://to.swang.googlepages.com/ICC2008LBSforMobilessimplifie`
   `dR2.pdf`
8. Steiniger, S., Neun, M., Edwardes, A.: University of Zurich,
   `http://www.geo.unizh.ch/publications/cartouche/`
   `lbs_lecturenotes_steinigeretal2006.pdf` [Cited: May 26, 2010]
9. Proximity Marketing Guide (2008),
   `http://www.mobilefx.com`,
   `http://www.mobilefx.com/web/documents/presentations/`
   `mobileFX_Proximity_Marketing_Guide.pdf` [Cited: May 20, 2010]

Inverse Square Law Based Solution for Data Aggregation Routing Using Survival Analysis in Wireless Sensor Networks

Khaja Muhaiyadeen A., Hari Narayanan R., Shelton Paul Infant C., and Rajesh G.

Department of Information Technology, Anna University, Chennai
{khaja.it,hari.zlatan,sheltonpaul89,raajiimegce}@gmail.com

Abstract. Wireless Sensor Network is a group of specialized transducers with a communications infrastructure intended to monitor and record conditions at diverse locations. Wireless Sensor networks have major power constraints. In order to prolong the lifetime of the sensor nodes, the sensor data should efficiently reach the base station and there should be a reduction in message transmission, which consumes the majority of the battery power. Aggregation of data at intermediate sensor nodes helps in saving the energy that would be spent if the nodes send directly to the base station. This paper proposes an efficient way based on inverse-square law along with survival analysis for aggregating data without the formation of an explicit structure. Our evaluation of performance shows a considerable decrease in the number of transmissions required to carry the sensed data to the base station. By using our approach, it is possible to minimize power usage of sensor nodes effectively.

Keywords: Inverse Square law, Survival Analysis, Kaplan-Meier estimator, Enhanced Random Delay, Wireless Sensor Networks.

1 Introduction

Wireless Sensor Network (WSN) consists of spatially distributed autonomous sensors to cooperatively monitor physical or environmental conditions, such as temperature, sound, vibration, pressure, motion or pollutants. Wireless sensor networks are now used in many civilian application areas, including environment and habitat monitoring, health applications, home automation, and traffic control. Size and cost constraints on sensor nodes result in corresponding constraints on resources such as energy, memory, computational speed and bandwidth. Specific applications for WSNs include habitat monitoring, object tracking, nuclear reactor control, fire detection, and traffic monitoring. In a typical application, a WSN is scattered in a region where it is meant to collect data through its sensor nodes. Since the sensor nodes cannot be recharged, the sensed data should reach the base station through multi-hop routing. Many approaches were common. Mostly, the sensor network is grouped into clusters or a tree like structure and data moves up hierarchically to the base station. Here those nodes in top of the hierarchy, gets affected more. In order to handle this, we propose the structure-less approach where data gets aggregated quickly. Two step framework is used. In first, node that is more probable to contain data is found and

N. Meghanathan et al. (Eds.): CCSIT 2011, Part II, CCIS 132, pp. 573–583, 2011.
© Springer-Verlag Berlin Heidelberg 2011

then the time for which a node must wait for data to arrive from other nodes is found. We show the gain in performance by means of the reduction in number of transmissions in the network. Finally, our simulation results will also substantiate our claim of the gain in performance.

2 Related Work

All of the previous work done can be broadly classified into 2 categories viz structured approach and structure less approach. This section delves deeper into the various approaches proposed in these categories.

2.1 Structured Approach

Rumor routing [1] routes the queries to nodes that observed a particular event rather than flooding, but maintaining agents and event-tables are sometimes infeasible. In [2], a protocol called *Low Energy Adaptive Clustering Hierarchy (LEACH)* forms cluster and randomly selects clusterheads and rotates this role to evenly distribute the load among nodes. In [3], *Power-Efficient Gathering in Sensor Information Systems* enhancement of *LEACH,* where nodes communicate only with their closest neighbors and once the turns of all the nodes are over, a new round will start. All the structured approaches results in fixed delay, which would be intolerable in large network deployments.

2.2 Structure-Less Approach

Studying the effect of the changing network topology is essential for analyzing the performance of structure less algorithms. [4] proposes a *Distributed Random Grouping(DRG)* algorithm that uses a probabilistic grouping to answer aggregate queries like computation of sum, average, maximum, minimum, etc. Through randomization, all values will progressively converge to the correct aggregate value (the average, maximum, minimum, etc.) in this method. The disadvantage with this approach is that it involves periodic and frequent transfer of message exchange between the nodes of a group. [5] proposed a novel data aggregation protocol for event based applications via 2 mechanisms namely *Data Aware Anycast (DAA)* at the MAC layer and *Randomized Waiting (RW)* at the application layer. DAA mechanism used RTS and CTS packet transmissions in order to determine whether the neighbor node has data. Since sensor nodes need to wait for data from other nodes, RW was proposed where each node chooses a random delay value within a maximum delay τ. We call this as *Structure Free Data Aggregation (SFDA)* and compare our approach with SFDA to show the improvement in performance.

3 Problem Formulation

Since we are primarily concerned with a structure less network, our aim here is to find a neighbor node within its communication range which is most probable to contain data and given that a node has sensed data, it needs to know how long it should wait for data from other nodes.

3.1 Neighbor Node Detection

In order to detect which node is most probable to contain data, we propose a prediction based approach. [5] proposed DAA method for the same problem of finding the neighbor node with data. The main problem with this approach is that it uses RTS and CTS packet transmissions for every data transmission. This can induce a serious load and can reduce the lifetime of sensor nodes considerably. Hence, we propose an approach which does not involve any kind of communication between the nodes. Each node analyses the collected upstream nodes data and calculates a probability value and using this probability value, it decides the node for which it has to forward data.

Inverse-Square Law. In physics, an Inverse-Square Law is any physical law stating that some physical quantity or strength is inversely proportional to the square of the distance from the source of that physical quantity.

This law is very suitable for our environment since all electromagnetic waves has to obey the inverse square law. Since we do not know the position of the source, we take the position of node with highest sensed value as the position of source, as the node is closest to the source. The value sensed by the sensor node which is at a particular distance from the event is analogous to the intensity value at that distance from the source. Next, we need to determine the rate at which the sensed value changes with respect to the distance. If we obtain this, then we can predict the most probable sensed value for the downstream nodes. The Inverse-Square Law is,

$$I = \frac{k}{r^2} \tag{1}$$

Where I is Intensity, r is distance from source and k is a constant. Differentiating (1) gives the rate at which the sensed value changes with respect to distance.

$$\frac{dI}{dr} = -2K_m r^{-3} \tag{2}$$

The negative sign indicates that the intensity decreases with respect to distance. Here K_m represents the mean value of K for all upstream nodes.

$$K_m = \frac{\sum_{j=1}^{N} I_j r_j^2}{N} \tag{3}$$

From this, we can determine the rate at which the intensity has varied with respect to distance for all the upstream nodes. It is most likely to vary at the same rate for downstream nodes also.

Survival Analysis (SA). It is a branch of statistics which deals with death in biological organisms and failure in mechanical systems with respect to time t. We correlate this to our environment where we define the survival function S(r) as the probability that data is sensed by a node which is beyond distance r. It is defined as,

$$S(r) = P(R > r) \tag{4}$$

Similar to the lifetime distribution function of SA, we define the *Intensity distribution function*, which is a compliment of the survival function $S(r)$, as

$$F(r) = P(R \leq r) = 1 - S(r) \tag{5}$$

The above equation (5) indicates the probability that data is sensed by a sensor node that is located at distance r or below. *Event density function* which denotes the rate of data sensed with respect to distance is given by

$$f(r) = F'(r) = \frac{d}{dr} F(r) = 2K_m r^{-3} \tag{6}$$

Kaplan Meier Estimator (KPE) is a probabilistic measure of SA which denotes the probability that a living being survives up to some point of time. In other words, it denotes the probability that $P(S \leq t)$. For our environment,
   According to KPE,

$$S^{\wedge}(r_i) = \prod_{x \leq r_i} \left(1 - m^{\wedge}(x)\right) \tag{7}$$

Here, Hazard function $m^{\wedge}(x)$ is defined as the event rate at time t conditional on survival until time t or later (i.e., $T \geq t$). For our environment is given by,

$$m^{\wedge}(x) = \frac{d(x)}{n(x)} \tag{8}$$

Where $d(x)$ is number of nodes without event detection and $n(x)$ is number of events under study. We now calculate the probability that data exists in the next downstream node. The probability that data don't exists in next downstream node is,

$$P(R \leq r_0 + r/R > r_0) = \frac{P(r_0 < R \leq r_0 + r)}{P(R > r_0)}$$

$$= \frac{\int_{r_0}^{r_0+r} f(r)dr}{S(r_0)} \tag{9}$$

The node with the least probability is chosen as the node that is most probable to have data. We then send data to that node and data aggregation is most probably achieved.

3.2 Delay Calculation

Once a node has collected data, it needs to know how long it should wait for data to come from its downstream nodes. In SFDA, they used a randomized waiting scheme wherein each node takes a random delay value within a certain maximum delay value. Deterministically assigning the waiting time to nodes such that nodes closer to the sink wait longer can avoid the problem but results in a fixed delay for all packets, which would be intolerable in large network deployments. Therefore, randomized waiting scheme is the optimal approach for assigning delay values to the sensor nodes.
   However, we propose Enhanced Random Delay (ERD), a subtle difference to that approach wherein, instead of making the maximum delay value fixed for the entire

network, we make the maximum delay value dependent on the distance of the node from the sink. This provides an improvement in performance because of lesser probability for a node to choose a delay value that will make it wait longer than is necessary.

4 Performance Analysis

In order to evaluate the performance of our approach, we cannot use the number of aggregation points as the metric because the packets may be aggregated after travelling many hops. Expected number of transmissions is the correct metric for evaluating the performance of our algorithm.

4.1 Expected Number of Transmissions

In this section, we will first calculate the probability for the packet to get aggregated at a node. After this, we will calculate the expected number of transmissions. In SFDA [5], they assume that the delay chosen by each node is distinct from each other. Using this assumption, they calculate the expected number of transmissions in the network. In a practical situation, each node is independent of each other i.e., each node chooses a random number that is independent of the random value chosen by another node. So, in the worst case, we compare the expected number of transmissions in the network of our approach with that of theirs.

Consider a chain topology of nodes from v_0 to v_n where v_0 is the sink and all nodes have data to send. Let the number of nodes in the network be 7. Let Y be the discrete random variable representing the number of hops a packet has been forwarded before it is aggregated. As an example, for 7 nodes shown, the node v_n can chooses its delay so that its sending order (l) ranges from 1 to 6, and the node v_{n-h} can take its order (k) from 2 to 7. The remaining $(h-1)$ nodes in between take delay values in l^{h-1} ways. The number of ways N_o in which the nodes from v_n to v_{n-h} take their delay values is therefore,

$$N_o = \sum_{k=2}^{n} \sum_{l=1}^{k-1} l^{h-1}, if\ 0 < h < n \qquad (10)$$

The number of ways in which the remaining $(n-h)$ nodes takes their order is $n^{n-(h+1)}$, and the total number of ways of assigning orders is n^n. For $h = n$, the nodes other than v_n takes same or lower delay value compared to v_n. Therefore, the probability that the packet gets aggregated after h hops is,

$$P(Y = h) = \begin{cases} \dfrac{N_o}{n^{h+1}}, if\ 0 < h < n \\ \dfrac{\sum_{h=1}^{n} h^{n-1}}{n^n}, if\ h = n \end{cases} \qquad (11)$$

The expected value $E(Y)$ for node v_n can now be calculated as,

$$E(Y) = \sum_{h=1}^{n} h \times P(Y = h) \qquad (12)$$

Then, the expected number of transmissions E_o for the whole network would be,

$$E_o = n \times E(Y)$$

$$= \sum_{h=1}^{n-1} h \times \left[\frac{N_o}{n^h}\right] + \frac{\sum_{h=1}^{n} h^{n-1}}{n^{n-2}} \qquad (13)$$

In the above described method, the maximum allowed delay value for all nodes is chosen as τ. In our approach, we fix the maximum delay for each node based on the node's distance from the sink. The node will choose a random delay within that fixed maximum delay. Obviously, since we reduce the limit of delay value for each node, nodes farther from the sink will choose a lower delay than the nodes that are closer to the sink thereby attaining early aggregation. An example is shown in fig. 1.

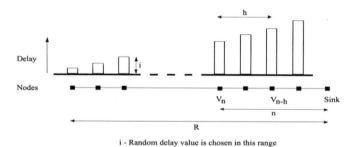

i - Random delay value is chosen in this range

Fig. 1. Nodes choosing random delay as per ERD

Let i be the maximum delay allotted for a node in the network, which decreases proportional to the radius of the network. A node v_n chooses a random delay within that allocated i value. Here i value is taken discrete for calculation purpose. Node v_{n-h} chooses a random delay within $i + h$.

The node in between v_n and v_{n-h} should chose delay less than or equal to i value, so that the packet generated in node v_n gets aggregated in node v_{n-h}. Let N_p denote the number of ways in which the nodes from v_n to v_{n-h} takes its order.

$$N_p = \sum_{k=2}^{i+h} \sum_{j=1}^{\min(i,k-1)} j^{h-1}, 1 < i < R \qquad (14)$$

The number of ways in which the remaining nodes from v_{n-h} to sink takes its order will be, $^R P_{i+h}$ and the total number of ways of assigning delay values is $^R P_{i-1}$. For $i = 1$, the case will be different. The packet from the farthest node's data will be aggregated to a node only if all the nodes between them choose same i value. Then, the probability that the packet gets aggregated after h hops is,

$$P(Y = h) = \begin{cases} \dfrac{N_p \times (i - 1)!}{(i + h)!}, & if\ 1 < i < R \\[2mm] \dfrac{h}{(h + 1)!}, & if\ i = 1 \end{cases} \tag{15}$$

The expected value $E_1(Y)$ for the case $i > 1$ is,

$$E_1(Y) = \sum_{h=1}^{R-1} h \times P(Y = h) \tag{16}$$

The expected value $E_2(Y)$ for the case $i = 1$ is,

$$E_2(Y) = \sum_{h=1}^{R} h \times P(Y = h) \tag{17}$$

Then, using (16) and (17), the expected number of transmissions E_p for the whole network would be,

$$E_p = \sum_{i=2}^{R} E_1(Y) + E_2(Y)$$

$$= \sum_{i=2}^{R} \left[\sum_{h=1}^{R-1} \frac{h(i - 1)!}{(i + h)!} \times N_p \right] + \sum_{h=1}^{R} \frac{h^2}{(h + 1)!} \tag{18}$$

For increasing network size, the expected number of transmissions in the ERD decreases drastically compared to the SFDA approach.

4.2 Intel Lab Data

We evaluated our approach based on dataset from Intel Berkeley Research Lab [6] where the sensory data was generated by light sensors. In addition, since the lab area is small we set the radio range to 8 meters that makes most of the sensors connected. In the simulation, the OMNeT++ 4.0 simulator is used along with the Intel lab data for calculation.

Maximum Delay (MD). The number of transmissions for the Intel-Lab network is compared with varying MD in the network. For increase in MD, the total number of transmissions in the network should decrease. From the graph Fig. 2, it is shown that, the proposed approach performs better than SFDA approach. On average, the number of transmissions decreases by 9.1 percent.

Weighted Delay (WD). The *weighted delay* is the average delay experienced by a packet reaching the sink weighted by number of contributing sources for that packet. For increase in MD, the average WD also increases. It can be seen from Fig. 3 that, the average WD decreases in the ERD compared to SFDA except at 2s and 2.8s MDs.

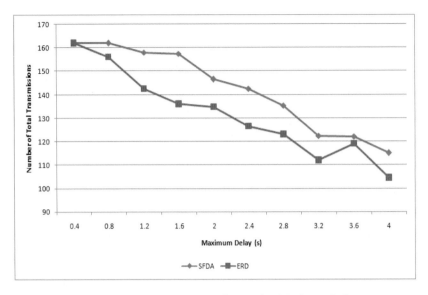

Fig. 2. Number of Transmissions for Varying Maximum Delays

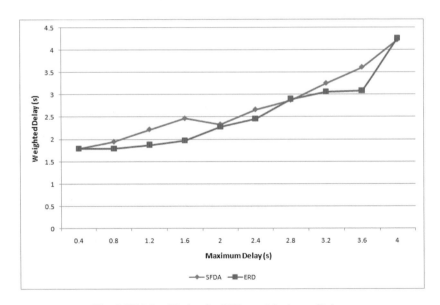

Fig. 3. Weighted Delay for Different Maximum Delays

5   Performance Evaluation

The OMNeT++ 4.0 simulator is used along with MiXiM simulation framework to provide mobility among the events. The nodes are arranged in a grid topology with inter-node separation of 30 m between the sensor nodes.

5.1 Simulation Scenario

The Packet Aggregation Ratio (PAR) is used as metric to compare different protocols. PAR determines how effective a protocol is in aggregating packets and is (*Number of nodes in which a packet gets aggregated*) / (*Number of nodes through which packet is transmitted to sink*). PAR will be in the range 0 to 1. Maximum the value of ratio determines the packet is effectively aggregated in the route. Table.1 shows the various default parameters used in the simulation.

Table 1. Default Parameters Used in the Simulation

Parameters	Values
Network Topology	300 m x 300 m
Data Rate	38.4 Kbps
Communication Range	55 m
Mobility Model	ConstSpeedMobility
Packet Size	50 bytes
Sensing Interval	10 s
Event Size	50 m to 200 m
Internode Separation	30 m
Event Moving Speed	10 m/s
Maximum Delay	0.8 s to 4 s

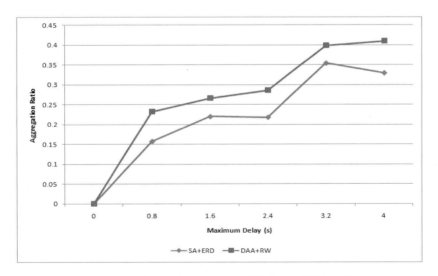

Fig. 4. Aggregation Ratio vs Different Maximum Waiting Times

Maximum Delay. For increase in MD, the total number of transmissions in the network should decrease. From Fig. 4, it is shown that the aggregation ratio increases with MD. The SA+ERD also provides performance almost equal to DAA. For applications that are not tolerant to delay, the proposed approach provides improved performance compared to SFDA.

Event Size (ES). Fig. 5 shows the results for different event sizes. The number of transmitted and received packets increases as the ES increases because more nodes are sensing the event. When the event size increases, more nodes are sending packets, and packets have more chances to be aggregated. Therefore, aggregation ratio increases with event size. The performance of the SA+ERD approach decreases only slightly compared to DAA.

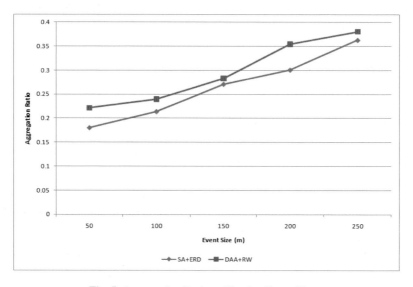

Fig. 5. Aggregation Ratio vs Varying Event Sizes

6   Conclusion

In this paper, we proposed a cost-effective solution for data aggregation without forming any explicit structure in the network. Instead of spending more energy in communication, SA, KME along with the use of inverse-square law finds the neighbor node that is more probable to contain data. Using the ERD method, the unwanted message transmissions are further reduced by finding the random delay within a fixed delay. From extensive simulation results, it is shown that SA+ERD exhibits almost equal performance to SFDA by minimizing energy consumption and unnecessary message transmissions.

References

1. Braginsky, D., Estrin, D.: Rumor Routing Algorithm for Sensor Networks. In: Proceedings of the First Workshop on Sensor Networks and Applications (WSNA), Atlanta, GA (October 2002)
2. Heinzelman, W., Chandrakasan, A., Balakrishnan, H.: Energy Efficient Communication Protocol for Wireless Microsensor Networks. In: Proceedings of the 33rd Hawaii International Conference on System Sciences, HICSS 2000 (January 2000)

3. Lindsey, S., Raghavendra, C.: PEGASIS: Power-Efficient Gathering in Sensor Information Systems. In: IEEE Aerospace Conference Proceedings, vol. 3(9-16), pp. 1125–1130 (2002)
4. Chen, J.-Y., Hu, J.: Analysis of Distributed Random Grouping for Aggregate Computation on Wireless Sensor Networks with Randomly Changing Graphs. IEEE Transactions On Parallel And Distributed Systems 19(8) (August 2008)
5. Fan, K.-W., Liu, S., Sinha, P.: Structure-Free Data Aggregation in Sensor Networks. IEEE Transactions On Mobile Computing 6(8) (August 2007)
6. Intel Berkeley Research Lab Sensor data,
   http://db.csail.mit.edu/labdata/labdata.html

System Implementation of Pushing the Battery Life and Performance Information of an Internal Pacemaker to the Handheld Devices via Bluetooth Version 3.0 + H.S

Balasundaram Subbusundaram[1] and Gayathri S.[2]

[1] Dept. of Electronics and Communication Engineering
Sri Venkateswara College of Engineering Sriperumbudur, Tamil Nadu, India
zealbala@gmail.com
[2] Dept. of Information Technology, RMD Engineering College, Tamil Nadu, India
gayathri.ram2008@gmail.com

Abstract. A pacemaker is a device that helps regulate the rhythm of the heart as well as the rate at which it beats. Since an internal pacemaker works on inbuilt battery, an experienced physician will interact with the pacemaker inside the patient using a pacemaker programmer to know information about the battery life and performance which is tedious and not possible at all times. So we have designed a system wherein a Bluetooth Version3.0 +High Speed (H.S) circuitry along with a logical circuitry is attached to the pacemaker's circuit. The logical circuitry will send processed data about the battery level and performance to the Bluetooth circuitry which in turn will push that information to the patients handheld device which might be devices such as mobile phones, PDA's, laptops, palmtops, etc., Almost everyone today has a mobile phone and Bluetooth has already become a standard inclusion on even the most basic mobile phones, student laptops and PDAs thus making the implementation quite easy.

Keywords: Bluetooth; Pacemaker; Battery life information; Performance information; handheld Device.

1 Introduction

A pacemaker is a device that helps regulate the rhythm of the heart as well as the rate at which it beats. A pacemaker with the help of inbuilt-batteries sends electrical impulses to the heart which helps it pump blood to different parts of the body properly. The pacemaker consists of an electrode which is placed next to the heart wall and small electrical charges travel through the helical lead to the heart. It may be used temporarily, such as after an open heart surgery, or placed permanently, with a minimally invasive procedure. Those pacemakers which are placed inside the heart are called internal pacemakers.

Since an internal pacemaker operates on battery, there is every possibility for the life of a battery to come down, and when the battery has to be replaced. However it is not easy to check the battery level by the patient, hence a trained physician is required, who would generally interact with the pacemaker using a pacemaker

N. Meghanathan et al. (Eds.): CCSIT 2011, Part II, CCIS 132, pp. 584–594, 2011.

programmer available at the hospitals. Removing the pacemaker from the body involves the patient having to go through a micro surgery and thus is a painful process and when the batteries have to be changed, it is purely based on an approximate date and not very accurate. Thus we propose a method using Bluetooth technology Version 3.0 + High Speed [1] [3] for checking the performance and battery level without the help of pacemaker programmer. Bluetooth is a low power communications device operating in the ISM frequency band between 2.4 and. 2.485 GHz .We install

- a Bluetooth device
- a battery level indicator software
- a test software for checking the performance to the existing internal pacemaker and thus monitor the battery levels and performance.

This paper consists of seven sections wherein section two explains the block diagram of the proposed system, section three elaborates the working of the sensors and the modules required for pushing data via Bluetooth Version3.0 + High Speed (H.S), section four explains the steps in pushing data from the pacemaker system to the handheld device, section five depicts the results along with the simulations, section six and seven conclude the paper by describing the disadvantages and the areas of future research.

2   Block Diagram of the System

Modern pacemakers are capable of adapting to a wide range of sensor information relating to the physiological needs and/or the physical activity of the patient. In our system there are two major categories of information from the sensors, the first type of information is about the battery life of the pacemaker and the second type is about the performance of the pacemaker. The system is based on a pacemaker having a demand pulse generator, which is sensitive to the measured parameter. Block diagram of Pacemaker with Bluetooth circuitry is shown Figure 1.

A.   Controlling Algorithm

This is an algorithm in the pacemaker, which is able to adjust the pacemaker response in accordance with the measured quantity of few body parameters measured by sensors. Modern rate-responsive [2] (also called frequency-response) pacemakers are capable of adapting to a wide range of sensor information relating to the physiological needs or the physical activity of the patient.

B.   Physiological Sensors

A sensor system consists of a device to measure some relevant parameter. In our case we measure few body parameters [6] like, body motion, respiration rate, pH, and blood pressure etc. In addition to this we also have the following.

C.   Battery Level Check Sensor

A circuitry is employed to check the battery level when it reaches below a certain threshold value; an alarm is triggered to activate Bluetooth circuitry.

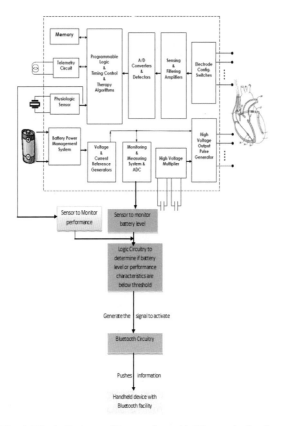

Fig. 1. Block diagram of Pacemaker with Bluetooth circuitry

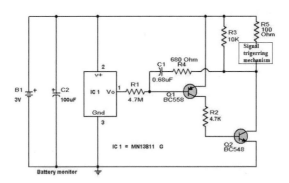

Fig. 2. Battery Level Check sensor

D. Performance Check Sensor

This runs test software periodically to check if all the parts of the pacemaker are functioning in proper order. If any discrepancies arise, the logic circuitry will report an immediate notification by signaling to the Bluetooth circuitry present inside the pacemaker. Data (report) is pushed via Bluetooth circuitry inside the pacemaker to the handheld device so that the necessary replacement can be done soon.

E. Logic Circuitry

This block runs a set of software modules after comparing the values generated by the sensor system with a predefined threshold value. The compared values are logically tested and the results are generated. These generated results will be transmitted via Bluetooth V3.0 +HS to the patient through his/her handheld device.

F. Bluetooth Circuitry

This is activated by the signal sent by either battery level check sensor or performance check sensor. Once activated, it pushes the data (battery level information or performance information) to the handheld device (using Bluetooth 3.0+HS) so that the necessary action can be taken soon.

G. Handheld Devices

They act as communication mediums between the patient and the pacemaker. They essentially are monitors which receive the information from the Bluetooth and display it for the benefit of the patient (to interpret it). The handheld devices may be mobile phones, PDA's, laptops, palmtops, etc.

H. Power Source

A pacemaker utilizes the energy stored in batteries to stimulate the heart. Pacing is the most significant drain on the pulse generator power source. The battery [4] capacity is commonly measured in units of charge (ampere hours). Many factors will affect the longevity of the battery, including primary device settings like pulse amplitude and duration and pacing rate. An ideal pulse generator battery should have a high energy density, low self-discharge rate, and sufficient energy reserve between early signs of depletion and full depletion to allow for safe replacement of the device.

I. Electrodes

The electrical connection between the heart and the implanted pulse generator is provided by an implantable electrode catheter called lead.

J. Sensing and Filtering Amplifier

The sense amplifier plays a fundamental role in providing information about the current state of the heart [2]. A sense amplifier and its subsequent detection circuitry, together called the front-end [2], derive only a single event (characterized by a binary pulse) and feed this to a microcontroller that decides on the appropriate pacing therapy to be delivered by the stimulator.

3 Working of the System

The cardiac sensing outputs generated by the controlling algorithm is digitized by the ADC using the successive approximation architecture .This digitized output is given to the sensing and filtering amplifiers which derives a single event and feed it to a microcontroller that decides on the appropriate pacing therapy to be delivered by the stimulator. It provides the current state information about the heart. This output is given to electrode configuration switches.

A. Battery level Check Sensor

Figure 2 is a circuit for battery monitor. The figure shows a basic battery level monitoring circuit that produces a signal through a signal triggering mechanism when the battery voltage drops below a predetermined voltage. The circuit is based on Panasonic's IC MN13811G and an efficient pulse triggering mechanism based on transistors Q1&Q2.Here when the battery voltage drops below 2.4 V the output of the IC is activated and the pulse is triggered. This circuit here is an ideal one for monitoring the level of all types of 3V batteries. The circuit is power efficient with an idle current drawing as less as 1 uA, and a current drawing while flashing as less as 20uA. If a trip point other than 2.4 V is required, IC MN13811 series are available with different trip point voltages(from 2.4V t0 4.8V) i.e. MN13811G to MN13811U and when the battery level reaches below a certain prefixed threshold value a signal is triggered by the circuit to activate the Bluetooth V3.0 +H.S circuitry. This circuitry gets activated only when it is triggered by a signal (to prevent battery wastage), which is also the advantage of using Bluetooth V3.0 +H.S technology. This battery information is sent by the device to the handheld device.

B. Performance Sensor

It runs a test software program to ensure that various parts of the pacemaker like the timing circuitry, detectors, sensing and filtering amplifiers etc are working correctly by automatically giving sample inputs and checking the outputs by matching them against sample outputs previously obtained. After the test is performed a signal is generated to activate the Bluetooth device in order to send the information to the handheld device of the patient.

C. Modules in the Bluetooth Circuitry

There are four software modules in our system:

- Bluetooth Information push module.
- Server side Bluetooth module.
- Client side module.
- Dynamic URL advertisement generator.

Bluetooth Information module and server side Bluetooth module, which handles data transfer processes, are located in the front end servers. Client side module is pushed by Bluetooth Information module and runs in customer's handheld device. Dynamic URL advertisement generator, placed in the front end servers, produces a Jar file containing a URL pointing to an advertisement webpage.

Functions of the four modules are described as follows.

D. Bluetooth Information Push Module

This module will periodically push information (battery level and performance) to the pre-paired handheld device with Bluetooth turned on [5]. If the push succeeds, the information is displayed on the monitor of the device, based on which interpretation can be done. If the push is rejected by some handheld device, the Bluetooth address of the device is logged and set with a reset timer in a denial device list which will be referred for the next push. Therefore, the device will not receive files pushed from the module for some period of time. If the timer is up the associated device will be removed from the list. When Bluetooth Information Push Module is running, it will receive Bluetooth device addresses which are discovered by front end servers. This module will check the addresses with database to see if they are pre-registered, that is, whether the addresses have associated with members' username and password. Registration is required only once.

E. Server Side Bluetooth Module

As counterpart of client side member registration module, this module will receive the registration information sent from User's device and check it with database to see whether this is the one pre-paired with the Bluetooth in the pacemaker. This module will notify handheld devices of the registration status will avoid hacking.

F. Client Side Module

This module can be automatically installed and run in a Java-enable device. Patients use this module to register their handheld devices by inputting their username and password. The username/password and the associated Bluetooth device address are sent to server side Bluetooth member registration module to complete the one-time registration of the handheld device. After the handheld device has been registered, Bluetooth Information push module will use its Bluetooth device address to identify the handheld device unique to the patient.

G. Dynamic URL Pacemaker information Generator

This module provides an alternative to lead the patient to access the pacemaker information. The information is prepared on a website rather than pushing them; and this module is used to create a Jar file containing the URL of the website. The Jar file will be pushed to patient's handheld device on which the jar file can be executed and bring the URL to the browser of the handheld device. Thus, patients can browse their pacemaker information on their handheld devices.

H. High voltage output system

To stimulate the heart muscle (e.g. initiate a heart beat), a high-voltage output pulse is delivered to the heart through the pacing leads. Multiplying the battery voltage is needed to generate the necessary high voltage. A Voltage multiplier circuit is used is generate the necessary high voltage. The amplitude and pulse width of the high voltage output pulse is customized for the Patients. A High Voltage DAC is used.

4   Flow Chart of Push Mechanism and Program Logics

Information push module is expounded as follows.

   (i)   There are two pushing modes in Bluetooth Information push module: One is automatic push and the other is manual push. Any one mode can be selected automatic push or manual push depending on requirements.

- Automatic Push: Program [3] continuously pushes information according to a predefined sequence within a period of time that is adjustable.
- Manual Push: Manually push specific information such as status of a particular sensor S at a time whenever the user (patient) wants to check.

Let the information be contained in a file F.

(ii) Search Bluetooth [5] devices around the front end servers; put the Bluetooth [3] devices being found in a device list. From the list choose consecutively one device which will go through the steps (iii) to (vi) processes described below. We define the chosen device as D (Device).

(iii) If device D is shown in the denial device list, that means the device has rejected receiving file. If the reset timer is expired then remove the device D from the denial device list.

(iv) If device D is not in the denial device list, then check whether it is registered or not.

- If registered it checks with database to see if device D has received file F.
- If not registered: Transmit "Client Side Member Registration Module" to device D. This allows the patient to register [1] from any handheld device to know information about his/her pacemaker.

(v) If the registered device D has received the file F, then stop pushing the file F to device D.

(vi) If the registered [5] device D rejects receiving file F, then system will not push any file to device D within a period of time which is adjustable.

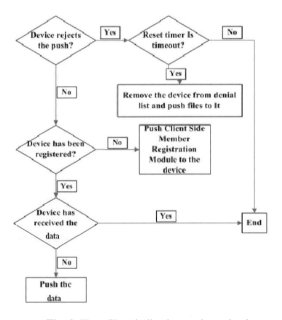

Fig. 3. Flow Chart indicating push mechanism

5 Results

Figure 4 indicating the Simulation Result1 shows that the battery level and performance check information are readily gathered in order to be sent to the hand held
device.

Fig. 4. Simulation Figure 1

Fig. 5. Simulation Figure 2

Figure 5 indicating the Simulation result 2 shows that the gathered data being successfully sent to the paired Bluetooth device. Due to the unavailability of Bluetooth V3.0+HS device and its respective simulation software, a general software was used along with V2.0 was used for testing.

Table 1. Comparison of Technologies

Technical Specifications	Bluetooth v2.1 + EDR	Bluetooth v3.0 + HS
Radio frequency	2.4 GHz	2.4 GHz and 5 GHz
Distance/Range	10 meters	10 meters
Over the air data rate	1-3 Mbps	up to 54 Mbps
Application throughput	0.7-2.1 Mbps	up to 24 Mbps
Nodes/Active slaves	7 / 16,777,184	Same as 2.1 + EDR
Security	64b/128b and application layer user defined	128b AES
Robustness	Adaptive fast frequency hopping, FEC, fast ACK	CSMA/CA with collision detection, ARQ, FEC, CRC
Latency (from a non connected state) Total time to send data (det.battery life)	100ms	Same as 2.1 + EDR with AMP Less than 2.1 + EDR with UCD
Government regulation	Worldwide	Same as 2.1 + EDR
Certification body	Bluetooth SIG	Same as 2.1 + EDR
Voice capable	Yes	Same as 2.1 + EDR
Network topology	Scatternet	Same as 2.1 + EDR
Power consumption	1 as the reference	< 1
Service discovery	Yes	Same as 2.1 + EDR
Profile concept	Yes	Same as 2.1 + EDR
Primary use cases	Mobile phones, gaming, headsets, stereo audio streaming, automotive, PCs, etc.	Same as 2.1 + EDR plus bulk data transfer, synchronization and video streaming

A.   Advantages

There are many advantages in embedding a Bluetooth 3.0+HS circuit in a pacemaker. It is simple, cheap and easy to implement by making only a few changes to the present design. Since we are using Bluetooth 3.0 +HS where HS means high speed, where the data is transferred at great speeds which involves minimum utilization of time and power. Also, Bluetooth 3.0, reduces wastage of battery, since, only after it gets activated it starts consuming power, till it completes transmitting the information to the handheld device. It also works alongside the demand pacemaker. No special device or circuitry is required for power conservation since Bluetooth V3.0 +H.S already comes with an inbuilt power conservation mechanism (from its architecture). Also Bluetooth does not interfere with the normal operation of a pacemaker and hence is safe for usage. Instrumentation and implementation cost on the consumer's side is practically zero, since most of the handheld devices come with inbuilt Bluetooth system.

Bluetooth Version3.0 is simply called as "Bluetooth Version 3.0 + High Speed", this is because it is an improvement over Version2.1 featuring

- High speed
- High power saving capabilities
- Robustness
- High security
- Extended P.A.N

while retaining rest of the features of V2.1.Refer Table 1. Comparison between Bluetooth technologies V3.0 +H.S and V2.1 + E.D.R This proposed system will replace the pacemaker programmer used in hospitals, and will help the patients to analyze the battery life and performance by themselves using their handheld devices such as mobile phones, PDA's, laptops, palmtops, etc.

6 Bottle Neck and Future Work

Though it offers numerous advantages, this technology has a few drawbacks too which can be overcome, possibly, in the near future. Since Bluetooth 3.0 is an emerging technology, testing software's used for Bluetooth 3.0 are still under the process of construction. One another drawback is that all existing pacemaker architectures have to be modified to accommodate BluetoothV3.0 +H.S. This might take some time but gradual evolving, as always is the case, will happen over time.

Future work can be extended to view a live streaming video on the areas of malfunction inside the pacemaker using wireless technologies. Pacemaker must be accessible through other wireless technologies like wifi, wimax etc.

7 Conclusion

Instruments that can check pacemaker battery levels or performance and functionality are possessed only by doctors and in major hospitals. For a normal patient to check his/her pacemaker information we propose to implement an easy, cheap and simple mechanism using Bluetooth. This system is highly advantageous and at the same time economic too. It is very simple to implement and the Bluetooth circuitry does not interfere with the pacemaker's normal operation in any way and thus is an easier alternative to locating the nearest hospital, every time a pacemaker check up is required.

References

[1] Bluetooth SIG, "Bluetooth Basics"
[2] Sandro, A.P., Hadda, D., Richar, D., Houben, P.M., Serdijn, W.R.A.: The Evolution of Pacemakers

[3] Chen, Y.-L., Chou, H.-J., Lin, C.-P., Lin, H.-T., Yuan, S.-M., Liu, Y.-C.: Blueg. A New Blog-like P2P System built on Bluetooth, Master Thesis of Computer Science and Engineering, National Chiao Tung University (June 2006)

[4] Wong, L.S.Y., Okamoto, R., Ahn, J.: A Very Low Power CMOS Mixed-Signal IC for Implantable Pacemaker Applications, St. Jude Medical, Cardiac Rhythm Management Division, Sunnyvale, CA

[5] Hopkins, B.: Part 1: File transfer with JSR-82 and OBEX

[6] Chow, A.W.C., Buxton, A.E. (eds.): Implantable Cardiac Pacemakers and Defibrillators

[7] Yeh, N.-S.: Linux Bluetooth Protocol Stack/BlueZ on SCAN Device. In: Computer and Communication, CEPS, vol. 107, pp. 38–47 (March 2004)

[8] Chatschik, B.: An overview of the Bluetooth wireless technology. IEEE Communications Magazine 39(12), 86–94 (2001)

[9] Yorozu, Y., Hirano, M., Oka, K., Tagawa, Y.: Electron spectroscopy studies on magneto-optical media and plastic substrate interface. IEEE Transl. J. Magn. Japan 2, 740–741 (1987); [Digests 9th Annual Conf. Magnetics Japan, p. 301, 1982]

[10] Khandpur, R.S.: Biomedical Instrumentation Technology and Applications

Cross-Layer Analyses of QoS Parameters in Wireless Sensor Networks

Alireza Masoum, Nirvana Meratnia, Arta Dilo,
Zahra Taghikhaki, and Paul J.M. Havinga

University of Twente, Department of Computer Science,
Pervasive Systems Group, 7500 AE Enschede, The Netherlands
{a.masoum,n.meratnia,a.dilo,
z.taghikhaki,p.j.m.havinga}@utwente.nl

Abstract. Providing reliable and timely information is one of the important tasks of wireless sensor networks. To this end, recently quality of service (QoS) satisfying end users and matching WSN constrains, has become an important research topic. However, majority of research in this area has overlooked the fact that ensuring quality of service requires a cross-layer approach spanning through all layers of the protocol stack. In this paper, we study QoS parameters and requirements in WSNs in application, data management and physical levels and analyze their cross-layer effects using simulations.

Keywords: Quality of service, WSN, network layers.

1 Introduction

Wireless sensor networks (WSNs) are new revolutionary monitoring platforms. A wireless sensor network is composed of many tiny, low-cost and low-power devices called sensor nodes. A large number of sensor nodes are deployed in an environment to monitor a physical phenomenon, reason about collected data, execute light processes, and send either raw data or processed information to a sink node.

Wireless sensor networks differ dramatically from the traditional wireless networks due to their specific nature, limited resources (in terms of power, memory and processing capacity), low node and network reliability and dynamic network topology [9]. These networks do not use end-to-end communication. This means that when nodes send data to the sink, each node only connects to its neighboring nodes [5]. In WSN relay nodes can themselves generate data. Environmental and inner-network parameters such as node failure or link failure may cause changes in network topology [9]. These specific aspects also generally prevent many solutions of wireless networks to be directly applicable to the wireless sensor networks. For instance, most of current quality of service (QoS) methods in wireless ad-hoc networks are based on end-to-end path discovery, resource reservation along the discovered path, and path recovery in case of topology changes [15]. Integrated and differential services are examples of these methods [17].

Compared to applications of wireless ad-hoc networks, WSN applications pose additional requirements on the quality of service (QoS). Providing acceptable QoS over

N. Meghanathan et al. (Eds.): CCSIT 2011, Part II, CCIS 132, pp. 595–605, 2011.
© Springer-Verlag Berlin Heidelberg 2011

WSN requires not only considering resource constraints of individual nodes and entire network but also physical node failure, communication unreliability, and dynamic network performance. In typical warehouse applications with time sensitive goods, for instance, sensor nodes need to report goods condition such as humidity or temperature in a timely and reliable fashion. When some unwanted conditions such as goods spoiling or extreme temperature changes occur, sensors must immediately inform the sink and possibly generate an alarm. If the sink receives data with delay, then the situation may not be controllable. Delay in data transmission from sensors to the sink as well as packet loss occurring during the course of transmission may potentially deteriorate performance of the system. Such delays and information loss cannot be tolerated in many safety-critical applications of WSNs [17].

Although QoS requirements are application-dependent, many applications are concerned about reliability, real-timeness, robustness, trustworthiness, and adaptability. Various QoS metrics may be used to measure the degree of satisfaction of these requirements. In this paper, we present a cross-layer analysis of QoS parameters and requirements in the field of WSNs. The remainder of this paper is organized as follows: The most important challenges for QoS in WSN are discussed in Section 2, while related work is presented in Section 3. QoS parameters for application, data management and physical levels are defined in Section 4. Effects of QoS parameters of different levels of the protocol stack are discussed and presented through simulation in Section 5 and 6. Section 7 closes the paper with conclusions.

2 QoS Challenges in WSN

Special characteristics of WSNs cause some limitations for QoS support. These limitations include [5,11,15]:

2.1 Resource Limitation

This constraint includes, among others, energy, bandwidth, memory, buffer size, processing power and transmission power. Therefore, QoS support methods need to be energy efficient, simple, and computationally light. They also need to provide bandwidth guarantees.

2.2 Data Redundancy

In WSN, it is possible to have similar data from nodes that sense similar phenomena. While redundant data can improve data reliability, sensing, transmitting and processing consume more energy. Reliable data aggregation or compression can decrease data redundancy but complicates QoS design.

2.3 Network Dynamics

Node failure, link failure, node mobility, etc., can change the network topology. Unpredictable condition of the environment in which nodes are deployed can also result in frequent change of the network topology. Such dynamicity complicates proper design of QoS support techniques.

2.4 Energy Balancing

Wireless sensor nodes have different types and periods of activities. This means that some nodes have to remain active for long periods of time while others have low activity and are mostly in sleep mode. Being in active mode requires energy. Therefore, the longer the active period, the more energy is spent. This may result in energy depletion of some of the active nodes and create holes in networks. An effective energy balancing and distribution mechanism or energy harvesting technique can greatly increase network lifetime. However, it also complicates the design of effective QoS support techniques.

2.5 Different Sampling Frequency

WSN applications may have different requirements in terms of sampling rate of various sensors. Due to the fact that sampling rate directly affects energy consumption and data quality, among others, designing a QoS support mechanism that satisfies both long network lifetime and high data quality would be challenging.

In what follows, we present various parameters used for QoS support and different techniques to ensure them.

3 Related Work

It seems that there is no single universally accepted set of QoS parameters, as different researchers have considered different QoS parameters. In [1] end-to-end delay is defined as the QoS parameter and a routing protocol is proposed to guarantee a least-cost, delay-constrained path for real-time data transmission. The protocol uses a link cost function which calculates connectivity parameters such as nodes reserved energy, transmission power and error rate. He et al. [6] have also considered end-to-end delay as a QoS parameter and propose a protocol called SPEED to decrease it. SPEED maintains a desired delivery speed across the network through combination of feedback control and non-deterministic QoS-aware geographic forwarding.

Authors of [14] define delay and packet loss as QoS parameters. The objective of their QoS-aware routing protocol QSR is to provide bi-directional routes based on the QoS required by the heterogeneous traffic including shortest time, highest average energy and robust routes. The design philosophy of the QSR protocol is based on ants searching for food.

Iyer et al. [7] define QoS as a sensor network resolution or optimum number of active sensors sending information to the sink. The main idea of their approach is to prolong network lifetime by powering on and off enough number of sensor nodes to collect sufficient data at the sink.

There are also researchers who consider area coverage as the QoS parameter. They detect how to best cover an area such that no hole exists and all unwanted events are detected [10]. Akyildiz et al. [3] mention that QoS is composed of latency, packet loss rate and data rate. Xia et al. [16] have proposed a fuzzy logic control based QoS management for wireless sensor and actuator networks (WSANs). They use deadline miss ratio for data transmission as a metric to measure the QoS of WSAN. For adjusting sampling period of a relevant sensor and keeping the deadline miss ratio at a desired level, they use a fuzzy logic controller. In this way, QoS requirements with respect to timeliness, reliability, and robustness can be satisfied.

Koubâa et al. [8] define a Hidden-Node Avoidance Mechanism (H-NAMe) for WSNs. Hidden-node collisions affect four QoS metrics, namely, throughput, transfer delay, energy, and reliability. The proposed mechanism eliminates hidden node collisions in synchronized single or multiple cluster WSNs using a contention-based MAC protocol. It follows a proactive approach through the creation of hidden-node interference- free node groups and node cluster groups.

4   QoS Requirements and Parameters

In this section we present QoS parameters on three different levels of the protocol stack: application, data management and physical level.

4.1 Application Level Parameters

Usually, lower level QoS requirements are determined by considering application level parameters. Requirements in this level are specified by users. Based on [5, 11,15], we define QoS requirements at the application level to be:

- **System lifetime:** is the time that first node in the network consumes its energy completely and dies. Some authors define system lifetime as the time from system deployment up to the time when failure occurs to the extent that network cannot satisfy users' requirements anymore [12].
- **Information latency:** For the continuous and event-based applications of WSNs, information latency refers to the period between event detection at the nodes and receiving event data at the sink [3]. In on-demand applications of WSNs, information latency is defined as the time period between sending a query and the time of receiving the response [15].
- **Detection probability:** is defined as a probability of detecting real world events and reporting them to the user.
- **Data quality:** relates to accuracy of collected data. Data accuracy refers to the degree of corresponding reported data to real value.
- **Data resolution:** outlines the required data density temporally or spatially. Sampling rate parameter defines data resolution in temporal scale while sensor density determines the spatial resolution [14].

4.2 Data Management Level Parameters

Various operations may occur in the data processing level. These operations may be applied on the sensed or buffered data of the nodes. Data management level can be divided into two parts: (i) data placement and discovery [18] and (ii) in network data processing [14,18]. Data placement and discovery unit stores acquired data and allows users to search and retrieve data (also known as data discovery). QoS parameters of this part include:

- **Error rate:** is amount of error in data during data placement and discovery operation at the sink or intermediate nodes.
- **Loss rate:** refers to the percentage of lost data through data placement and discovery operations.
- **Communication cost:** is related to the consumed energy for data placement and discovery operations.
- **Discovery latency:** is defined as the time taken for data querying and data retrieval.
- **Replacement latency:** is the time required to send data to the destination nodes.

QoS parameters of the in-network processing part can be defined as:

- **Computation cost:** is the energy consumption of the data processing.
- **Data abstraction:** is the amount of processed data for real world phenomena representation.
- **Data accuracy:** is accuracy of the processed data.
- **Processing latency:** it shows the real amount of processing speed.

4.3 Physical Level Parameters

The physical level consists of wireless unit, processor and sensing unit. Parameters of these units are interconnected. Wireless unit parameters include channel speed, coding and radio frequency power. Processing unit parameters include processing speed, computation power, and memory capacity. Sensing unit parameters include sampling, frequency, sensing power and sensing range. We further investigate the following physical level QoS parameters:

- **Sampling rate:** is number of measurements taken from the environment at a specific time interval.
- **Transmission rate:** is number of transmissions of sensed data from a node towards the sink at a specific time interval.
- **Queue size:** is the maximum number of packets that can be stored in a queue. In other words, it is the maximum capacity of a queue.
- **Number of nodes:** is number of deployed nodes to monitor an environment.

5 QoS Parameters Effects

Defined parameters in previous section directly affect each other. This means that improving QoS in one level may improve or worsen QoS parameters of the other levels. In this section we investigate the relations between these parameters.

5.1 Effect of Data Management Level Parameters on Application Level

Data loss can decrease the probability of event detection and data quality. Therefore, error rate and loss rate during data placement and discovery operations can influence the event detection probability and data quality.

Discovery and placement latency have direct effect on information latency. For the system lifetime parameter, communication and computation costs are the essential parameters. Decreasing the consumed energy for communication and processing in each node, improves system lifetime [14].

In the data processing section, processing latency affects information latency in application level. Some methods such as compression algorithms or improving processing power can improve the processing latency and information latency [13].

Finally, data abstraction has direct relation with data resolution.

5.2 Effect of Physical Level Parameters on Application and Management Level

In wireless unit, channel speed affects the throughput parameter. Coding methods as well as radio frequency power and transmission rate influence the throughput, system lifetime, connectivity robustness and data quality parameters. In Sensing unit, measurement accuracy and sampling rate have impact on data accuracy, data quality, and resolution. They have direct effect on the sample volume, which growth increases the throughput and decreases the network lifetime. In processing unit, processing speed, computation power and queue size have impact on processing latency and computation cost parameters of data management level, which on their side affect the information latency and system lifetime parameters in the application level.

6   Cross-Layer Analysis of QoS Parameters

In previous sections we defined QoS parameters for application, data management and physical levels and explained their effects on each other. In this section, we present cross-layer effects application, management, and physical layers using simulation. We consider lifetime, information latency, and data resolution parameters of the application level, error rate and loss rate of the data management level, and sampling rate, transmission rate, number of nodes and queue size parameters of the physical level.

For simulation we use Ptolemy simulator [2]. The $50 \times 50 \text{m}^2$ simulation area contains one sink node and 35 sensor nodes being randomly deployed. We assume 25m communication range for the nodes and different sampling and transmission rates. Network topology is star, and sink node is located at the center of the deployment area. Basic energy level of each node is 5J. Transmission and reception power are 0.0495W and 0.0288W, respectively. Sensing power is 0.015W. Simulations are repeated 10 times and the duration of each simulation is one day.

We consider a scenario, in which sensor nodes monitor temperature condition of environment and each node senses data in dedicated times and sends them to the sink periodically.

6.1   Impact of Physical Level Parameters on Application Level Parameters

Sampling rate defines the amount of sensed data. Higher sampling rate means smaller sampling time intervals. This may lead to faster detection of environmental changes. Higher sampling rate means that sensed data becomes closer to the real data. This improves data resolution parameter in the application layer as well. These theoretical hypotheses are also confirmed through simulation. However growing sampling rate can reduce lifetime, because nodes sense and then send more data per time unit and their energy is depleted. It can be seen from Figure 1(a) that by increasing sampling rate, energy consumption in each node increases. On the other side, transmitting more data to the sink causes more energy consumption. Figure 1(b) shows effects of both transmission and sampling rates on energy consumption.

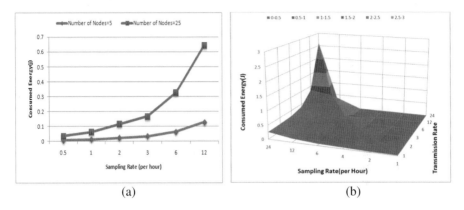

(a)   (b)

Fig. 1. Effect of (a) sampling rate on energy consumption, (b) sampling rate and transmission rate on energy consumption

Figure 2(a) shows the effect of different sampling rates on data resolution. By increasing number of nodes and number of transmissions, data resolution will be increased. The generated data need to be inserted into queue to be processed later. As it can be seen from Figure 2(b), increase of transmission rate leads to increase of information latency.

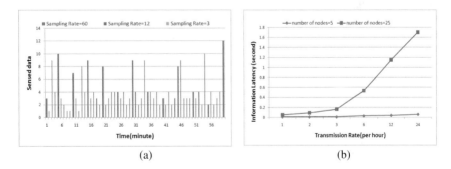

(a)   (b)

Fig. 2. Effect of (a) sampling rate on data resolution (b) transmission rate on information latency

6.2 Impact of Data Management Level Parameters on Application Level

The increase of sampling rate makes collected data to be closer to the real data and consequently leads to lower data representation error, as it can be seen in Figure 3(a).

This figure shows the impact of sampling rate on error rate for different number of nodes. Compared to 5 nodes, 25 nodes generate more data traffic. Figure 3(b) shows the effect for a wider range of network densities, shown by the number of nodes. Higher number of nodes increases the number of transmissions and produces more traffic in the network, which causes congestion and increases the loss rate. On the other side, increased congestion diminishes the number of received data packets at the sink node and result in higher error rate. This effect is also tested against three different transmission rates.

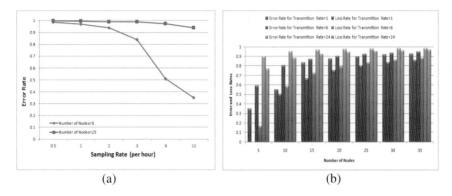

(a)   (b)

Fig. 3. Effect of sampling and transmission rate on (a) error rate and (b) loss rate for different number of nodes

Figure 4 shows the combined effect of sampling rate and transmission rate on error rate for two different networks, with 5 and 25 nodes.

Queue size is another parameter that can influence QoS in the application layer. Considering a fixed queue size, the increase of the number of transmissions results in a faster filling up of the queue. When rate of traffic generation is higher than the queue size, packet loss occurs. Due to producing more data in the network, data has to wait in the queue and so delay increases. After a while, nodes queue will be overloaded, thus some packets will be dropped and loss rate will increase as well. Thus sink node receives less data, which in turn leads to higher error rate. These effects are shown in Figure 5.

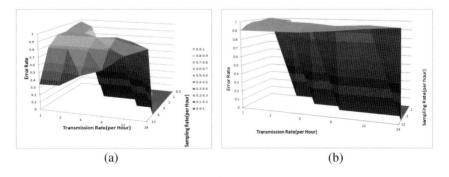

(a)   (b)

Fig. 4. Effect of sampling and transmission rate on error rate for (a) 5 nodes (b) 25 nodes

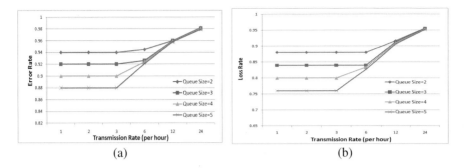

Fig. 5. Effect of queue size on (a) error rate and (b) loss rate

6.3 Impact of Cross Layer on Application and Data Management Level

Now that we have analyzed the effects of QoS parameters of different levels, it is time to determine the trade-offs between them.

Figure 6(a) shows the effect of transmission rate on energy consumption, which determines the system lifetime parameter from the application level and on loss rate parameter from the data management level. Higher transmission rate means higher energy consumption for each node and the whole network, therefore decreased network lifetime. On the other side, a high transmission rate means low delay in sending data, thus improves information latency. However, by increasing the number of transmissions, network traffic will be increased and more packets will be lost. This will then cause information latency due to delay in packet retransmission. This effect can be seen in Figure 6(b).

Figure 7 shows the effect of transmission rate on detection probability parameter from the application level and loss rate from the management level. Increasing transmission rate impacts the relation between queue processing time and the amount of generated traffic. By increasing the volume of traffic in a time unit, the queue processing mechanism cannot process the entire queue quickly. Therefore, the queue will be full and the received packets will be dropped. This causes more loss rate and decreases detection probability.

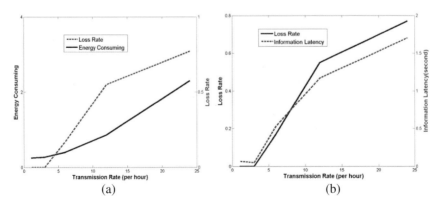

Fig. 6. Trade-off between (a) loss rate and energy consuming (b) loss rate and information latency

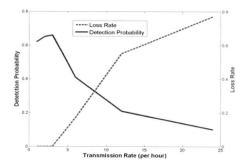

Fig. 7. Trade-off between detection probability and loss rate

7 Conclusions

This paper presented QoS parameters and requirements at different levels of the protocol stack for WSN applications. After providing definitions for each of these parameters, effects of QoS parameters of physical and data management levels on application level QoS were investigated. Simulation results helped in defining the trade-offs between various cross-layer QoS parameters.

Acknowledgments. The work presented in this paper is supported by FREE project that is funded as part of the Innovation programme PointOne organized by SenterNovem, the Netherlands.

References

1. Akayya, K., Younis, M.: An Energy-Aware QoS Routing Protocol for Wireless Sensor Networks. In: 23rd International Conference on Distributed Computing Systems Workshops (ICDCSW 2003), USA, pp. 710–715 (2003)
2. Ptolemy Project, http://ptolemy.eecs.berkeley.edu/
3. Akyildiz, I.F., Melodia, T., Chowdhury, K.R.: A Survey on Wireless Multimedia Sensor Networks. Computer Networks 51(4), 921–960 (2007)
4. Arici, T., Gedik, B., Altunbasak, T., Liu, L.: PINCO: a Pipelined In-Network Compression Scheme for Data Collection in Wireless Sensor Networks. In: Proc. of 12th International Conference on Computer Communications and Networks (IEEE ICCCN 2003), Dallas, Texas, USA, pp. 539–544 (2003)
5. Chen, D., Varshney, P.K.: QoS Support in Wireless Sensor Networks: A Survey. In: Proc. of the International Conference on Wireless Networks (ICWN 2004), Las Vegas, Nevada, USA, pp. 227–233 (2004)
6. He, T., Stankovic, J.A., Lu, C., Abdelzaher, T.: SPEED: A stateless protocol for real-time communication in sensor networks. In: International Conference on Distributed Computing Systems (ICDCS 2003), USA, pp. 46–55 (2003)
7. Iyer, A., Kleinrock, L.: QoS Control for Sensor Networks. In: Proc. of IEEE International Conference on Communications (ICC 2003), Alaska, USA, pp. 517–521 (2003)

8. Koubâa, A., Severino, R., Alves, M., Tovar, E.: Improving Quality-of-Service in Wireless Sensor Networks by Mitigating Hidden-Node Collisions. In: Technical Report, IPP-HURRAY! Polytechnic Institute of Porto, ISEP-IPP (2009), http://www.hurray.isep.ipp.pt

9. Martínez, F., García, A.B., Corredor, I., López, L., Hernández, V., Dasilva, A.: QoS in Wireless Sensor Network: Survey and Approach. In: IEEE/ACM EATIS (2007)

10. Meguerdichian, S., Koushanfar, F., Potkonjak, M., Srivastava, M.B.: Coverage Problems in Wireless Ad-hoc Sensor Networks. In: Proc. of IEEE Infocom, Alaska, USA, pp. 1380–1387 (2001)

11. Perillo, M., Heinzelman, W.: Providing Application QoS through Intelligent Sensor Management. In: 1st IEEE International Workshop on Sensor Network Protocols and Applications (SNPA 2003), pp. 93–101 (2003)

12. Phoha, S., LaPorta, T., Griffin, C.: Sensor Network Operations. A John Wiley & Sons, USA (2006)

13. Sorooshi, M.: QoS challenges in wireless sensor networks. MS Thesis, Computer engineering department, Sharif University of Technology (2007)

14. Su, W.: Enabling Quality-of-Service Applications in Sensor Networks. PHD Thesis Presented to School of Electrical and Computer Engineering, Georgia Institute of Technology, USA (2004)

15. Wang, Y., Liu, X., Yin, J.: Requirements of Quality of Service in Wireless Sensor Network. In: Proc. of the International Conference on Networking, International Conference on Systems and International Conference on Mobile Communications and Learning Technologies (ICN/ICONS/MCL 2006), USA, pp. 116–121 (2006)

16. Xia, F., Zhao, W.H., Sun, Y.X., Tian, Y.C.: Fuzzy Logic Control Based QoS Management in Wireless Sensor/Actuator Networks. In: Sensors 2007, vol. 7(12), pp. 3179–3191 (2007)

17. Xia, F.: QoS Challenges and Opportunities in Wireless Sensor/Actuator Networks. Sensors 8(2), 1099–1110 (2008)

18. Ye, F., Luo, H., Cheng, J., Lu, S., Zhang, L.: A Two-tier Data Dissemination Model for Large-scale Wireless Sensor Networks. In: Proc. of 8th Annual International Conference on Mobile Computing and Networking (ACM MobiCom 2002), Georgia, USA, pp. 148–152 (2002)

Optimum Routing Approach vs. Least Overhead Routing Approach for Minimum Hop Routing in Mobile Ad hoc Networks

Natarajan Meghanathan

Jackson State University
Jackson, MS 39217, USA
natarajan.meghanathan@jsums.edu

Abstract. Proactive routing protocols for mobile ad hoc networks (MANETs) follow on Optimum Routing Approach (ORA) to choose and use the optimal route at any time instant. On the other hand, on-demand routing protocols for MANETs have been traditionally designed using the Least Overhead Routing Approach (LORA) wherein a route determined using broadcast flooding-based route discovery is used as long as exists. With LROA, a route determined to be the best optimal route based on a particular route selection metric, may later become sub-optimal, and could be still used, if exists. In this paper, we evaluate the impact of the ORA and LORA strategies on minimum hop routing. Our hypothesis is that the LORA strategy could yield routes with a larger time-averaged hop count when compared to the minimum hop count of routes determined using the ORA strategy. We evaluate the two routing strategies under diverse conditions of network density, node mobility and mobility models such as the Random Waypoint model, City Section model and the Manhattan model. Simulation results illustrate that the hop count of routes maintained according to the LORA strategy is at most 12% greater than that incurred with the ORA strategy. The Random Waypoint model under the LORA strategy incurs the lowest hop count per path and the largest increase in hop count vis-à-vis the ORA strategy; on the other hand, the Manhattan model incurs a larger hop count per path and the smallest increase in hop count.

Keywords: Optimum Routing Approach (ORA), Least Overhead Routing Approach (LORA), Mobility Model, Hop Count, Mobile Ad hoc Networks.

1 Introduction

A mobile ad hoc network (MANET) is a dynamic distributed system of wireless nodes that move independently of each other. Routes in MANETs are often multi-hop in nature due to the limited transmission range of the battery-operated wireless nodes. MANET routing protocols are of two types [1][2]: proactive and reactive. Proactive routing protocols determine routes between every pair of nodes in the network, irrespective of their requirement. Reactive or on-demand routing protocols determine

N. Meghanathan et al. (Eds.): CCSIT 2011, Part II, CCIS 132, pp. 606–616, 2011.

routes between any pair of nodes only if data needs to be transferred between the two nodes and no route is known between the two nodes. Proactive routing protocols always tend to maintain optimum routes between every source-destination (*s-d*) pair and this strategy is called the Optimum Routing Approach (ORA) [1][3]. In this pursuit, each node periodically exchanges its routing table and link state information with other nodes in the network, thus generating a significantly larger control overhead. On the other hand, reactive routing protocols use a Least Overhead Routing Approach (LORA) [1][3] wherein an *s-d* route is discovered through a global broadcast flooding-based route discovery process and the discovered route is used as long as it exists. With node mobility, an *s-d* route determined to be optimal at a particular time instant need not remain optimal in the subsequent time instants, even though the route may continue to exist. Thus, with LORA, it is possible that the routing protocols continue to send data packets through sub-optimal routes. On the other hand, with ORA, even though, we could send data packets at the best possible route at any time instant, the cost of periodically discovering such a route may be significantly high. In dynamically changing network topologies, reactive on-demand routing protocols have been preferred over proactive protocols with respect to the routing control overhead incurred [4][5].

The objective of this paper is to study the impact of adopting the ORA and LORA strategies for minimum hop routing in MANETs. Minimum hop routing is a very widely adopted route selection principle of MANET routing protocols, belonging to both proactive and reactive categories. As ORA determines the best optimal route at any time instant, our hypothesis is that the hop count of minimum hop routes discovered under the LORA strategy would be greater than those discovered under the ORA strategy. We determine the percentage difference in the hop count of minimum hop *s-d* paths determined under the two strategies. We conduct extensive simulations under two different network densities and three different mobility models with three different levels of node mobility. The three mobility models [6] used are the Random Waypoint model, City Section model and Manhattan model. Even though, performance comparison studies of individual proactive vs. reactive routing protocols, an extensive simulation based analysis on the impact of the ORA and LORA strategies on the minimum hop count of routes (adopted by the proactive and reactive routing protocols) has not been conducted in the literature and therein lies our contribution through this paper.

The rest of the paper is organized as follows: Section 2 discusses the algorithms employed for simulating minimum hop routing under the ORA and LORA strategies and also illustrates an example highlighting the difference between the two strategies and their impact on the hop count of *s-d* paths. Section 3 reviews the three different mobility models used in the simulations. Section 4 describes the simulation environment and presents the simulation results for hop count per *s-d* path, path lifetime and network connectivity. Section 5 concludes the paper and lists future work. Throughout the paper, the terms 'node' and 'vertex', 'edge' and 'link', 'path' and 'route' are used interchangeably. They mean the same.

2   Minimum Hop Routing under the ORA and LORA Strategies

We use the notion of a mobile graph [7] defined as the sequence $G_M = G_1G_2 \ldots G_T$ of static graphs that represent the network topology changes over the time scale T, representing the simulation time. We sample the network topology periodically, for every 0.25 seconds, which in reality could be the instants of data packet origination at the source. Each of the static graphs is a unit disk graph [8] of nodes and edges, wherein there exists an edge if and only if the Euclidean distance between the two constituent end nodes of the edge is within the transmission range of the nodes. We assume every node operates at a fixed transmission range, R.

Input: Static Graph $G = (V, E)$, source s, destination d
Auxiliary Variables/Initialization: *Nodes-Explored* = Φ; *FIFO-Queue* = Φ;
$\qquad\qquad\qquad\qquad\qquad$ ∀ node $v \in V$, *Parent* (v) = NULL
Begin Algorithm *BFS* (G, s, d)
$\quad$ *Nodes-Explored* = *Nodes-Explored* U $\{s\}$
$\quad$ *FIFO-Queue* = *FIFO-Queue* U $\{s\}$
$\quad$ **while** (|*FIFO-Queue*| > 0) **do**
$\quad\quad$ node u = Dequeue(*FIFO-Queue*) //extract the first node
$\quad\quad$ **for** (every edge (u, v)) **do** // i.e. every neighbor v of u
$\quad\quad\quad$ **if** ($v \notin$ *Nodes-Explored*) **then**
$\quad\quad\quad\quad$ *Nodes-Explored* = *Nodes-Explored* U $\{v\}$
$\quad\quad\quad\quad$ *FIFO-Queue* = *FIFO-Queue* U $\{v\}$
$\quad\quad\quad\quad$ *Parent* (v) = u
$\quad\quad\quad$ **end if**
$\quad\quad$ **end for**
$\quad$ **end while**
$\quad$ **if** (| *Nodes-Explored* | = | V |) **then**
$\quad\quad$ Path P_{d-s} = $\{d\}$
$\quad\quad$ *temp-node* = d
$\quad\quad$ **while** (*Parent* (*temp-node*) != NULL) **do**
$\quad\quad\quad$ P_{d-s} = P_{d-s} U $\{Parent\ (temp\text{-}node)\}$
$\quad\quad\quad$ *temp-node* = *Parent* (*temp-node*)
$\quad\quad$ **end while**
$\quad\quad$ Path P_{s-d} = reverse(P_{d-s})
$\quad\quad$ **return** P_{s-d}
$\quad$ **end if**
$\quad$ **else**
$\quad\quad$ **return** NULL // no s-d path
$\quad$ **end if**

End Algorithm BFS

Fig. 1. Breadth First Search (BFS) Algorithm to Determine Minimum Hop s-d Path

Input: $G_M = G_1 G_2 \ldots G_T$, source s, destination d
Auxiliary Variable: i, Path P_{s-d}
Initialization: $i=1$; P_{s-d} = NULL
Begin *ORA-MinHopPaths*
   while $(i \leq T)$ **do**
      Path P_{s-d} = BFS(G_i, s, d)
      $i = i + 1$
   end while
End *ORA-MinHopPaths*

Fig. 2. Pseudo Code to Determine Minimum Hop *s-d* Paths under the ORA Strategy

Input: $G_M = G_1 G_2 \ldots G_T$, source s, destination d
Auxiliary Variables: i, j, Path P_{s-d}
Initialization: $i=1$; $j=1$; P_{s-d} = NULL
Begin *LORA-MinHopPaths*
   while $(i \leq T)$ **do**

     if $(P_{s-d}$!= NULL$)$ **then**
       for every edge (u, v) in P_{s-d} **do**
         if $(\,(u, v)$ does not exist in $G_i)$ **then**
           P_{s-d} = NULL
         end if
       end for
     end if

     if $(P_{s-d}$ = NULL$)$ **then**
      Path P_{s-d} = BFS(G_i, s, d)
     end if
   $i = i + 1$

   end while

End *LORA-MinHopPaths*

Fig. 3. Pseudo Code to Determine Minimum Hop *s-d* Paths under the LORA Strategy

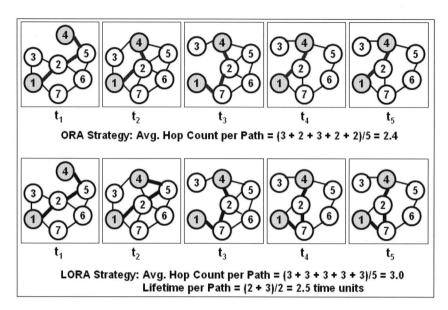

Fig. 4. Example for use of ORA and LORA Strategies for Minimum Hop Routing

For the ORA strategy, we determine the sequence of minimum hop s-d paths between a source node s and a destination node d by running the Breadth First Search (BFS) algorithm [9], starting from the source node s, on each of the static graphs of the mobile graph generated over the entire time period of the simulation. In the case of LORA, if we don't know a path from source s to destination d in static graph G_i, we run BFS, starting from node s, on G_i and determine the minimum hop path $P_{s\text{-}d}$ from s to d. For subsequent static graphs G_{i+1}, G_{i+2}, ..., we simply test the presence of path $P_{s\text{-}d}$. We validate the existence of a path $P_{s\text{-}d}$ in static graph G_j by testing the existence of every constituent edge of $P_{s\text{-}d}$ in G_j. If every constituent edge of $P_{s\text{-}d}$ exists in G_j, then the path $P_{s\text{-}d}$ exists in G_j. Otherwise, we run BFS on G_j, starting from the source s, and determine a new s-d path $P_{s\text{-}d}$. This procedure is repeated until the end of the simulation time. The pseudo code for BFS is given in Figure 1 and the pseudo code of our algorithms to determine the minimum hop paths under the ORA and LORA strategies is given in Figures 2 and 3 respectively.

Figure 4 is an example to illustrate the difference between the ORA and LORA strategies with respect to minimum hop routing. We sample the network topology for five consecutive instants of time as shown. The source and destination node IDs are 1 and 4 respectively. We notice that under the LORA strategy, we could use path {1 – 2 – 4 – 5} for time instants t_1 and t_2 and path {1 – 7 – 2 – 4} for time instants t_3, t_4 and t_5 respectively. The paths {1 – 2 – 4 – 5} and {1 – 7 – 2 – 4} appear to be the best possible minimum hop paths at the time of discovery, i.e., at time instants t_1 and t_3 respectively. Nevertheless, after each of these paths is chosen at a particular time instant, we notice the emergence of relatively shorter paths (i.e., with a lower hop count) in the static graphs captured at subsequent time instants. But it is not possible to use these paths under the LORA strategy. With ORA, the strategy is to capture the minimum hop paths at every time instant.

3   Review of Mobility Models

All the three mobility models used in this paper assume that the network is confined within fixed boundary conditions. The Random Waypoint mobility model assumes that the nodes can move anywhere within a network region. The City Section and the Manhattan mobility models assume the network to be divided into grids: square blocks of identical block length. The network is thus composed of a number of horizontal and vertical streets. Each street has two lanes, one for each direction (north and south direction for vertical streets, east and west direction for horizontal streets). A node is allowed to move only along the grids of horizontal and vertical streets.

According to the Random Waypoint model, the nodes are initially assumed to be placed at random locations in the network. The movement of each node is independent of the other nodes in the network. The mobility of a particular node is described as follows: The node chooses a random target location to move. The velocity with which the node moves to this chosen location is uniformly randomly selected from the interval $[v_{min},...,v_{max}]$. The node moves in a straight line (in a particular direction) to the chosen location with the chosen velocity. After reaching the target location, the node may stop there for a certain time called the *pause time*. The node then continues to choose another target location and moves to that location with a new velocity chosen again from $[v_{min},...,v_{max}]$. The selection of each target location and a velocity to move to that location is independent of the current node location and the velocity with which the node reached that location.

In both the City Section and Manhattan model, the nodes are assumed to be initially randomly placed in the street intersections. For the City Section model, each street (i.e., one side of a square block) is assumed to have a particular speed limit. Based on this speed limit and block length, one can determine the time it would take to move in the street. Each node placed at a particular street intersection chooses a random target street intersection to move. The node moves to the chosen street intersection on a path with the least amount of travel time. If two or more paths incur the same amount of least travel time, the tie is broken arbitrarily. After reaching the targeted street intersection, the node may stay there for a pause time and again choose a random street intersection to move. Each node independently repeats this procedure.

For the Manhattan model, the movement of a node is decided one street at a time. To start with, each node has equal chance (i.e., probability) of choosing any of the streets leading from its initial location. After a node begins to move in the chosen direction and reaches the next street intersection, the subsequent street in which the node will move is chosen probabilistically. If a node can continue to move in the same direction or can also change directions, then the node has 50% chance of continuing in the same direction, 25% chance of turning to the east/north and 25% chance of turning to the west/south, depending on the direction of the previous movement. If a node has only two options, then the node has an equal (50%) chance of exploring either of the two options. If a node has only one option to move (this occurs when the node reaches any of the four corners of the network), then the node has no other choice except to explore that option.

4 Simulations

Simulations have been conducted in a discrete-event simulator implemented by the author in Java. Network dimensions are 1000m x 1000m. For the Random Waypoint (RWP) mobility model, we assume the nodes can move anywhere within the network. For the City Section (CS) and Manhattan (Manh) mobility models, we assume the network is divided into grids: square blocks of length (side) 100m. The network is thus basically composed of a number of horizontal and vertical streets. Each street has two lanes, one for each direction (north and south direction for vertical streets, east and west direction for horizontal streets). A node is allowed to move only along the grids of horizontal and vertical streets. The wireless transmission range of a node is 250m. The network density is varied by performing the simulations with 50 (low density) and 100 (high density) nodes. The node velocity values used for each of the three mobility models are 2.5 m/s (about 5 miles per hour), 12.5 m/s (about 30 miles per hour) and 25 m/s (about 60 miles per hour), representing scenarios of low, moderate and high node mobility respectively. For the Random Waypoint mobility model, we assume $v_{min} = v_{max}$.

We obtain a centralized view of the network topology by generating mobility trace files for 1000 seconds under each of the three mobility models. The network topology is sampled for every 0.25 seconds to generate the static graphs and the mobile graph. Two nodes a and b are assumed to have a bi-directional link at time t, if the Euclidean distance between them at time t (derived using the locations of the nodes from the mobility trace file) is less than or equal to the wireless transmission range of the nodes. Each data point in Figures 5 through 8 and in Tables I to III is an average computed over 5 mobility trace files and 20 randomly selected s-d pairs from each of the mobility trace files. The starting time of each s-d session is uniformly distributed between 1 to 20 seconds. The following performance metrics are evaluated:

- Percentage Network Connectivity: The percentage network connectivity indicates the probability of finding an s-d path between any source s and destination d in networks for a given density and a mobility model. Measured over all the s-d sessions of a simulation run, this metric is the ratio of the number of static graphs in which there is an s-d path to the total number of static graphs in the mobile graph.

- Average Route Lifetime: The average route lifetime is the average of the lifetime of all the static paths of an s-d session, averaged over all the s-d sessions.

- Average Hop Count: The average hop count is the time averaged hop count of a mobile path for an s-d session, averaged over all the s-d sessions. The time averaged hop count for an s-d session is measured as the sum of the products of the number of hops per static s-d path and the lifetime of the static s-d path divided by the number of static graphs in which there existed a static s-d path. For example, if a mobile path spanning over 10 static graphs comprises of a 2-hop static path p_1, a 3-hop static path p_2, and a 2-hop static path p_3, with each existing for 2, 3 and 5 seconds respectively, then the time-averaged hop count of the mobile path would be $(2*2 + 3*3 + 2*5) / 10 = 2.3$.

4.1 Percentage Network Connectivity

The percentage network connectivity (refer Figures 5 and 6) is not dependent on the routing strategy (ORA or LORA) and is dependent only on the mobility model, the level of node mobility and network density. It is quite natural to observe that for a given mobility model and level of node mobility, the percentage network connectivity increases with increase in network density. In low density networks (50 nodes), the Random Waypoint model provided the largest network connectivity for a given level of node mobility; the City Section and Manhattan models yielded a relatively lower network connectivity, differing as large as by 11% . This can be attributed to the constrained motion of the nodes only along the streets of the network. On the other hand, as we increase the network density (100 node scenarios), the City Section model and/or the Manhattan model yielded network connectivity equal or larger than that incurred with the Random Waypoint model. As more nodes are added to the streets, the probability of finding source-destination routes at any point of time increases significantly. For a given network density, the network connectivity provided by each of the three mobility models almost remained the same for different values of node velocity. Hence, network connectivity is mainly influenced by the number of nodes in the network and their initial random distribution. The randomness associated with the mobility models ensure that node velocity is not a significant factor influencing network connectivity.

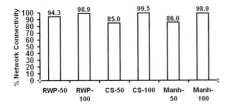
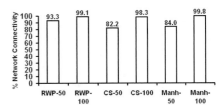

Fig. 5. % Network Connectivity (v_{max} = 2.5 m/s)   **Fig. 6.** % Network Connectivity (v_{max} = 25 m/s)

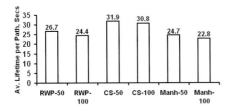
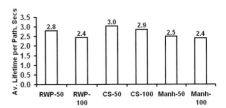

Fig. 7. Lifetime per Route (v_{max} = 2.5 m/s)   **Fig. 8.** Lifetime per Route (v_{max} = 25 m/s)

4.2 Route Lifetime

The average lifetime (Figures 7 and 8) is measured only for routes discovered under the LORA strategy as routes are determined for every static graph under the ORA strategy. With LORA, a route is used as long as it exists. The average lifetime of minimum hop routes is mainly influenced by node velocity and to a lesser extent by the mobility model and network density, in this order. For a given node velocity and network density, minimum hop routes determined under the City Section model had the largest lifetime and those determined under the Manhattan model had the smallest lifetime except the scenario of 100 nodes with 12.5 m/s velocity, wherein the Random Waypoint model yielded routes with the lowest average lifetime. For a given node velocity, the difference in the average lifetime of routes between the City Section model and the other two mobility models increases with increase in network density. The City Section model yielded a route lifetime that is 8-20% and 17-26% more than that discovered under the RWP model in low and high density networks respectively. Compared to the Manhattan model, the City Section model yielded routes that have 15-30% and 12-35% larger lifetime in low and high density networks respectively. For a given mobility model, the route lifetime decreases proportionately with increase in node velocity. As we increase the node velocity from 2.5 m/s to 25 m/s, the average lifetime of minimum hop routes determined under a particular mobility model approximately reduced to $1/10^{th}$ of the value incurred at low node velocity.

4.3 Hop Count of Minimum Hop Routes

For each mobility model, node velocity and network density, minimum hop routes discovered under the LORA strategy has a larger hop count than those discovered under the ORA strategy. But, the increase in the hop count is not substantial and is within 12%. Thus, if the on-demand MANET routing protocols based on LORA are designed meticulously with minimum hop routing as the primary routing principle, they could discover routes that have at most 12% larger hop count than those discovered by the ORA-based proactive routing protocols. The maximum increase in the hop count under the LORA strategy vis-à-vis the ORA strategy is observed with the RWP model and the lowest increase in the hop count is observed with the Manhattan model. However, with regards to the absolute values of the hop count, the minimum hop routes determined under the RWP model have the smallest hop count and those determined under the Manhattan model have the largest hop count.

Table 1. Average Hop Count per *s-d* Path under Random Waypoint Mobility Model

Node Velocity	50 Node Network			100 Node Network		
	ORA	LORA	% Increase	ORA	LORA	% Increase
2.5 m/s	2.36	2.63	11.51	2.27	2.50	10.40
12.5 m/s	2.40	2.65	10.14	2.36	2.58	9.46
25 m/s	2.40	2.63	9.44	2.31	2.52	9.31

For a given mobility model, the hop count of the minimum hop routes determined for a particular network density does not seem to be much influenced with different levels of node mobility. For a given mobility model and node velocity, under both the ORA and LORA strategies, the average hop count of minimum hop routes decreases with increase in network density. This is because, with a larger number of nodes in the network, there is a larger probability of finding an *s-d* path involving only fewer nodes that lie on the path from the source to the destination. The decrease in the hop count of minimum hop routes with increase in network density is very much appreciable for the Manhattan model compared to the other two mobility models.

Table 2. Average Hop Count per *s-d* Path under City Section Mobility Model

Node Velocity	50 Node Network			100 Node Network		
	ORA	LORA	% Increase	ORA	LORA	% Increase
2.5 m/s	2.66	2.86	7.51	2.45	2.71	10.40
12.5 m/s	2.85	3.07	7.66	2.70	2.93	8.68
25 m/s	2.83	3.04	7.39	2.60	2.82	8.47

Table 3. Average Hop Count per *s-d* Path under Manhattan Mobility Model

Node Velocity	50 Node Network			100 Node Network		
	ORA	LORA	% Increase	ORA	LORA	% Increase
2.5 m/s	3.31	3.60	8.81	3.08	3.34	8.38
12.5 m/s	3.37	3.60	6.90	3.00	3.26	8.60
25 m/s	3.51	3.74	6.60	3.03	3.27	7.94

5 Conclusions and Future Work

Our hypothesis that there would be difference in the hop count of minimum hop routes discovered under the ORA and LORA strategies has been observed to be true through extensive simulations, the results of which are summarized in Tables 1, 2 and 3. However, the difference is not significantly high and is within 6-12%, depending mainly on the mobility model employed and to a lesser extent on network density and the level of node mobility. With respect to absolute values, the Random Waypoint model yields minimum hop routes with the smallest hop count and the Manhattan model yields minimum hop routes with the largest hop count. With respect to the increase in the hop count of minimum hop routes due to the use of LORA strategy vis-à-vis the ORA strategy, we observe that the Random Waypoint model incurs the maximum increase and the Manhattan model incurs the smallest increase. The City Section model is ranked in between the two mobility models with regards to the absolute value of the hop count and the relative increase in the hop count with the LORA strategy. With regards to the route lifetime, the minimum hop routes determined under the City Section model are relatively more stable (i.e. have larger lifetime) compared to the other two mobility models. As future work, we will be extending this study and will study the impact of ORA vs. LORA strategy and the three mobility models on minimum-hop based multicast routing, minimum-link based multicast routing as well as node-disjoint and link-disjoint multi-path routing for MANETs.

References

1. Abolhasan, M., Wysocki, T., Dutkiewicz, E.: A Review of Routing Protocols for Mobile Ad hoc Networks. Ad hoc Networks 2(1), 1–22 (2004)
2. Meghanathan, N.: Survey and Taxonomy of Unicast Routing Protocols for Mobile Ad hoc Networks. The International Journal on Applications of Graph Theory in Wireless Ad hoc Networks and Sensor Networks 1(1), 1–21 (2009)
3. Siva Ram Murthy, C., Manoj, B.S.: Ad hoc Wireless Networks – Architectures and Protocols. Prentice Hall, USA (2004)
4. Broch, J., Maltz, D.A., Johnson, D.B., Hu, Y.C., Jetcheva, J.: A Performance Comparison of Multi-hop Wireless Ad hoc Network Routing Protocols. In: The 4th International Conference on Mobile Computing and Networking, pp. 85–97. ACM, Dallas (1998)
5. Johansson, P., Larsson, T., Hedman, N., Mielczarek, B., Degermark, M.: Scenario-based Performance Analysis of Routing Protocols for Mobile Ad hoc Networks. In: The 5th International Conference on Mobile Computing and Networking, pp. 195–206. ACM, Seattle (1999)
6. Camp, T., Boleng, J., Davies, V.: A Survey of Mobility Models for Ad Hoc Network Research. Wireless Communication and Mobile Computing 2(5), 483–502 (2002)
7. Farago, A., Syrotiuk, V.R.: MERIT – A Scalable Approach for Protocol Assessment. Mobile Networks and Applications 8(5), 567–577 (2003)
8. Kuhn, F., Moscibroda, T., Wattenhofer, R.: Unit Disk Graph Approximation. In: Joint Workshop on Foundations of Mobile Computing, pp. 17–23. ACM, Philadelphia (2004)
9. Cormen, T.H., Leiserson, C.E., Rivest, R.L., Stein, C.: Introduction to Algorithms, 2nd edn. MIT Press/ McGraw Hill, New York (2001)

Architecture for High Density RFID Inventory System in Internet of Things

Jain Atishay[1] and Tanwer Ashish[2]

[1] Computer Science Department, Thapar University, Patiala–147001, India
[2] Electronics and Communication Department, Thapar University, Patiala–147001, India
{atishay811,ashishtanwer}@gmail.com

Abstract. This paper proposes a novel architecture of Internet of Things (IOT) implemented using RFID. Our proposed architecture solves the problem of over-loading as the load on the RFID Tag reader is the total number of changed objects rather than the actual number of objects present. Our architecture is based on EPCglobal Network with some assumptions and modifications. We have discussed in details the components and working of our model. We have also discussed the physical implementation of our model taking the examples of two sample applications one for the retail system and other for smart home applications and their performance results have been tabulated and represented graphically.

Keywords: Internet of Things, RFID, Smart Home Application, Retail system.

1 Introduction

RFID is the new generation Auto ID technology that uses wireless communication to uniquely identify and track an object. It was invented in 1948 and was first-used during the IInd World War by the US Army for identification of friend or foe (IFF) aircrafts. RFID is widely used across a multitude of industry sectors and applications like airline baggage tracking, automated vehicle identification and toll collection. A RFID system basically consists of a Tag, a Reader and an antenna. The RFID Tag is basically a transponder with a silicon microchip for storing large amounts of data. Tags can be either active or passive. Passive tags are read only, gains its power from that generated by a reader. and reading range is typically shorter up to 30 feet (3 meters) and the data storage capacity is comparatively less (96/128 bits) as compared to active tags. Active tags have both read/write capability and are powered by means of battery. This battery-supplied power enables data to be read and written on to a tag and thus gives it a greater reading range up to 300 feet (100 meters) and large data storage capacity (128 KB). Some popular frequency ranges or RFID and their applications are given in Table1.

There are a number of existing (ISO) and proposed RFID standards (EPC Global) that have different data content, use different protocols and have different applications as shown in Table 2. With the adoption of Gen 2 ePC (UHF) standards, the adoption of RFID systems is now a major tool for supply chain management.

N. Meghanathan et al. (Eds.): CCSIT 2011, Part II, CCIS 132, pp. 617–626, 2011.
© Springer-Verlag Berlin Heidelberg 2011

Table 1. Ranges and Applications of RFID

Frequency Range	Characteristics	Applications
Low Frequency 125 – 300 kHz	Short range (To 18 inches) Low reading speed	Livestock ID Reusable containers
High Frequency 13.56 MHz	Medium range (3-10 feet) Medium reading speed	Access Control Airline Baggage ID Library automation
Ultra High Frequency 400 MHz–1 GHz	High range (10 – 30 feet) High reading speed Orientation sensitive	Supply chain management & Container Tracking
Microwave Frequency > 1 GHz	Medium range (10+ feet)	Automated Toll Collection Vehicle Identification

Table 2. RFID Standards

Specification	Description	Frequency
ePC UHF Class O	64-bit factory programmed	900 MHz
ePC UHF Class 1	96/128 bit one-time programmable	860-930 MHz
ePC HF Class 1	96/128 bit one-time programmable	13.56 MHz
ePC UHF Gen 2	96/128 bit one-time-Programmable	860-960 MHz
ISO 18000-3	Item Management	13.56 MHz
ISO 18000-4	Item Management	2.4 GHz
ISO 18000-6	Item Management	860-960 MHz

The RFID reader can be

1. Fixed RFID reader like UHF standard
2. Multi antenna RFID reader for supporting several appliances
3. Handheld mobile RFID (MRFID) readers

The internet of Things (IOT) is a networked interconnection of objects. It is global expansion wireless Electronic Product Code (EPC) network implemented through RFID tags [3] or QR Codes.An EPC number essentially contains:

1. Header, which identifies the length, type, structure, version and generation of EPC
2. Manager Number, which identifies the company or company entity
3. Object Class, refers to a stock keeping unit or product SKU
4. Serial Number, which identifies a specific item of the Object Class being tagged.

2 Background

EPCglobal has developed the Object Name Service (ONS) [4], a mechanism which makes use of the Domain Name System (DNS) protocol [5] to discover information about a product and related services from the Electronic Product Code (EPC) and is used for the resource addressing of Internet of Things. The EPC is first encoded to a Fully Qualified Domain Name (FQDN), then existing DNS infrastructure is used to query for additional information. This procedure makes use of the Name Authority Pointer (NAPTR) DNS record [6], which is also used by E.164 NUmber Mapping (ENUM) [7]. Ubiquitous ID Center (uID Center) brings forward similar resource addressing service named uCode Resolution Protocol (uCodeRP) [8], which also utilizes the protocol similar to DNS.

We are proposing ONS based a novel architecture of Internet of Things (IOT) implemented using RFID network. Our proposed architecture solves the problem of over-loading as the load on the RFID Tag reader is the total number of changed objects rather than the actual number of objects present as described in Section-2.

3 RFID Network Architecture

EPCglobal is a joint venture between GS1 (formerly EAN International) and GS1 US (formerly Uniform Code Council). The organization has created worldwide standard for EPC, RFID and the use of the Internet to share data via the EPCglobal Network.

Fig 1 shows the EPCglobal Network Standards given by EPCglobal. EPCglobal Network has following components.

3.1 Tags (Transponder) with EPC

Tags follow coding standard of EPC tag information. The EPC coding scheme provides differentiating codes [1] for each object of RFID network. Air interface protocol (GEN 2 AIP) regulates communication between the reader and the tag). Tag data translation protocols converts EPC information to Internet compatible format.

3.2 EPC Enabled Reader (Interrogator/Scanner)

Reader follows standard reader protocol to exchange data between EPC-capable middleware Reader management specifications are used to configuration readers.

3.3 Object Naming Service (ONS)

ONS is the network service system, similar to the DNS. This server will contain all EPC numbers and their associated IP addresses. ONS points out the specific EPC-IS server where the information being queried. It has standard security specifications and API.

3.4 EPC Information Service (EPC-IS)

EPC-IS is a software component to communicate with the EPCglobal Network and the ONS server. It stores the information processed by EPC middleware and query related information. EPCIS protocols manage storing and accessing of EPC information via the EPCglobal Network).

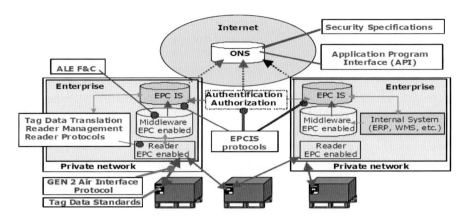

Fig. 1. EPCglobal Network Standards (Source: GS1 Germany/EPCglobal)

3.5 EPC Middleware (Savant)

Program module or service with a series of specific attributes, which is integrated by users to meet their specific needs. The most important part of EPC middleware is Filter and collection Application Level Events (F&C ALE).

Our proposed RFID based Internet of Things network architecture is based on the original EPCglobal Network architecture and has some specializations as explained below:

1. RFID Tags

The RFID tags are attached to each object that is to be identified as shown in Fig 3 (a). The RFID tags used for our purpose are passive and are in inactive state and need to be woken up by a wake-up call when in radio range of an active Tag Reader.

2. Tag readers (Master and Slave)

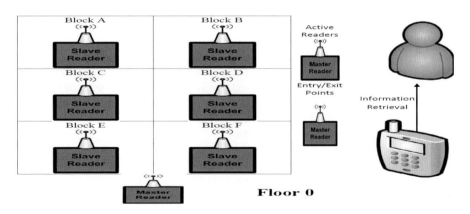

Fig. 2. Placement of Master and Slave Tag Readers at Floor 0 of a Building having 6 Blocks (A-F)

Our system has two types of Tag Readers –Master reader and Slave reader [2]. The master reader is a conventional powerful fixed active reader with a direct fixed or wireless connection. It initiates a read process in the slave reader and wakes up any passive tags for power-up or any other service initiation. In addition, it collects the item-level information and forwards it to the back-end for further processing. Fig 2 shows the placement of Master and Slave Tag Readers. The Master Tag readers are placed at entry/exit points while Slave Tag Readers are in Blocks.

3. The Master reader

It communicates with both ONS and Inventory database in two different states as shown in Fig 3 (b). The proposed database is used for inventory management in the system with many records. It is responsible for maintaining information as cache for reading purposes.

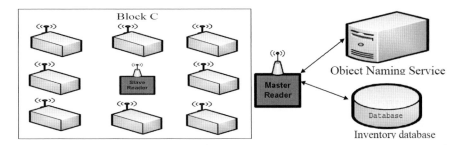

Fig. 3. (a) Block Structure (b) Communication of Master reader with ONS and Inventory database

We have made following assumption in proposing our system architecture:

1. The number of RFID objects in the block is very large
2. The objects are stationary within a region except for when they are brought in and out of the region
3. The movement of objects within a region is not present once the object is made stationary
4. There are a fixed number of entry/exit points within the region. The movement of objects are only to get in and out of the region
5. Each object has a unique RFID that can be interpreted at the Object Name Server (ONS).

4   Network Working

The objects labeled with the RFID tags will be located within the closed region divided into blocks each of which having a slave reader to identify the items whose RFID tags can be activated by the slave reader. This slave reader will in normal working situation be in inactive state. The slave readers will be connected to a master reader which would act like an aggregation server for the slave reader readings and will pass the information the ONS and used the inventory database for caching. The connection of the slave to the master reader can be wireless, direct wired or switched with redundant cabling based on the use case. The slave readers located at the entry/exit point will remain active and function as the primary readers for data update.

4.1 Case I Initial Setup / Refresh

The initial setup will consist of the master reader instructing the slave readers to active state (by sending wake-up call) one by one which in return will force the RFID tags of all the objects in the state space (region) into the active state (by their wake-up calls). The slave readers will transmit the read RFID tags to the master reader which will, with the help of the ONS cache the location of the objects in the inventory server. The field will include the RFID, the object description, the user identification number (in case it is different from the RFID) as in the case of a local repository of the ONS. Alongside this, the location as well as the block number of the objects will be saved.

4.2 Case II Reading

The reading of a tag involves getting the data from the inventory database and returning the information.

4.3 Case III Removal of Object

In case of removal of object, the active readers the exit points will activate the RFID tags. These RFID tags will send the information to the readers which will match it inside the inventory database. The deletion of information can occur directly from the inventory database for the object. In case of an object absent, it indicates that the data inside the database needs refresh.

4.4 Case IV Addition of Object

The addition of object to the system through the entry points will involve the wakeup of the RFID tag by the entry points. The entry point reader will inform the master to wake up the corresponding slave to a reading state where it reads active tags but does not transmit the Wake-up Calls. The newly entered object will be in the active state and will be transmitting the RFID information. This can be used to track its new location by the slave readers without activating the other objects and thus preventing energy wastage or clatter.

5 Application in Shopping Mall or Retail Shop

Market studies indicate that companies with current RFID deployments are pursuing and achieving significant business benefits. For RFID deployment according to our architecture, we need to separate different products in different blocks each with different Slave Reader. We can use different rooms for different blocks as discussed in Smart Home Application. We put active master readers at billing desk, entry and exits points. The slave readers are placed in different blocks and elsewhere for location identification. We should use different Tag read orientations for minimum interference and optimizing performance. The commonly used read orientations in retail are horizontal, vertical and End-on inlay orientations as shown in Fig 4. There is wide variation on percentage of read accuracy depending on inlay type.

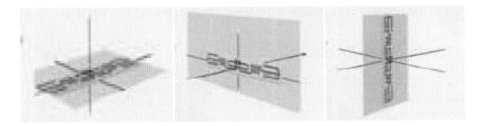

Fig. 4. Orientation of Tags (a) End-on (b) Horizontal (c) Vertical

Fig. 5. Retail shop with different products placed different blocks and monitored by their Slave Readers

Fig 5 shows an example of clothing shop with clothing rack wit hanging clothes (top) with vertical tag orientation, jeans (bottom left) with end-on inlay orientation and shoeboxes (bottom right) with horizontal inlay orientation. For our architecture to function correctly the location of all objects within the shopping mart must be fixed. The objects of one block are not permitted to be shifted or placed in other block. The relative movement of objects within a mart should be negligible.

For a retail shop, a major concern is to detect theft and inventory pile. We can easily avoid such situations by providing customers a PII (personally identifiable information) number and that can be associated with tag identification (EPC) numbers.

For Checking Out, as mentioned above, we have placed Master Tag Reader at billing desk and Entry and Exit points of each block. All checkouts are done by Master Tag reader by scanning EPC numbers of object Tags. The master Tag reader scans the first item and then its quantity, instead to scanning each item individually. After checkout, the Tags are usually deactivated to avoid their further interference. The theft is detected by continuously scanning EPC numbers at entry or exit points.

6 Performance Results

For the retail shop application, the performance curves (Inlay read percentage) as function of read distance for different orientations of Tags are shown in Table 3 and corresponding Fig 6.

Table 3. Inlay Read Performance (%)

Reading Distance (in ft)	Inlay Read Performance %		
	Shoebox	Hanging	Jeans
1	100%	100%	100%
2	100%	100%	95%
3	100%	95%	80%
4	100%	90%	70%
5	100%	80%	60%
6	100%	75%	50%

The curves show that the read performance horizontal tags (in Shoebox) is better than the performance of Vertical tags (hanging clothes) when distance is more than 3 feet. The end-on orientation (for jeans) performance is least, even at distance of 2 feet from the reader. A hundred percent read rate is possible in a variety of situations as shown in Fig 7.

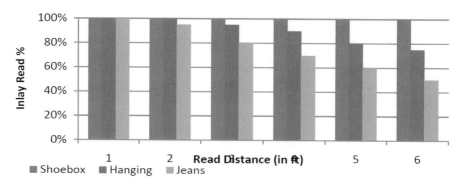

Fig. 6. Configuration Variation Effects: Inlay read performance for varying arrangements

For the implementation of our architecture the performance characteristics of master and slave RDIF tag readers should be shown in Table 4 and corresponding

Fig 7. As shown in figure, the number of tags read by slave reader should decrease steeply with increase in reading distance so that two slave tag reader cannot interfere with each other. On the other hand, the master tag reader should have long range so that it can make connection with all the slave readers.

Table 4. Reading Performance (%) of Master and Slave Tag Readers

Reading Distance (in ft)	Tags Read by Master Reader	Tags Read by Slave Reader
1	100%	100%
2	100%	80%
3	95%	55%
4	90%	45%
5	85%	35%
6	80%	20%

The higher range of master readers as illustrated in the figure is a prime requirement for the system to be effective. No object entering the system should be able to skip the master reader. Ideal placement for the master reader would be overhead or along the sides of the entry/exit points. The sphere of 100% reading performance should cover the entire area of these points. Additional readers networked as one can be used to boost performance. The performance curve indicates that the slave reader should also be placed to make blocks (Fig 3a) keeping them at 2-3 feet from each other. This range largely depends on the tag density (here 20 tags/feet) for higher density increases clutter and disturbance. Also for slave readers, the density refers to the number of active tags within range rather than all tags, in case of which, there could be 1-2 tags in a slow moving system within the range of a tag reader.

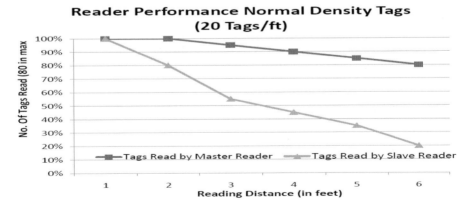

Fig. 7. Reading Performance comparison of master and Slave Tag Readers

7 Conclusion

RFID offers new levels of visibility for companies that want to track physical items between locations. In the retail supply chain, the goods tagged at the point of manufacture can now be traced from the factory to the shop floor, providing a real time view of inventory for all supply chain partners. Internet of Things (IOT) is future network of all objects and it can be implemented using RFID. Its standards are given by EPCglobal. Our proposed architecture is based on EPCglobal Network with some assumptions and modifications. It solves the problem of over-loading as the load on the RFID Tag reader is the total number of changed objects rather than the actual number of objects present. We have also discussed the way to implement our architecture for sample applications like retail system and smart home. Future work in this system could be to incorporate a means for tracking movement of objects within the system. Another extension could be to provide a placement criterion for the slave readers, which in the current architecture use the overlapping structure similar to the placement of wireless access point for internet access. The major difference in the systems is the size of the slave readers which is much smaller, with smaller ranges as compared to access points. Also, slave readers can be arranged without wired connections to contact and share information wirelessly over the network. Awareness of RFID technology and Internet of Things concept can benefit industry and home automation globally.

References

[1] Yan, B., Huang, G.: Supply Chain Information Transmission based on RFID and Internet of Things, see its ref. 1, 6, 7
[2] Darianian, M., Michael, M.P.: Smart Home Mobile RFID-based Internet-Of-Things Systems and Services
[3] A Model Supporting Any Product Code Standard for the Resource Addressing in the Internet of Things
[4] EPCglobal Inc., Object Name Service (ONS) Version 1.0, EPCglobal, US (October 2005)
[5] Albitz, P., Liu, C.: DNS and BIND, 4th edn. O'Reilly & Associates, Sebastopol (2001)
[6] Mealling, M., Daniel, R.: The Naming Authority Pointer (NAPTR) DNS Resource Record, RFC 2915, IETF (September 2000)
[7] Faltstrom, P.: E.164 number and DNS, IETF RFC2916 (September 2000)
[8] Minegishi, K.: On ucode Resolution Server Connection Tests. In: TRONWARE, vol. 84, pp. 71–73 (2003)

A Relative Study of MANET and VANET: Its Applications, Broadcasting Approaches and Challenging Issues

Ajit Singh[1], Mukesh Kumar[1], Rahul Rishi[1], and D.K. Madan[2]

[1] Department of Computer Science and Engineering
[2] Department of Mathematics
The Technological Institute of Textile and Science,
Bhiwani, Haryana, India
{ajit713,drmukeshji}@gmail.com,
{rahulrishi,dk_madaan}@rediffmail.com

Abstract. Mobile Ad hoc Networks (MANET) and Vehicular Ad hoc Networks (VANET) are the most promising fields of research and development of wireless network. VANET is one the most challenging flavor of MANET due to high and unpredictable dynamic topology, frequent disconnections and life threatening issues. The present paper emphasizes the importance of studying VANET as a separate discipline although it is a part of MANET. This paper presents a relative study of MANET and VANET and also describes whether the approaches and protocol applicable to MANET are equally applicable to VANET or not.

Keywords: VANET, MANET, Unicasting, Multicasting, Broadcasting, Geocasting.

1 Introduction

Since last decade, Mobile Ad hoc Networks are one of the key factors in the revolutionary field of wireless communication. These are self organized and self monitored ad hoc networks of PDAs, laptops or mobile nodes which are used for instant communication during disaster relief, emergency situations, information sharing and in military operations. MANET possess a lot of features such as dynamic topology, limited physical security, energy and power constraints. A Vehicular Ad hoc networks is a form of MANET, to provide communications among nearby vehicles and nearby fixed roadside equipment [12, 6]. The main objective of VANET is to provide safety and comfort to passengers. Each vehicle is integrated with VANET device that can receive and relay messages through wireless network such as traffic information, road block, parking, location tracking, fuel station and weather information [12, 7]. VANET are also known as Intelligent Vehicular Ad hoc Networks as it provides information in an intelligent way. It is one of the self organized and distributed network having characteristics as dynamic topology, no battery constraint, bandwidth constraint and limited physical security [1]. The paper is organized in the following sections. In section 2 features, applications and

N. Meghanathan et al. (Eds.): CCSIT 2011, Part II, CCIS 132, pp. 627–632, 2011.
© Springer-Verlag Berlin Heidelberg 2011

broadcasting approaches of MANET are given. In section 3 existing routing protocols and security aspects of MANET are discussed. In section 4 features, applications and broadcasting approaches of VANET are given. In section 5 routing protocols and security aspects of VANET are discussed and In section 6 challenging issues are given. Finally, conclusion is given.

2   Features, Applications and Broadcastig Approaches of Mobile Adhoc Networks

According to IETF RFC 2501, [2, 5] MANET have several features which can be classified as:

- *Dynamic topology*: Free movements of node cause a dynamic environment in its position.
- *Bandwidth constraint*: Variable low capacity links exist as compared to wireless network which are more susceptible to external noise, interference and signal attenuation effects.
- *Energy constrained operations*: A mobile node possess a battery of finite power, so it is very difficult to save electricity in the context of depletion system design.
- *Limited physical security*: MANET is more vulnerable to attacks like man in middle attacks, spoofing, eaves-dropping, denial of service and so on. These all occur due to decentralization.

2.1   Applications of MANET

[7, 13]Due to less infrastructure and easy deployment their applicability is scalable to be used:

- For military and battlefield operations.
- For disaster relief operations such as tsunami, earthquake, flood, fire etc.
- Meetings or Conventions in which people wish to quickly share information.
- Emergency search and rescue operations, recovery and human networking.
- Localized advertising and shopping
- Coverage extension

2.2   Broadcasting Approaches in MANET

In MANET [6], a number of broadcasting approaches on the basis of cardinality of destination set:

- *Unicasting*: Sending a message from a source to a single destination.
- *Multicating*: Sending a message from a source to a set of destinations.
- Broadcasting: Flooding of messages from a source to all other nodes in the specified network.
- *Geocasting*: Sending a message from a source to all nodes inside a geographical region.

3   Existing Routing Protocols and Security Aspects in MANET

In MANET, routing protocols are broadly classified in three ways on the basis of different broadcasting approaches, network latency and congestion control as:

•   *Flat Routing*: It comprises table driven (proactive) and on demand (reactive) routing protocols like WRP, DSDV, AODV etc [3, 10].
•   *Hierarchical Routing*: This comprises hybrid of proactive and reactive protocols in respect of hierarchical manner like ZRP, CGSR etc [3, 10].
•   *Geographical Assisted Routing*: It comprises GPS assisted devices along with geographical routers. In this all nodes send their geographical location to the routers and collect updated location of their neighbors from geographic routers such as LAR, GPSR etc [3, 10].

3.1   Security Aspects in MANET

Security in MANET is one of the critical issues and difficult to achieve due to decentralization, self organized, self monitored and ad hoc nature of network [11].

MANET are more vulnerable to two types of attacks mainly active and passive attacks like denial of service, eavesdropping, spoofing, routing table overflow, replay attack, black hole etc. In order to provide security solutions, MANET routing protocols mainly rely on protocol enhancement and cryptographic approaches [10].

4   Features, Application of Broadcasting Approaches of Vehicular Adhoc Networks

Being a part of MANET, features of VANET are different in some respects according to [7, 13]:

•   Dynamic topologies
•   Self organized, self monitored and decentralized
•   No battery constraint
•   Initially low market penetration ratios
•   Potentially unbounded network sizes
•   Bandwidth constraint
•   Potential support from infrastructure
•   Abundant resources as computation power and battery power.
•   Limited physical security

4.1   Applications of VANET

The applications of VANET are mainly based on level of comfort and safety of passengers besides commercial utilization as:

•   *Safety applications*: These applications assist the drivers in handling the unpredictable events or danger by actively monitoring nearby traffic environment through message exchanges. Safety applications are intersection collision warning, post crash warning, emergency electronics brake lights, road condition information, traffic signal violation, emergency warning signals and location tracking [7].

• *Comfort applications*: These applications enhance the degree of convenience of drivers and traffic efficiency by sharing traffic information's among roadway infrastructure and ongoing vehicles. Comfort applications are congested road notifications, parking availability notifications, parking spot locator, weather information's, gas and oil station information, electronic toll collection and so on [7].

• *Commercial applications*: These applications boost up driver satisfaction along with entertainment by providing various types of communication services. Commercial applications are service announcements as food malls and shopping complexes, map downloads internet connectivity, group communications and road side service finder [7].

4.2 Broadcasting Approaches in VANET

In VANET [13, 1], broadcasting is the most prominent technique used for sharing information and it is used to establish and maintain the route by using a number of protocols. Different broadcasting schemes for VANET are:

• *Urban Multihop Broadcast* which solve the broadcast storm, hidden and exposed node problem without sharing information among the neighbor's nodes.

• *Multihop Vehicular Broadcast* which broadcast information to other vehicle and store in its local database for future safety. These techniques also assist for congestion detection and backfire algorithm.

5 Routing Protocols and Security Aspects in VANET

In VANET [14], the routing protocols are classified on the basis of broadcasting techniques such as:

• *Topological based routing protocols*: These routing protocols use links information that exists in the network to perform packet forwarding .These are further divided into proactive and reactive protocols like FSR, TORA etc.

• *Position based routing protocols*: These protocols share the property of using geographic positioning information in order to select the next forwarding hops. The packet is sent without any map knowledge to one hop neighbor which is closest to destination. Position based routing is divided in two types: Position based greedy V2V protocol, Delay tolerant Protocol.

• *Broadcasting routing protocols*: These are mainly employed when message need to be disseminated to the vehicle beyond the transmission range. Broadcast sends a packet to all nodes in the network by using flooding. This ensures the delivery of packets but bandwidth is wasted and node receives duplicates. Broadcasting protocols are BROADCOMM, V-TRADE etc.

• *Geocast routing protocols*: These are basically a location based multicast routing whose aim is to deliver the packet   from source node to all other nodes within a specified geographical region. The various geocast routing protocols are DG-CASTOR, DRG etc [8, 1].

5.1 Security Aspects in VANET

Security is one of main concerning challenges in VANET according to the network perspective. Vehicle safety applications are among the major drivers of VANET, where the peoples life is at stake. There is no doubt that it is one of most promising research field in wireless network but suffers from a number of attacks as bogus information, denial of services, masquerade ID disclosure, wrong position information, sybil attack and packet dropping. Security management mainly depends on digital signature and key management [9, 4].

6 Challenging Issues in MANETS and VANETS

The major challenges faced by MANET architecture are classified according to [2, 5]:

• Incorporation among mobile devices, ad hoc routers and embedded sensors in existing protocols.
• Unreliability end to end delivery services.
• A number of existing vulnerabilities such as denial of services, spoofing, man in middle attack etc.
• Dynamic topology
• Hidden terminal problem
• Device discovery and route maintenance
• Limited resources
• Bandwidth optimization
• Non scalability of routing protocols
• Poor transmission quality
• Lack of central coordinator

There are a number of challenges faced by today's VANET architecture according to [7, 13, 1]:

• Low tolerance for errors as the information as the information conveyed over a VANET may affect life or death decision.
• A number of security holes exists which leads to disaster. As an attacker can easily misuse the traffic control management.
• Frequent disconnections due to high mobility of vehicles.
• Non scalable routing protocol
• Secure key distribution facing several significant challenges because vehicles are manufactured by different companies, so installing key at the company site would require coordination and interoperability between manufactures.
• Dynamic topologies
• Bandwidth constraint
• Hidden terminals problems

7 Conclusion

Ad hoc networks is the most talked about term in wireless technologies which provide the vision of "anytime, anywhere" communication. The current scenario is more inclined towards VANET due to sudden rise of tragic and safety issues in driving. New applications call for both bandwidth and capacity of network by using higher frequency and better spatial spectrum reuse. This paper concluded that security being one of the challenging tasks in ad hoc network but in VANET it becomes more critical where malicious information may decide life or death decision. So security concern and other challenging issues will encourage researchers to contribute in most exciting future research area.

References

[1] Saha, A.K., Johnson, D.B.: Modelling mobility for vehicular ad hoc networks. In: Proceeding of ACM International Workshop on Vehicular Ad Hoc Networks, pp. 91–92 (2004)
[2] Corson, M.: Information RFC 2501 MANET Performance issues (January 1999)
[3] Royer, E.M., Toh, C.-K.: A review of Current routing protocols for Ad Hoc Mobile Wireless
[4] Dotzer, F.: Privacy issues in vehicular ad hoc networks (2005)
[5] Ilyas, M.: The hand book of ad hoc wireless networks. CRC press LLC, Boca Raton (2003); Larsson, T., Hedman, N.: Routing Protocols in Wireless Ad Hoc Networks: A simulation study, Master Thesis Lulea University of Technology, Stockholm (1998)
[6] Wu, J., Dai, F.: Broadcasting in Ad Hoc Networks: Based on Self-Pruning. In: Twenty Second Annual Joint Conferences of IEEE Computer and Communication Socities, IEEE INFOCOM 2003 (2003)
[7] Luo, J., Hubaux, J.-P.: A Survey of Inter-Vehicle Communication Technical report (2004)
[8] Kevin, C.L., Lee, U., Gerla, M.: Survey of Routing Protocols in Vehicular Ad Hoc Networks in Car 2 Car communication consortium
[9] Raya, M., Hubaux, J.P.: The Security of Vehicular Ad Hoc Networks. In: SANS 2005, November 7. ACM, New York (2007)
[10] Yousefi, S., Bastani, S., Fathy, M.: On the Performance of Safety Message Dissemination in Vehicular Ad Hoc Networks. In: IEEE Fourth European Conference on Universal Multiservice Networks, European (2007)
[11] Zhou, L., Haas, Z.J.: Securing Ad Hoc Networks. Cornell University, Ithica (1999), http://www.cs.cornell.edu/home/Idzhou/adhoc
[12] Basagni, S., et al. (eds.): Mobile Ad Hoc Networking. IEEE Press, Los Alamitos (2003)
[13] Wang, Y., Li, F.: Vehicular Ad Hoc Networks. In: Guide to Wireless Ad Hoc Networks, Compute Communication and Networks, doi:10.1007/978-1-84800328-6-20
[14] Haas, Z.: A new routing Protocol for reconfigurable wireless networks. In: Proceeding of the IEEE International Conferences on Universal Personal Communications (ICUPC 1997) (October 1997)

Adaptive Threshold Based on Group Decisions for Distributed Spectrum Sensing in Cognitive Adhoc Networks

Rajagopal Sreenivasan, G.V.K. Sasirekha, and Jyotsna Bapat

International Institute of Information Technology, Bangalore
rajagopal.s@iiitb.net, {sasirekha,jbapat}@iiitb.ac.in

Abstract. The Dynamic Spectrum Access in Cognitive Radios (CRs) calls for efficient and accurate spectrum sensing mechanism that provides the CR network with current spectral occupancy information. For a CR using energy detection for spectrum sensing, accurate estimate of Signal to Noise Ratio (SNR) at the receiver is crucial for determination of the decision threshold and ultimately the correct decision. In practical situations, SNR (and hence threshold) estimation is sub optimum resulting in high probability of decision error. Optimum threshold value in absence of reliable SNR estimate can be determined adaptively using a training signal. This training signal adds an overhead to the bandwidth requirements and necessitates frequent retraining in time varying channel conditions. In this paper, we propose an innovative cooperative spectrum sensing technique for Cognitive Adhoc Networks wherein spectral occupancy decisions from other CRs in the group are combined and used as a training signal to intelligently adapt the local decision threshold, making the threshold independent of local SNR measurement inaccuracies. Simulations in presence of Rayleigh fading channels show probability of decision errors reduce significantly as compared with other distributed spectrum sensing techniques.

Keywords: Group Intelligence, Cognitive Ad-hoc Networks, Dynamic Spectrum Access, Cooperating Spectrum Sensing.

1 Introduction

Cognitive Radio has been considered a promising technology that would address the conflicting situation of scarcity of the electromagnetic radio spectrum and under utilization of spectrum in many places [1]. Opportunistic Spectrum Access (OSA) is one of the solutions proposed to address this problem. A Cognitive Radio (CR) that is aware of its surroundings may be able to access these un-utilized spectrum bands (referred to as spectrum holes) opportunistically, without affecting the performance of the licensed user, also referred to as the Primary User (PU). Given its potential, the cognitive radio systems have been described as "disruptive but unobtrusive technology" [1]. Cognitive Adhoc Networks (CANs) comprise of several CRs connected in adhoc manner usually having a common control channel as shown in figure 1.

N. Meghanathan et al. (Eds.): CCSIT 2011, Part II, CCIS 132, pp. 633–644, 2011.
© Springer-Verlag Berlin Heidelberg 2011

In CANs, spectral awareness may be achieved by sensing the spectrum either in standalone or in distributed fashion. Local spectrum sensing and data fusion method employed by the distributed sensing techniques form the key technologies required to achieve OSA. Commonly used spectrum sensing techniques include energy detection, matched filter, cyclo-stationarity based feature extraction etc. [2]. Energy detection based spectrum sensing techniques have been used extensively due to their ease of implementation and speed of operation. The binary decision provided by the energy detection device indicating spectral occupancy is based on a pre-defined threshold, which depends on the signal and noise power measurements. This threshold needs to balance between the probability of false alarms and probability of detection.

In time varying channel conditions, the threshold should be updated continually based on the changing signal strength. Optimal threshold in such conditions can be determined dynamically using learning or adaptation technique as seen in [3]. Training sequence consists of spectrum status of the PU for learning, which is an overhead to the bandwidth. Mobility of the transmitter and receiver means changing channel conditions making the results achieved from training worthless after a small duration. Other adaptive techniques such as floating threshold, floating/fixed threshold, double floating thresholds based on SNR measurements have been proposed in [4-6].

In this paper, we propose a new threshold adaptation technique which uses group decisions as a training signal, for distributed spectrum sensing in a Cognitive Adhoc Network (CAN). The scenario is as shown in Figure 1. It is assumed that the CRs in the network are closely placed and sense the presence of different PUs that are at a

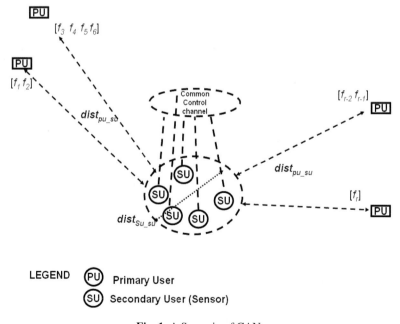

Fig. 1. A Scenario of CAN

larger distance, i.e dist_SU_SU << dist_PU_SU. Each CR adjusts its threshold in such a way that its local decisions about spectral occupancy are more "like" the global decisions. Because of the usage of this global knowledge, it is expected that the local decision will be relatively immune to the inaccuracies in the signal power measurements. The data fusion techniques used could be simple Majority logic or Likelihood Ratio Test based [8].

Remainder of the paper is organized as follows. Section 2 describes the system model under the considered scenario. Section 3 describes the proposed adaptive threshold method. Simulation model with results are described in section 4. Finally the conclusions and future work are presented.

2 System Model

In this section, the local spectral sensing technique and the data fusion techniques as applied to the scenario under consideration are discussed in detail. The proposed adaptation of local threshold is discussed in next section.

2.1 Local Spectrum Sensing: Energy Detection

Energy detection has been the technique of choice for local spectrum sensing due to its lower complexity, ease of implementation and faster decision making capability. While energy detection techniques can be implemented in different ways [8], for purpose of this work, the focus is on the binary decision (primary user present or absent) provided by the energy detector, rather than the technique itself.

Figure 2 shows the block diagram of an energy detector system [9]. Output of the band-pass filter (with bandwidth W) is followed by a squaring device and integrator to measure the received signal energy over the observation interval of T seconds. Output is normalized by the noise spectral density N_0 to obtain Y, which is compared with a decision threshold   to make the spectral occupancy decision. Same can be formulated as a binary hypothesis testing problem, where H_0 corresponds to the case where PU is absent and H_1 corresponds to PU being present.

$$Y \underset{<}{\overset{>}{\underset{H_0}{\overset{H_1}{}}}} \lambda \tag{1}$$

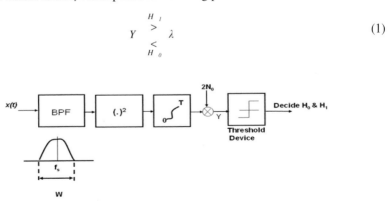

Fig. 2. Energy Detection

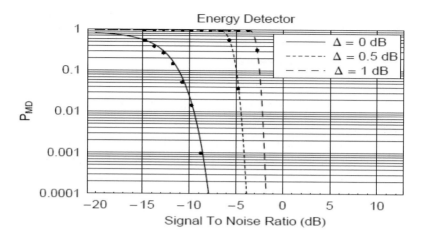

Fig. 3. Pm Versus SNR: Static Threshold (replicated from Reference [7]]

The normalized output Y has central and non-central chi-square distributions under H_0 and H_1, respectively, each with 2m degrees of freedom, where m is an integer number denoting the time-bandwidth product WT and γ is the signal to noise ratio. The distribution of random variable Y under the two hypotheses is as shown in equation (2)

$$f_{Y|H_0}(y) = \frac{y^{m-1}e^{-y/2}}{\Gamma(m)2^m}$$

$$f_{Y|H_1}(y) = \frac{y^{m-1}e^{-(y+2m\gamma)/2}}{\Gamma(m)2^m}\,_0F_1(m,\frac{m\gamma y}{2}) \tag{2}$$

$\Gamma(.)$ is the gamma function and $_0F_1(.,.)$ is the confluent hyper geometric limit function. The performance of a spectral sensing technique can be expressed in terms of probability of detection (P_d) and probability of false alarm (P_f). P_f is the measure of lost opportunity by the SU where the spectral band is falsely declared as occupied, while P_d is the measure of ability of the SU to use the white spaces without interfering with the PU. Higher P_d is essential for the SU to be able to use the licensed band. The need to maximize P_d conflicts with the requirement for a lesser P_f. The decision threshold should be chosen such that P_f is minimized while guaranteeing P_d above a certain level. For the detector shown in figure 2, the expressions for P_d and P_f have been derived in literature as shown below.

$$P_d = P\{Y > \lambda \,|\, H_1\} = Q_m(\sqrt{2m\gamma},\sqrt{\lambda})$$

$$P_f = P\{Y > \lambda \,|\, H_0\} = \frac{\Gamma(m,\lambda/2)}{\Gamma(m)} \overset{\Delta}{=} G_m(\lambda) \tag{3}$$

$$\Gamma(a,b) = \int t^{a-1}e^{-t}dt$$

Γ (a,b) is the incomplete gamma function and $Q_m(.;.)$ is the generalized Marcum function. More details can be found in [9]. Decision threshold that minimizes the probability of error ($P_e = P_f + (1 - P_d)$), can be obtained by solving the equation below for a given SNR (γ) and time-bandwidth product m.

$$\frac{\lambda^{(m-1)/2}}{I_{m-1}\left(\sqrt{2m\gamma\lambda}\right)} = \frac{\Gamma(m)}{(2m\gamma)^{(m-1)/2}} e^{-m\gamma}.2^{m-1} \tag{4}$$

The performance of a spectrum sensing scheme is limited by the signal power at the sensor. Error in the signal and noise power estimation will result in incorrect threshold estimation and effectively higher probability of error. Figure 3 (reproduced from [7]) shows the performance of the energy detector under noise uncertainty, for large values of m. It can be seen that with no noise uncertainty, the energy detector can perform well at negative SNR values. However, the performance degrades sharply with errors in noise estimation. In practice, an energy detection device must estimate the operating SNR conditions and use them to determine the decision threshold. Due to time varying channel conditions and inherent uncertainty associated with the estimation process, the estimated SNR and the threshold chosen is sub-optimum; resulting in large decision errors. The performance can be improved by updating the threshold using information about the local noise and signal power [5-6].

Such adaptation can compensate for local changes in SNR and improve on the performance of the energy detector. However, in "hidden node" situations, the SU is likely to make incorrect decision with only local measurements at its disposal.

2.2 Distributed Sensing and Data Fusion

Hidden node conditions can be better handled using spatial diversity or the so-called cooperative or distributed spectrum sensing [9, 10]. In the CAN scenario under consideration, SUs in the network broadcast their spectral decisions over the common control channel (figure 1). Each SU then can use these decisions, along with its own estimation to make a more accurate decision about the spectral occupancy. Spatial diversity between different SUs is expected to provide considerable performance improvements in the presence of hidden nodes and channel fading.

Decisions from the different SUs can be combined using simple logical techniques such as AND, OR or majority logic. These techniques treat decisions from all SUs equally, without taking into account the fact that some SUs may be in lower fading zone, and hence more reliable than others. As a result, the performance improvement is minimal. Considerable improvement can be obtained if each SU transmits its reliability information (P_d and P_f) along with spectral occupancy information (+1 for occupied and -1 for not). This information would be used to combine the data using log-likelihood test based (LLRT) data fusion rule [10, 12]. With N active SUs in the network, LLRT is

$$\sum_{S^+} log_e \frac{P_{di}}{P_{fi}} + \sum_{S^-} log_e \frac{(1 - P_{fi})}{(1 - P_{di})} + log \frac{P_1}{P_0} \underset{H0}{\overset{H1}{\underset{<}{>}}} 0 \tag{5}$$

The local decision of the ith SU is denoted by d_i. and S$^+$ indicates subset with occupancy result $d_i=1$ and S$^-$ with result $d_i=-1$. P_1 and P_0 are the prior probability of the presence & absence of PU signals [10]. Decision from each SU is weighed based on its reliability. This technique has been shown to be optimum technique for data fusion provided correct estimates of the local probabilities are available. As a result, distributed spectrum sensing with adaptive weighing of the local decisions before fusion has been the general approach so far for performance improvements [11,13].

3 Adaptive Threshold Based on Group Decision

The proposed adaptive threshold system is as shown in figure 4. The input, output and the desired signals for the adaptive system are as described below:

Input: Y_t, output of the energy detector at time instance t.

Desired Output: Decision d_t made using available decisions from other SUs in the group. The decision may be obtained using majority logic or Log Likelihood Ratio test (if information about P_d and P_f is available). This is a hard decision, limited to +1 or 0 at instance t. 1 indicating presence of PU and vice versa.

Output: Output of the adaptive system is the local soft decision z_t obtained using current threshold λ_t, where λ_t is the current estimate of threshold. z_t is limited to a closed interval [0, 1]. The decision device is a scaled sigmoid function. Larger the difference between the received signal and the threshold, closer is the output to +1 or 0.

The error is defined as the difference between the output of the decision device and the global decision. The threshold λ_t is updated such that the error is minimized in the mean square sense. The update takes place every time instance "t", where t is the sampling period of the energy detection device.

Update Algorithm:

$$e_t = d_t - z_t$$

$$\lambda_{t+1} = \lambda_t - \mu \frac{\partial E\left(e_t^2\right)}{\partial \lambda_t}$$

$$z_t = f\left(Y_t - \lambda_t\right) = \frac{1}{1 - e^{-\beta(Y_t - \lambda_t)}}$$

$$E(e_t^2) \approx e_t^2$$

$$\frac{\partial e_t^2}{\partial \lambda_t} = 2e_t \frac{\partial e_t}{\partial \lambda_t} = 2e_t \frac{\partial(d_t - z_t)}{\partial \lambda_t} = -2e_t \frac{\partial z_t}{\partial \lambda_t}$$

$$\frac{\partial z_t}{\partial \lambda_t} = \frac{\partial f(Y_t - \lambda_t)}{\partial \lambda_t} = -\beta f(Y_t - \lambda_t)\left[1 - f(Y_t - \lambda_t)\right]$$

$$\frac{\partial z_t}{\partial \lambda_t} = -\beta z_t (1 - z_t)$$

$$\frac{\partial e_t^2}{\partial \lambda_t} = -2e_t \frac{\partial z_t}{\partial \lambda_t} = 2e_t \beta z_t (1 - z_t)$$

Update

$$\lambda_{t+1} = \lambda_t - \mu_1 \frac{\partial e_t^2}{\partial \lambda_t} = \lambda_t - 2\mu_1 \beta e_t z_t (1 - z_t)$$

$$\mu = \mu_1 \beta$$

$$\lambda_{t+1} = \lambda_t - \mu_1 \frac{\partial e_t^2}{\partial \lambda_t} = \lambda_t - 2\mu e_t z_t (1 - z_t)$$

(6)

At each time instance t, the updated threshold λ_{t+1} is used to make the hard decision about the spectral occupancy decision. It can be seen from the update equation that, the threshold remains relatively unchanged in two situations:

- When the error $e_t \sim 0$, indicating that the local decision is in agreement with the global decision.
- When output of the decision device is close to 1 or 0. This indicates saturation of the sigmoid function or large distance between the input and the threshold.

Thus, the update is slow when local decision is in agreement with global decision (the training signal) and when local SNR is high, implying higher confidence in local decisions.

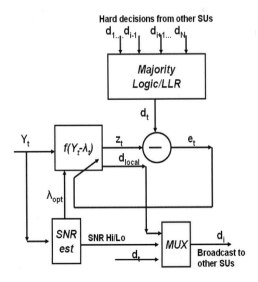

Fig. 4. System model at an 'i'th SU

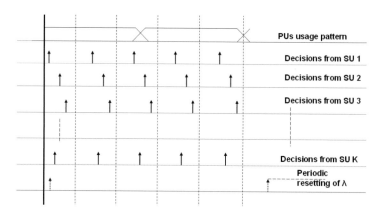

Fig. 5. Event Diagram at an SU

However, in case of "hidden node" situations, the local signal strength may be very poor, resulting in a strong "no" decision ($z_t \sim 0$). In this case, local decision is deemed not reliable, and instead the global decision is used.

The event diagram of the scanning process is depicted in figure 5. Each SU scans the spectrum continually, generates a hard decision on the presence/absence of the PU and broadcasts this information to the entire network. The SUs senses the spectrum and transmit the hard decision at least once in a T_s second frame and at the end of which data fusion is performed to obtain the desired signal (global decision) d_t. The spectrum sensing and broadcasting by each SU is asynchronous in nature. Each SU uses the available information from other SUs to generate global decision or the training signal. Since the SUs scan asynchronously, the training signal may vary for each SU.

The decision threshold at each SU is re-calibrated periodically based on the estimated local SNR at that instant. This periodic resetting process prevents accumulation of errors in the feedback system.

4 Simulation Environment and Results

The simulated Cognitive Radio Network scenario consists of 'N' SUs and one PU. The PU goes on and off randomly. Each SU scans the spectrum periodically, generates a hard decision on the presence or absence of the PU and broadcasts this information to the entire network every T_s seconds. The SUs face Rayleigh fading and Additive White Gaussian Noise (AWGN). At the ith SU, the threshold is updated based on the decisions received from other N-1 SUs in the network, as per equation (6). This updated threshold is used to make the local decision about spectral occupancy. This local decision is compared with ground-truth to determine the probability of error. The results from individual SUs are compared with those obtained using simple majority logic data fusion. Other set of results are obtained by using the optimum LLRT based data fusion technique. For LLRT based data fusion, each node must broadcast its hard decision along with reliability information (P_d and P_f). This information is used to make a decision about the channel occupancy, which serves as the training signal from the adaptive process. Since LLRT based data fusion technique is superior to majority logic, the training signal is more reliable, and as a result, the adaptive technique performs better. In both cases, the adaptive technique achieves lower probability of missed detection than using a static threshold.

Figure 6 shows simulation results using 10 SUs. The average operating SNR for the SUs is 5 dB with a variance of 10 dB. The SNR estimate error at the SUs is 5 dB.

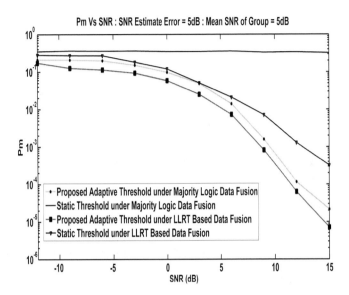

Fig. 6. P_m Vs SNR with SNR Estimate Error=5dB, Mean SNR of Group= 5dB

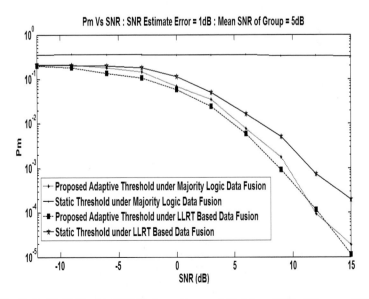

Fig. 7. P_m Vs SNR with SNR Estimate Error = 1dB, Mean SNR of Group = 5dB

In the first case, it assumed that each SU broadcasts its hard decision and the training signal for each SU is obtained by using majority logic decision. In the second case, knowledge of (P_d, P_f) for each SU is assumed and training signal is obtained using LLRT. It can be seen that the proposed adaptive technique outperforms the corresponding distributed decision technique. The gain is substantial as the local SNR increases, and the method always performs as well as the corresponding distributed decision method.

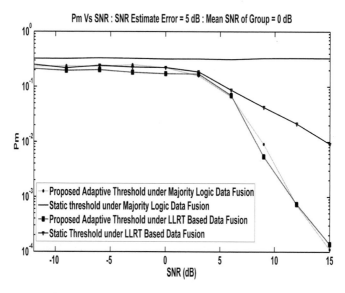

Fig. 8. P_m Vs SNR with SNR Estimate Error = 5dB, Mean SNR of Group = 0dB

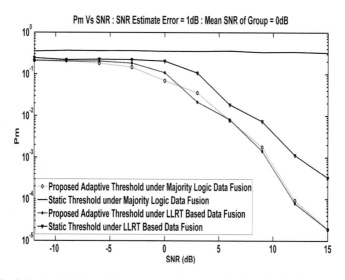

Fig. 9. P_m Vs SNR with SNR Estimate Error = 1dB, Mean SNR of Group = 0dB

Figure 7 shows the simulation results under same conditions as before, except here the error in SNR estimation is smaller; 1 dB. It can be see that the method is relatively insensitive to SNR estimation error and continues to perform better than the distributed sensing methods. Figures 8 and 9 show similar results under lower average SNR conditions (0 dB). P_f was assumed to be 0.1 for all simulations.

The performance is depicted in terms of P_m versus SNR, which is a methodology to access the performance of a given spectrum sensing mechanism [14]. The lowest SNR for a particular targeted reliability is the metric to compare sensing mechanisms.

5 Conclusions

In this paper, an adaptive thresholding mechanism based on group decision in the distributed spectrum sensing scenario of cognitive adhoc networks has been proposed. The proposed technique has the ability to perform better than the majority logic and LLRT methods, at the cost of extra computation at the SU. The concept of adapting the local threshold to synchronize with the global decision makes the process relatively insensitive to SNR estimation errors and hidden node issues. Weightage given to the self decision in high SNR conditions helps in handling primary user emulation attacks and bit errors in the common control channel. Further investigations to quantify these advantages need to be carried out.

References

1. Haykins, S.: Cognitive radio: Brain-Empowered Wireless Communication. IEEE Journal on Selected Areas in Communications 23(2), 201–220 (2005)
2. Akyildiz, F., Lee, W., Vuran, M., Mohanty, S.: NeXt generation/dynamic spectrum access/cognitive radio wireless networks: A survey. Computer Networks (2006)
3. Gong, S., et al.: Threhold-Learning in Local Spectrum of Cognitive radio, http://202.194.20.8/proc/VTC09Spring/DATA/03-02-05.PDF
4. Kadhim, D.J., Gong, S., Liu, W., Cheng, W.: Optimization of Cooperation Sensing Spectrum Performance. In: 2009 International Conference on Communications and Mobile Computing (2009)
5. Lee, J.-W., Kim, J.-H., Oh, H.-J., Hwang, S.-H.: Energy Detector using Adaptive-Fixed Thresholds in Cognitive Radio Systems. In: Proceedings of APCC 2008, IEICE 2008 SB 0083 (2008)
6. Vu-Van, H., Koo, I.: Cooperative Spectrum Sensing with Double Adaptive Energy Thresholds and Relaying Users in Cognitive Radio. In: 2010 Sixth Advanced International Conference on Telecommunications (2010)
7. Shellhammer, S.J.: Spectrum Sensing in IEEE 802.22, http://www.eurasip.org/Proceedings/Ext/CIP2008/../1569094657.pdf
8. Cabric, D., Tkachenko, A., Brodersen, R.W.: Experimental Study of Spectrum Sensing based on Energy Detection and Network Cooperation. TAPAS 222 archive; Proceedings of the First International Workshop on Technology and Policy for Accessing Spectrum, Boston, Massachusetts, Article No. 12 (2006) ISBN:1-59593-510-X
9. Ghasemi, A., Sousa, E.S.: Opportunistic Spectrum Access in Fading Channels Through Collaborative Sensing. Journal of Communications 2(2) (March 2007)

10. Chen, L., Wang, J., Li, S.: An adaptive Cooperative Spectrum Sensing Scheme Based on the Optimal Data Fusion Rule. In: IEEE ISWCS (2007)
11. Ansari, N., Hou, E., Zhu, B., Chen, J.: Adaptive Fusion by Reinforcement Learning for Distributed Detection Systems. IEEE Transactions on Aerospace and Electronic Systems 32(2) (April 1996)
12. Chair, Z., Varshney, P.K.: Optimal Data Fusion in Multiple Sensor Detection Systems. IEEE Transactions on Aerospace and Electronic Systems AES-22(1), 98–101 (1986)
13. Mansouri, N., Fathi, M.: Simple counting rule for optimal data fusion. In: Proceedings of 2003 IEEE Conference on Control Applications, CCA 2003, vol. 2, pp. 1186–1191 (June 2003) ISBN: 0-7803-7729-X
14. Arshad, K., Imran, M.A., Moessner, K.: Collaborative SpectrumSensing Optimisation Algorithms for Cognitive Radio Networks. International Journal of Digital Multimedia Broadcasting 2010, Article ID 424036, doi:10.1155/2010/424036

A Distributed Mobility-Adaptive and Energy Driven Clustering Algorithm for MANETs Using Strong Degree

T.N. Janakiraman and Senthil Thilak A.

Department of Mathematics, National Institute of Technology,
Tiruchirapalli - 620015, Tamil Nadu, India
janaki@nitt.edu, asthilak23@gmail.com

Abstract. In this paper, we propose a new distributed weighted clustering algorithm for MANETs by introducing a new graph parameter called strong degree defined based on the quality of neighbors of a node. The proposed algorithm is a cluster-head based algorithm. The parameters are so chosen to ensure high connectivity, cluster stability and energy efficient communication among nodes of high dynamic nature. This paper deals with the design and complexity analysis of the algorithm and we discuss the different cases which cause topology change and the behavior of our algorithm in these cases.

Keywords: MANET, Strong degree, Connectivity, Cluster Stability.

1 Introduction

Mobile Ad hoc Networks [MANETs], also called as multi-hop/peer-to-peer networks are those formed by a series of autonomous mobile hosts interlinked by means of bandwidth-constrained wireless links with limited battery power. Ad hoc networks, as their name indicates, are unpredictable with frequently changing topology. Each node has a circular transmission range and those nodes which lie within this range alone can communicate with this node. The transmission range of all the nodes can either be uniform or may vary and the nodes may either be of similar or of dissimilar nature. If the transmission range of all the nodes is uniform or the nodes are of same nature, i.e., they are of same architecture then the network is termed as a Homogeneous network. Otherwise, it is referred to as a heterogeneous network. As the network is highly decentralized, all network activities including topology discovery, keeping track of topological changes, transmitting and maintaining routing information and efficient usage of battery power must be executed and monitored by the nodes themselves. But, because of their nature, executing these control functions becomes a bottle-neck. To overcome this problem and to communicate messages among nodes having no permanent bonding, it is essential to set up a virtual backbone, which is accomplished by the process of clustering. Clustering is the process of grouping nodes based on certain strategies and the above mentioned functions can either be distributed among the nodes in each cluster or performed by the leader nodes/Cluster-heads of each cluster rather than distributing throughout the network. This reduces, to a great extent,

N. Meghanathan et al. (Eds.): CCSIT 2011, Part II, CCIS 132, pp. 645–655, 2011.
© Springer-Verlag Berlin Heidelberg 2011

the information exchange between the network nodes and the information to be maintained by each node thereby reducing the overheads incurred. Several clustering algorithms are available for MANETs [1], [12], [15], [18], [21]. Particularly, classified as mobility-only-based algorithms [5], [13], [16], power-only-based [2], [18], [19] and combination-based algorithms [7-9], [18], [21], [22]. The algorithm proposed here is a combination-based algorithm.

The paper is organized as follows. The required definitions and graph theoretic terminologies are given in section 2 and section 3 outlines a review of the existing clustering algorithms. Section 4 includes the ideas which led to the proposed algorithm and the objectives of the algorithm. Section 5 gives the description and section 6, the analysis of the algorithm. Section 7 says how the clusters can be ranked based on their cluster members. Finally, section 8 concludes the paper.

2 Basic Definitions and Terminologies

The network considered here is assumed to be homogeneous. Hence, from now on, by a network, we mean a Homogeneous Mobile Ad Hoc Network unless otherwise specified.

2.1 Graph Theory *vs.* MANET

A graph G is an ordered pair *(V, E)*, where V is a non-empty set of nodes and E is the set of edges/links between different pairs of nodes in V. To represent any given network using a graph, say G, the set of all nodes in the network is taken as the node set V, where two nodes are made adjacent, if the corresponding two nodes are within the transmission range of each other. The graph G thus obtained is referred to as the *underlying graph or the network graph*. For any two nodes u and v in G, *d(u,v)* denotes the least number of hops to move from u to v and vice versa and is referred to as the *Hop-distance* between u and v and *ed(u,v)* denotes the Euclidean distance between u and v. Thus, in a homogeneous network, for a given transmission range r, two nodes u and v can communicate with each other if and only if $ed(u, v) \leq r$. For a given node u, *N(u)* denotes the set of neighbors of u, i.e., *N(u)* is the set of those nodes which are 1-hop away from u and its cardinality is defined as the *degree* of u, denoted by *deg(u)*. The hop-distance between u and its farthest node in G is called the *eccentricity of u* in G and is denoted by *ecc(u)*, i.e., $ecc(u) = \max_{v \in V(G)} \{d(u,v)\}$.

2.2 Categorizations of Neighbors of a Node

Given a node u, the nodes closer to u receive stronger signals and those far apart from u get weaker signals. Based on this notion, we classify the neighbors of a node as shown in Fig. 1. A node v is said to be a *strong neighbor* of a node u, if $0 \leq ed(u, v) \leq r/2$. A node v is said to be a *medium neighbor* of u, if $r/2 < ed(u, v) \leq 3r/4$ and a *weak neighbor* of u, if $3r/4 < ed(u, v) \leq r$.

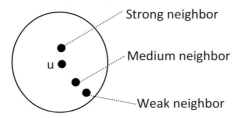

Fig. 1. Three types of neighbors of node u

3 Prior Work

As mentioned earlier, clustering is essential to set up a virtual backbone. Further, to provide an optimal cost effective communication, the amount of information maintained by each node (essential for controlling and routing) is reduced to a certain extent by providing a hierarchical network organization, facilitated by clustering. Several clustering procedures are available in the literature and are categorized in different ways. One such classification is Cluster-Head (CH) based and Non-Cluster-Head (NCH) based clustering algorithms [10], [21]. The algorithm proposed here is a CH based algorithm. So, few of the related CH based algorithms are discussed below.

Lowest ID Heuristic (LID). In the LID heuristic proposed by Baker and Ephremides [3], [4], each node is assigned a unique identifier (ID). The cluster-heads (CHs) are those with smaller ids compared to their neighbors and their respective neighbors are the respective cluster members (CMs). The major drawback of this algorithm is that it causes inconvenient re-clustering and undesired CH changes. Secondly, the smaller ID nodes suffer from severe battery drainage leading to short lifespan. Also, as the id needn't be assigned based on any practical constraint, the election of CHs is not meaningful.

Highest Degree Heuristic (HD). HD heuristic proposed by Gerla et al. [11], [17] is based on the connectivity between a node and its neighbors. If a node has higher connectivity value than its neighbors, then it is elected as a CH and its neighbors are declared as its CMs. Any tie in CH election is broken by node IDs. But, the algorithm doesn't restrict the number of nodes that can be handled by a CH. So, the heads run out of power very quickly.

Mobility-only-based Clustering Algorithms. The algorithm MOBIC given by Basu et al. [5] follows the same procedure as in LID heuristic except that the node ID in LID is replaced by a relative mobility metric value M [5]. Hence, it has all the drawbacks of LID. The same problem is met with the MobDHop clustering algorithm given by Er and Seah [13].

Power-only-based Clustering Algorithms. The algorithms given in [18], [19] consider battery power as the only system parameter for electing CHs. But, as the mobility of nodes is not considered in the election, the possibility of re-clustering is still high when elected CHs have high mobility.

T.N. Janakiraman and A. Senthil Thilak
Combination-based Clustering Algorithms. Chatterjee et al. [7], [8], Choi and Woo [9] have given clustering algorithms using multiple-metrics, where mobility and battery power are used as two important metrics together with other parameters. In these algorithms, while computing mobility metric, the node positions are obtained using GPS, the accuracy of which is not ideal for fine computing and the operations of which could drain the battery power quickly. Chatterjee et al., in [7], [8], used the cumulative time period for which a node acts as a CH for computing battery power. But, this cannot accurately reflect the current level of battery power [20]. Choi and Woo [9] used consumed battery power as a metric for computing battery power.
In this paper, we consider three important parameters, namely, *battery power, mobility measure and strong degree*. Most of the existing algorithms use node degree as an important parameter, where all the strong, medium and weak neighbors of a node contribute for the highest degree of that node. But, there may be some nodes, say, u and v such that the number of strong neighbors of u is less than that of v and the number of medium (and weak) neighbors of u is greater than that of v with deg(u) > deg(v). Thus, as per the strategies used in the existing algorithms, on comparing u and v, u becomes eligible for CH election, even though it has lesser number of strong neighbors than v. But, at a later instant, due to mobility, the node u may lose its eligibility of remaining as a CH. This makes the cluster structure less stable requiring re-affiliations and sometimes re-clustering.
Considering such a situation, we've defined a new degree called strong degree and this is included as one of the main parameters in the proposed algorithm. Apart from this, we also include the mobility of the nodes and the battery power for CH election. For, if a CH is allowed to continue its status for a longer period, then it will lead to battery drainage and hence we should continue with re-affiliation or re-clustering. Hence, to avoid excessive usage of a CH, battery power is considered for selecting cluster heads. With these three parameters, the algorithm is developed with the following objectives.
1. The network nodes are partitioned into clusters of various sizes.
2. The clusters have to be stable as long as possible, but, without excessive battery drainage.
3. The cluster formation and maintenance overhead should be minimized.
4. The CHs should not be overloaded. The load is to be distributed among all the nodes in the network during cluster formation and maintenance.
5. Re-affiliations should be minimized and re-clustering should be avoided as much as possible. At times of necessity, re-affiliations are allowed instead of re-clustering to reduce the cost of cluster maintenance.
6. The algorithm should overcome the problem of scalability.

5   Proposed Algorithm-Strong Degree Based Distributed Weighted Clustering Algorithm (SD_DWCA)

5.1   Metrics

Strong Degree. Let $G = (V, E)$ be a given network graph and $u \in V(G)$. Then, the *Strong neighbor set* of u, denoted by *SN(u)*, is the set of all strong neighbors of u. i.e., $SN(u)=\{v \in N(u): 0 \le ed(u, v) \le r/2\}$. The cardinality of *SN(u)* is defined as the *strong degree* of u and is denoted by $d_{sn}(u)$. Analogously, *the medium neighbor set* (denoted by *MN(u)*) and *weak neighbor set* (denoted by *WN(u)*) are defined using definitions given in section 2.2. The *medium degree ($d_{mn}(u)$)* and *weak degree ($d_{wn}(u)$)* of u are defined to be the cardinality of the sets *MN(u)* and *WN(u)* respectively.

It is to be noted that $deg(u) = d_{sn}(u) + d_{mn}(u) + d_{wn}(u)$.

Mobility Metric. We adopt the mobility measure defined by Xing et al. [20]. For each node u, after receiving two successive hello messages from its 1-hop neighbors, the relative mobility metric with respect to each of its 1-hop neighbor v is computed using (1). The relative mobility metric of u with respect to v is denoted by $R_v(u)$.

$$R_v(u) = \frac{r_{1v}}{r_{2v}}. \tag{1}$$

where, r_{1v}, r_{2v} denote the two successive signal strengths received by u from v which can be read from RSS indicator. Depending on whether $r_{1v} < r_{2v}$ or $r_{1v} > r_{2v}$ or $r_{1v} = r_{2v}$, we can say whether the nodes are moving closer to each other or moving away from each other or either they do not move at all or move with the same speed in the same direction. The root mean square deviation of these values taken from the value 1 (as given in (2)) is used as the mobility measure of u, denoted by M(u).

$$M(u) = \sqrt{\frac{\sum\limits_{v \in N(u)} (R_v(u) - \overline{R}(u))^2}{deg(u)}}, \tag{2}$$

where $\overline{R}(u) = 1$. In the CH election procedure, to maintain the stability of elected CHs, the CHs are expected not to move away from their CMs. Hence, the value $R_v(u)$ of each node u with respect to each of its neighbors is preferred to be less than or equal to 1 and therefore $\overline{R}(u) = 1$, instead of actual mean. Suppose, some neighbor of u has sent more than two periodical hello messages, but u didn't receive two of them successively or u received only one of them, then that neighbor is excluded in the weight calculation of u. This is because, that particular neighbor of u might have moved away from u, i.e., might be a weak neighbor of u or there might be signal attenuation.

Power Metric. To consider the battery level of each mobile node and to ensure that the cluster-heads are not excessively utilized, we use a metric denoted by RE(u), residual energy of node u. If IE(u) and CE(u) denote respectively, the initial energy and consumed battery power of u, then RE(u) = IE(u) – CE(u). To compute this, each node records its remaining battery power after sending and receiving every message.

5.2 Node Weight

To elect CHs, each node is initially assigned a weight computed using formula (3).

$$w(u) = \alpha_1 d_{sn}(u) + \alpha_2 [1 / M (u)] + \alpha_3 RE(u). \tag{3}$$

The constants α_1, α_2 and α_3 in (3) denote the weighing factors. In almost all related applications, it is natural to give equal weightage to all the three parameters. So we choose the values of the three weighing factors as 1/3, so that their sum is unity. The weighing factors can also be varied as per application requirements.

The algorithm includes two phases, namely, cluster formation and cluster maintenance as explained below.

5.3 Cluster Formation

It is assumed that all nodes are free to move in any direction with uniform speed and the status of each node is initially set to *"UNKNOWN"*.

Initial Cluster Formation
Step 1: Each node periodically sends and receives hello messages containing node id, position etc., at a predefined broadcast interval (BI). The received signal strength and the time stamp are also recorded.
Step 2: Each node computes its own weight after a fixed duration. This time gap is specified to allow the hello messages to be sent and received by each node from all its neighbors. If a node fails to receive two successive hello messages after a neighbor has sent atleast three messages, then the neighbor is excluded in weight computation.
Step 3: Each node broadcasts its weight to all its neighbors
Step 4: Each node compares its weight with that of its neighbors. If it is maximum, then the node declares itself as a CH and sends a message *CLUSTER_INFO* together with its node id, to all its neighbors.
Step 5: On receiving the message *CLUSTER_INFO*, if the current status of the receiving node is *UNKNOWN*, then it becomes a CM of the sender and stores the sender's id as its CH id and in turn broadcasts the message to all its neighbors. In case, it is already a CM of another cluster and if the weight of its CH is less than that of the sender, then it changes its affiliation, i.e., changes its CH id as the id of the sender.
Step 6: Finally, the clusters generated are obtained as output.
Step 7: After making all comparisons, nodes still in the status of *UNKNOWN* are collected separately and are termed as "Critical nodes". The critical nodes are then subjected to an adjustment procedure.

Formation of Adjusted Clusters. Let C denote the set of critical nodes obtained after initial cluster formation. If some (atleast two) of the critical nodes are adjacent, then they are allowed to form a cluster on their own, among which, the one with higher weight is chosen as CH and the rest as CMs. If still there are left out nodes, then they become CHs on their own. In most of the existing algorithms, if there is any node left uncovered, then either re-clustering takes place [7], [8] or the nodes are themselves declared as CHs [9]. But, in the proposed algorithm, the nodes are grouped as far as possible, thereby reducing the number of clusters generated.

5.4   Cluster Maintenance

In general, the position in the terrain and status of the nodes (CH/CM/Critical node, in our case) at the time of cluster formation will change in due course, because of nodes' mobility. Hence, to provide a valid hierarchical structuring so as to facilitate an efficient routing, it is necessary to consider this topology change and discuss the behavior of the clustering procedure in such cases. This leads to the cluster maintenance phase. The change in the initial topology may be due to node failure or addition of a new node into network or link failure or link establishment.

Case i: Node Failure. As per our clustering procedure, a node failure means either the drainage of battery power below a fixed threshold value or complete exhaustion of battery power. Generally, the idea of clustering is adopted for proper utilization of resources of nodes during data transmission. The CHs are allowed to play a key role than the non-cluster heads, leading to higher usage of battery power by CHs rather than the other nodes. So, we assume that only the CHs have a greater chance of getting drained out quickly and we deal with the failure of CHs. To avoid CHs being overloaded or to avoid excessive usage of battery by a subset of the nodes, we fix a threshold value for battery power. During cluster formation, each CH periodically checks whether its residual energy is above the threshold value. When it goes below the threshold value, the CH sends a resignation message and all the nodes in the cluster should affiliate themselves to other existing clusters. So, each CM of such a cluster will send a *find_CH* message to its neighboring CHs. Any CH which receives this message will in turn send an acknowledgement message to the sender. If a sending node receives a CH acknowledgement message from more than one node, then it gets attached to the one having higher weight. When a node gets completely drained out, it will be isolated from communication. But, the periodical check up of available battery power of the maximum utilized nodes will avoid such a situation as far as possible. This also increases the network life time.

Case ii: Node Addition. There is a chance for a new node entering into the network. In such a case, the newly added node should attach itself to an existing cluster. Hence, after identifying its neighbors, it broadcasts the *find_CH* message and fixes its appropriate status as explained in the previous case.

Case iii: Link failure. There is also a possibility for the nodes which are already grouped into some cluster to move outside the cluster boundary. Such a node sends a *find_CH* message and gets attached to some existing cluster as in case i.

Case iv: Link establishment. When there is a possibility for nodes moving outside their existing cluster boundary, the same will move closer to some other cluster boundary. This will induce new link establishments and also continuous movement of the nodes will also induce frequent link establishments and failures. To handle new link establishments, each CH should periodically update its neighbor table. If a CH finds a new node in its neighbor table, it checks whether its weight is greater than that of the new node. If so, it continues its status and adds the new neighbor as its CM. If not, it will check in its neighbor table whether there are many (quantified as atleast two) nodes which are common neighbors of both the existing CH and the newly added neighbor, then the current CH will interchange its role with the newly added neighbor. The nodes in the current cluster, which are non-neighbors of the newly elected CH, will get attached to the appropriate neighboring clusters by passing *find_CH* messages.

Remark. If an execution of the above clustering procedure yields no critical nodes, then the clustering is said to be a *perfect clustering*. On the other hand, if there are some critical nodes left out and the number of critical nodes can be reduced to zero by the adjustment procedure, then the clustering is said to be a *fairly perfect clustering*.

6   Complexity Analysis

To perform the analysis, it is assumed that the continuous run time of the algorithm is divided into discrete time steps. Here, one time step is defined as the time duration for the sending of a message (control packets) by a sender and a complete processing of it by the recipient [6]. The approach adopted in this paper is motivated by the theoretical analysis of DMAC made in [6], [13]. It is also assumed that any message transmitted by a sender is successfully received and processed by all its recipients in one time step. We compute the total overhead (message/time) incurred in three steps as follows: Overhead due to hello protocols, cluster formation and cluster maintenance.

Let M_H (T_H), M_{CF} (T_{CF}) and M_{CM} (T_{CM}) denote the message (time) complexities due to hello protocol, cluster formation, cluster maintenance respectively and M and T denote the overall message and time complexities respectively. Then the total message complexity of the algorithm is the sum of M_H, M_{CF} and M_{CM}. Similarly, T is the total of T_H, T_{CF} and T_{CM}.

6.1   Overhead Due to Hello Protocols

Each node periodically broadcasts the hello messages to keep track of its knowledge about its neighbors, at a fixed predefined interval BI. Thus, the frequency of hello messages broadcast by a node is T/BI, where T is the total running time of the algorithm. Hence, on the whole, N*(T/BI) hello messages are to be transmitted, for the entire set of nodes to maintain their neighbor data and so the message complexity due to hello protocols is $M_H = \Theta(N)$, as (T/BI) is a fixed constant. By our assumption, it takes one time step for the transmission of hello messages by each node and successful reception of it by all its neighbors. Hence, totally N time steps are required for successful transmission and reception. Thus, $T_H = \Theta(N)$.

6.2   Overhead Due to Cluster Formation

Cluster formation is done by invoking the two procedures in section 5.3. Suppose that there are N_c clusters and C_r critical nodes before the execution of adjustment procedure. Then, the total number of CMs in the network will be $N - N_c - C_r$.

Initially, during cluster formation, each node computes its weight in constant time and broadcasts to its neighbors, so that $M_1 = N * \Theta(1)$. The respective neighbors store this received weight info in their neighbor table for further comparison in one time step, so that $T_1 = N * \Theta(1)$. Upon receiving this weight info, each node compares its weight with that of its neighbors and decides whether it is maximum. If maximum, it broadcasts a *CLUSTER_INFO* message to its neighbors. But, this message broadcast is done only by the CHs. Therefore, if N_c is the total number of clusters generated, then $N_c * \Theta(1)$ *CLUSTER_INFO* messages are transmitted, i.e., $M_2 = N_c * \Theta(1)$. Each node upon receiving this *CLUSTER_INFO* decides its role as whether to become a CM of the sender (if its current status is *UNKNOWN*) or change its affiliation (if already a CM) or to retain/change its status based on weight comparison (in case, it is already a CH). This takes one time step for each node, i.e., $T_2 = N_c * \Theta(1)$. After this decision making process, each CM broadcasts its CH id to all its neighbors and the neighbors store this info for further processing. Hence, $M_3 = (N - N_c - C_r) * \Theta(1) = T_3$.

Regarding the adjustment procedure, the critical nodes which decide to become as CHs will send *CLUSTER_INFO* messages to their neighbors. In the worst case, all the critical nodes can become as CHs so that C_r messages are transmitted and $M_4 = C_r * \Theta(1) = T_4$.

Thus, the total message and time complexities due to cluster formation are given by, $M_{CF} = N * \Theta(1) + N_c * \Theta(1) + (N - N_c - C_r) * \Theta(1) + C_r * \Theta(1) = \Theta(N)$ and $T_{CF} = T_1 + T_2 + T_3 + T_4 = \Theta(N)$. Suppose Δ_{max} is the maximum number of neighbors of the nodes in the network, then each cluster may contain at the most Δ_{max} CMs and hence in the worst case, we have totally $N/(\Delta_{max} + 1)$ clusters/CHs and $N*(\Delta_{max} / (\Delta_{max} + 1))$ CMs. Here, Δ_{max} can be a constant or a function of N. If it is constant, then $M_2 = M_3 = \Theta(N)$.

6.3 Overhead Due to Cluster Maintenance

The maintenance phase is invoked in any of the four situations discussed in section 5.4. But, in all these cases, the nodes adjust themselves by sending either a *find_CH* message or a resignation message. The resignation message is sent only by the CHs going beyond their battery limit and the message complexity for such transmission is $\Theta(\Delta_{max})$. On the whole, in the worst case, such a message can be transmitted by all the CHs to their respective neighbors. But, this is equivalent to invoking the clustering procedure again. The *find_CH* message is broadcast in all the four cases.

Case i will lead to m broadcasts, where m is the number of CMs attached to the resigned CH. Case ii will lead to n_a broadcasts, where n_a denotes the number of newly added nodes, (one message corresponding to each newly added node). Case iii will cause two broadcasts, because any link failure will lead to change of status of two nodes joined by the link. Similarly, in Case iv, there will be two broadcasts for each newly added link. Thus, the total number of *find_CH* broadcasts is $m + n_a + (2*l_f) + (2*l_a)$, where l_f, l_a denote respectively the number of link failures and link establishments.

7 Ranking of Clusters

While generating clusters using the procedure given in section 5.3, the neighbors of the CH which are considered to be CMs may be either strong neighbors or medium or weak neighbors. Based on this criterion, it is possible to rank the clusters.

If all the CMs in a cluster are strong neighbors of that CH, then the connectivity in this case will be strong enough and the CH can retain its status for a longer period. But, this will not cause the problem of quick battery drainage, because of the strategy followed in assigning node weights. Thus, the clusters generated with the above features are ranked as the topmost (in terms of stability) clusters and termed as *Strong or Balanced Clusters*. A cluster with all its CMs as medium neighbors is termed as a *Medium or Semi-balanced Cluster* and the one with all its CMs as weak neighbors is ranked as a *Weak or Unbalanced Cluster*. There may be cases in which the CMs are combinations of strong, medium and weak neighbors and such clusters are termed as *Intermediate Clusters*. In due course, because of the dynamic nature of our network, these Clusters can change into any of the above mentioned three types of clusters.

8 Conclusion

In the networks considered here, we allow mobility of the nodes in all possible directions. Hence, a node which is a weak neighbor at an instant may become a medium or strong neighbor at a later instant. Similarly, a medium neighbor may either become a strong or a weak neighbor and this leads to re-election of CHs. But, this situation can be avoided as much as possible by the choice of our mobility metric. Thus, the algorithm is reliable even for high speed networks. It is evident from the adjustment procedures given in section 5.3 that to reduce the number of critical nodes, we adopt re-affiliation rather than re-clustering and this greatly reduces the cost of cluster maintenance. Thus, the proposed algorithm is efficient in terms of both execution and maintenance.

References

1. Abbasi, A.A., Buhari, M.I., Badhusha, M.A.: Clustering Heuristics in Wireless Networks: A survey. In: Proc. 20th European Conference on Modelling and Simulation (2006)
2. Aoudjit, R., Lalam, M., Zoughi, A.M., Belkadi, M., Daoui, M.: Load Balancing: An Approach Based on Clustering in Ad Hoc Networks. J. Computing and Information Technology 17(2), 177–184 (2009)
3. Baker, D.J., Ephremides, A.: A distributed algorithm for organizing mobile radio telecommunication networks. In: 2nd International Conference on Distributed Computer Systems, pp. 476–483. IEEE Press, France (1981)
4. Baker, D.J., Ephremides, A.: The architectural organization of a mobile radio networks via a distributed algorithm. IEEE Transactions on Communications COM-29(11), 1694–1701 (1981)
5. Basu, P., Khan, N., Little, T.D.C.: A mobility based metric for clustering in mobile ad hoc networks. In: Proc. of IEEE ICDCS, Phoenix, Arizona, USA, pp. 413–418 (2001)

6. Bettstetter, C., Konig, S.: On the message and time complexity of a distributed mobility-adaptive clustering algorithm in wireless ad hoc networks. In: Proc. 4th European Wireless, Florence, Italy, pp. 128–134 (2002)
7. Chatterjee, M., Das, S.K., Turgut, D.: A Weight Based Distributed Clustering Algorithm for Mobile ad hoc Networks. In: Prasanna, V.K., Vajapeyam, S., Valero, M. (eds.) HiPC 2000. LNCS, vol. 1970, pp. 511–521. Springer, Heidelberg (2000)
8. Chatterjee, M., Das, S.K., Turgut, D.: WCA: A Weighted Clustering Algorithm for Mobile Ad Hoc Networks. In: Cluster Computing, vol. 5, pp. 193–204. Kluwer Academic Publishers, The Netherlands (2002)
9. Choi, W., Woo, M.: A Distributed Weighted Clustering Algorithm for Mobile Ad hoc Networks. In: Proc. of AICT/ICIW 2006. IEEE, Los Alamitos (2006)
10. Francis, S.J., Rajsingh, E.B.: Performance Analysis of Clustering Protocols in Mobile Ad Hoc Networks. J. Computer Science 4(3), 192–204 (2008)
11. Gerla, M., Tsai, J.T.C.: Multi-cluster, mobile, multimedia radio network. Wireless Networks 1(3), 255–265 (1995)
12. Hincapié, R.C., Correa, B.A., Ospina, L.: Survey on clustering Techniques for mobile ad hoc networks. IEEE, Los Alamitos (2006)
13. Inn Inn, E.R., Winston, K.G.S.: Performance Analysis of Mobility-based d-Hop (MobDHop) Clustering Algorithm for Mobile Ad Hoc Networks. Elsevier Comput. Networks 50, 3339–3375 (2006)
14. Inn Inn, E.R., Winston, K.G.S.: Clustering overhead and convergence time analysis of the mobility-based multi-hop clustering algorithm for mobile ad hoc networks. In: Proc. 11th Int. Conference on Parallel and Distributed Systems (ICPADS 2005), pp. 1144–1155 (2005)
15. Johansson, T., Carr-Matyčková, L.: On Clustering in Ad Hoc Networks. In: Proc. Vehicular Tech. Conf. Fall, Swedish National Computer Networking Workshop (2003)
16. McDonald, A.B., Znathi, T.F.: A Mobility-based framework for adaptive clustering in wireless ad hoc networks. IEEE Journal on Selected Areas in Communications 17(8), 1466–1487 (1999)
17. Parekh, A.K.: Selecting routers in ad-hoc wireless networks. In: Proc. SB/IEEE International Telecommunications Symposium (1994)
18. Gajurel, S.: Multi-Criteria Clustering (2006)
19. Sheu, P.R., Wang, C.W.: A Stable Clustering Algorithm based on Battery Power for Mobile Ad Hoc Networks. Tamkang Journal of Science and Engineering 9(3), 233–242 (2006)
20. Xing, Z., Gruenwald, L., Phang, K.K.: A Robust Clustering Algorithm for Mobile Ad Hoc Networks. In: Handbook of Research on Next Generation Networks and Ubiquitous Computing (December 2008)
21. Yu, J.Y., Chong, P.H.J.: A Survey of Clustering Schemes for Mobile Ad Hoc Networks. IEEE Communications Surveys and Tutorials, First Quarter 7(1), 32–47 (2005)
22. Yang, W., Zhang, G.: A Weight-based clustering algorithm for mobile Ad hoc networks. In: Proc. 3rd Int. Conf. on Wireless and Mobile Communications (2007)

Dynamic Sink Placement in Wireless Sensor Networks

Parisa D. Hossein Zadeh, Christian Schlegel, and Mike H. MacGregor

Dept. of Electrical and Computer Engineering, Dept. of Computing Science,
University of Alberta
{dehlehho,schlegel,macg}@ualberta.ca

Abstract. Wireless sensor networks consist of a distributed set of sensor nodes
that cooperatively monitor physical or environmental conditions, and send their
data to a "sink" node over multihop wireless links. Since the main constraint in
wireless sensor networks is limited energy supply at the sensor nodes, it is
important to deploy the sink at a position with respect to the area of interest, a
specific area that is of more interest to the end-user, such that total energy
consumption is minimized. In this paper we propose a new dynamic approach
to find the optimal position for the sink with the goal of reducing the total
energy consumption which has a direct effect on the network's lifetime. A
related problem is that the nodes neighboring the sink suffer more rapid energy
depletion due to high transit traffic. This situation can be mitigated by
relocating the sink occasionally. In this work we propose an algorithm based on
exhaustive search to find the initial optimal sink location, and to relocate the
sink when appropriate. This exhaustive search is intended as a standard by
which other more efficient and practically useful algorithms can be judged. We
also investigate the effects of various additional constraints on the solutions
from exhaustive search.

Keywords: Sink Placement, Sink Relocation, Topology Control.

1 Introduction

Wireless sensor networks consist of a large number of sensor devices each with
limited energy, processing and communication capabilities. The nodes communicate
over a multihop wireless network. The large number of physically dispersed nodes
makes it highly impractical, and sometimes impossible, to replace batteries. A typical
task for sensor nodes is to cooperatively gather data from the surrounding
environment and send the collected data to a "sink". Generally, the sink is a
distinguished node with higher energy reserves. The sink processes the data received
from the sensor nodes and forwards it to an end-user. Due to the scarce energy
reserves in the other nodes many studies have focused on energy-aware solutions in
order to increase the network's lifetime. Although energy is consumed by several
tasks in wireless sensor networks, the most energy intensive task is communication
[1]. In the case of small networks, the sensor nodes may be able to send data directly
to the sink. However in large networks multihop communication is required with

N. Meghanathan et al. (Eds.): CCSIT 2011, Part II, CCIS 132, pp. 656–666, 2011.
© Springer-Verlag Berlin Heidelberg 2011

intermediate sensor nodes cooperating to forward data to the sink. It is crucial to find the optimal position for the sink because correct placement of the sink has a direct and significant effect on energy consumption in the network [2].

In some networks, data from a specific area of network is critical. This might be the front line in a battlefield, a portion of a forest supporting a colony of animals or the location of a fire in a city. Sensor data that originates in the area of interest is more important than that from other sensors. The data should reach the sink successfully with low average delay. Nevertheless, the position of the sink in such networks is crucial as far as energy consumption is concerned. In this paper, we propose an algorithm for sink placement. Nodes close to the sink will be heavily involved in data forwarding and thus their energy reserves will be depleted rather quickly [3]. Therefore, sink relocation must be taken into account. Such a sink could be a laptop computer inside the backpack of a rescue worker. The sink may or may not include an uplink to a backbone network. This investigation recognizes that possibility, but we have not as yet pursued its further implications.

To the best of our knowledge the problem of placing and relocating a sink relative to an area of interest has not been investigated previously. The goal of most published work is to find the optimal location for the sink according to initial energy resources and the density of sensor nodes. Past research has considered the energy consumption of the whole network. However our goal is to find the position for the sink relative to the area of interest that minimizes total energy consumption while maintaining the reserve energy in each node at or above a given threshold. Moreover, we relocate the sink over time to preserve energy reserves in the nodes.

The paper is organized as follows. Section 2 presents a review of related solutions to sink placement in wireless sensor networks. In Section 3, we describe our proposed algorithm for sink positioning and relocation. Section 4 presents simulation results for our approach in different network situations. Finally, we conclude the paper in section 5 and discuss future work.

2 Related Work

In the past, most researchers focused on minimizing energy consumption [4,5] or maximizing data aggregation [6,7]. Recently, several papers [3,8,9] report work on sink placement and mainly design the network to ensure coverage and connectivity. However none of these papers considered sink placement relative to an area of interest.

In [1] the authors use a mathematical model to place the sink based on the traffic flow and a cluster infrastructure. Here, the sink calculates the amount of traffic arriving at its one-hop neighbors and moves in the direction of the gradient. However, the proposed approach relies on local information that might result in isolating the sink from the network by moving it to a place without sensor nodes. Many solutions for sink placement based on clustering have been proposed in the literature [4,8,10,11]. The approach in [8] is to place the sink at the centre of mass of the sensor nodes. If there are multiple sinks, multiple clusters are created. The drawback of this approach is that the number of clusters depends on the number of sinks in network, and a priori knowledge about the number of sinks is needed without having a global view of the network.

In [3] the authors propose repositioning the sink to find a new optimal location according to traffic density and the transmission energy of the sink's neighbors. They have shown that sink repositioning reduces the average energy consumed per transmitted data packet. They also argue that network throughput increases. They have studied both cases of unconstrained and constrained network traffic to avoid packet loss in real-time traffic. None of the previous papers in the literature aims to find the optimal position for the sink while considering the importance of a specific area of interest. In this paper we explore the idea of positioning and relocating the sink relative to an area of interest in order to manage the energy consumption.

2 Our Approach

In this paper we propose a sink placement algorithm that has the goal of minimizing total energy consumption in a wireless sensor network containing a known area of interest. In addition, in order to validate our results we have considered various types of areas of interest. We have considered placing the area of interest in the centre, corner and side of the network. We have also considered different transmission rates and sizes for the area of interest.

In the following, we begin by presenting an algorithm based on exhaustive search. We then examine the consequences of adding various constraints on the allowable positions of the sink. The results from exhaustive search must, of course, result in the global minimum energy consumption. Adding constraints to this search must increase energy consumption, and we are interested in the magnitude of these increases. Exhaustive search is relied on here as an expedient way to explore the effects of arbitrary side-constraints that could be very difficult to add to a more efficient method. We recognize the need for efficient, practical algorithms and anticipate developing them once we have completed this initial survey.

2.1 Sink Placement

Multihop forwarding must be used if the sink is situated at a significant distance relative to the sensor nodes. This results in energy consumption in all intermediate nodes for message reception and transmission.

Let e_{mn} denote the energy consumed when node (m,n) transmits data to the sink s_{ij}. U_{mnij} denotes all the sensor nodes along a shortest path to the sink. We use Dijkstra's algorithm for finding shortest paths. In the case of multihop communication, e_{mn} would be the total consumed energy of contributor nodes for all nodes in set U_{mnij}. Fig. 1 shows such a communications setup:

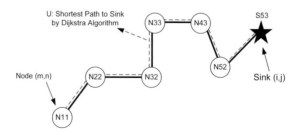

Fig. 1. Multihop communication in a wireless sensor network

In this example, set U_{mnij} includes:

$$U_{mnij} = U_{1,1,5,3} = \{\mathcal{N}_{11}, \mathcal{N}_{22}, \mathcal{N}_{32}, \mathcal{N}_{33}, \mathcal{N}_{43}, \mathcal{N}_{52}\} \tag{1}$$

$e_{1,1}$ is obtained as:

$$e_{\mathcal{N}_{mn} \to S_{ij}} = \sum_{\mathcal{N}_{kl} \in U} e_{\mathcal{N}_{kl}} \tag{2}$$

In the expression below, let $N \times N$ denotes the number of sensor nodes in the entire network. α_{mn} stands for weight of each sensor node $\mathcal{N}_{mn}$. In this work, we assume the weight of a node is its transmission rate. This parameter could alternatively be used to represent other node characteristics, such as its importance, etc.

Once we have deployed the sink somewhere in the network, all nodes start transmitting data to the sink over their shortest paths. The energy reserve of every node which contributed to the data transmission is reduced appropriately. Then the total energy consumption of placing the sink at location (i,j) is:

$$E_{ij} = \sum_{m=1}^{N} \sum_{n=1}^{N} b_{mn} e_{\mathcal{N}_{mn} \to S_{ij}} \tag{3}$$

Equation (3) is used to calculate the energy consumptions of all possible locations for the sink. By placing the sink in all possible locations in network, we will have a matrix of total energy consumptions E_{ij} which is denoted by E.

$$E = [E_{ij}]_{nn} \tag{4}$$

Let S_{ij}^0 denote the initial optimum position of the sink, and let W be the set of alive nodes in the network. Using (2) S_{ij}^0 is obtained as:

$$S_{ij}^0 = arg \min_{S_{ij}} \{ E, W \} \tag{5}$$

Our results show that the algorithm finds an optimum location for the sink, and not surprisingly this is close to the area of interest. Therefore, data originated by nodes inside the area of interest reaches the sink quickly and reliably while causing minimum energy consumption as they transit the network. As the transmission rate of the nodes in the area of interest increases (in other words, as the importance of nodes inside the area of interest increases) the algorithm tends to choose positions for the sink towards the centre of the area of interest. This trend is beneficial in decreasing the total energy consumption in the network.

However, placing the sink statically in one position will cause nodes nearby the sink to run out of energy quickly as they are the most heavily utilized nodes in the network. In this case, the sink will be isolated from the network. In some cases, the sink's nearest neighbors are located in the area of interest. These nodes need even more long-term support in terms of energy because they are both originating and forwarding data. To reflect this, each node in the area of interest is assigned a threshold energy value $\mathcal{T}_{hs}$ assumed equal for all nodes located inside the area of interest. Here, "hs" denotes the area of interest, or "hot spot". The value of the threshold can be defined according to node physical resources such as battery capacity.

We set $\mathcal{T}_{hs}$ as the average energy required for a node in the hot spot to communicate with the sink, with the sink in its initial position:

$$\mathcal{T}_{hs} = \frac{\sum_{m,n \in hs} e^0_{mn}}{n_{hs}} \qquad (6)$$

where:

- $\mathcal{T}_{hs}$ is the threshold value for nodes located in the area of interest,
- e^0_{mn} is the energy consumption of nodes (m,n) for communicating with the sink in initial sink placement,
- hs is the set of the indices of the nodes in the area of interest,
- n_{hs} is the number of nodes in the area of interest.

In order to calculate $\mathcal{T}_{hs}$, we put the sink at its initial optimum position in the network without considering any threshold value, and compute the average of energy consumption of the nodes in the area of interest for sending data to the sink. Then, we use this value as $\mathcal{T}_{hs}$ and find an optimum position for the sink subject to the condition that every node in the area of interest can send a message to the sink using less energy than $\mathcal{T}_{hs}$. If the features of the area of interest such as its location, size or transmission rate change, the algorithm calculates the new $\mathcal{T}_{hs}$ value. In order to calculate the new $\mathcal{T}_{hs}$ value, the algorithm locates the sink at the optimum position based on the new features of the area of interest, and computes the average energy which nodes in the area of interest use to communicate with the sink. This value is considered the new $\mathcal{T}_{hs}$ until any of the features of the area of interest changes. The pseudocode of $\mathcal{T}_{hs}$ calculation is shown in Table 1.

Table 1. Pseudocode of $\mathcal{T}_{hs}$ threshold

If (Area of Interest's location is changed)
Or
(Area of Interest's size is changed)
Or
(Area of Interest's transmission rate is changed)
Then
Add the new features to the network status
Run Sink Placement algorithm (Equation 5)
$\mathcal{T}'_{hs} = \frac{\sum_{m,n \in hs} e_{mn}}{n_{hs}}$
$\mathcal{T}_{hs} = \mathcal{T}'_{hs}$

Using (6), we define a new optimal location for the sink, $S^*_\mathcal{T}$:

$$S^*_\mathcal{T} = arg \min_{S^*_{ij}}\{ E \mid e_{ij \in hs} \leq \mathcal{T}_{hs}, \quad w \} \qquad (7)$$

where,

- E is the matrix of total energy consumptions related to locating the sink in all positions,
- $S^*_\mathcal{T}$ is an optimum position of the sink which satisfies the threshold.

Equation (7) selects the position for the sink which minimizes the total energy consumption for each node to send a message to the sink. The selected position must meet the threshold condition of the nodes in the area of interest. It is not surprising to see slightly higher total energy consumption in the network after adding $\mathcal{T}_{hs}$ as a parameter of the optimization. Setting the threshold value is necessary to keep nodes in the area of interest safe from rapid energy depletion.

2.1 Sink Relocation

Once the sink has been in place for a while at the chosen optimal position, the energy levels in neighboring sensor nodes will be reduced. We propose to relocate the sink from time to time to prevent this pattern of energy depletion from partitioning the network. We assume that the sink can move to any location in the area covered by the network. Relocating the sink is complicated by the following factors. First, there exist an infinite number of locations in the network where the sink can be placed. Second, in every search step all the energy-aware routes that become possible must be considered. We also need to decide exactly when to move the sink.

We consider two different cases. First, we recall that the sink is being moved to avoid energy depletion in its neighbors. Therefore, we define a threshold value equal to a specific number of depleted nodes around the sink. We move the sink before this threshold is exceeded. Fig. 2 shows the relocation of the sink in order to meet the threshold value. Leaving the sink where it is first placed will result in longer paths from other nodes that are communicating with the sink due to presence of some depleted nodes around the sink. We find that our algorithm avoids this undesirable situation by relocating the sink and keeps the total energy consumption low.

The following notation is used in deriving the condition for sink relocation:

- $\mathcal{D}$: the set of depleted nodes nearby the sink
- $\mathcal{W}$: the set of alive nodes in the network
- $S_T^{*(i)}$: new optimal location for sink

The sink relocation can be defined in (8) as:

$$S_T^{*(i)} = arg\min_{S_{ij}^*}\{ E \mid e_{ij \in hs} \leq \mathcal{T}_{hs}, \mathcal{W} - \mathcal{D} \} \tag{8}$$

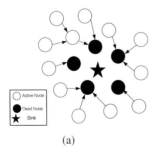 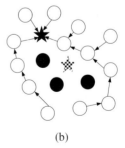

(a)   (b)

Fig. 2. (a) Depletion of all nodes nearby sink resulted in isolating the sink from network. (b) Sink is relocated to a new position. Other nodes' messages can reach the sink while keeping total energy consumption low.

Another reason to relocate the sink is that in practical situations, the area of interest may move from one place in the network to another. However, if the sink stays in its previous location regardless of changes in the location of the area of interest, then after a while the end-user is likely to lose contact with some of the nodes in the area of interest. Therefore, we developed another algorithm in which the sink tracks the location of the area of interest. This reduces the total energy consumption while maintaining a high rate of successful data transmission. If either or both of the two relocation conditions are met, the algorithm for sink placement is called with the input of updated network conditions and the output as a new coordinate S_{ij} for the sink. Table 2 Shows the Pseudocode for the sink relocation process.

Table 2. Sink relocation pseudocode

If (Area of Interest has moved)
Or
If (too many sink's nearby nodes depleted)
Then remove depleted nodes from consideration
Run Sink Placement algorithm (Equation 8)
Relocate S_{ij}

3   Simulation Results

We implemented a simulator in Matlab and evaluated the performance of our proposed algorithm. Then we compared the results of different scenarios. In our experiments, the sensor network consisted of 100 nodes deployed in a 10×10 square meter grid-shaped area.

The communication range of the sensor nodes was such that each node could communicate with its one-hop horizontal and vertical neighbors. We assumed that the energy used for transmitting one bit is twice the energy needed to receive a bit [12]. Every sensor consumed one unit of energy for each data transmission and reception.

The sink is assumed to know its own location and the location of the area of interest. The sink is assumed to have enough energy to broadcast a message containing its location to all the sensor nodes in the network. We used Dijkstra's algorithm to find a shortest path from each node to the sink. The threshold value for sink relocation was defined as 75% depleted nodes, and the energy threshold T_{hs} for nodes inside the area of interest was calculated by taking the average value of consumed energy for the nodes inside the area.

We ran the simulations under different network conditions while considering various characteristics for the nodes and the area of interest. These included the transmission rates, which we set at two, five and ten data transmissions per second for nodes inside the area of interest while considering one data transmission per second for all other nodes. We located the area of interest at the centre, corner and side of the network, and tried one hope and two hop lengths for the area of interest.

3.1   Performance Results

In this section, we present the performance results from our simulation. As noted, we evaluated the performance of our algorithm by placing the area of interest at different locations with different sizes, and for each case we considered three different transmission rates for nodes within the area. Fig. 3 illustrates the optimal sink placements found by our algorithm. Fig. 3.e gives the legend for the related figures. Fig. 3.a and 3.b show the placements of the sink when the area of interest is located at the side of network while increasing the area's data transmission rate and size respectively. Fig. 3.c shows the case when the area of interest is placed at the corner of network. It is interesting to note that the sink's position at the centre of the network is never changed in Fig. 3.d. Obviously, this is caused by the symmetric shape of the network in this case. Comparing the energy consumption of the network when using our proposed algorithm to the case of placing the sink without considering the area of interest, we find a significant reduction.

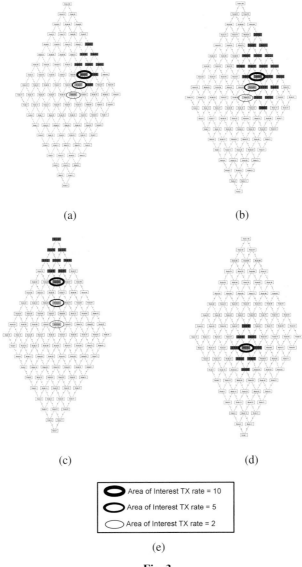

(a)   (b)

(c)   (d)

Area of Interest TX rate = 10
Area of Interest TX rate = 5
Area of Interest TX rate = 2

(e)

Fig. 3.

Recall that setting the threshold for nodes in the area of interest, $\mathcal{T}_{hs}$, avoids depleting those nodes. Fig. 4 shows the situation when the area of interest is placed at the corner of the network while we set $\mathcal{T}_{hs}$ equal to 50 units of energy and transmission rate for nodes inside the interesting area is set to 5. The sink tends to move away from the area of interest.

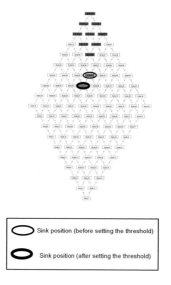

Fig. 4. Effect of threshold on sink position

Fig. 5 presents the results without and then with taking into account the threshold, $\mathcal{T}_{hs}$. The results of sink placement simulation show that energy consumption before setting the threshold was 1644 units of energy while after having threshold for nodes in the area of interest the energy consumption increases slightly to 1800 units of energy. As can be seen from the results, the value for the case of considering threshold is higher than placement of the sink regardless of threshold. This is because the sink is positioned further away in contrast to situations without any threshold. Using the threshold, results in data transiting longer paths to reach the sink. The goal is to respect the threshold $\mathcal{T}_{hs}$ of the nodes in the area of interest. The algorithm tries to keep the consumed energy as low as possible. Other experiments with different conditions give similar results.

Moreover, the algorithm relocates the sink if the number of depleted nodes around the sink exceeds a threshold value. This value is set to 75% of all nearby nodes in our experiments. These sensor nodes are not necessarily nodes in the area of interest - they could be any node in the network. It is reasonable to move the sink after depletion of ¾ nearby nodes because we assumed each sensor node can communicate directly with its four horizontal and vertical neighbors. First the algorithm finds the optimal sink position. This yields a total energy consumption of 1800 units of energy. However, sink optimum static placement allows depletion of ¾ of neighbors and leads to 1830 units of energy. Therefore, we do dynamic sink placement to avoid neighbor depletion. The new position for the sink is selected by running our relocation algorithm while we do not take into account the depleted nodes in this decision. The relocation algorithm finds a new position for the sink after reevaluating the overall network traffic flow. The result is to locate the sink in a position which leads to a lower total energy consumption. The new value for the total energy consumption is even less than the static placement of the sink because the new position of the sink in this case is closer to the area of interest. We achieved reduction in total energy consumption to 1755 units of energy.

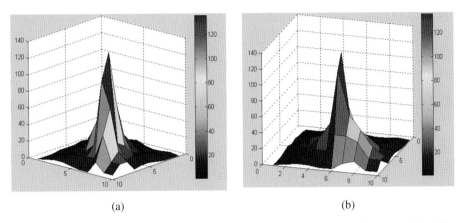

(a)   (b)

Fig. 5. (a) Before Threshold, Total Energy Consumption=1644 units of energy. (b) After Threshold, Total Energy Consumption=1800 units of energy.

Another condition which makes the algorithm relocate the sink to a new position is when the location of the area of interest changes. In order to evaluate our algorithm, first we placed the area of interest at the west corner of the network. We used the algorithm to find the optimal position for the sink, and this resulted in total energy consumption of 1800 units of energy. Then, we moved the area of interest to the east corner of the network while keeping the sink's location unchanged. Total energy consumption increased to 2124 units of energy. By relocating the sink to a new optimum location with respect to the new location of the area of interest we obtained 7% reduction in total energy consumption from 2124 to 1971 units of energy. Therefore, careful sink relocation can prevent the loss of connectivity to the sink and also significantly reduce energy consumption compared to the case where the position of sink is static. These results confirm that our algorithm enhances the network performance by repositioning the sink. However, sink repositioning must be controlled carefully as it can result in slightly higher energy consumption in if we set too high a value for the threshold $\mathcal{T}_{hs}$.

4 Conclusions

In this paper, we propose a new approach for sink placement and relocation relative to a known area of interest. The sink is placed to minimize the total energy consumption while considering different features of the area of interest, such as its size, location and data transmission rate. Our algorithm considers the features of the area of interest as well as the importance of this area in order to position the sink in a place where the network consumes the least energy. As discussed, placing the sink statically in a position once and for all will result in depleting the energy of the sink's neighbors. Our algorithm takes into account the problem of early depletion of these nodes by relocating the sink to a new position whenever the nodes around the sink pass below a threshold value for remaining energy. Furthermore, the algorithm relocates the sink whenever the location of the area of interest changes. Our future plan is to develop an algorithm more efficient than exhaustive search. Another research challenge is to develop a method to estimate the position and extent of an area of interest based on traffic or other measureable quantities. We also plan to extend this work to the case of multiple sinks in large networks.

References

[1] Vincze, Z., Vida, R., Vidacs, A.: Deploying multiple sinks in multi-hop wireless sensor networks. In: IEEE International Conference on Pervasive Services, July 15-20, pp. 55–63 (2007)
[2] Friedmann, L., Boukhatem, L.: Efficient multi-sink relocation in wireless sensor network. In: ICNS, Third International Conference on Networking and Services, 2007, June 19-25, p. 90 (2007)
[3] Younis, M., Bangad, M., Akkaya, K.: Base-station repositioning for optimized performance of sensor networks. In: IEEE Vehicular Technology Conference, VTC 2003, October 6-9, vol. 5, pp. 2956–2960 (2003)
[4] Seema, B., Coyle, E.J.: An energy efficient hierarchical clustering algorithm for wireless sensor networks. In: INFOCOM 2003, Twenty-Second Annual Joint Conference of the IEEE Computer and Communications Societies, March 30-April 3, vol. 3, pp. 1713–1723 (2003)
[5] Chen, B., Jamieson, K., Balakrishnan, H., Morris, R.: Span: An energy-efficient coordination algorithm for topology maintenance in ad hoc wireless networks. Wireless Networks 8(5), 481–494 (2002)
[6] Silberstein, A., Munagala, K., Yang, J.: Energy-efficient monitoring of extreme values in sensor networks. In: Proc. of the 2006 ACM SIGMOD International Conference on Management of Data, Chicago, IL, USA, pp. 169–180 (2006)
[7] Chatterjea, S., Havinga, P.: A dynamic data aggregation scheme for wireless sensor networks. In: ProRISC 2003, Veldhoven, Netherlands (November 2003)
[8] Oyman, E.I., Ersoy, C.: Multiple sink network design problem in large scale wireless sensor networks. In: 2004 IEEE International Conference on Communications, June 20-24, vol. 6, pp. 3663–3667 (2004)
[9] Qiu, L., Chandra, R., Jain, K., Mahdian, M.: Optimizing the placement of integration points in multi-hop wireless networks. In: Proceedings of the International Conference on Network Protocols (ICNP), Berlin, Germany, pp. 271–282 (October 2004)
[10] Ghiasi, S., et al.: Optimal energy aware clustering in sensor networks. Sensors Magazine 19(2), 258–269 (2002)
[11] Safwat, A., Hassanein, H., Mouftah, H.T.: Power-aware fair infrastructure formation for wireless mobile ad hoc communications. In: IEEE GLOBECOM 2001, vol. 5, pp. 2832–2836 (November 2001)
[12] Texas Instruments, Low-Cost Low-Power Sub- 1 GHz RF Transceiver, SWRS038C datasheet (May 2008)

Author Index

Printing: Mercedes-Druck, Berlin
Binding: Stein+Lehmann, Berlin